The Shelly Cashman Series®

Microsoft® Office 365®

Outlook® 2021

Comprehensive

The
Shelly Cashman
Series®

Microsoft® Office 365®
Outlook® 2021

Comprehensive

Cengage

Australia • Brazil • Canada • Mexico • Singapore • United Kingdom • United States

Cengage

Shelly Cashman Series® Microsoft® Office 365® & Outlook® 2021 Comprehensive
Corinne Hoisington

SVP, Product: Erin Joyner
VP, Product: Thais Alencar
Product Director: Mark Santee
Senior Product Manager: Amy Savino
Product Assistant: Ciara Horne
Learning Designer: Zenya Molnar
Senior Content Manager: Anne Orgren
Digital Delivery Quality Partner: Jim Vaughey
Developmental Editor: Lisa Ruffolo
VP, Product Marketing: Jason Sakos
Director, Product Marketing: Danaë April
Executive Product Marketing Manager: Jill Staut
IP Analyst: Ann Hoffman
IP Project Manager: Ilakkiya Jayagopi
Production Service: Lumina Datamatics, Inc.
Designer: Erin Griffin
Cover Image Source: Volanthevist/Getty Images

Mac Users: If you're working through this product using a Mac, some of the steps may vary. Additional information for Mac users is included with the Data files for this product.

Disclaimer: This text is intended for instructional purposes only; data is fictional and does not belong to any real persons or companies.

Disclaimer: The material in this text was written using Microsoft Windows 10 and Office 365 Professional Plus and was Quality Assurance tested before the publication date. As Microsoft continually updates the Windows 10 operating system and Office 365, your software experience may vary slightly from what is presented in the printed text.

Library of Congress Control Number: 2022910298

Student Edition ISBN: 978-0-357-67721-6
Looseleaf available as part of a digital bundle

Cengage
200 Pier 4 Boulevard
Boston, MA 02210
USA

Cengage is a leading provider of customized learning solutions with employees residing in nearly 40 different countries and sales in more than 125 countries around the world. Find your local representative at **www.cengage.com.**

To learn more about Cengage platforms and services, register or access your online learning solution, or purchase materials for your course, visit **www.cengage.com.**

Notice to the Reader

Printed in the United States of America
Print Number: 01 Print Year: 2022

Brief Contents

Contents

Getting to Know Microsoft Office Versions

Cengage is proud to bring you the next edition of Microsoft Office. This edition was designed to provide a robust learning experience that is not dependent upon a specific version of Office.

Microsoft supports several versions of Office:

- **Office 365:** A cloud-based subscription service that delivers Microsoft's most up-to-date, feature-rich, modern productivity tools direct to your device. There are variations of Office 365 for business, educational, and personal use. Office 365 offers extra online storage and cloud-connected features, as well as updates with the latest features, fixes, and security updates.
- **Office 2021:** Microsoft's "on-premises" version of the Office apps, available for both PCs and Macs, offered as a static, one-time purchase and outside of the subscription model.
- **Office Online:** A free, simplified version of Office web applications (Word, Excel, PowerPoint, and OneNote) that facilitates creating and editing files collaboratively.

Office 365 (the subscription model) and Office 2021 (the one-time purchase model) had only slight differences between them at the time this content was developed. Over time, Office 365's cloud interface will continuously update, offering new application features and functions, while Office 2021 will remain static. Therefore, your onscreen experience may differ from what you see in this product. For example, the more advanced features and functionalities covered in this product may not be available in Office Online or may have updated from what you see in Office 2021.

For more information on the differences between Office 365, Office 2021, and Office Online, please visit the Microsoft Support site.

Cengage is committed to providing high-quality learning solutions for you to gain the knowledge and skills that will empower you throughout your educational and professional careers.

Thank you for using our product, and we look forward to exploring the future of Microsoft Office with you!

1 Managing Email Messages with Outlook

Objectives

After completing this module, you will be able to:

- Add a Microsoft account to Outlook
- Set language preferences and sensitivity levels
- Apply a theme
- Compose, address, and send an email message
- Read aloud, translate, and dictate your messages
- Open, read, print, and close an email message
- Preview and save a file attachment
- Reply to an email message
- Check spelling as you type an email message
- Attach a file from recent items to an outgoing email
- Forward an email message
- Copy another person when sending an email message
- Create and move messages into a folder
- Delete an email message
- View the mailbox size

What Is Outlook?

The Office application, **Microsoft Outlook**, helps you organize and manage your communications, contacts, schedules, and tasks. **Email** (short for **electronic mail**) is the transmission of messages and files between your PC, Mac, or mobile device, over a network. An **email client**, such as Microsoft Outlook, is an app that allows you to compose, dictate, send, receive, store, and delete email messages. Outlook can access mail servers in a local network, such as your school's network, or on a remote network, such as the Internet. Finally, you can use Outlook to streamline your messages so that you easily can find and respond to them later.

To use Outlook, you must have an email account. An **email account** is an electronic mailbox you receive from an **email service provider**, which is an organization that provides servers for routing and storing email messages. Your employer or school could set up an email account for you, or you can do so yourself through your Internet service provider (ISP) or using a web application such as a Microsoft account, Google Gmail, or iCloud Mail. Outlook does not create or issue email accounts; it merely provides you with access to them. When you have an email account, you also have an **email address**, which identifies your email account on a network so you can send and receive email messages.

Project: Composing and Sending Email Messages

The project in this module follows the general guidelines for using Outlook to compose, dictate, open, and reply to email messages, as shown in Figure 1–1. To communicate with individuals and groups, you typically send or receive some kind of message. Texting, posting, tweeting, and email are examples of ways to communicate a message. Email is a convenient way to send information to multiple people at once.

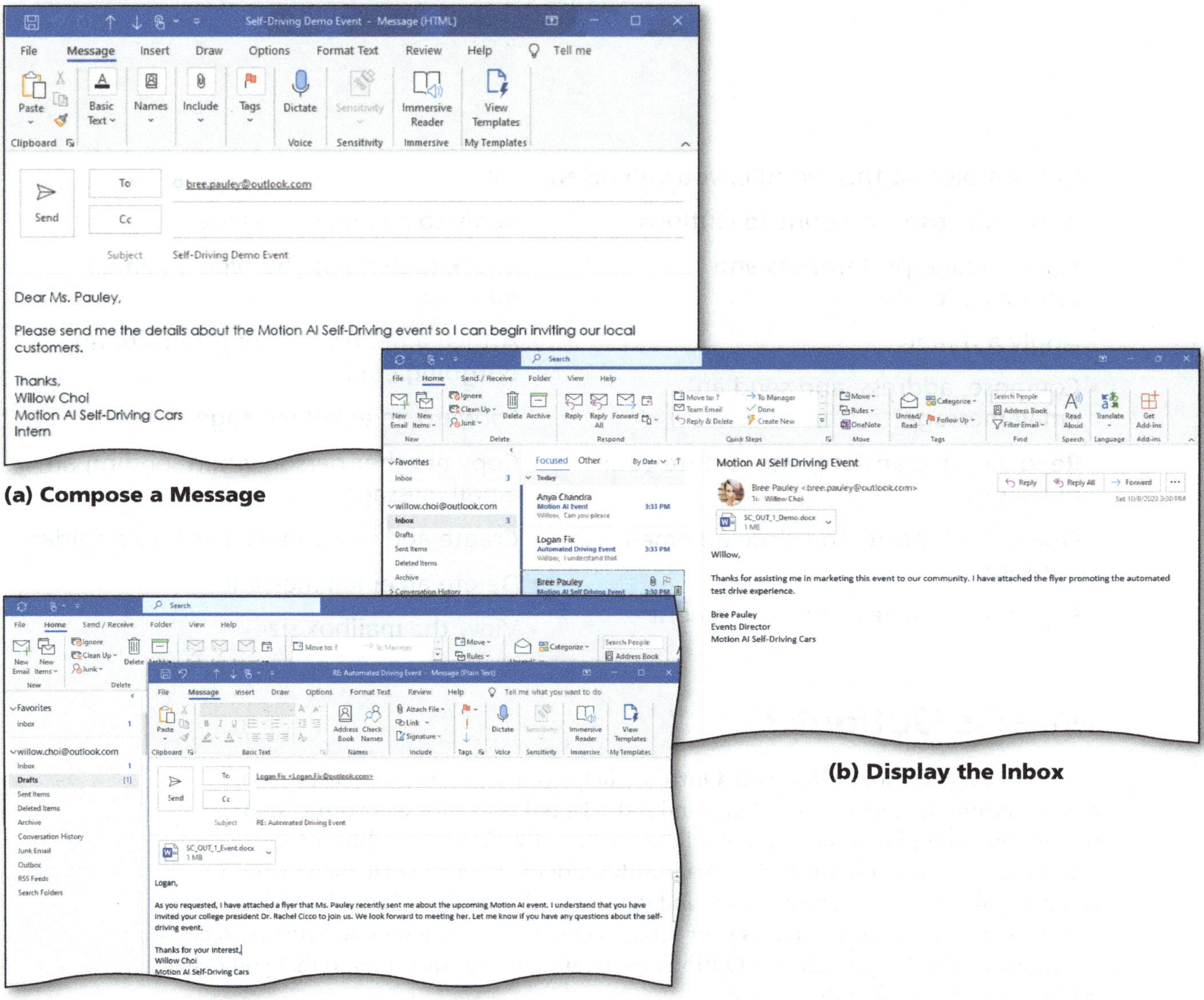

(a) Compose a Message

(b) Display the Inbox

(c) Reply and Attach a File to a Message

Look Studio/Shutterstock.com

Figure 1–1

Willow Choi, an intern at the Motion AI Self-Driving Cars company, uses Outlook to connect with the customers, staff, and others interested in self-driving vehicles. This module uses Microsoft Outlook to compose, dictate, send, read, reply to, and forward email messages regarding an upcoming demo event in October.

Willow has been asked by Bree Pauley, the Motion AI events director, to coordinate the self-driving demonstration. Using Outlook, Willow reads email messages from others at Motion AI and from local contacts regarding the demo event and customer experience opportunities. She replies to email messages and includes a document containing a flyer about the demo. To organize messages, she also creates folders and then stores the messages in those folders.

In this module, you will learn how to perform basic email messaging tasks. You will perform the following general activities as you progress through this module:

1. Configure the account options.
2. Compose and send an email message.
3. View and print an email message.
4. Reply to an email message.
5. Attach a file to an email message.
6. Organize email messages in folders.

To Start Outlook

If you are using a computer to step through the project in this module and you want your screens to match the figures in this book, you should change your screen's resolution to 1366 × 768.

The following steps, which assume Windows 11 is running, use the Start menu to start Outlook based on a typical installation. You may need to ask your instructor how to start Outlook on your computer.

1. Click the Start button on the Windows 11 taskbar to display the Start menu.
2. Scroll to and then click Outlook in the apps list to run Outlook.
3. If the Outlook window is not maximized, click the Maximize button on its title bar to maximize the window.

Setting Up Outlook

Many computer users have an email account from an online email service provider such as Outlook.com or Gmail.com and another email account at work or school. You can add many types of email accounts to Outlook, including an Office 365 account as shown in Figure 1–2, and Gmail, Yahoo, iCloud, and Exchange accounts. Instead of using a web app for your online email account and another app for your school account, you can use the Outlook client (installed version of Outlook) to access all of your email messages in a single location. Outlook provides cloud storage for storing information such as email messages, calendars, contacts, and tasks. When you access your email in Outlook, you can take advantage of a full set of features that include dictation, predictive text, translation, and having Outlook read your email aloud to you. You can read your downloaded messages offline and set options to organize your messages in a way that is logical and convenient for you.

CONSIDER THIS

What should I do if I do not have an email address?
Use a browser such as Microsoft Edge to go to the Outlook.com or Gmail.com website. Look for a Create an Account link or button, click it, and then follow the instructions to create an account, which includes creating an email address.

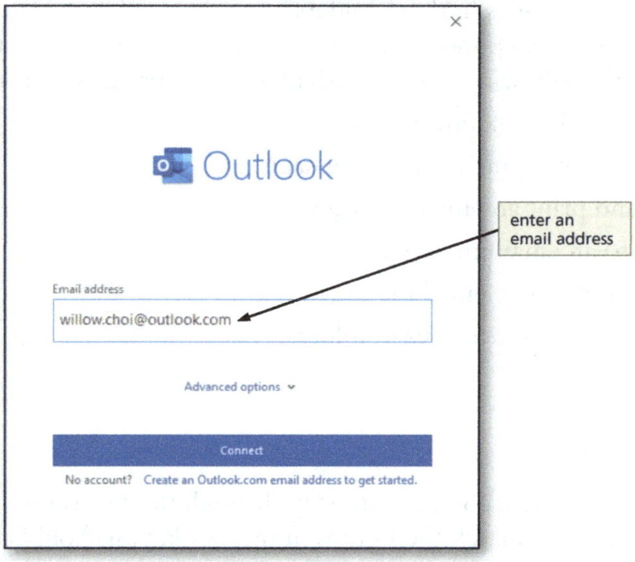

Figure 1–2

Parts of an Email Address

An email address is divided into two parts. The first part contains a **user name**, which is a combination of characters that identifies a specific user. The last part is a **domain name**, which is the name associated with a specific Internet address and is assigned by your email service provider. A user name must be different from other user names in the same domain. For example, the outlook.com domain can have only one user named Willow.Choi. An email address contains an @ (pronounced *at*) symbol to separate the user name from the domain name. Figure 1–3 shows an email address for Willow Choi, which would be read as Willow dot Choi at outlook dot com.

Figure 1–3

To Add an Email Account

You can add one or more of your email accounts to Outlook. For most accounts, Outlook automatically detects and configures the account after you type your name, email address, and password. Add an email account to Outlook when you are working on your personal or home computer only. You do not want your personal information or email messages on a public computer. Although most people add an email account the first time Outlook runs, you can add email accounts at any time. This module assumes you already set up an email account in Outlook. If you choose to add an email account to Outlook, you would use the following steps.

1. Click the File tab, and then click Add Account.
2. Click the Email address box, and then enter your full email address to associate your email address with the account.
3. Click the Connect button and then select the type of account, such as Outlook .com, in the Advanced setup window.
4. Click the Password text box, and then enter your password to verify the password to your email account.
5. Click the Retype password box, and then enter your password again to confirm your password.
6. Click the Finish button to add your email account.

To Change from the Simplified Ribbon to the Classic Ribbon

When you first open Microsoft Outlook, the **Simplified ribbon** (single-row) is displayed to dedicate more screen space to viewing your email than the traditional Classic ribbon as shown in Figure 1–4. The Simplified ribbon includes the most frequently used features. You can expand it to access the full set of commands on the Classic three-line ribbon. This module uses the full Classic ribbon. If you need to change the Simplified ribbon to Classic ribbon, you would use the following steps.

You may see a different ribbon using Office 2021 rather than Office 365.

1. Click the Ribbon Display Options arrow on the right side of the Simplified ribbon and then click Classic Ribbon to display the Classic ribbon.

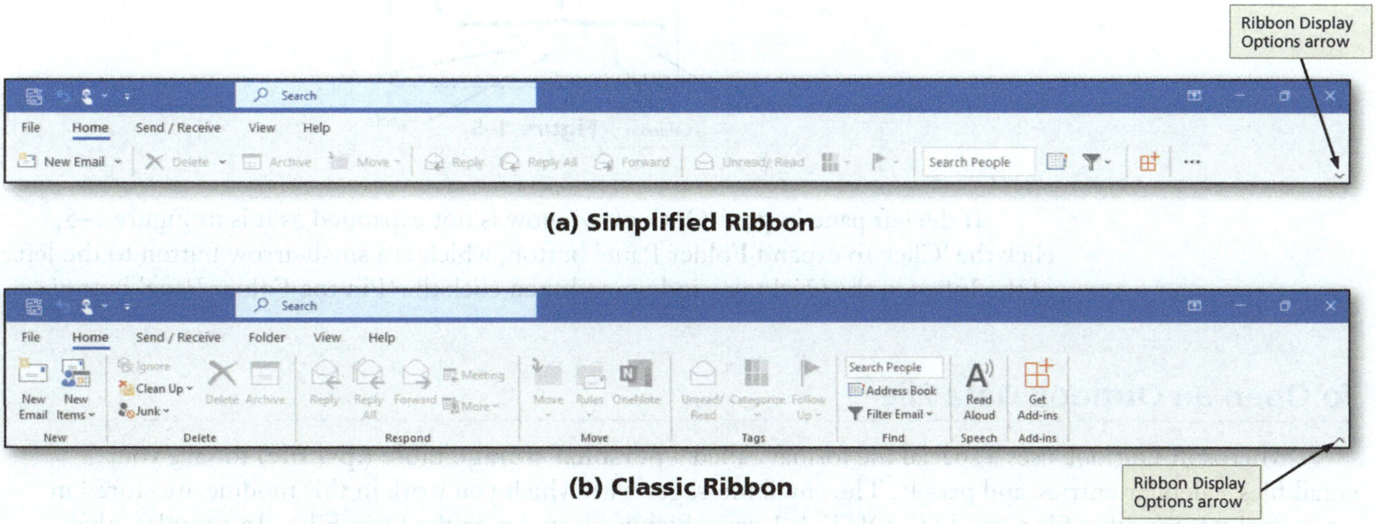

(a) Simplified Ribbon

(b) Classic Ribbon

Figure 1–4

CONSIDER THIS

How do you remove an email account in Outlook?

- Click the File tab on the ribbon.
- Click the Account Settings button, and then click Account Settings to display the Account Settings dialog box.
- Click the account you want to remove, and then click Remove.
- In the Account Settings dialog box, click the Yes button.

The Navigation Pane and Navigation Bar

The Navigation pane appears on the left side of the Outlook window and is how you switch between the different areas of Outlook, such as Mail, Calendar, People, Tasks, and Notes. The lower-left corner of the screen provides a Navigation bar that displays small icons representing Mail, Calendar, People, and Tasks as shown in Figure 1–5.

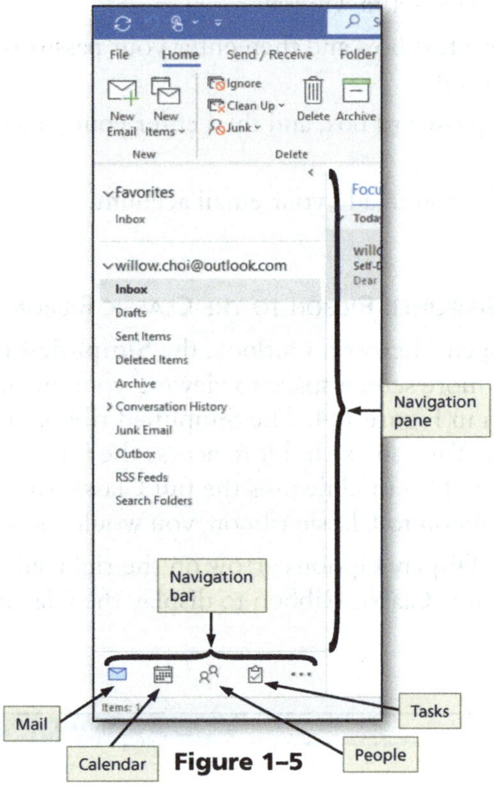

Figure 1–5

If the left pane in your Outlook window is not expanded as it is in Figure 1–5, click the 'Click to expand Folder Pane' button, which is a small arrow button to the left of the Inbox in the Outlook window, and then click the 'Pin the Folder Pane' button.

To Open an Outlook Data File

Microsoft Outlook uses a special file format called a **personal storage table (.pst file)** to save your email files, calendar entries, and people. The email messages with which you work in this module are stored in a personal storage table file named SC_OUT_1-1.pst, which is located with the Data Files. To complete this assignment, you will be required to use the Data Files. Please contact your instructor for information about accessing the Data Files. In this example, SC_OUT_1-1.pst contains a Willow mailbox and is located in the Module folder in the Outlook1 folder in the Data Files folder. The following steps open the SC_OUT_1-1 .pst file in Outlook, display the Inbox for the Willow mailbox, and then make your Willow mailbox match the figures in this module. ***Why?*** *Importing a .pst file allows you to move your email and other Outlook information to another computer.*

1

- Click File on the ribbon to open Backstage view.
- Click the Open & Export tab in Backstage view to display the Open gallery (Figure 1–6).

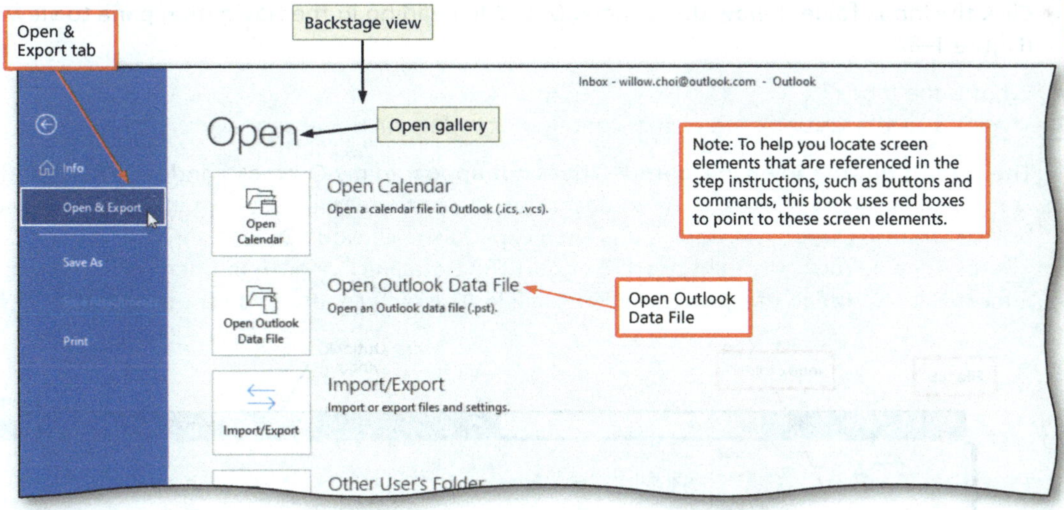

Figure 1–6

2

- Click Open Outlook Data File to display the Open Outlook Data File dialog box.
- Navigate to the mailbox location (in this case, the Module folder in the Outlook1 folder in the Data Files folder) (Figure 1–7).

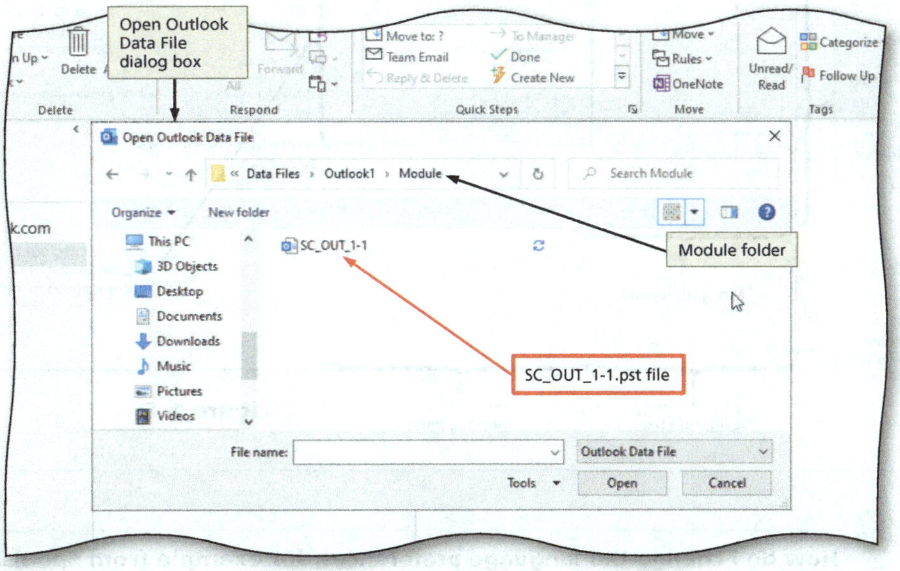

Figure 1–7

3

- Click SC_OUT_1-1.pst to select the file, and then click OK (Open Outlook Data File dialog box) to open the mailbox in your Outlook window.
- If necessary, click the right-pointing arrow next to the Outlook Data File mailbox in the Navigation pane to expand the folders.

- Click the Inbox folder below the Outlook Data File heading in the Navigation pane to view Willow's Inbox (Figure 1–8).

Q&A

What is the Inbox?
The Inbox is the Outlook folder that contains incoming email messages.

The contact photo shown in Figure 1–8 does not appear in my Outlook window. What should I do?
Outlook needs to synchronize the contact photos with the email addresses in the Willow mailbox. Click the Close button to close Outlook, restart it, and then expand the Outlook Data File in the Navigation pane to have the photos appear. You also might need to import the Data File rather than opening it. In Step 2 on this page, click Import/Export instead of Open Outlook Data File. The pictures are also part of the student files.

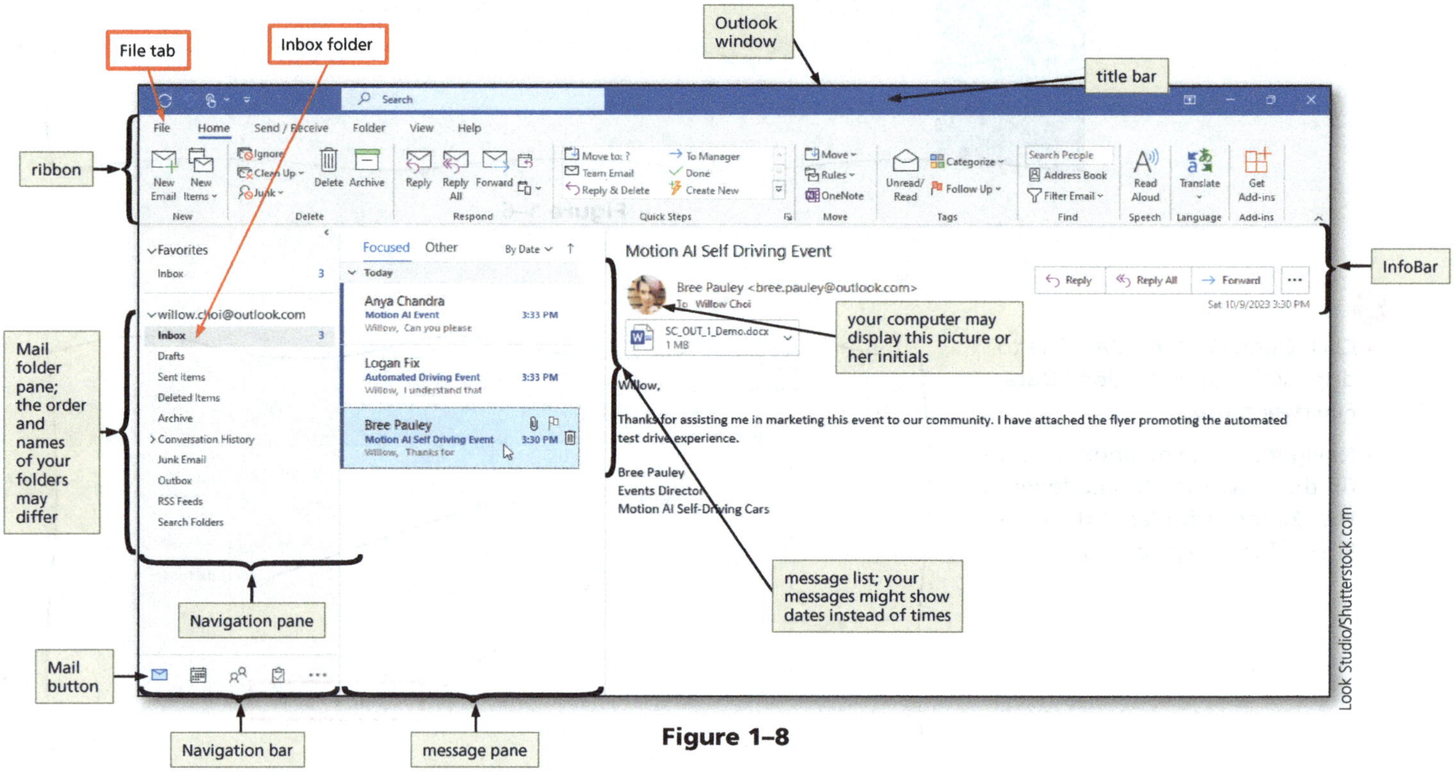

Figure 1–8

CONSIDER THIS

How do I change the language preferences, for example from Spanish to English?

- Click File on the ribbon to open Backstage view.
- Click the Options tab in Backstage view to display the Outlook Options dialog box.
- In the left pane, click Language (Outlook Options dialog box) to display the Language options.
- In the Office authoring languages and proofing section, click the 'Add a Language' button to display a list of editing languages that can be added to Outlook.
- If necessary, scroll the list and then click English (United States) to set the default editing language. Otherwise, click the Cancel button to close the list.

To Set the Sensitivity Level for All New Messages

The **Sensitivity level** of a message advises the recipient on how to treat the contents of the message. Sensitivity levels are Normal, Personal, Private, and Confidential. Changing the Sensitivity setting in the Outlook Options dialog box changes the default Sensitivity level of all messages created afterward. ***Why?*** *For example, if you set the Sensitivity level of a message to Confidential, the information should not be disclosed to anyone except the recipient.* The following steps set the default Sensitivity level.

1

- Click File on the ribbon to open Backstage view (Figure 1–9).

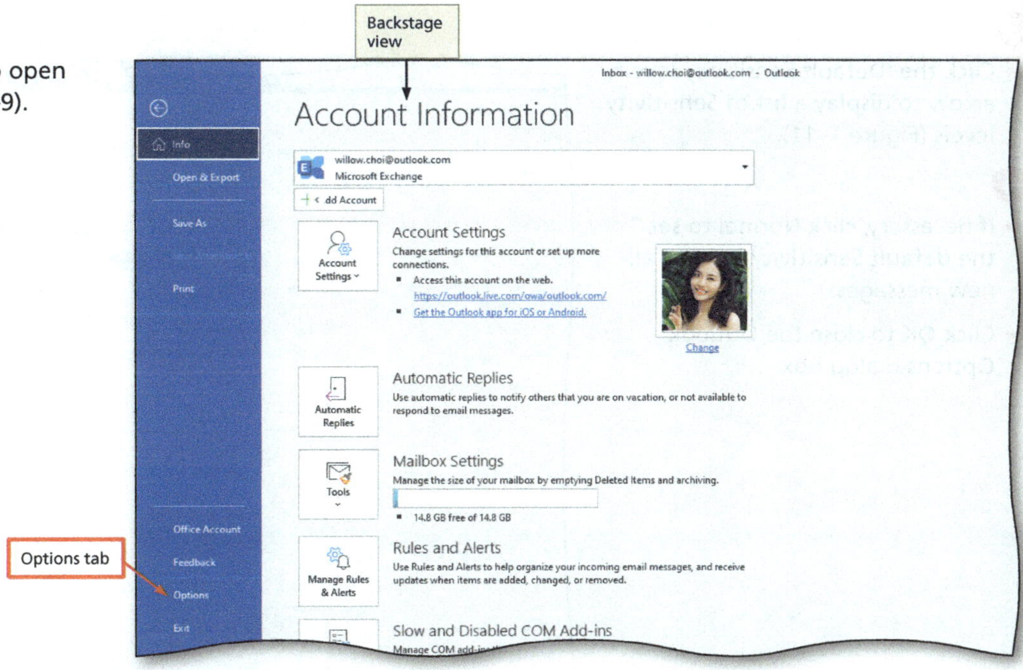

Figure 1–9

2

- Click the Options tab in Backstage view to display the Outlook Options dialog box.
- In the left pane, click Mail (Outlook Options dialog box) to display the Mail options.
- Drag the scroll bar to display the Send messages area (Figure 1–10).

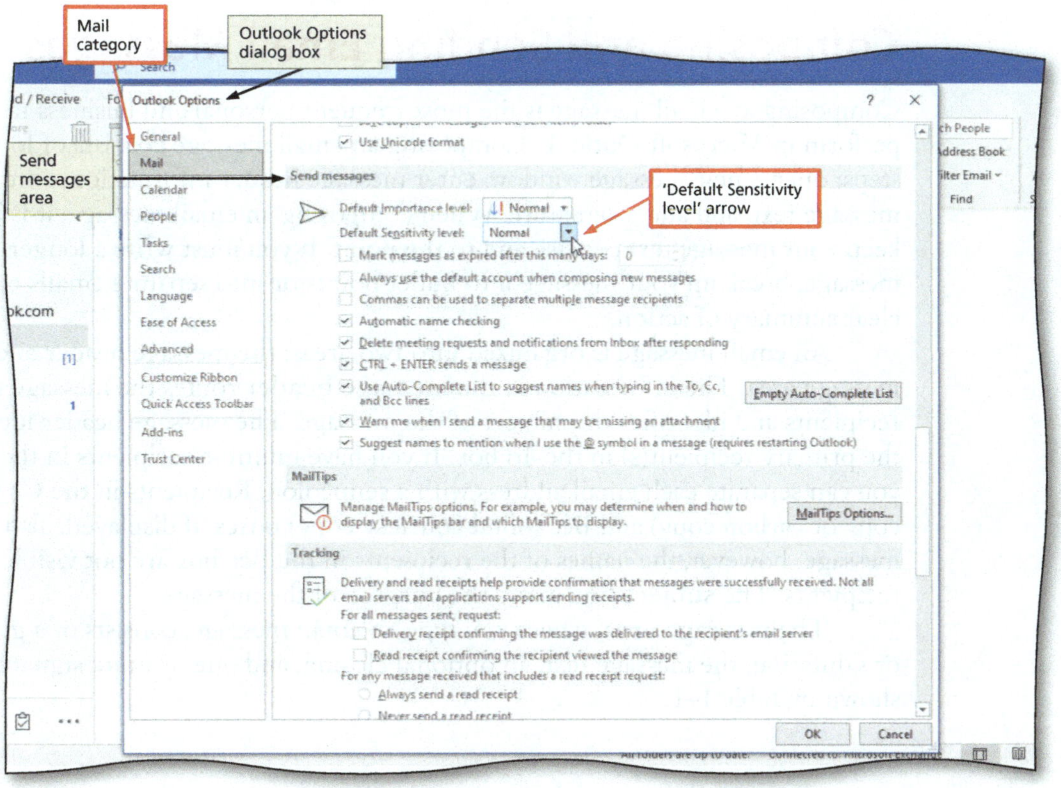

Figure 1–10

3

- Click the 'Default Sensitivity level' arrow to display a list of Sensitivity levels (Figure 1–11).

4

- If necessary, click Normal to set the default Sensitivity level of all new messages.
- Click OK to close the Outlook Options dialog box.

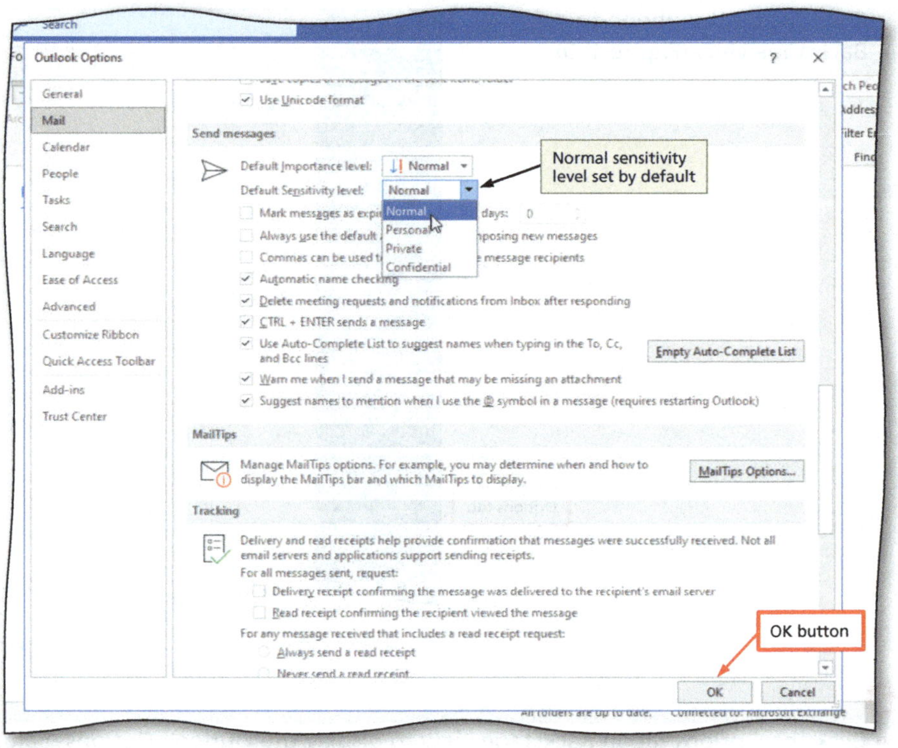

Figure 1–11

Composing and Sending Email Messages

Composing an email message is the most frequent personal and business task you perform in Microsoft Outlook. Composing an email message consists of four basic steps: open a new message window, enter message header information, enter the message text, and add a signature. When composing an email message, it is best to keep your message text concise and to the point. If you must write a longer, detailed message, break up your message into bullet points or into separate emails each with a clear summary of action.

An email message is organized into two areas: the message header and the message area. The information in the **message header** routes the message to its recipients and identifies the subject of the message. The message header identifies the primary recipient(s) in the To box. If you have multiple recipients in the To box, you can separate each email address with a semicolon. Recipients in the Cc (courtesy copy or carbon copy) and Bcc (blind courtesy copy) boxes, if displayed, also receive the message; however, the names of the recipients in the Bcc box are not visible to other recipients. The **subject line** states the purpose of the message.

The **message area**, where you type an email message, consists of a greeting line or salutation, the message text, an optional closing, and one or more signature lines as shown in Table 1–1.

Table 1–1 Message Area Parts

Part	Description
Greeting line or salutation	Sets the tone of the message and can be formal or informal, depending on the nature of the message. You can use a colon (:) or comma (,) at the end of the greeting line.
Message text	Informs the recipient or requests information.
Closing	Informs the recipient or requests information. A closing line is an end to the message using courtesy words such as *Thank you* or *Regards*. Because the closing is most appropriate for formal email messages, it is optional.
Signature line(s)	Identifies the sender and may contain additional information, such as a job title, business name, and phone number(s). In a signature, the name usually is provided on one line followed by other information listed on separate lines.

CONSIDER THIS

How can I make sure everyone can read the email messages I compose?

- Consider accessibility when composing email messages. For example, left-align message text to make sure everyone can scan the text naturally. If you include a picture, provide a caption or alt text (alternative text) that describes the image. To add alt text, select the picture, and then click the Alt Text button (Picture Format tab | Accessibility group).

To Compose an Email Message

An email message from Willow Choi, the intern at Motion AI Self-Driving Cars, requests information about the self-driving demo event from the events director, Bree Pauley. The following steps compose a new email message. ***Why?*** *Composing email messages is a direct and efficient method to connect with personal and professional contacts.*

1

- Click the New Email button (Home tab | New group) to open the Untitled – Message (HTML) window (Figure 1–12).

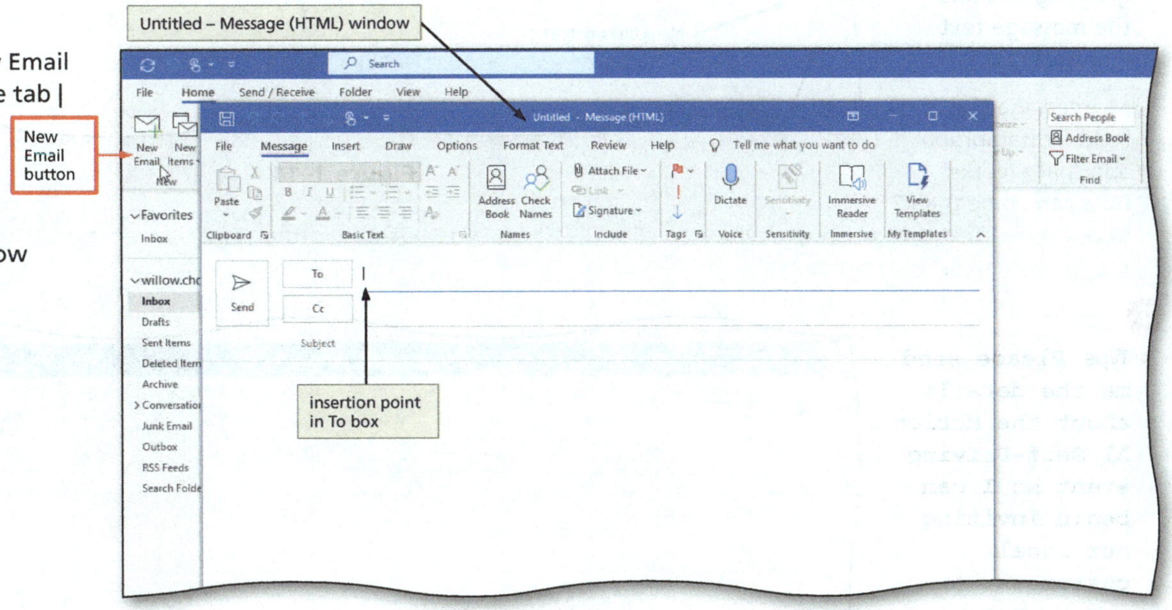

Figure 1–12

2

- Type **bree.pauley@outlook.com** (with no spaces) in the To box to enter the email address of the recipient.
- Click the Subject box, and then type **Self-Driving Demo Event** to enter the subject line.
- Press TAB to move the insertion point into the message area (Figure 1–13).

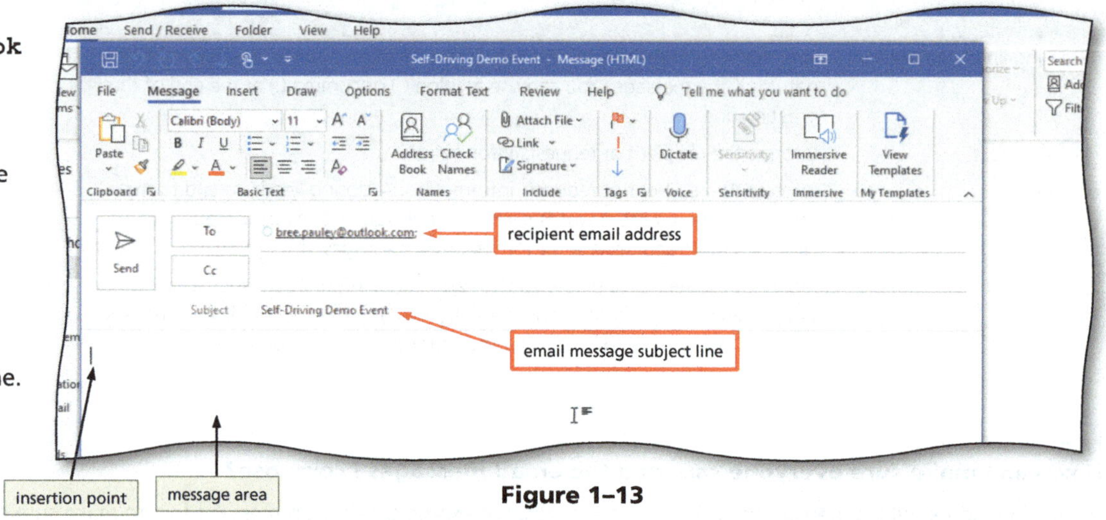

Figure 1–13

3

- Type **Dear Ms. Pauley,** as the greeting line.
- Press ENTER to move the insertion point to the beginning of the next line.
- Press ENTER again to insert a blank line between the greeting line and the message text (Figure 1–14).

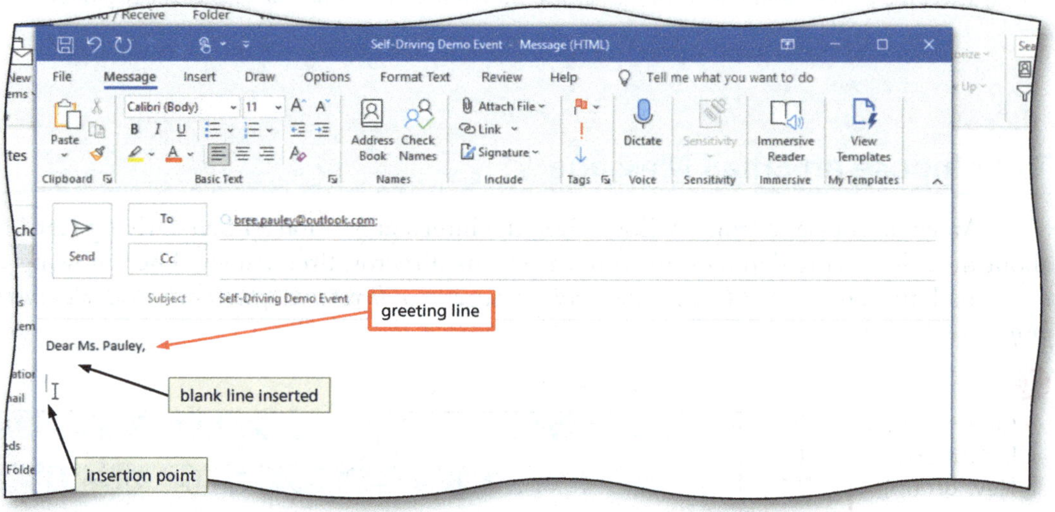

Figure 1–14

Q&A My message text includes paragraph and space marks. How can I hide them?

Click Format Text on the ribbon, and then click the Show/Hide button (Format Text tab | Paragraph group) to hide the paragraph and space marks.

4

- Type **Please send me the details about the Motion AI Self-Driving event so I can begin inviting our local customers.** to enter the message text.
- Press ENTER two times to insert a blank line below the message text (Figure 1–15).

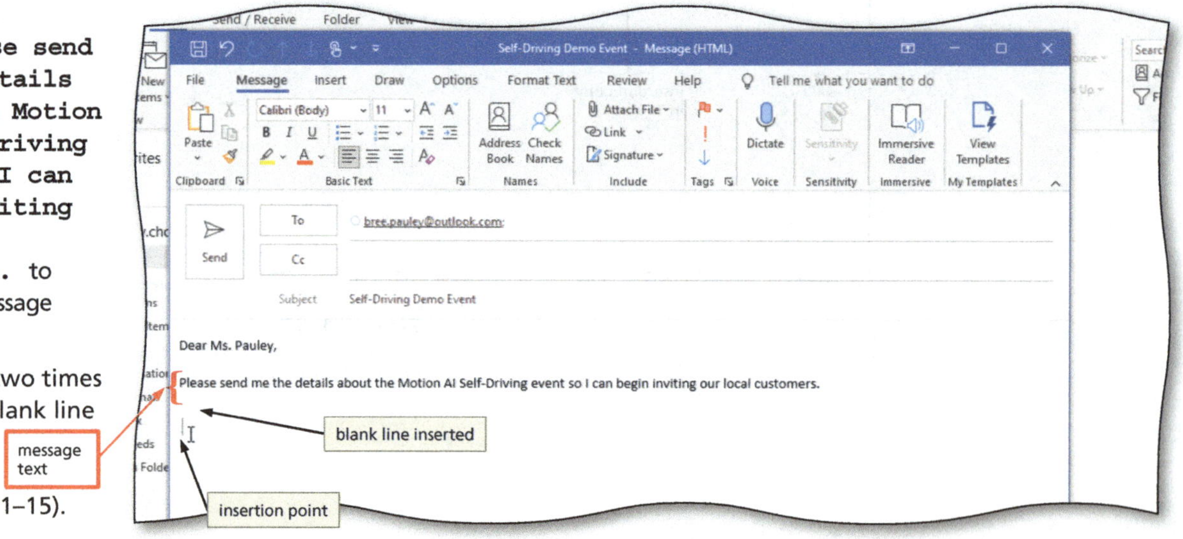

Figure 1–15

5

- Type **Thanks,** to enter the closing for the message.
- Press ENTER to move the insertion point to the next line.
- Type **Willow Choi** as the first line of the signature.
- Press ENTER to move the insertion point to the next line.
- Type **Motion AI Self-Driving Cars** as the second line of the signature.
- Press ENTER to move the insertion point to the next line.
- Type **Intern** as the third line of the signature (Figure 1–16).

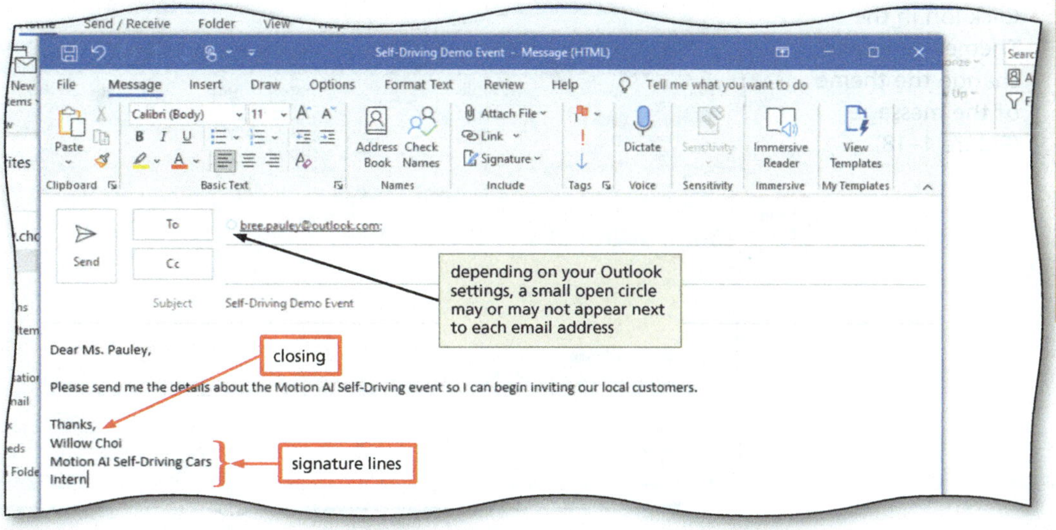

Figure 1–16

Other Ways

1. Click Inbox folder, press CTRL+N

To Apply a Theme

An Outlook theme can give an email message instant style and personality. Each theme provides a unique set of colors, fonts, and effects. The following steps apply a theme to the message. ***Why?*** *Themes give your organization's communications a modern, professional look using subtle styles.*

1

- Click Options on the ribbon to display the Options tab.
- Click the Themes button (Options tab | Themes group) to display the Themes gallery.
- Point to Ion in the Themes gallery to display a Live Preview of the theme (Figure 1–17).

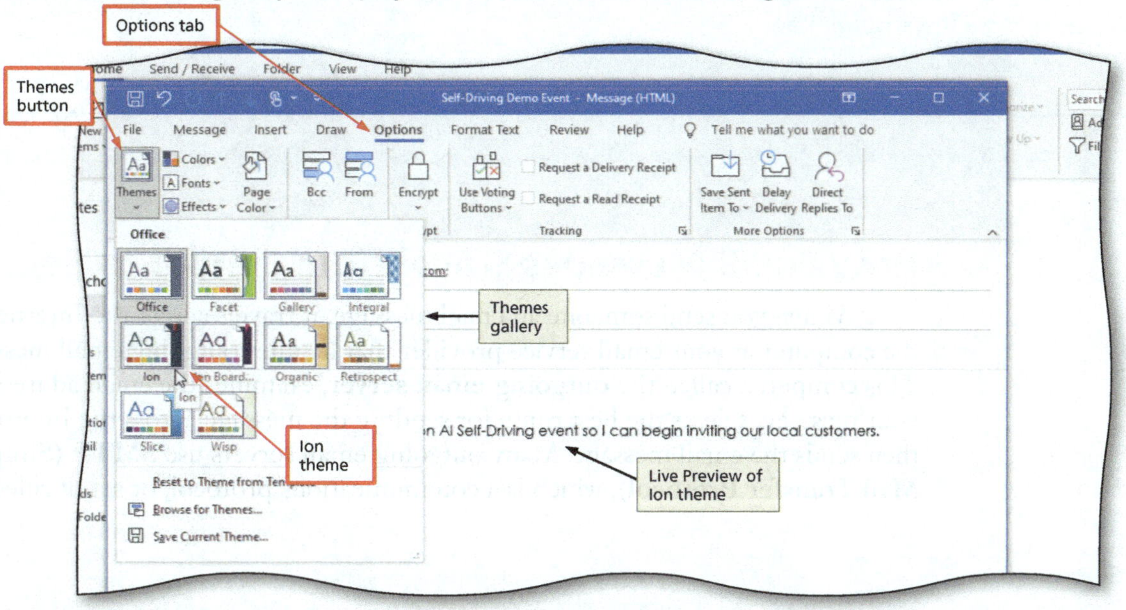

Figure 1–17

2

- Click Ion in the Themes gallery to change the theme of the message (Figure 1–18).

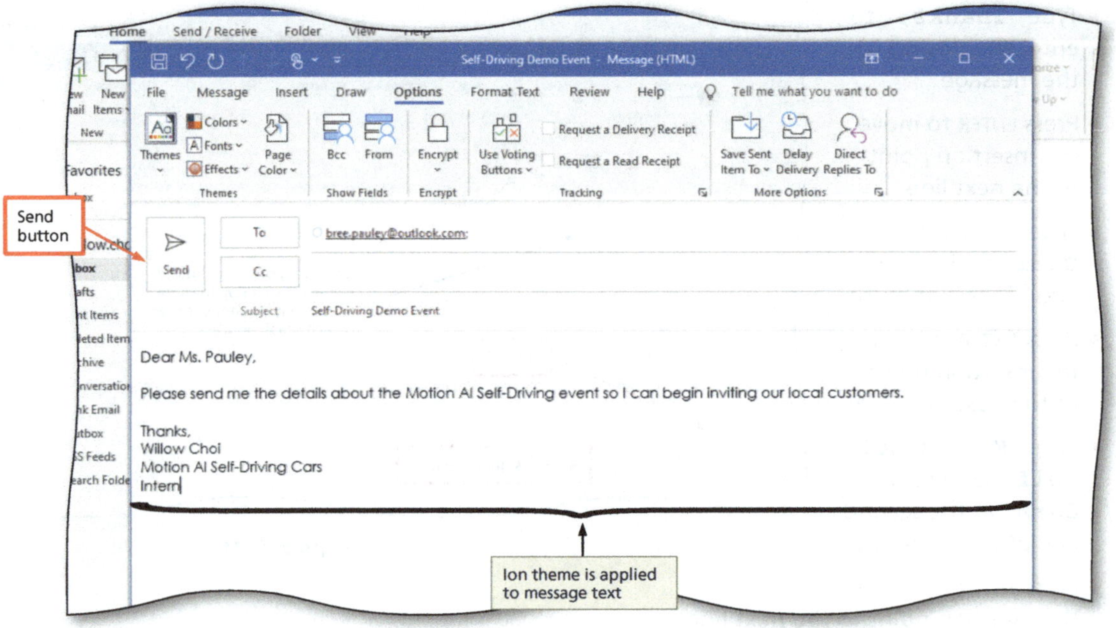

Figure 1–18

To Send an Email Message

The following step sends the completed email message to the recipient. ***Why?*** *After you complete a message, you send it to the recipient, who typically receives the message in seconds.*

1

- Click the Send button in the message header to send the email message and close the message window.

Q&A

What happened to the email message?
Outlook automatically sends email messages to their recipient(s) when you click Send in a new message window if you have your own email account set up.

Why did I get an error message that stated that 'No valid email accounts are configured. Add an account to send email'?
If you do not have an email account set up in Outlook, you cannot connect to the Internet to send the email. Click Cancel to close the error message.

Other Ways

1. Press ALT+S

How Email Messages Travel from Sender to Receiver

When you send someone an email message, it travels across the Internet to the computer at your email service provider that handles outgoing email messages. This computer, called the **outgoing email server**, examines the email address on your message, selects the best route for sending the message across the Internet, and then sends the email message. Many outgoing email servers use **SMTP (Simple Mail Transfer Protocol)**, which is a communications protocol, or set of rules for communicating with other computers. An email program such as Outlook contacts the outgoing email server and then transfers the email message(s) in its Outbox to that server. If the email program cannot contact the outgoing email server, the email message(s) remains in the Outbox until the program can connect to the server.

As an email message travels across the Internet, routers direct the email message to a computer at your recipient's email service provider that handles incoming email messages. A **router** is a device that forwards data on a network. The computer handling incoming email messages, called the incoming email server, stores the email message(s) until your recipient uses an email program such as Outlook to retrieve the email message(s). Some email servers use **POP3**, the latest version of **Post Office Protocol (POP)**, a communications protocol for incoming email, or **IMAP**, which stands for **Internet Message Access Protocol**. Figure 1–19 shows how an email message may travel from a sender to a receiver.

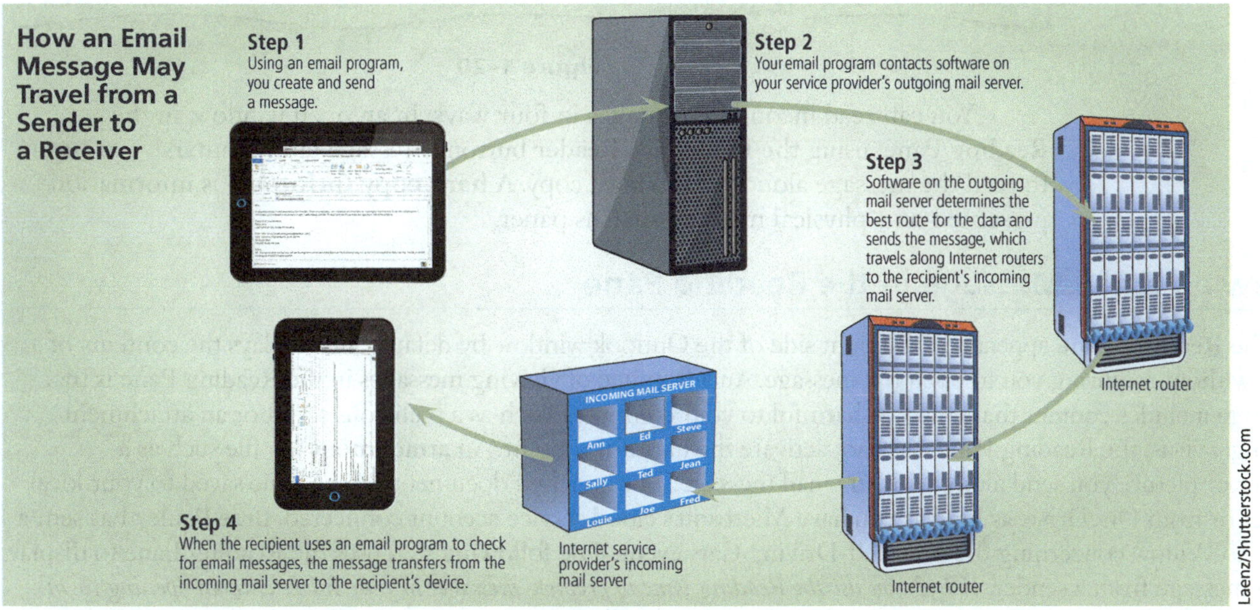

Figure 1–19

BTW

Know the Sender

If you receive an email message from someone you do not know, you should not open it because it might trigger a virus. Unsolicited email messages, known as **spam** or **junk email**, are email messages sent from an unknown sender to many email accounts, usually advertising a product or service such as low-interest loans or free credit reports. Do not click a hyperlink in an email message from an unknown sender. A **hyperlink** is a word, phrase, symbol, or picture in an email message or on a webpage that, when clicked, directs you to another document or website.

Working with Incoming Messages

When you receive email messages, Outlook directs them to your Inbox and displays them in the **message pane**, which lists the contents of the selected folder (Figure 1–20). The list of messages displayed in the message pane is called the **message list**. An unread (unopened) email message in the message list includes a blue vertical bar in front of the message and displays the subject text and time of arrival in a blue bold font. The blue number next to the Inbox folder shows how many unread messages are stored in the Inbox. The email messages on your computer may be different from those in Figure 1–20.

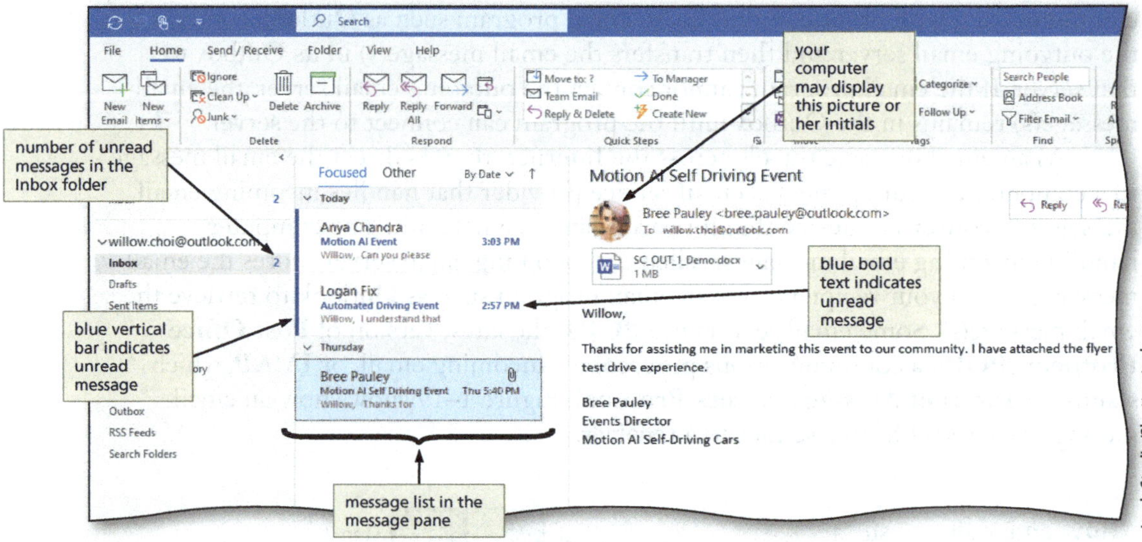

Figure 1–20

You can read incoming messages in four ways: in an open window, in the Reading Pane, using the Immersive Reader button (Message tab | Immersive group) to read the message aloud, or as a hard copy. A **hard copy (printout)** is information presented on a physical medium such as paper.

To View an Email Message in the Reading Pane

The **Reading Pane** appears on the right side of the Outlook window by default and displays the contents of a message without requiring you to open the message. An advantage of viewing messages in the Reading Pane is that if a message includes content that could be harmful to your computer, such as a malicious script or an attachment containing a virus, the Reading Pane does not activate the harmful content. An **attachment** is a file such as a document or picture you send along with an email message. The attached document can be a file saved to your local computer or from OneDrive, as long as you have Microsoft's cloud service account connected. Bree Pauley has sent a response to Willow concerning the next Self-Driving Cars event. The following step uses the Reading Pane to display an email message from a sender. ***Why?** You use the Reading Pane to preview messages in your Inbox without opening them.*

1

- Click the message header from Bree Pauley in the Inbox message list to select the email message and display its contents in the Reading Pane (Figure 1–21).

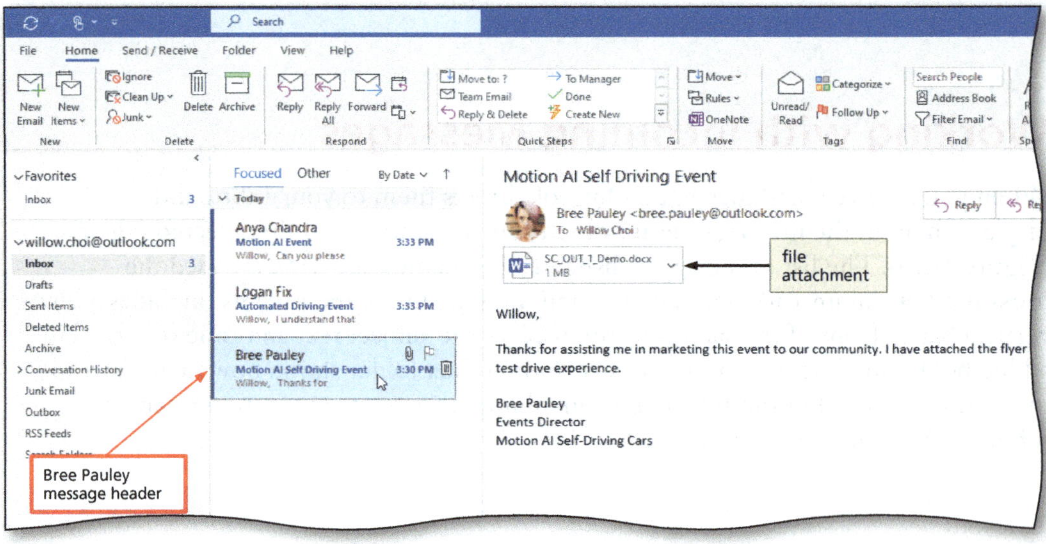

Figure 1–21

Q&A What happens to the message header when I select another message?
Outlook automatically marks messages as read after you preview the message in the Reading Pane and select another message to view. A read message is displayed in the message list without a vertical blue line or bold text.

To Open, Listen to, and Translate an Email Message in a Window

The following steps display and read aloud an email message from a sender in a window. ***Why?*** *To fully evaluate an email message and use additional Outlook tools for working with messages, you display the email message in a window.*

1

- Double-click the Bree Pauley message in the message list to display the selected email message in its own window (Figure 1–22).

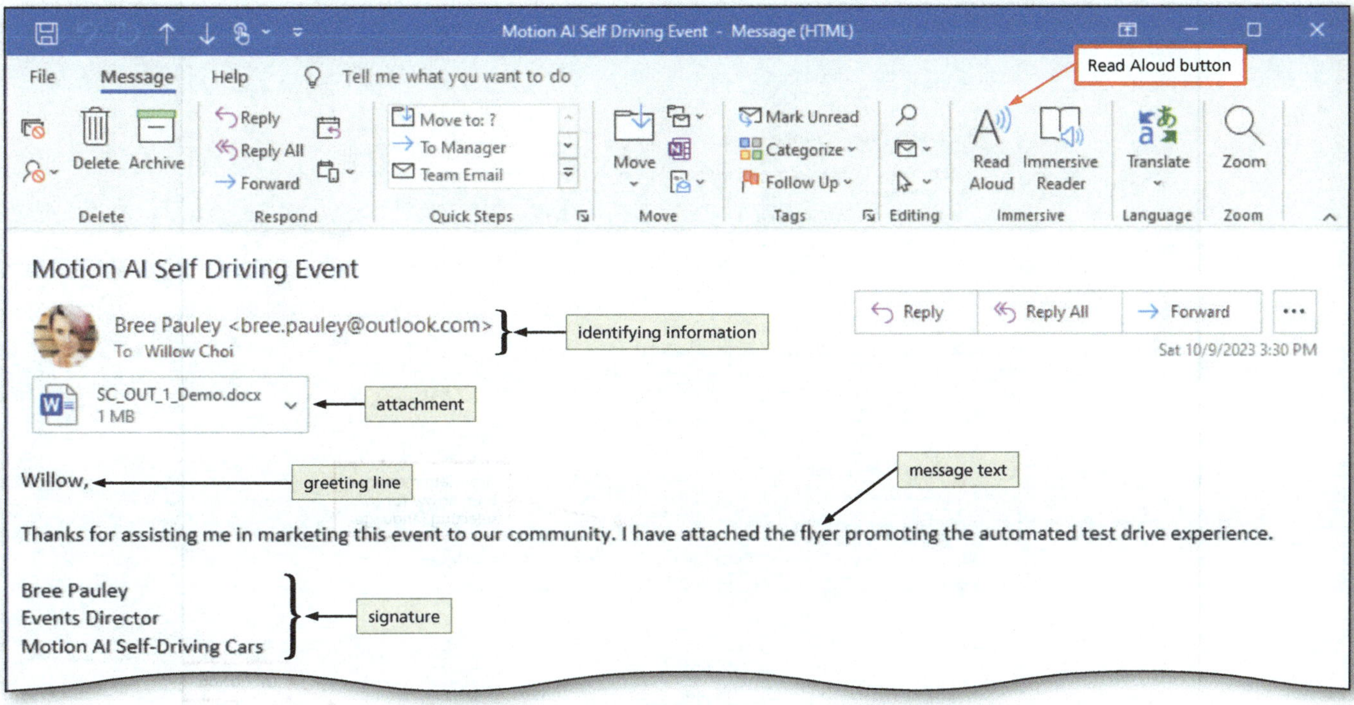

Figure 1–22

2

- Turn on your computer speakers. Click the Read Aloud button (Message tab | Immersive group) to hear the email message being read to you aloud.

3

- Click the Translate button (Message tab | Language group) to display the translate options (Figure 1–23).

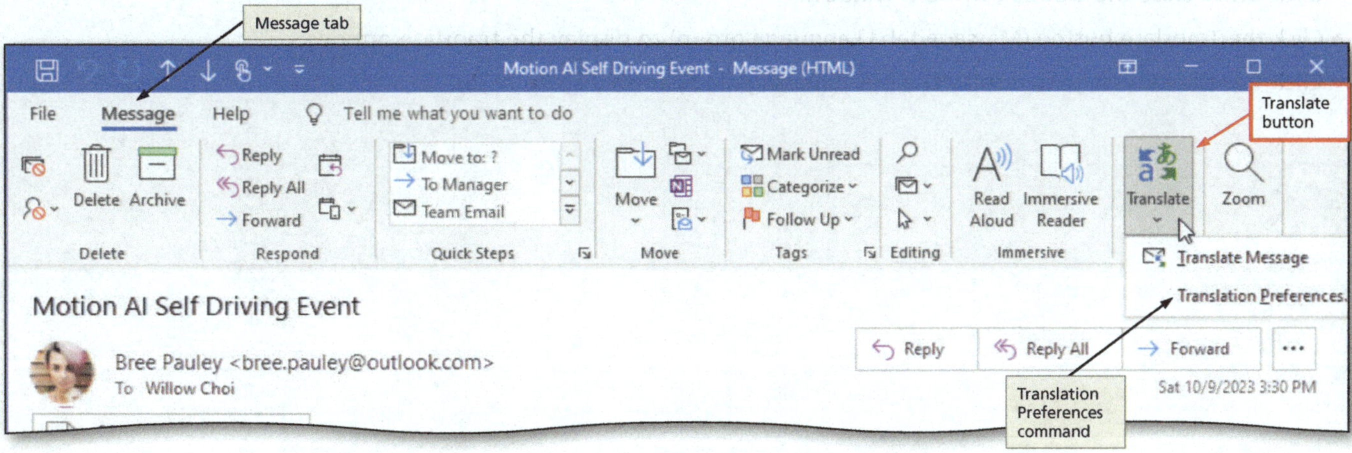

Figure 1–23

4

- Click Translation Preferences to open the Outlook Options window (Figure 1–24).

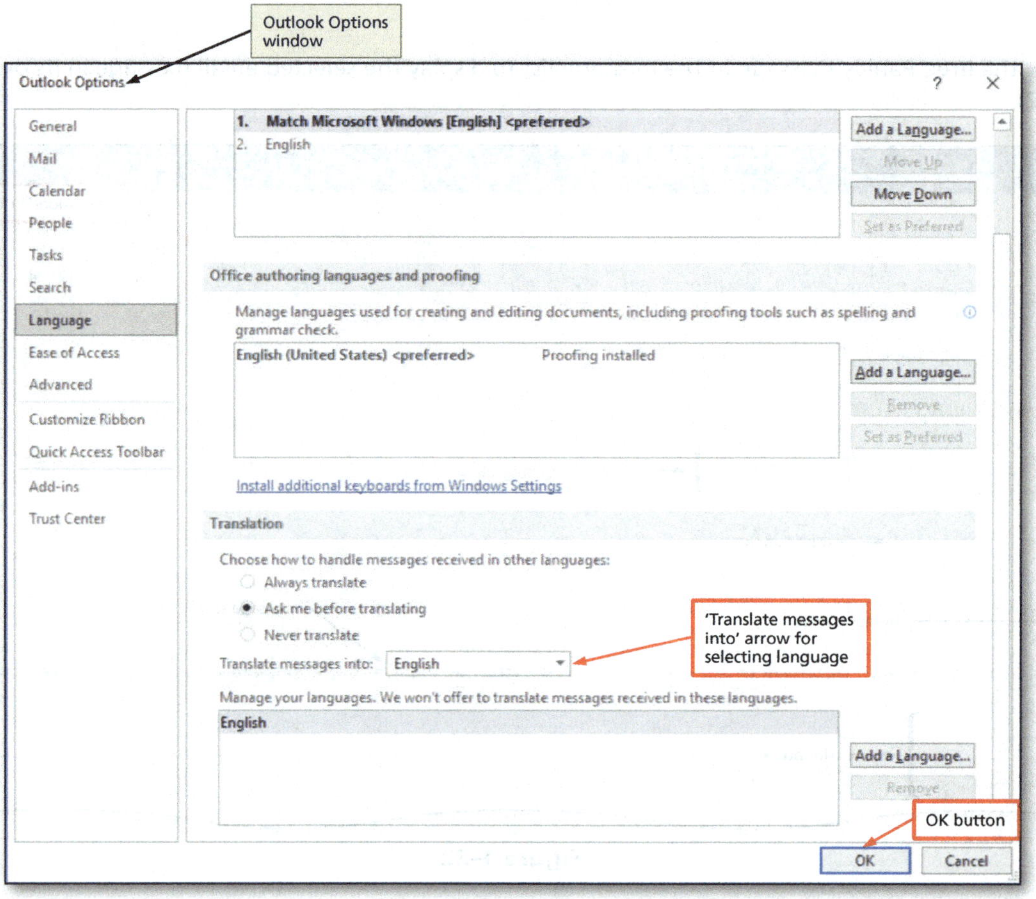

Figure 1–24

5

- Click the 'Translate messages into' arrow to display a list of languages that can be added to Outlook.
- If necessary, scroll the list and then click Spanish to add the Spanish language for translation purposes.
- Click OK to close the Outlook Options window.
- Click the Translate button (Message tab | Language group) to display the translate options.
- Click Translate Message to display the email message in Spanish (Figure 1–25).

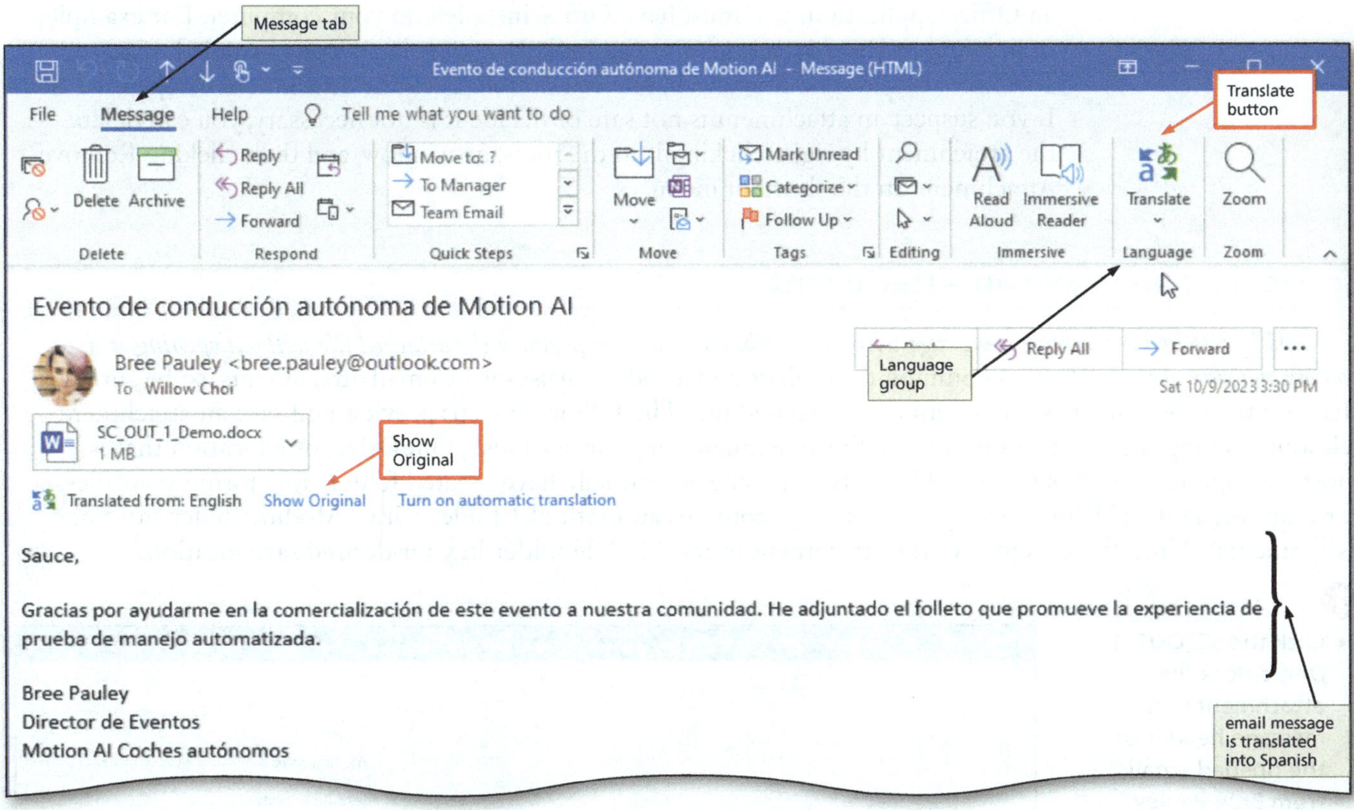

Figure 1–25

6

- Click Show Original to return the message back to English.

Opening Attachments

Email messages that include attachments are identified by a paper clip icon in the message list. Users typically attach a file to an email message to provide additional information to the recipient. An attachment in a message can appear in a line below the subject line or in the message body. To help protect your computer, Outlook does not allow you to receive files as attachments if they are a certain file type, such as .exe (executable) or .js (JavaScript), because of their potential for introducing a virus into your computer. When Outlook blocks a suspicious attachment in a message, the blocked file appears in the InfoBar at the top of your message. An **InfoBar** is a banner displayed at the top of an email message that indicates whether an email message has been replied to or forwarded.

The **Attachment Preview** feature in Outlook allows you to preview an attachment you receive in an email message from either the Reading Pane in an unopened message or the message area of an opened message. Outlook has built-in previewers for several file types, such as other Office programs, pictures, text, and webpages. Outlook includes attachment previewers that work with other Microsoft Office programs so that users can preview an attachment without opening it. These attachment previewers are turned on by default. To preview an attached file created in an Office application, you must have Office installed on your computer. For example, to preview an Excel attachment in Outlook, you must have Excel installed. If an attachment cannot be previewed, you can double-click the attachment to open the file. If you suspect an attachment is not safe or decide it is not necessary, you can delete the attachment by right-clicking it in the message window, and then clicking Remove Attachment on the shortcut menu.

To Preview and Save an Attachment

Why? *When you receive a message with an attachment, you can preview the attached file without opening it if you are not sure of the contents.* A common transmission method of viruses is by email attachments, so be sure that you trust the sender before opening an attached file. The following steps preview and save an attachment without opening the file. You should save the attachment on your hard disk, OneDrive, or a location that is most appropriate to your situation. These steps assume you already have created folders for storing your files, for example, a CIS 101 folder (for your class) that contains an Outlook1 folder with a Module folder (for your assignments). Thus, these steps save the attachment in the Module folder in your desired save location.

1

- Click the SC_OUT_1_Demo.docx file attachment in the message header of the opened email from Bree Pauley to preview the attachment within Outlook (Figure 1–26).

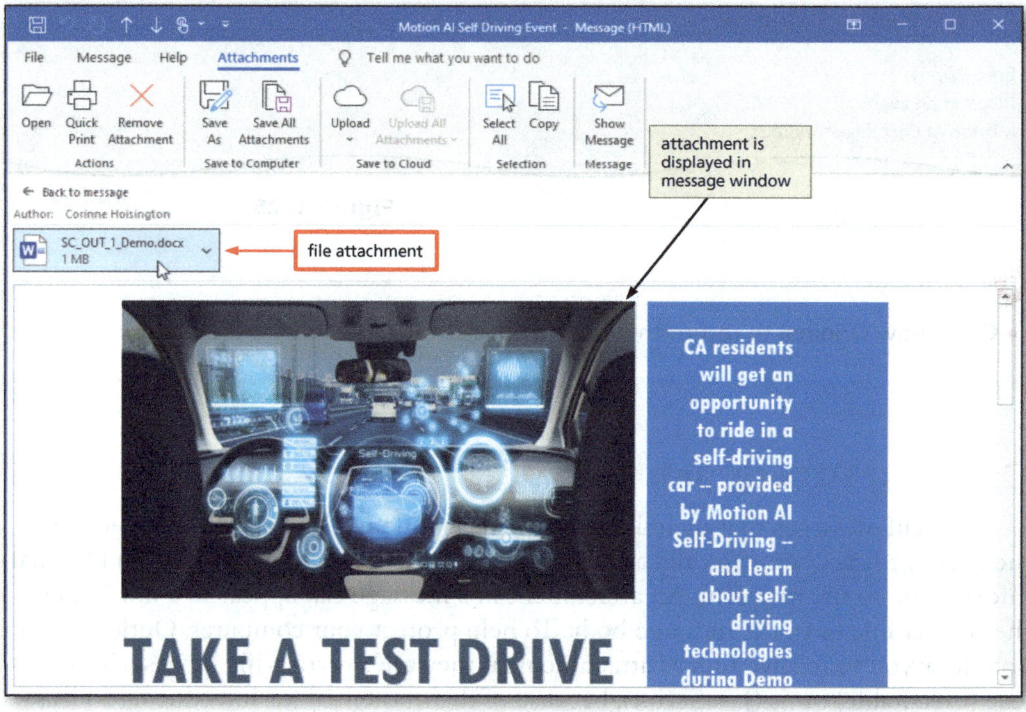

metamorworks/Shutterstock.com

Figure 1–26

2

- Click the Save As button (Attachments tab | Save to Computer group) to display the Save Attachment dialog box.
- Navigate to the desired save location (in this case, the Module folder in your Outlook1 folder or your class folder on your computer or OneDrive).
- Change the file name to `SC_OUT_1_Event`, and, if requested by your instructor, add your last name to the end of the file name (Figure 1–27).

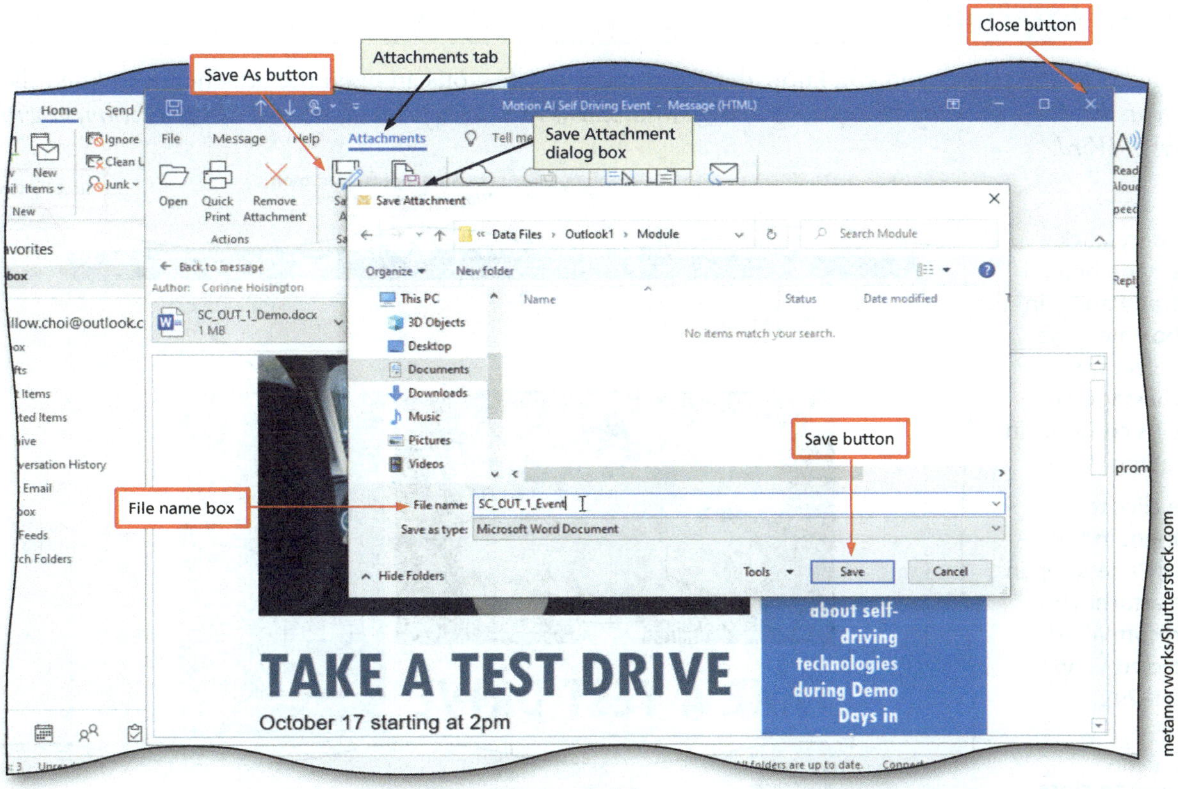

metamorworks/Shutterstock.com

Figure 1–27

3

- Click the Save button (Save Attachment dialog box) to save the document in the selected folder in the selected location with the entered file name.
- Click Close to close the attachment preview window and email message (Figure 1–28).

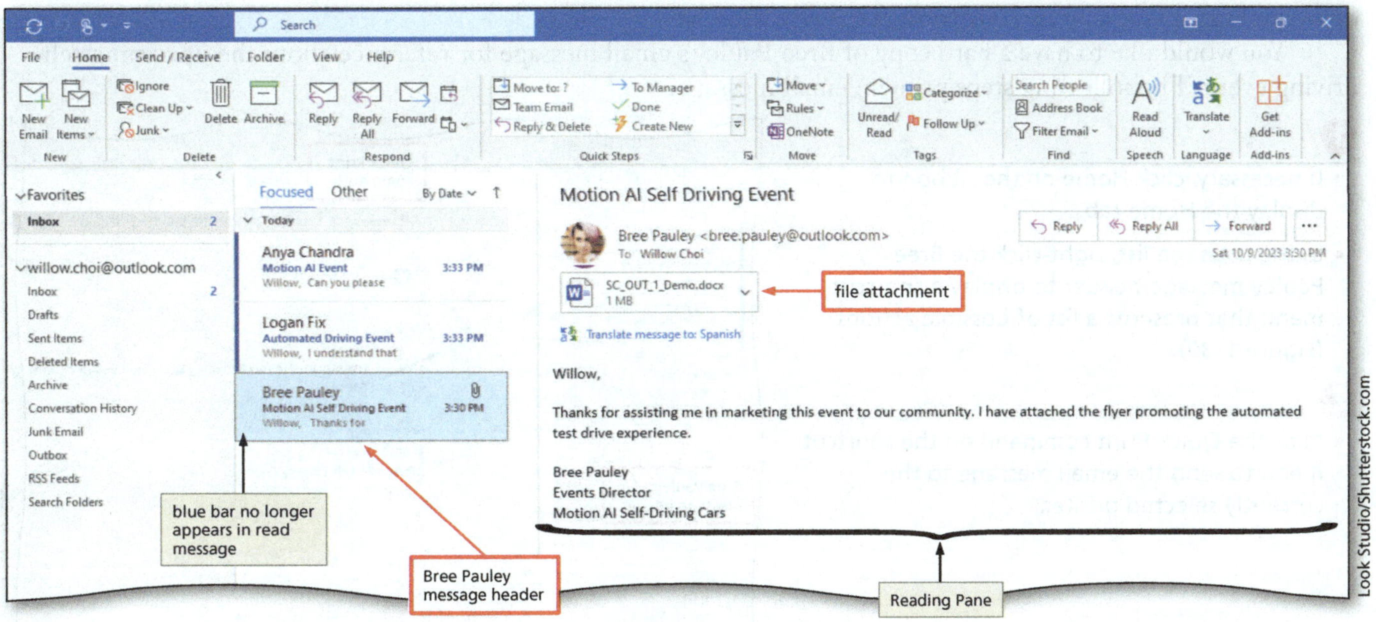

Look Studio/Shutterstock.com

Figure 1–28

To Open an Attachment

If you know the sender and you know the attachment is safe, you can open the attached file. The following steps open an attachment. ***Why?*** *By opening a Word attachment in Microsoft Word, you can edit the document with the full features of Word.*

1

- If necessary, click the message header from Bree Pauley in the Inbox message list to select the email message and display its contents in the Reading Pane.
- Double-click the attachment in the Reading Pane to open the file attachment in Microsoft Word in Protected View (Figure 1–29).

2

- Click Close to close the Word file.

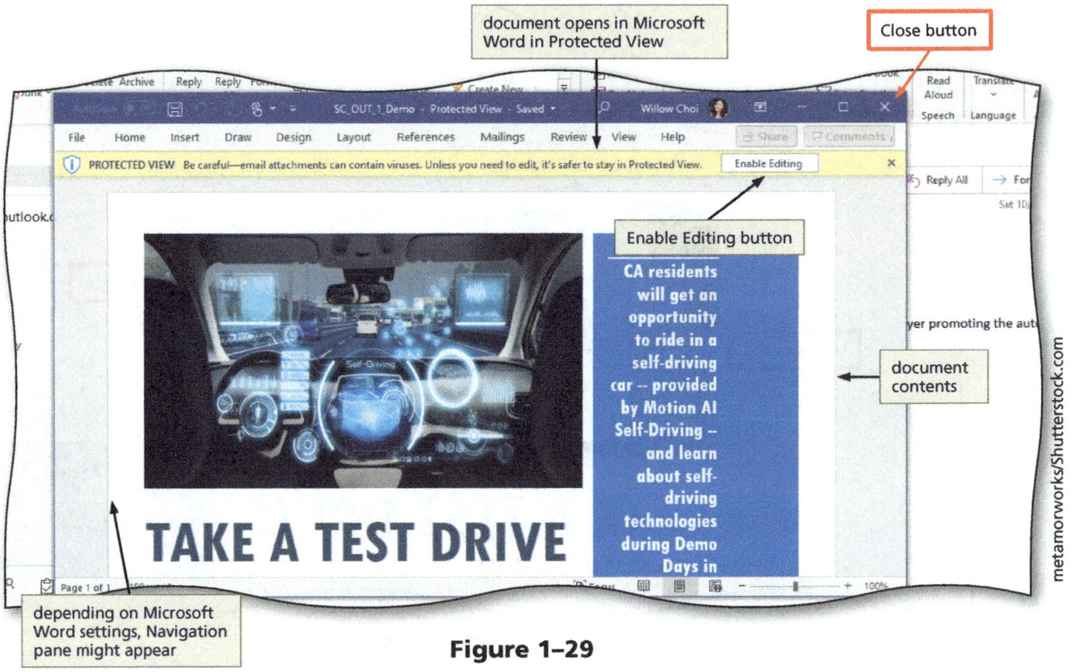

Figure 1–29

To Print an Email Message

Occasionally, you may want to print the contents of an email message. ***Why?*** *A hard copy of an email message can serve as reference material if your storage medium becomes corrupted and you need to view the message when your computer is not readily available.* A printed copy of an email message also serves as a **backup**, which is an additional copy of a file or message that you store for safekeeping. You can print the contents of an email message from an open message window or directly from the Inbox window.

You would like to have a hard copy of Bree Pauley's email message for reference about the upcoming self-driving event. The following steps print an email message.

1

- If necessary, click Home on the ribbon to display the Home tab.
- In the message list, right-click the Bree Pauley message header to display a shortcut menu that presents a list of possible actions (Figure 1–30).

2

- Click the Quick Print command on the shortcut menu to send the email message to the currently selected printer.

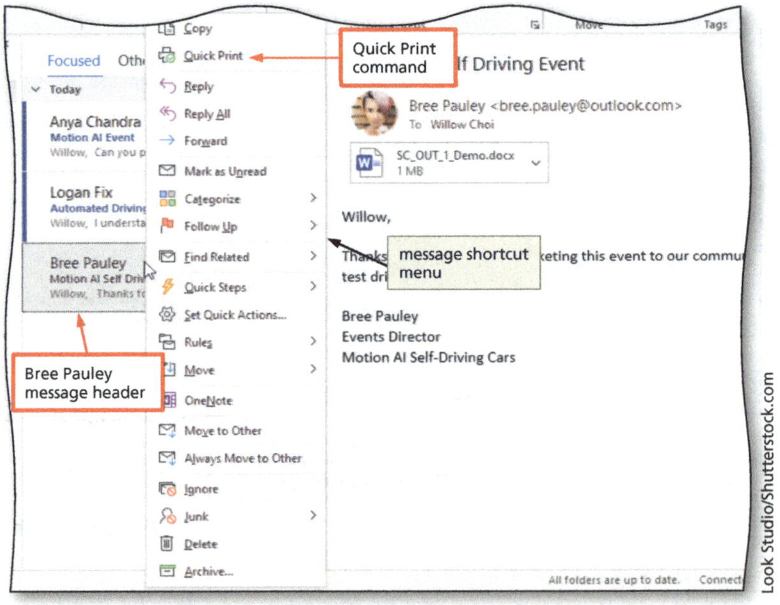

Figure 1–30

CONSIDER THIS

How do I reposition the Reading Pane using the Search tool?

- Click the Search box on the title bar, and then type **Reading Pane**.
- Click the Reading Pane matching text option to display the Reading Pane options.
- Click Bottom in the Reading Pane options to place the Reading Pane for all mail folders at the bottom of the window.
- Using the ribbon, click the Reading Pane button (View tab | Layout group) to display the Reading Pane gallery.
- Click Right in the Reading Pane gallery to return the Reading Pane to the right side of the Outlook window for all mail folders.

Responding to Messages

When you receive a message, you can send a reply to the sender. You also have the option to forward the message to additional people.

CONSIDER THIS

How should a formal business response differ from a close friend's response?

- An email response you send to an instructor, coworker, or client should be more formal than the one you send to a close friend. For example, conversational language to a friend, such as "Can't wait to hang out!" is not appropriate in professional email messages.
- A formal email message should be businesslike and get to the point quickly. An informal email is more conversational and friendly.
- Most professionals are required to sign a contract with their employer that states that the company has the right to access anything on the employee's work computer, so do not send personal email messages using company email services.
- All standard grammar rules apply, such as punctuation, capitalization, and spelling, no matter the audience.

When responding to email messages, you have three options in Outlook: Reply, Reply All, or Forward. Table 1–2 lists the response options and their actions.

Table 1–2 Outlook Response Options

Response Option	Action
Reply	Opens the RE: reply window and sends a reply to the person who sent the message.
Reply All	Opens the RE: reply window and sends a reply to everyone listed in the message header.
Forward	Opens the FW: message window and sends a copy of the selected message to additional people, if you want to share information with others. The original message text is included in the message window.

You reply to messages you already have received. You can forward an email message to additional recipients to share information with others. Based on the situation, you should request permission from the sender before forwarding a message in case the sender intended the original message to remain private. When forwarding, you send the message to someone other than the original sender of the message. A reply sends the message to the person who sent the message.

To Reply to an Email Message

When you reply to an email message, the email address of the sender is inserted in the To box automatically. If you select Reply All, the To box automatically includes the sender and the other people who originally received the message (except for those who originally received a Bcc message).

In an email message, a local instructor named Logan Fix has requested that Willow send information about the self-driving event. The following steps reply to an email message. ***Why?*** *When replying to a colleague, responding in a professional manner in an email message indicates how serious you are about your role and enhances your reputation within the organization.*

1

- Click Home on the ribbon to display the Home tab.
- Click the Logan Fix message header in the message list to select it and display its contents in the Reading Pane (Figure 1–31).

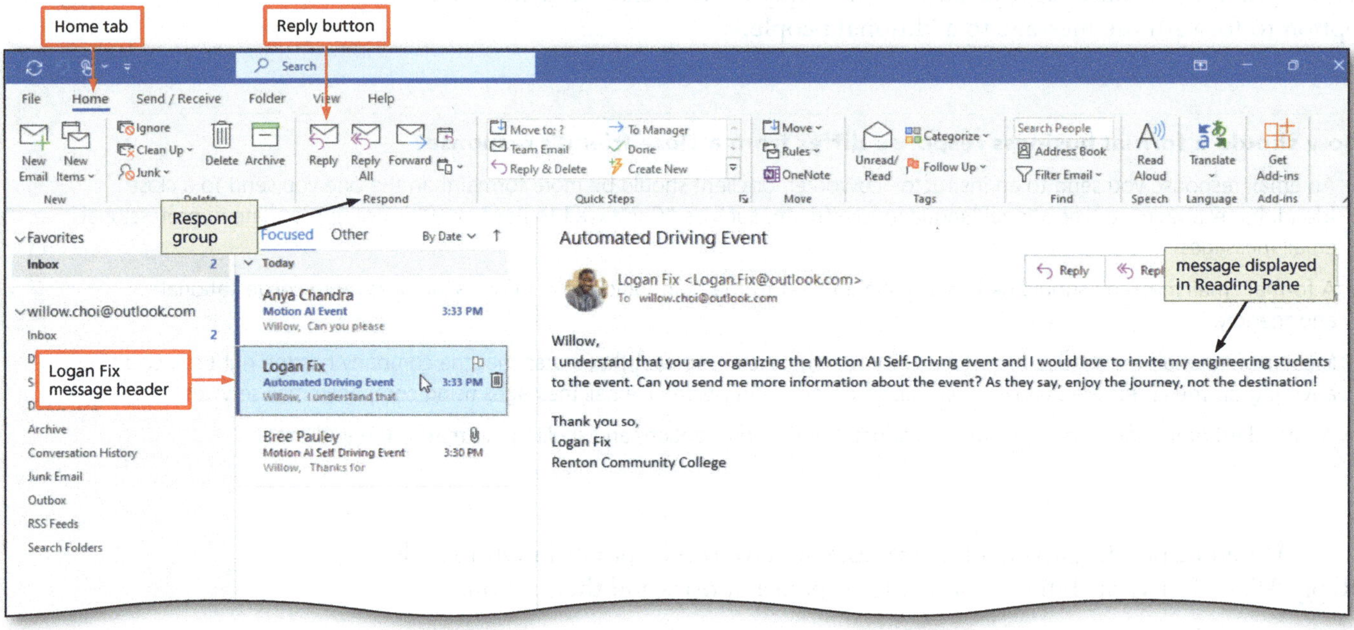

Monkey Business Images/Shutterstock.com

Figure 1–31

2

- Click the Reply button (Home tab | Respond group) to reply to the message in the Reading Pane (Figure 1–32).

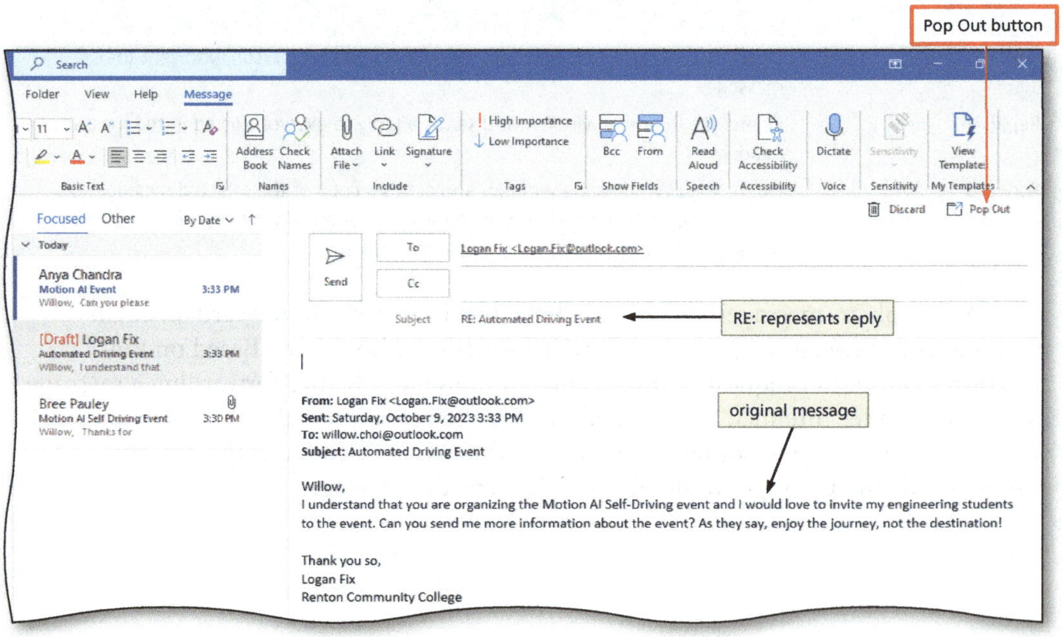

Figure 1–32

3

- Click the Pop Out button to display the RE: Automated Driving Event - Message (HTML) window (Figure 1–33).

Q&A Why does RE: appear at the beginning of the subject line and in the title bar?
The RE: indicates this message is a reply to another message. The subject of the original message appears after the RE:.

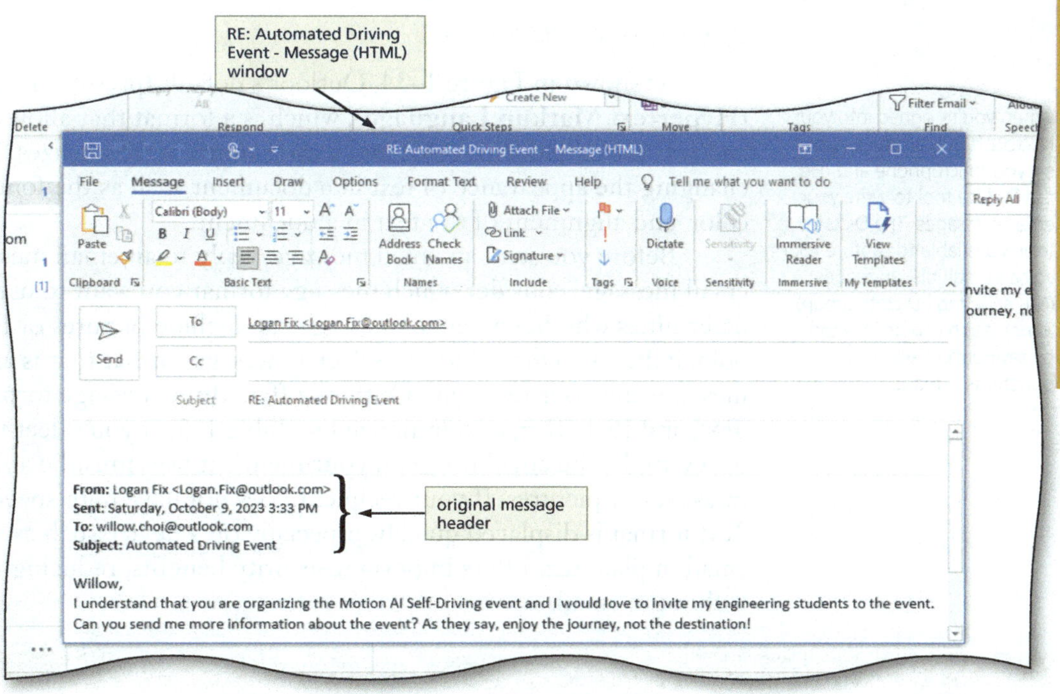

Figure 1–33

4

- If necessary, click the message area below the message header to position the insertion point at the top of the message area.
- Type **`Logan,`** as the greeting line.
- Press ENTER two times to insert a blank line between the greeting line and the message text.
- Type **`As you requested, I have attached a flyer that Ms. Pauley recently sent me about the upcoming Motion AI event.`** to enter the message text.
- Press ENTER two times to insert a blank line between the message text and the closing.
- Type **`Thanks for your interest,`** as the closing, and then press ENTER to move the insertion point to the next line.
- Type **`Willow Choi`** as signature line 1, and then press ENTER to move the insertion point to the next line.
- Type **`Motion AI Self-Driving Cars`** as signature line 2, and then press ENTER to move the insertion point to the next line.
- Type **`Intern`** as signature line 3 (Figure 1–34).

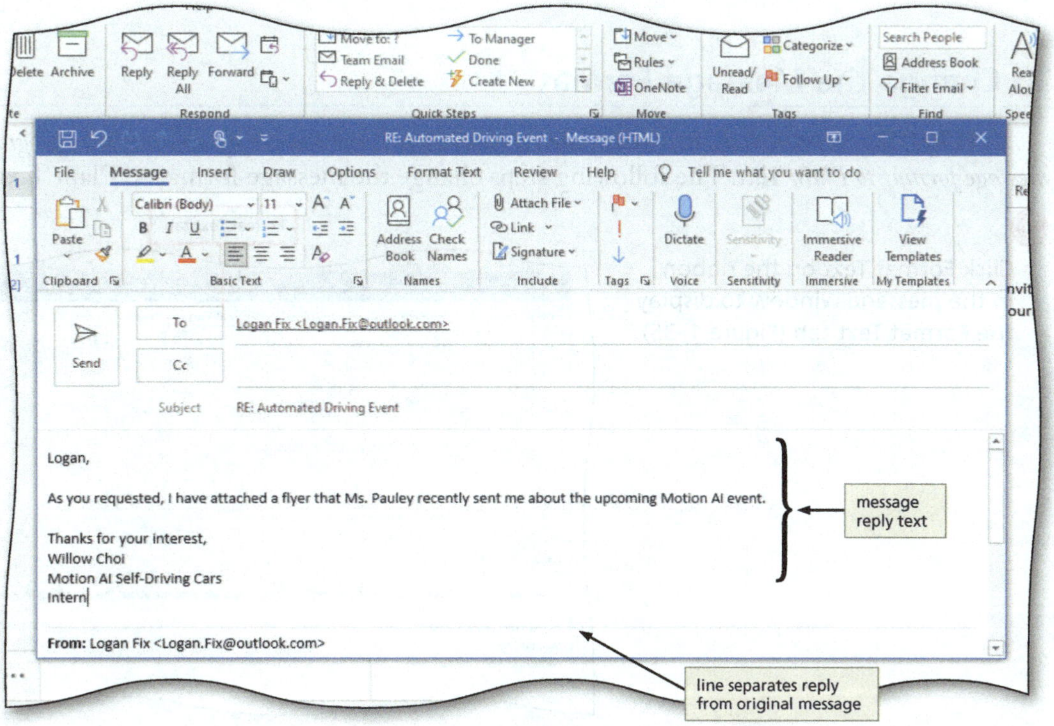

Figure 1–34

BTW
Dictating Email Messages
When you're signed into your Microsoft 365 account, turn on your microphone and use the Dictate tool to write your email messages. The Dictate tool is available to capture your voice in multiple languages (Message tab | Dictate group). Punctuation can be inserted by saying the name of the punctuation mark.

Message Formats

As shown in Figure 1–34, Outlook's default (preset) message format is **HTML (Hypertext Markup Language)**, which is a format that allows you to view pictures and text formatted with color and various fonts and font sizes. **Formatting** refers to changing the appearance of text in a document such as the font (typeface), font size, color, and alignment of the text in a document.

Before you send an email message, reply to an email message, or forward an email message, consider which message format you want to use. A **message format** determines whether an email message can include pictures or formatted text, such as bold, italic, and colored fonts. Select a message format that is appropriate for your message and your recipient. Outlook offers three message formats: HTML, Plain Text, and Rich Text, as summarized in Table 1–3. If you select the HTML format, for example, the email program your recipient uses must be able to display formatted messages or pictures. If your recipient does not have high speed connectivity, a Plain Text format is displayed quickly, especially on a device such as a smartphone. Reading email in plain text offers important security benefits, reducing the possibility of a virus within the email.

Table 1–3 Message Formats

Message Format	Description
HTML	HTML is the default format for new messages in Outlook. HTML lets you include pictures and basic formatting, such as text formatting, numbering, bullets, and alignment. HTML is the recommended format for Internet mail because the more popular email programs use it.
Plain Text	Plain Text format is recognized by all email programs and is the most likely format to be allowed through a company's virus-filtering program. Plain Text does not support basic formatting, such as bold, italic, colored fonts, or other text formatting. It also does not support pictures displayed directly in the message.
Rich Text	Rich Text Format (RTF) is a Microsoft format that only the latest versions of **Microsoft Exchange** (a Microsoft message system that includes an email program and a mail server) and Outlook recognize. RTF supports more formats than HTML or Plain Text; it also supports hyperlinks. A hyperlink can be text, a picture, or other object that is displayed in an email message.

To Change the Message Format

***Why?** You want to make sure that your reply message is not blocked by an antivirus program, so you will change the message format to Plain Text.* The following steps change the message format to Plain Text.

1

- Click Format Text on the ribbon in the message window to display the Format Text tab (Figure 1–35).

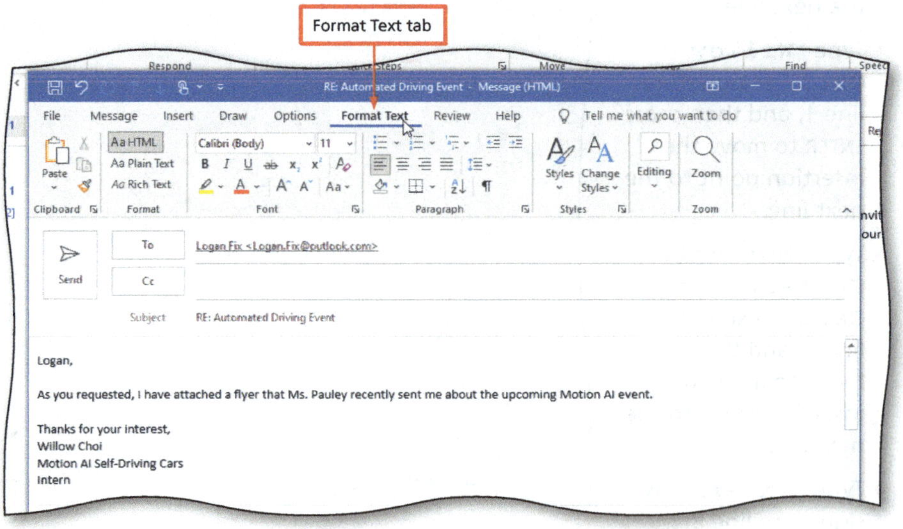

Figure 1–35

2

- Click the Plain Text button (Format Text tab | Format group) to select the Plain Text message format, which removes all formatting in the message.
- When the Microsoft Outlook Compatibility Checker dialog box is displayed, click the Continue button to change the formatted text to plain text (Figure 1–36).

Q&A What happened to the line separating the existing message and the new message?
When Plain Text is selected as the message format, all formatting such as text color, font type, lines, themes, and size is removed.

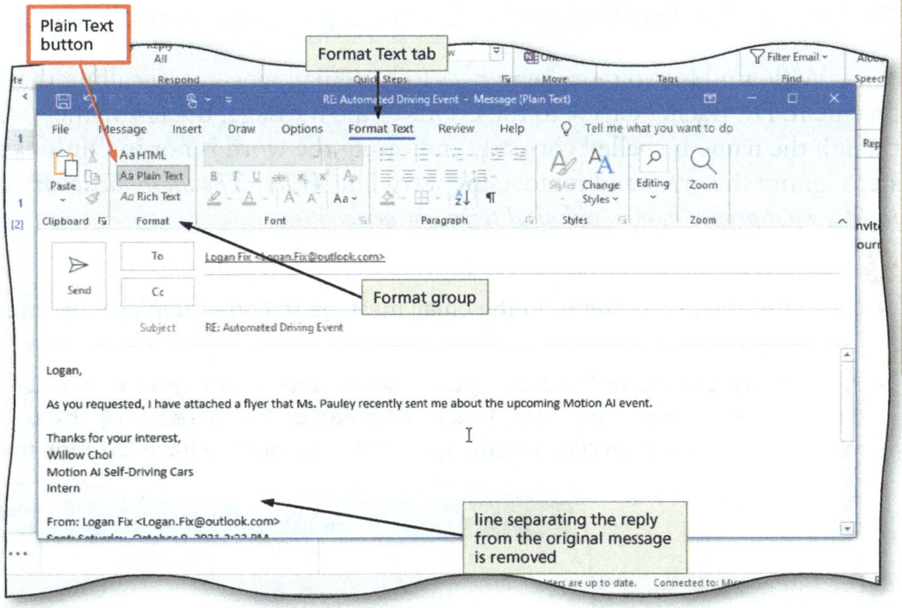

Figure 1–36

Checking Spelling and Grammar

Outlook checks your message for possible spelling and grammar errors as you type and flags any potential errors in the message text. A wavy underline means the flagged text is not in Outlook's main dictionary because it is a proper name or misspelled. A double underline indicates the text may be incorrect grammatically or that the text may contain a contextual spelling error such as the misuse of homophones (words that are pronounced the same but have different spellings or meanings, such as one and won). Although you can check the entire message for spelling and grammar errors at once, you also can check these flagged errors as they appear on the screen.

A flagged word is not necessarily misspelled. For example, many names, abbreviations, and specialized terms are not in Outlook's main dictionary. In these cases, you instruct Outlook to ignore the flagged word. As you type, Outlook also detects duplicate words while checking for spelling errors. For example, if your email message contains the phrase *to the the store*, Outlook places a wavy underline below the second occurrence of the word, *the*.

BTW
Misspelled Words in an Email Message
When you misspell words in a professional email message, your clients may think you are just sending a quick message and not giving the email your full attention when responding.

BTW
Original Message in Replies
Many email users prefer to reply to a message without including the original email message along with their response. To remove the original message from all email replies, click File to open Backstage view, and then click the Options tab. Click Mail to display the Mail options. In the Replies and forwards section, click the 'When replying to a message box' arrow, select the 'Do not include original message' option, and then click OK.

To Check the Spelling of a Correctly Typed Word

Willow adds two more sentences to her email message, recalling that Logan has invited his college president, Dr. Rachel Cicco, to the event. In the message, the last name of Cicco has a wavy line below it even though the name is spelled correctly, indicating the word is not in Outlook's main dictionary. The following steps ignore the error and remove the wavy line. ***Why?*** *The main dictionary contains most common words, but does not include most proper names, technical terms, or acronyms.*

1

- Click after the first sentence in the email message to Logan to place the insertion point, and then press SPACEBAR to insert a space.
- Type `I understand that you have invited your college president Dr. Rachel Cicco to join us. We look forward to meeting her.` to enter a second sentence in the message text, and then click a blank spot in the window to have Outlook mark a spelling error (Figure 1–37).

Q&A Why does Outlook flag "Cicco" as a spelling error even though the last name is spelled correctly?
Outlook flags any word that is not in its main dictionary.

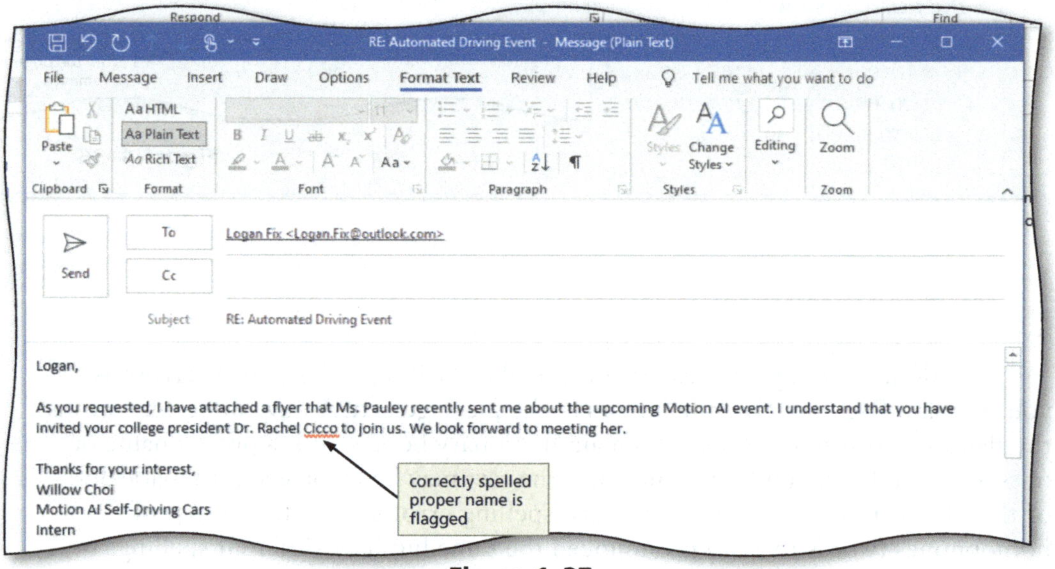

Figure 1–37

2

- Right-click the wavy line below the proper name to display a shortcut menu that presents a list of suggested spelling corrections for the flagged word (in this case, the last name) (Figure 1–38).

Q&A What if Outlook does not flag my spelling and grammar errors with wavy underlines?
To verify that the check spelling and grammar as you type features are enabled, click the File tab on the ribbon to open Backstage view and then click Options to display the Outlook Options dialog box. Click Mail (Outlook Options dialog box) and click the Editor Options button to display the Editor Options dialog box. In the 'When correcting spelling in Outlook' section, ensure the 'Check spelling as you type' check box contains a check mark. Click OK two times to close each open dialog box.

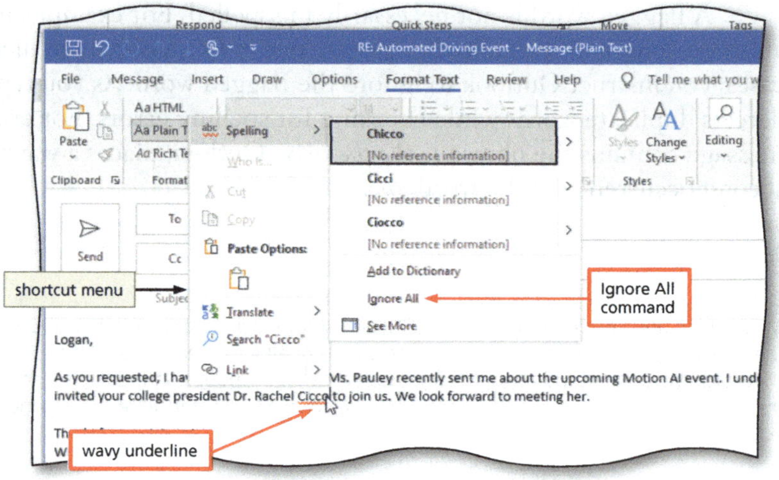

Figure 1–38

3

- Click Ignore All on the shortcut menu to ignore this flagged error, close the shortcut menu, and remove the wavy line beneath the proper name.

To Check the Spelling of Misspelled Text

In the following steps, the word *event* is misspelled intentionally as *evnt* to illustrate Outlook's check spelling as you type feature. If you are performing the steps in this project, your email message may contain different misspelled words, depending on the accuracy of your typing. The following steps check the spelling of a misspelled word. ***Why?*** *The way you present yourself in email messages contributes to the way you are perceived, so you should be sure to proofread and check the spelling of all communications.*

1

- Click after the third sentence in the email message to Logan to place the insertion point, and then press SPACEBAR to insert a space.
- Type **Let me know if you have any questions about the self-driving evnt.** to complete the message text, and then press SPACEBAR so that a wavy line appears below the misspelled word (Figure 1–39).

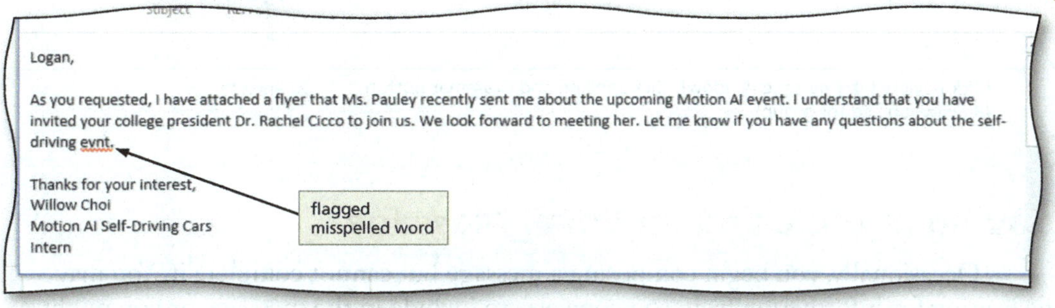

Figure 1–39

Q&A When I was typing the third sentence starting with "Let me", why did gray text automatically display the text "know if you" automatically?

Outlook can suggest words or phrases as you compose messages using AI (artificial intelligence). If you are typing and suggested text appears that you want to accept, press TAB to accept the text predictions.

2

- Right-click the flagged word (evnt, in this case) to display a shortcut menu that presents a list of suggested spelling corrections and contextual definition for the flagged word (Figure 1–40).

Q&A What should I do if the correction I want to use is not listed on the shortcut menu?

You can click outside the shortcut menu to close it and then re-enter the correct word.

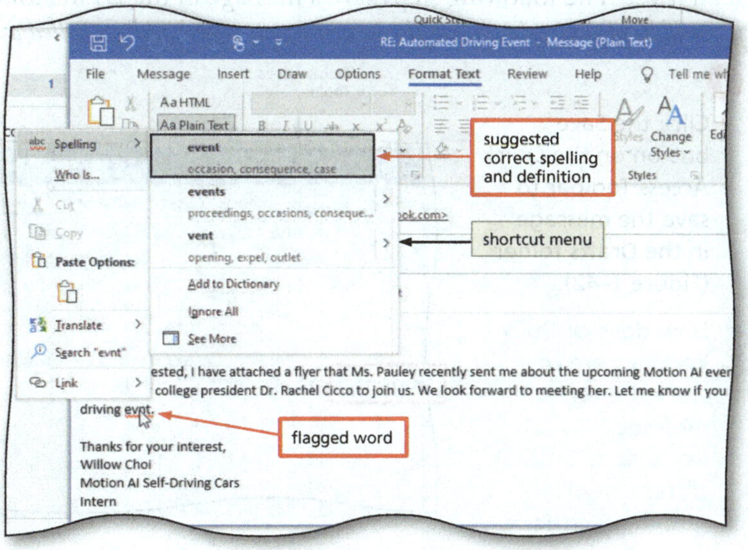

Figure 1–40

3

- Click the correct spelling on the shortcut menu (in this case, event) to replace the misspelled word in the email message with the correctly spelled word (Figure 1–41).

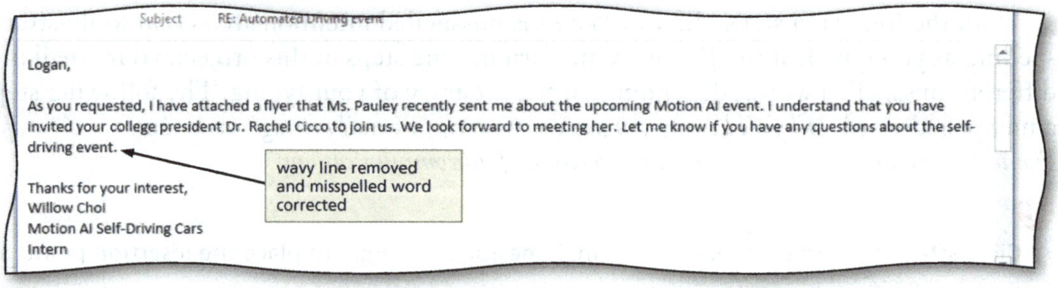

Figure 1–41

Other Ways

1. Click Review tab (message window), click Spelling and Grammar button (Review tab | Editor group)
2. Press F7

Saving and Closing an Email Message

Occasionally, you begin composing a message but cannot complete it. You may be waiting for information from someone else to include in the message, or you might prefer to rewrite the message later after you have time to evaluate its content. One option is to save the message, which stores the message in the Drafts folder for your email account until you are ready to send it. The Drafts folder is the default location for all saved messages. Later, you can reopen the message, finish writing it, and then send it.

To Save and Close an Email Message without Sending It

The self-driving event information that Logan Fix requested has been drafted, but Willow is not ready to send it yet. The following steps save a message in the Drafts folder for completion at a later time. ***Why?*** *If you are in the middle of composing a lengthy or important email and get called away, you can save your work so you can resume it later.*

1

- Click the Save button on the Quick Access Toolbar to save the message in the Drafts folder (Figure 1–42).

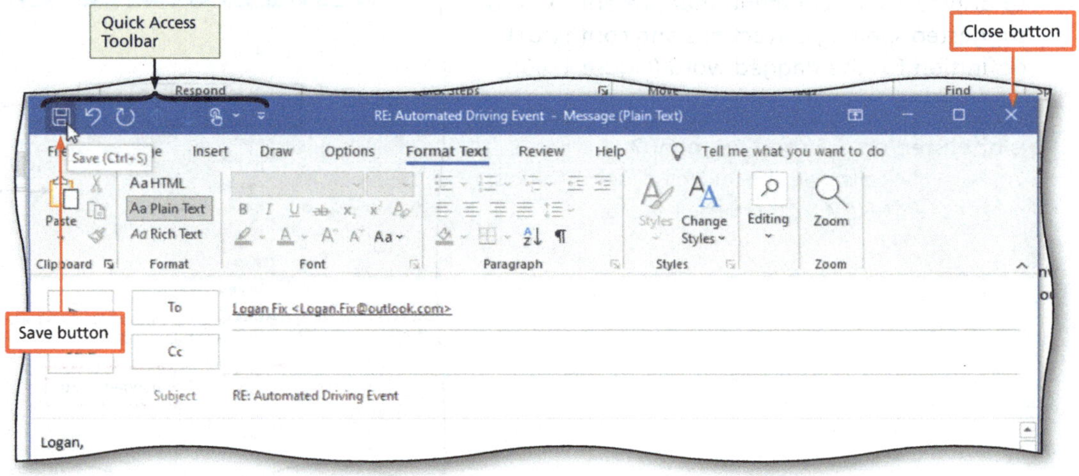

Figure 1–42

Q&A

How does Outlook know where to store the saved message?
By default, Outlook stores saved messages in the Drafts folder for your email account.

Can I save the message to a location other than the Drafts folder?
To save the message to the Outlook student folder, click the File tab on the ribbon to open Backstage view, and then click Save As in Backstage view to display the Save As dialog box. Navigate to the Outlook student folder. In the File name text box, type the name of the message file and then click the Save button. The message is saved with the extension .msg, which represents an Outlook message.

What should I do if the message window does not display the Quick Access Toolbar?
Click the File tab and then click Save.

2

- Click the Close button on the title bar to close the RE: Automated Driving Event – Message (Plain Text) window (Figure 1–43).

Q&A What should I do if Outlook did not save the message in the Drafts folder?
Click the Home tab, click the Move button, click Other Folder, select the Drafts folder for Willow Choi's Outlook Data File, and then click OK.

How do I know when a message is a draft rather than an incoming message?
The message appears in the message list with [Draft] displayed in red.

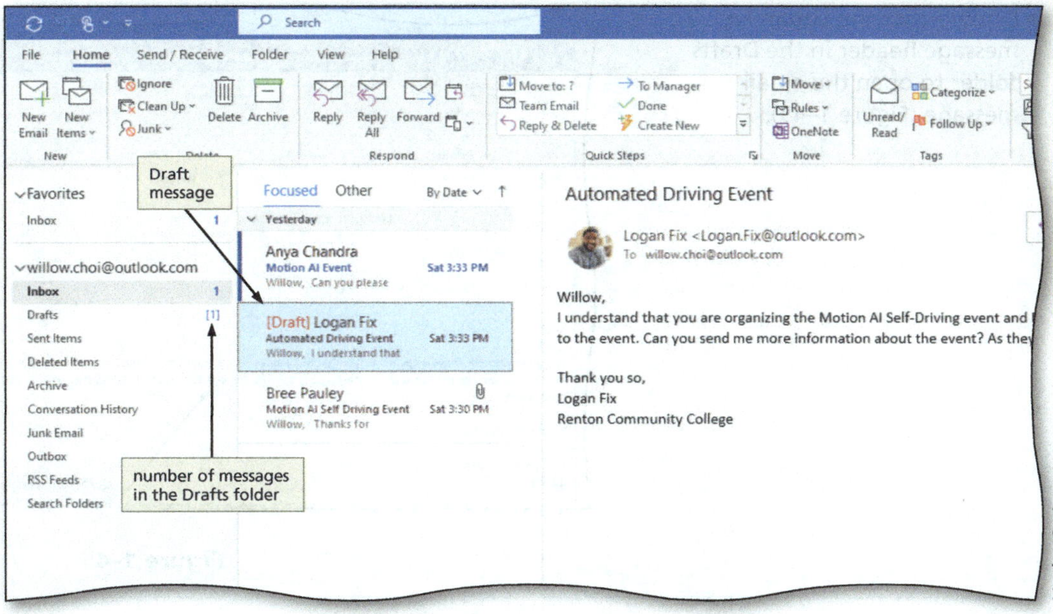

Figure 1–43

Monkey Business Images /Shutterstock.com

To Open a Saved Email Message

The following steps open the message saved in the Drafts folder. ***Why?** By default, Outlook saves any email message in the Drafts folder every three minutes.* You can also save a message and reopen it later.

1

- Click the Drafts folder in the Navigation pane to display the message header for the Logan Fix email message in the message list (Figure 1–44).

Q&A What should I do if the message does not appear in my Drafts folder?
If the message does not appear in the Drafts folder, return to the Inbox, and then click the message header in the message pane.

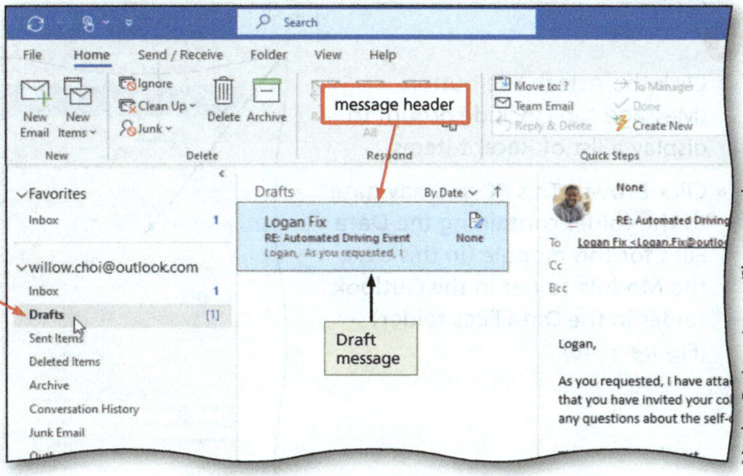

Figure 1–44

Monkey Business Images/Shutterstock.com

2

- Double-click the Logan Fix message header in the Drafts folder to open the email message (Figure 1–45).

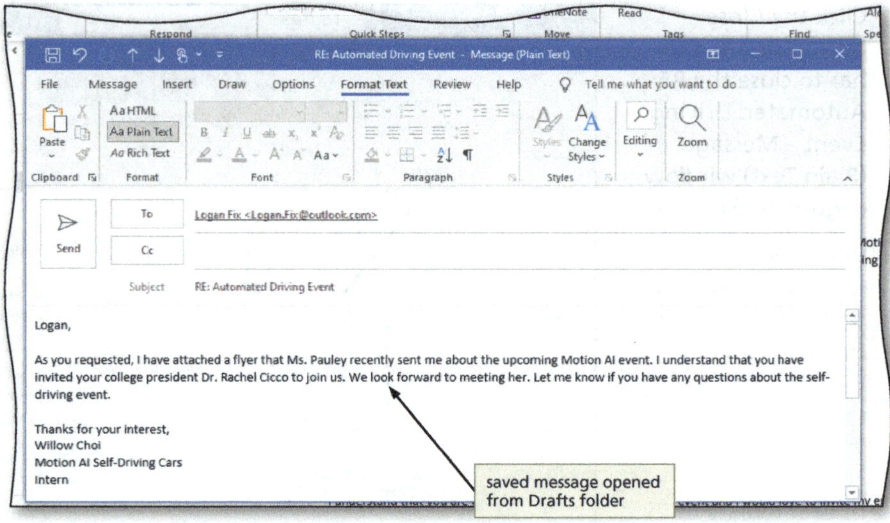

Figure 1–45

To Attach a File to an Email Message

To share a file such as a photo, flyer, or business document through email, you attach the file to an email message. Outlook does not have a predefined file size limit for attachments, but an email service provider may restrict the size of incoming attachments or the size of the email mailbox. Very large email attachments may be rejected by the recipient's email service provider and returned to the sender as undeliverable. Consider storing large files in OneDrive and sharing a link to the file within an email.

Before you send the email message to Logan, you need to attach a file of a flyer describing the informational meeting about the event. The file may be listed on a Recent Items listing when the Attach File button is clicked, or you can browse web locations or the local PC for the file attachment(s). The following steps attach a file to an email message. ***Why?*** *Attaching a file to an email message provides additional information to a recipient.*

1

- Click the Attach File button (Message tab | Include group) to display a list of Recent Items.
- Click Browse This PC and navigate to the folder containing the Data Files for this module (in this case, the Module folder in the Outlook1 folder in the Data Files folder) (Figure 1–46).

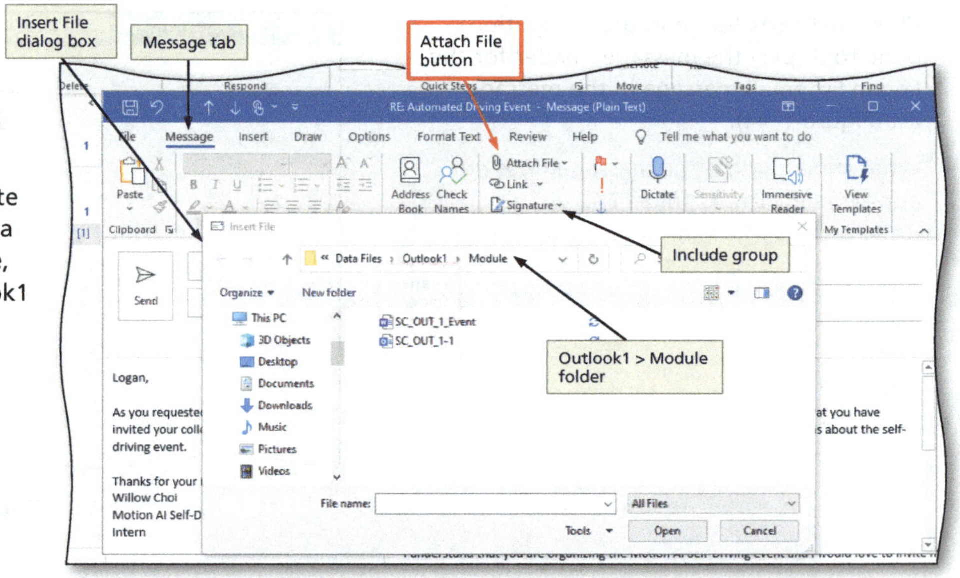

Figure 1–46

2

- Click the document SC_OUT_1_Event.docx to select the file to attach.
- Click the Insert button (Insert File dialog box) to attach the selected file to the email message and close the Insert File dialog box (Figure 1–47).

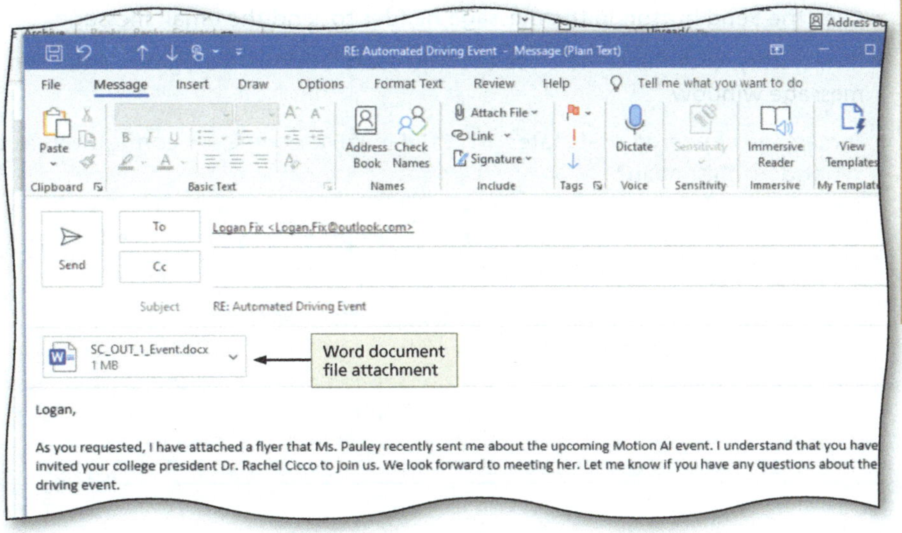

Figure 1–47

To Set Message Importance and Send the Message

Outlook provides the option to assign an **importance level** to a message, which indicates to the recipient the priority level of an email message. ***Why?*** *When you have a message that requires urgent attention, you can send the message with a high importance level.* The default importance level for all new messages is normal importance, but you can change the importance level to high or low, depending on the priority level of the email message. A message sent with **high importance** displays a red exclamation point in the message header and indicates to the recipient that the message requires a higher priority than other messages they might have received. The **low importance** option displays a blue arrow and indicates to the recipient a low priority for the message. The following steps set the high importance option for a single email message and to send the message.

1

- Click the High Importance button (Message tab | Tags group) to add a high importance level (a red exclamation point) to the email message (Figure 1–48).

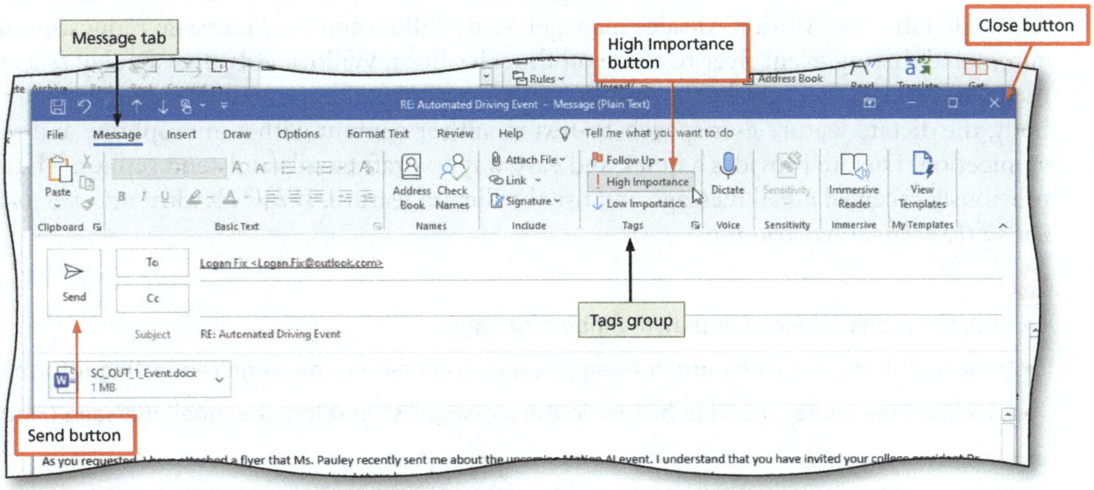

Figure 1–48

Q&A

When does a red exclamation point appear in a message with high importance?

The red exclamation point appears in the message header when the message is received.

How would I set a low importance to an email message?

Click the Low Importance button (Message tab | Tags group).

2

- Click the Send button in the message header to send the email message.
- If necessary, click Cancel to close the Microsoft Outlook dialog box and then click Close to close the message window.

Q&A

A message appeared that states 'No valid email accounts are configured. Add an account to send email'. What does this mean?

The SC_OUT_1-1.pst Data File is an Outlook Data File, which cannot send an email message. If you are using the SC_OUT_1-1.pst Data File, the sent message remains in the Drafts folder unless you configure an email account. You can set up and configure your own email address in Outlook to send an email message.

What happens to the actual email message after I send it?

After Outlook closes the message window, it stores the email message reply in the Outbox folder while it sends the message to the recipient. You might not see the message in the Outbox because Outlook usually stores it there only briefly. Next, Outlook moves the message to the Sent Items folder. The original message in the message list now shows an envelope icon with a purple arrow to indicate a reply was sent.

CONSIDER THIS

Can you place a tag in an email message that requests the recipient to respond within a certain time period?

- If you are sending an email message that requires a timely response, you can click the Follow Up button (Message tab | Tags group) to insert a flag icon indicating that the recipient should respond within a specified period of time.
- Based on your expected response time, you can select the Follow Up flag for Today, Tomorrow, This Week, Next Week, No Date, or Custom.

To Forward an Email Message and Add a Dictated Message

When you forward an email message, you resend a received or sent email message to another recipient. Anya Chandra, the Motion AI sales manager, sent Willow an email message requesting that she forward the automated driving event flyer to share on the sales floor. Willow adds Bree Pauley as a courtesy copy (cc) recipient to make her aware that Anya is receiving a copy of her email message. Instead of typing the message body, the dictate feature uses speech-to-text to author content with a microphone and reliable Internet connection. Dictate provides a quick and easy way to draft emails and send replies. The following steps forward a previously received email message and use the dictate feature. ***Why?*** *Forwarding sends an email to someone who was not on the original recipient list.*

1

- Click the Inbox folder to display the Inbox messages.
- Double-click the Anya Chandra message header and read her message requesting information about the event.
- Click the Bree Pauley message header in the message list to select the email message (Figure 1–49).

Q&A

Why do my message headers show times instead of dates?

Outlook shows today's messages with times in the headers and messages prior to today with dates in the headers.

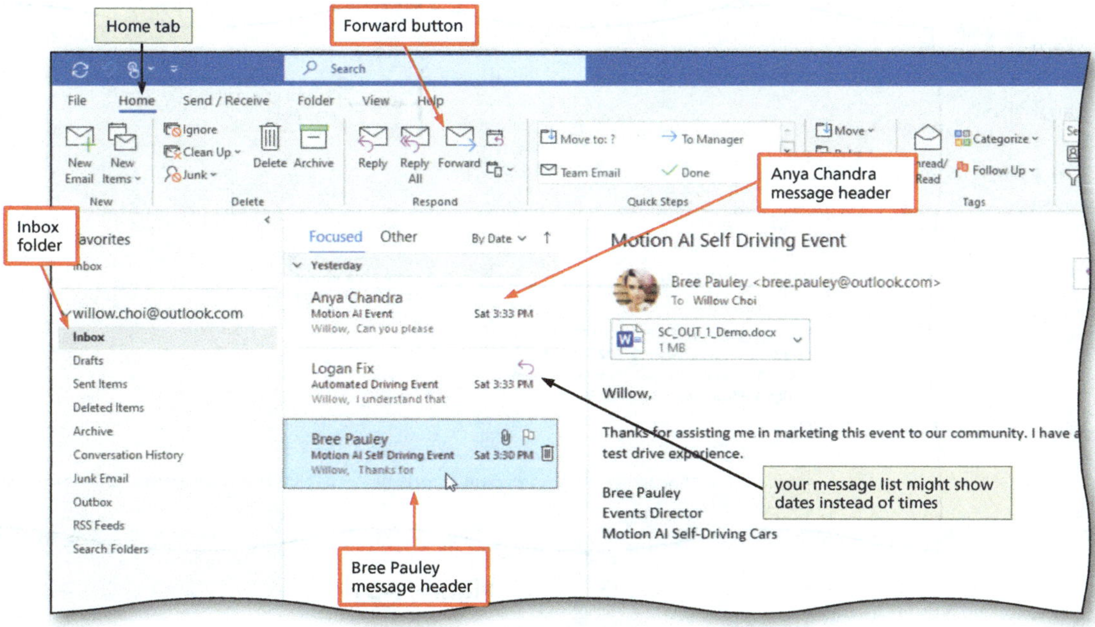

Look Studio/Shutterstock.com

Figure 1–49

2

- Click the Forward button (Home tab | Respond group) to display the message in the Reading Pane (Figure 1–50).

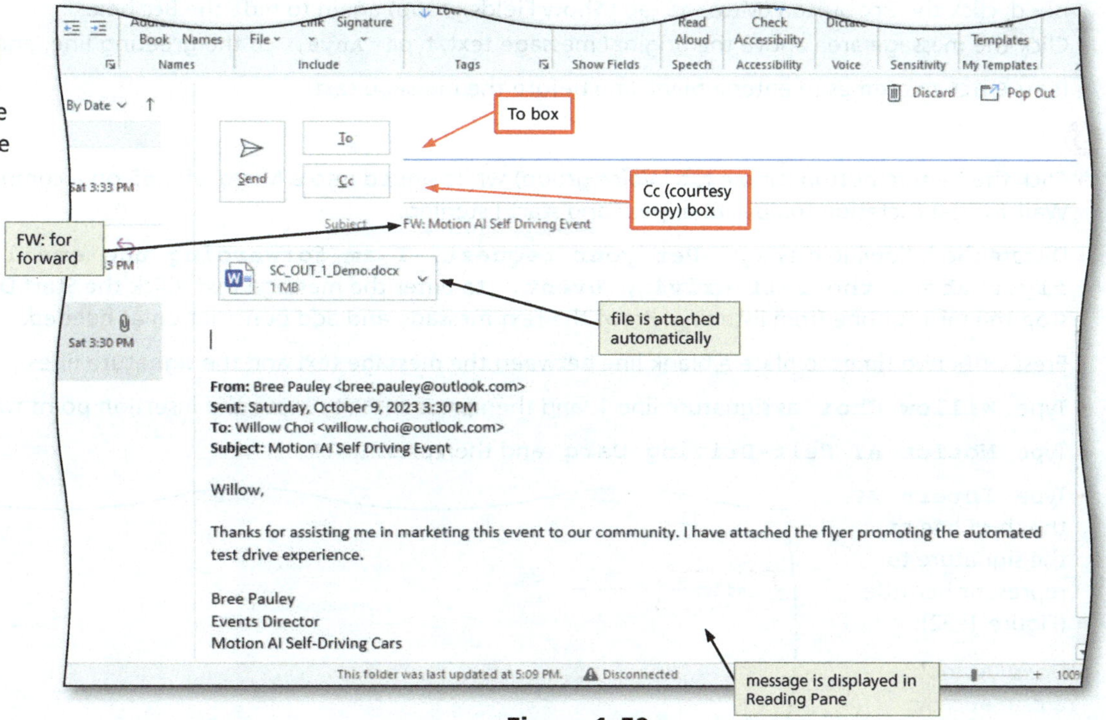

Figure 1–50

3

- Click the To box, and then type **anya.chandra@outlook.com** (with no spaces) as the recipient's email address.
- Click the Cc box, and then type **bree.pauley@outlook.com** (with no spaces) to send a courtesy copy to inform the original sender that you are forwarding her email message (Figure 1–51).

Q&A Why does the original message appear in the message area of the window?
By default, Outlook displays the original message below the new message area for all message replies and forwards.

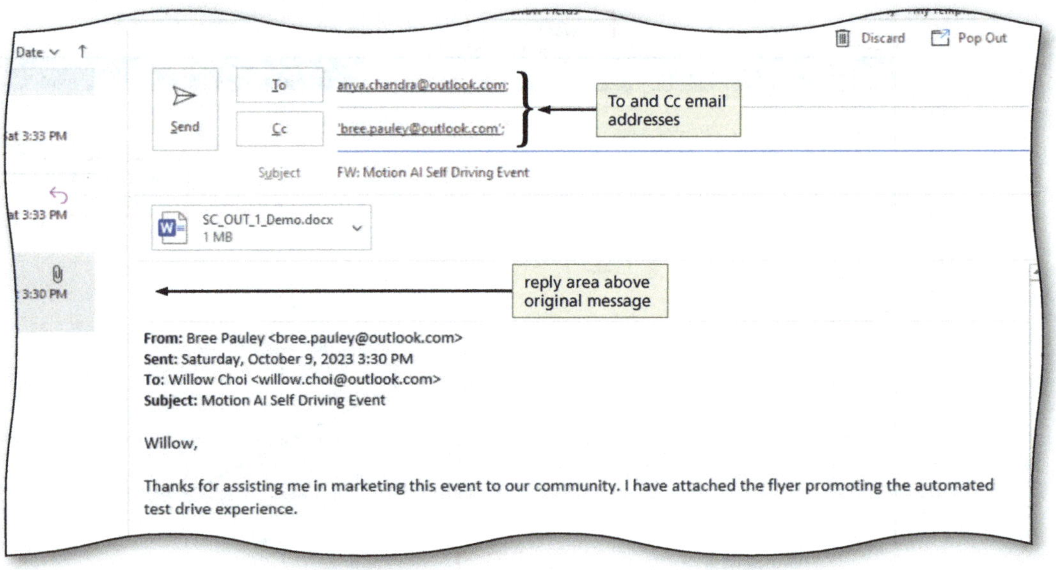

Figure 1–51

4

Experiment

- Click the Bcc button (Message tab | Show Fields group) to display the Bcc (Blind carbon copy) box. When you are finished, click the Bcc button (Message tab | Show Fields group) again to hide the Bcc box.
- Click the message area above the original message text, type `Anya,` as the greeting line, and then press SPACEBAR.
- Press ENTER two times to enter a blank line before the message text.

5

- Click the Dictate button (Home tab | Voice group) while signed into a Microsoft 365 on a computer with a mic. Wait for the Dictation toolbar to appear and start listening.
- Dictate the following message: `Per your request, I am forwarding the email and event flyer about the self-driving event.` to enter the message text. Click the Start Dictation button to stop the microphone from listening. Proof the text message and add punctuation as needed.
- Press ENTER two times to place a blank line between the message text and the signature lines.
- Type `Willow Choi` as signature line 1, and then press ENTER to move the insertion point to the next line.
- Type `Motion AI Self-Driving Cars` and then press ENTER.
- Type `Intern` as the third line of the signature to represent her title (Figure 1–52).

Q&A Does Outlook automatically forward the attachment to the recipient?
Yes. Outlook automatically adds the attachment to the forwarded message unless you choose to remove it.

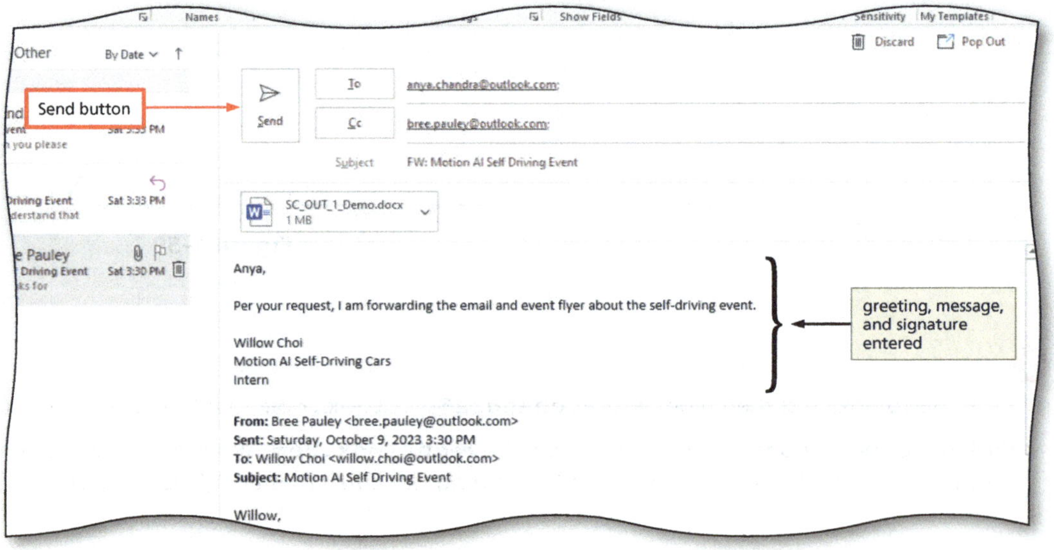

Figure 1–52

6

- Click the Send button in the message header to forward the message.
- If necessary, click Cancel to close the Microsoft Outlook dialog box.

Organizing Messages with Outlook Folders

To keep track of your email messages effectively, Outlook provides a basic set of **folders**, which are containers for storing Outlook items of a specific type, such as messages, appointments, or contacts. Email is supposed to help you be more efficient and save time, but if you do not manage it effectively, you can quickly become overloaded with messages. The Inbox is an email folder that stores your incoming email messages. Instead of leaving all of your incoming messages in the Inbox, you can create additional folders and then move messages to these new folders so you can organize and locate your messages easily.

To Create a New Folder in the Inbox Folder

By creating multiple folders within the Inbox folder, and then organizing messages in the new folders, you can find a specific email message easily. The following steps create a folder within the Inbox folder. ***Why?*** *Folders provide an efficient method for managing your email.*

1

- If necessary, click the Inbox folder to select it.
- Click Folder on the ribbon to display the Folder tab.
- Click the New Folder button (Folder tab | New group) to display the Create New Folder dialog box (Figure 1–53).

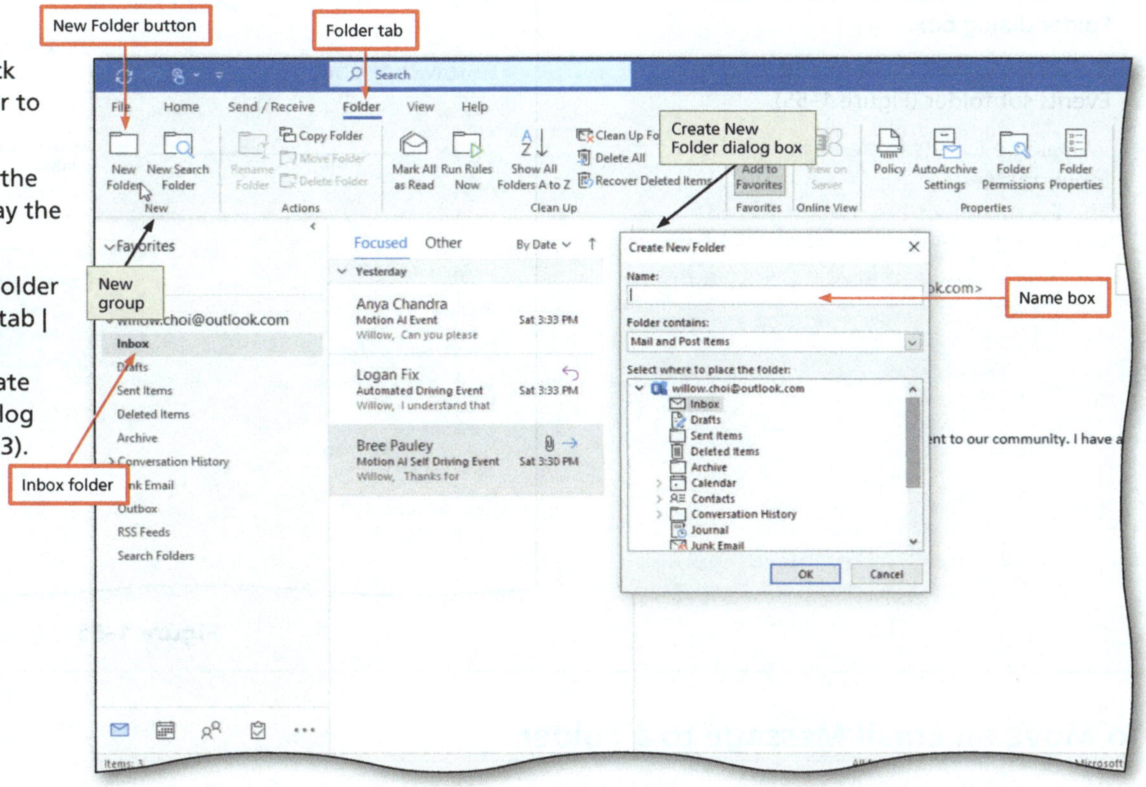

Figure 1–53

2

- Click the Name text box, and then type **`Events`** to name the folder within the Inbox folder.
- If necessary, click the Folder contains arrow, and then click 'Mail and Post Items' in the list to place only email messages in the new folder.
- If necessary, click Inbox in the 'Select where to place the folder' list to place the new folder within the Inbox folder (Figure 1–54).

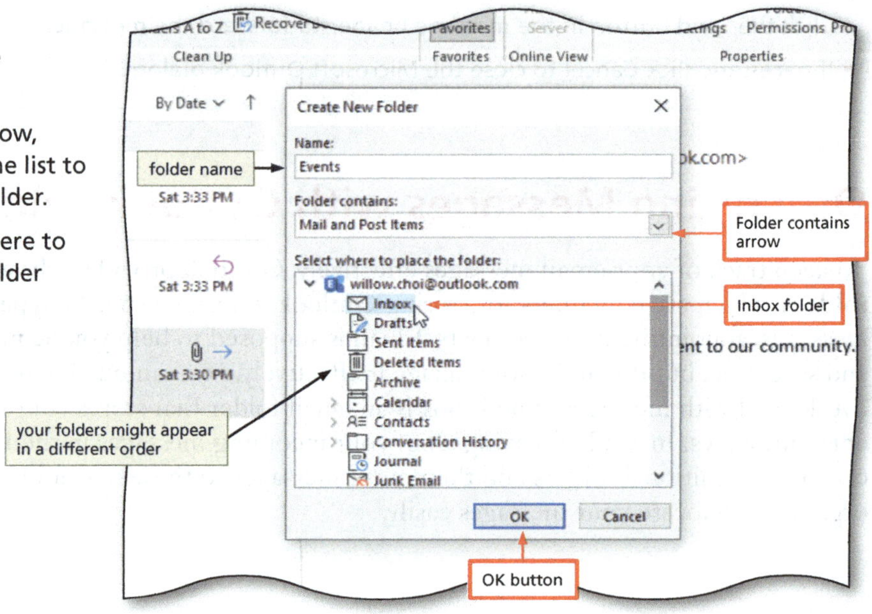

Figure 1–54

3

- Click OK to create the Events folder within the Inbox and close the Create New Folder dialog box.
- If necessary, click the Inbox to view the Events subfolder (Figure 1–55).

Q&A Why is the Events folder indented below the Inbox folder?
The Events folder is stored within the Inbox folder. Outlook indents the folder in the list to indicate that it is within the main folder.

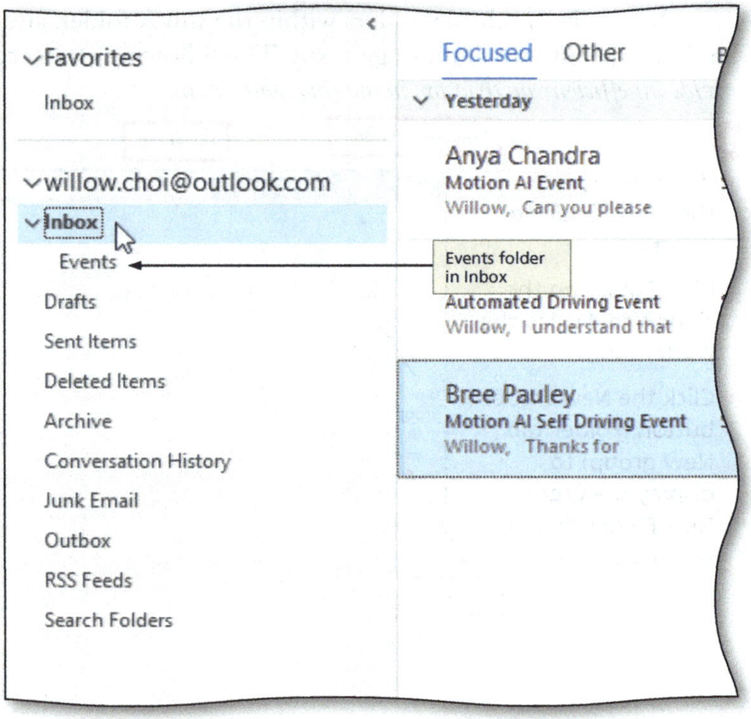

Figure 1–55

To Move an Email Message to a Folder

Organizing important email messages about the self-driving event into the Events folder saves time when you search through hundreds or thousands of email messages later. Specifically, you will move the message from Bree Pauley from the Inbox folder to the Events folder. In this case, the Inbox folder is called the source folder, and the Events folder is called the destination folder. A **source folder** is the location of the document or message to be moved or copied. A **destination folder** is the location where you want to move or copy the file or message. The following steps move an email message into a folder. ***Why?*** *By organizing your emails into topical folders, you can access your messages easily.*

1

- In the Inbox folder (source folder), click the Bree Pauley message header in the Inbox message list to select the email message.
- Click Home on the ribbon to display the Home tab.
- Click the Move button (Home tab | Move group) to display the Move menu (Figure 1–56).

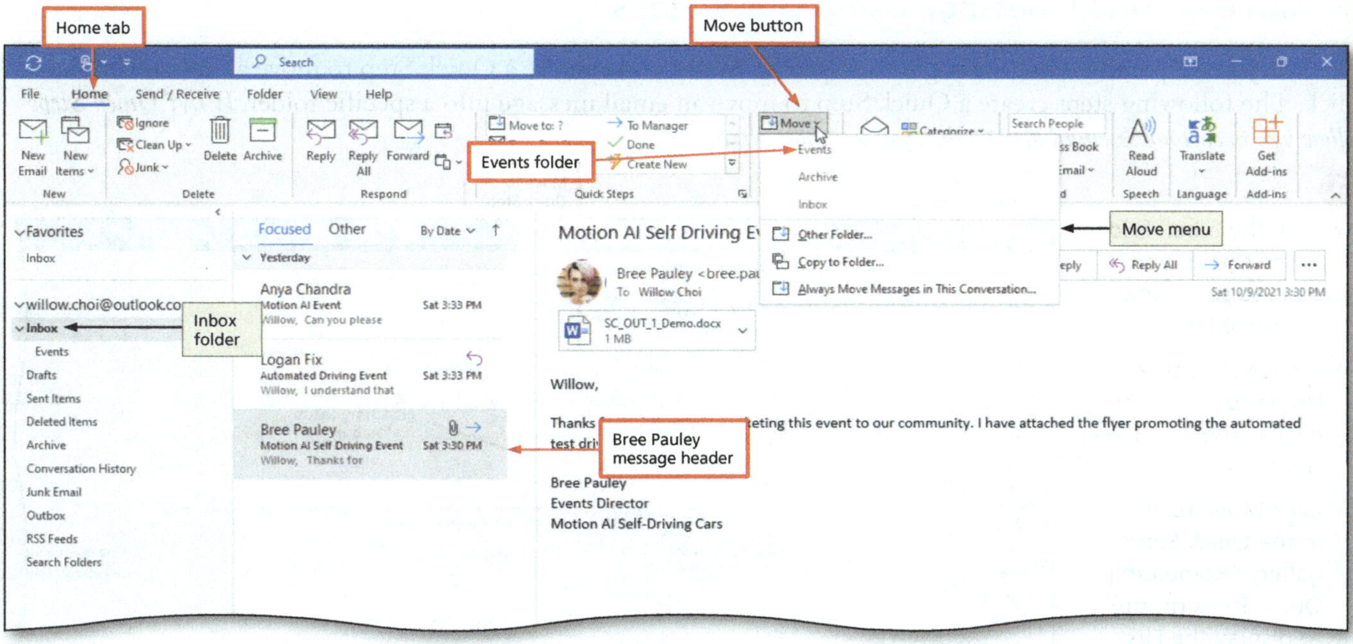

Look Studio/Shutterstock.com

Figure 1–56

2

- Click Events on the Move menu to move the selected message from the source folder (Inbox folder) to the destination folder (Events folder).
- In the Navigation pane, click the Events folder to display its contents (Figure 1–57).

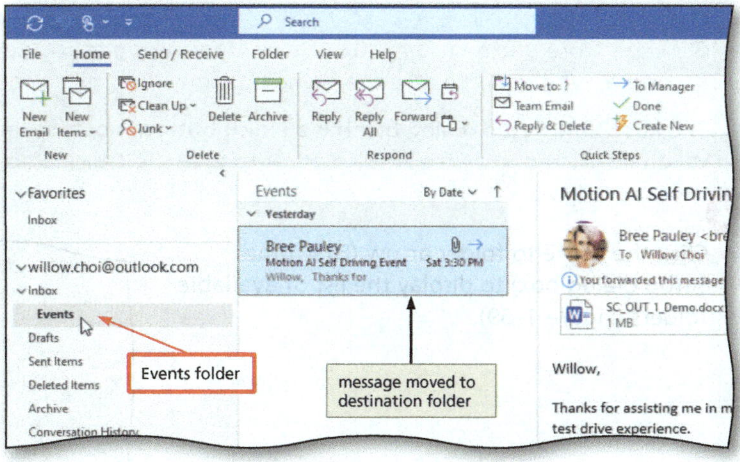

Look Studio/Shutterstock.com

Figure 1–57

Q&A

Can I move more than one message at a time?
Yes. Click the first message to select it. While holding CTRL, click additional messages to select them. Click the Move button (Home tab | Move group) and then click the destination folder to select it.

Can I copy the email messages instead of moving them?
Yes. Select the message(s) to copy, and then click the Move button (Home tab | Move group). Click Copy to Folder on the menu to display the Copy Items dialog box. Select the destination folder, and then click OK to copy the selected message to the destination folder.

Other Ways

1. Right-click selected message, point to Move, click folder
2. Click selected message, drag message into destination folder

Outlook Quick Steps

An Outlook feature called **Quick Steps** provides shortcuts to perform redundant tasks with a single keystroke. For example, you can move an email message to a folder using a one-click Quick Step. You can use the built-in Quick Steps to move a file to a folder, send email to your entire team, or reply to and then delete an email message.

To Move an Email Message Using Quick Steps

If you frequently move messages to a specific folder, you can use a Quick Step to move a message in one click. The following steps create a Quick Step to move an email message into a specific folder. ***Why?*** *Quick Steps allow you to customize email actions that you use most often.*

1

- Click the Inbox folder in the Navigation pane to select the Inbox folder.
- If necessary, click Home to display the Home tab.
- Click Move to: ? in the Quick Steps gallery (Home tab | Quick Steps group) to display the First Time Setup dialog box (Figure 1–58).

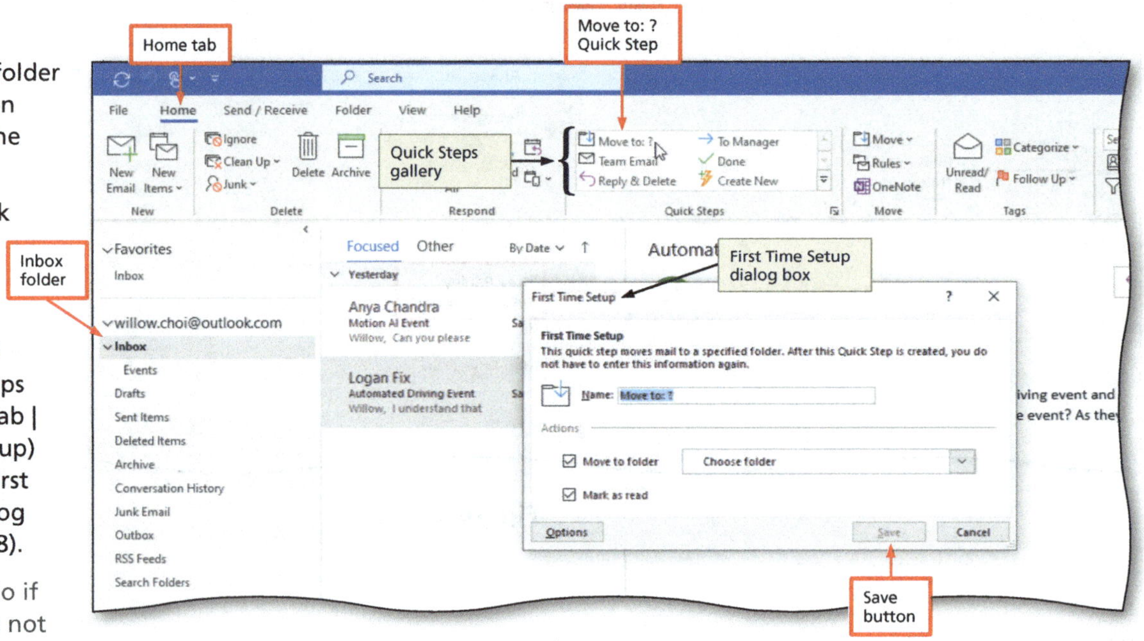

Figure 1–58

Q&A What should I do if Move to: ? does not appear on the Home tab?

Click the More button (Home tab | Quick Steps group), click New Quick Step, and then click Move to Folder. If necessary, type Move to: ? in the Name box.

The First Time Setup dialog box has a Finish button, not a Save button. What should I do?

When instructed, click the Finish button to save the Quick Step and display it in the Quick Steps gallery.

2

- Click the Move to folder arrow (First Time Setup dialog box) to display the list of available folders (Figure 1–59).

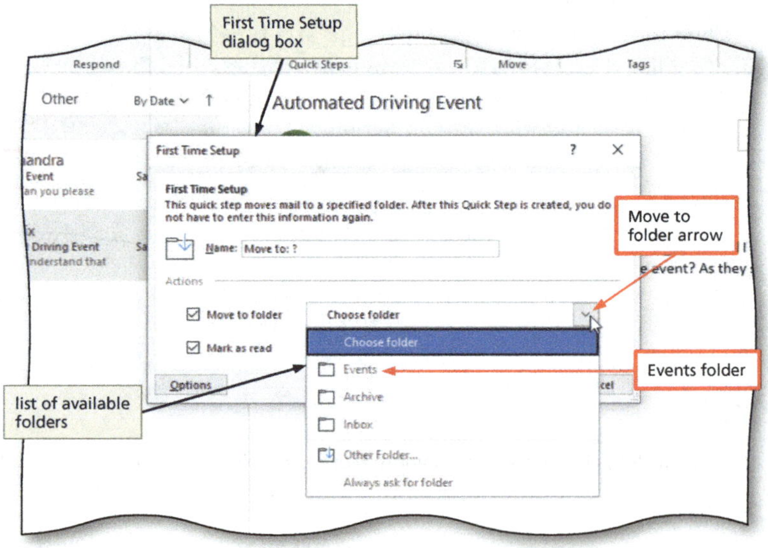

Figure 1–59

3

- Click the Events folder to create a Quick Step that moves a message to the specified folder.
- Click the Save button (First Time Setup dialog box) to save the Quick Step and display it in the Quick Steps gallery (Figure 1–60).

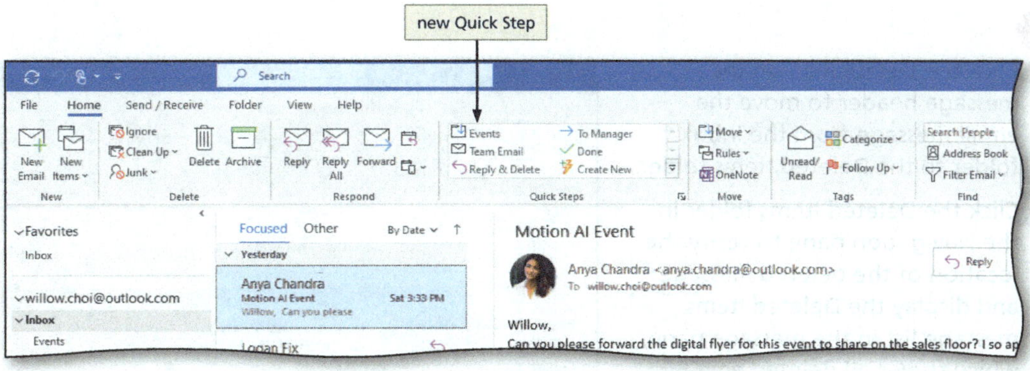

El Nariz/Shutterstock.com

Figure 1–60

4

- In the Inbox folder, click the Anya Chandra message header in the Inbox message list to select the email message.
- Click Events in the Quick Steps gallery (Home tab | Quick Steps group) to move the message to the Events folder.
- In the Navigation pane, click the Events folder to display its contents (Figure 1–61).

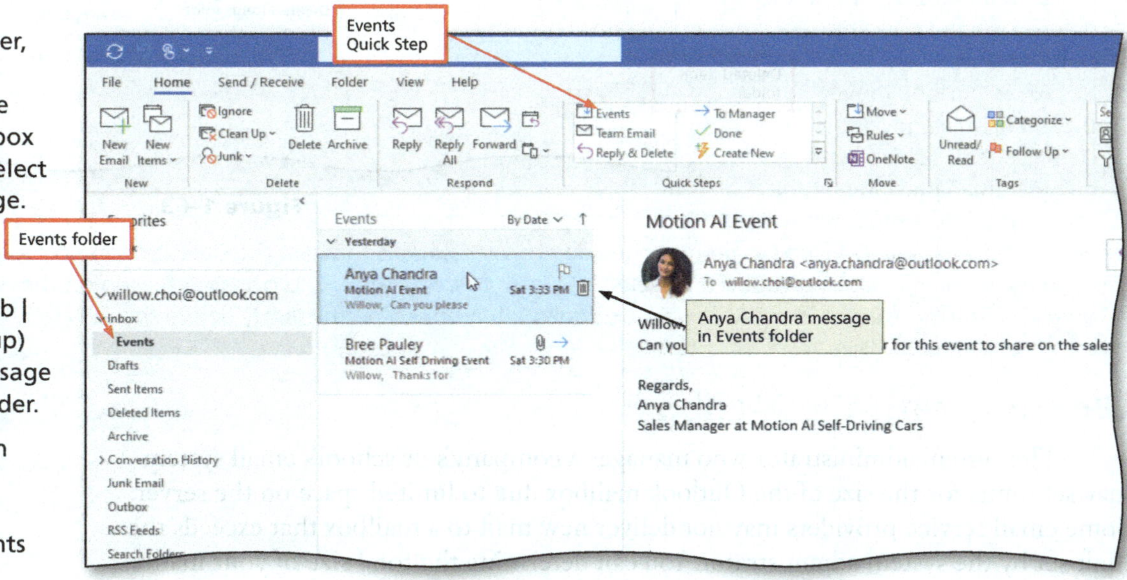

El Nariz/Shutterstock.com

Figure 1–61

To Delete an Email Message

When you delete a message from a folder, Outlook moves the message from the folder to the Deleted Items folder. For example, Willow no longer needs to keep the email message from Logan Fix in the Inbox and has decided to delete it. The following steps delete an email message. ***Why?** Delete messages you no longer need so you do not exceed the limits of your mailbox.*

1

- Click the Inbox folder in the Navigation pane to select the Inbox folder.
- Point to the Logan Fix message header in the message list to display the Delete icon (Figure 1–62).

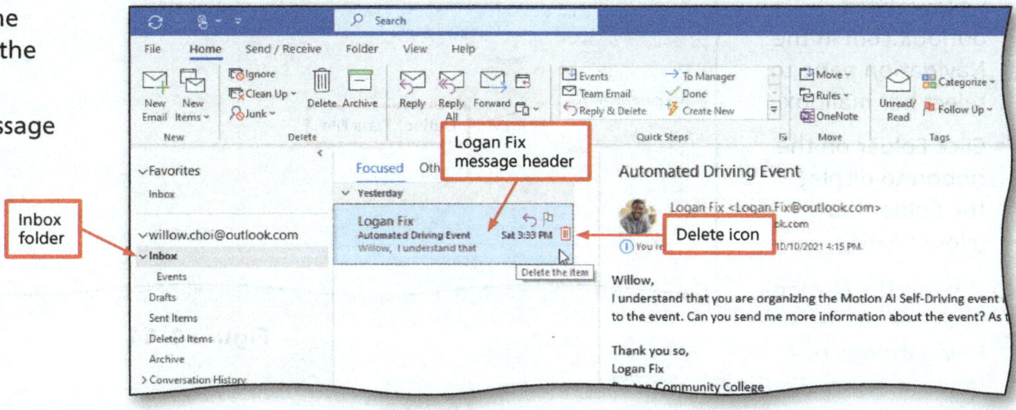

Monkey Business Images/Shutterstock.com

Figure 1–62

2

- Click the Delete icon on the message header to move the email message from the Inbox folder to the Deleted Items folder.
- Click the Deleted Items folder in the Navigation pane to verify the location of the deleted message and display the Deleted Items message list in the message pane, which shows all deleted email messages (Figure 1–63).

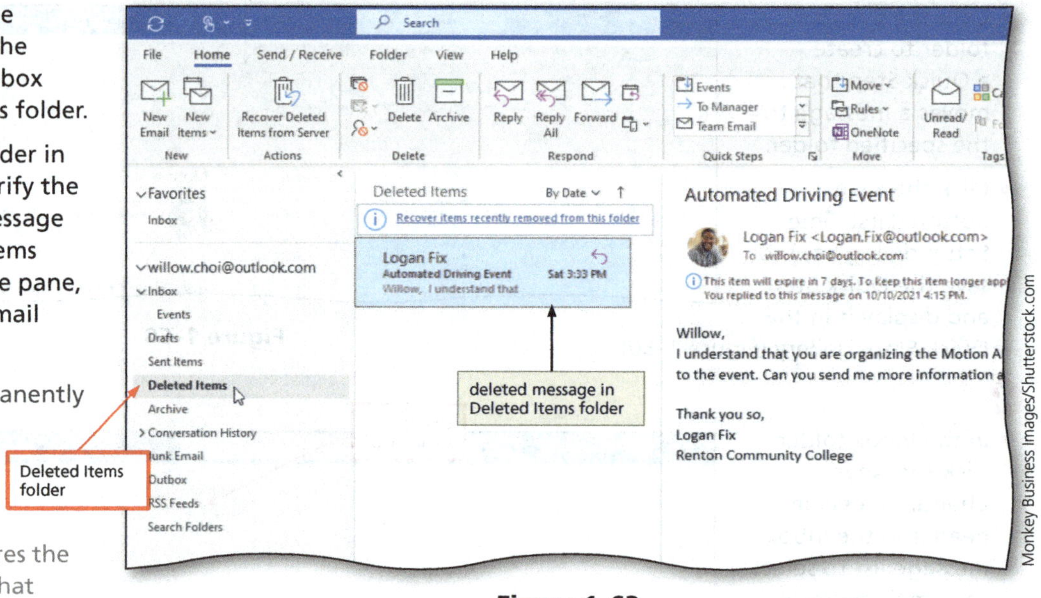

Figure 1–63

Q&A Is the email message permanently deleted when I click the Delete icon?

No. After Outlook moves the email message to the Deleted Items folder, it stores the deleted email message in that folder until you permanently delete the message. One way to permanently delete a message is to select the Deleted Items folder to view its contents in the message pane and then select the item to be deleted. Click the Delete icon on the message header and then click the Yes button in the Microsoft Outlook dialog box to permanently delete the selected item from Outlook.

Working with the Mailbox

The system administrator who manages a company's or school's email system may set limits for the size of the Outlook mailbox due to limited space on the server. Some email service providers may not deliver new mail to a mailbox that exceeds the limit set by the system administrator. You can determine the total size of your mailbox and other details about individual folders.

To View Mailbox Size

The following steps view the amount of space available in the mailbox. ***Why?*** *You can determine if you are close to your mailbox size limit.*

1

- Click the Outlook Data File indicated by the email address willow.choi@outlook.com in the Navigation pane to select her mailbox.
- Click Folder on the ribbon to display the Folder tab (Figure 1–64).

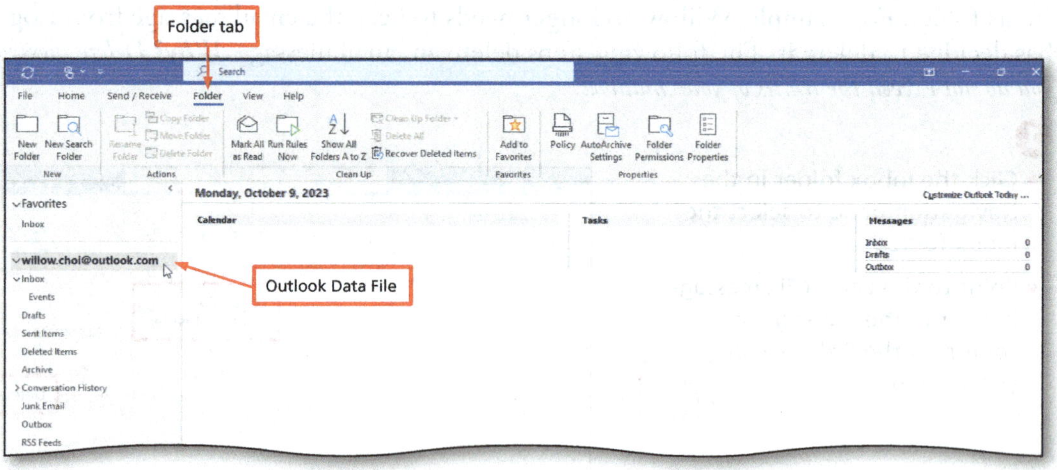

Figure 1–64

Q&A What is the Outlook Data File in the Navigation pane?

In this case, the Outlook Data File is the mailbox of Willow Choi.

2

- Click the Folder Properties button (Folder tab | Properties group) to display the Properties dialog box for the mailbox (Figure 1–65).

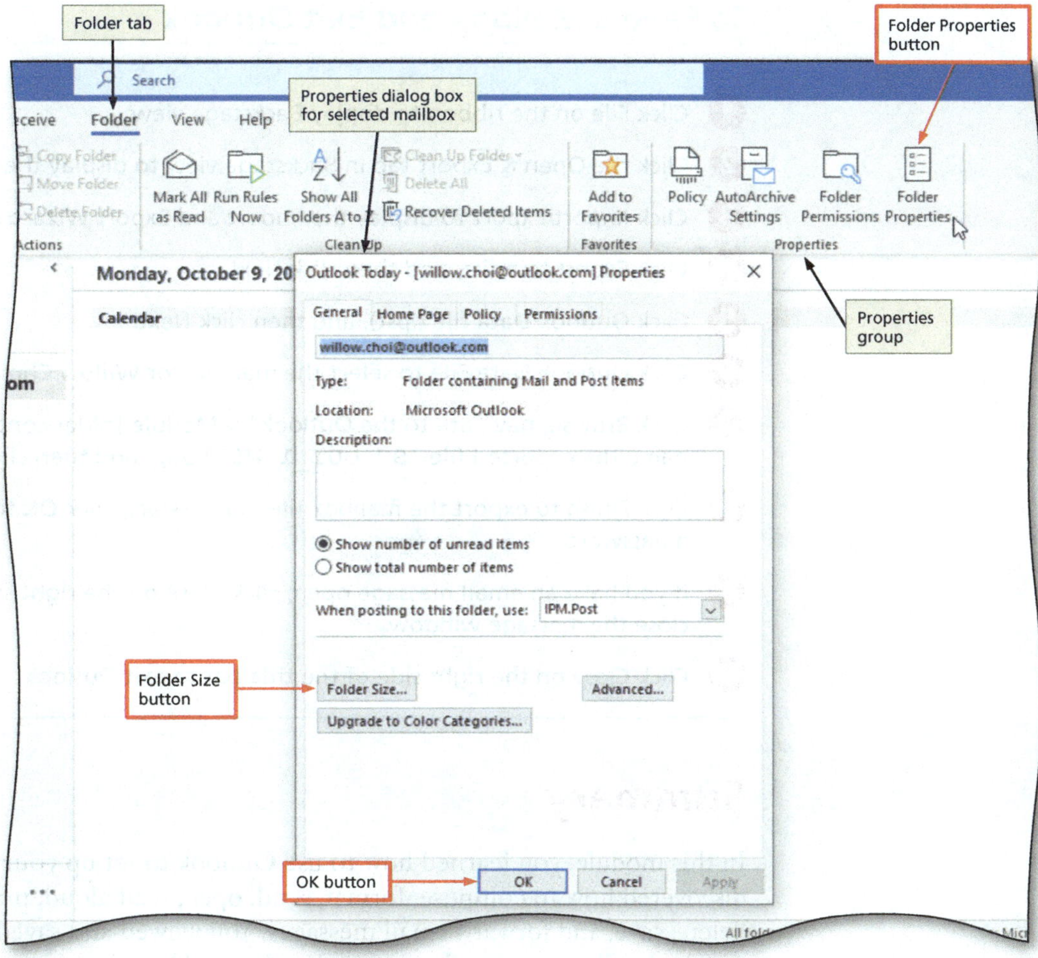

Figure 1–65

3

- Click the Folder Size button (mailbox Properties dialog box) to display the Folder Size dialog box (Figure 1–66).

4

- After viewing the folder sizes, click Close to close the Folder Size dialog box.
- Click OK to close the mailbox Properties dialog box.

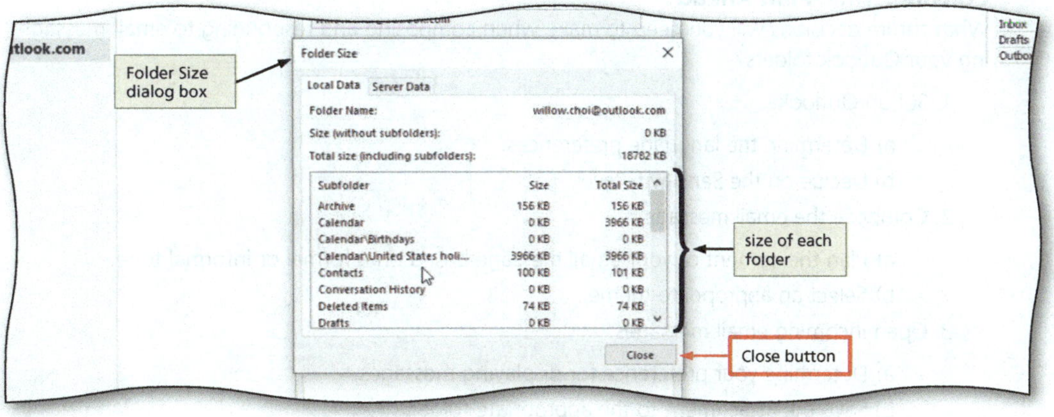

Figure 1–66

To Save a Mailbox and Exit Outlook

1. Click File on the ribbon to display Backstage view.
2. Click the Open & Export tab in Backstage view to display the Open gallery.
3. Click Import/Export to display the Import and Export Wizard dialog box.
4. Click Export to a file, and then click Next.
5. Click Outlook Data file (.pst), and then click Next.
6. Click Outlook Data File to select the mailbox for Willow Choi, and then click Next.
7. Click Browse, navigate to the Outlook1 > Module folder containing your Data Files, name the exported file **SC_OUT_1_Willow,** and then click OK.
8. Click Finish to export the mailbox file. If necessary, click OK to save the file without a password.
9. If you have an email message open, click Close on the right side of the title bar to close the message window.
10. Click Close on the right side of the title bar to exit Outlook.

Summary

In this module, you learned how to use Outlook to set up your email account. You discovered how to compose, format, send, open, read aloud, print, reply to, dictate, delete, save, and forward email messages. You viewed and saved file attachments and attached a file to an email message. You learned how to add a courtesy copy to an email message and set the sensitivity and importance of email messages. Finally, you created a folder in the Inbox and moved an email message to the new folder.

CONSIDER THIS

Consider This: Plan Ahead

What future decisions will you need to make when composing and responding to email messages, attaching files, and organizing your Outlook folders?

1. Set up Outlook.
    a) Determine the language preferences.
    b) Decide on the Sensitivity level.
2. Compose the email message.
    a) Plan the content of your email message based on a formal or informal tone.
    b) Select an appropriate theme.
3. Open incoming email messages.
    a) Determine your preference for displaying messages.
    b) Save the attachment to the appropriate folder.
4. Respond to messages.
    a) Plan your response to the incoming message.
    b) Correct errors and revise as necessary.
    c) Establish which file you will attach to your email message.
    d) Determine the importance level of the message.
5. Organize your Outlook folders.
    a) Establish your folder names.
    b) Plan where each email message should be stored.

Apply Your Knowledge

Reinforce the skills and apply the concepts you learned in this module.

Creating an Email with an Attachment

Note: To complete this assignment, you will be required to use the Data Files. Please contact your instructor for information about accessing the Data Files.

Instructions: Start Outlook. You are to send an email message addressed to your instructor with information about a periodic table assignment. You also attach an Excel workbook called Support_OUT_1_Periodic_Table.xlsx, which is located in the Data Files.

Perform the following tasks:

1. Compose a new email message addressed to your instructor and add your own email address as a courtesy copy address.
2. Type **`Periodic Table`** as the subject of the email message.
3. Type **`Greetings,`** as the greeting line. Check spelling as you type.
4. Enter the text shown in Figure 1–67 for the message text.

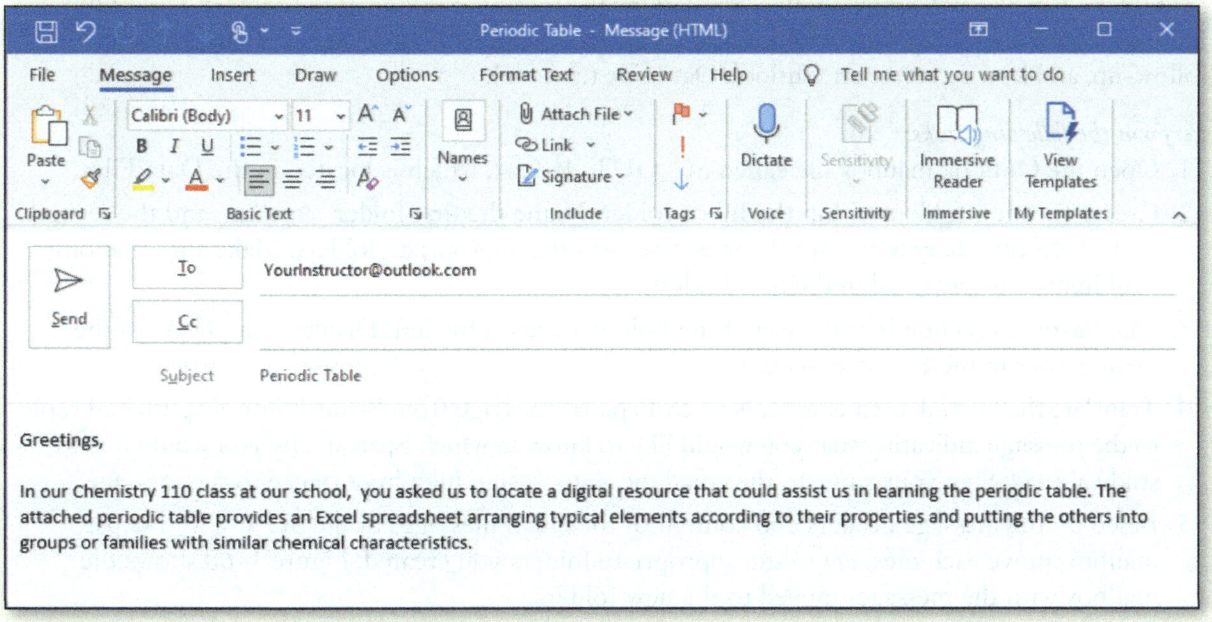

Figure 1–67

5. Type **`Thanks,`** as the closing line.
6. Enter your name as the first signature line.
7. Type **`Student of Your School`** as the second signature line.
8. If requested by your instructor, type your cell phone number as the third signature line.
9. Attach the Excel workbook called Support_OUT_1_Periodic_Table.xlsx, which is located in the Data Files, to the email message.
10. Click the File tab, and then click Save As. Save the message on your hard drive, OneDrive, or a location that is most appropriate to your situation using the file name **`SC_OUT_1_Periodic_Table`**.

Continued >

Apply Your Knowledge *continued*

11. Submit the email message in the format specified by your instructor.
12. Exit Outlook.
13. The attachment in the email message contained an Excel workbook. What file types are typically not allowed as a file attachment? Name at least two file types and explain why they are not allowed.

Extend Your Knowledge

Extend the skills you learned in this module and experiment with new skills. You may need to use Help to complete the assignment.

Organizing Email Messages

Note: To complete this assignment, you will be required to use the Data Files. Please contact your instructor for information about accessing the Data Files.

Instructions: Start Outlook. You are considering two study abroad opportunities next fall. You will create two folders, add a folder in the Favorites section, and then move messages into the appropriate folders. You also will apply a follow-up flag for the messages in one of the folders. Use Outlook Help to learn how to duplicate a folder in the Favorites section, how to add a flag to a message for follow-up, and how to create an Outlook Data File (.pst file).

Perform the following tasks:

1. Open the Outlook mailbox file called SC_OUT_1-2.pst, which is located in the Data Files.
2. Create two new folders within the Inbox folder. Name the first folder `Spain` and the second folder `South Korea`. Move the messages into the appropriate folders. Make sure that only mail items are contained in the new folders.
3. The Favorites section is at the top of the Folder Pane on the left. Display a duplicate of the Spain folder in the Favorites section.
4. Translate the "Estudiar en el extranjero en España" message from Spanish into English and reply to the message indicating that you would like to know in which Spanish city you would like to study abroad. Sign your name to the email message. Assign high importance to the message.
5. Based on the message headers and content of the email messages in the SC_OUT_1-2.pst mailbox, move each message to the appropriate folders you created. Figure 1–68 shows the mailbox with the messages moved to the new folders.

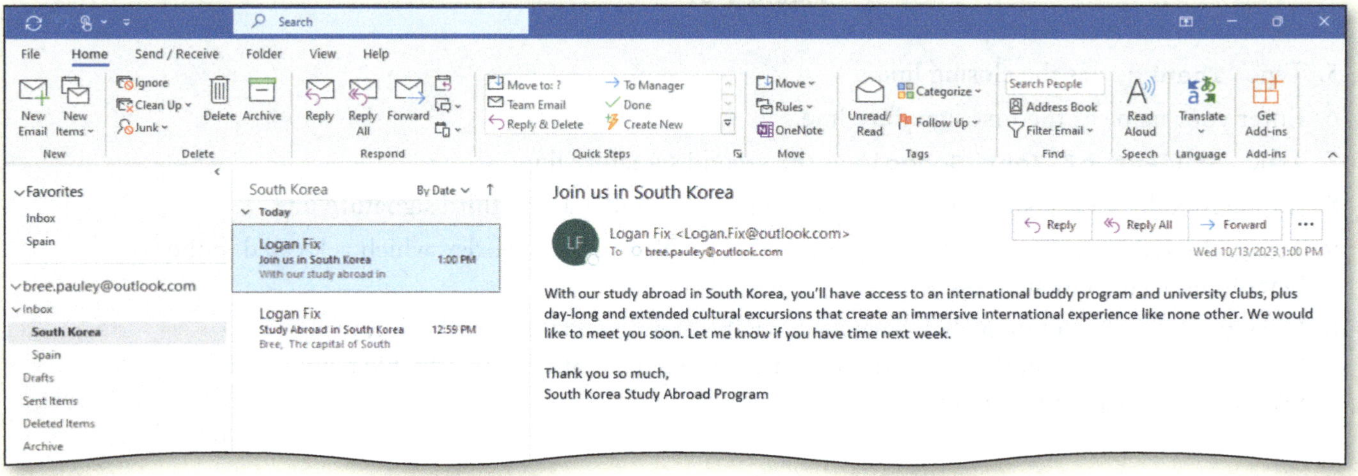

Figure 1–68

6. Export the Inbox mailbox to an Outlook Data File (.pst) on your hard drive, OneDrive, or a location that is most appropriate to your situation using the file name **SC_OUT_1_Abroad**, and then submit it in the format specified by your instructor.
7. Exit Outlook.
8. Saving your mailbox as a .pst file provides a backup copy of your email messages to submit to your instructor. What are other reasons for saving your mailbox as a .pst file?

Expand Your World

Create a solution that uses cloud or web technologies by learning and investigating on your own from general guidance.

Opening an Outlook.com Web-Based Email Message in the Outlook Client

Note: To complete this assignment, you will be required to use the Data Files. Please contact your instructor for information about accessing the Data Files.

Instructions: In your role in the Human Resources Department, you are presenting the topic, Work-Life Balance. Using Outlook, you compose the email message shown in Figure 1–69 and include a PowerPoint file attachment. Save the attachment from your Outlook.com account to your OneDrive and edit the PowerPoint slides as a web app. Share the PowerPoint slides by providing a link to your OneDrive. Sharing files in the cloud as links can eliminate large attachments and saves email storage space.

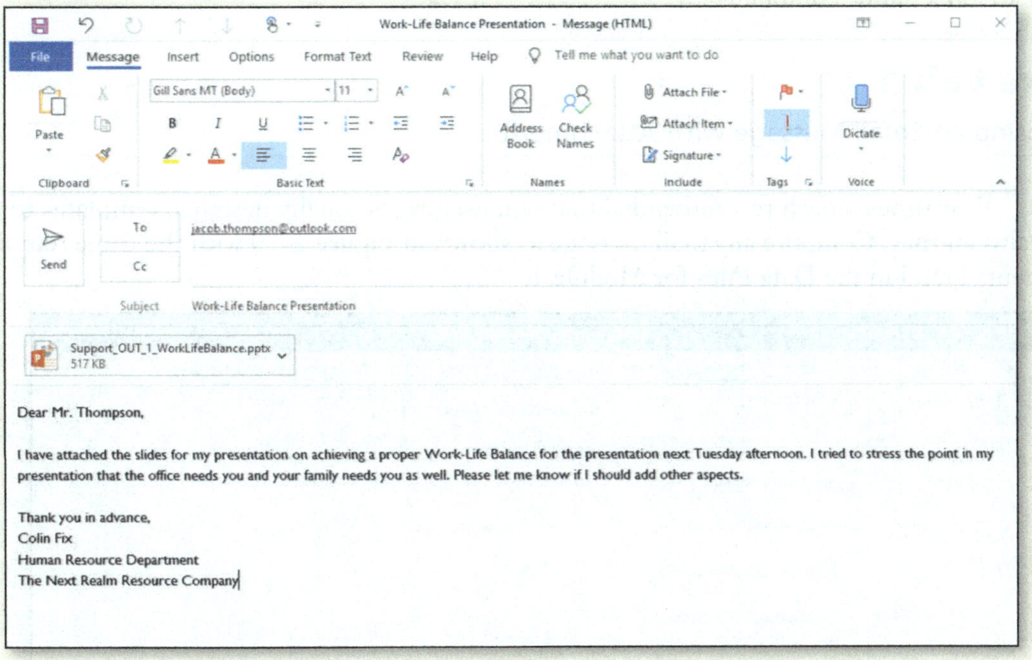

Figure 1–69

Perform the following tasks:

1. If necessary, create a Microsoft account at outlook.com.
2. Compose a new email message from the client program, Outlook (not Outlook.com). Address the email message to your Microsoft account with the subject and message text shown in Figure 1–69. Select a theme of your choice and write an email message about which theme you selected. Replace the signature with your name and school name.

Continued >

Expand Your World *continued*

3. Attach the PowerPoint presentation called Support_OUT_1_WorkLifeBalance.pptx, which is located in the Data Files, to the email message.
4. Open your Microsoft account at outlook.com. Open the email message that you sent from Outlook, and then click View online to view the PowerPoint file attachment.
5. Click Edit in Browser to edit the PowerPoint presentation in the Microsoft PowerPoint web app.
6. If requested by your instructor, change the name on the first slide to your name.
7. Add a fifth slide to the PowerPoint presentation showing the percentage of employees who telecommute to work and include a link to the information source. (*Hint:* Research this statistic on the web.)
8. Click the Insert tab, and then add an online picture about telecommuting to the fifth slide.
9. Click the File tab, and then click Share to share the PowerPoint file.
10. Click 'Share with people', and then type your instructor's email address and a short message describing how sharing a file by sending a link to your OneDrive can be easier than sending an attachment. Include your name at the end of the message.
11. Click the Send button to send the shared link of the completed PowerPoint file to your instructor.
12. Exit the PowerPoint web app, and then exit Outlook.
13. In this exercise, you sent an email message from the Outlook client to your web-based email service provider at outlook.com. What are the advantages of using a Microsoft account with Outlook on your personal computer and checking the same email address at outlook.com when you are on a public computer?

In the Lab 1

Composing an Email Message with Attachments

Problem: Your fitness coach recommended that you use professionally designed templates to track your health journey. Compose an email message as shown in Figure 1–70 with the three template attachments found in the Data Files for Module 1.

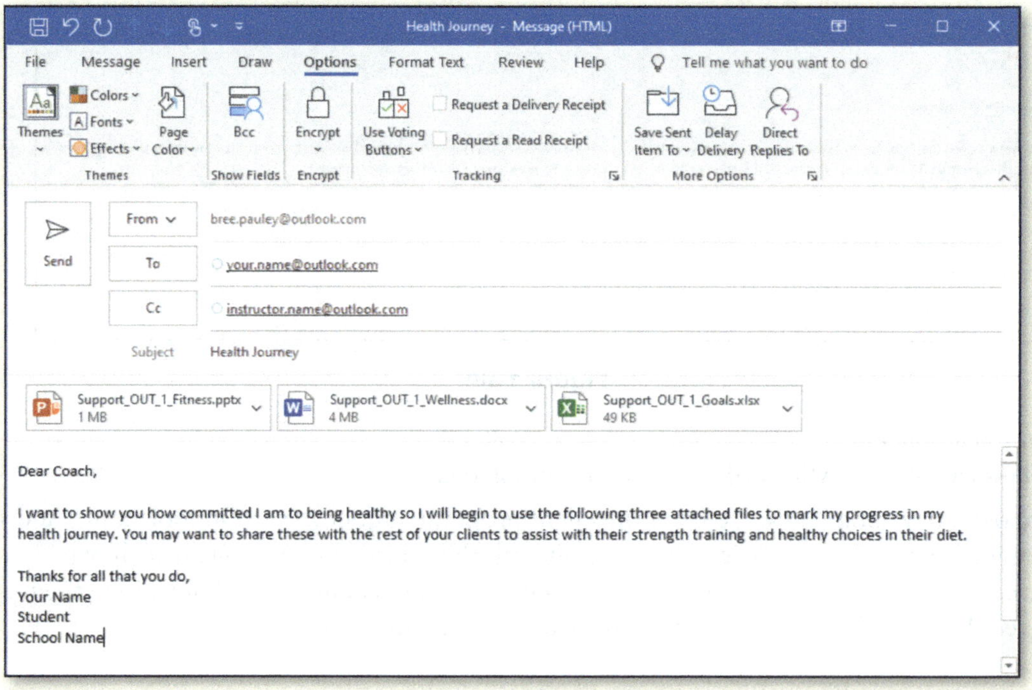

Figure 1–70

Perform the following tasks:

1. Compose a new email message. Address the message to yourself with a courtesy copy to your instructor.
2. Enter the subject, message text, and signature shown in Figure 1–70. Insert blank lines where they are shown in the figure. If Outlook flags any misspelled words as you type, check their spelling and correct them.
3. Change the theme of the email message to the Retrospect theme.
4. Change the signature to your name.
5. Attach the three files called Support_OUT_1_Fitness.pptx, Support_OUT_1_Wellness.docx, and Support_OUT_1_Goals.xlsx, which are located in the Data Files, to the email message.
6. Send the email message.
7. When you receive the message, open it, and then save the message on your hard drive, OneDrive, or a location that is most appropriate to your situation using the file name `SC_OUT_1_Health`. Submit the file in the format specified by your instructor.
8. Using one of your own email service providers, determine the maximum allowed mailbox size. Report the name of your email service provider, the maximum size, and whether you feel that is enough storage space.

In the Lab 2

Composing and Replying to an Email Message

Note: To complete this assignment, you will be required to use the Data Files. Please contact your instructor for information about accessing the Data Files.

Problem: You are in a new role at a tech start-up company. Your boss has asked you to represent your tech company at a large conference. Your first step is to ask your boss about the conference booth request form. You need to send the booth request form to your boss, ask the questions shown in the email message shown in Figure 1–71a, and then attach a file. Your boss responds to your email as shown in Figure 1–71b.

Perform the following tasks:

1. Create a new email message. Address the message to your instructor with a courtesy copy to yourself.
2. Enter the subject, message text, and signature shown in Figure 1–71a. Check spelling and grammar.
3. If requested by your instructor, change the address in the email message of the conference center to your own address.
4. Change the theme of the email message to the Wisp theme.
5. Change the importance of this email to high importance because you would like a response as soon as possible.
6. Attach the document called Support_OUT_1_BoothRequestForm.docx, which is located in the Data Files, to the email message. You do not need to fill out this form.
7. Send the email message and use the HTML format for the message.
8. When you receive the email message, move it to a new folder in your Inbox named `Tech Conference`.
9. Open the message in the Tech Conference folder, and then compose the reply. Figure 1–71b shows the reply from your boss. Reply using the text in the email message shown in Figure 1–71b. If Outlook flags any misspelled words as you type, check their spelling and correct them.

Continued >

In the Lab 2 *continued*

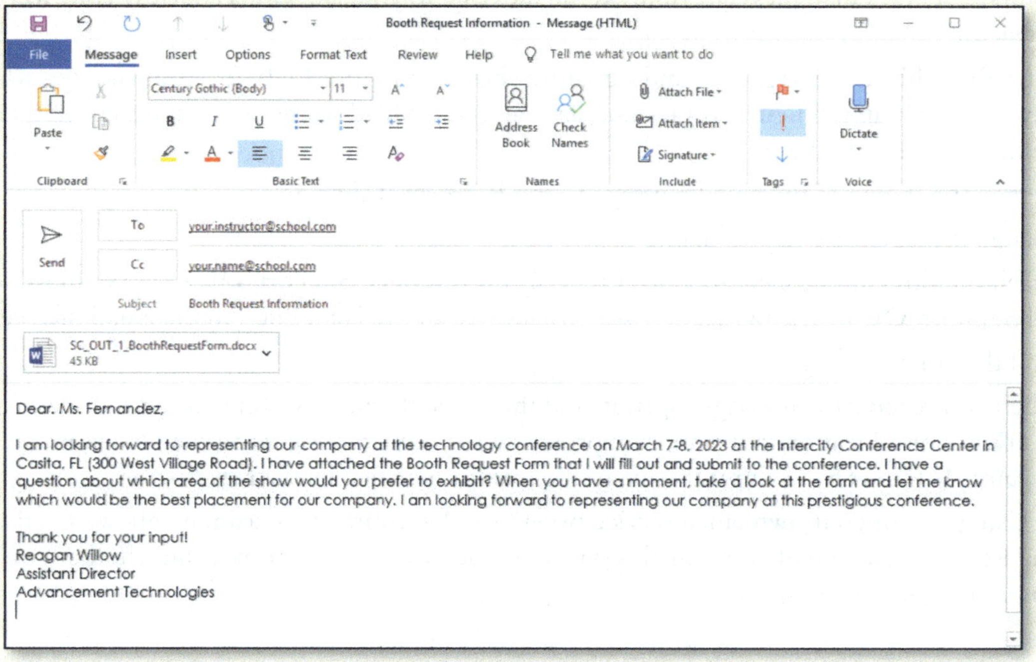

(a) Composed Email Message

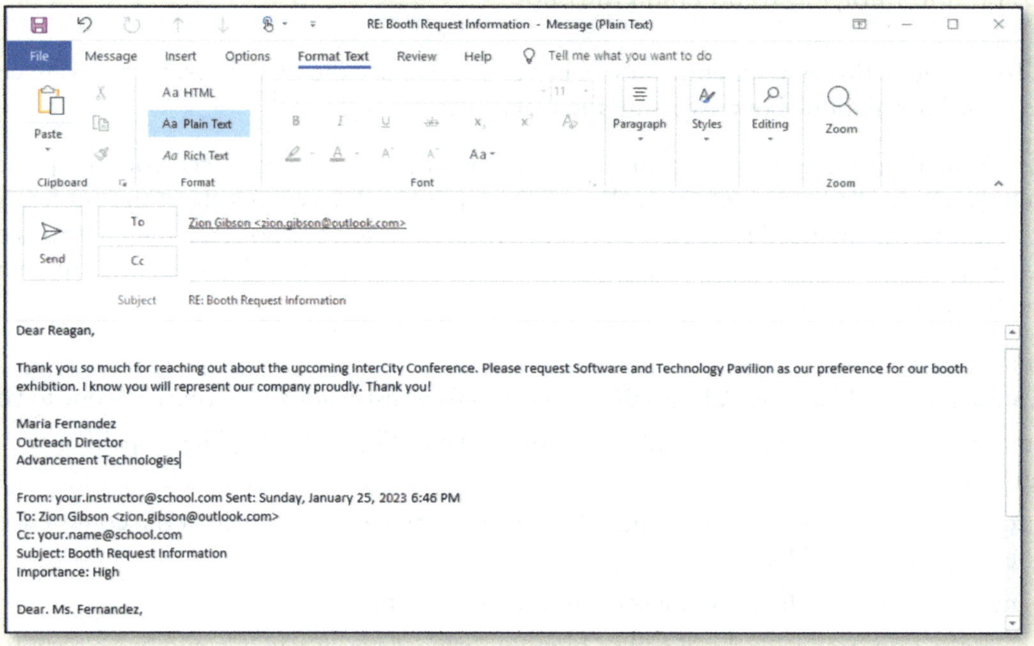

(b) Response to Email Message

Figure 1–71

10. If necessary, change the format of the email message to Plain Text, and then send the message to yourself.
11. When you receive the RE: Booth Request Information message, move it to the Tech Conference folder in your Inbox folder.

12. Select the original Booth Request Information message in the Sent Items folder. Save the message on your hard drive, OneDrive, or a location that is most appropriate to your situation using the file name `SC_OUT_1_Booth`. Submit the file in the format specified by your instructor.
13. Some conference websites do not include a phone number or a physical address. Why do you think that these business and conference sites only include an email address for correspondence?

In the Lab 3

Compose an Introductory Email Message to an Employer and Attach a File

Problem: For an upcoming job interview, your potential employer requests that you send an email message to introduce yourself. You compose a new introduction message and attach a PowerPoint file.

Part 1: The email message you write should be addressed to yourself and your instructor. Insert an appropriate subject line based on the content of your message. Write a paragraph of at least 50 words telling a potential employer about yourself (career path, past jobs, and so forth). Next, create a PowerPoint presentation with an opening slide with your picture and two additional slides with your academic and employment background with bulleted lists with your own information. Name this slide presentation My Background and attach it to the email message. Apply a theme other than the Office theme. Use the concepts and techniques presented in this module to create this email message. Be sure to check spelling and grammar before you send the message. Submit your assignment in the format specified by your instructor.

Part 2: You made several decisions while creating the email message in this assignment. When you decide on the subject of an email message, what considerations should you make? Why is it important that the email subject be eye-catching and informative? Why should you not use the following subject lines: LOL, Hey You, or Open This Now?

2 Managing Calendars with Outlook

Objectives

After completing this module, you will be able to:

- Describe the components of the Outlook Calendar
- Add a personal calendar to Outlook
- Add a city to the calendar Weather Bar list
- Navigate the calendar using the Date Navigator
- Display the calendar in various views
- Add national holidays to the default calendar
- Enter, save, move, edit, and delete appointments, Teams meetings, and events
- Organize your calendar with color categories
- Set the status of and a reminder for an appointment
- Import an iCalendar and view it in overlay mode
- Schedule and modify events
- Schedule live meetings and Teams online meetings
- Respond to meeting requests
- Peek at a calendar
- Print a calendar
- Save and share a calendar

Introduction to the Outlook Calendar

Plan your day, keep track of your deadlines, and increase your daily productivity. Whether you are a business professional, an entrepreneur, a student, or a community organizer, you can take advantage of the Outlook Calendar to schedule and manage appointments, events, and meetings. In particular, you can use Calendar to keep track of your class schedule and appointments and to schedule meetings. If you are traveling, you can view your calendar on your mobile phone or you can print a copy to keep with you. Use Outlook to view a daily, weekly, or monthly calendar.

In addition to using Calendar in your academic or professional life, it is helpful for scheduling personal time. Most people have multiple appointments to keep each day, week, or month. The Outlook Calendar can organize activity-related information in a structured, readable manner. You can create a calendar folder for a specific project and share it with your friends and professional colleagues.

BTW

Using Calendars

You can share your calendar with others online using OneDrive to make appointments, check free times, schedule meetings, and refer to contact information. This is especially useful when you are arranging and syncing events that depend on other people's schedules.

Project: Appointments, Events, and Meetings in Calendar

By creating a daily schedule to manage your time, you can stay organized and reduce your stress level. Managing your schedule using a calendar can increase productivity while maximizing free time. Outlook is the perfect tool to maintain both a professional and a personal schedule. The **Calendar** is the Outlook folder that contains your personal schedule of appointments, events, and meetings. In this project, Willow Choi, an intern of Motion AI Self-Driving Cars, sets up the basic features of Calendar to track her appointments, classes, work schedules, and meetings, both face-to-face and virtual, using Microsoft Teams (Figure 2–1).

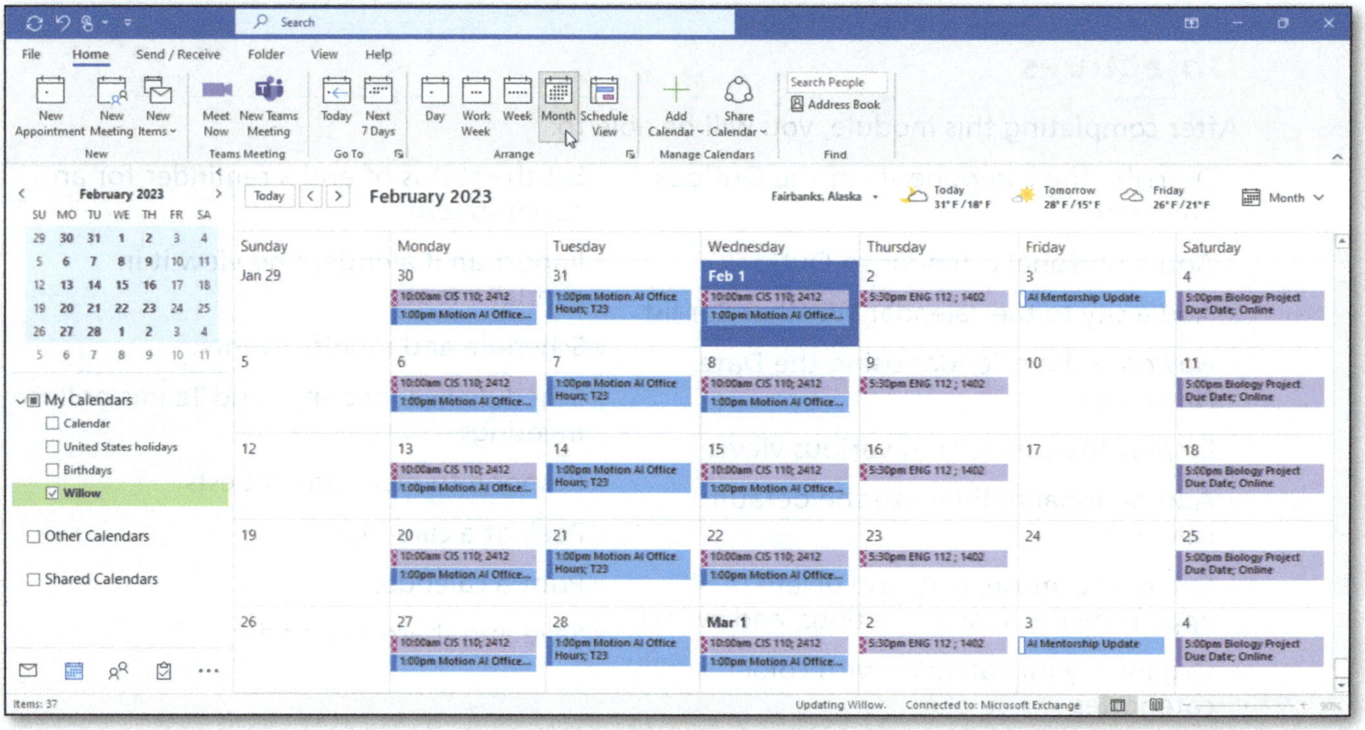

Figure 2–1

BTW

Deleting Items Permanently

Items you delete, including events and email messages, are stored in the Deleted Items folder in Mail view until you empty the folder by right-clicking the Deleted Items folder and then clicking Empty Folder on the shortcut menu.

People use a calendar to keep track of their schedules and to organize and manage their time. For students, a class list with room numbers and class times would be a good start toward managing their school schedule. For business professionals, the calendar is a dynamic tool that requires frequent updating to keep track of appointments and meetings. You also may want to keep track of personal items, such as doctor appointments, birthdays, and family gatherings.

In this module, you will learn how to perform basic calendar tasks. You will perform the following general activities as you progress through this module:

1. Configure the Calendar options.
2. Create and manage appointments.
3. Schedule events.
4. Schedule meetings.
5. Print a calendar.
6. Save and share a calendar.

Configuring the Outlook Calendar

When you start Outlook, Mail view appears. The Navigation bar displays four views: Mail, Calendar, People, and Tasks. By selecting Calendar, you can create a customized calendar to assist in scheduling your day, week, and month. Before scheduling your first calendar appointment, you can add a personal calendar and customize your settings to fit the way you work. Each day as you check your calendar for the day's events, the Weather Bar displays your local weather so you can determine whether you need an umbrella or dress professionally for work based on the climate. By adding national holidays to your Outlook calendar, you can make sure these dates are prominent in your calendar.

BTW

The Ribbon and Screen Resolution

Outlook may change how the groups and buttons within the groups appear on the ribbon, depending on the computer's screen resolution. Thus, your ribbon may look different from the ones in this book if you are using a screen resolution other than 1366 × 768.

CONSIDER THIS

What advantages does a digital calendar like Outlook provide compared to a paper planner or wall calendar?

A digital calendar provides access from any location by syncing your computer or smartphone with the cloud to view your appointments and meetings. You can view your schedule within an email meeting invitation. You can view more than one calendar at a time, share others' calendars, and overlay calendars to plan a meeting date with colleagues.

Using the Calendar Window

The Calendar window shown in Figure 2–2 includes a variety of features to help you work efficiently. It contains many elements similar to the windows in other Office programs, as well as some that are unique to Outlook. The main elements of the Calendar window are the Navigation pane and the appointment area.

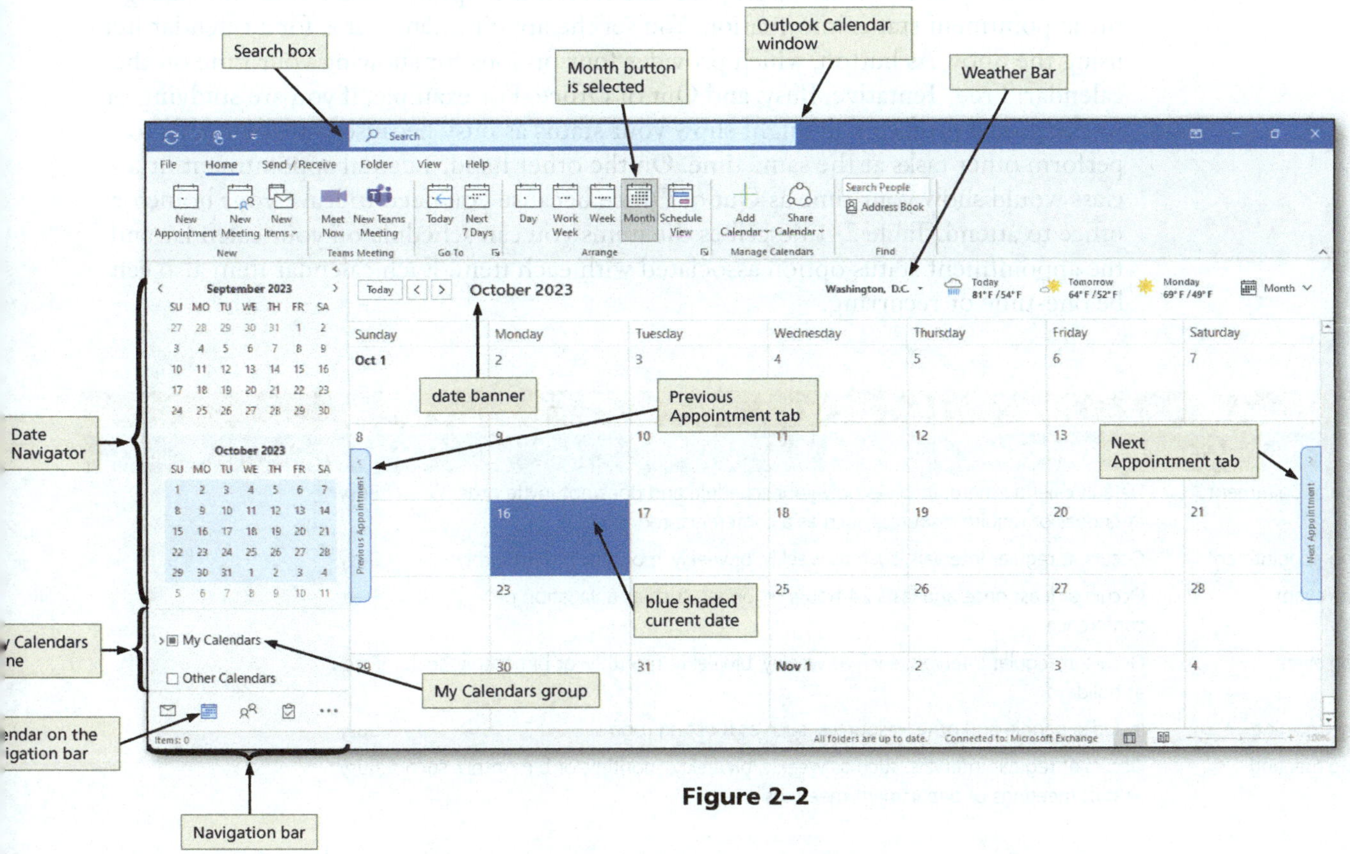

Figure 2–2

BTW
Searching for Calendar Items
To find a calendar item, click the Search box on the title bar, and then type a word or phrase that appears in the calendar item you are seeking. Items that contain the text you typed are listed with the search text highlighted. When you are finished, click the Close Search button (Search tab | Close group).

The Navigation pane includes two panes: the Date Navigator and the My Calendars pane. The **Date Navigator** contains the current month's calendar and the future month's calendar. The calendars on the Date Navigator display a blue box around the current date, scroll arrows to advance from one month to another, and bold for any dates on which an item is scheduled. The **My Calendars pane** lists available calendars; you can view them one at a time as a single calendar or view more than one calendar displayed side by side. The **appointment area** contains a date banner and a Weather Bar that shows today's weather in the selected city. The appointment area displays one-hour time slots split in half hours by default when viewing Calendar in Day, Work Week, or Week view. (The appointment area is not available in Month view.)

Identifying Calendar Items

An **item** is any element in Outlook that contains information. Examples of calendar items include appointments, events, and meetings. All calendar items start as an appointment. Outlook defines an **appointment**, such as a doctor's appointment, as an activity that does not involve other people or resources, such as conference rooms. Outlook defines an **event**, such as a seminar or vacation, as an activity that occurs at least once and lasts 24 hours or longer. An appointment becomes an event when you schedule it for the entire day. An annual event, such as a birthday, anniversary, or holiday, occurs yearly on a specific date. Events do not occupy time slots in the appointment area and, instead, are displayed in a banner below the day heading when viewing the calendar in Day, Work Week, or Week view. An appointment becomes a **meeting** when people and other resources, such as meeting rooms, are invited whether face-to-face or virtually.

When you create items on your calendar, it is helpful to show your time using the appointment status information. You set the appointment status for a calendar item using the Show As button, which provides four options for showing your time on the calendar: Free, Tentative, Busy, and Out of Office. For example, if you are studying or working on a project, you might show your status as busy because you are unable to perform other tasks at the same time. On the other hand, a dental appointment or a class would show your time as Out of Office because you need to leave your home or office to attend. Table 2–1 describes the items you can schedule on your calendar and the appointment status option associated with each item. Each calendar item also can be one-time or recurring.

Table 2–1 Calendar Items

Calendar Item	Description	Show As Default
One-time appointment	Default calendar item; involves only your schedule and does not invite other attendees or require resources such as a conference room	Busy
Recurring appointment	Occurs at regular intervals, such as weekly, biweekly, monthly, or bimonthly	Busy
One-time event	Occurs at least once and lasts 24 hours or longer, such as a vacation or conference	Free
Recurring event	Occurs at regular intervals, such as weekly, biweekly, monthly, or bimonthly, such as holidays	Free
One-time meeting	Includes people and other resources, such as meeting rooms	Busy
Recurring meeting	Occurs at regular intervals, such as weekly, biweekly, monthly, or bimonthly, such as staff meetings or department meetings	Busy

To Create a Calendar Folder

When you schedule an appointment, Outlook adds the appointment to the Calendar folder by default. Willow Choi plans to keep track of her intern business tasks at Motion AI as well as her personal and academic items instead of creating separate calendars for every aspect of her life. Users often create multiple calendars to keep personal items separate from academic or business items. As in other Outlook folders, such as the Inbox, you can create multiple folders within the Calendar folder that each contains one or more calendars. The following steps create a calendar to store your personal and school-related information separate from your default Calendar within the same calendar group. ***Why?*** *In certain situations, you may need to keep more than one calendar, such as one for business items and another for personal items.*

1

- Start Microsoft Outlook.
- Click Calendar on the Navigation bar to display the Outlook Calendar.
- Click Folder on the ribbon to display the Folder tab (Figure 2–3).

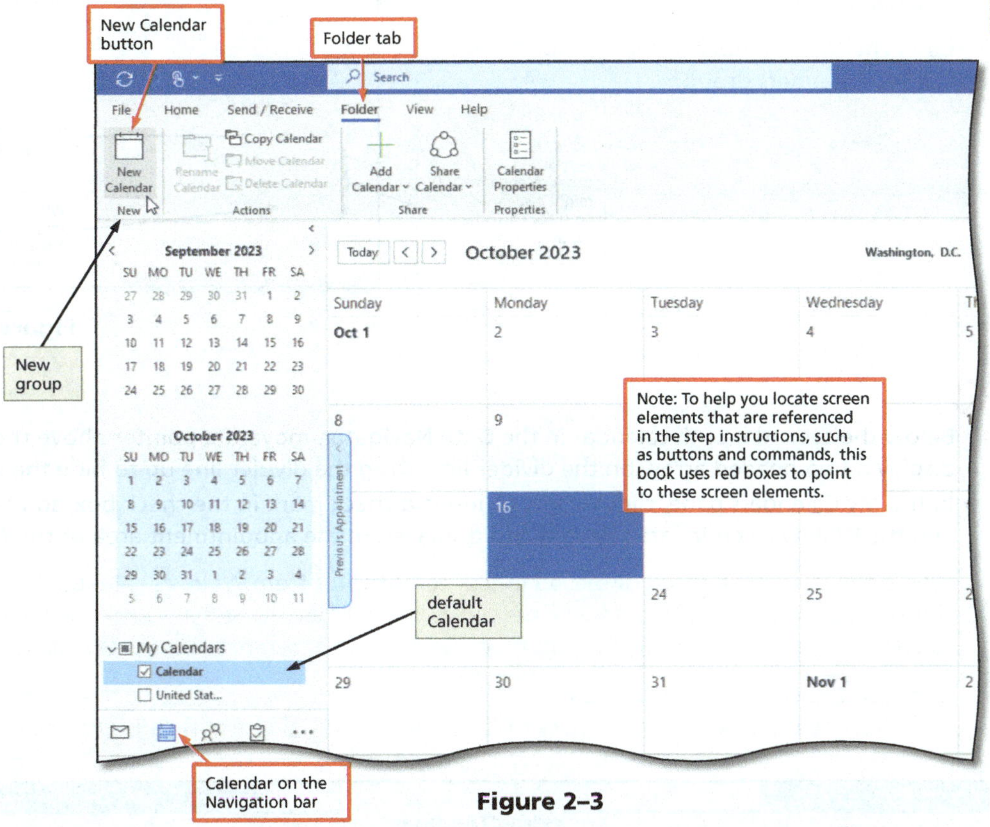

Figure 2–3

2

- Click the New Calendar button (Folder tab | New group) to display the Create New Folder dialog box.
- Type **Willow** in the Name box (Create New Folder dialog box) to enter a name for the new folder.
- Click the Folder contains arrow to display a list of items the folder will contain.
- If necessary, click Calendar Items to specify what the folder will contain.
- If necessary, click Calendar in the 'Select where to place the folder' list to specify where the folder will be stored (Figure 2–4).

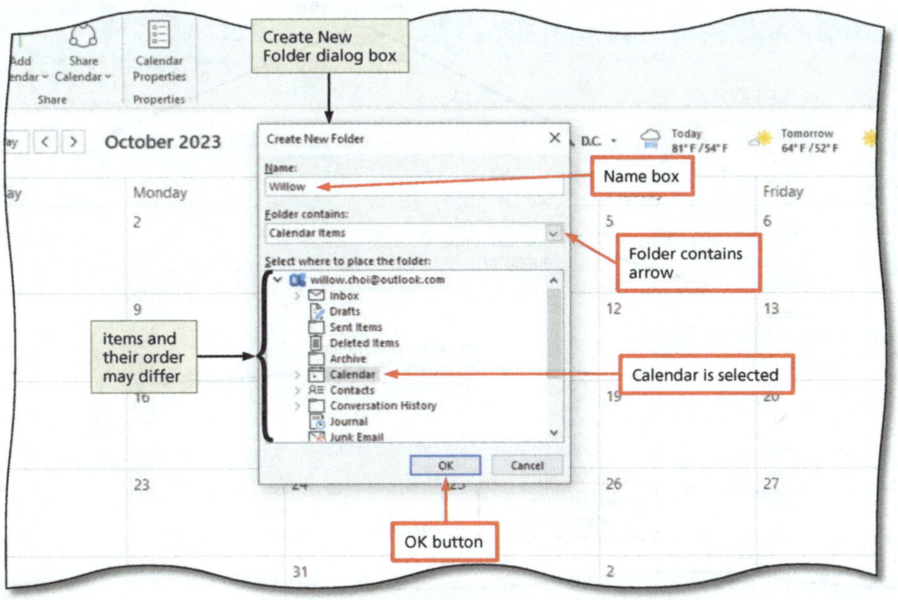

Figure 2–4

3

- Click OK to close the Create New Folder dialog box and add the new folder to the My Calendars group.
- Scroll the My Calendars pane to display the Willow calendar (Figure 2–5).

Q&A Why is the Willow calendar not displayed in the Outlook window?
Outlook does not automatically display the newly created calendar until you select it.

Can I change the order of the calendars listed in the My Calendars group?
Yes. Right-click a calendar and then click Move Up or Move Down on the shortcut menu.

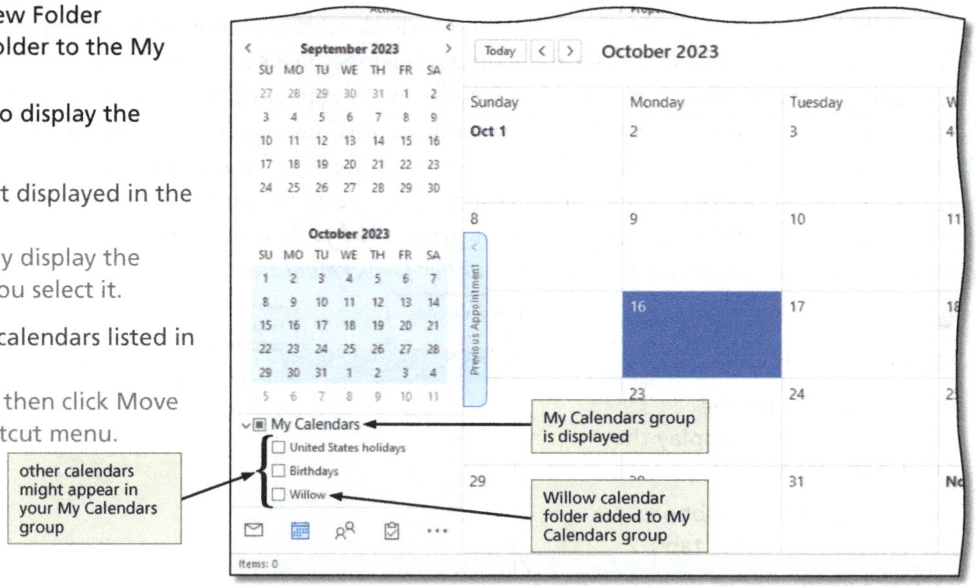

Figure 2–5

4

- Below the second month calendar in the Date Navigator, move the pointer above the My Calendars group to display a two-headed arrow on the divider line. Drag the divider line up to hide the second month calendar.
- In the My Calendars pane, click Willow to insert a check mark in the check box, so that both the default Calendar and the Willow calendar are selected and displayed in the appointment area of the Outlook window (Figure 2–6).

Q&A Why is the default calendar displayed in a different color from Willow's calendar?
Outlook automatically assigns a different color to each new calendar you create to make it easier to distinguish one calendar from the other. Your calendar colors might be different from those shown in Figure 2–6.

Can I select a color for the calendar?
Yes. Click the View tab, click the Color button (View tab | Color group), and then select a color from the Color gallery.

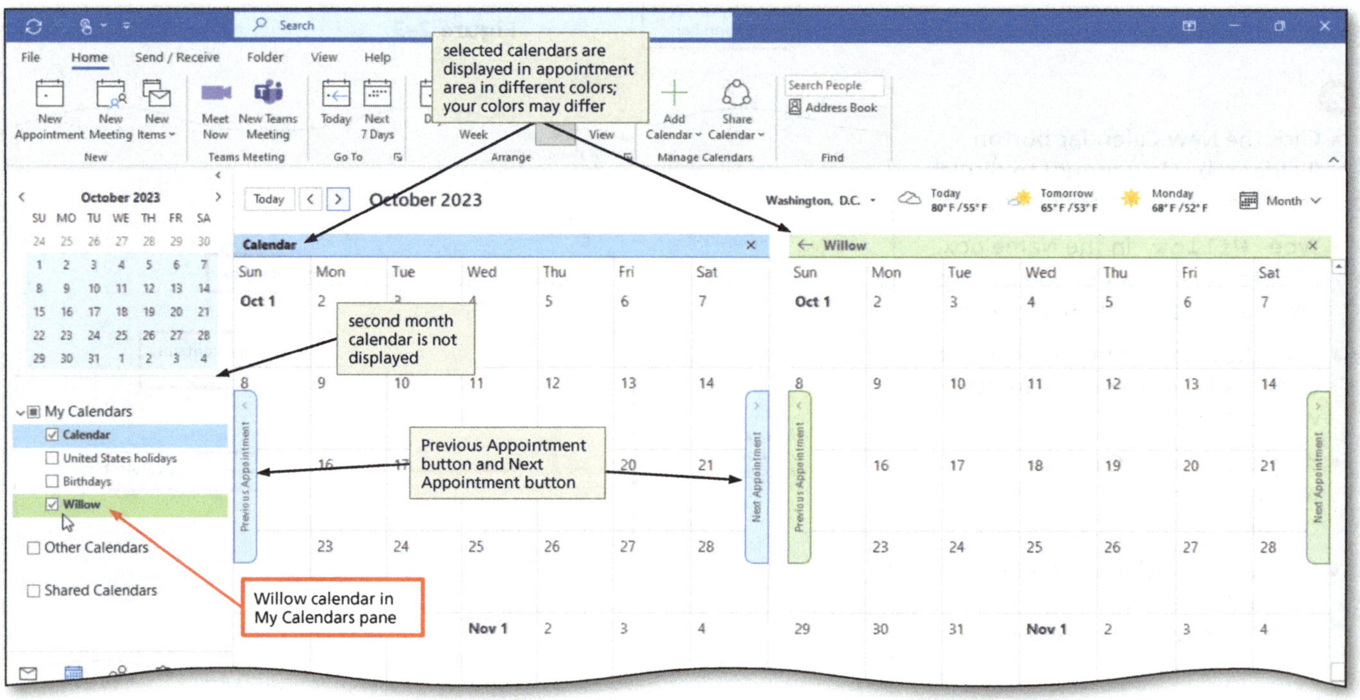

Figure 2–6

5

- Click Calendar in the My Calendars pane to remove the check mark from the Calendar check box so that the default calendar no longer is displayed in the appointment area.

Q&A What is the purpose of the tabs on each side of the appointment area?
The tabs are for navigating to the previous and next appointments.

Other Ways

1. Press CTRL+SHIFT+E

To Add a City to the Calendar Weather Bar

Outlook provides a Weather Bar so you can view the current three-day weather forecast when you open the calendar. By default, Washington, D.C. is displayed. When you click the forecast, further details appear such as the wind condition, humidity level, and precipitation, along with a link to a detailed weather forecast online. ***Why?*** *Each morning as you view your schedule, the Weather Bar informs you about the day's weather so you can plan your day accordingly.* The following steps add a city to the calendar Weather Bar to display the current forecast.

1

- Click the arrow to the right of the current city in the Weather Bar to display the Add Location command (Figure 2–7).

Q&A My Weather Bar does not appear in the calendar. What should I do?
Click the File tab to display Backstage view, click Options, and then click the Calendar category. Scroll down to the Weather section, and then click the Show weather on the calendar check box to insert a check mark.

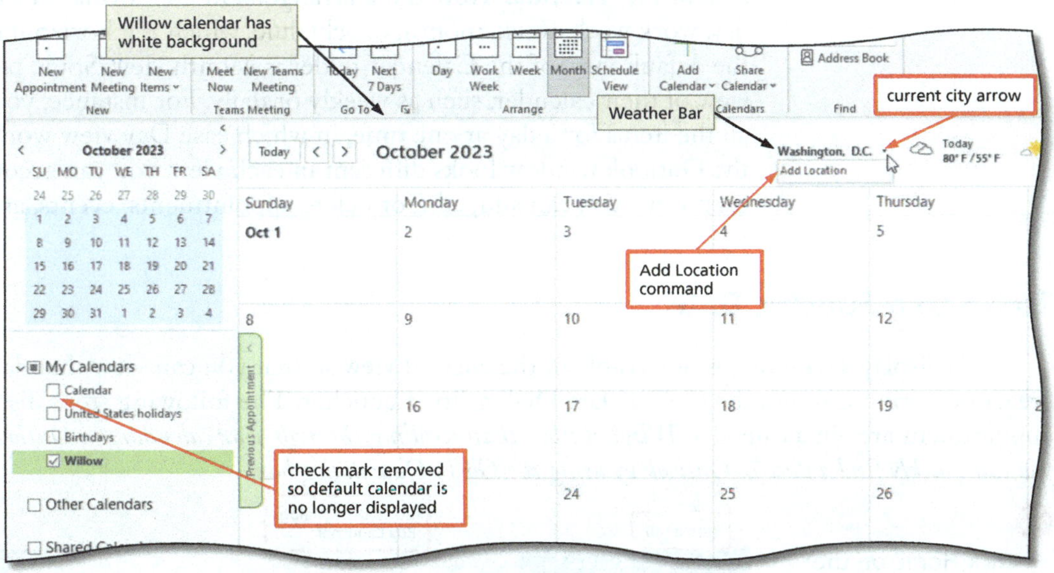

Figure 2–7

2

- Click Add Location to display a search box.
- Type **Fairbanks** and then click the magnifying glass to search for the city location (Figure 2–8).

Q&A Can I search for a city using a postal code?
Yes. Type the postal code to search for the location in the Weather Bar search box.

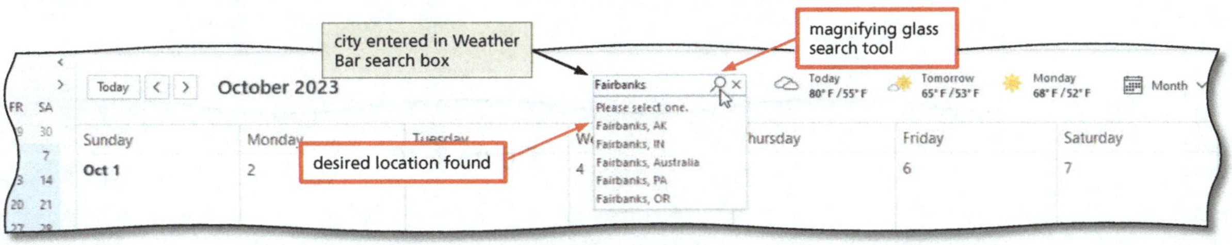

Figure 2–8

3

- Click Fairbanks, AK to select the location and display its three-day forecast in the Weather Bar (Figure 2–9).
- If requested by your instructor, replace Fairbanks, AK with your hometown in the Weather Bar.

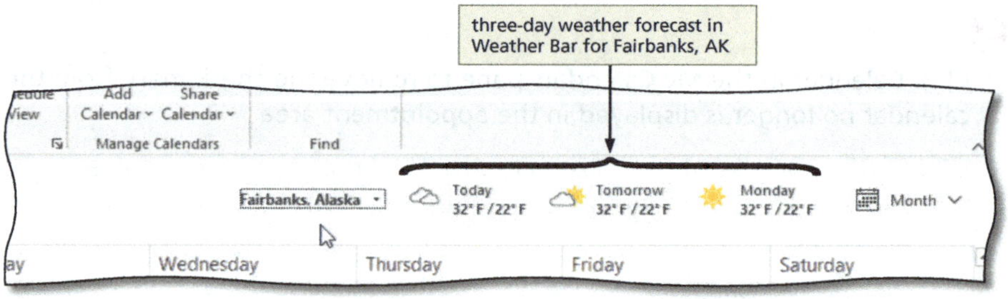

Figure 2–9

Q&A Why does my Weather Bar display the message 'Weather service is not available'?
Most likely, you are not connected to the Internet. You must have Internet connectivity to display the weather forecast.

Navigating the Calendar

Each Microsoft Outlook folder displays the items it contains in a layout called a view. The **calendar view** is the arrangement and format of the folder contents by day, work week, week, month, or schedule, which is a horizontal layout. Recall that the default view of the Calendar folder is Month view. Some people prefer a different view of their calendar, such as weekly or daily. For instance, you might want to view all the items for a day at one time, in which case Day view would work best. Although the Outlook window looks different in each view, you can accomplish the same tasks in each view: you can add, edit, or delete appointments, events, and meetings.

To Go to a Specific Date

To display a date that is not visible in the current view so that you can view that date in the appointment area, one option is to use the Go To Date Dialog Box Launcher. The following steps display a specific date in the appointment area in a calendar. ***Why?*** *Rather than scrolling through your calendars in Outlook to find a specific date, you can quickly find a date in Outlook by using the Go To Date dialog box.*

1

- Click Home on the ribbon to display the Home tab.
- Click the Go To Date Dialog Box Launcher (Home tab | Go To group) to display the Go To Date dialog box (Figure 2–10).

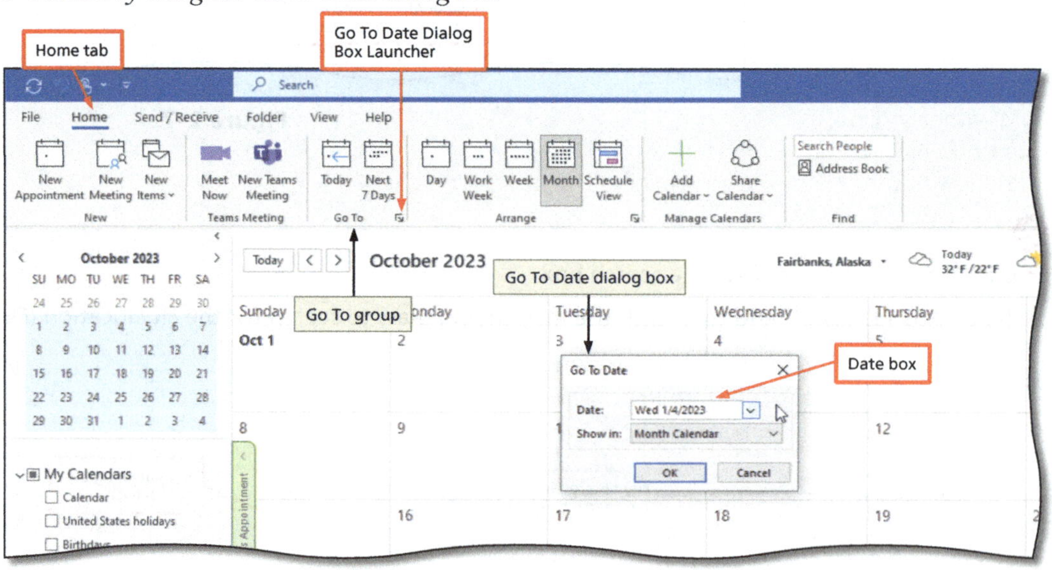

Figure 2–10

2

- Type **1/4/2023** in the Date box to enter the date you want to display in the current calendar.
- Click the Show in button, and then select Day Calendar to show the calendar in Day view (Figure 2–11).

Q&A Why did 'Wed' appear next to the date in the Date box?
Outlook automatically includes the day of the week (Wednesday, in this case) when you enter a date in the Date box.

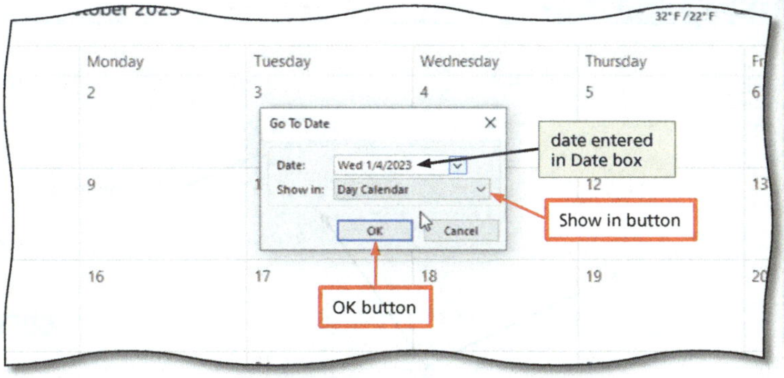

Figure 2–11

3

- Click OK to close the Go To Date dialog box and display the selected date in Day view (Figure 2–12).

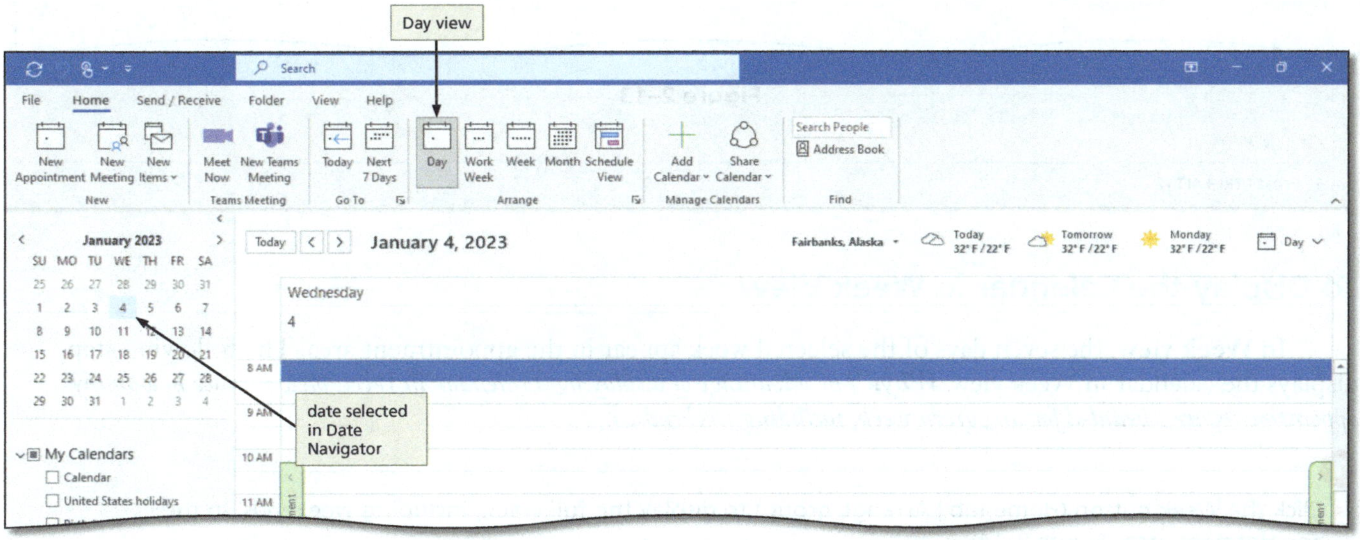

Figure 2–12

Other Ways

1. Press CTRL+G

To Display the Calendar in Work Week View

Why? In Outlook, you can display several calendar days at once so that you can see multiple appointments at the same time. **Work Week view** shows five workdays (Monday through Friday) in a columnar style. Hours that are not part of the default workday (8:00 AM – 5:00 PM) appear shaded when viewing the calendar in Day, Work Week, and Week view. The following step displays the calendar in Work Week view.

1

- Click the Work Week button (Home tab | Arrange group) to display the work week in the appointment area for the selected date (Figure 2–13).

Experiment

- Scroll up and down in Work Week view to see how the color changes to reflect hours outside the default workday.

Q&A Why are Monday through Friday highlighted on the Date Navigator?
The calendar days displayed in the appointment area are highlighted on the Date Navigator.

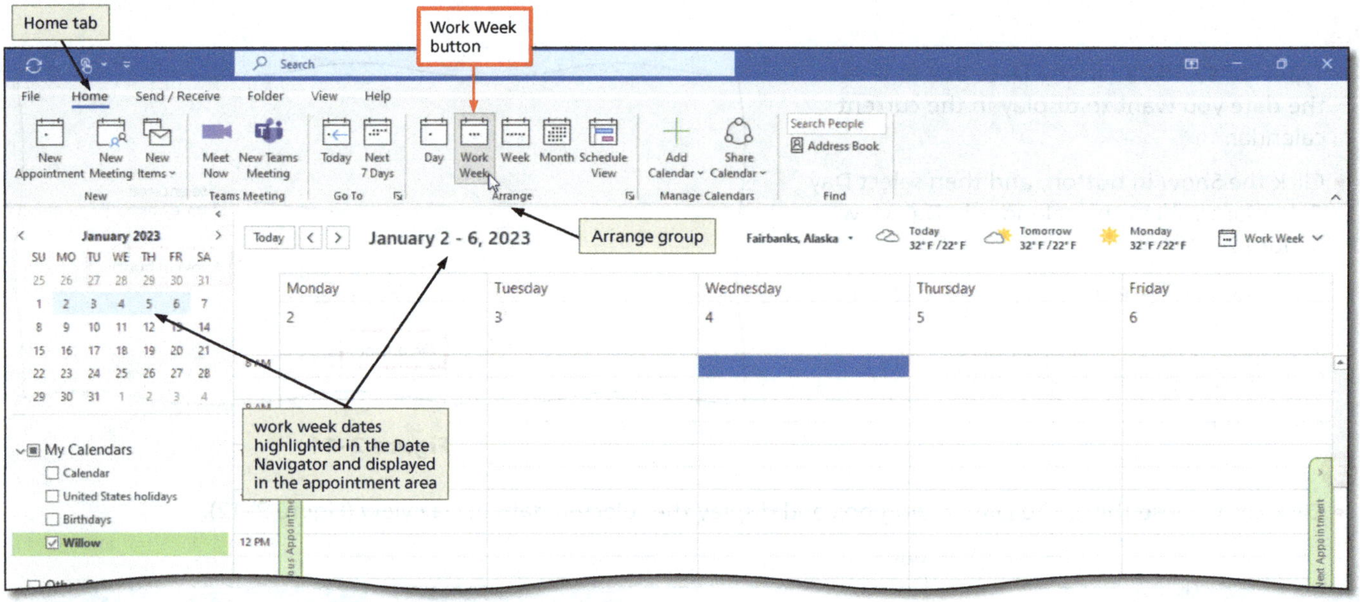

Figure 2–13

Other Ways

1. Press CTRL+ALT+2

To Display the Calendar in Week View

In **Week view**, the seven days of the selected week appear in the appointment area. The following step displays the calendar in Week view. ***Why?*** *The advantage of displaying a calendar in Week view is to see how many appointments are scheduled for any given week, including weekends.*

1

- Click the Week button (Home tab | Arrange group) to display the full week, including weekends, in the appointment area (Figure 2–14).

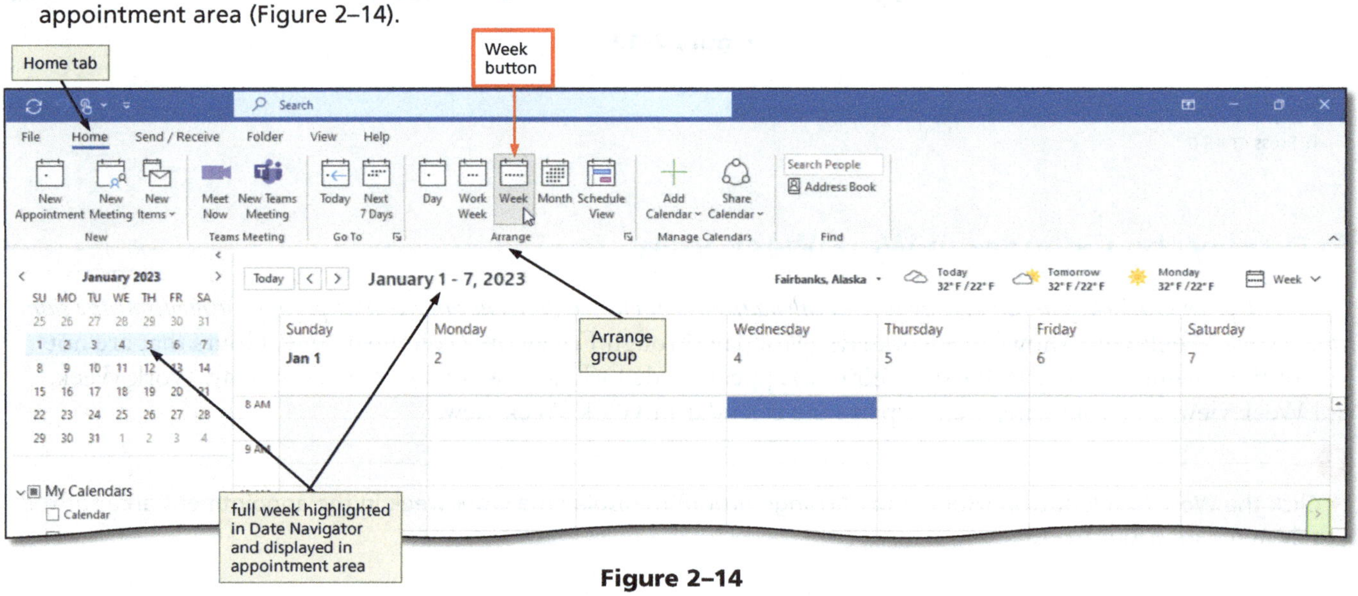

Figure 2–14

Other Ways

1. Press CTRL+ALT+3

To Display the Calendar in Month View

Month view resembles a standard monthly calendar page and displays a schedule for an entire month. Appointments can be displayed in each date in the calendar. The following step displays the calendar in Month view. ***Why?*** *By viewing the entire month without scrolling through individual appointments, you can see when you have an open day.*

1

- Click the Month button (Home tab | Arrange group) to display one full month in the appointment area (Figure 2–15).

Experiment

- By default, Month view displays dates from the beginning to the end of a calendar month. To select several weeks across two calendar months, click the Date Navigator and then drag to select the weeks you want to view.

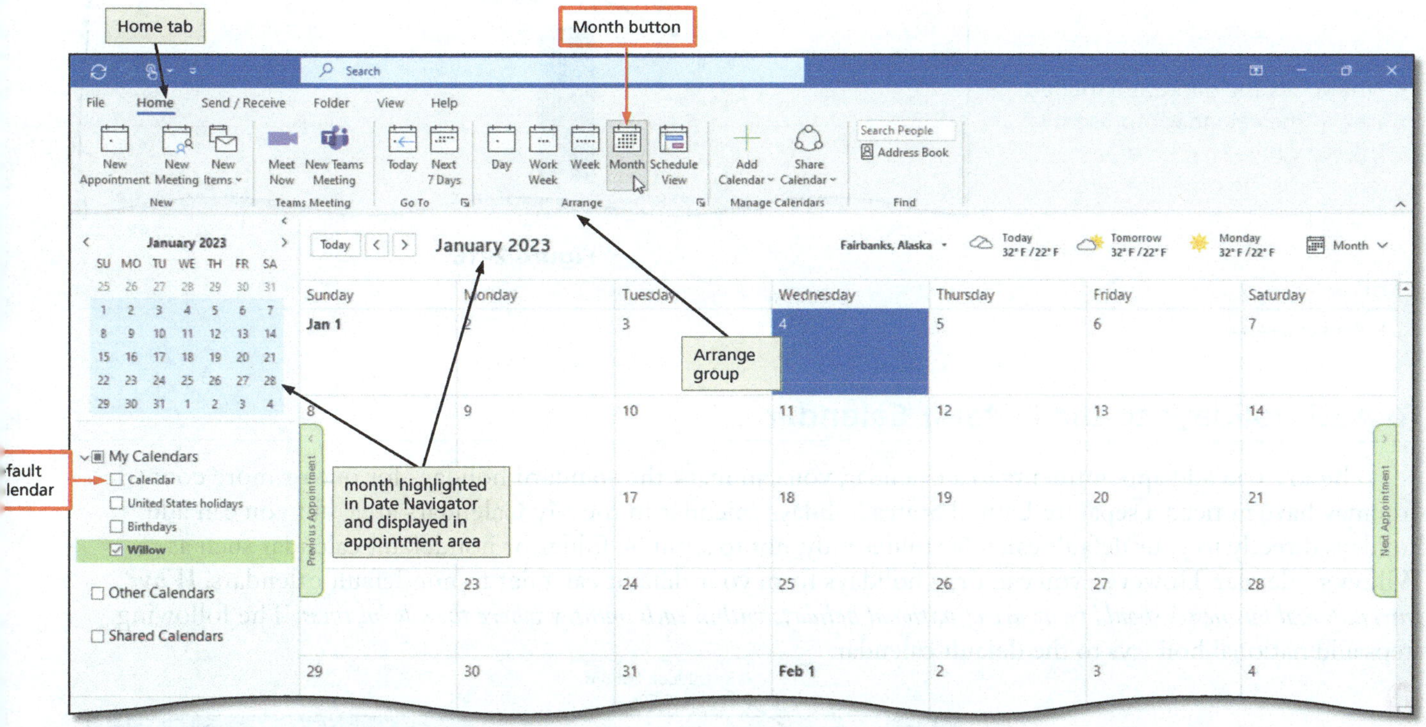

Figure 2–15

Other Ways

1. Press CTRL+ALT+4

To Display the Calendar in Schedule View

Schedule view allows you to view multiple calendars over the course of a single day in a horizontal layout to make scheduling meetings easier. The following steps display the default Calendar and the Willow calendar in Schedule view. ***Why?*** *Schedule view is useful when trying to see multiple calendars so that you can check for overlapping items.*

1

- Click Calendar (default Calendar) in the My Calendars pane to insert a check mark in the check box and to display both the default Calendar and Willow's calendar in the appointment area.
- Click the Schedule View button (Home tab | Arrange group) to display both calendars in Schedule view (Figure 2–16).

Q&A Why does Schedule view show a single day instead of multiple days?
Schedule view is designed to display one day at a time.

What does the dark blue shaded area in the calendar represent?
The dark blue shaded area represents the time slot selected in Day view.

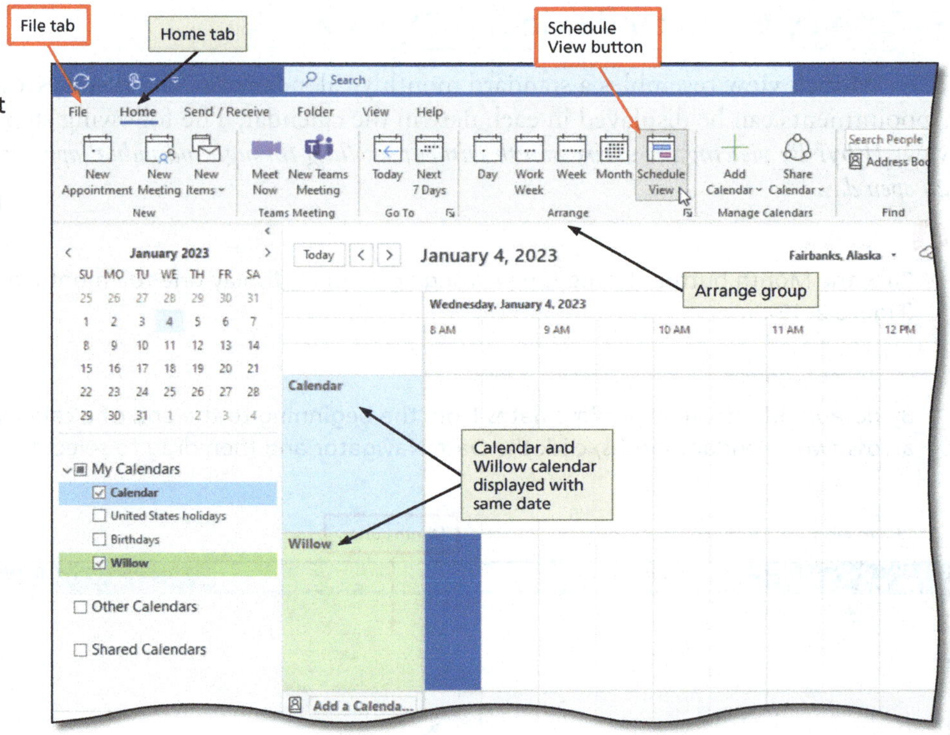

Figure 2–16

Other Ways

1. Press CTRL+ALT+5

To Add Holidays to the Default Calendar

Before you add appointments to a calendar, you can mark the standard holidays for one or more countries. You may have noticed a separate United States holidays calendar in the My Calendars area, but you can add holidays directly to your default calendar folder only, not to a public folder or nondefault calendar such as Willow's calendar. However, you can drag holidays from your default calendar to nondefault calendars. ***Why?*** *International businesses should be aware of national holidays within each country where they do business.* The following steps add national holidays to the default calendar.

1

- Click the File tab on the ribbon to open Backstage view.
- Click Options to display the Outlook Options dialog box.
- Click Calendar in the left pane to display the options in the Calendar category (Figure 2–17).

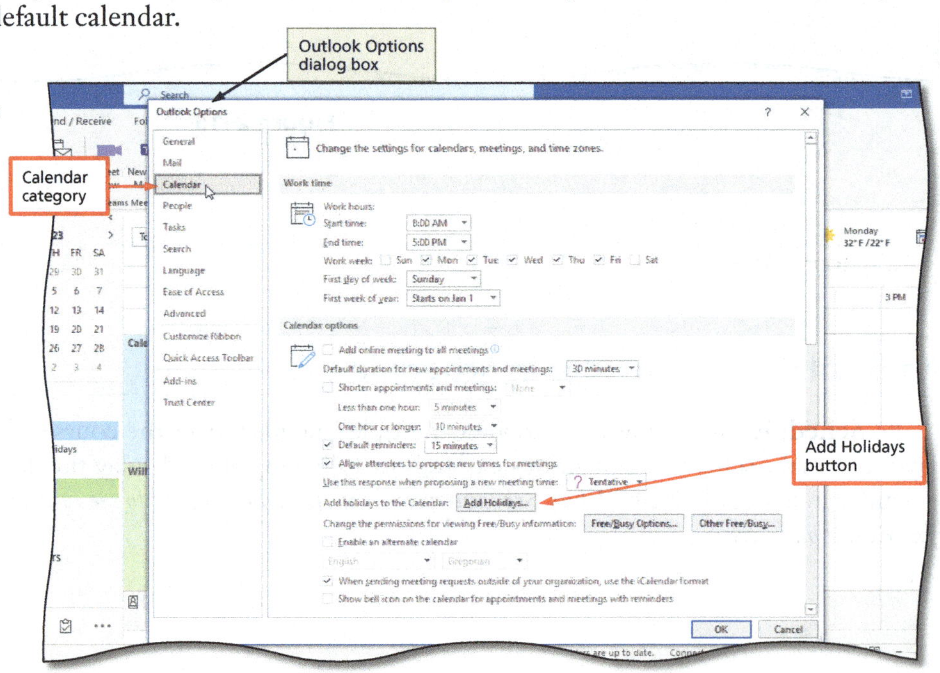

Figure 2–17

2

- Click the Add Holidays button to display the Add Holidays to Calendar dialog box (Figure 2–18).

Q&A Can I select multiple countries to display more than one set of national holidays?
Yes. You can select the holidays of multiple countries to display in the default calendar.

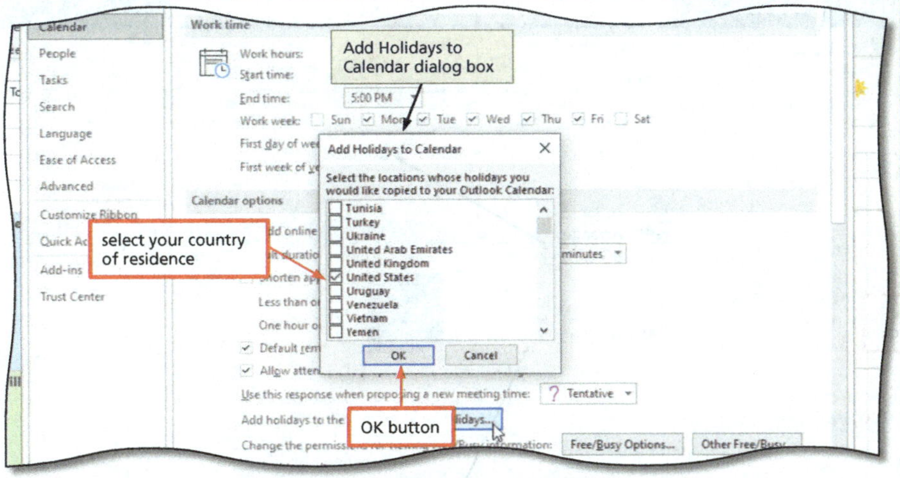

Figure 2–18

3

- If necessary, click the check box for your country of residence to add that country's national holidays to the default calendar.
- Click OK to close the dialog box, import the holidays, and display the confirmation message that the holidays were added to your calendar (Figure 2–19).

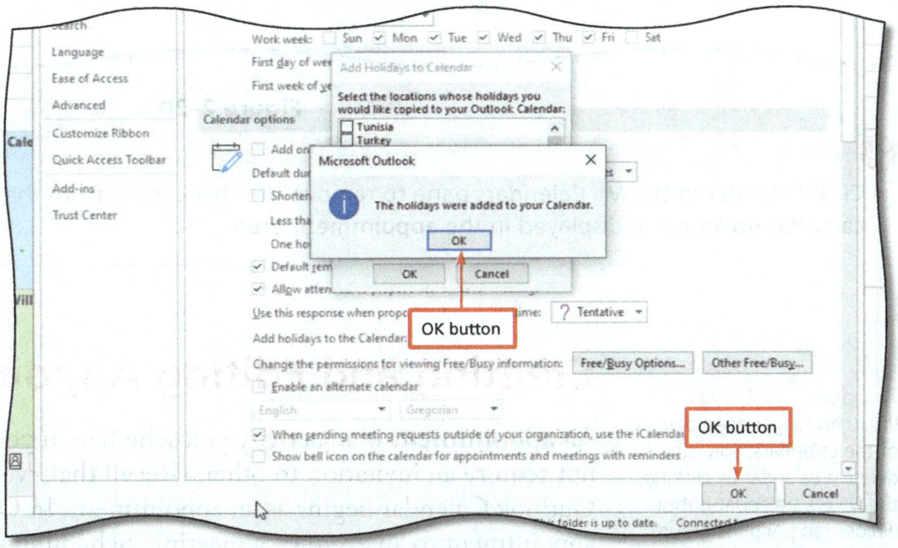

Figure 2–19

4

- Click OK to close the Microsoft Outlook dialog box and the Add Holidays to Calendar dialog box.
- Click OK to close the Outlook Options dialog box.
- Click the Month button (Home tab | Arrange group) to display both calendars in Month view in the appointment area (Figure 2–20).

Q&A The national holidays do not appear in Willow's calendar. Where are they displayed?
Holidays are displayed only in the default calendar.

Why are the national holidays on my default calendar different from Figure 2–20?
Your default calendar holiday dates might differ from those shown in Figure 2–20 if you selected a different country.

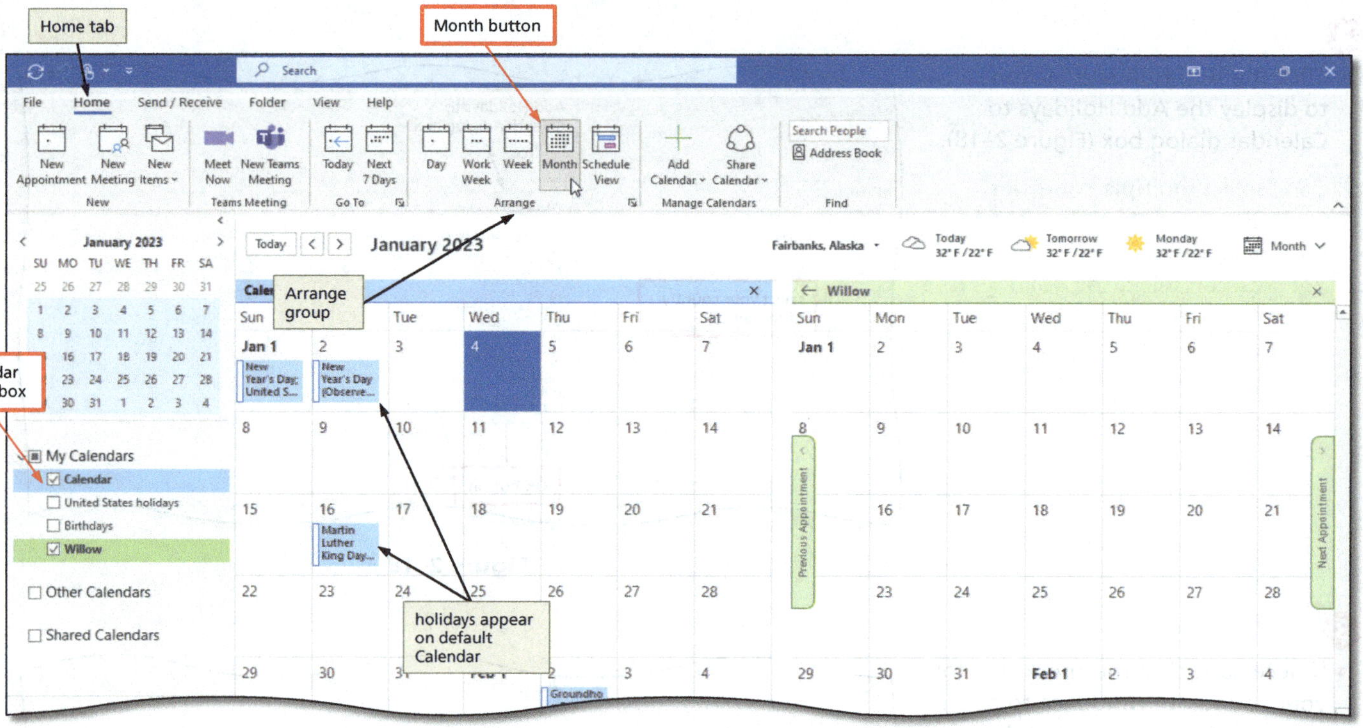

Figure 2–20

5

- Click Calendar in the My Calendars pane to remove the check mark from the Calendar check box so that the default calendar no longer is displayed in the appointment area.

BTW

Deleting a Calendar

If you no longer need one of the calendars, you can delete a calendar by clicking the Delete Calendar button (Folder tab | Actions group). Click the Yes button in the Microsoft Outlook dialog box to delete the folder. Outlook sends the deleted folder to the Deleted Items folder.

Creating and Editing Appointments

An **appointment** is an activity you schedule in your Outlook calendar that does not require an invitation to others. Recall that every calendar item you schedule in Outlook Calendar begins as an appointment. In Outlook, you easily can change an appointment to an event or a meeting. Scheduling a board meeting, dental visit, or a class schedule as a recurring appointment helps you successfully manage your activities and obligations. To better organize your appointments and meetings in your Outlook calendar, you can add color categories that let you scan and visually associate similar items. For example, you can set the color blue to represent your business meetings and the color green for doctor's appointments.

Creating Appointments in the Appointment Area

A **one-time appointment**, such as a concert event, conference call, or course exam date, is an appointment that occurs only once on a calendar. A **recurring appointment**, such as a class throughout an academic course, repeats on the calendar at regular intervals. Appointments can be created in two ways: using the appointment area, where you enter the appointment directly in the appropriate time slot, or using the Untitled - Appointment window, where you can enter more specific details about the appointment such as the location or address of the activity.

You can also create an appointment from an email message. In Mail view, drag an email message from the Inbox to the Calendar icon on the Navigation bar to open an Appointment window where you can enter appointment details.

To Create a One-Time Appointment Using the Appointment Area

When you click a day on the calendar in the Navigation pane, Outlook displays the calendar for the date selected in Day view in the appointment area. Day view shows a daily view of a specific date in half-hour increments. The following steps use the appointment area to create a one-time appointment for Willow's yearly dental cleaning. ***Why?*** *If you are scheduling a one-time activity such as a doctor's appointment, you can type directly in the appointment area because you do not need a detailed description.*

1

- Click and hold the month name January on the Date Navigator to display a list of months with the associated year (Figure 2–21).

Experiment

- View several dates that are not consecutive by clicking a date on the Date Navigator, holding down the CTRL key, and then clicking additional days.

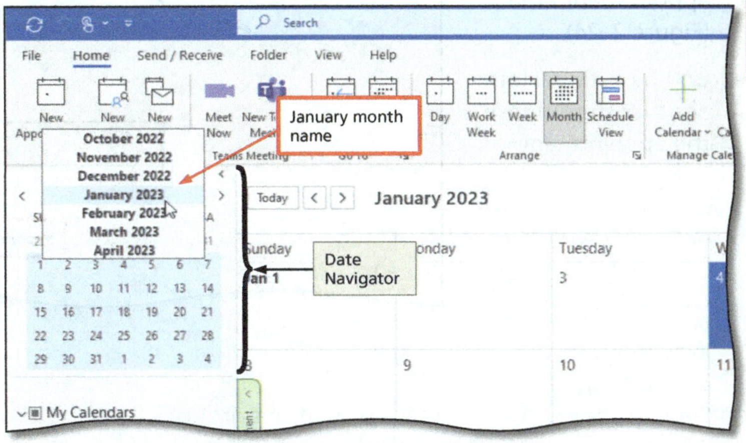

Figure 2–21

2

- If necessary, click January 2023 on the Date Navigator to display the selected month in the appointment area.
- Click 13 in the January 2023 calendar on the Date Navigator to display the selected date in the appointment area in Day view (Figure 2–22).

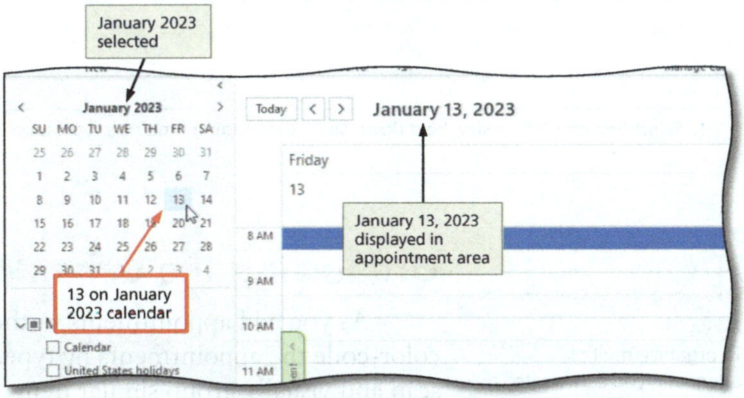

Figure 2–22

3

- Drag to select two half-hour increments from the 9:00 AM to the 10:00 AM time slot in the appointment area (Figure 2–23).

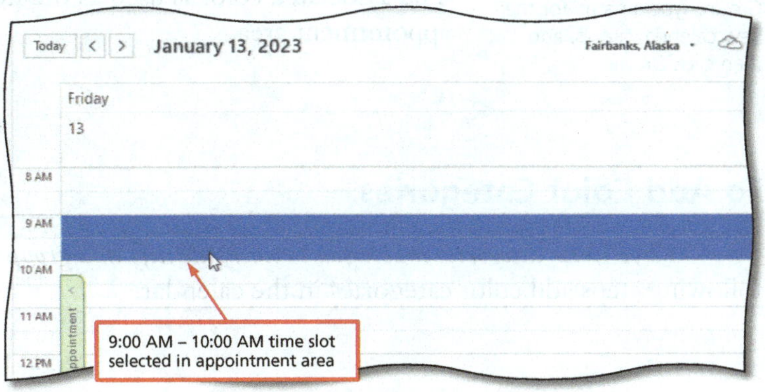

Figure 2–23

4

- Type **Dental Cleaning: Dr. Overby** as the appointment title and then press ENTER to enter the appointment in the appointment area (Figure 2–24).

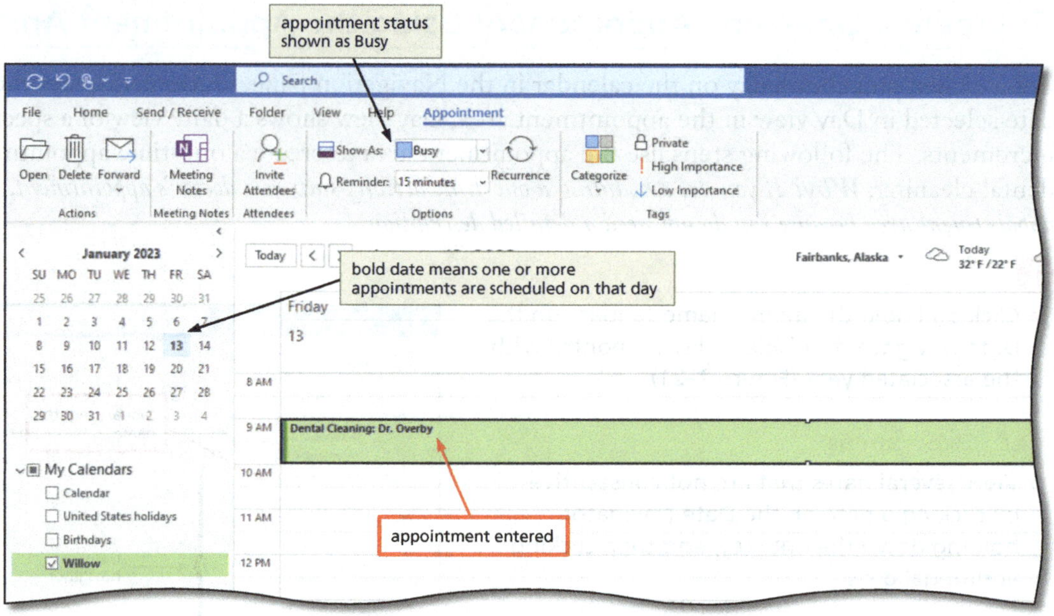

Figure 2–24

Q&A

Do I have to perform another step to save the appointment entry?

No, the appointment entry is saved automatically when you press ENTER.

Why is Busy displayed in the Show As box (Appointment tab | Options group)?

When you create an appointment, Outlook assigns your time as busy by default.

Why does the date of the dental cleaning appointment appear in bold on the Date Navigator?

Outlook displays in bold any date with a time allocated on your calendar as busy to indicate that you have something scheduled on that day.

Other Ways

1. Select beginning time slot, hold down SHIFT, click ending time slot, type appointment name, press ENTER

BTW

Adding a Calendar Group

To organize multiple calendars, you can create calendar groups. Click the Calendar Groups button (Home tab | Manage Calendars group) and then click Create New Calendar Group. Type a name for the new calendar group, and then click OK.

Organizing the Calendar with Color Categories

As you add appointments to the Outlook Calendar, you can use categories to color-code the appointments by type. Adding color categories allows you to quickly scan and visually group similar items such as classes or work-related appointments. For example, Willow can assign her work tasks to a blue category, doctor's appointments to green, classes to orange, and all friends- and family-related activities to purple. After associating each category with a color, she can categorize each appointment. The associated color is used as the item's background color on the calendar in the appointment area.

To Add Color Categories

Why? *Color categories enable you to easily identify and group associated items in the Outlook Calendar.* The following steps add color categories in the calendar.

1

- Click the Categorize button (Appointment tab | Tags group) to display the Categorize list of color categories (Figure 2–25).

Q&A Can you use color categories for any type of email account?

No. If you use a Microsoft account as your Outlook email account, you can take advantage of categories and other special features.

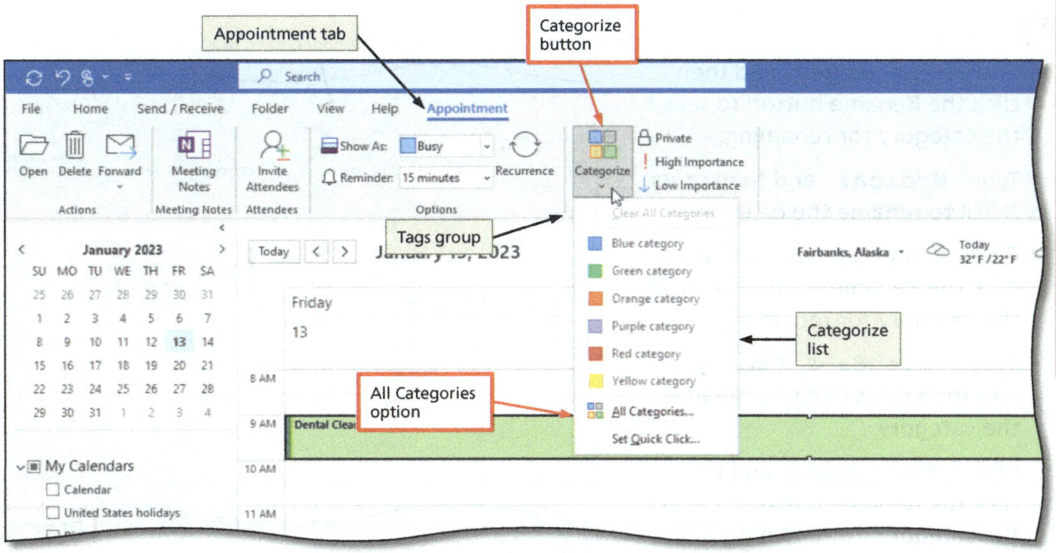

Figure 2–25

2

- Click All Categories to display the Color Categories dialog box (Figure 2–26).

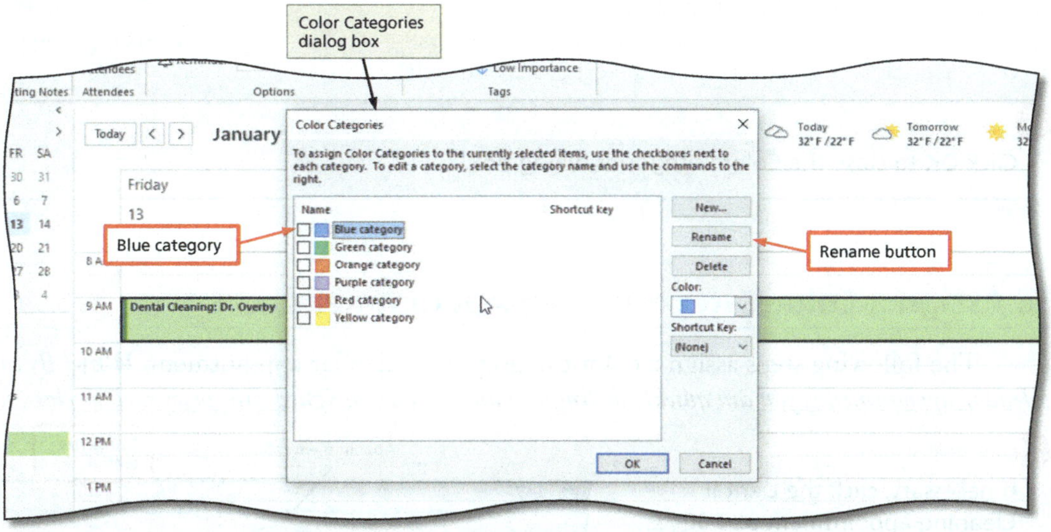

Figure 2–26

3

- If necessary, click Blue category to select the category.
- Click the Rename button to select the category for renaming.
- Type **`Work`** and then press ENTER to rename the category (Figure 2–27).

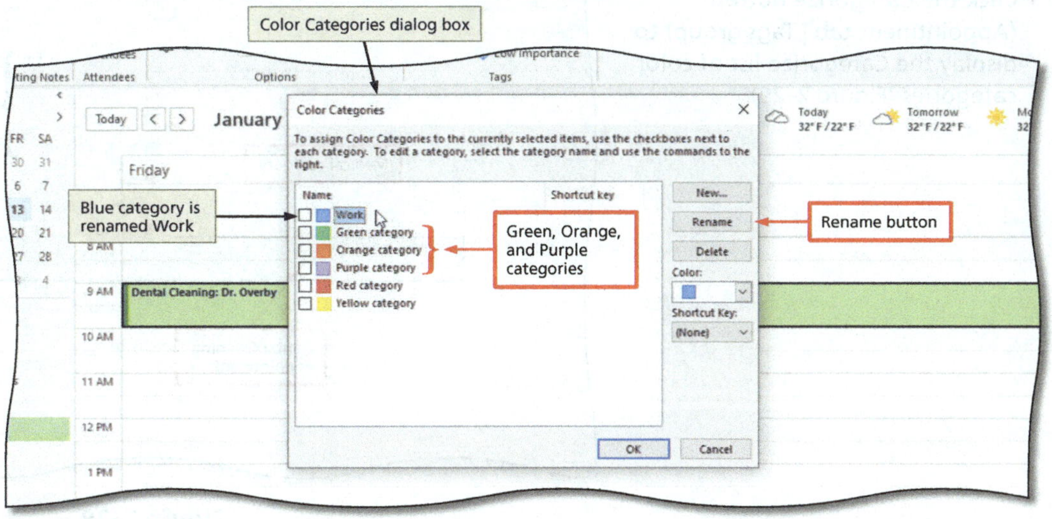

Figure 2–27

4

- Click Green category, and then click the Rename button to select the category for renaming.
- Type **Medical** and then press ENTER to rename the category.
- Click Orange category, and then click the Rename button to select the category for renaming.
- Type **Friends & Family** and then press ENTER to rename the category.
- Click Purple category, and then click the Rename button to select the category for renaming.
- Type **Classes** and then press ENTER to rename the category (Figure 2–28).

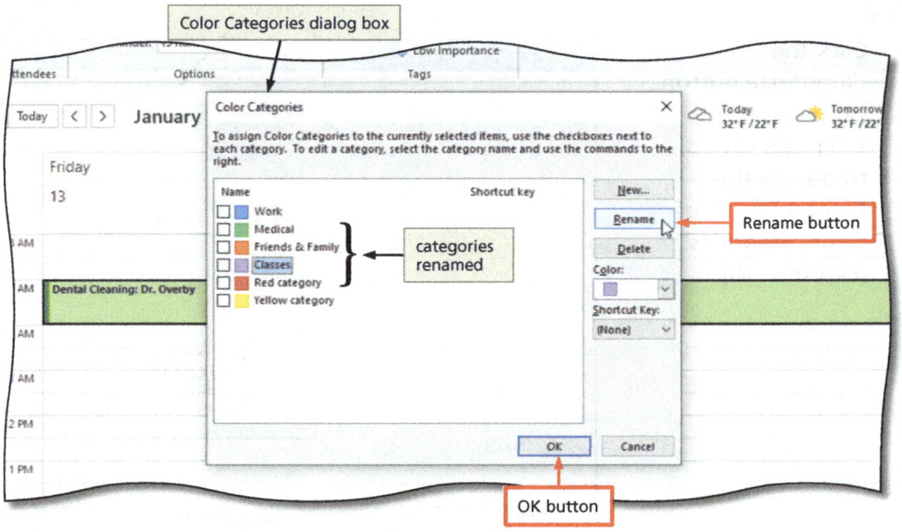

Figure 2–28

Q&A How many color categories can I set?
You can assign 15 color categories in the Outlook Calendar. Click the New button in the Color Categories dialog box to select colors not shown in the dialog box by default.

5

- Click OK to close the Color Categories dialog box.

To Assign a Color Category to an Appointment

The following steps assign a color category to a calendar appointment. ***Why?*** *By color coding your Outlook calendar appointments, you can quickly distinguish among your assigned categories such as class, work, or birthday.*

1

- If necessary, click the Dental Cleaning appointment at 9:00 AM to select the appointment.
- Click the Categorize button (Appointment tab | Tags group) to display the Categorize list of color categories (Figure 2–29).

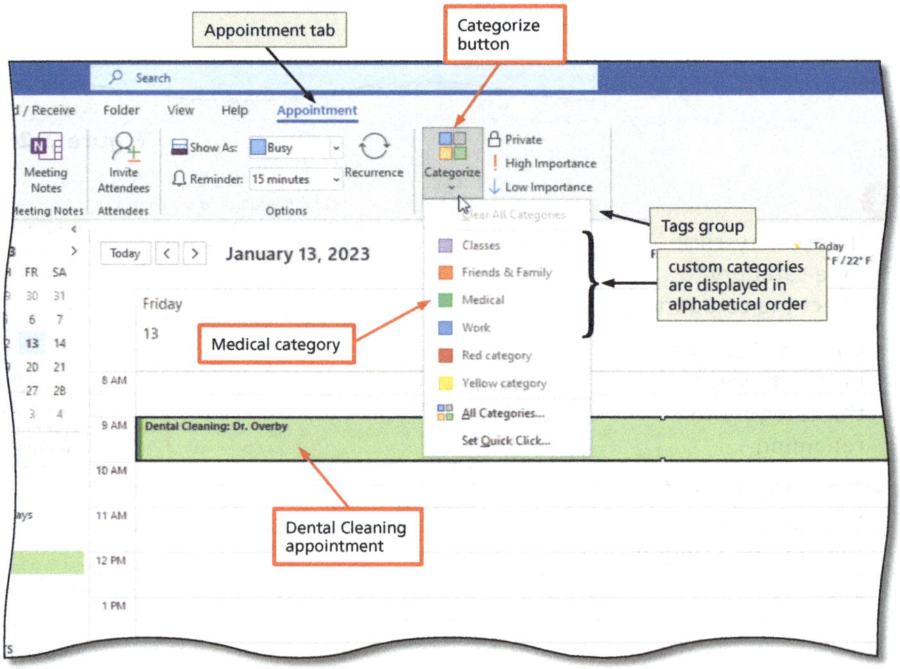

Figure 2–29

2

- Click the green Medical category to display the selected appointment with a medium-green background (Figure 2–30).

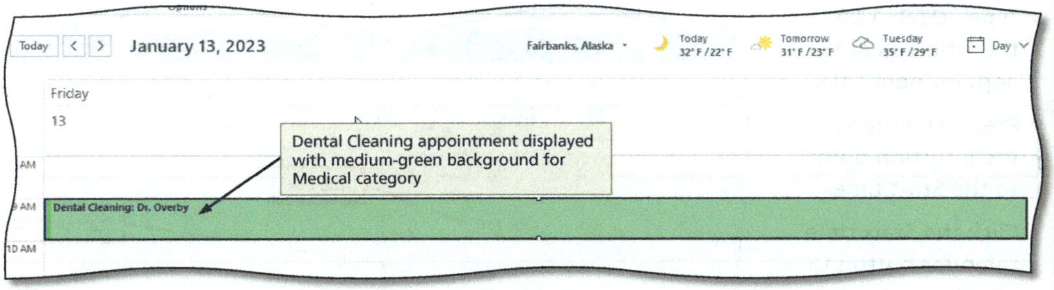

Figure 2–30

Creating Appointments Using the Appointment Window

Another way to create an appointment is by using the Appointment window, which provides additional options for entering an appointment, such as the location of the appointment, a recurrence pattern, and whether the meeting is an online Teams meeting. Part of Microsoft 365, **Microsoft Teams** is a meetings app that provides a workspace for real-time collaboration and communication, meetings, and file and app sharing.

When you set a **recurrence pattern**, Outlook schedules the appointment on the calendar at regular intervals for a designated period of time, such as a class that Willow takes for an entire semester on Tuesdays and Thursdays.

Outlook also allows you to configure a **reminder**, similar to an alarm clock reminder, which is an alert window that briefly appears on your screen to remind you of an upcoming appointment. You also can set a chime or other sound to play as part of the reminder.

Another option when creating an appointment is to set the **appointment status**, which is how the time for a calendar item is marked on your calendar. The default appointment status setting is Busy, as indicated in the previous steps, but you can change the status to reflect your availability as appropriate.

BTW

Entering Locations

As you enter calendar items using the Appointment window, you can include location information by clicking the Location arrow and selecting a location on the list.

To Create an Appointment Using the Appointment Window

Why? *Instead of directly entering an appointment in the appointment area, you can specify various details such as the location by using the Appointment window.* To schedule an appointment such as Willow's CIS 110 computer class that meets repeatedly over the semester in a particular room on campus, you decide to use the Appointment window. If you have a meeting across the world's time zones, you can set time zones, which you can use to specify the time zones for the start and end times of the appointment. The following steps create an appointment using the Appointment window.

1

- Click Home on the ribbon to display the Home tab.
- Click the New Appointment button (Home tab | New group) to open the Untitled - Appointment window (Figure 2–31).

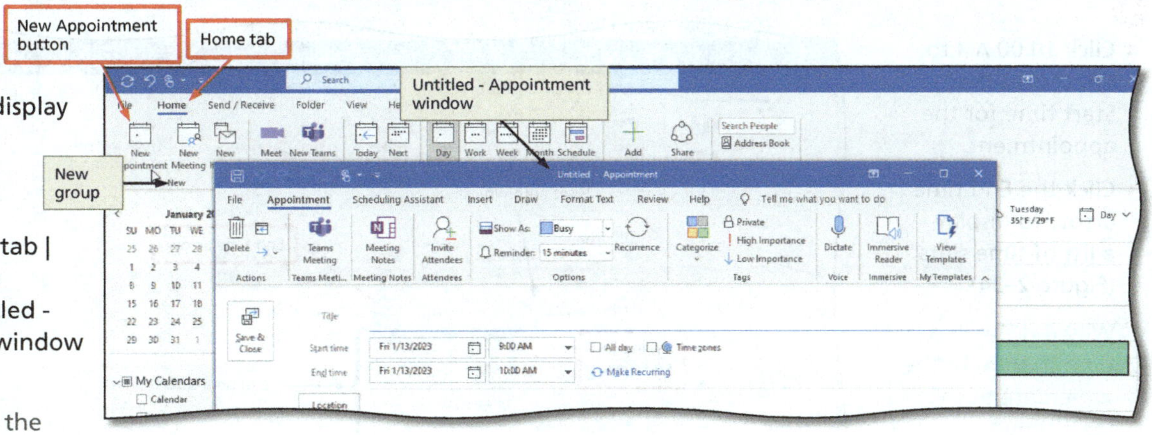

Figure 2–31

Q&A How can I hide the ribbon in the Untitled - Appointment window?

If the ribbon is expanded, click the Collapse the Ribbon button in the lower-right corner of the ribbon. Double-click a tab to expand the ribbon again.

2

- Type `CIS 110` in the Title box as the appointment title.
- Press TAB to move the insertion point to the Start time.
- Click the Start time calendar button to display a calendar for the current month (Figure 2–32).

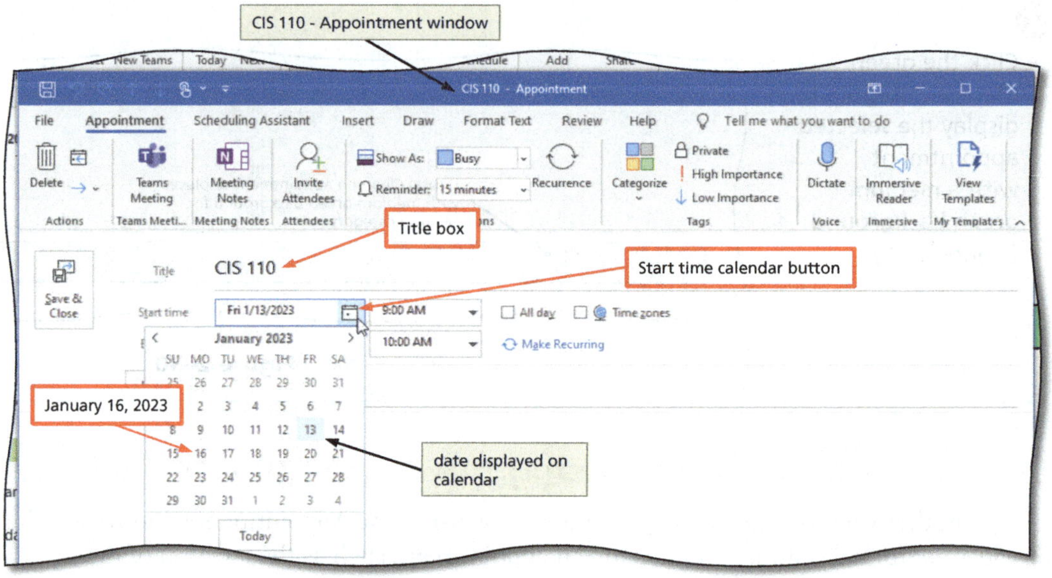

Figure 2–32

Q&A Why did the title of the window change from Untitled - Appointment to CIS 110 - Appointment?
The title bar displays the name of the appointment. Because the name of the appointment has changed, the name on the title bar also changes.

Why are the date and time already specified?
When you start to create a new appointment, Outlook sets the start and end times using the time selected in the appointment area.

3

- Click 16 on the calendar to select the next CIS 110 class as January 16, 2023.
- Click the Start time arrow to display a list of time slots (Figure 2–33).

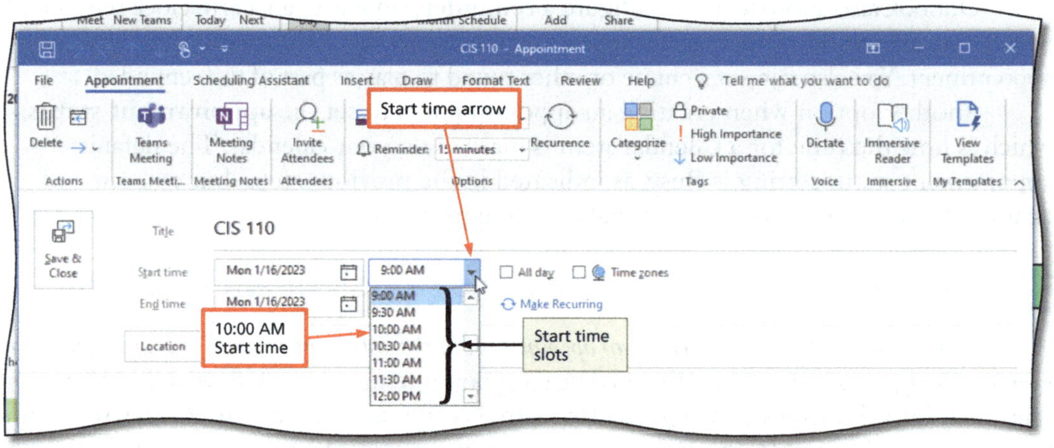

Figure 2–33

4

- Click 10:00 AM to select it as the Start time for the appointment.
- Click the End time arrow to display a list of time slots (Figure 2–34).

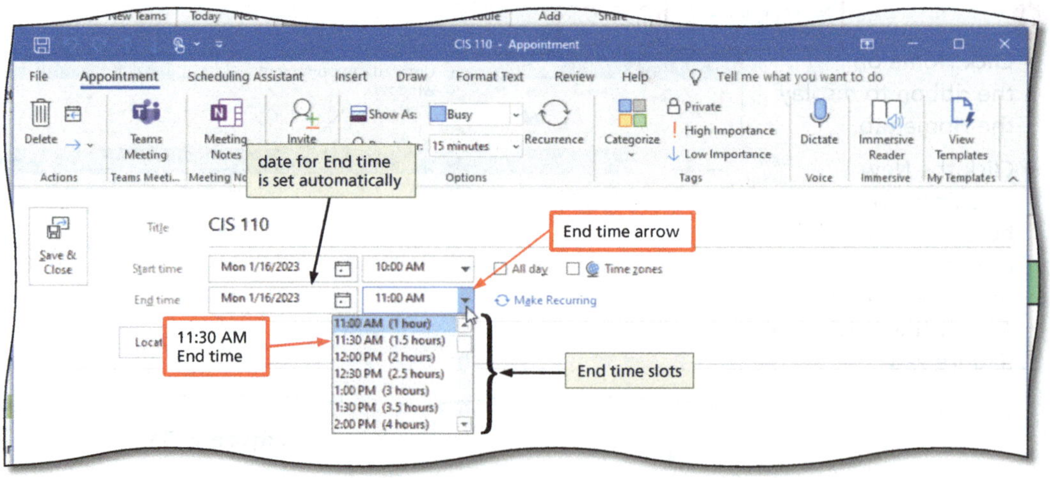

Figure 2–34

Q&A Why did the End time change to the same date as the Start time?
Outlook automatically sets appointments to occur during a single day.

Q&A Why does the second end time list have a duration for each time?
Outlook automatically displays the duration next to the end time to help you set the length of the appointment.

5

- Click 11:30 AM (1.5 hours) to select it as the End time for the appointment.
- Click the Location box and type **2412** as the room number of the class (Figure 2–35).

Q&A Why did local addresses starting with 2412 appear when I typed in the room number 2412?
Outlook automatically attempts to find street address locations when connected to the Internet for the Location.

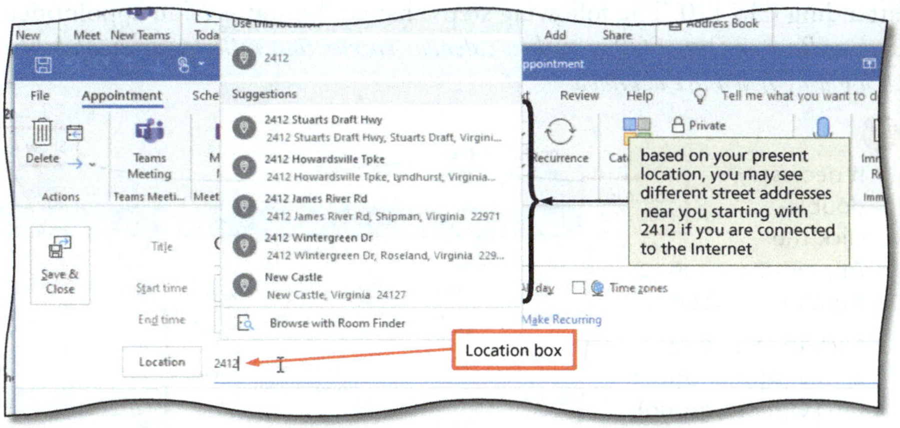

Figure 2–35

Other Ways

1. Press CTRL+SHIFT+A

Setting Appointment Options

When creating appointments on the Outlook calendar, you can set a number of options that determine how the appointment is handled. Table 2–2 lists the options available when creating an item on your calendar.

Table 2–2 Calendar Window Options

Option	Description
Show As	Indicates your availability on a specific date and time; if you want to show others your availability when they schedule a meeting with you during a specific time, this must be set accurately
Reminder	Alerts you at a specific time prior to the item's occurrence
Recurrence	If an item on your calendar repeats at regularly scheduled intervals, set the recurring options so that you only have to enter the item once on your calendar

Outlook provides five options for indicating your availability on the Calendar, as described in Table 2–3.

Table 2–3 Calendar Item Status Options

Calendar Item Status Option	Description
Free	Shows time with a white bar in Day, Week, Work Week, or Month view
Working Elsewhere	Shows time with a white bar with dots in Day, Week, Work Week, or Month view while working remotely
Tentative	Shows time with a slashed bar in Day, Week, Work Week, or Month view
Busy	Shows time with a slashed bar in Day, Week, Work Week, or Month view
Out of Office	Shows time with a purple bar in Day, Week, Work Week, or Month view

BTW
Time Zones
Use the Time Zones button (Appointment tab | Options group) to specify a time zone for the start and end times of an appointment.

To Change the Status of an Appointment

To make sure your time is displayed accurately on the calendar, you can change the appointment status from the default of Busy to Out of Office, meaning Willow is not in the Motion AI office during class time while attending CIS 110. The following steps change the status of an appointment. ***Why?*** *You can display time indicators such as Busy or Out of Office to show calendar entries that reflect your availability. If you share your calendar, others can see at a glance if you are available.*

1

- If necessary, double-click the Appointment tab to expand the ribbon.
- Click the Show As arrow (Appointment tab | Options group) in the CIS 110 appointment to display the Show As list of appointment status options (Figure 2–36).

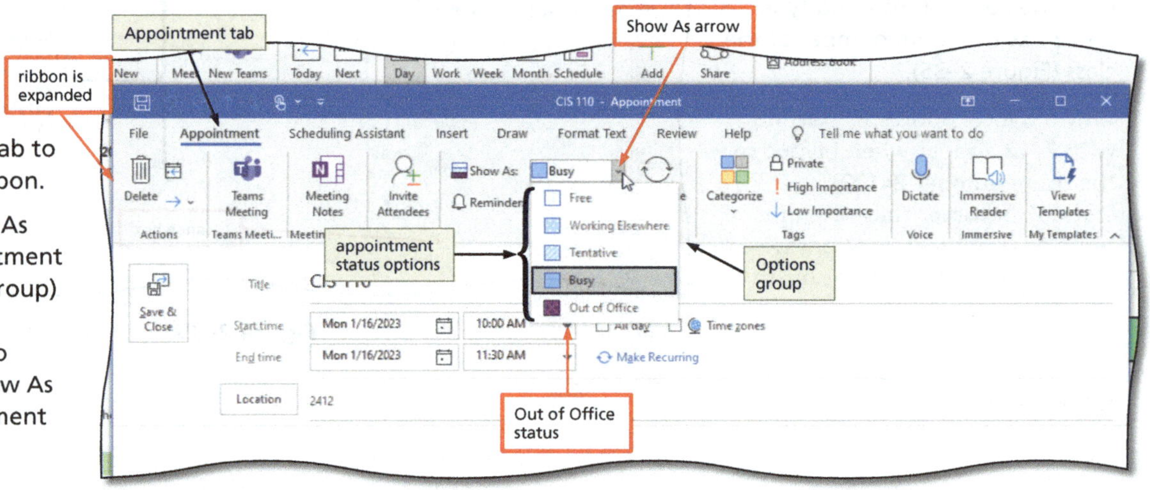

Figure 2–36

2

- Click Out of Office to change the appointment status (Figure 2–37).

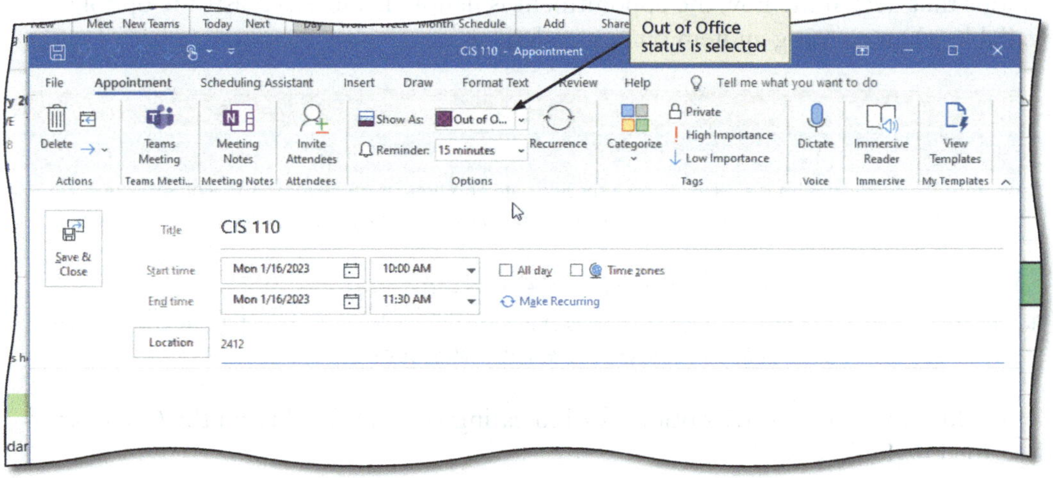

Figure 2–37

To Set a Reminder for an Appointment

With the start and end dates and times for the class set and the appointment status selected, Willow wants to schedule a reminder so that she does not forget class. ***Why?*** *Your Outlook Calendar can be your personal alarm clock by displaying reminders of your appointments with options such as snooze and dismiss.* When the reminder is displayed, you can open the appointment for further review. The following steps set a 30-minute reminder for an appointment.

1

- Click the Reminder arrow (Appointment tab | Options group) to display the Reminder list of available reminder intervals (Figure 2–38).

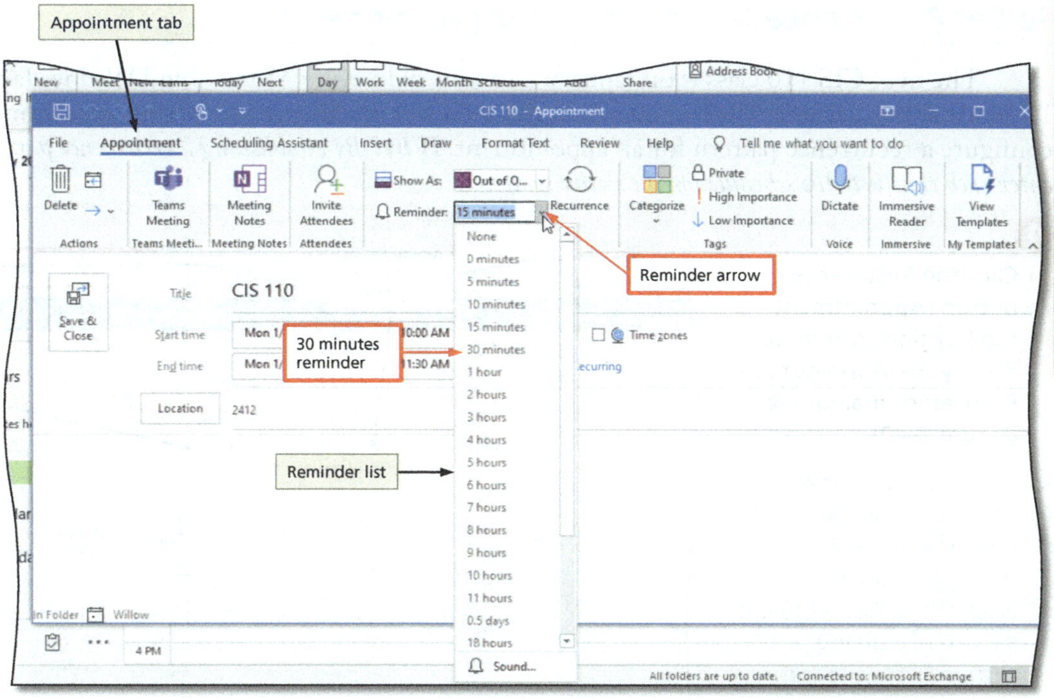

Figure 2–38

2

- Click 30 minutes to set a reminder for 30 minutes prior to the start time of the appointment (Figure 2–39).

Q&A Why was the reminder time originally scheduled for 15 minutes?
Fifteen minutes is the default reminder time. However, you can increase or decrease the default reminder time.

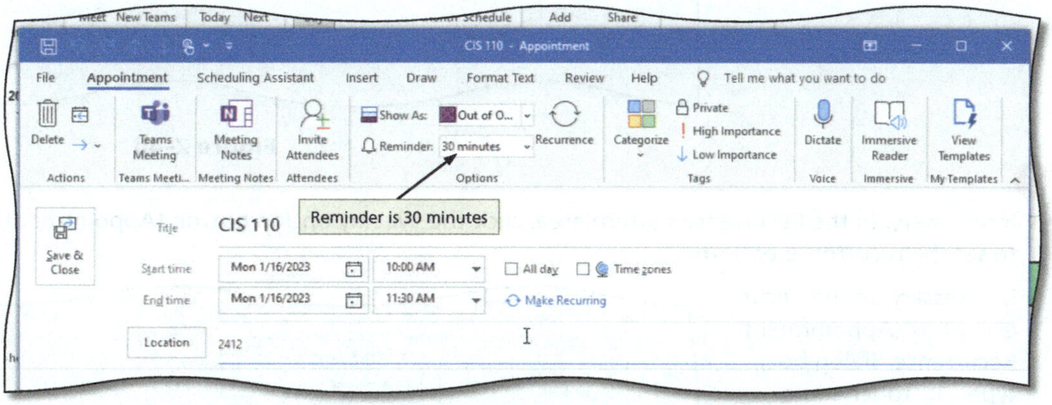

Figure 2–39

CONSIDER THIS

Can you customize the sound that is played when a reminder is displayed?

- When you click the Reminder arrow (Appointment tab | Options group), click Sound to open the Reminder Sound dialog box.
- Click the Browse button, and then select the sound .wav file that you want played.
- Click the Open button. Click OK to select the custom reminder sound.
- A reminder time must be selected before the Sound command appears.

Creating Recurring Appointments

Many appointments are recurring appointments, meaning they happen at regular intervals for a designated period of time. The recurring appointment is configured with a recurrence pattern designating the rate of recurrence, for example, weekly, and on what day(s) of the week the appointment occurs.

To Set Recurrence Options for an Appointment

The next CIS 110 class is on January 16 and is held every Monday and Wednesday from 10:00 AM to 11:30 AM at regular intervals for the rest of the semester, making it a recurring appointment. The following steps configure a recurrence pattern for an appointment. ***Why?*** *By establishing a recurrence pattern, you do not have to enter each class into the schedule for the entire semester.*

1

- Click the Recurrence button (Appointment tab | Options group) to display the Appointment Recurrence dialog box (Figure 2–40).

Q&A Why are the start and end times and the duration already set in the Appointment time area of the Appointment Recurrence dialog box?
Outlook uses the settings you already selected for the appointment.

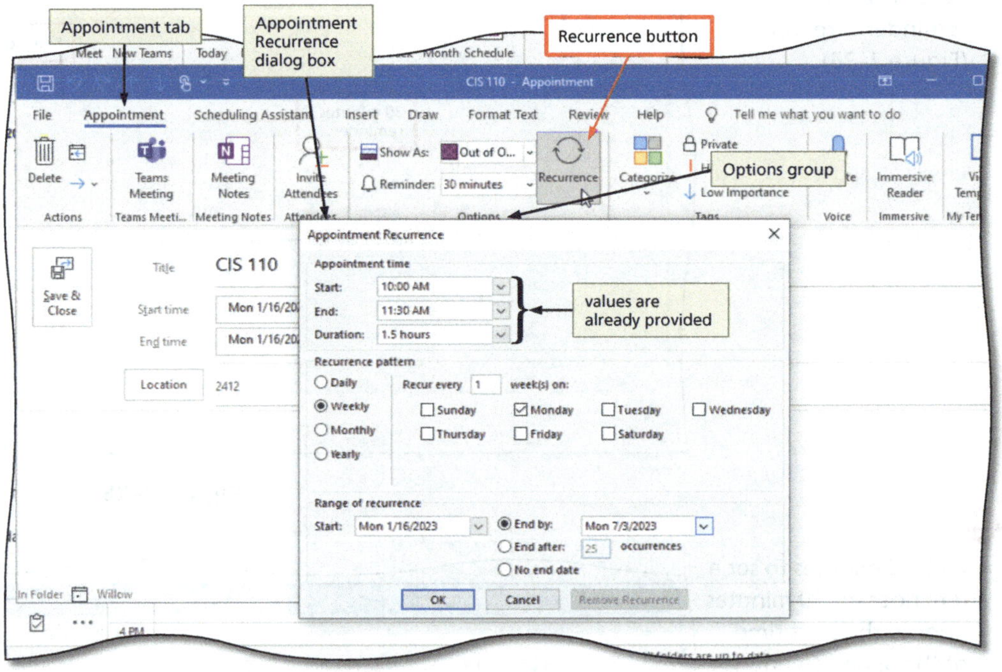

Figure 2–40

2

- If necessary, in the Recurrence pattern area, click the Weekly option button (Appointment Recurrence dialog box) to set the recurrence pattern.
- If necessary, in the Recur every box (Appointment Recurrence dialog box), type `1` to schedule the frequency of the recurrence pattern.
- Click Wednesday to insert a check mark in the check box and to schedule the class two times per week (in this case, Monday and Wednesday) (Figure 2–41).

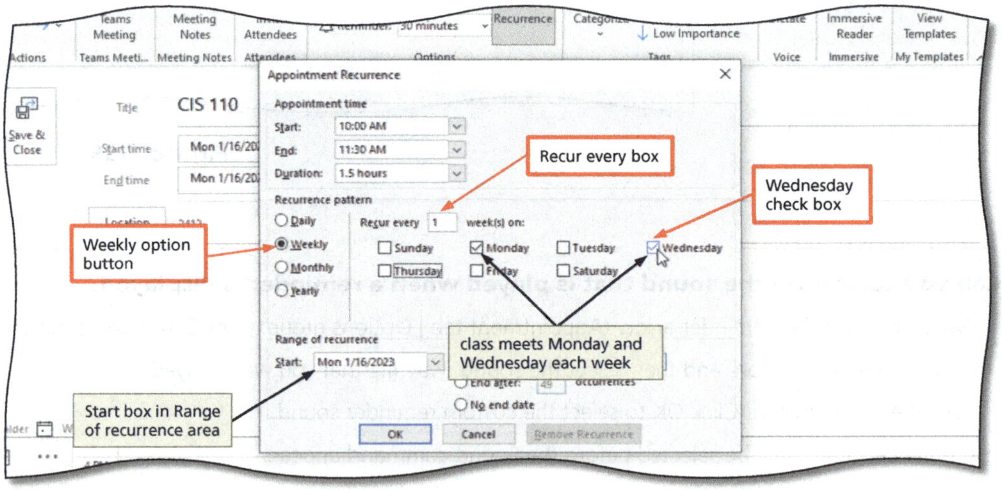

Figure 2–41

Q&A Why is the Monday check box already selected in the Recurrence pattern area?
Monday is already selected because the class starts on that day of the week.

Why does the Start box in the 'Range of recurrence' area contain a date?
When you display the Appointment Recurrence dialog box, Outlook automatically sets the range of recurrence with the date the appointment starts.

3

- In the Range of recurrence area, click the End by option button (Appointment Recurrence dialog box), and then press TAB to select the End by box.
- Type **5/11/2023** as the day the class ends to replace the displayed end date with a new date (Figure 2–42).

Q&A What if I do not know the end date, but I know how many times the class meets?
You can click the End after option button and then type the number of times the class meets in the End after box.

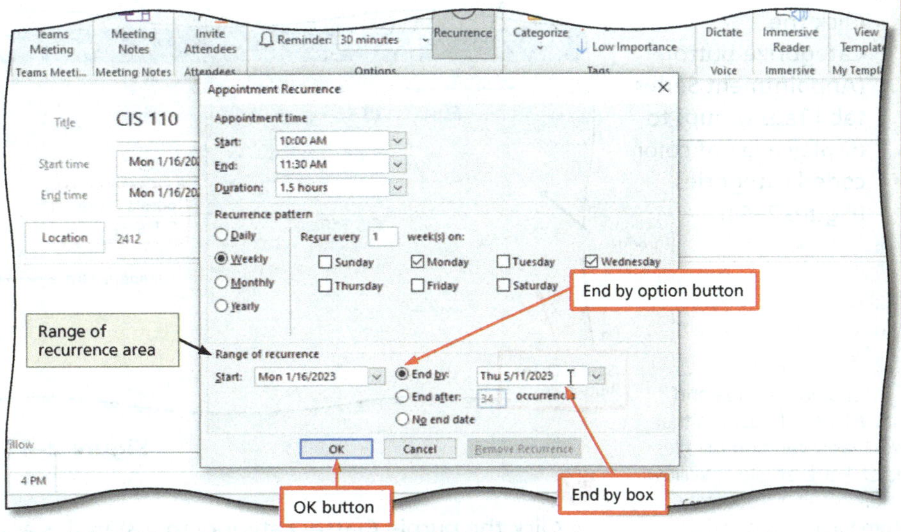

Figure 2–42

4

- Click OK to close the Appointment Recurrence dialog box and set the recurrence pattern (Figure 2–43).

Q&A Why did the Appointment tab change to the Appointment Series tab?
When you set a recurrence pattern, the tab name changes to reflect that you are working with a series of appointments.

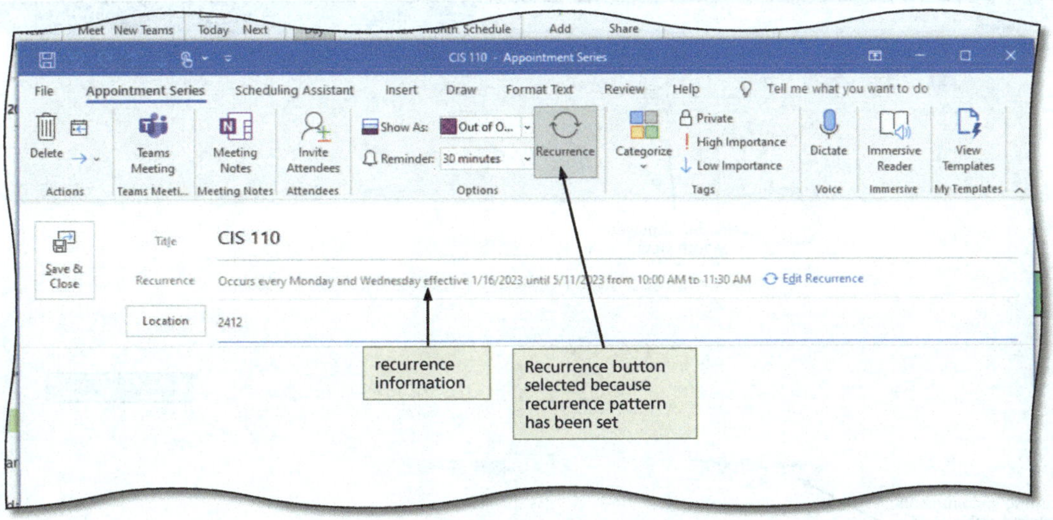

Figure 2–43

To Save an Appointment

With the details entered for the CIS 110 class, you can assign the appointment to a color category and then save the appointment. The following steps categorize the appointment, save the appointment series, and close the window. ***Why?*** *By changing the color-coded category and saving the appointment, your recurring appointment is scheduled.*

1

- Click the Categorize button (Appointment Series tab | Tags group) to display a list of color-coded categories (Figure 2–44).

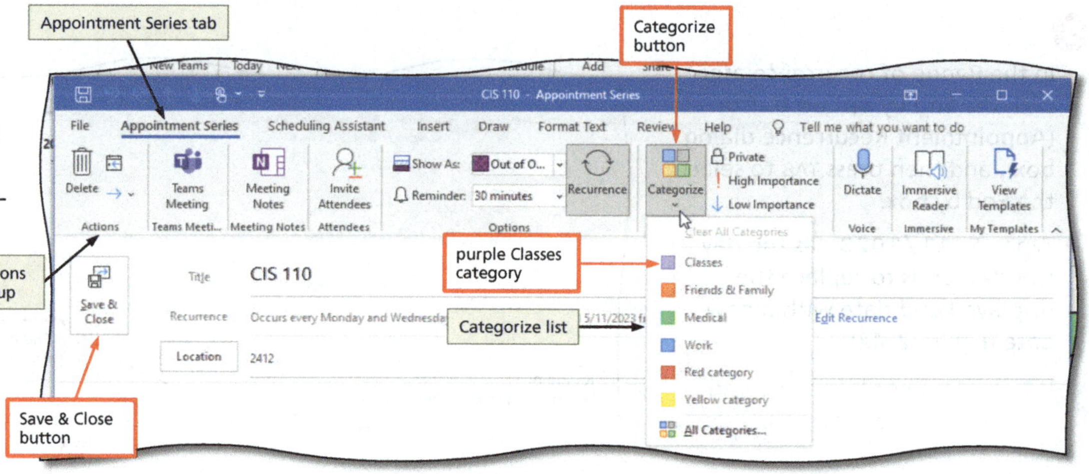

Figure 2–44

BTW

Organizing Files and Folders

You should organize and store files in folders so that you easily can find the files later. For example, if Willow is taking an introductory computer class called CIS 110, a good practice would be to save all Outlook files in an Outlook folder in a CIS 110 folder.

2

- Click the purple Classes category to assign this appointment to a category.
- Click the Save & Close button (Appointment Series tab | Actions group) to save the recurring appointment on the calendar and close the window.
- Click Home on the ribbon to display the Home tab.
- Click the Month button (Home tab | Arrange group) to display the calendar in Month view (Figure 2–45).

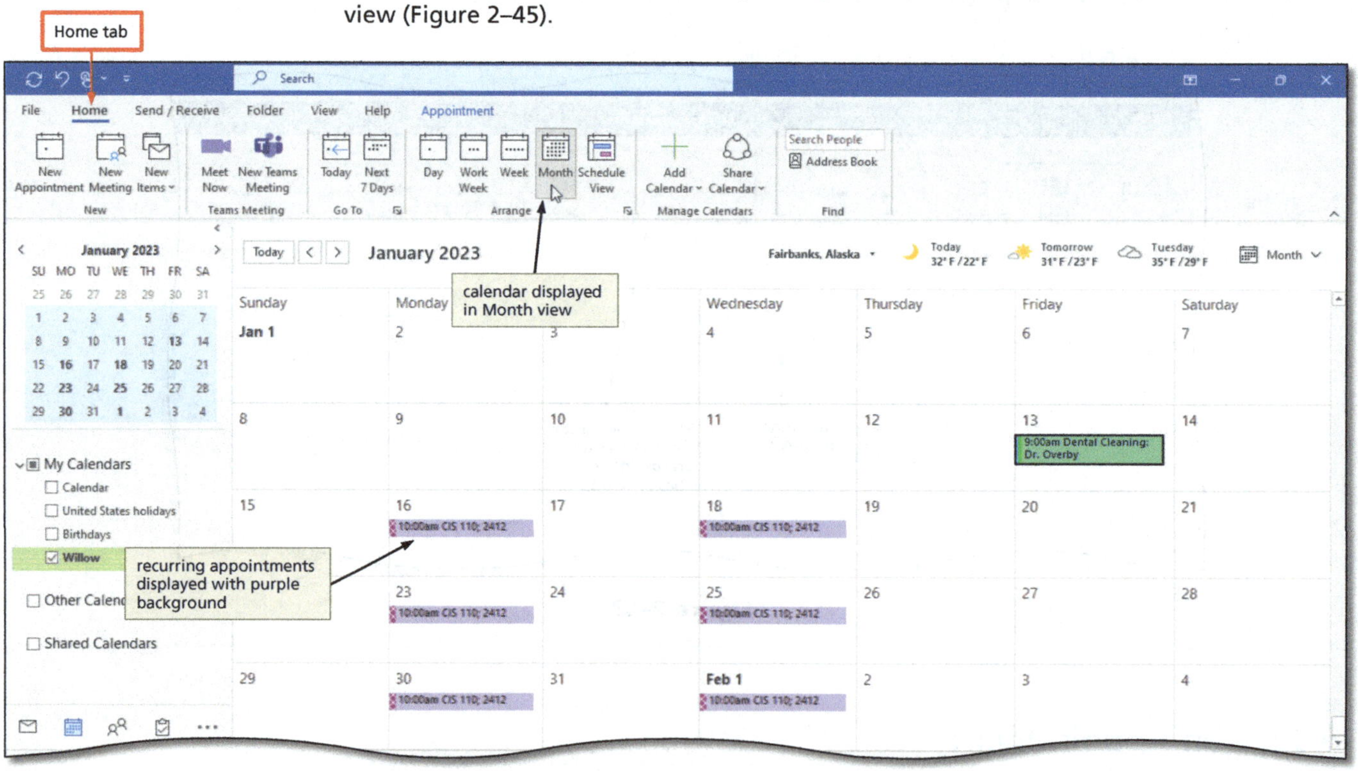

Figure 2–45

To Add More Recurring Appointments

With the CIS 110 class appointment series created, the next step is to create recurring appointments for the remainder of Willow's class and work schedule using the appointment information in Table 2–4. The following steps create the remaining class schedule using the Appointment window. ***Why?*** *By adding your full schedule to the Outlook calendar, you will not miss any important appointments.*

Table 2–4 Recurring Appointments

Appointment	Start Date	End Date	Start Time	End Time	Show As	Reminder	Recurrence	Category
ENG 112	1/19/2023	Set in Recurrence	5:30 PM	8:30 PM	Out of Office	30 minutes	Weekly, every Thursday; end by Thursday, 5/11/2023	Classes
Biology Project Due Date	2/04/2023	Set in Recurrence	5:00 PM	5:00 PM	Busy	1 day	Weekly, every Saturday; end by Saturday, 5/6/2023	Classes
Motion AI Office Hours	1/02/2023	Set in Recurrence	1:00 PM	5:00 PM	Busy	15 minutes	Weekly, every Monday, Tuesday, & Wednesday; end by Wednesday 5/10/2023	Work

1. If necessary, click Home to display the Home tab.
2. Click the New Appointment button (Home tab | New group) to open the Appointment window.
3. Type **ENG 112** as the appointment title.
4. Select January 19, 2023 to set the start date.
5. Select the start time as 5:30 PM and the end time as 8:30 PM.
6. Type **1402** as the location.
7. If necessary, expand the ribbon and select the Show As arrow to display the list of appointment status options, and then click the option shown in Table 2–4.
8. Select the Reminder arrow to display the list of time slots, and then click the option shown in Table 2–4.
9. Click the Recurrence button (Appointment tab | Options group), set the recurrence pattern shown in Table 2–4, and then click OK to close the Appointment Recurrence window.
10. Click the Categorize button (Appointment Series tab | Tags group) and select the color-coded category shown in Table 2–4.
11. Click the Save & Close button to close the Appointment Series window.
12. Repeat Steps 1 through 11 to add the information shown in the second and third rows of Table 2–4 (Figure 2–46).

Q&A

Why is the Appointment Series tab displayed instead of the Appointment tab?
The Appointment Series tab is displayed when you select an appointment that is part of a series. This tab provides tools for working with recurring appointments.

What if I have appointments that recur other than weekly?
You can set daily, weekly, monthly, or yearly recurrence patterns in the Appointment Recurrence dialog box. A recurring appointment can be set to have no end date, to end after a certain number of occurrences, or to end by a certain date.

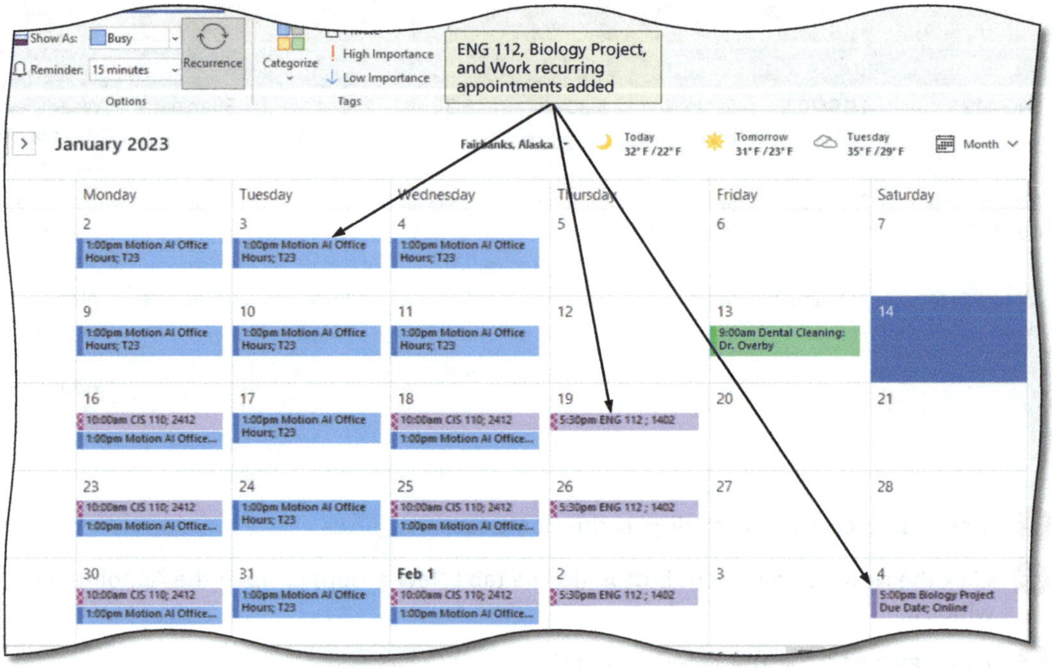

Figure 2–46

BTW
Outlook Help
At any time while using Outlook, you can find answers to questions and display information about various topics through Outlook Help. Used properly, this form of assistance can increase your productivity and reduce your frustrations by minimizing the time you spend learning how to use Outlook.

Creating a Teams Meeting

The Teams Meeting add-in is automatically installed for users who have Microsoft Teams and Office 365 installed on their computer. Users will see the Teams Meeting add-in on the Outlook Calendar ribbon. In this ever-changing world, remote meetings from home offices and travel locations are common in business. To book an Outlook Teams meeting, you do not have to open Teams. When you create an Outlook Teams meeting, the meeting request changes to include a location of "Microsoft Teams Meeting" and a link in the body of the request that attendees can click to join the meeting. This link is automatically added into Teams as well.

Using Natural Language Phrasing

In the previous steps, you entered dates and times in the Appointment window using standard numeric entries, such as 2/8/2023. You also can specify appointment dates and times using natural language. A **natural language phrase** is a phrase closely resembling how people speak during normal conversation. For example, you can type a phrase, such as "next Thursday" or "two weeks from yesterday," or you can type a single word, such as "midnight," and Outlook will calculate the correct date and time relative to the current date and time on the computer's system clock.

Outlook also can convert abbreviations and ordinal numbers into complete words and dates. For example, you can type "Feb" instead of "February" or "the first of May" instead of "5/1." Outlook's Calendar also can convert words such as "yesterday" and "tomorrow" and the names of holidays that occur on the same date each year, such as Valentine's Day. Table 2–5 lists various natural language options.

Table 2–5 Natural Language Options

Category	Examples
Dates Spelled Out	June twenty-third, March 17th, first of May This Fri, next Sat, three days from now
Times Spelled Out	Noon, midnight Nine o'clock AM, five-twenty
Descriptions of Times and Dates	Now Yesterday, today, tomorrow
Holidays	Cinco de Mayo Christmas Day, Christmas Eve
Formulas for dates and times	10/15/2023 + 12d converts the date to 10/27/2023; use *d* for day, *m* for month, or *y* for year and add that amount of time to any date

To Create a Teams Meeting Appointment Date and Time Using Natural Language Phrases

Using a natural language phrase, you can make a Teams meeting appointment for a Motion AI mentor meeting with a friend, Bree Pauley, next Friday at 2:00 PM. The following steps create an appointment using natural language phrases for the date and time. ***Why?*** *If you are not sure of the exact date for next Tuesday or 36 days from now, you can use a natural language phrase.*

1

- Click the New Teams Meeting button (Home tab | Teams Meeting group) to open the Untitled - Meeting window.
- Type **Mentor Meeting** in the Title box.
- Press TAB to select the Required box, and then type **bree.pauley@outlook.com** to enter the email address of a required meeting invitee.
- Press TAB twice to select the first Start time box, and then type **next friday** to enter the start date (Figure 2–47).

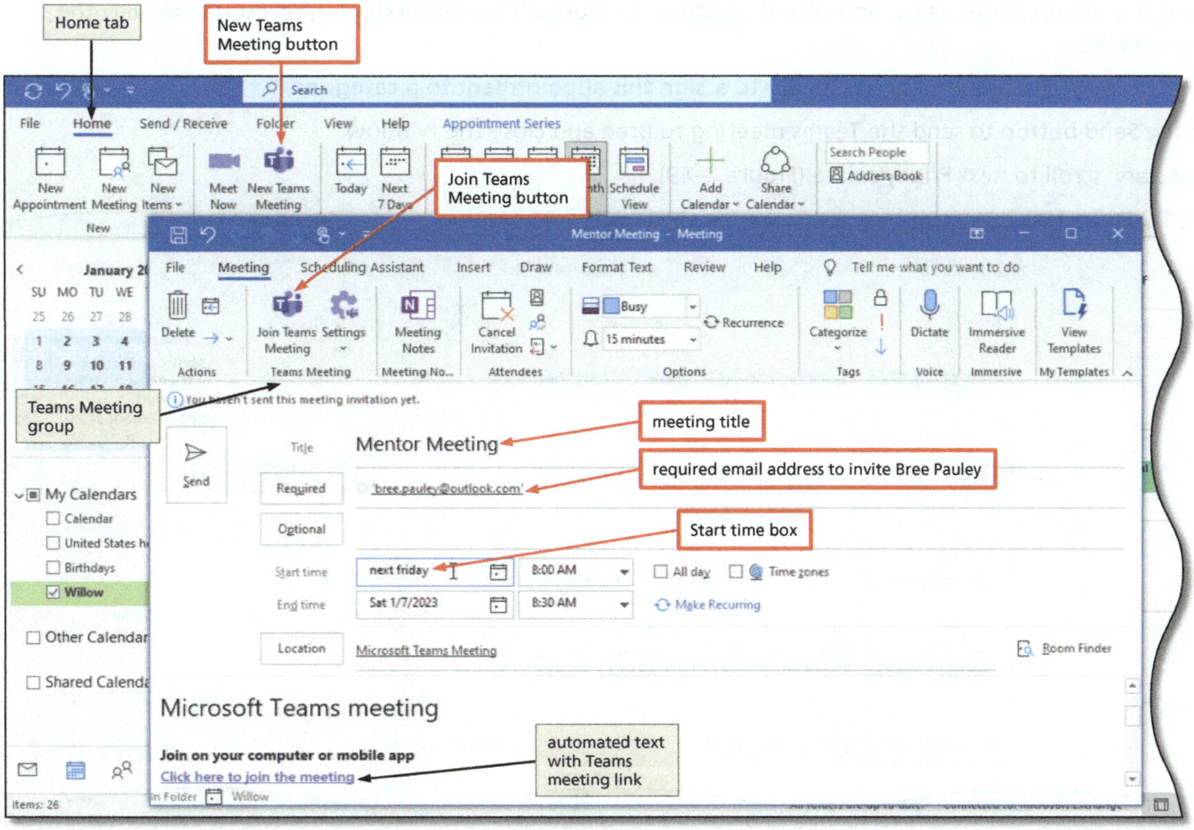

Figure 2–47

2

- Press TAB twice to convert the phrase to a start date and to select the second Start time box.
- Type **two PM** as the time in the second Start time box to enter the start time (Figure 2–48).

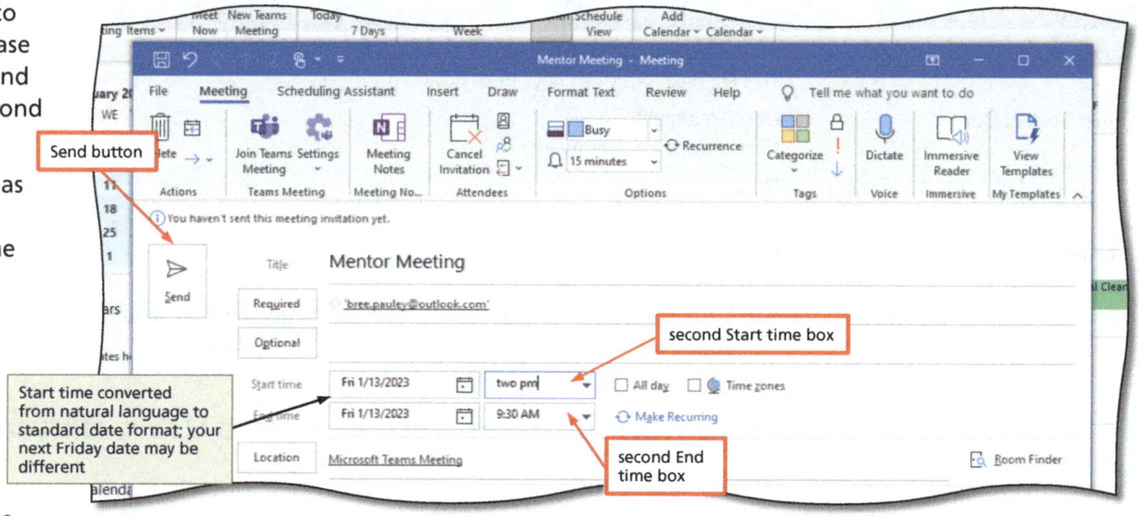

Figure 2–48

Q&A

Do I need to use proper capitalization when entering natural language phrases?

No. Outlook converts the text to the proper date or time, regardless of the capitalization.

Why did the text change to a numeric date when I pressed TAB?

If you enter the date using natural language phrasing, Outlook converts typed text to the correct date format based on the actual date when you click to move the insertion point to a different box.

3

- Press TAB three times to convert the Start time entry to 2:00 PM.
- Type **three PM** as the time in the second End time box.
- Press ENTER to convert the end time text to 3:00 PM.
- Expand the ribbon, if necessary, and click the Categorize button (Meeting tab | Tags group) to display the Categorize list.
- Click the orange Friends & Family category to assign this appointment to a category.
- Click the Send button to send the Teams meeting to Bree and close the window.
- If necessary, scroll to next Friday's date (Figure 2–49).

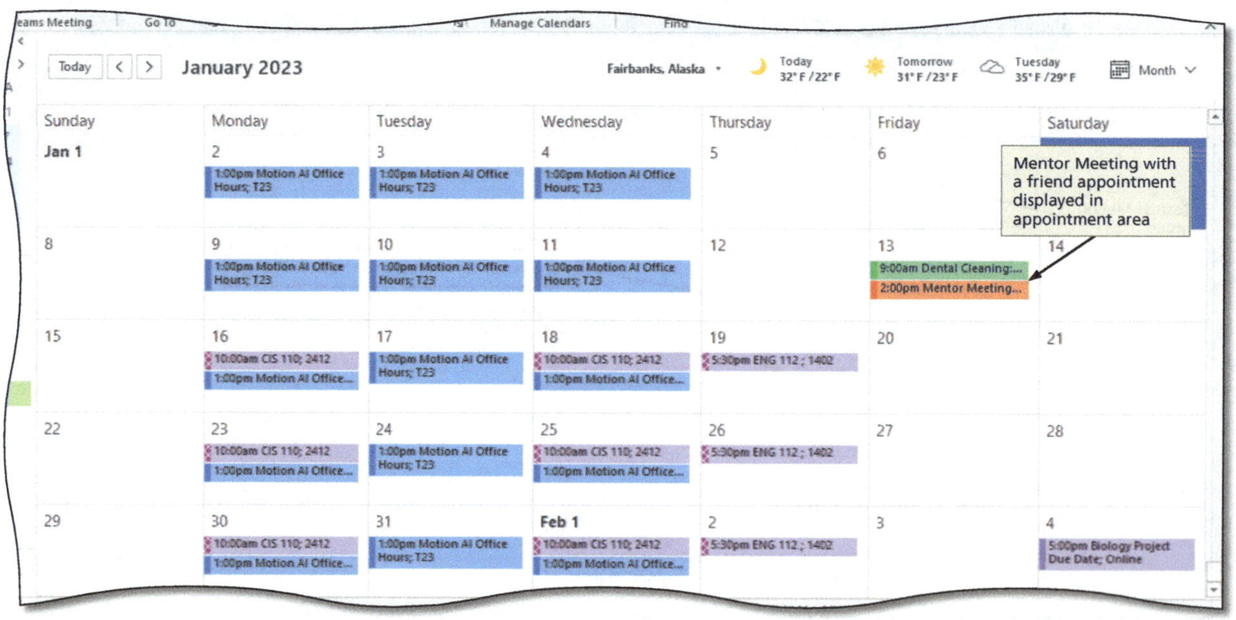

Figure 2–49

Editing Appointments

Schedules often need to be rearranged, so Outlook provides several ways to edit appointments. You can change the title or location by clicking the appointment and editing the information directly in the appointment area. You can change the title, location, date, or time by double-clicking the appointment and making corrections using the Appointment window. You can specify whether all occurrences in a series of recurring appointments need to be changed, or only a single occurrence should be altered.

BTW

Emailing Calendar Items

To send a calendar item to someone else, click the item, such as an appointment, and then click the Forward button (Appointment tab | Actions group). Enter the email address of the recipient and send the message.

To Move an Appointment to a Different Time on the Same Day

Suppose that you cannot attend the Dental Cleaning appointment at 9:00 AM on January 13, 2023. The appointment needs to be rescheduled to 11:00 AM for the same amount of time. The following step moves an appointment to a new time slot. ***Why?*** *Instead of deleting and then retyping the appointment, you can drag it to a new time slot.*

1

- If necessary, click a scroll arrow on the Calendar in the Navigation pane until January 2023 is displayed in the calendar on the Date Navigator.
- Click 13 in the January 2023 calendar on the Date Navigator to display the selected date in the appointment area.
- Drag the Dental Cleaning appointment from 9:00 AM to the 11:00 AM time slot on the same day to reschedule the appointment (Figure 2–50).

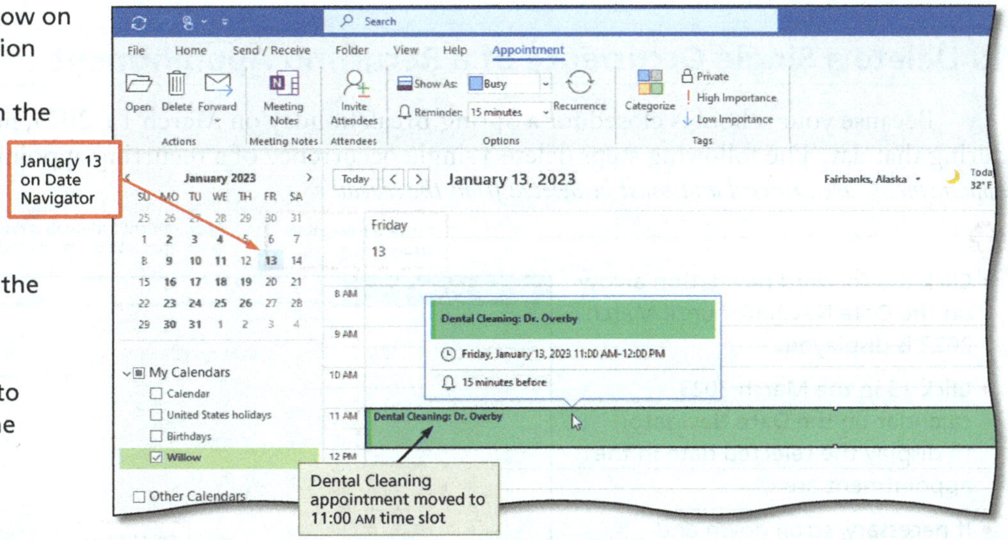

Figure 2–50

Other Ways

1. Double-click appointment, change time
2. Press CTRL+O, change time

BTW

Moving a Recurring Appointment

If you move a recurring appointment, you move only the selected instance of the appointment. To move all instances of a recurring appointment, open the appointment, click the Recurrence button (Appointment Series tab | Options group), and then change the recurrence pattern.

To Move an Appointment to a Different Date

Why? *If you are moving an appointment to a new date at the same time, you can drag the appointment to the new date on the Date Navigator instead of retyping it.* The following step moves an appointment to a new date in the same time slot.

1

- Drag the Dental Cleaning appointment on January 13, 2023 to January 20, 2023 on the Date Navigator to move the appointment to a new date (Figure 2–51).

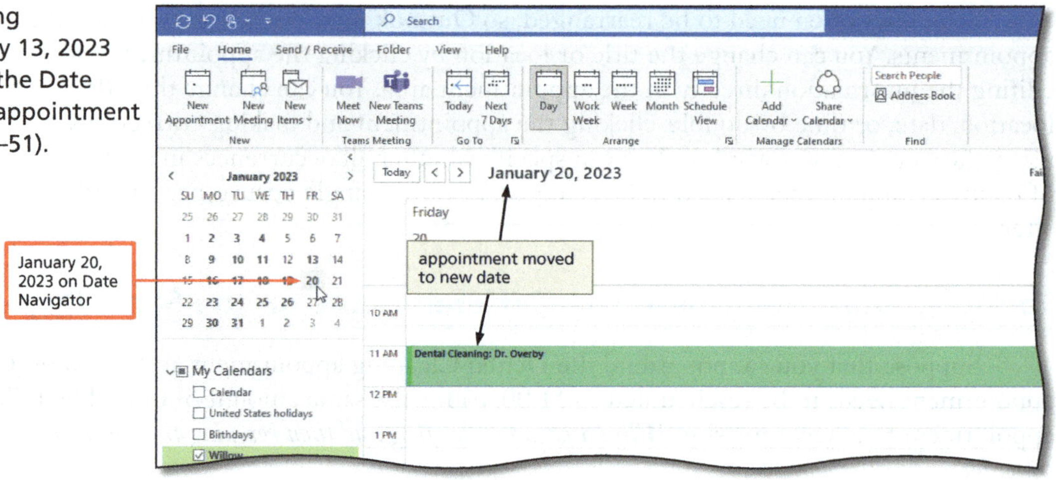

Figure 2–51

To Delete a Single Occurrence of a Recurring Appointment

Because your school is closed for a Spring Break holiday on March 13, 2023, no classes will meet during that day. The following steps delete a single occurrence of a recurring appointment. ***Why?*** *Occasionally, appointments are canceled and must be deleted from the schedule.*

1

- Click the forward navigation arrow on the Date Navigator until March 2023 is displayed.
- Click 13 in the March 2023 calendar on the Date Navigator to display the selected date in the appointment area.
- If necessary, scroll down and click the class, CIS 110, scheduled for March 13, 2023, to select the appointment and display the Appointment Series tab (Figure 2–52).

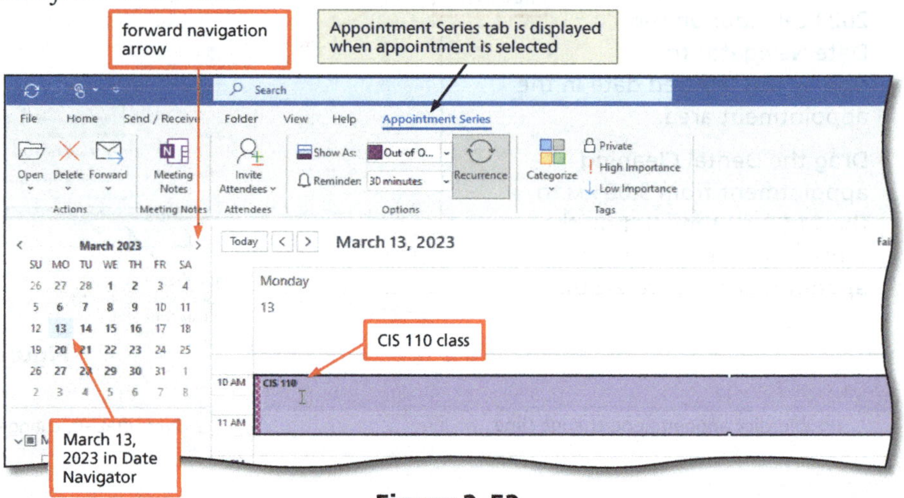

Figure 2–52

2

- Click the Delete button (Appointment Series tab | Actions group) to display the Delete list (Figure 2–53).

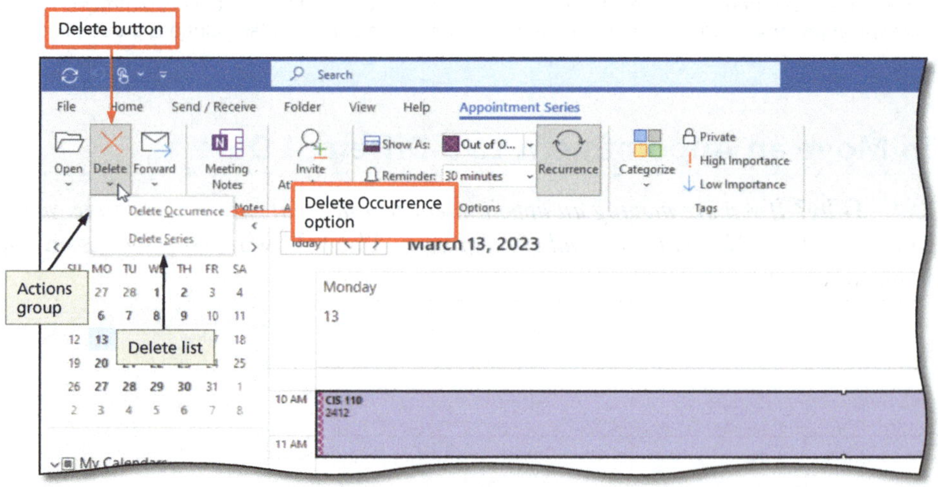

Figure 2–53

3

- Click Delete Occurrence on the Delete list to delete only the selected occurrence (single appointment) from the calendar.
- Click the Month button (Home tab | Arrange group) to display Month view (Figure 2–54).

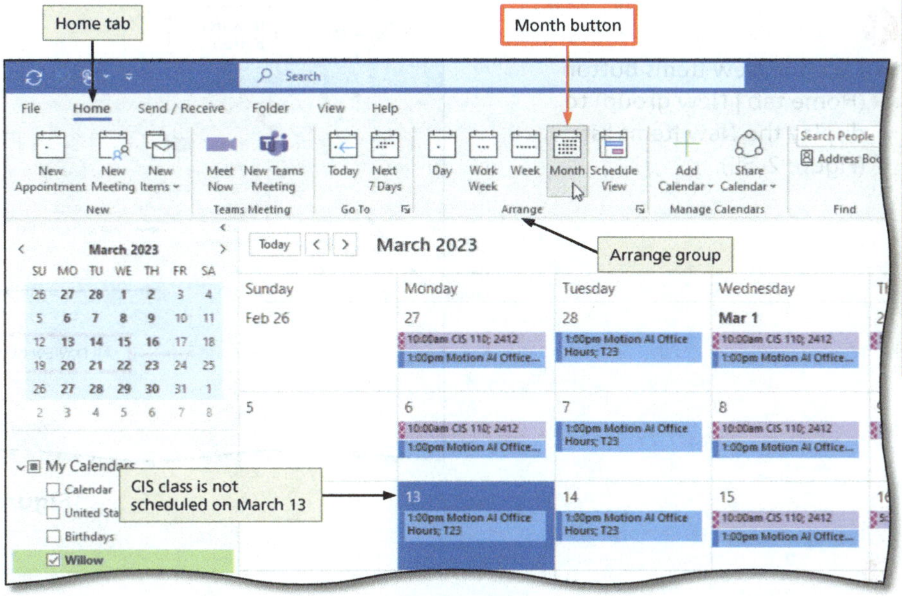

Figure 2–54

Other Ways

1. Click appointment, press DELETE, click Delete this occurrence, click OK
2. Right-click appointment, click Delete on shortcut menu, click Delete Occurrence

Break Point: If you want to take a break, this is a good place to do so. To resume later, continue to follow the steps from this location forward.

Scheduling Events

Similar to appointments, events are activities that last 24 hours or longer. Examples of events include seminars, vacations, birthdays, and anniversaries. Events can be one-time or recurring and differ from appointments in one primary way—they do not appear in individual time slots in the appointment area. Instead, the event description appears in a small banner below the day heading. As with an appointment, the event status can be free, busy, tentative, or out of the office and categorized according to the type of event. An all-day appointment displays your time as busy when viewed by other people, but an event or annual event displays your time as free. By default, all-day events occur from midnight to midnight.

To Create a One-Time Event in the Appointment Window

The Motion AI Self-Driving Event is on January 28, but Willow is assisting with the setup starting on January 27, so she wants to block out both days for the event. Because the Motion AI event will last for a couple days, Outlook will schedule it as an event. *Why? An event represents an appointment that is scheduled over a period of days such as a conference.* Willow will be busy both days, so she decides to show her time for the event as Out of Office. The following steps create an event on the calendar.

1

- Click the New Items button (Home tab | New group) to display the New Items list (Figure 2–55).

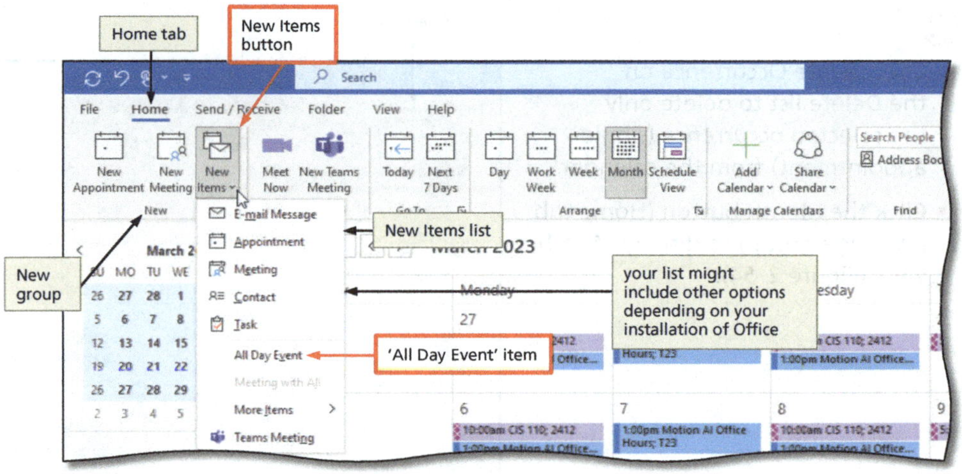

Figure 2–55

2

- Click 'All Day Event' to open the Untitled - Event window and expand the ribbon, if necessary.
- Type **`Motion AI Self-Driving Event`** in the Title box.
- Click the Start time calendar button to display the Start time calendar.
- If necessary, display the January 2023 calendar.
- Click 27 in the January 2023 calendar to display Fri 1/27/2023 as the day the event setup begins (Figure 2–56).

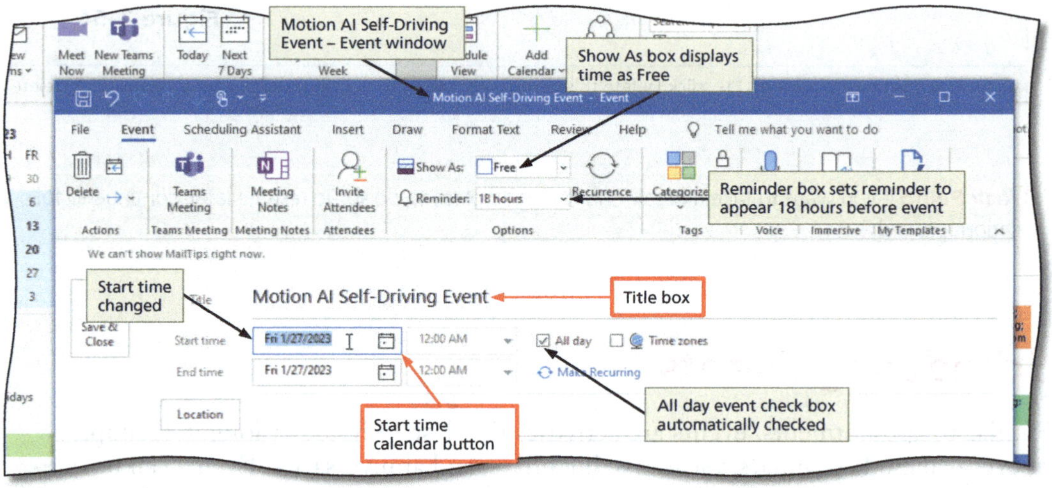

Figure 2–56

Q&A Can I create an event by checking the 'All day' check box in an appointment?
Yes. Click the New Appointment button (Home tab | New group) and then click 'All day' to create an event.

3

- Click the End time calendar button to display the End time calendar.
- Click 28 in the January 2023 calendar to set the end date.
- Move the insertion point to the Location box and type **`Lodo Center`** as the location of the event.
- Click the Show As arrow (Event tab | Options group) to display the Show As list of event status options.
- Click Out of Office to set the event status.
- Click the Categorize button (Event tab | Tags group) to display the Categorize list of color categories.

- Click Work to assign the event to a category (Figure 2–57).

Q&A Why does the Show As box originally display the time as Free?
The default Show As appointment status for events is Free because events do not occupy blocks of time during the day on the calendar.

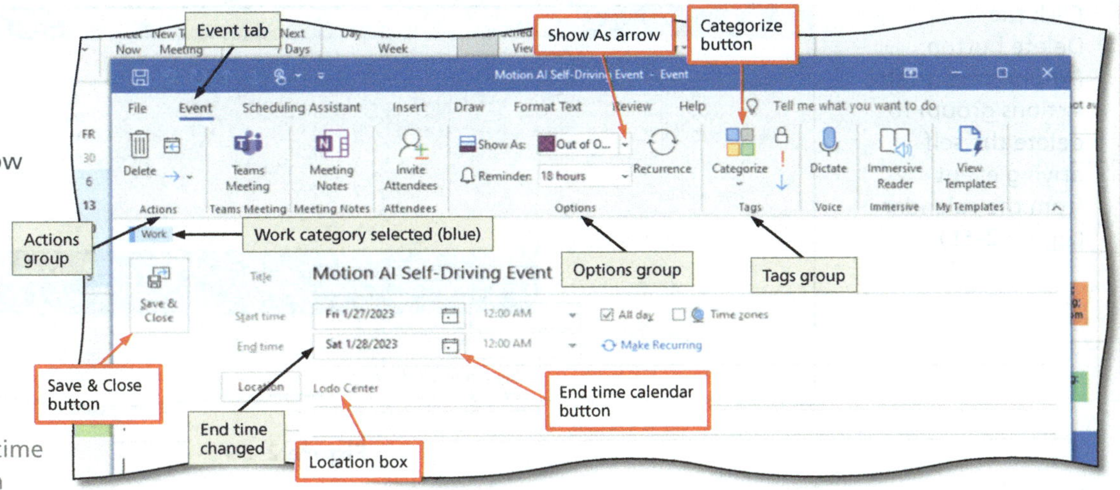

Figure 2–57

4

- Click the Save & Close button to save the event and close the window.
- Click 27 in the January 2023 calendar on the Date Navigator to display the selected date in the appointment area (Figure 2–58).

Q&A Why is the Motion AI Self-Driving event displayed at the top of Day view of the calendar?
Events do not occupy time slots on Day view of the calendar, so they appear as banners at the top of the calendar on the day they occur.

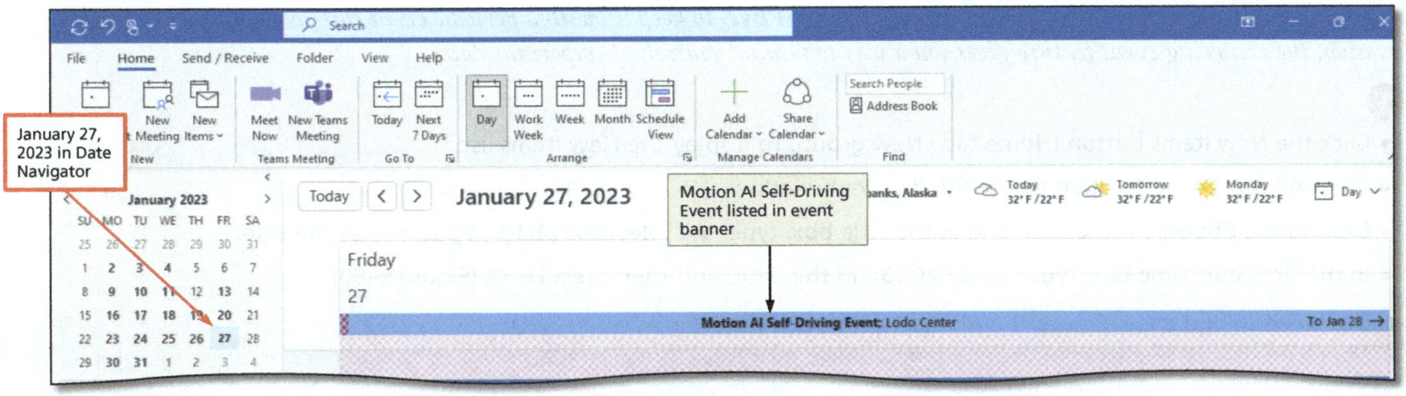

Figure 2–58

To Delete a One-Time Event

Bree Pauley, the Motion AI events director, decides that the Motion AI Self-Driving event must be cancelled due to a conflict with another event in the local area. The following step deletes an event from your calendar. ***Why?*** *Because the schedule has changed, the Motion AI Self-Driving event is cancelled but will be rescheduled later in the spring.*

1

- Click the Motion AI Self-Driving Event banner in the appointment area of the calendar to select it and to display the Appointment tab on the ribbon.

- Click the Delete button (Appointment tab | Actions group) to delete the self-driving event from the calendar (Figure 2–59).

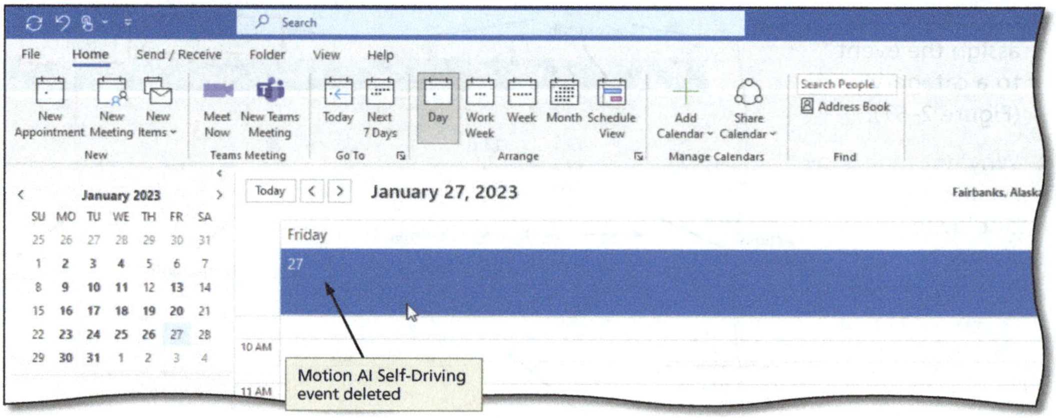

Figure 2–59

Other Ways

1. Select event, press DELETE

To Create a Recurring Event Using the Appointment Window

A recurring event is similar to a recurring appointment in that it occurs at regular intervals on your calendar. However, editing a recurring event is slightly different from editing one-time events. You can specify whether all occurrences in a series of recurring events need to be changed, or if a single occurrence should be altered.

On the first day of each month, the Motion AI website highlights an AI mentorship opportunity. Willow wants to add the dates to the calendar to keep track of when to prepare the website. The following steps create a recurring event for the AI mentorship opportunity. ***Why?*** *To keep up with a periodic event such as a monthly or weekly occasion, the recurring event feature gives you a way to remind yourself of important dates.*

1

- Click the New Items button (Home tab | New group) to display the New Items list.
- Click 'All Day Event' to open the Untitled - Event window.
- Expand the ribbon, if necessary, and in the Title box, type **AI Mentorship Update** as the title.
- In the first Start time box, type **2/1/2023** as the date, and then press ENTER (Figure 2–60).

Q&A Do I need to add a location to the AI Mentorship Update event?

No, an event such as a website update, Teams online meeting, payday, or marketing campaign does not have a location.

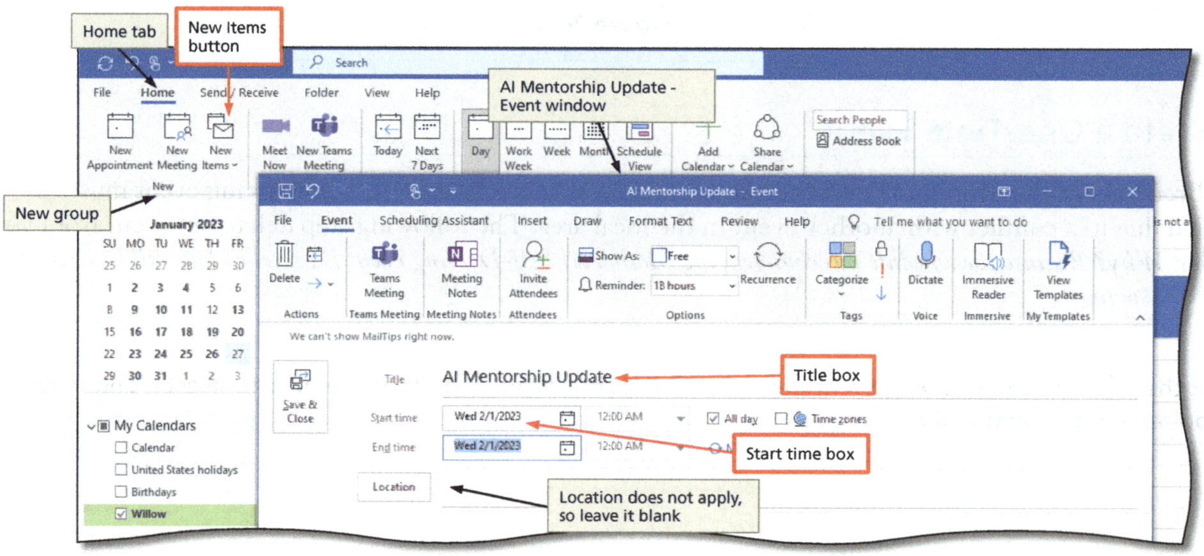

Figure 2–60

2

- Click the Recurrence button (Event tab | Options group) to display the Appointment Recurrence dialog box.
- In the Recurrence pattern section, click the Monthly option button to set the Recurrence pattern to Monthly.
- If necessary, in the Day box, type 1 to have the event appear on the calendar at the first of each month.
- If necessary, in the Range of recurrence section, click the 'No end date' option button so that the event remains on the calendar indefinitely (Figure 2–61).

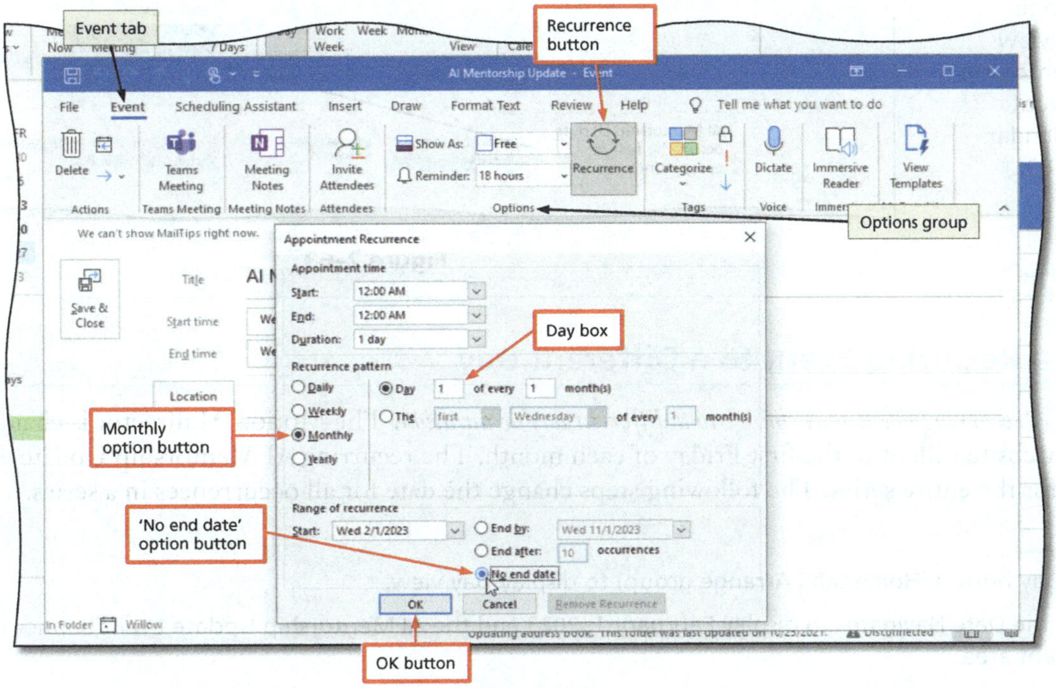

Figure 2–61

3

- Click OK to accept the recurrence settings and close the Appointment Recurrence dialog box.
- Click the Reminder arrow (Recurring Event tab | Options group) to display the Reminder list of reminder time slots.
- Click None, if necessary, to remove the reminder from the event.
- Click the Categorize button (Recurring Event tab | Tags group) to display the Categorize list of color categories.
- Click the blue Work category to assign the event to a category (Figure 2–62).

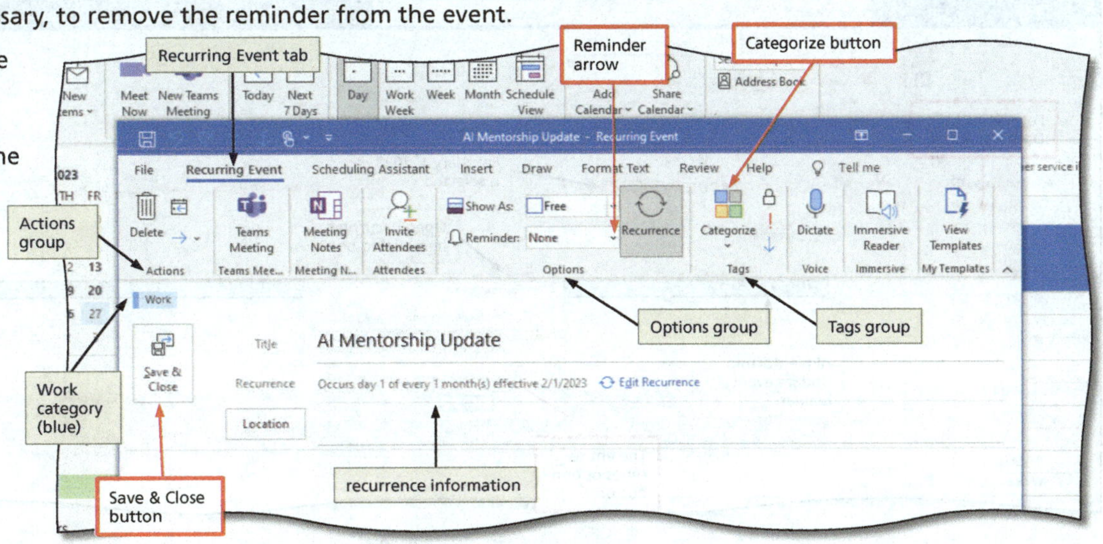

Figure 2–62

4

- Click the Save & Close button to save the event and close the window.
- Click the Month button (Home tab | Arrange group) to view the AI Mentorship Update event on the calendar (Figure 2–63).

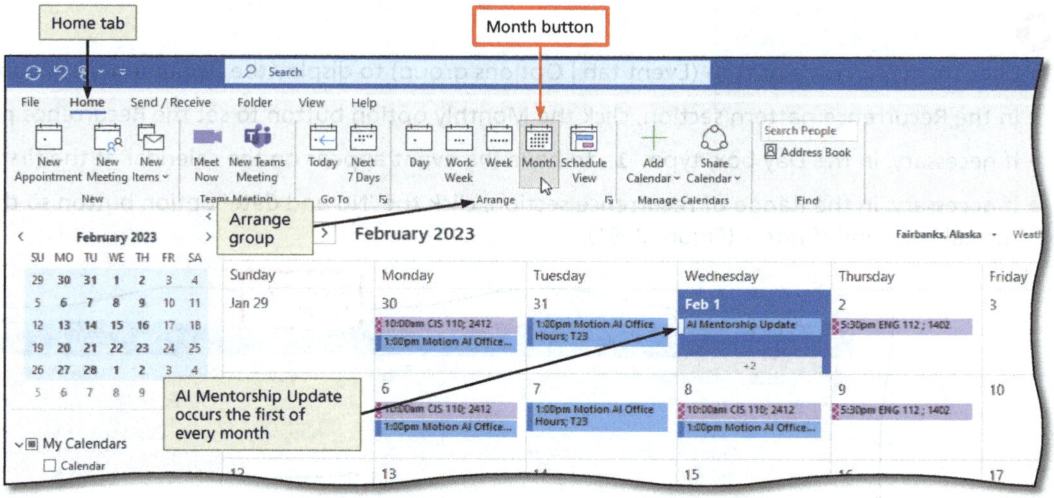

Figure 2–63

To Move a Recurring Event to a Different Day

***Why?** A recurring event may change to a different day or duration.* The Motion AI director is changing the mentorship website rollout to the first Friday of each month. The recurring AI Mentorship Update event must be changed for the entire series. The following steps change the date for all occurrences in a series.

1

- Click the Day button (Home tab | Arrange group) to display Day view.
- Click 1 on the Date Navigator to display February 1, 2023 and the AI Mentorship Update event banner in the appointment area.
- In the appointment area, double-click the AI Mentorship Update event banner to select it and to display the Open Recurring Item dialog box (Figure 2–64).

Q&A What does the double arrow symbol on the right side of the event banner represent?
The event appears in the Outlook calendar with a double arrow symbol to show that it is a recurring appointment.

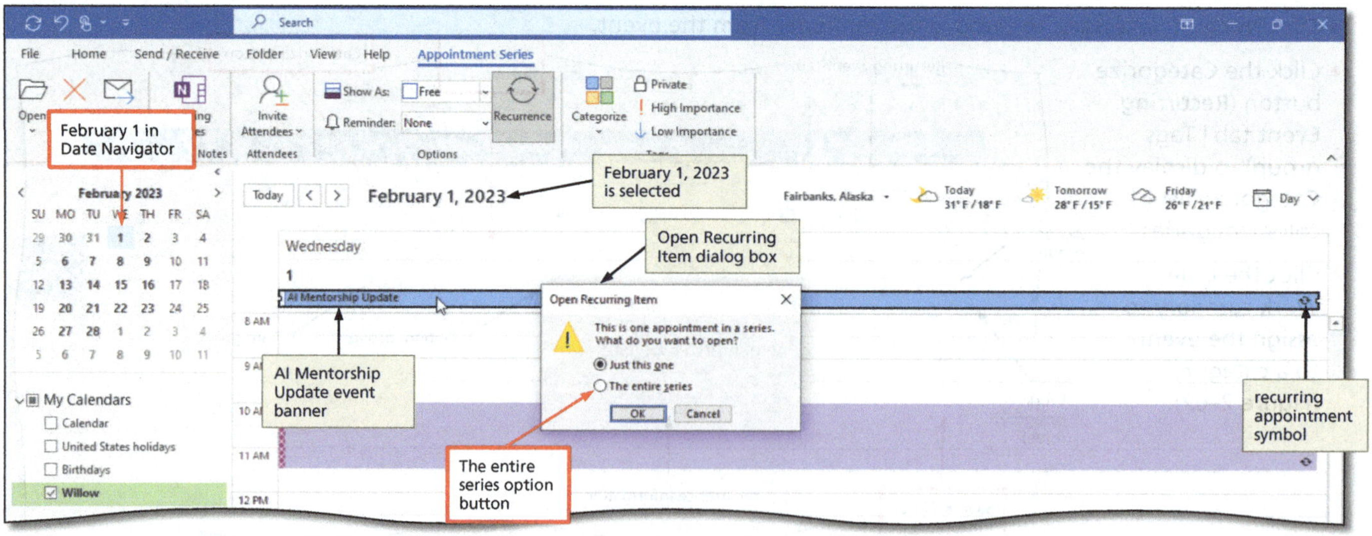

Figure 2–64

2

- Click the 'The entire series' option button and then click OK to display the AI Mentorship Update - Recurring Event window.
- Click the Recurrence button (Recurring Event tab | Options group).
- Click the second option button 'The first Wednesday of every 1 month(s)' to change the recurrence pattern.

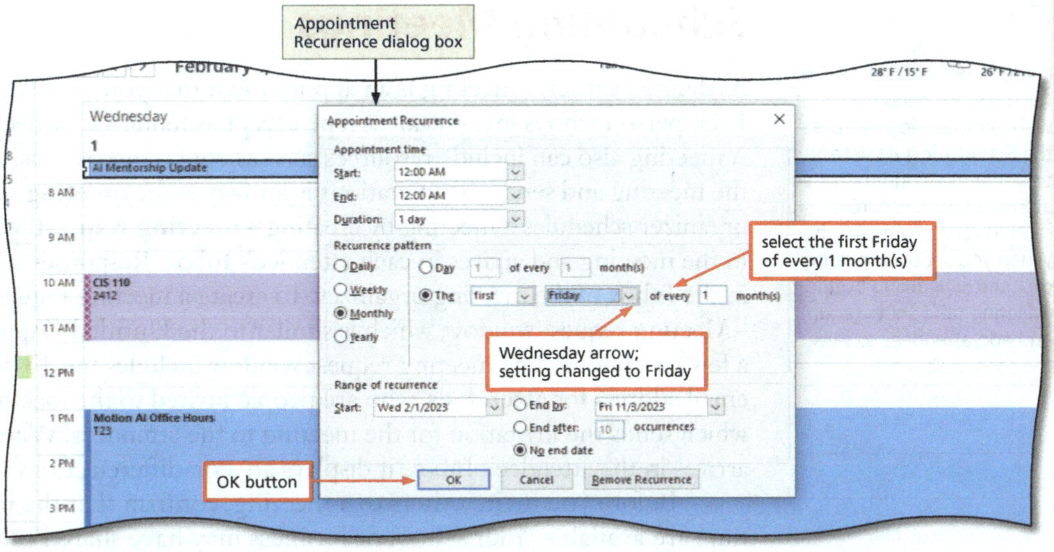

Figure 2–65

- Click the Wednesday arrow and then click Friday to set the recurrence to the first Friday of each month (Figure 2–65).

3

- Click OK to close the Appointment Recurrence dialog box and change the event day.
- Click the Save & Close button to save the event.
- Click the Month button (Home tab | Arrange group) to view the full month calendar (Figure 2–66).

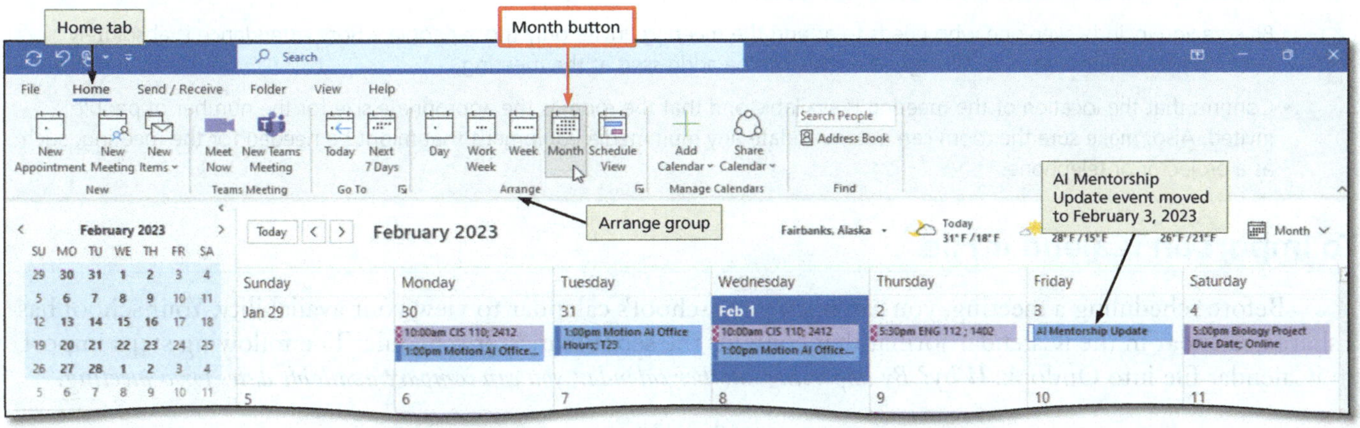

Figure 2–66

Other Ways

1. Double-click event, click entire series option button, click Recurrence button
2. Click event, press CTRL+O, click entire series option button, click Recurrence button

To Delete a Recurring Event

Deleting a recurring event is similar to deleting a recurring appointment. If you choose to delete a recurring event, you would use the following steps.

1. Click the scroll arrow on the Date Navigator to display the date of the event.
2. Click the event to display the Calendar Tools Appointment Series tab.
3. Click the Delete button (Calendar Tools Appointment Series tab | Actions group) to display the Delete menu.
4. Click Delete Series on the Delete menu to delete the event from the calendar.

BTW
Scheduling Assistant
If you have Microsoft 365 or Microsoft Exchange account with Outlook, you can use the **Scheduling Assistant** to find a meeting time when attendees and resources, such as rooms, are available. When you set up a meeting, click the Scheduling button (Meeting tab | Show group) and add attendees to view their schedules.

Scheduling Meetings

As defined earlier, a meeting is an appointment that you invite other people to attend. Each person who is invited can accept, accept as tentative, or decline a meeting request. A meeting also can include resources such as conference rooms. The person who creates the meeting and sends the invitations is known as the **meeting organizer**. The meeting organizer schedules a meeting by creating a **meeting request**, which is an email invitation to the meeting and arrives in each attendee's Inbox. Responses to a meeting request arrive in the Inbox of the meeting organizer. To create a meeting request, you use the Untitled - Meeting request window, which is similar to the Untitled - Appointment window with a few exceptions. The meeting request window includes the To box, where you enter an email address for **attendees**, who are people invited to the meeting, and the Send button, which sends the invitation for the meeting to the attendees. When a meeting request arrives in the attendee's Inbox, it displays an icon different from an email message icon.

Before you invite others to a meeting, confirm that the meeting date and time are available. Your school or business may have shared calendars that can be downloaded to your Outlook calendar. This shared calendar may be an iCalendar with an .ics file extension. An **iCalendar** represents a universal calendar format used by several email and calendar programs, including Microsoft Outlook, Google Calendar, and Apple iCal. The iCalendar format enables users to publish and share calendar information on the web and by email.

CONSIDER THIS

Before I send out a meeting request, how can I set the groundwork for an effective meeting?

- Import other calendars to compare everyone's schedule.
- Prepare an agenda stating the purpose of the meeting.
- Be sure you include everyone who needs to attend the meeting. Invite only those people whose attendance is absolutely necessary to ensure that all of the agenda items can be addressed at the meeting.
- Confirm that the location of the meeting is available and that the room is the appropriate size for the number of people invited. Also, make sure the room can accommodate any multimedia equipment that might be needed for the meeting, such as a projector or telephone.

To Import an iCalendar File

Before scheduling a meeting, you can open your school's calendar to view your availability. Your school has a shared calendar in the iCalendar format that contains the school's master schedule. The following steps import an iCalendar file into Outlook. ***Why?*** *By importing another calendar, you can compare available dates for a meeting.*

1

- Click the File tab on the ribbon to open Backstage view.
- Click Open & Export to display the Open gallery (Figure 2–67).

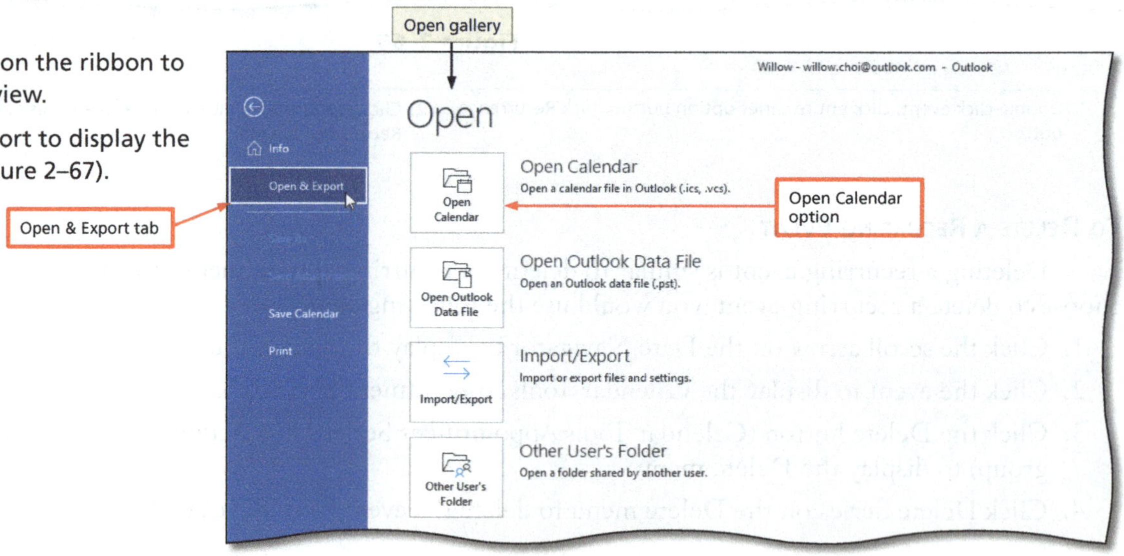

Figure 2–67

2

- Click Open Calendar in the Open gallery to display the Open Calendar dialog box.
- Navigate to the mailbox location (in this case, the Module folder in the Outlook2 folder in the Data Files folder) (Figure 2–68).

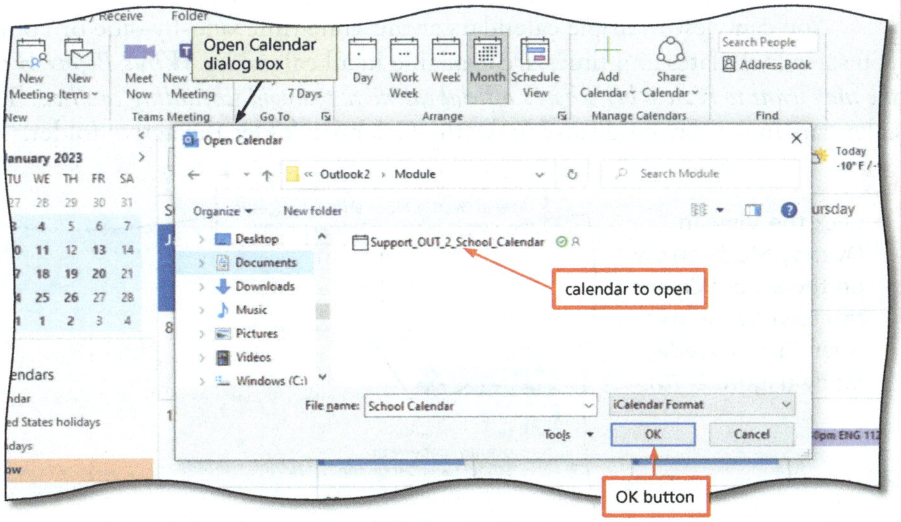

Figure 2–68

3

- Click Support_OUT_2_School_Calendar to select the file, and then click the OK button (Open Calendar dialog box). If you are asked whether you want to open this new calendar as a new calendar or to import its items into your calendar, click the Open as New button to open the calendar, which appears as School Calendar next to Willow's calendar in the appointment area (Figure 2–69).

Q&A

Why is the School Calendar not displayed in the My Calendars group?

Outlook organizes multiple calendars in groups. If you frequently work with a set of calendars, you can view them in groups. When you open an iCalendar, it initially might appear in an Other Calendars group.

The School Calendar is not displayed in the appointment area. What should I do?

Click the School Calendar check box in the My Calendars area. If the School Calendar overlays Willow's calendar, click the View in Side-by-Side Mode arrow on the School Calendar.

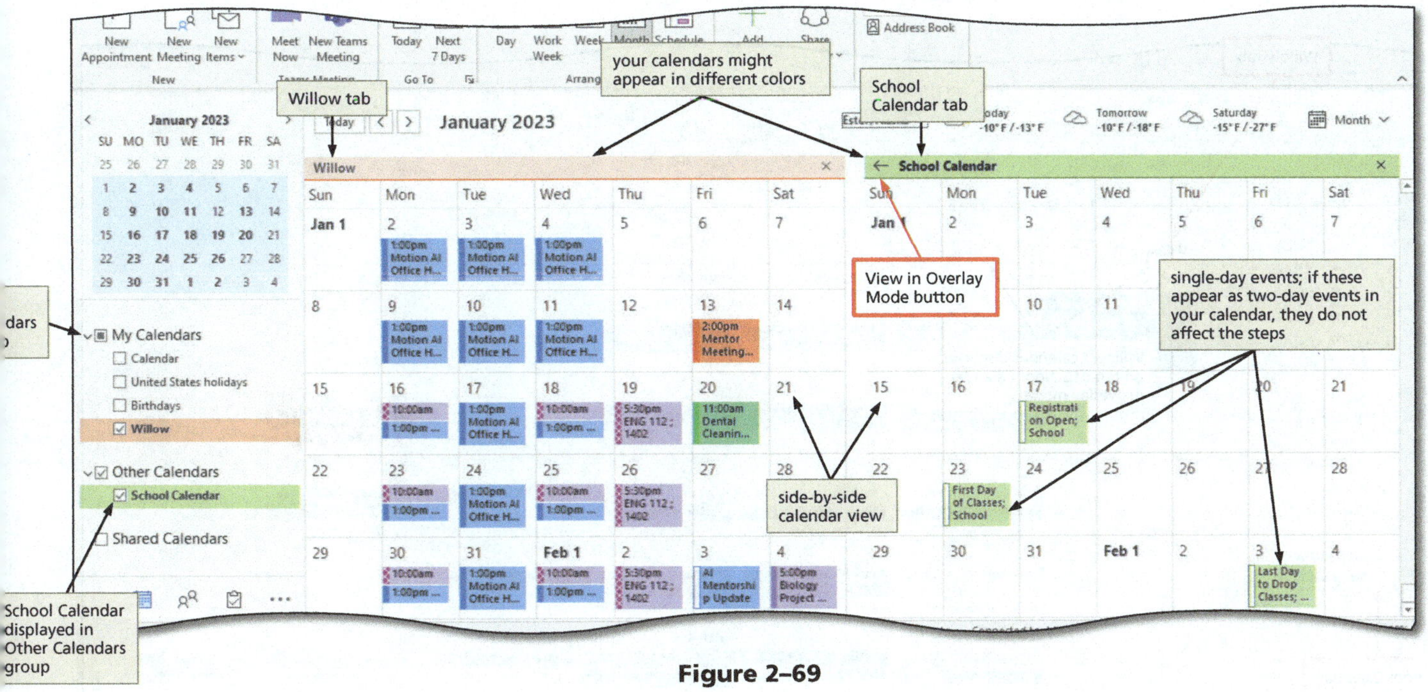

Figure 2–69

To View Calendars in the Overlay Mode

You can view multiple calendars at the same time side-by-side or combined into an overlay view to help you see which dates and times are available in all calendars. ***Why?*** *Before Willow schedules a meeting on her calendar, she may want to review her school's official calendar to avoid scheduling conflicts.* The following steps display both calendars in overlay mode and make the Calendar folder the active folder.

1

- Click the View in Overlay Mode arrow on the School Calendar tab to view the two calendars in overlay mode (Figure 2–70).

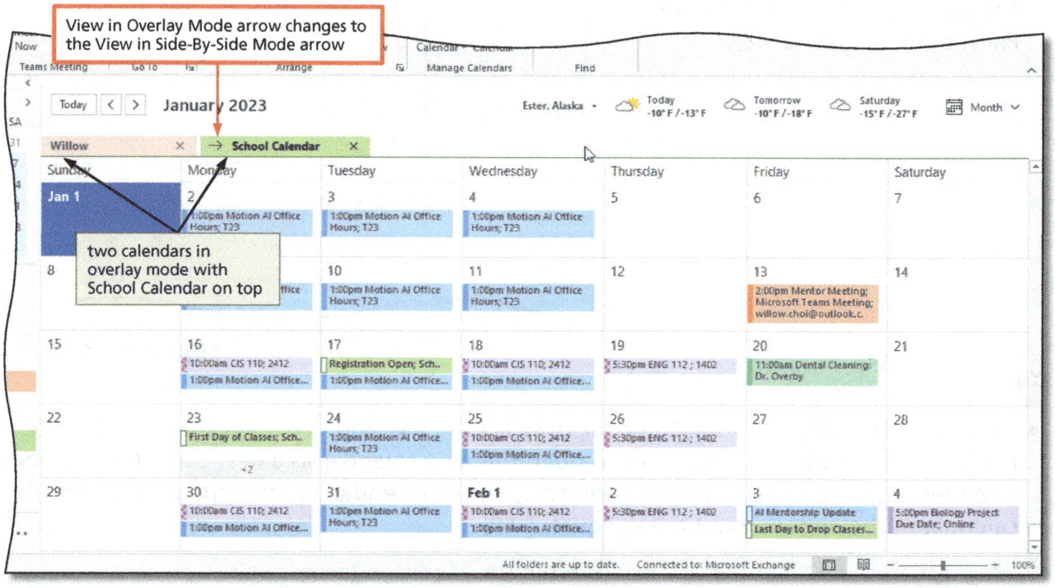

Figure 2–70

2

- Click the Willow tab to display the Willow calendar in front of School Calendar and Willow's calendar items displayed in bolded text on the calendar (Figure 2–71).

Q&A What happens if I click the arrow on Willow's calendar at this point?
Outlook again displays the calendars side by side.

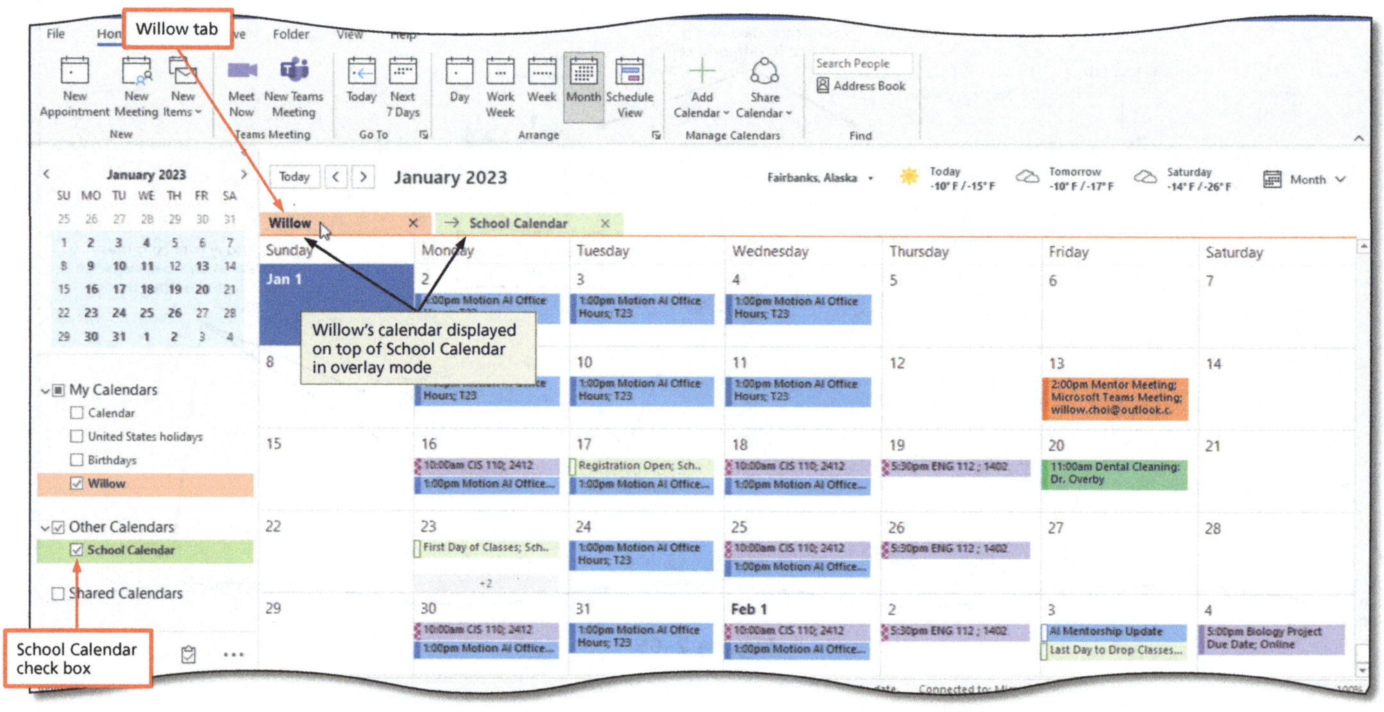

Figure 2–71

To View and Dock the Peek Calendar

The Outlook Navigation bar provides a **Peek** feature, a pop-up window that provides access to email, calendar, people, and tasks. ***Why?*** *Using the Peek feature, you can take a quick glance at your schedule without having to rearrange windows or lose your train of thought.* When you hover over Calendar in the Navigation pane, a Peek calendar of the current month opens and the current date is highlighted with a blue background. The Peek calendar can be docked in the right pane of the calendar. Appointments and meetings scheduled for today appear below the calendar. The following steps view, dock, and remove the Peek calendar.

1

- Click the School Calendar check box in the Navigation pane to remove the School Calendar from the Outlook window.
- Point to the Calendar icon on the Navigation bar to display the Peek calendar with today's appointments or meetings (Figure 2–72).

Q&A Why do I not see any appointments or meetings in the Peek calendar?

If you do not have any appointments or meetings today in the default Calendar, the Peek calendar does not display any calendar items.

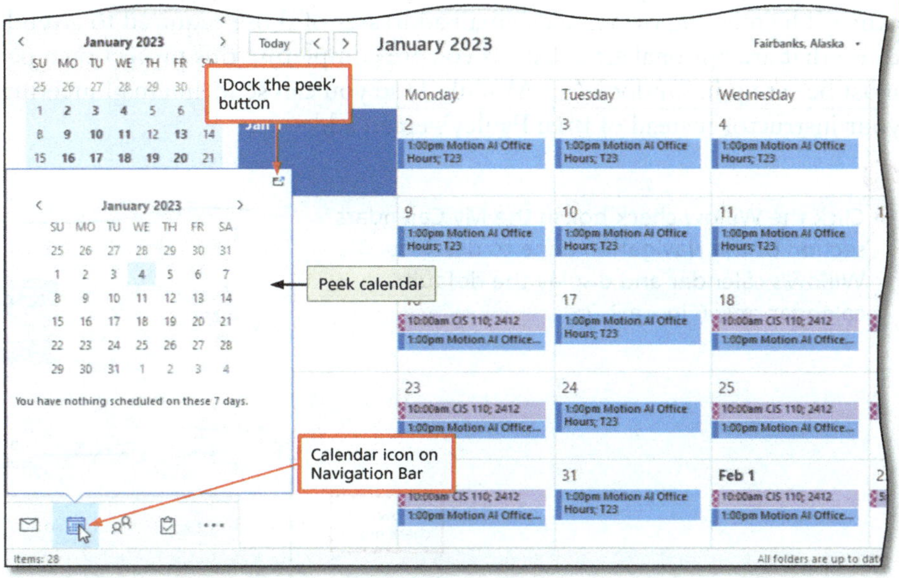

Figure 2–72

2

- Click the 'Dock the peek' button to dock the Peek calendar in the right pane of the Outlook window (Figure 2–73).

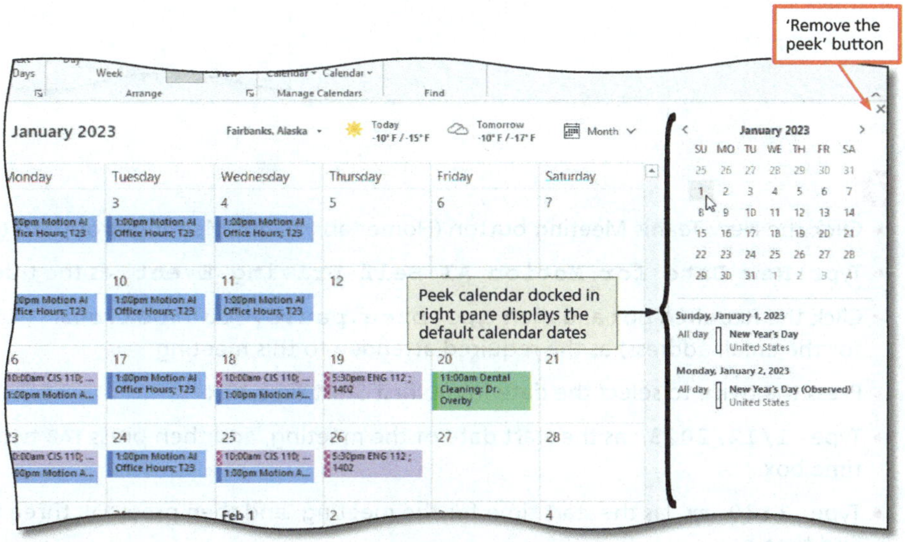

Figure 2–73

3

- Click the 'Remove the peek' button on the docked Peek calendar to remove the Peek calendar.

BTW

Room Finder

Some features in Outlook require a Microsoft Exchange Server account. **Exchange** is a collaborative communications server that many organizations use. Microsoft 365 includes Exchange Online, and some Internet hosting providers offer Exchange accounts. If you use a Microsoft Exchange account, you can click Rooms to check availability and reserve rooms when you select a location in the Location box. A feature called the **Room Finder** assists you in locating times for your meeting when most attendees are available. To select a meeting time, click a time suggestion in the Room Finder pane in the Suggested times section, or pick a time on the free/busy calendar.

To Create and Send a Meeting Request

Willow needs to meet with Bree Pauley to discuss rescheduling the Motion AI Self-Driving event. Rather than send an email message requesting the meeting, she decides to use Outlook Calendar to create this meeting. The meeting can either be face-to-face or a Teams online conference. You can create a Microsoft Teams meetings directly from within Outlook, without having to book them through the Teams app. The Teams meeting is displayed on both the Outlook calendar and the calendar within the Teams app. ***Why?*** *To find the best time to meet with other people, request a meeting, and keep track of the meeting date in your Inbox, you can send a Teams meeting request in Outlook.* Meetings can be scheduled on your default calendar or supplemental calendars. The following steps display the default calendar, create a meeting request, and send an invitation to the accounting office. The meeting owner adds email addresses of those required to attend the meeting and email addresses of those that are optional attendees. If you are completing this project on a personal computer, your email address must be set up in Outlook (see Module 1) so you can send an email meeting invitation. Use the email address of your instructor instead of Bree Pauley's email address.

1

- Click the Willow check box in the My Calendars section of the Navigation pane to deselect Willow's calendar and display the default calendar only (Figure 2–74).

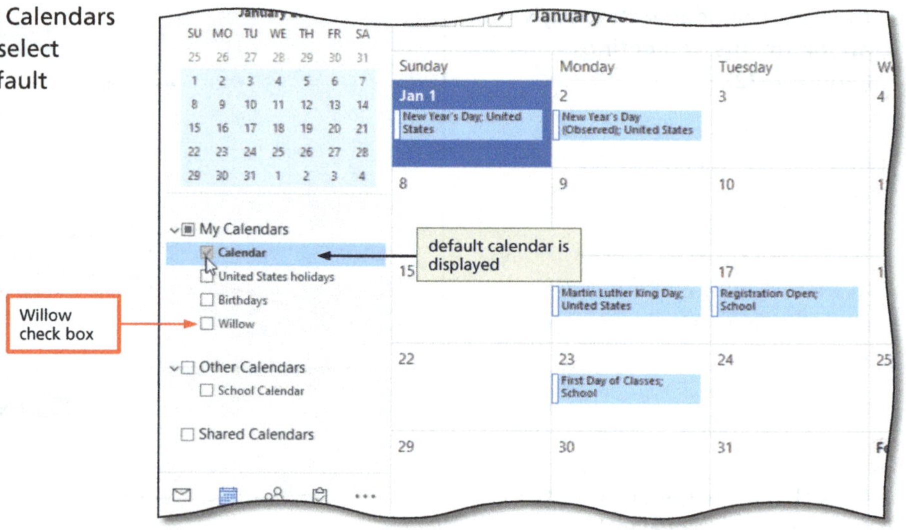

Figure 2–74

2

- Click the New Teams Meeting button (Home tab | Teams Meeting group) to open the Untitled - Meeting window.
- Type **`New Date for Motion AI Self-Driving Event`** as the title of the meeting.
- Click the Required box and then type **`bree.pauley@outlook.com`** (substitute your instructor's email address for the email address) as the required attendee to this meeting.
- Press TAB twice to select the date in the first Start time box.
- Type **`1/12/2023`** as the start date of the meeting, and then press TAB twice to select the time in the second Start time box.
- Type **`1:30 PM`** as the start time for the meeting, and then press TAB three times to select the time in the second End time box.
- Type **`2:30 PM`** as the end time for the meeting (Figure 2–75).

Q&A

The date in the End time box changed to Fri 1/13/2023. Should I change it?
Yes, change the End time to Thu 1/12/2023 to create a one-hour meeting.

Why does the message header include the text, "You haven't sent this meeting invitation yet"?
This notice reminds you that you have not yet sent the invitation to the meeting. If you review this invitation after sending it, the notice no longer appears.

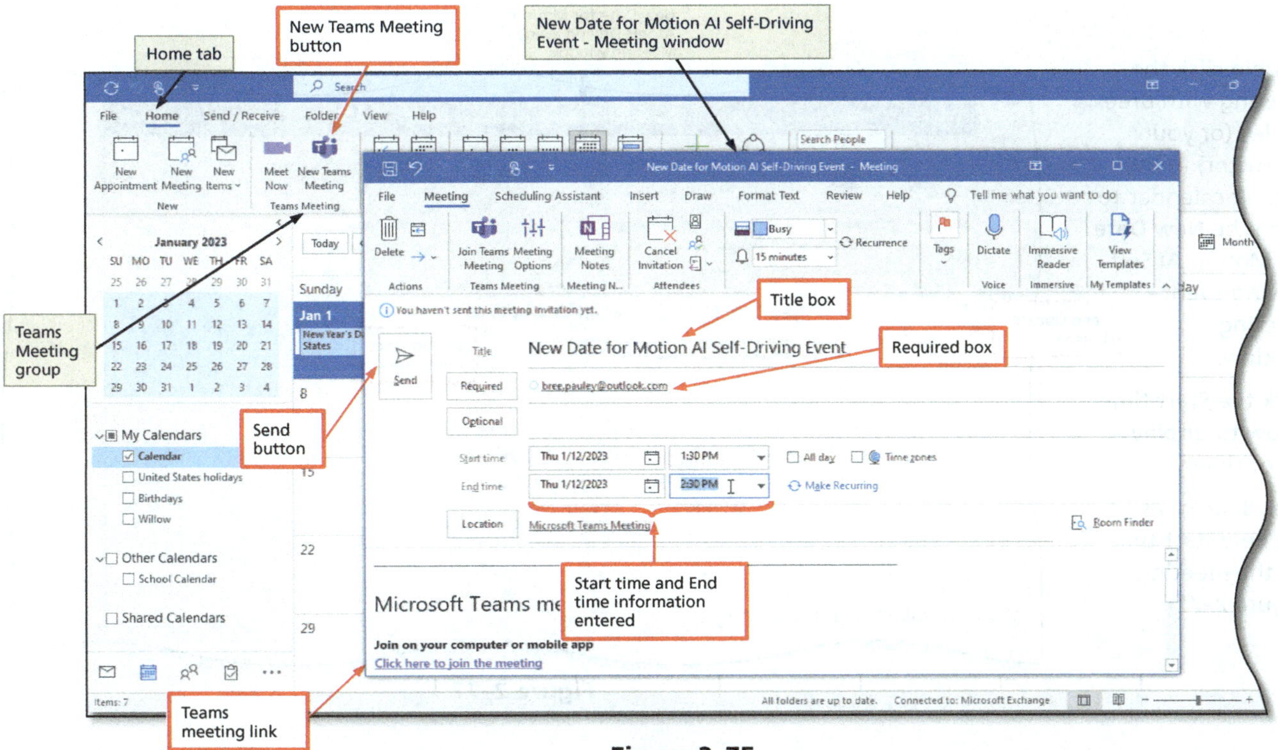

Figure 2–75

3

- Click the Send button to send the invitation and add the meeting to the calendar.
- If necessary, add an email account to Outlook to send the invitation to view the meeting on the calendar (Figure 2–76).

Q&A When I sent the meeting request, an error message appeared that states "No valid email accounts are configured." Why did I get this error message?
A meeting request sends an email to each of the invitees. You must have an email account set up in Outlook to send the meeting request.

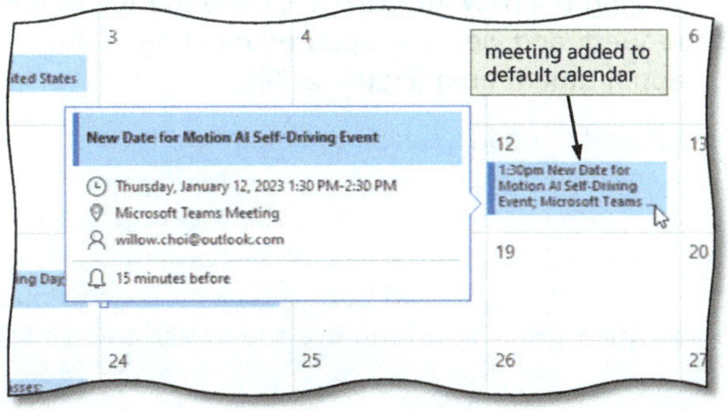

Figure 2–76

To Change the Time of a Meeting and Send an Update

Your schedule has changed, which means you need to change the time of the meeting about the self-driving event and send an update about the change. Though an attendee can propose a new time, only the originator (owner) can change or delete the meeting. ***Why?*** *You can update any meeting request to add or remove attendees or resources, change the meeting to a recurring series, or move the meeting to a different date or time.* The following steps change the time of the meeting and send an update to the attendee. If you are completing this project on a personal computer, your email account must be set up in Outlook (see Module 1) to be able to view the meeting request.

1

- Double-click the meeting with Bree Pauley (or your instructor) in the default calendar to open the New Date for Motion AI Self-Driving Event - Meeting window.
- Click the Start time arrow to display a list of times.
- Click 3:30 PM as the new start time for the meeting (Figure 2–77).

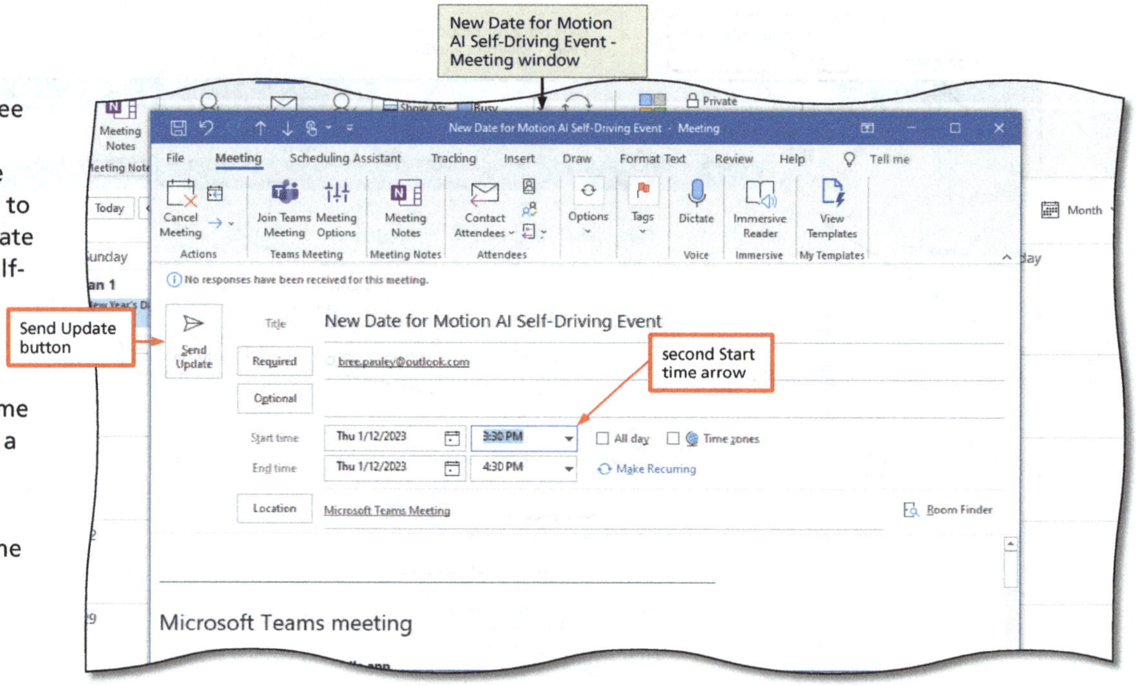

Figure 2–77

2

- Click the Send Update button in the message header to send the new information, close the Teams meeting request, and view the updated meeting in the appointment area (Figure 2–78).

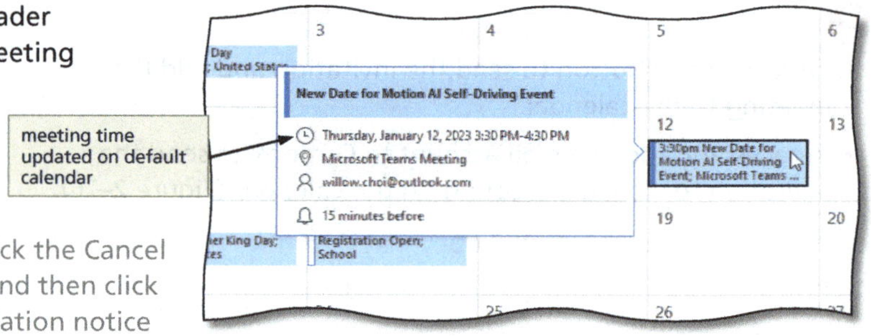

Figure 2–78

Q&A

What if I need to cancel the meeting?

To remove a meeting, click the meeting in the appointment area to display the Meeting tab, click the Cancel Meeting button (Meeting tab | Actions group), and then click the Send Cancellation button to send the cancellation notice to the attendee and remove the meeting from the calendar.

Other Ways

1. Drag meeting to new time, click 'Save changes and send update,' click OK, click Send Update

To Reply to a Meeting Request

Bree Pauley has received Willow's meeting request in an email message. Outlook allows invitees to choose from four response options: Accept, Tentative, Decline, or Propose New Time. ***Why?*** *Providing response options makes it easy for invitees to reply to a meeting request.* The following steps accept the meeting request. If you have a meeting request in your personal email that is set up using Outlook, substitute your meeting request in the following steps. If you do not have any meeting requests, read these steps without performing them.

1

- Click Mail on the Navigation bar to display the Inbox folder.
- Double-click the email message header to open the meeting invitation (Figure 2–79).

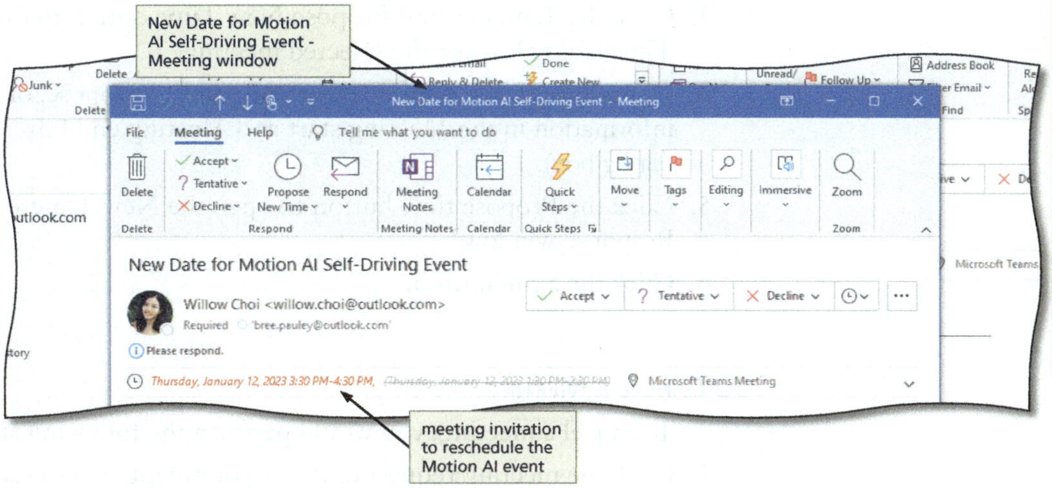

Makistock/Shutterstock.com

Figure 2–79

2

- Click the Accept button to display the options for accepting the meeting (Figure 2–80).

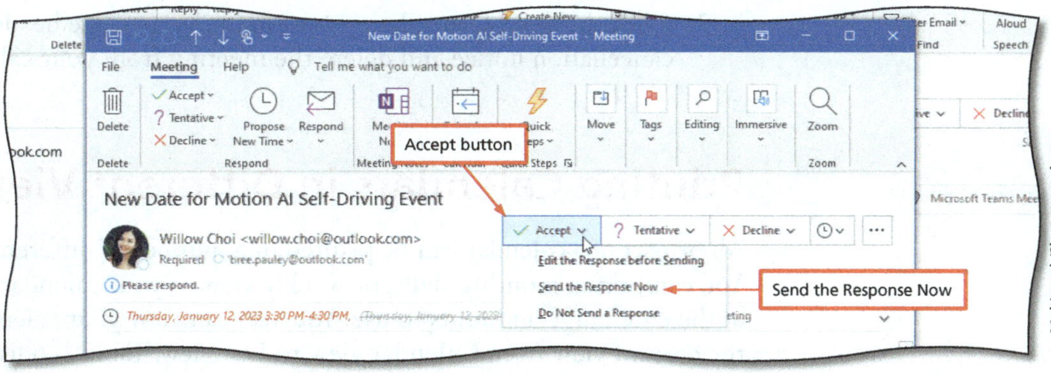

Makistock/Shutterstock.com

Figure 2–80

3

- Click Send the Response Now to send the accept response and add the meeting to the calendar.

Q&A

What happened to the meeting invitation in the Inbox?

When you accept or tentatively accept a meeting request, the invitation is deleted from the Inbox and the meeting is added to your calendar. The meeting response is in the Sent Items folder.

What happens when I decline a meeting request?

When a meeting request is declined, it is removed from your Inbox and the meeting is not added to your calendar. The reply is placed in the Sent Items folder.

To Propose a New Meeting Time

When you receive a meeting invitation, you can propose a new time if the original time is not available in your calendar. When you propose a new time, a proposal is sent to the meeting originator via email, indicating that you tentatively accept the request, but propose the meeting be held at a different time or on a different date. To propose a new time for a meeting, you would perform the following steps.

1. Click the appropriate meeting request to display the Meeting Occurrence tab on the ribbon.
2. Click the Propose New Time button (Meeting Occurrence tab | Respond group) to display the Occurrence menu.

3. Click the Tentative and Propose New Time option to display the Propose New Time dialog box for the selected meeting.
4. Drag through the time slot that you want to propose, or enter the appropriate information in the Meeting start and Meeting end boxes (Propose New Time dialog box).
5. Click the Propose time button to open the New Time Proposed - Meeting Response window.
6. Click the Send button.

To Cancel a Meeting

To cancel a meeting, you would perform the following steps.

1. Click the meeting request in the appointment area to select the meeting and display the Meeting tab on the ribbon.
2. Click the Cancel Meeting button (Meeting tab | Actions group) to open the window for the selected meeting.
3. Click the Send Cancellation button in the message header to send the cancellation notice and delete the meeting from your calendar.

Printing Calendars in Different Views

All or part of a calendar can be printed in a number of different views, or **print styles**. You can print a monthly, daily, or weekly view of your calendar and select options such as the date range and fonts to use. You also can view your calendar in a list by changing the current view from Calendar view to List view. Table 2–6 lists the print styles available for printing your calendar from Calendar view.

Table 2–6 Print Styles for Calendar View

Print Style	Description
Daily	Prints a daily appointment schedule for a specific date including one day per page, a daily task list, an area for notes, and a two-month calendar
Weekly Agenda	Prints a seven-day weekly calendar with one week per page and a two-month calendar
Weekly Calendar	Prints a seven-day weekly calendar with one week per page and an hourly schedule, similar to the Daily style
Monthly	Prints five weeks per page of a particular month or date range
Tri-fold	Prints a page for each day, including a daily task list and a weekly schedule
Calendar Details	Prints a list of calendar items and supporting details

To Print the Calendar in Weekly Calendar Style

Willow would like to print her calendar for a hard copy of her first week of classes. ***Why?*** *Printing a calendar enables you to keep or distribute the calendar in a form that can be read or viewed, but cannot be edited.* The following steps print a calendar in a weekly calendar style.

1

- Click Calendar on the Navigation bar to display the Outlook calendar.
- If necessary, click the Willow check box to display Willow's calendar.
- If necessary, click the other check boxes to close the other calendars.
- Click the Go To Date Dialog Box Launcher (Home tab | Go To group) to display the Go To Date dialog box.
- Type `2/1/2023` in the Date box to select that date.
- If necessary, click the Show in button, and then click Month Calendar to show Month view in the appointment area (Figure 2–81).

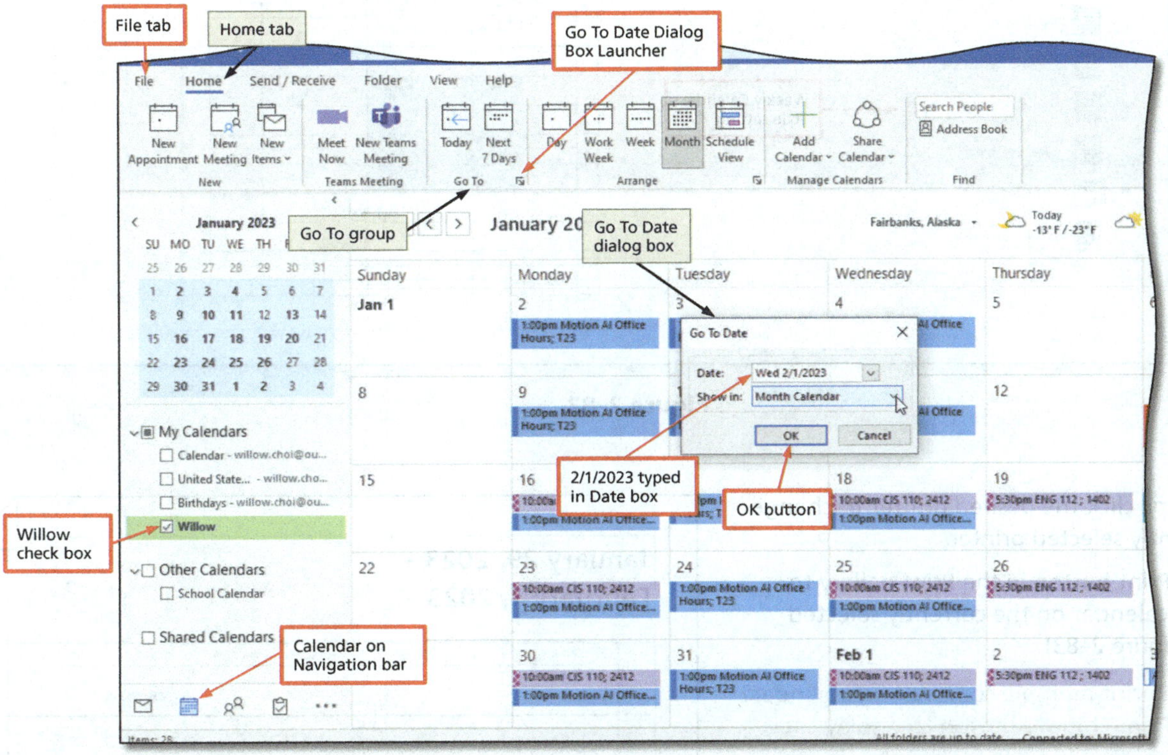

Figure 2–81

2

- Click OK to close the Go To Date dialog box.
- Click File on the ribbon to open Backstage view.
- Click the Print tab in Backstage view to display the Print gallery.
- Click Weekly Calendar Style in the Settings list to preview how the printed calendar will look in Weekly Calendar Style (Figure 2–82).

Experiment

- Click the other settings to preview the different print styles. When finished, select Weekly Calendar Style.

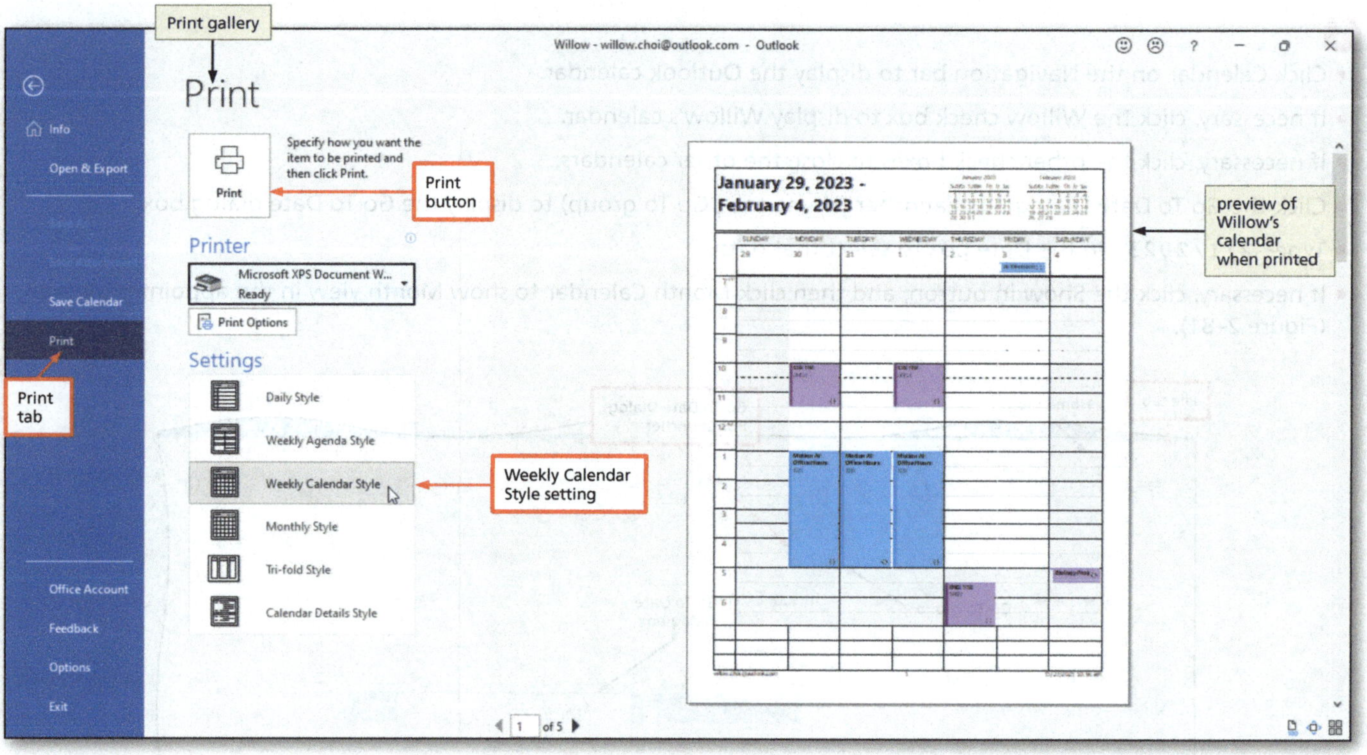

Figure 2–82

3

- If necessary, click the desired printer to change the currently selected printer.
- Click the Print button in the Print gallery to print the calendar on the currently selected printer (Figure 2–83).

Q&A

How can I print multiple copies of my calendar?

Click the Print Options button to display the Print dialog box, increase the number in the Number of copies box, and then click the Print button to send the calendar to the printer and return to the calendar.

What if I decide not to print the calendar at this time?

Click File on the ribbon to close Backstage view and return to the Calendar window.

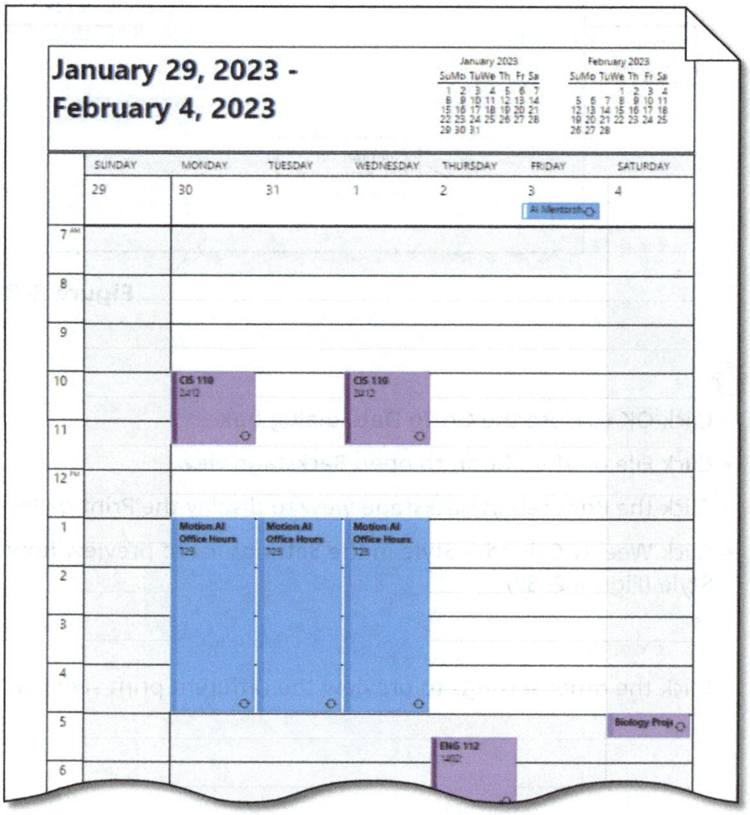

Figure 2–83

Other Ways

1. Press CTRL+P, press ENTER

To Change the Calendar View to List View

By default, the Outlook calendar is displayed in Calendar view, but other options include List view, which displays the calendar as a table with each row containing a unique calendar item. ***Why?*** *To display all of your calendar appointments, events, and meetings, change the current Calendar view to List view.* The following steps change the view from Calendar view to List view.

1

- Click View on the ribbon to display the View tab.
- Click the Change View button (View tab | Current View group) to display the Change View gallery (Figure 2–84).

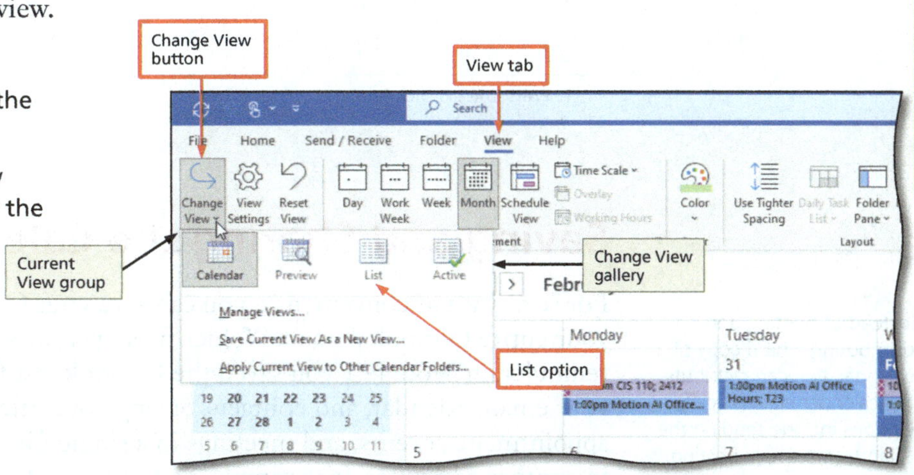

Figure 2–84

2

- Click List in the Change View gallery to display a list of calendar items in the appointment area (Figure 2–85).

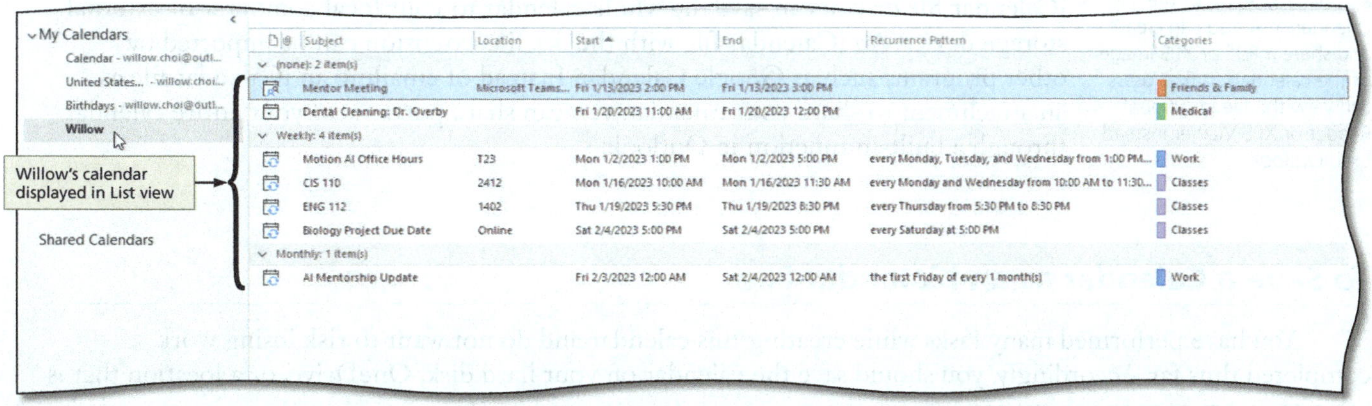

Figure 2–85

BTW
Changing Settings before Printing
To change the margins, page orientation, or paper size before printing, click the Print Options button in the Print gallery and then click the Page Setup button to display the Page Setup: Table Style dialog box.

To Print the Calendar in List View

To print a list of your calendar items in a table, print the List view display. The following steps print the calendar in Table style.

1. Click File on the ribbon to open Backstage view.
2. Click the Print tab in Backstage view to display the Print gallery.
3. Click the Table Style option in the Settings list to preview the calendar in Table Style.
4. If necessary, click the Printer box to display a list of available printer options, and then click the desired printer to change the selected printer.

5 Click the Print button to send the list of appointments to the selected printer.

Q&A When I change the view from List view to Calendar view, why does the Calendar display the current date and not the date I printed?
The calendar always displays the current date when you change from List view to Calendar view.

Other Ways

1. Press CTRL+P, click Print

BTW
Distributing a Calendar
Instead of printing and distributing a hard copy of a calendar, you can distribute the calendar electronically. Options include sending the calendar via email; posting it on cloud storage (such as OneDrive) and sharing the file with others; posting it on a social networking site, blog, or other website; and sharing a link associated with an online location of the calendar. You also can create and share a PDF or XPS image of the calendar, so that users can view the file in Acrobat Reader or XPS Viewer instead of in Outlook.

Saving and Sharing the Calendar

For security and convenience, you can save your Outlook calendar by backing up your entire Outlook personal folder files (.pst) or an individual calendar (.ics). As a reminder, in Module 1 you saved the Outlook .pst file, which contained a backup of your email, calendar, and contacts. Saving your calendar file allows you to back up your appointments, events, and meetings in a single file. You can then move your calendar to another computer, for example, and continue to schedule items there. Besides saving your calendar, you can share it with others, whether they use Outlook or not. Finally, scheduling a meeting with someone who cannot see your calendar can be difficult, so you can share your calendar through email.

With Outlook, each appointment, task, or contact can be saved as a separate iCalendar file or you can save the whole calendar to your local computer or external storage device. An iCalendar file with the .ics file extension can be imported by other programs such as Google Calendar. Instead of emailing an iCalendar file as an attachment to share your calendar, you can share portions of your entire calendar through a built-in function in Outlook.

To Save a Calendar as an iCalendar File

You have performed many tasks while creating this calendar and do not want to risk losing work completed thus far. Accordingly, you should save the calendar on your hard disk, OneDrive, or a location that is most appropriate to your situation.

The following steps assume you already have created folders for storing your files, for example, a CIS folder (for your class) that contains an Outlook folder (for your assignments). These steps save the calendar in the Module folder in the Outlook2 folder on your desired save location, such as the CIS > Outlook folder on your hard drive.

Why? *By saving a copy of your calendar to an iCalendar format, you can back up or share your calendar with your business colleagues or friends.* The following steps save a calendar.

1

- Click File on the ribbon to display Backstage view.
- Click the Save Calendar tab to display the Save As dialog box.
- Type **SC_OUT_2_Willow_Calendar** in the File name box to provide a file name.

- Navigate to the desired save location (in this case, the Module folder in Outlook2 folder of your Data Files folder) (Figure 2–86).

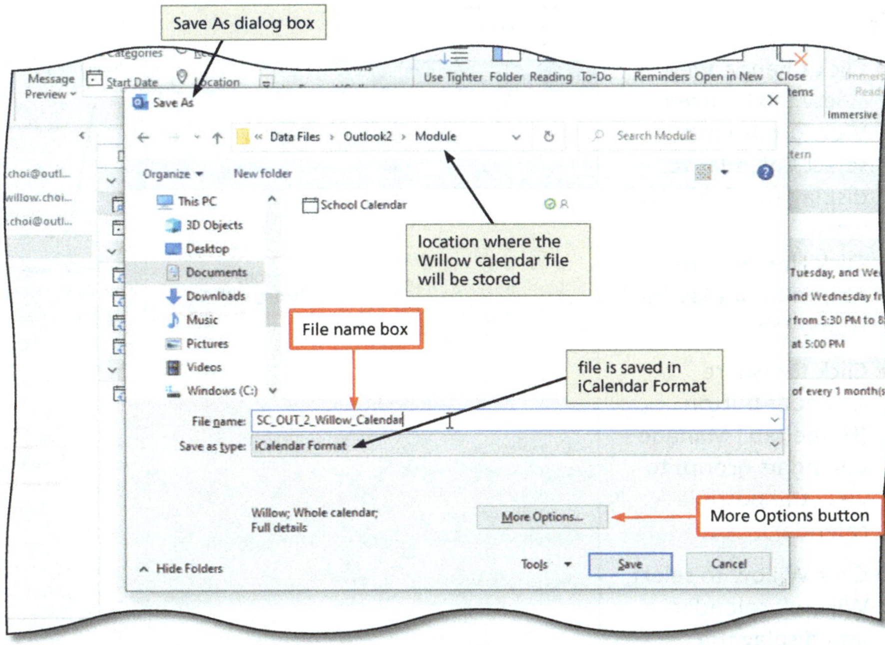

Figure 2–86

2

- Click the More Options button to display the Save As dialog box.
- Click the Date Range arrow to display the Date Range list (Figure 2–87).

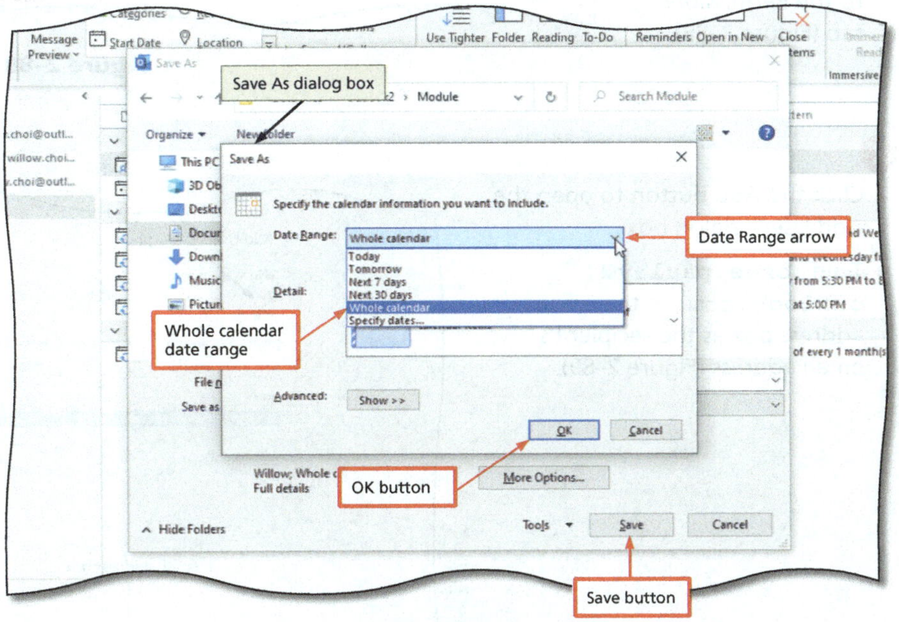

Figure 2–87

3

- If necessary, click Whole calendar on the Date Range list to save the calendar's full details.
- Click OK (Save As dialog box) to specify the whole calendar date range.
- Click the Save button (Save As dialog box) to save the calendar as an iCalendar file in the selected location.

To Share a Calendar

Bree Pauley needs to meet with Willow to reschedule the self-driving event. She requests a copy of Willow's calendar. ***Why?*** *Willow can send a copy of her calendar in an email message directly from Outlook to inform Bree Pauley when she is available for a meeting.* The following steps share a calendar by forwarding the selected calendar. These steps assume you have an email account set up in Outlook.

1

- Click Change View (View tab | Current View group) and select Calendar to display the Calendar view.
- Click Home on the ribbon to display the Home tab.
- Click the Share Calendar button (Home tab | Manage Calendars group) to view the possible calendars.
- Click Willow to select Willow's calendar and display the Willow Properties dialog box opened to the Permissions tab (Figure 2–88).

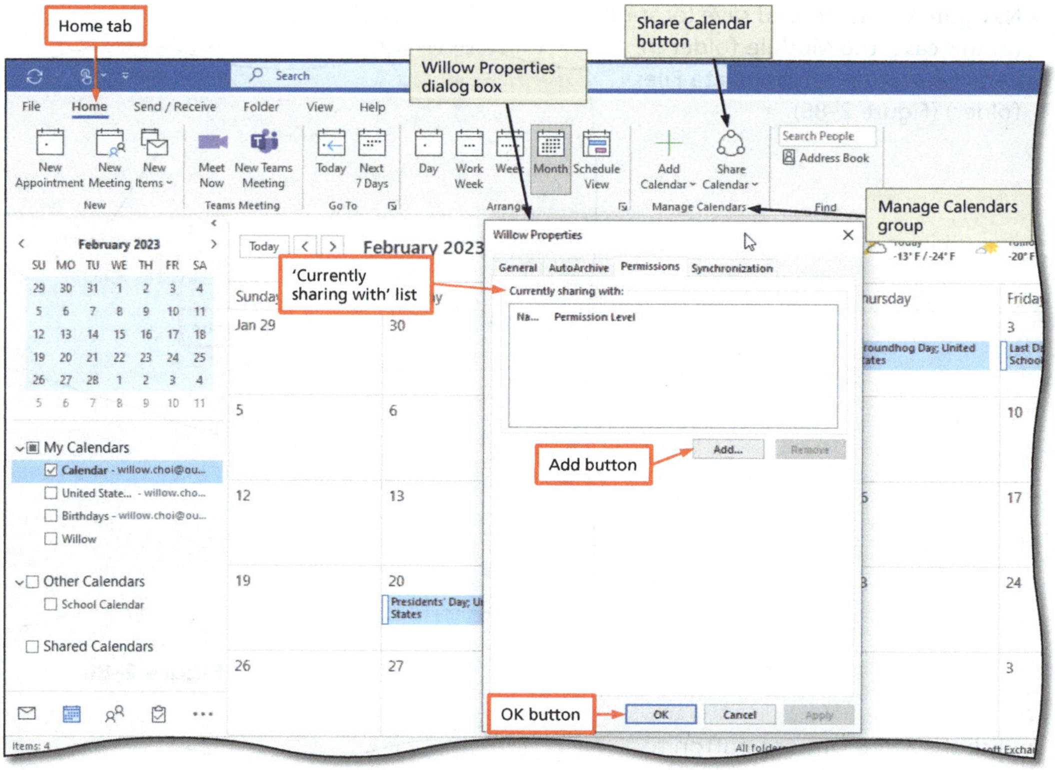

Figure 2–88

2

- Click the Add button to open the Add Users dialog box.
- Type **bree.pauley@outlook.com** in the email address box as the recipient's email address (Figure 2–89).

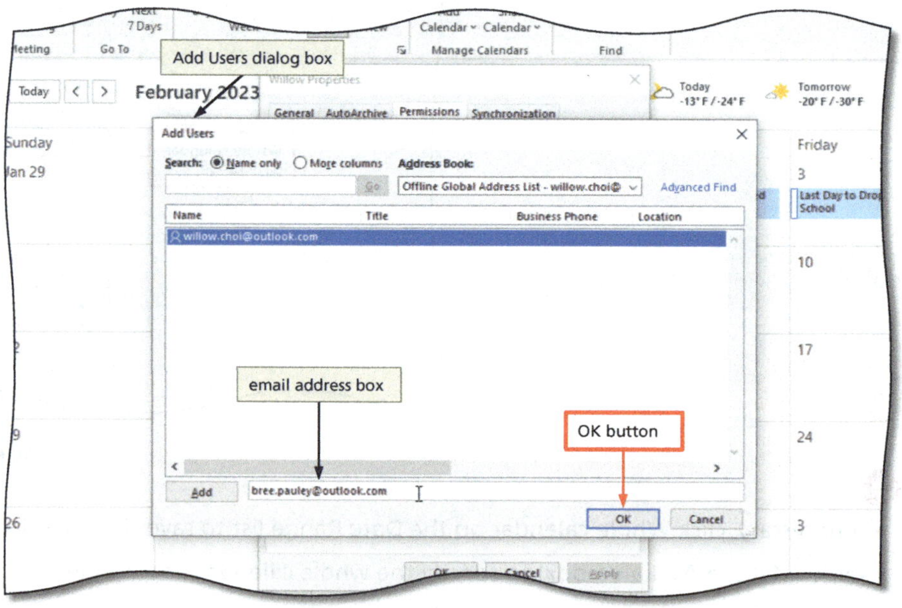

Figure 2–89

3

- Click the OK button to add Bree Pauley's email address to the 'Currently sharing with' list on the Permission tab (Figure 2–90).

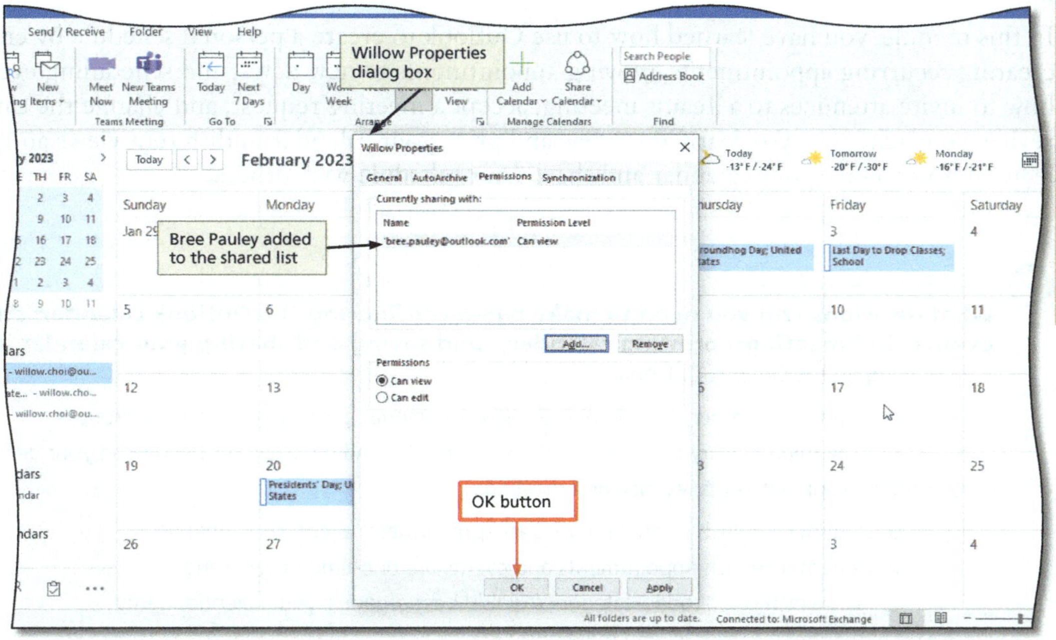

Figure 2–90

4

- Click the OK button to share your iCalendar with the email message recipient. Ms. Pauley is sent an email automatically (Figure 2–91).

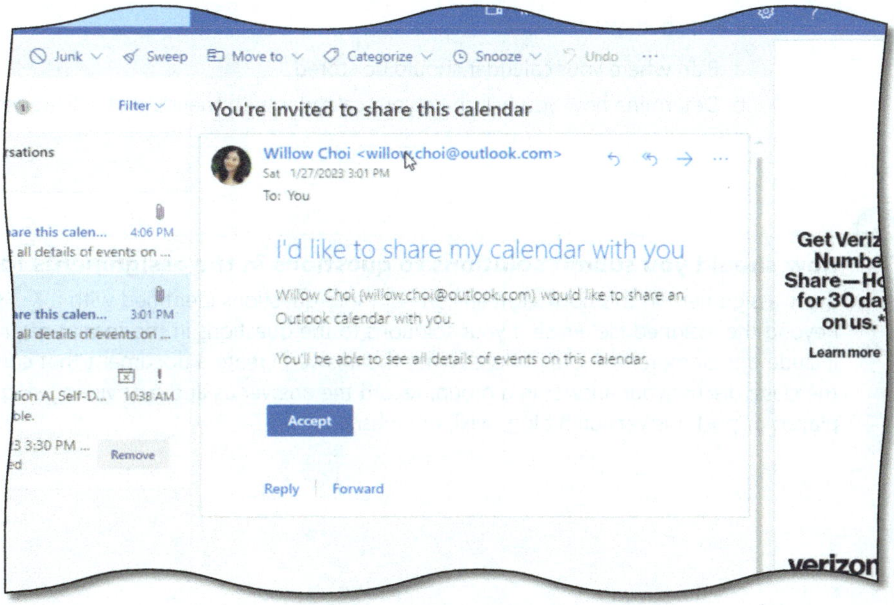

Figure 2–91

5

- Exit Outlook.

Summary

In this module, you have learned how to use Outlook to create a personal schedule by entering appointments, creating recurring appointments, moving appointments to new dates, and scheduling events. You also learned how to invite attendees to a Teams meeting, accept a meeting request, and change the time of a meeting. To review your schedule, you learned to view and print your calendar in different views and print styles. Finally, you learned how to save your calendar and share your schedule with others.

CONSIDER THIS

What decisions will you need to make when configuring the Outlook calendar; scheduling appointments, events, and meetings; printing calendars; and saving and sharing your calendar in the future?

1. Configure the Outlook Calendar:
    a. Determine the purpose of your calendar—personal, professional, or for a group.
    b. Determine the city displayed on the Weather Bar and if you prefer holidays in your default calendar.
2. Schedule appointments, events, and meetings:
    a. Determine if each calendar item is an appointment, event, or a meeting.
    b. Determine which appointments and events are one-time or recurring.
    c. Plan which color-coded categories would best organize your calendar items.
3. Edit appointments, events, and meetings:
    a. Update the details of your calendar items as your schedule changes.
    b. Respond to meeting requests.
4. Print your calendar:
    a. Plan which calendar style would best fit your needs.
5. Save and share your calendar:
    a. Plan where your calendar should be stored.
    b. Determine how you will share your calendar with friends and colleagues.

CONSIDER THIS

How should you submit solutions to questions in the assignments identified with a symbol?

Every assignment in this book contains one or more questions identified with a symbol. These questions require you to think beyond the assigned file. Present your solutions to the questions in the format required by your instructor. Possible formats may include one or more of these options: write the answer; create a document that contains the answer; present your answer to the class; discuss your answer in a group; record the answer as audio or video using a webcam, smartphone, or portable media player; or post answers on a blog, wiki, or website.

Apply Your Knowledge

Reinforce the skills and apply the concepts you learned in this module.

Updating a Calendar

Note: To complete this assignment, you will be required to use the Data Files. Please contact your instructor for information about accessing the Data Files.

Instructions: Start Outlook. You are updating your school's Athletic Events iCalendar, which is located in the Data Files, by revising the scheduled activities.

Perform the following tasks:

1. Open the SC_OUT_2-1.ics calendar file from the Data Files.
2. Display only this iCalendar in the Outlook Calendar window. Use Month view to display the calendar for March 2023.
3. Add a weekly **`Game Video Review`** appointment for every Tuesday from March 7, 2023 to May 9, 2023, starting at 1 PM and lasting for one hour in MLK Hall.
4. Create two color categories for Booster Meetings (red) and Coach Meetings (blue).
5. Change the Coach and Assistant's Meeting to one hour earlier with the same duration and color categorize the meeting only to blue. Change the location to Tirrell Room 28.
6. Change the Baseball Booster's meeting to March 13 at the same time. Assign this calendar event to a color category.
7. Reschedule the March Madness Bracket meeting to a recurring time on Fridays starting on February 24 and ending on March 24.
8. Add a Teams meeting for the Division League Coach's Conference from March 6 to March 8 and make it an all-day event. Assign this calendar event to a color category. Insert your email address as the required email address.
9. Add a monthly appointment that adds a **`Twitter Announcement`** at 9:00 AM for 30 minutes about Booster Meeting Updates the first Tuesday of each month starting in February 2023 for 12 months and color categorize the appointment.
10. If requested by your instructor, change the location of the Coach and Assistant's Meeting from the Tirrell Room 28 to a room named after your birth city.
11. Save the Calendar as **`SC_OUT_2_Athletic_Events_Calendar`** and submit the iCalendar in the format specified by your instructor.
12. Print the final calendar in Month view for March 2023 to a Microsoft Print to PDF or to paper as specified by your instructor, shown in Figure 2–92, and then submit the printout to your instructor.

Continued >

Apply Your Knowledge *continued*

13. Delete this calendar from Outlook and exit Outlook.
14. Most calendar programs save files with the .ics format. Why is it convenient that most calendar programs use the same format?

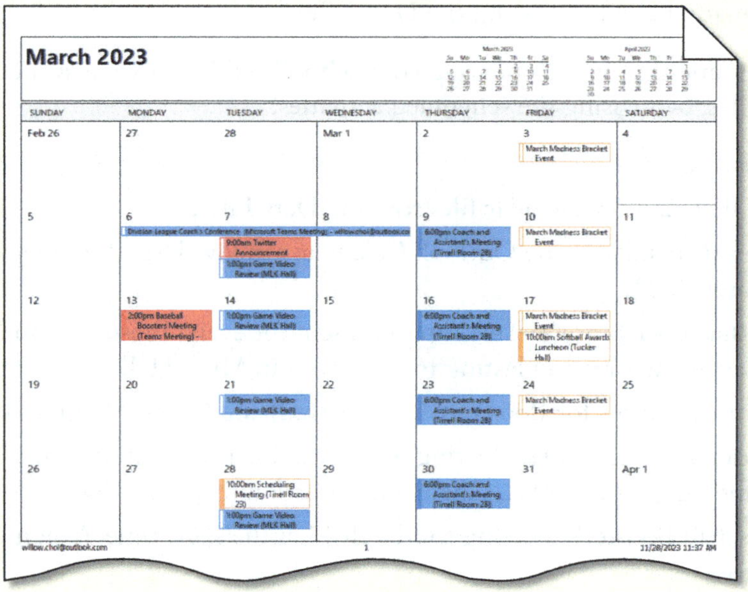

Figure 2–92

Extend Your Knowledge

Extend the skills you learned in this module and experiment with new skills. You may need to use Help to complete the assignment.

Creating and Sharing a Calendar

Instructions: Start Outlook. You work as a charge nurse at Centra Medical Hospital. Create a new calendar to share your availability for open cases. Use Outlook Help to learn how to create a calendar group, change the color of the calendar, and create a private appointment.

Perform the following tasks:

1. Create a blank calendar named **Neonatal Research** and then move it to a new calendar group named **Centra** within the Other Calendars group.
2. Change the color of the entire calendar to light teal.
3. Add a recurring **Case Reporting** appointment from 8:00 AM to 9:30 AM on Wednesday and Friday beginning on June 14, 2023 and continuing for 22 occurrences in the Naomi Room.
4. Create an event named **Pediatric Conference** starting on June 24, 2023 at the Western Conference Center lasting four days from this Saturday to Tuesday.
5. Add a recurring **Hemoglobin Reports Due** event at 4 PM starting on June 30 and lasting for 12 months on the last day of each month in the location of Records Office.
6. If requested by your instructor, change the Weather Bar to display weather information for your hometown. The completed calendar is shown in Figure 2–93.

7. Save the Calendar file as **SC_OUT_2_Neonatal_Research** and submit the iCalendar in the format specified by your instructor.
8. Exit Outlook.
9. Think about the reason you might share your Outlook Calendar. In the case of sharing your work schedule with others at your company, why would a digital calendar be more helpful instead of a paper schedule?

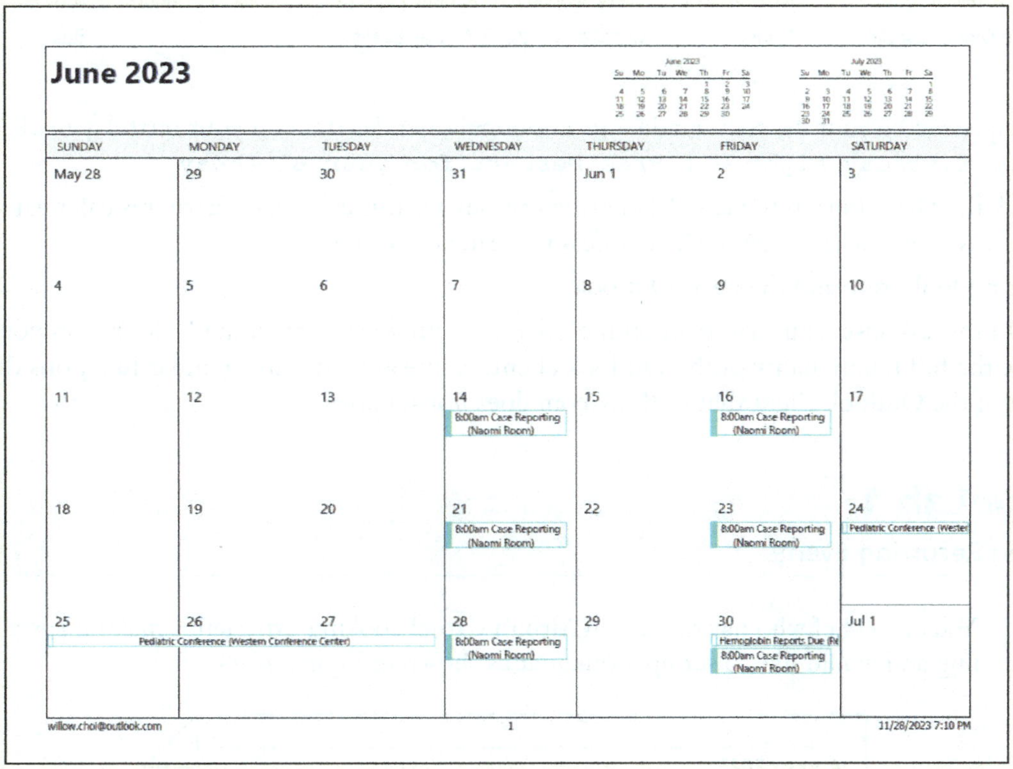

Figure 2–93

Expand Your World

Create a solution that uses cloud or web technologies by learning and investigating on your own from general guidance.

Opening a Web-Based Calendar in the Outlook Client

Instructions: In your role as a social media manager for a restaurant chain named Saffron Cafe, you market the restaurant chain on social media by posting to Facebook, Twitter, and Instagram. Use the calendar dates shown in Table 2–7 to create an online calendar at Outlook.com using your Microsoft account. Share the online calendar with your instructor. Using Outlook, open the online calendar and print the calendar in the Outlook client. Sharing your calendar in the cloud as a link allows anyone to see it, such as the restaurant's management, even if they do not have their own calendar established.

Perform the following tasks:

1. If necessary, create a Microsoft account at outlook.com.
2. Open the calendar option at outlook.com and add a calendar with the name **Social Media for Saffron Cafe Calendar.**
3. Open the Social Media for Saffron Cafe Calendar only and add the items shown in Table 2–7 to the online calendar.

Continued >

Expand Your World *continued*

Table 2–7 Social Media for Saffron Cafe Calendar Items

Description	Recurrence	Due Date	Availability
Saffron Dinner	Monthly	First Saturday in October 2023 until the end of the year	Free
Loyalty Customer Dinner 20% Off	Monthly	First day of each month starting October 2023 at 5PM–9PM, never ends	Free
Vegetarian Special	Mondays	Every Monday in October 2023 from 6:00 PM for 3 hours	Busy
Halloween Dinner Special	None	October 31, 2023 All Day Event	Busy

4. If requested by your instructor, add a promotional calendar item on your birthday in 2023 titled **`Birthday Night – 1 Free Dessert for your Birthday`**.
5. Click the Share button to view the sharing options for this calendar. Share this calendar with your instructor with a view-only to access this calendar online.
6. Exit outlook.com, and then exit Outlook.
7. In this exercise, you shared an online calendar with your instructor. Outlook.com does not have the full functionality of the Outlook client. Name at least four calendar functions that are part of the Outlook client that outlook.com does not support.

In the Lab 1

Creating Recurring Events

Problem: You are a chef who has started an Airbnb virtual cooking experience making pasta for team-building and would like to set up a calendar as shown in Figure 2–94.

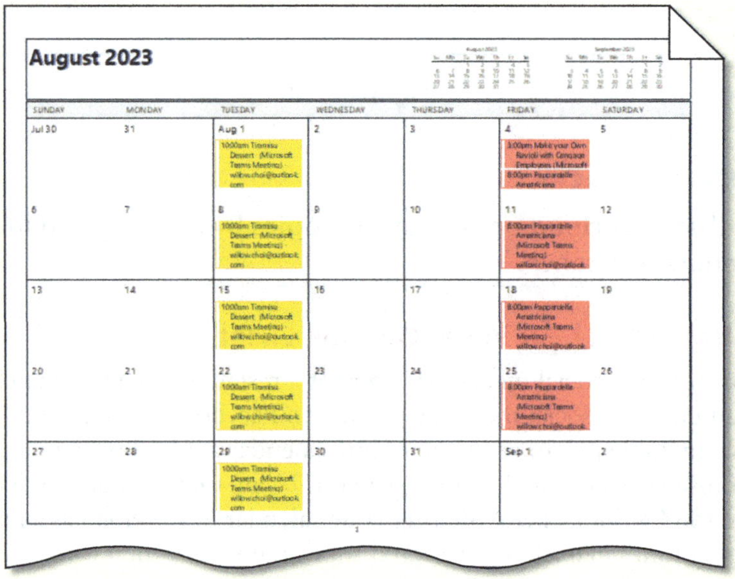

Figure 2–94

Perform the following tasks:

1. Create a calendar named **`Airbnb Virtual Experience Calendar`** in Outlook.
2. Create the events in the calendar in the year 2023, using the information listed in Table 2–8.
3. For each event, create a Teams meeting and place your email address in the Required box.

Table 2–8 AirBnb Chef Virtual Experiences

Calendar Item	Due Date	Category	Color Code
Make your Own Ravioli with Cengage Employees	First Friday of each month at 3:00 PM for 2 hours	Pasta	Red
Tiramisu Dessert	Every Tuesday at 10:00 AM for three hours (except December)	Dessert	Yellow
Pappardelle Amatriciana	Every Friday in June, July, and August at 8:00 PM for two hours	Pasta	Red
Pici Carbonara with Russell Employees	Feb 14, March 17, and April 3 at 1:00 PM for two hours	Pasta	Red
Pumpkin Gnocchi	Oct 24 – Oct 31 at 7:00 PM for 1.5 hours	Potato	Warm gray
Cannoli Sicilian Dessert	Every day in December except Dec 24 and Dec 25 at 10:00 AM for two hours	Dessert	Red, Yellow

4. For each event, show the time as Free.
5. For each event, set the reminder to one day.
6. If requested by your instructor, add your own menu choice for an Italian cooking experience on your birthday as an event in your 2023 calendar.
7. Save the calendar as an .ics file using the name `SC_OUT_2_Airbnb_Calendar` and submit it in a format specified by your instructor.
8. Print the month of August using the Monthly Style as shown in Figure 2–94, and submit it in a format specified by your instructor.
9. A calendar can keep you organized. In the case of scheduling your reserved dates, why might you want to share this calendar on your virtual experience's customer-facing website?

In the Lab 2

Creating a Blogger Calendar

Problem: You are a local TikTok video blogger who reviews local activities for your hometown. By taking the time to develop a plan for your event visits, as shown in Figure 2–95, you will remember to produce regular reviews for your local blog.

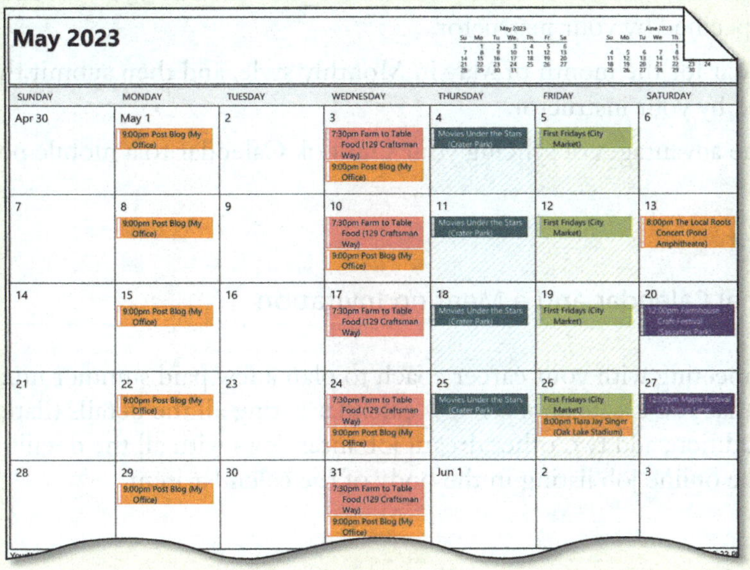

Figure 2–95

Continued >

In the Lab 2 *continued*

Instructions: Open Outlook. Perform the following tasks:

1. Create a calendar named **TikTok Calendar** in Outlook.
2. Create the appointments in the calendar, using the information listed in Table 2–9.

Table 2–9 Local Events Table

Event	Location	Event Date	Category	Color Code
First Fridays	City Market	All Fridays in May–August	Cultural	Lime green
The Local Roots Concert	Pond Amphitheatre	May 13, 2023 from 8:00 PM to 10:00 PM	Music	Orange
Maple Festival	12 Syrup Lane	May 27, 2023 from 12:00 PM to 3:00 PM	Festival	Dark purple
Farmhouse Craft Festival	Sassafras Park	May 20, 2023 from 12:00 PM to 3:00 PM	Festival	Dark purple
Farm to Table Food	129 Craftsman Way	Wednesdays in May	Restaurant	Red
Tiara Jay Singer	Oak Lake Stadium	May 26, 2023 from 8:00 PM to 10:00 PM	Music	Orange
Movies Under the Stars	Crater Park	Every Thursday night in May	Other	Teal

3. For each event in the table, set the reminder as two hours before the event.
4. For each event, show the time as Tentative.
5. Set each restaurant dinner for 7:30 PM for two hours, concerts at 8:00 PM for two hours, and festivals at noon for three hours.
6. For each Monday and Wednesday throughout the month of May 2023, add a recurring appointment. Enter **Post Blog** as the title. For location, enter **My Office**. Show the time as Busy. The appointment should start at 9:00 PM and end two hours later. Add all of the color-coded categories shown in Table 2–9 and set a 10-minute reminder.
7. Delete the one occurrence of the recurring appointment for your blog on May 17.
8. If requested by your instructor, change your Weather Bar to show the weather for your hometown.
9. Save the calendar as an .ics file using the name **SC_OUT_2_Blogger_Calendar** and submit it in a format specified by your instructor.
10. Print the calendar for the month of May in Monthly style, and then submit the printout in the format specified by your instructor.
11. What are the advantages of syncing your Outlook Calendar to a mobile phone?

In the Lab 3

Creating a Personal Calendar and a Meeting Invitation

Problem: You are meeting with your career coach to plan a few paid summer internship interviews. She has requested that you create an interview calendar listing all the details (date, time, opportunity, and pay). In addition, add two other dream job interviews with all the details and the link of where you found the online job listing in the body of the calendar item.

Instructions: Open Outlook. Perform the following tasks:

1. Create a calendar named **`Internship Calendar`** in Outlook.
2. Add the meetings shown in Table 2–10 to the calendar and then send an invitation for the first meeting to your instructor. Enter the pay in the body of the calendar item. All the interviews are held at the North HR Suite. Send a meeting invitation to yourself.

Table 2–10 Interview Calendar Meetings

Opportunity	Date	Time	Show As	Reminder	Pay	Category
Alphabet Human Resource Analyst	April 4	1:00 PM – 2:00 PM	Out of Office	3 days	$33 per hour	Summer Only (dark orange)
Venmo Human Resource Temp	April 11	12:00 PM – 2:00 PM	Tentative	30 minutes	$27 per hour	Part-Time (lavender)
Microsoft Store Human Resource Insurance	April 6	9:00 AM 1.5 hours	Tentative	1 day	Negotiable	Summer Only (dark orange)

3. Research online and add two interviews for dream jobs for you in the calendar based on your present career pathway. Schedule the interviews for the second week of April and include the details and the web link to actual job listings in the body of the calendar item.
4. Save your calendar as an iCalendar named **`SC_OUT_2_Internship_Calendar`**. Submit your assignment in the format specified by your instructor.

Part 2: If you receive a meeting request, you can respond in several ways. What are the four ways to respond to a meeting request? You can add comments with each of these responses. Provide comments to each of the four meeting request responses explaining why you can or cannot attend the meeting with your advisor.

3 Managing Contacts and Personal Contact Information with Outlook

Objectives

After completing this module, you will be able to:

- Create a new contact
- Create a contact from an email message
- Modify a contact
- Add a contact photo
- Delete a contact
- Manipulate attachments to contacts
- Display contacts in different views
- Sort a contact list
- Find contacts using complete or partial information
- Find contacts from any Outlook folder
- Create a contact group
- Modify a contact group
- Add and remove names in a contact group
- Preview a contact list
- Print a contact list

Introduction to Outlook Contacts

To keep track of your colleagues, friends, family, and others with whom you communicate, you can use Outlook to create contact lists and contact groups. A **contact list** lets you record information about people, such as their email address, phone number, birthday, physical address, and photo. Each person's information is stored in a **contact record** in the contact list. If you have several colleagues at work who you email frequently, you can add them to a **contact group**. You then can send email messages to all of your colleagues using the contact group rather than having to select each contact individually.

BTW

The Ribbon and Screen Resolution

Outlook may change how the groups and buttons within the groups appear on the ribbon, depending on the computer or mobile device's screen resolution. Thus, your ribbon may look different from the ones in this book if you are using a screen resolution other than 1366 × 768.

Project: Contact List with Groups

People and businesses create contact lists to keep track of people who are important to them or their business. A contact list may contain groups so that several contacts can be identified with a group name rather than individual contact names. Managing your contacts using a contact list can increase productivity greatly.

The project in this module follows general guidelines and uses Outlook to create the contact list shown in Figure 3–1. This contact list displays individual contacts and contact groups in a business card layout. In this layout, the individual contacts present essential information, such as the name, affiliation, and email address of the contact. A photograph of each contact helps you associate a face to a name. The contact groups display the name of the group, have a group label, and include a different graphic from the individual contacts.

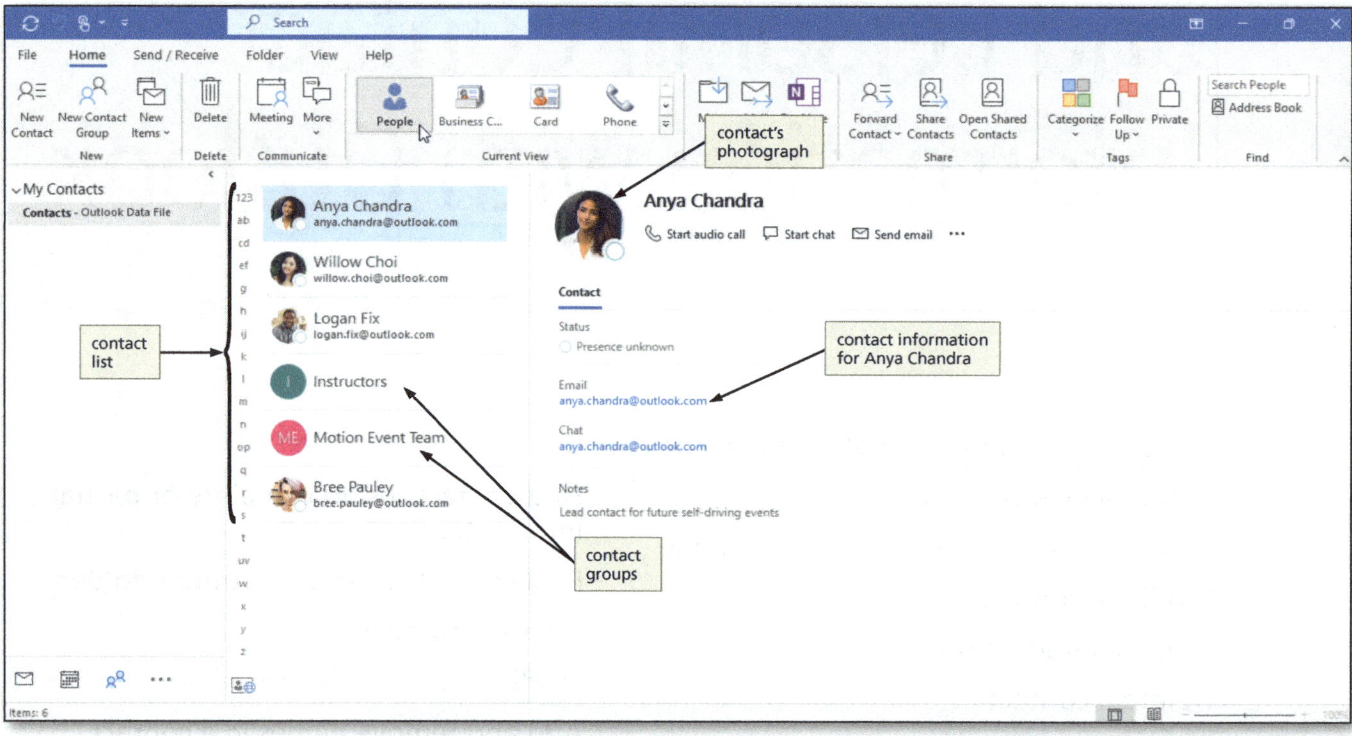

Figure 3–1

In this module, you will learn how to perform basic contact management tasks. The following list identifies general activities you will perform as you progress through this module:

1. Create a new contact.
2. Modify a contact.
3. Change the view of contacts.
4. Find a contact.
5. Create a contact group.
6. Print the contact list.

Creating a Contact List

The first step in creating a contact list is to enter information such as names, email addresses, and phone numbers for the people you communicate with regularly. After you enter and save contact information, that information is available as you compose email messages. You can type the first few letters of a contact's name into an email message, and Outlook will fill in the rest of the email address for you. If you are working on a mobile device that can make and receive phone calls, you can also use contact information to call someone on your contact list.

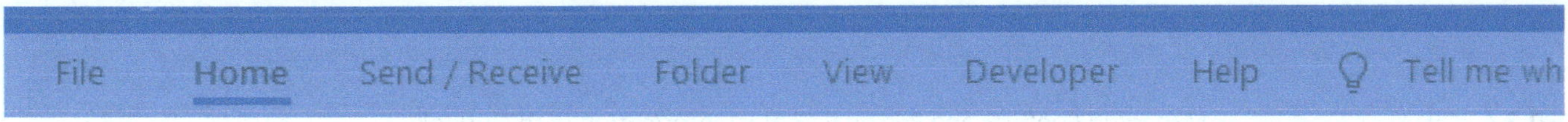

What advantages does an Outlook contact list provide for marketing a new business such as an Etsy Online Store?

Creating a contact list of your customer contacts lets you reach more people who can help your business grow by becoming repeat customers and spreading the word about your business. An Etsy store owner can keep an email address mailing list so that customers can keep up with the latest products and deals. For example, the online store might send monthly email messages to advertise specials for those who follow their products, such as 15 percent off a special vintage item or personalized gift.

CONSIDER THIS

Contacts Window

The Contacts window shown in Figure 3–2 includes a variety of features to help you work efficiently with a contact list. The Contacts window contains many elements similar to the windows in other Office programs, as well as some elements that are unique to Outlook. The main elements of the Contacts window are the My Contacts pane, the contact list, and the People pane.

BTW

Using More Than One Outlook Data File

If you have multiple email accounts or Data Files set up in Outlook, you may need to remove the email accounts or Data Files to practice the steps in this module. To remove an account, click the File tab, click Account Settings, and then click Account Settings. Select the email account and then click the Remove button to remove the email account.

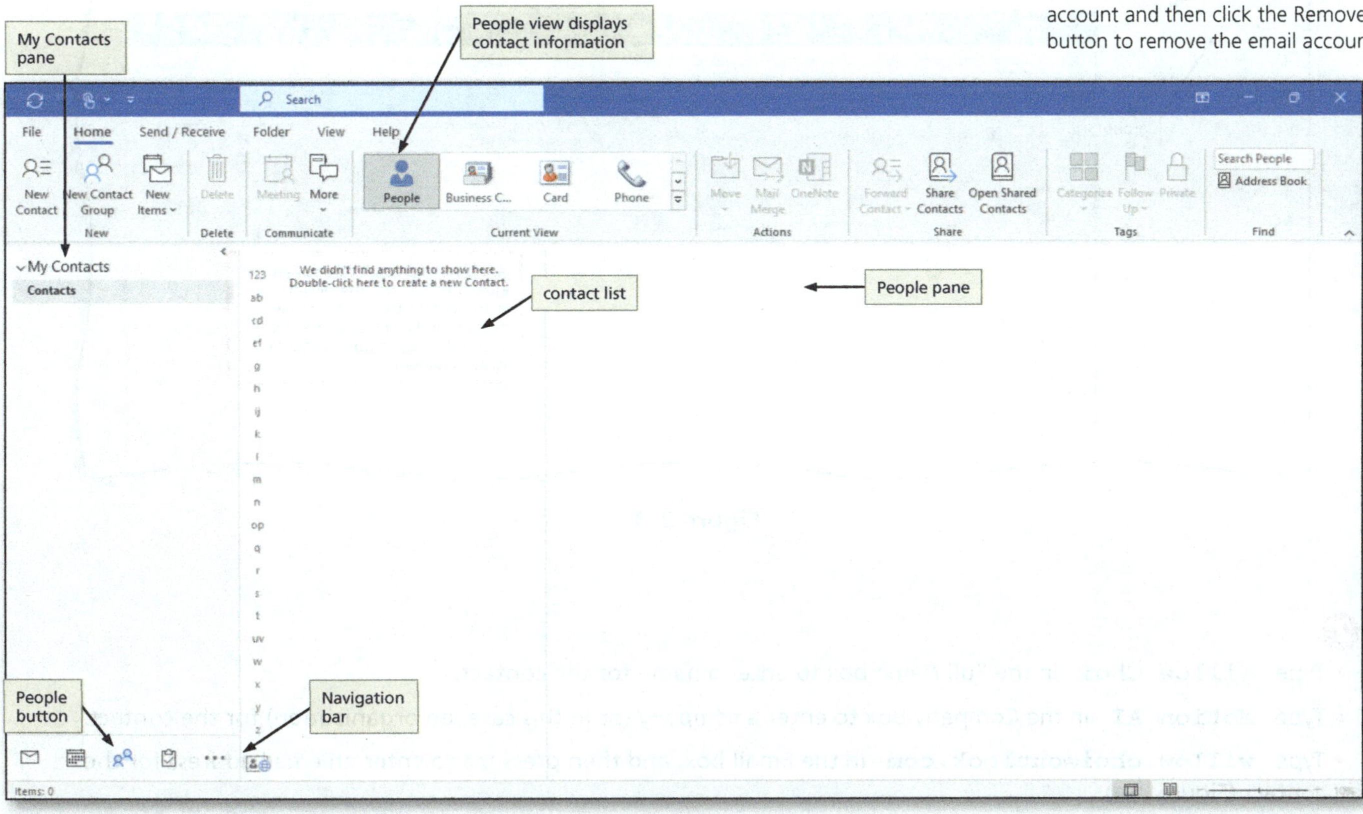

Figure 3–2

To Create a New Contact

To create the contact list in this module, you start by adding Willow Choi as the first contact. In Modules 1 and 2, you set up Willow's email account and calendar in Outlook. When you create or update a contact, you add the contact's name, company name, email address, and other information, such as a Twitter username. The following steps create a new contact in People view. ***Why?*** *To organize the contact information of your friends, clients, and colleagues, you should keep an Outlook contact list to communicate efficiently without having to search for information in multiple locations. Willow is adding herself to her contact list to organize her contact information in a central place.*

To perform the steps, you will be required to use the Data Files. Please contact your instructor for information about accessing the Data Files.

1

- Start Outlook and open the SC_OUT_3-1.pst Outlook Data File from the Data Files for Module 3.
- Click People (shown in Figure 3–2) on the Navigation bar to display the Outlook Contacts.
- Click the New Contact button (Home tab | New group) to display the Untitled - Contact window (Figure 3–3).

Q&A What should I do if I have more than one Outlook data file open in the Navigation pane?
Open only the SC_OUT_3-1.pst Outlook data file, which appears as Outlook Data File in the Navigation pane. Close any other Outlook data files open in the Navigation pane, and then repeat Step 1.

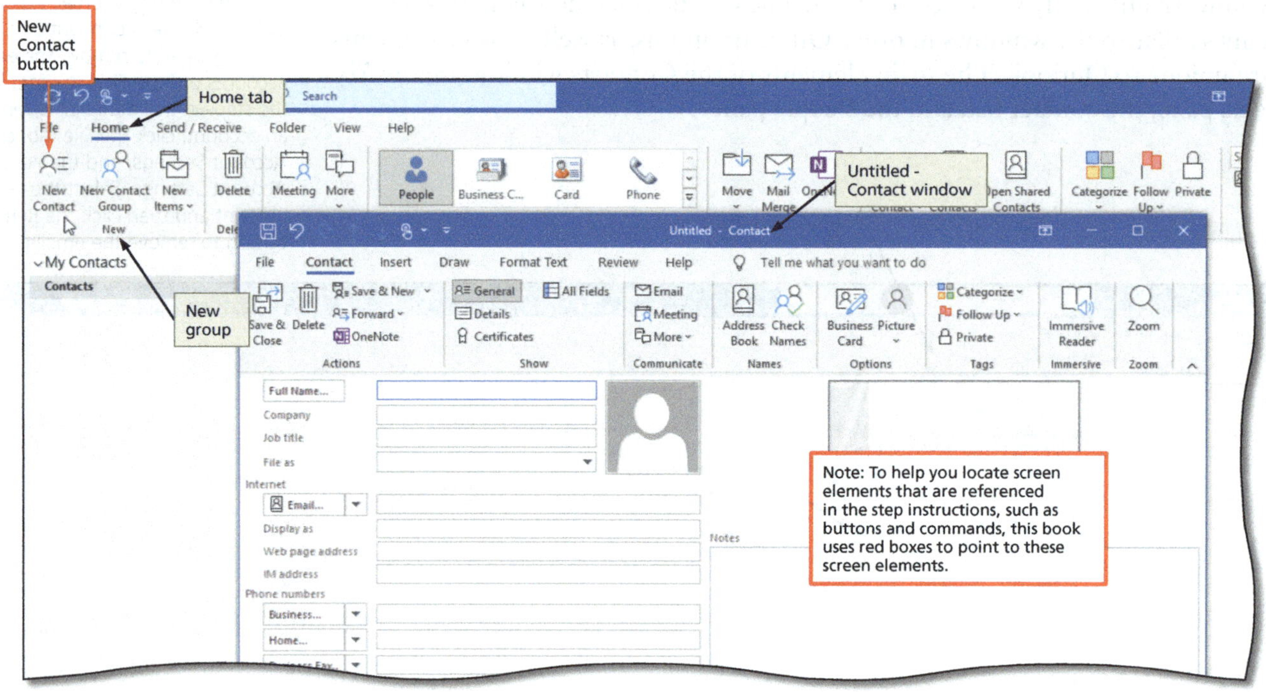

Figure 3–3

2

- Type **Willow Choi** in the Full Name box to enter a name for the contact.
- Type **Motion AI** in the Company box to enter a company (or in this case, an organization) for the contact.
- Type **willow.choi@outlook.com** in the Email box, and then press TAB to enter an email address for the contact (Figure 3–4).

Q&A Why did the title of the Contact window change after I entered the name?
As soon as you enter the name, Outlook updates the Contact window title to reflect the information you have entered. Outlook also displays the name in the File as box. The contact is not saved, however; only the window title and File as boxes are updated.

Can I add information to other fields for a contact?
Yes. As long as you have the information, you can fill out the fields accordingly. You even can add fields besides those listed by clicking the All Fields button (Contact tab | Show group).

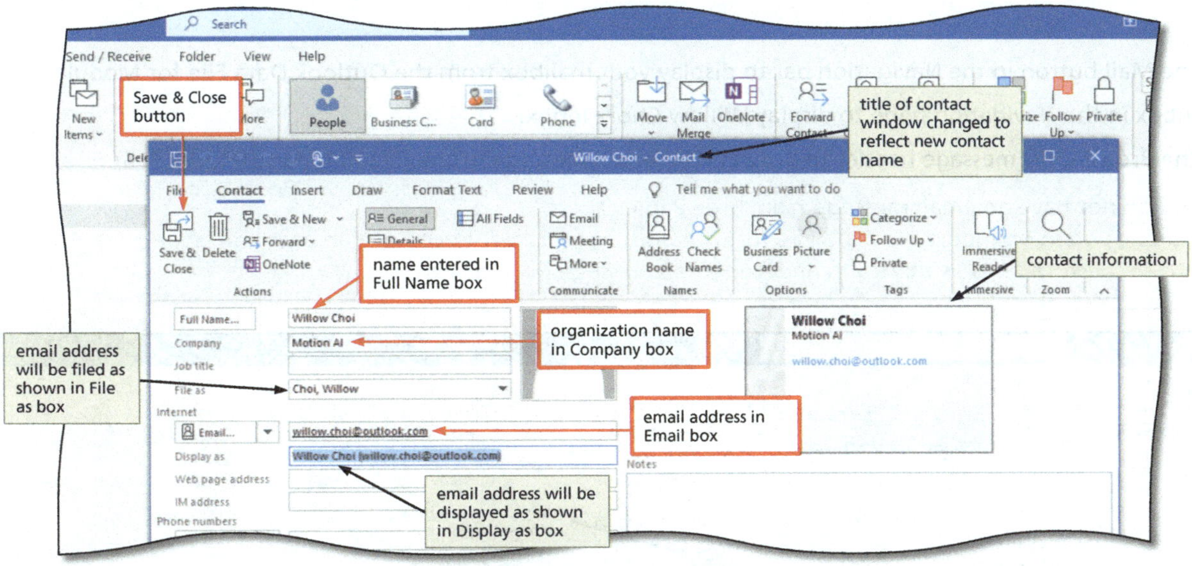

Figure 3–4

3

- Click the Save & Close button (Contact tab | Actions group) (shown in Figure 3–4) to save the contact record and close the Contact window (Figure 3–5).

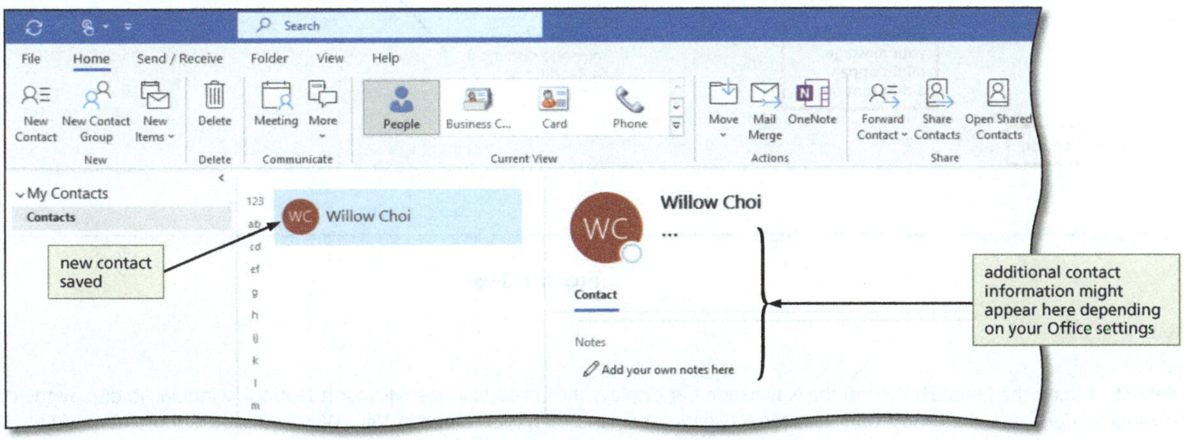

Figure 3–5

Other Ways

1. Right-click contact list, click New Contact
2. Press CTRL+SHIFT+C

To Create Contacts from Email Messages

Willow frequently emails Bree Pauley, the marketing director of Motion AI. In addition, as an intern, Willow contacts one of her colleagues named Anya Chandra, who is assisting at the next self-driving event. Creating contacts for Bree and Anya will simplify communications for Willow. Outlook can create a contact based on the information located within email messages. The following steps create contacts from email messages. ***Why?*** *You can quickly add a contact from an email message to keep better track of the sender's information. If you type the first few letters of a contact's name into a new email message, Outlook fills in the email address for you.*

1

- Click the Mail button in the Navigation bar to display your mailbox from the Outlook Data File for Module 3.
- Click Inbox in the Navigation pane to display Willow Choi's Inbox.
- Click the Bree Pauley message header to preview the email message in the Reading pane (Figure 3–6).

Q&A What if I do not have an email message from Bree Pauley?
If you did not open or import the Data File for this module, you might not have an email message from Bree Pauley. In that case, perform these steps using another email message in your mailbox.

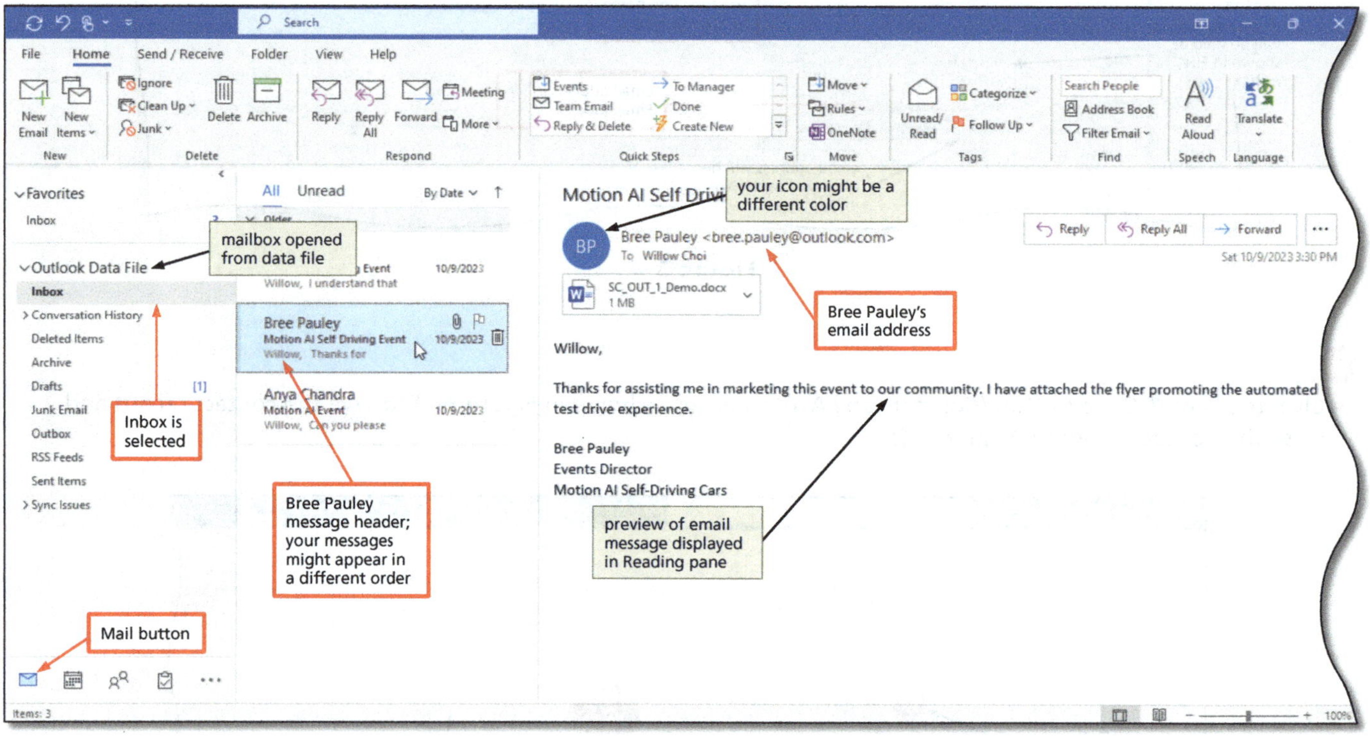

Figure 3–6

BTW
Contacts Window
By default, clicking the People button in the Navigation bar displays the contacts in the Microsoft Outlook window. To display the contacts in a new window, right-click the People button in the Navigation bar, and then click 'Open in New Window' on the shortcut menu.

2

- Right-click Bree Pauley's email address (shown in Figure 3–6) in the message header of the Reading pane to display a shortcut menu (Figure 3–7).

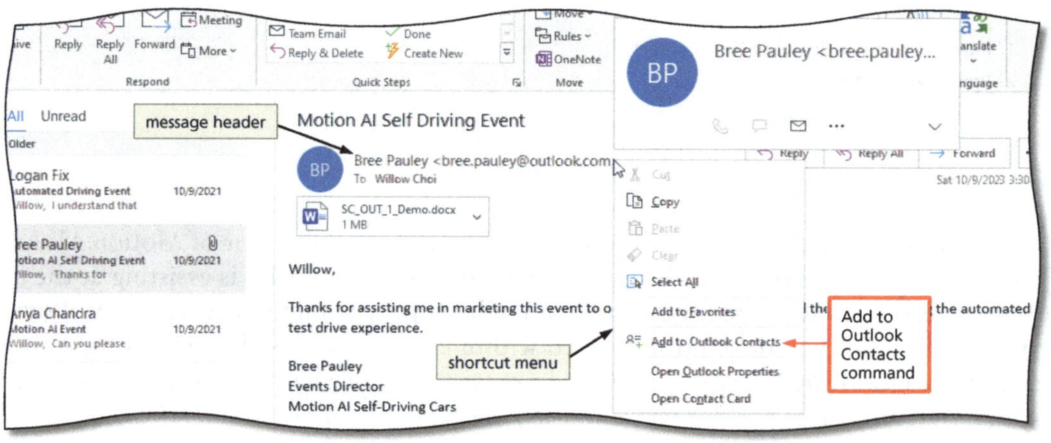

Figure 3–7

3

- Click 'Add to Outlook Contacts' (shown in Figure 3–7) to display the contact window (Figure 3–8).

Q&A Why does the contact window already have Bree Pauley's name and email address entered into the Name and Email boxes?
Outlook automatically detects the name and the email address for the contact from the existing email message.

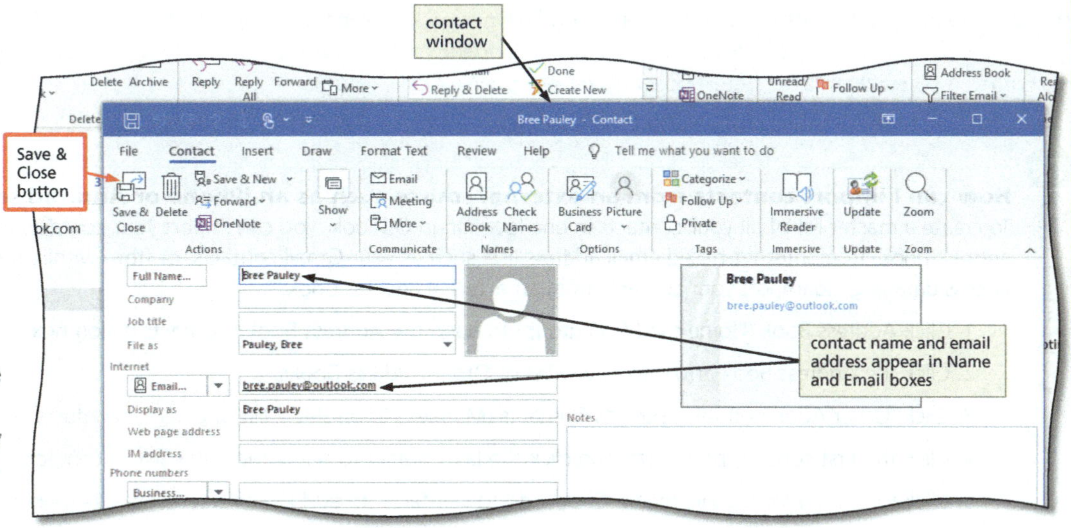

Figure 3–8

4

- Click the Save & Close button (shown in Figure 3–8) in the contact window to save the contact.
- Click the Anya Chandra message header to preview the email message in the Reading pane.
- Right-click Anya Chandra's email address in the message header of the Reading pane to display a shortcut menu.
- Click 'Add to Outlook Contacts' to display the contact window.
- Click the Save & Close button in the contact window to save the contact and close the contact window.
- Click the Mail button in the Navigation bar to display your mailbox from the Outlook Data File and add Logan Fix as a contact using logan.fix@outlook.com as the email address.
- Click People in the Navigation bar to display your contact list, including the new contacts for Bree Pauley, Anya Chandra, and Logan Fix (Figure 3–9).

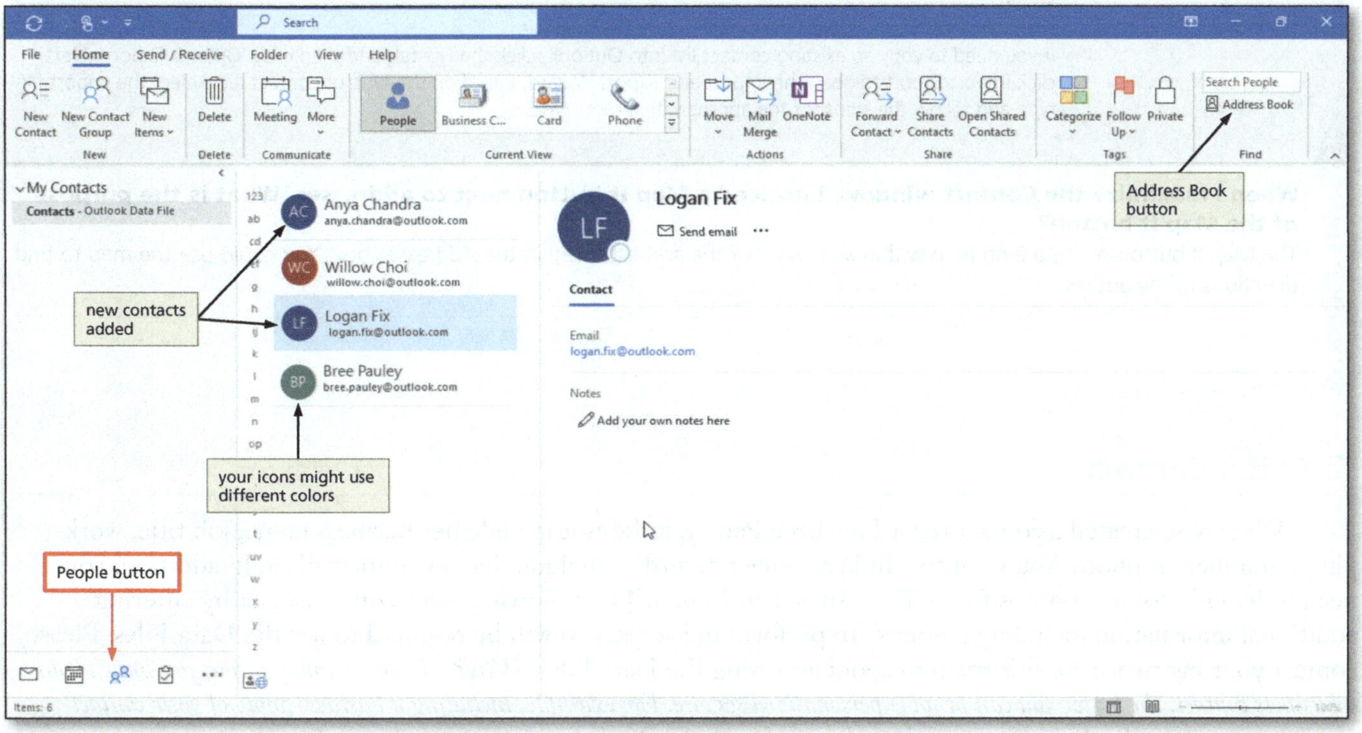

Figure 3–9

Q&A

Can I add more details such as a phone number or work number to the contact window?
You always can add more information such as another email address or photo to the contact window when you create a contact or later when you have more time.

CONSIDER THIS

How can I import contacts from an external source such as an iPhone or Android smartphone?
To create a master list of all your contacts in one location in Outlook, you can import your contacts from your smartphone's address book, from Internet-based email address lists such as your Gmail contacts, or from within another program such as an Access database. To import your contacts from an external address book:

1. Click Address Book (Home tab | Find group) to open the Address Book: Contacts dialog box.
2. Click the Address Book arrow to view a list of Other Address Books.
3. Click 'Other Address Books, such as Contacts (Mobile)', to display a list of external contacts.
4. Click the first contact, press SHIFT, and click the last contact to select the entire list of contacts.
5. Click File to display the File menu. Click 'Add to Contacts' to add the selected contacts to your Outlook contact list.
6. Click Close to close the Address Book: Contacts dialog box.

BTW
Organizing Files and Folders
You should organize and store files in folders so that you easily can find the files later. For example, if you are taking an introductory technology class called CIS 101, a good practice would be to save all Outlook files in an Outlook folder in a CIS 101 folder.

Editing a Contact

After setting up your contact list, you need to keep the information current and add new information, such as a new work phone number, Twitter account username, or picture, to help you interact with your contact. You can attach one or more files to a contact to store documents, tables, pictures, or clip art, for example, along with their contact information. If your colleagues transfer to other companies, remove contact information that you no longer need unless you will continue to interact with them on a regular basis.

BTW
Importing Contacts from External Sources
If you need to copy an existing contact list into Outlook, click the File tab and then click 'Open & Export'. Next, click Import/Export to open the Import and Export Wizard. Based on the type of contact file, select the import file type and follow the steps for the appropriate import type.

CONSIDER THIS

When I maximize the Contact window, I noticed a Map It button next to addresses. What is the purpose of the Map It button?
The Map It button opens a Bing map within a browser of the address listed in the Addresses box. You could use the map to find directions to the address.

To Edit a Contact

When you created a contact record for Bree Pauley, it did not include her business name, job title, work phone number, or photo. You want to edit her contact record to include the new information. In addition, you need to include contact photos for Willow, Anya, and Logan. The following steps edit a contact by entering additional information including pictures. To perform the steps, you will be required to use the Data Files. Please contact your instructor for information about accessing the Data Files. ***Why?*** *The more information you have about a business contact, the better you can provide personalized service. For example, including a business photo of your contact associates a name with a face. A company logo also could be used instead of a professional photo.*

1

- Double-click the Bree Pauley contact to display the Bree Pauley - Contact window.
- Type `Motion AI` in the Company box to enter an organization name for the contact.
- Type `Marketing Manager` in the Job title box to enter an organization name for the contact.
- In the Phone numbers section, type `(951) 555-3330` in the Business box, and then press ENTER to enter a business phone number for the contact (Figure 3–10).

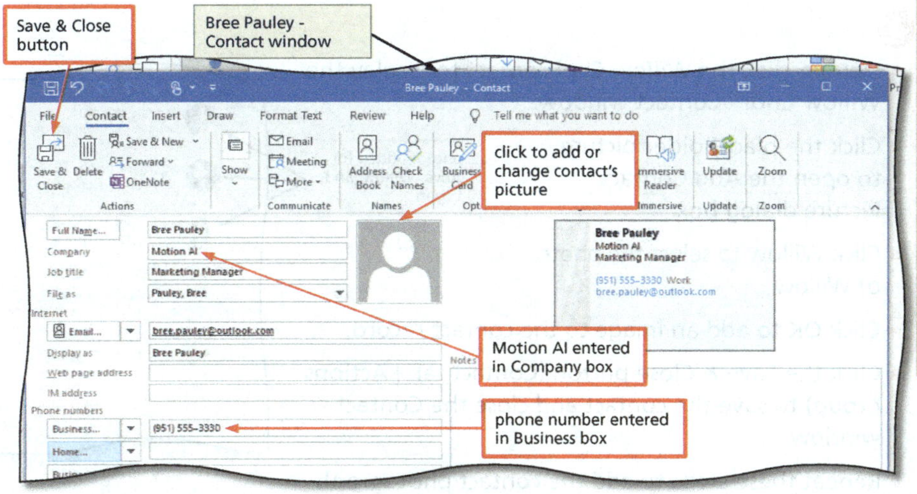

Figure 3–10

2

- Click the placeholder picture to open the Add Contact Picture dialog box.
- Navigate to the file location, in this case, the Module folder in the Outlook3 folder provided with the Data Files.
- Click Bree to select the photo of Bree Pauley (Figure 3–11).

Q&A What if I only see filenames and not actual pictures of the contacts?
An image is displayed only if the Large or Medium icons view is set for the dialog box.

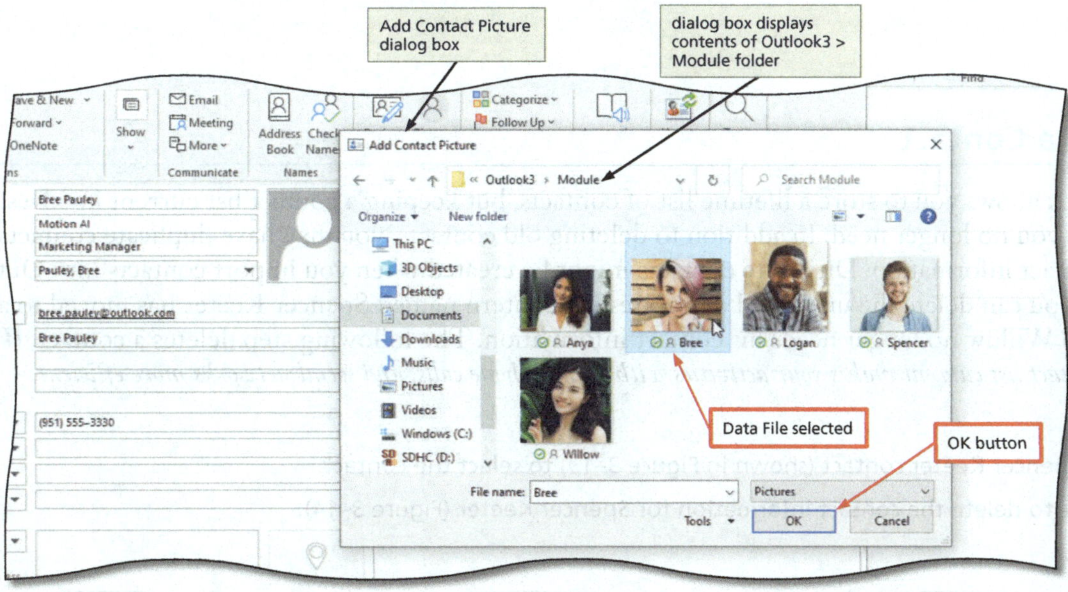

Figure 3–11

El Nariz/Shutterstock.com; Look Studio/Shutterstock.com; Cookie Studio/Shutterstock.com; Monkey Business Images/Shutterstock.com; Look Studio/Shutterstock.com; Makistock/Shutterstock.com

3

- Click OK (shown in Figure 3–11) to add an image to the contact record.
- Click the Save & Close button (Contact tab | Actions group) to save the contact and close the Contact window (Figure 3–12).

Figure 3–12

Look Studio/Shutterstock.com

4

- Double-click the Willow Choi contact to display the Willow Choi - Contact window.
- Click the placeholder picture to open the Add Contact Picture dialog box.
- Click Willow to select the photo of Willow.
- Click OK to add an image to the contact record.
- Click the Save & Close button (Contact tab | Actions group) to save the contact and close the Contact window.
- Repeat these steps to add the contact photograph named Anya for the Anya Chandra contact.
- Repeat these steps to add the contact photograph named Logan for the Logan Fix contact.
- Add one more contact name, `Spencer Keeter`, with the email address `spencer.keeter@outlook.com`, company `Motion AI`, Job title `Intern`, and a contact photograph named Spencer (Figure 3–13).

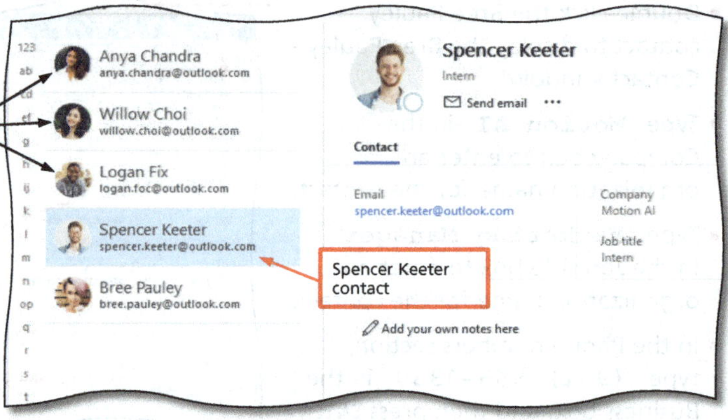

El Nariz/Shutterstock.com; Look Studio/Shutterstock.com; Monkey Business Images/Shutterstock.com; Cookie Studio/Shutterstock.com; Makistock/Shutterstock.com

Figure 3–13

CONSIDER THIS

Do I have to add actual pictures of every client?

You may not have access to images of every client, but consider adding at least a company logo, which could assist you in making a mental note of where the client is employed.

To Delete a Contact

Outlook allows you to store a lifetime list of contacts, but keeping a contact list current involves deleting contacts that you no longer need. In addition to deleting old contacts, you may have duplicate contacts that have the same contact information. Duplicate contacts might be created when you import contacts into Outlook. In this case, you can delete the unwanted duplicates. The intern named Spencer Keeter has moved to another company and Willow no longer needs his contact information. The following step deletes a contact. ***Why?*** *Keeping a contact list current makes your activities with email, phone calls, and social networks more efficient.*

1

- Click the Spencer Keeter contact (shown in Figure 3–13) to select the contact.
- Press DELETE to delete the contact information for Spencer Keeter (Figure 3–14).

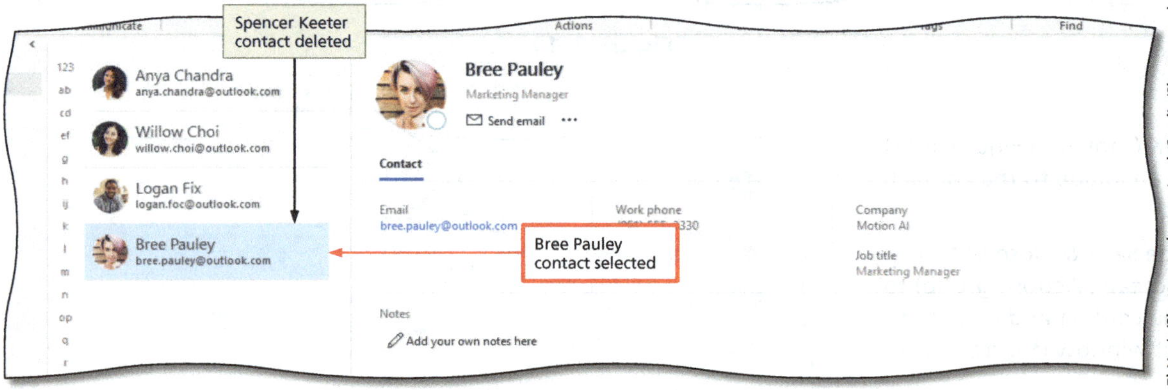

El Nariz/Shutterstock.com; Look Studio/Shutterstock.com; Monkey Business Images/Shutterstock.com; Makistock/Shutterstock.com

Figure 3–14

Other Ways

1. Click contact, click Delete (Home tab | Delete group)
2. Right-click contact, click Delete

To Add an Attachment to a Contact

Logan Fix sent you a resume from one of his students (Cameron Von Hausen), who plans to apply for a position at Motion AI. You want to attach the resume document to his contact record. ***Why?*** *Including this document as part of his contact record will help you find the document easily.* Any files you attach to a contact are displayed in the Notes section of the Contact window. You can also insert items such as financial spreadsheets, pictures, and meeting slides to the Notes section. The following steps add an attachment to a contact.

1

- Double-click the Logan Fix contact to display the Logan Fix - Contact window.
- Click Insert on the ribbon to display the Insert tab (Figure 3–15).

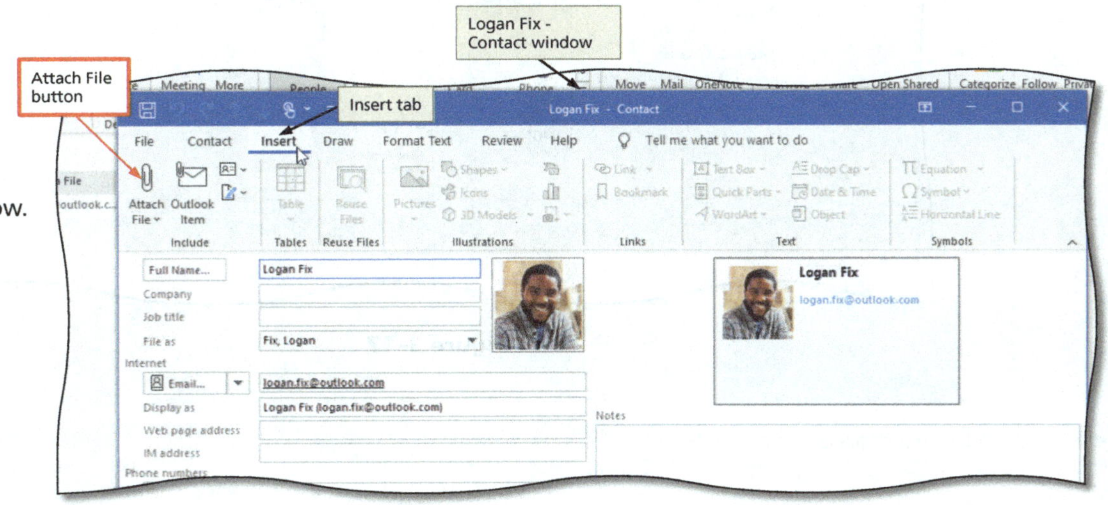

Figure 3–15

2

- Click the Attach File button (Insert tab | Include group) to display a list of Recent Items.
- Click 'Browse This PC' to display the Insert File dialog box.
- If necessary, navigate to the file location, in this case, the Module folder in the Outlook3 folder provided with the Data Files.
- Click 'Von Hausen Resume' to select the Word document (Figure 3–16).

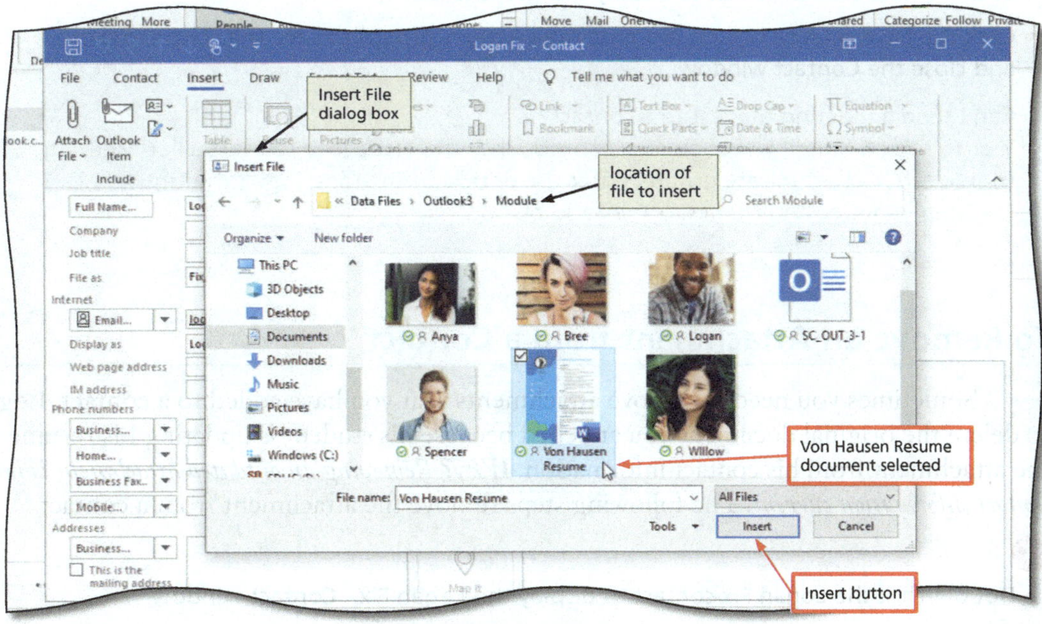

Figure 3–16

3

- Click the Insert button (Insert File dialog box) to attach the document to the contact record in the Notes area (Figure 3–17).

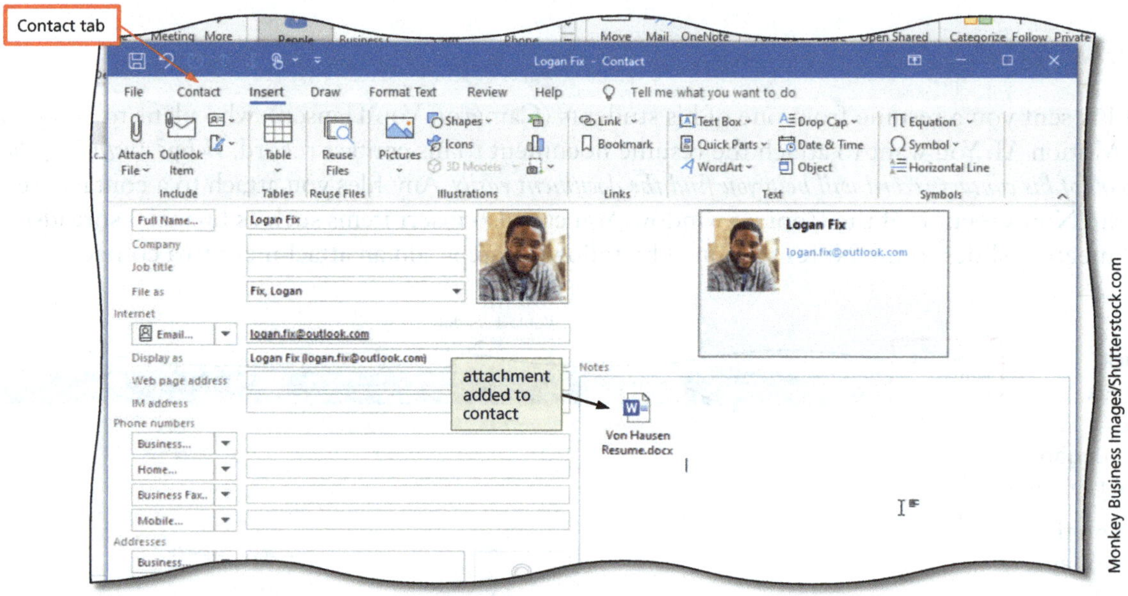

Figure 3–17

Q&A

Can I add more than one attachment?
Yes. You can add as many attachments as you want.

How do I view an attachment after I have added it?
Open the contact and then double-click the attachment to open it.

4

- Click Contact on the ribbon to display the Contact tab.
- Click the Save & Close button (Contact tab | Actions group) to save the contact record and close the Contact window.

Q&A

Can I send a meeting request to a contact?
Yes. To send a meeting request to a contact, click the contact to select it, click Meeting (Home tab | Communicate group), enter the details of the meeting in the Untitled - Meeting window, and then click the Send button.

BTW

Changing an Attachment

If you need to change an attachment to another file within a contact, select the original file and then click the Insert tab on the ribbon. Click Attach File and select the new attachment. Because the original file was selected before attaching the new file, the new file replaces the original file. If the original file were not selected, Outlook would add the new file while keeping the original file.

To Remove an Attachment from a Contact

Sometimes you need to remove attachments that you have added to a contact. Logan Fix has asked you to delete the original document you attached because his student is updating his resume. You need to remove the attachment from his contact information. ***Why?*** *Removing an outdated attachment is important to keeping your contact information current.* The following steps remove the attachment from a contact.

1

- Double-click the Logan Fix contact to display the Logan Fix - Contact window.

• Click the Von Hausen Resume document to select it (Figure 3–18).

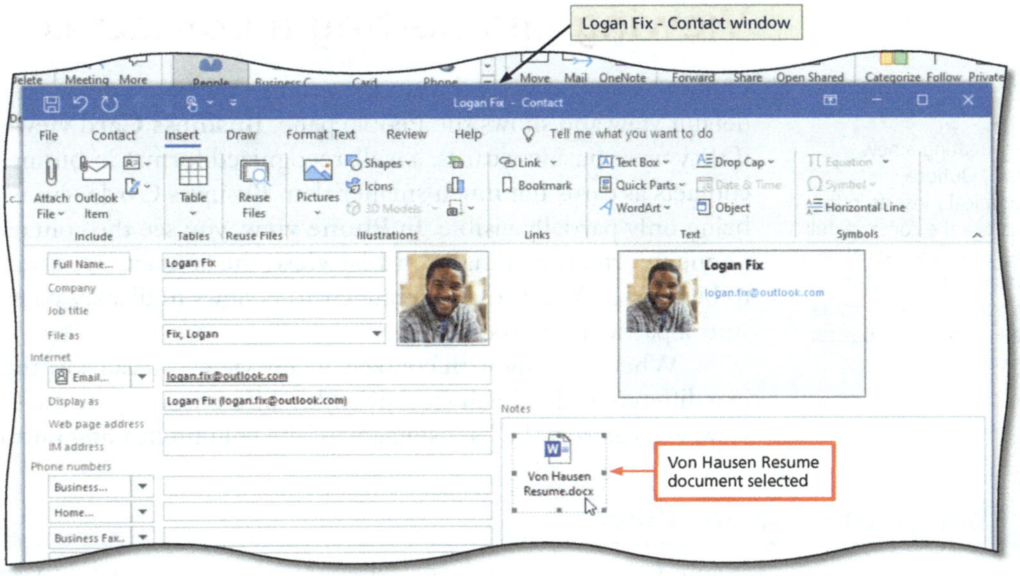

Monkey Business Images/Shutterstock.com

Figure 3–18

2

• Press DELETE to remove the attachment (Figure 3–19).

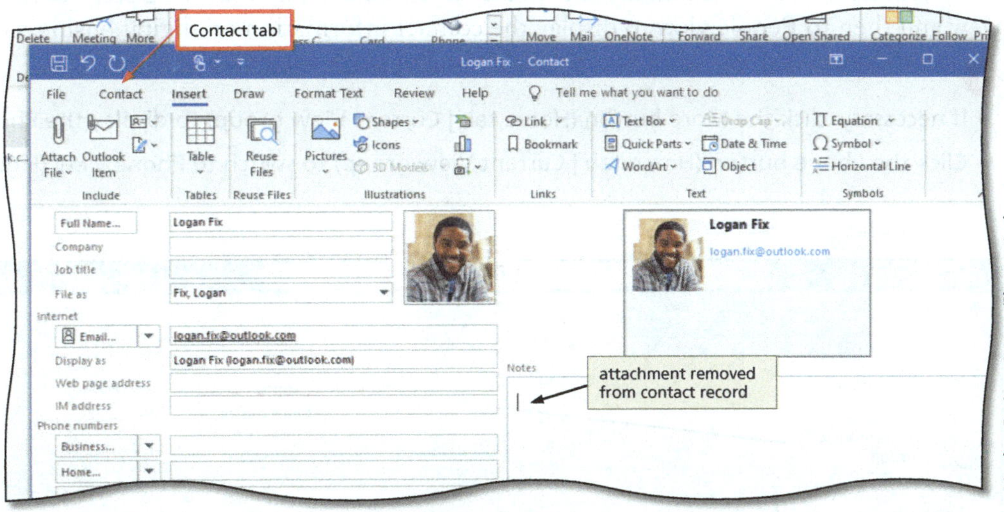

Monkey Business Images/Shutterstock.com

Figure 3–19

3

• Click the Save & Close button (Contact tab | Actions group) to save the contact and close the Contact window.

Other Ways

1. Click file icon, click Delete (Contact tab | Actions group)

CONSIDER THIS

How can I tag a contact to include a color-coded category or follow-up flag to remind me to follow up with a contact later?

To search through your contacts more efficiently, add color-coded categories such as a green tag to remind you of a new intern in Motion AI, for example. You may want to tag a contact with a Follow Up Tomorrow flag to remind you to email that person in the next day. To add a tag to a contact:

1. Double-click a contact in the contact list to display the Contact window.
2. Click Categorize or Follow Up (Contact tab | Tags group) to display a list of color-coded categories or follow-up flags.
3. Click the color-coded category or follow-up flag that you want to use. You can use multiple tags on each contact if needed.

Viewing and Sorting a Contact List

BTW
Filing Contacts
When creating a new contact, Outlook automatically inserts in the File as box the contact's full name, usually in Last Name, First Name format. Outlook sorts contacts on the value stored in the File as box for each contact.

Outlook supports several ways for you to view your contact list. **People view** is the default view and shows the People pane. **Business Card view** displays the contacts as if they were business cards, a well-recognized format in business. **Card view** shows the contacts as cards but much smaller than Business Card view, with most information being only partially visible. In **Phone view**, you see the contacts in a list displaying phone information. Finally, in **List view**, the contacts are arranged in a list according to businesses. You also can create custom views to display your contacts in a way that suits a particular purpose.

When working with contacts in any view, you can sort the contacts to display them in a different order. Each view provides different sort options. For example, in Phone view, you can sort the list using any of the column heading buttons that are displayed.

To Change the Current View

People view provides useful information, but the other views also can be helpful. Changing the view sometimes can help you find a contact's information more quickly. Use Phone view, for example, when you are looking for a contact's phone number in a long list. ***Why?*** *Phone view provides a tabular layout with each contact in one row, and each column containing one contact's information.* The following steps change the current view to Phone view and then to People view to display the contact information on digital business cards.

1

- If necessary, click the More button (Home tab | Current View group) to display the Phone button.
- Click the Phone button (Home tab | Current View group) to switch to Phone view (Figure 3–20).

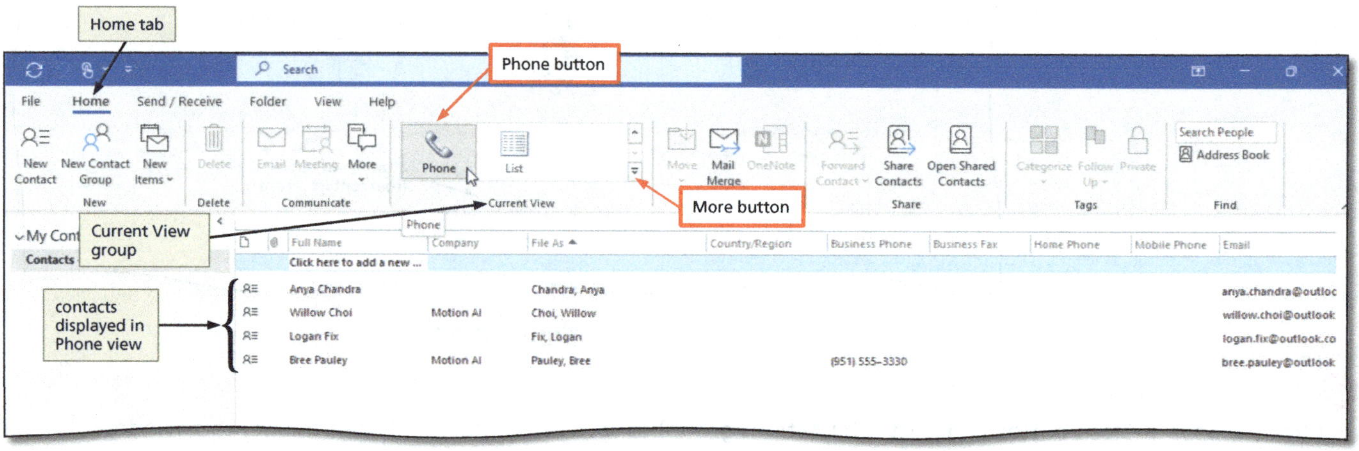

Figure 3–20

2

- If necessary, click the More button (Home tab | Current View group), and then click Business Card to switch to Business Card view (Figure 3–21).

Q&A What if the More button is not displayed in the Current View group?
You likely are using a lower resolution than 1366 × 768, so the ribbon hides additional buttons. Click the Business Card button in the Current View group to switch to Business Card view.

Experiment

- Click the other views in the Current View group to view the contacts in other arrangements. When you are finished, click Business Card to return to Business Card view.

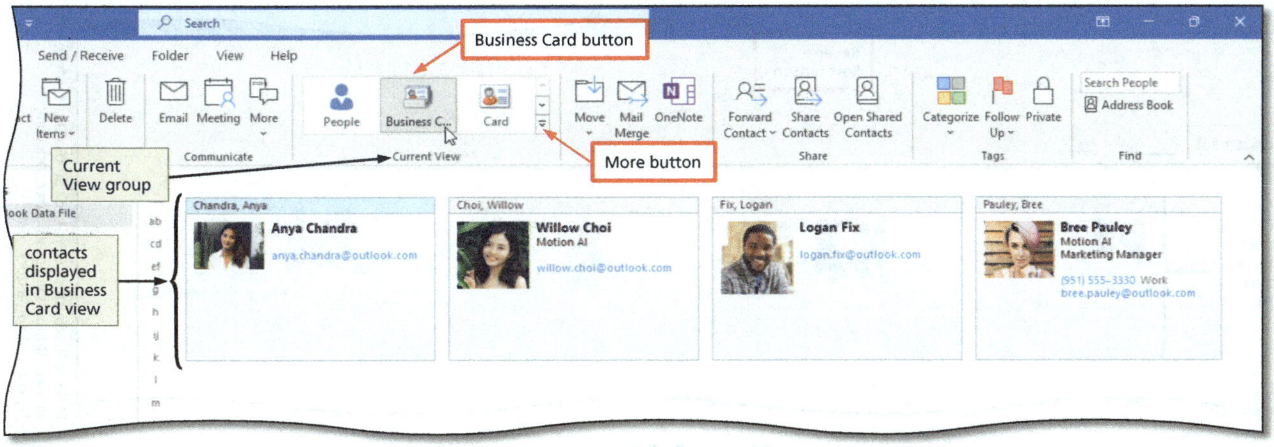

Figure 3–21

To Sort Contacts

Business Card view lists contacts in alphabetical order by default; however, you can sort the contacts to view them in reverse order. ***Why?*** *Reverse order is especially helpful if you want to quickly open a record for a contact at the end of a long contact list.* The following steps sort the contact list in reverse order, and then switch back to alphabetical order.

1

- Click View on the ribbon to display the View tab.
- Click the Reverse Sort button (View tab | Arrangement group) to display the contact list in reverse alphabetical order (Figure 3–22).

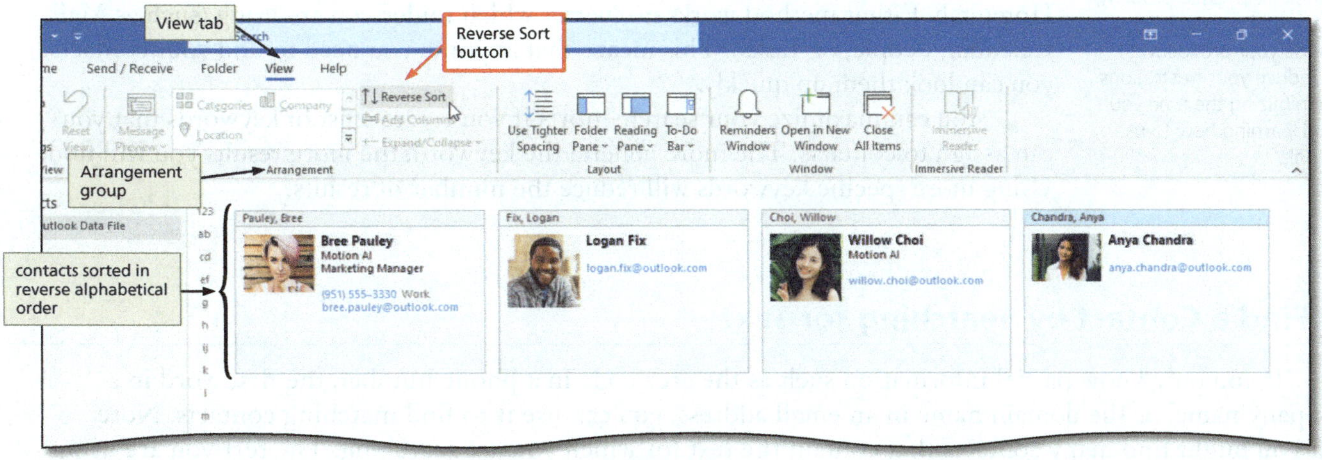

Figure 3–22

2

- Click the Reverse Sort button (View tab | Arrangement group) to display the contact list in the original order (Figure 3–23).

Figure 3–23

Break Point: If you want to take a break, this is a good place to do so. To resume later, continue to follow the steps from this location forward.

Using Search to Find a Contact

BTW

Outlook Help

At any time while using Outlook, you can find answers to questions and display information about various topics through Outlook Help. Used properly, this form of assistance can increase your productivity and reduce your frustrations by minimizing the time you spend learning how to use Outlook.

Over time, contact lists can grow quite large, making them difficult to navigate. In addition, you sometimes may not remember details about a contact you want to find. For example, you may remember that someone works for a particular company, but not their name. Alternatively, you may remember a phone number but nothing else. If this happens, you can use the Search box on the title bar to search your contact list.

You also can find contacts using the Search People box in the Find group on the Home tab. Either method works no matter which folder you are using (such as Mail, Calendar, People, or Tasks). This means that anytime you need to find your contacts, you can look them up quickly.

You can maximize your search efforts if you create a list of keywords that you can assign to contacts. The more general the keyword, the more results you will find. Using more specific keywords will reduce the number of results.

To Find a Contact by Searching for Text

If you only know partial information such as the area code in a phone number, the first word in a company name, or the domain name in an email address, you can use it to find matching contacts. Note that you might find many contacts that contain the text for which you are searching. The text you are using as the search term could be part of an email address, a school name, or a Twitter username, for example. Therefore, you may have to examine the results further. The following steps find all contacts that contain the text, motion. ***Why?*** *To save time, you can search for text or tags such as the company name Motion to locate the correct contact(s) quickly.*

1

- Click the Search box on the title bar to display the Search tab and a list of Suggested Actions (Figure 3–24).

Q&A

Why is the Search tab displayed when I click the Search box?

The Search tab contains buttons and commands that can help you search contacts.

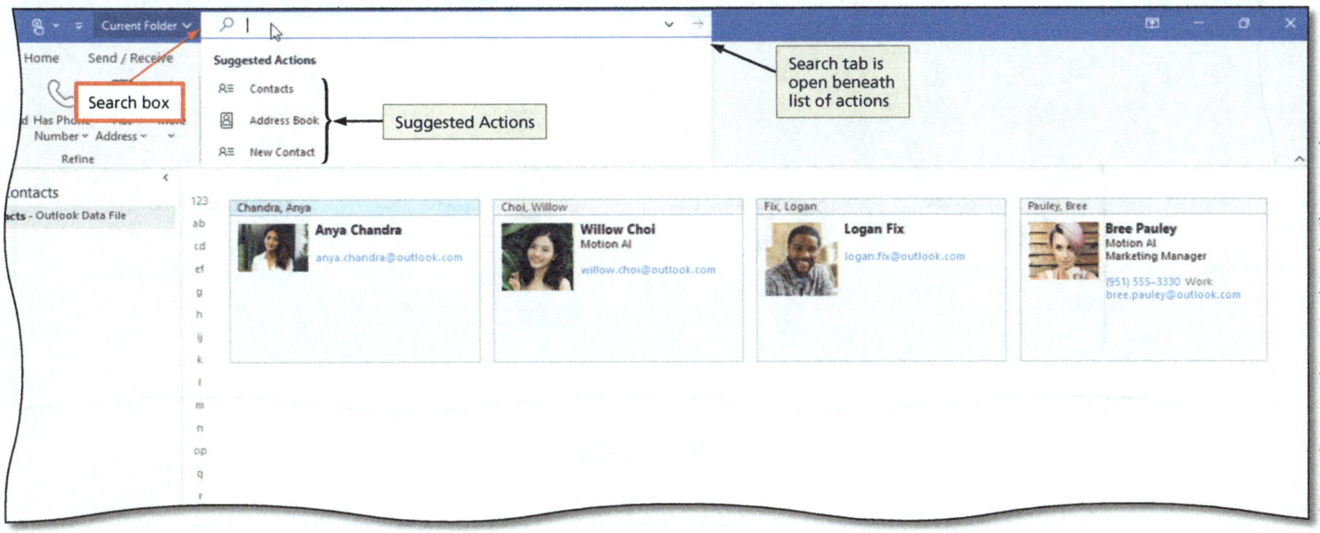

Figure 3–24

2

- Type **motion** in the Search box and press ENTER to search for all contacts containing the text, motion (Figure 3–25).

Q&A Can I modify a search further after getting the initial results?
Certainly. You can use the Search tab to refine your search by specifying a name or phone number, for example. You also can expand the search to include all of the Outlook folders.

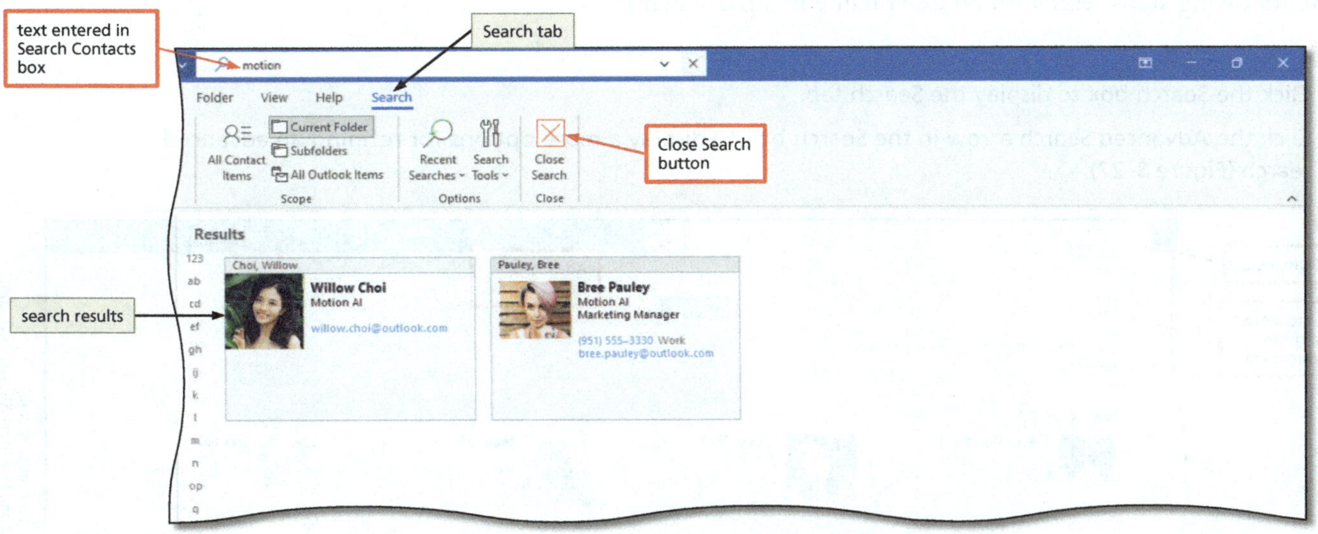

Figure 3–25

3

- Click the Close Search button (shown in Figure 3–25) (Search tab | Close group) to close the search and return to the Contacts window (Figure 3–26).

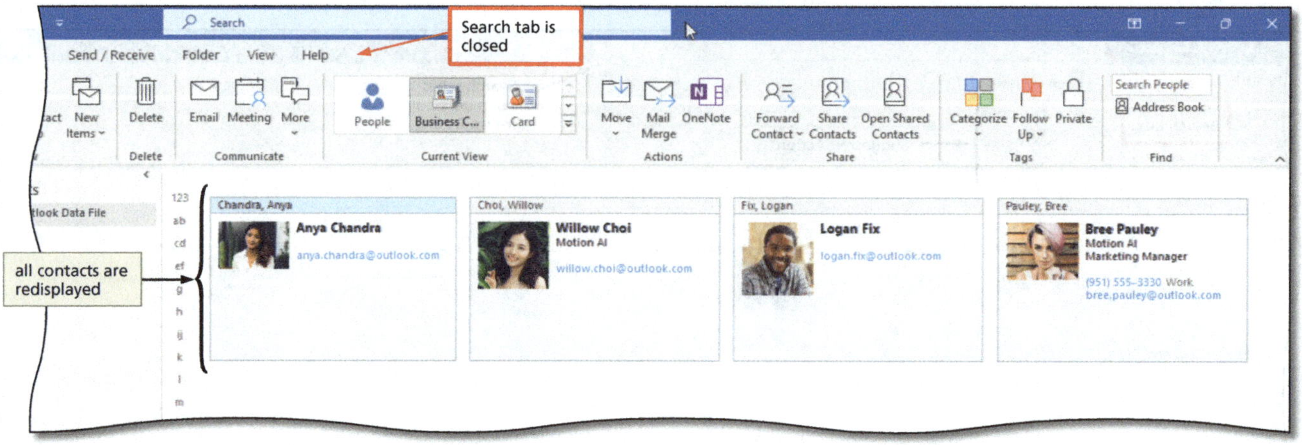

Figure 3–26

Other Ways

1. Press CTRL+E

To Refine an Advanced Search

If you type a full name or email address in the Search box, you will find your contact, but the information need not be only in the Email field or the Company field. The results might contain contacts where the name or email address is part of the Notes field, for example. In that case, you can find a contact by searching only a particular field. ***Why?*** *The results will contain only contacts with the search term in the specified field. No contacts will appear that contain the search term in a different field.*

You want to update the Anya Chandra contact record by searching only the Full Name field. The following steps search for an exact name in a particular field.

1

- Click the Search box to display the Search tab.
- Click the Advanced Search arrow in the Search box to display a more options for refining an advanced search (Figure 3–27).

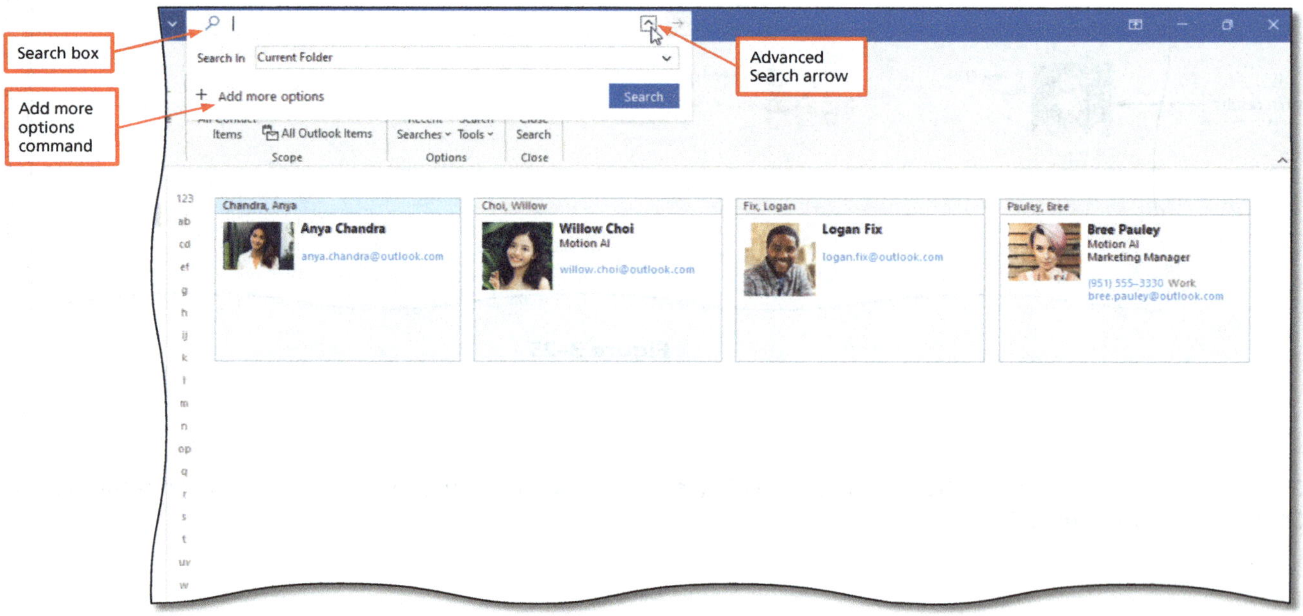

Figure 3–27

2

- Click + Add more options to display the Advanced Search Options dialog box.
- Click the Full Name check box to select the Full Name search option (Figure 3–28).

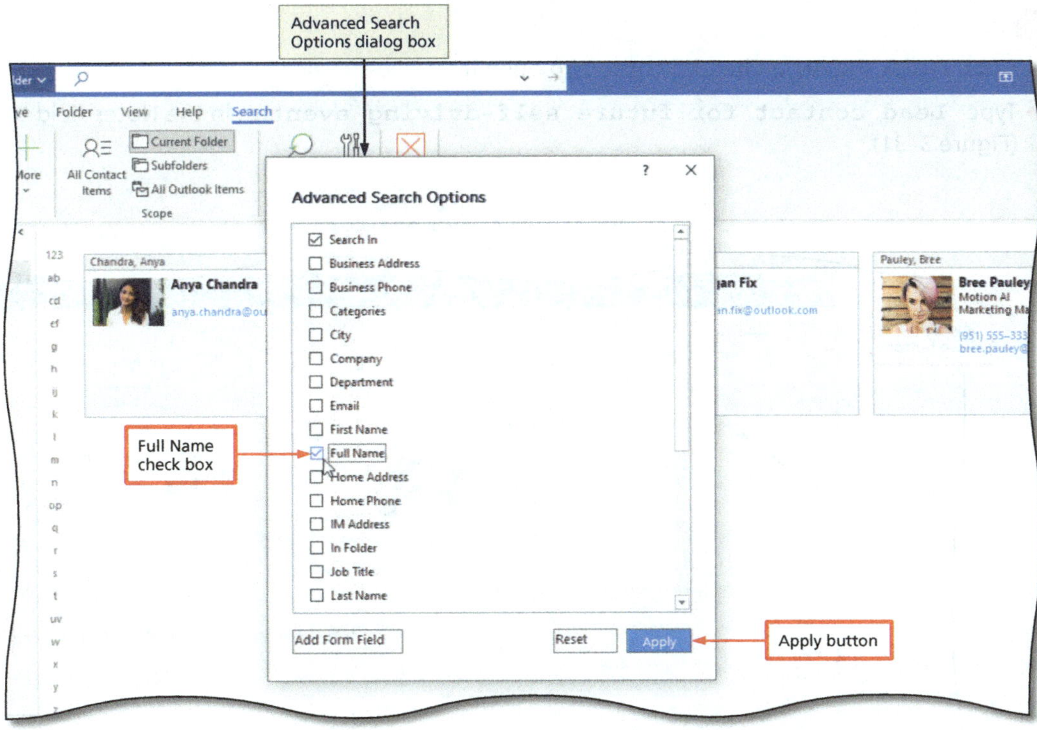

Figure 3–28

3

- Click the Apply button in the Advanced Search Options dialog box to add the Full Name search option to the Search box.
- Type **Anya Chandra** in the Full Name box to search for the Anya Chandra contact (Figure 3–29).

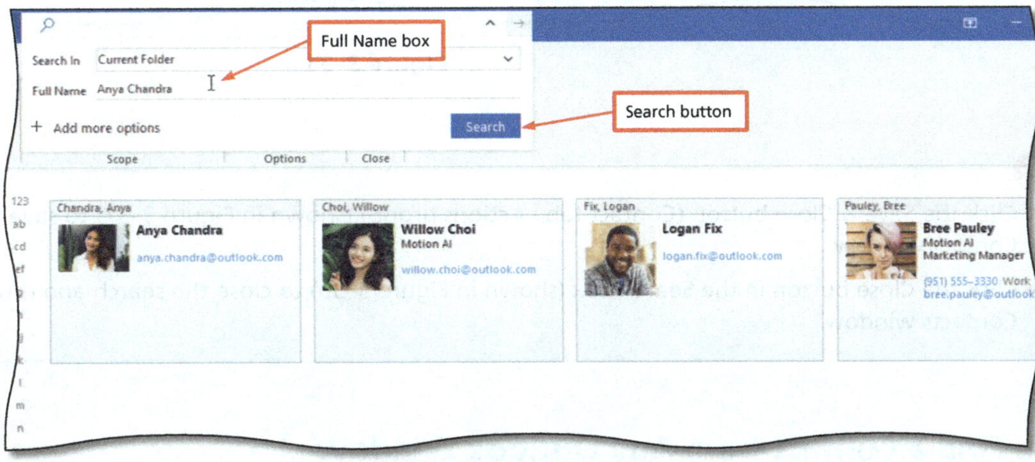

Figure 3–29

4

- Click the Search button to display the search results (Figure 3–30).

Q&A Why might Outlook display search results that do not seem to contain the search text?
When you perform a search, Outlook searches all specified fields for a match. However, the matching fields might not be displayed in the list of search results, although the contact record does contain the search text.

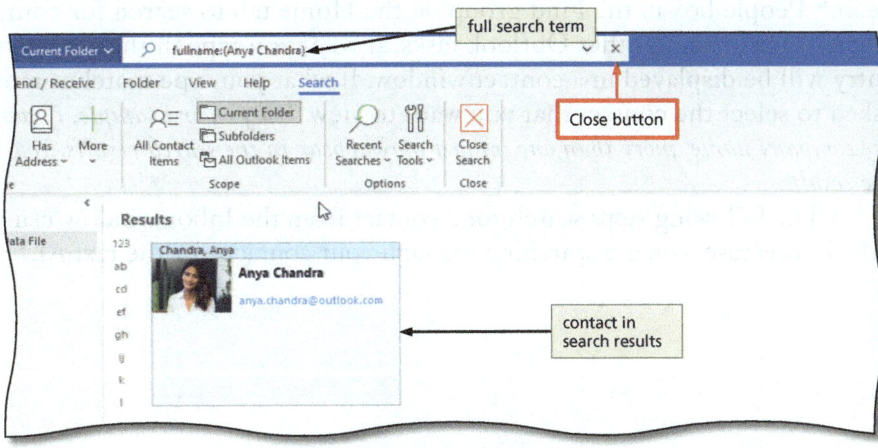

Figure 3–30

5

- Double-click the Anya Chandra contact to open it.
- Type **`Lead contact for future self-driving events`** in the Notes field to update the contact (Figure 3–31).

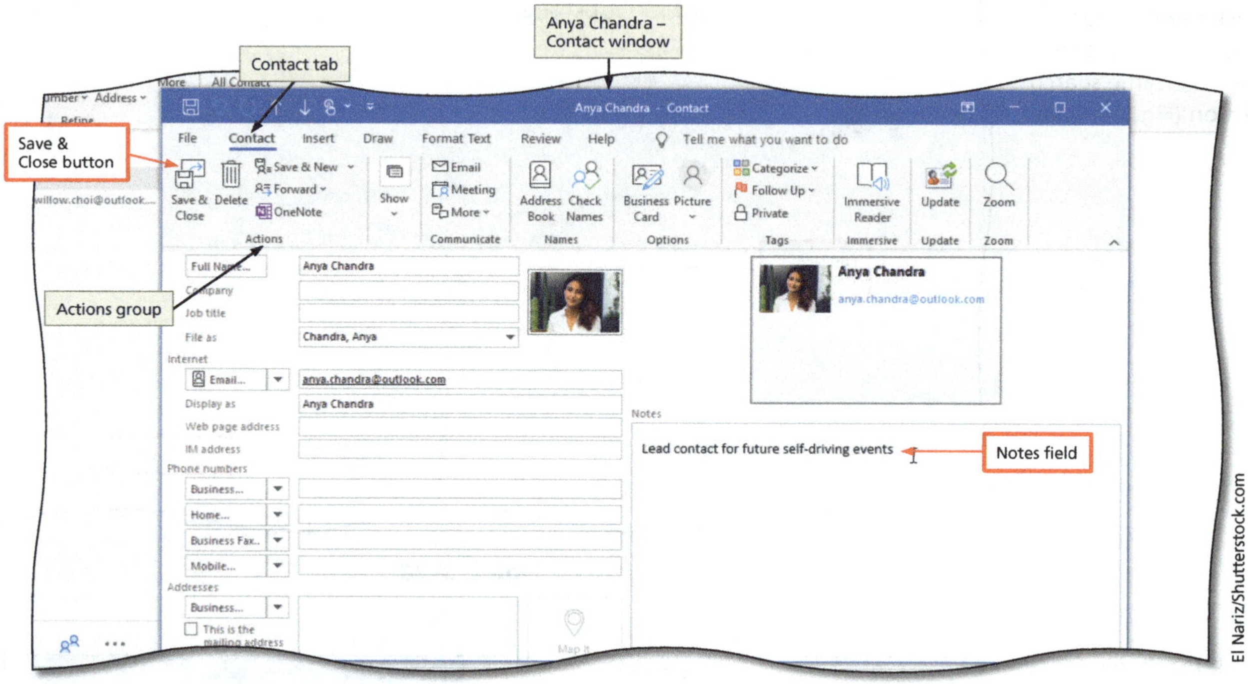

Figure 3–31

6

- Click the Save & Close button (Contact tab | Actions group) (shown in Figure 3–31) to save the contact and close the Contact window.
- Click the Close button in the Search box (shown in Figure 3–30) to close the search and return to the Contacts window.

To Find a Contact from Any Outlook Window

You do not have to be working in the Contacts window to search for contacts. You can use the Search People box in the Find group on the Home tab to search for contacts when you are working with email or performing other Outlook tasks. If what you type in the search box matches a single contact, that entry will be displayed in a contact window. If what you type matches more than one entry, you will be asked to select the contact that you want to view. ***Why?*** *For example, if you search for a contact using part of the company name, more than one contact may appear in the search results. You then can select a single contact from the results.*

The following steps search for a contact from the Inbox window using only part of the company name or title. In this case, you are searching through your contacts for the text AI.

1

- Click the Mail button on the Navigation bar to display the mailbox for the Outlook Data File.
- Click the Inbox folder, if necessary, to display the Inbox (Figure 3–32).

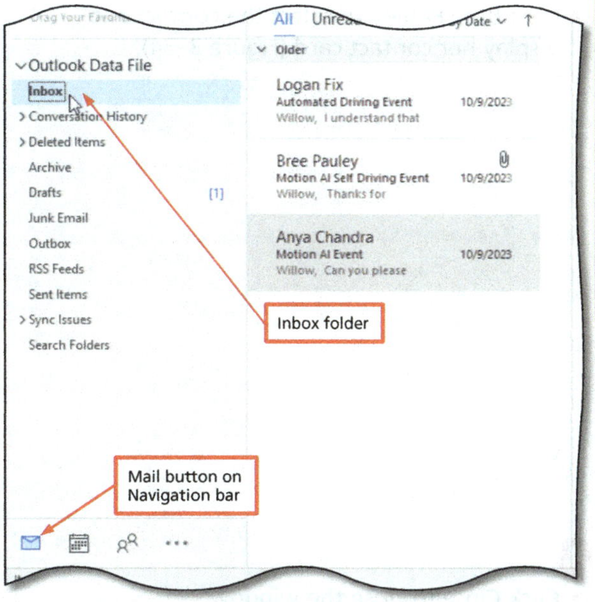

Figure 3–32

2

- Type **AI** in the Search People box (Home tab | Find group) to search for contacts containing the search text (Figure 3–33).

Q&A Outlook searched a different Outlook data file instead of the SC_OUT_3-1.pst file in the Outlook3 > Module folder. What should I do?
Open only the SC_OUT_3-1.pst Outlook data file, which appears as Outlook Data File in the Navigation pane. Close any other Outlook data file open in the Navigation pane, and then repeat the steps. You can make an Outlook data file the default by clicking the File tab, the Account Settings button, Account Settings, the Data Files tab, select the appropriate Outlook data file, and then click Set as Default.

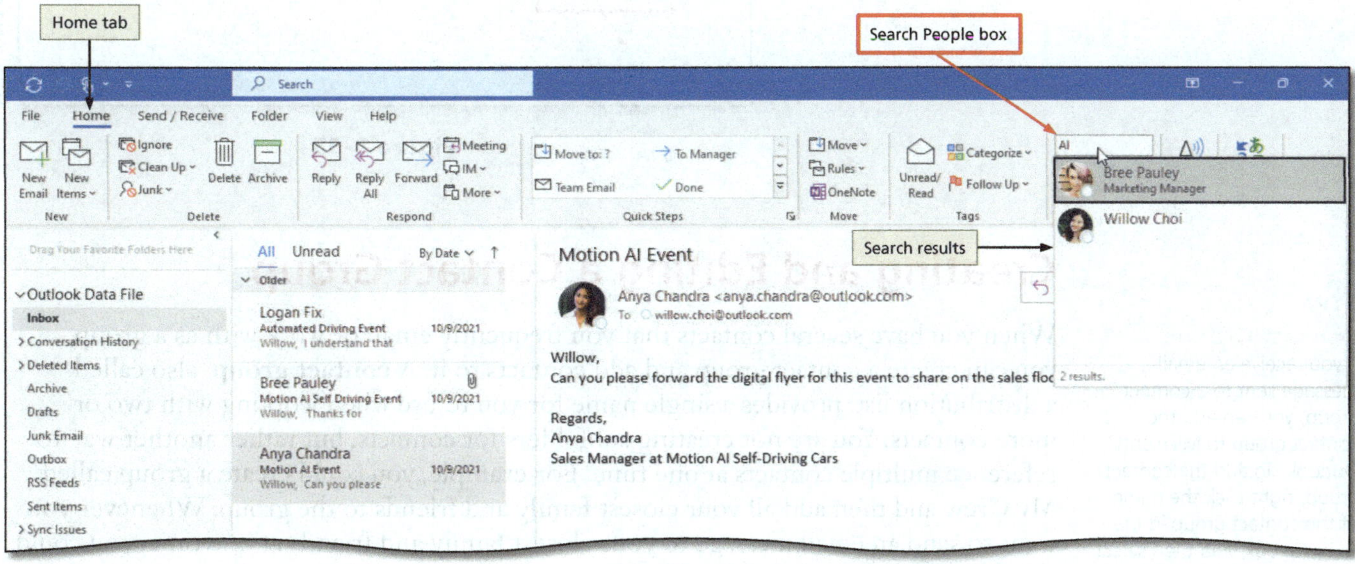

Figure 3–33

El Nariz/Shutterstock.com; Look Studio/Shutterstock.com; Makistock/Shutterstock.com

3

- Click Bree Pauley to select the contact and display her contact card (Figure 3–34).

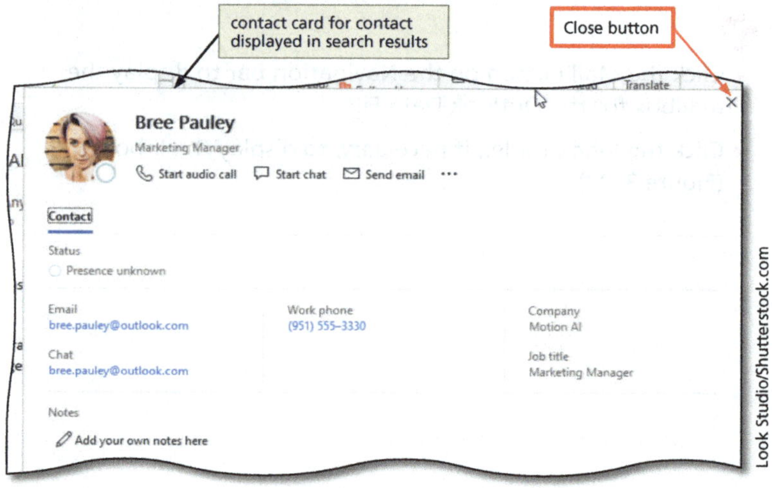

Figure 3–34

4

- Click Close to close the window.
- Click the People button on the Navigation bar to return to the Contacts window (Figure 3–35).

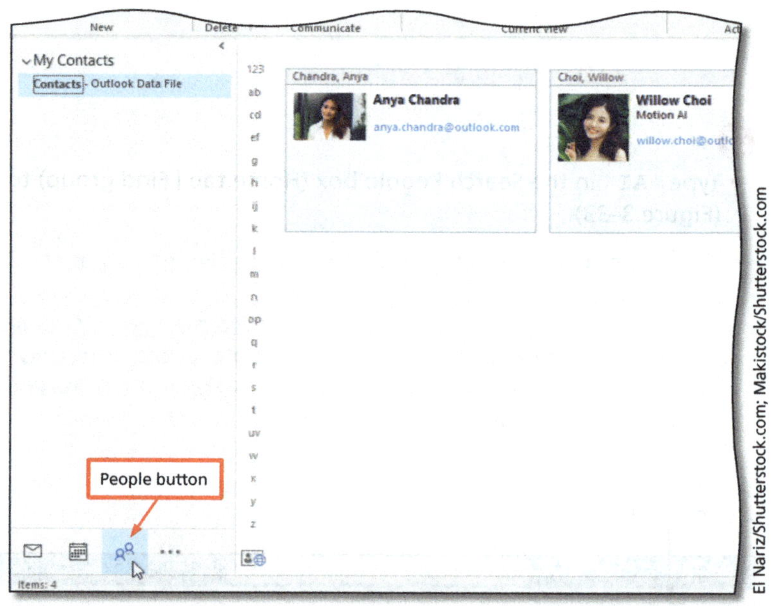

Figure 3–35

Creating and Editing a Contact Group

When you have several contacts that you frequently email or work with as a group, you can create a contact group and add contacts to it. A **contact group**, also called a distribution list, provides a single name for you to use when working with two or more contacts. You are not creating subfolders for contacts, but rather another way to reference multiple contacts at one time. For example, you could create a group called My Crew and then add all your closest family and friends to the group. Whenever you want to send an email message to your closest family and friends at one time, you could enter the contact group name, My Crew, as the recipient of the email message, and every contact in the group would receive the email message.

BTW

Contact Groups

If you receive an email message sent to a contact group, you can add the contact group to Microsoft Outlook. To add the contact group, right-click the name of the contact group in the To or Cc box, and then select Add to Outlook Contacts.

To Create a Contact Group from Existing Contacts

Why? *A message sent to a contact group goes to all recipients listed in the group. If your contact list gets too cluttered, you can use a contact group to communicate with friends, family, and coworkers more quickly.* When creating contact groups, you choose the name for your contact group and then add the contacts you want to have in the group. To quickly send out an email to all the stakeholders within Motion AI, you want to create a group of all the members who are part of your contact list named Motion Event Team. The following steps create a contact group and then add the related contacts to the group.

1

- Click the 'New Contact Group' button (Home tab | New group) to display the Untitled - Contact Group window (Figure 3–36).

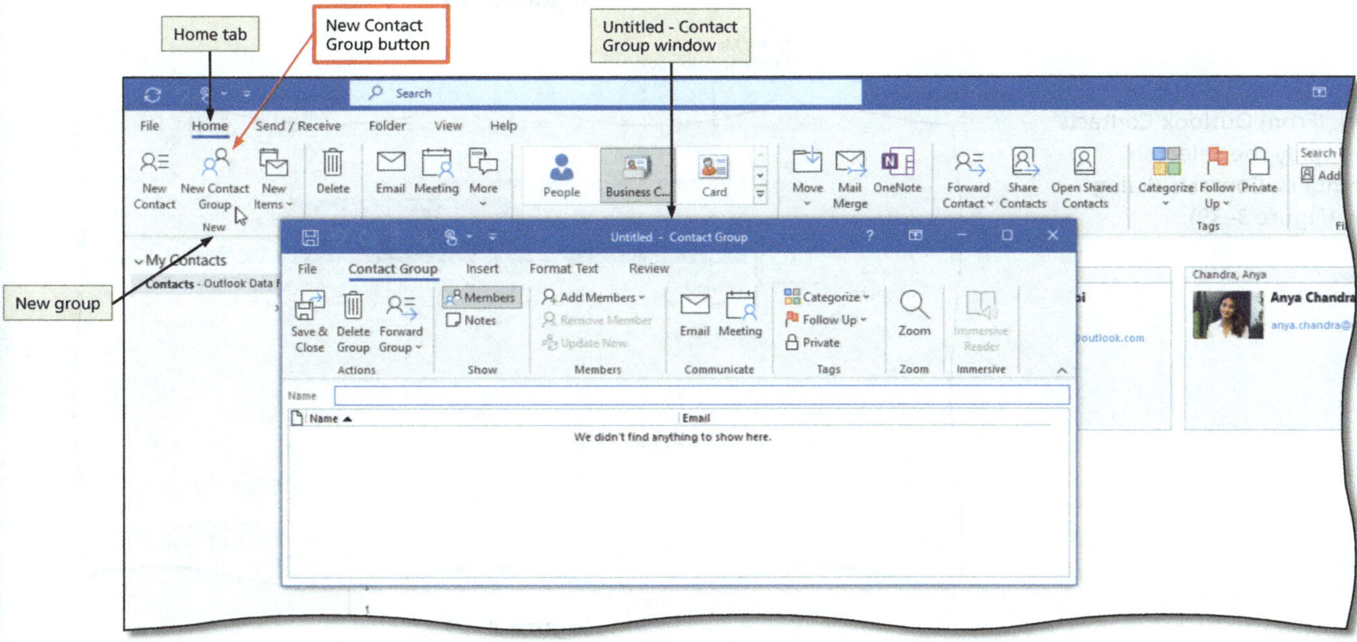

El Nariz/Shutterstock.com

Figure 3–36

2

- Type `Motion Event Team` in the Name box to enter a name for the group (Figure 3–37).

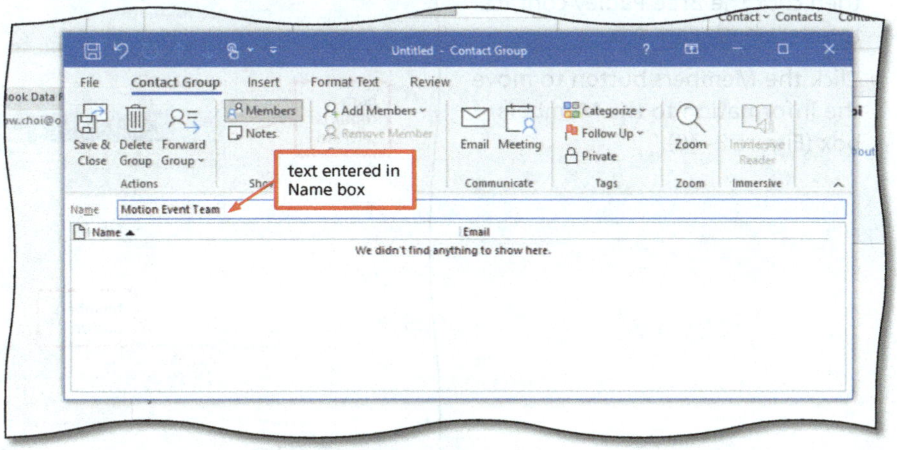

Figure 3–37

3

- Click the Add Members button (Contact Group tab | Members group) to display the Add Members menu (Figure 3–38).

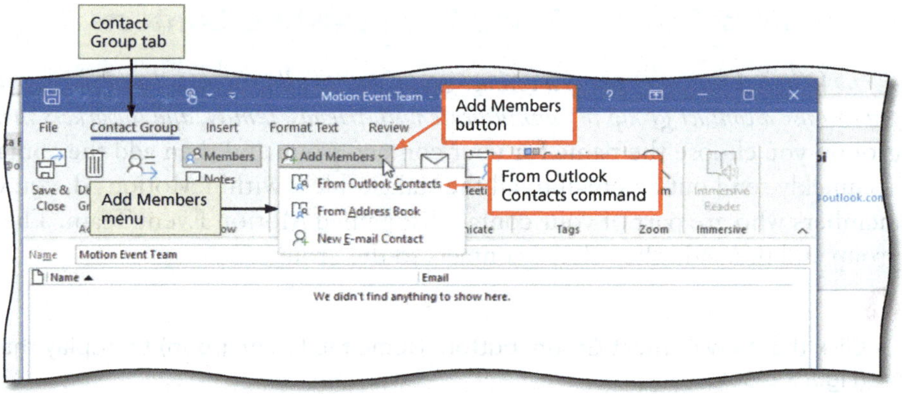

Figure 3–38

4

- Click 'From Outlook Contacts' to display the Select Members: Contacts dialog box (Figure 3–39).

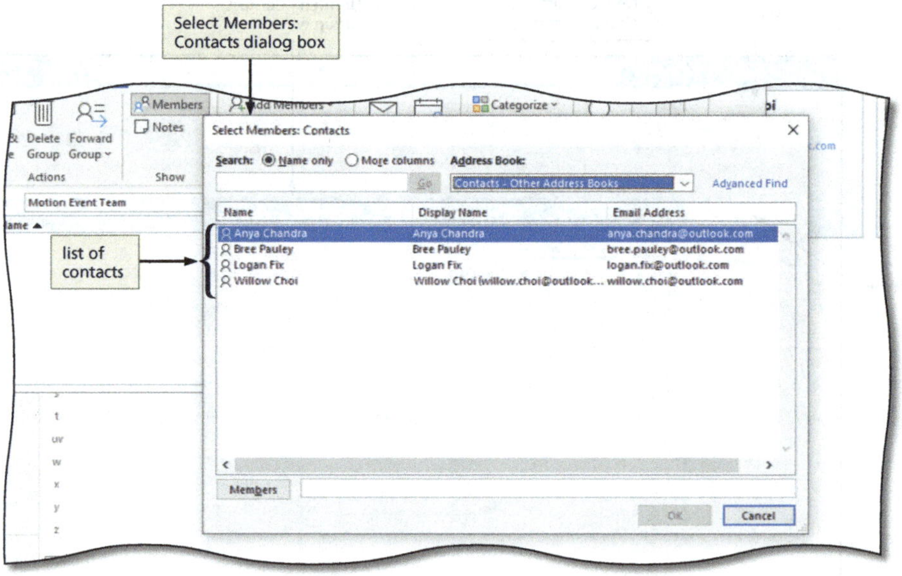

Figure 3–39

5

- Click the Anya Chandra contact to select it, press and hold CTRL, and then click the Bree Pauley contact to select both contacts.
- Click the Members button to move the information to the Members box (Figure 3–40).

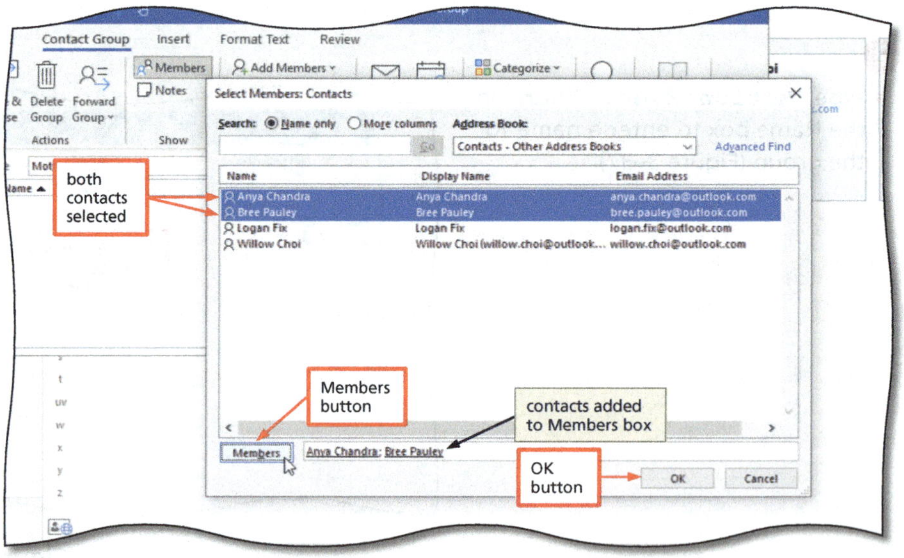

Figure 3–40

6

- Click OK to add the contacts to the group (Figure 3–41).

Q&A What if I add the wrong member(s) to the contact group?
In the Contact Group window, select the member you want to remove, and then click the Remove Member button (Contact Group tab | Members group). Next, repeat Steps 3–6 to add any missing members.

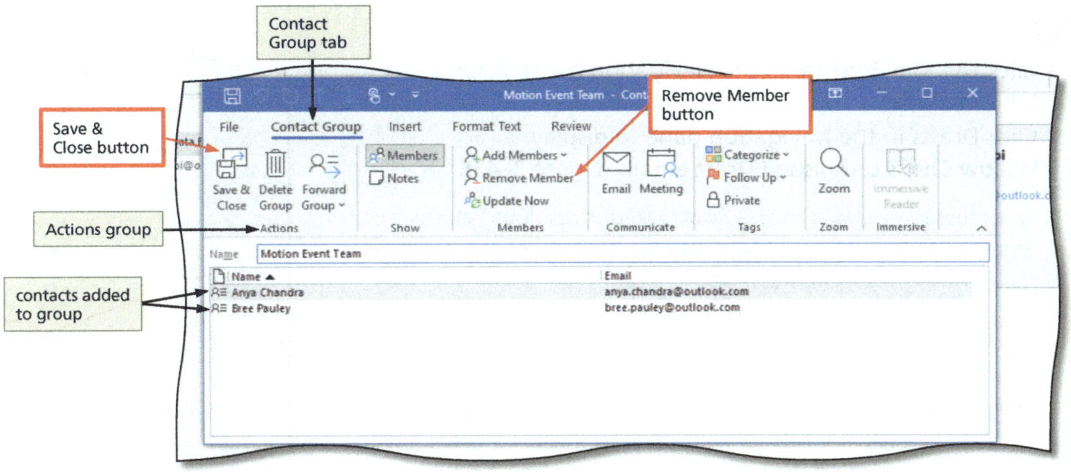

Figure 3–41

7

- Click the Save & Close button (Contact Group tab | Actions group) to save the contact group and close the window (Figure 3–42).

Q&A Why are the contacts and the group displayed in the Contacts window?
You use a contact group to send email messages to a set of contacts using the group name; it does not replace or move the existing contacts.

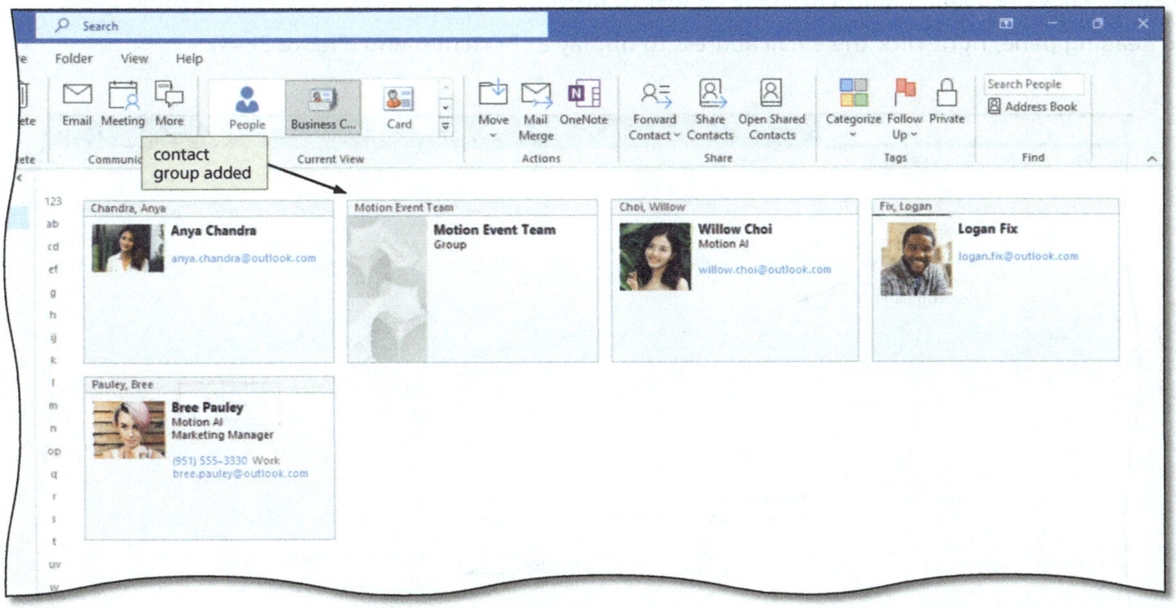

Figure 3–42

El Nariz/Shutterstock.com; Look Studio/Shutterstock.com; Monkey Business Images/Shutterstock.com; Makistock/Shutterstock.com

To Create a Contact Group from an Existing Email Message

Outlook allows you to create a group for individuals who are not in your contact list but have sent you an email message. To do this, you copy a name from an email message and then paste the name in the Select Members dialog box when creating the group. Willow had started an email that is in the Drafts folder to a local instructor named Samuel Marks. The following steps create a contact group named Instructors and then add a member by using information in an email message to Samuel Marks. ***Why?** You can create a group and add a new contact right after writing or receiving an email.*

1

- Click the Mail button on the Navigation bar to display your mailbox.
- Click Drafts in the Navigation pane to display Willow Choi's unfinished Draft emails (Figure 3–43).

Q&A The message header in the Drafts folder displays Willow's email address instead of samuel.marks@outlook.com. Do I have the right email message?
Yes. Your Drafts folder is set to display the email address in the From field instead of the To field. To change it, click View on the ribbon, click View Settings (View tab | Current View group), and then click Columns (Advanced View Settings: Compact dialog box). Click To in the Available columns list, click Add, click Move Up until "To" appears before "Subject," and then click OK (Show Columns dialog box). Click OK (Advanced View Settings: Compact dialog box).

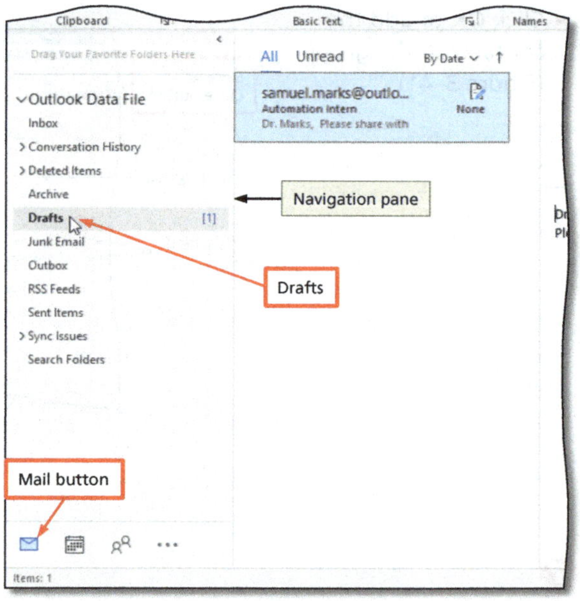

Figure 3–43

2

- If necessary, click the Samuel Marks message header to preview the email message in the Reading pane.
- In the Reading pane, right-click the email address to display a shortcut menu (Figure 3–44).

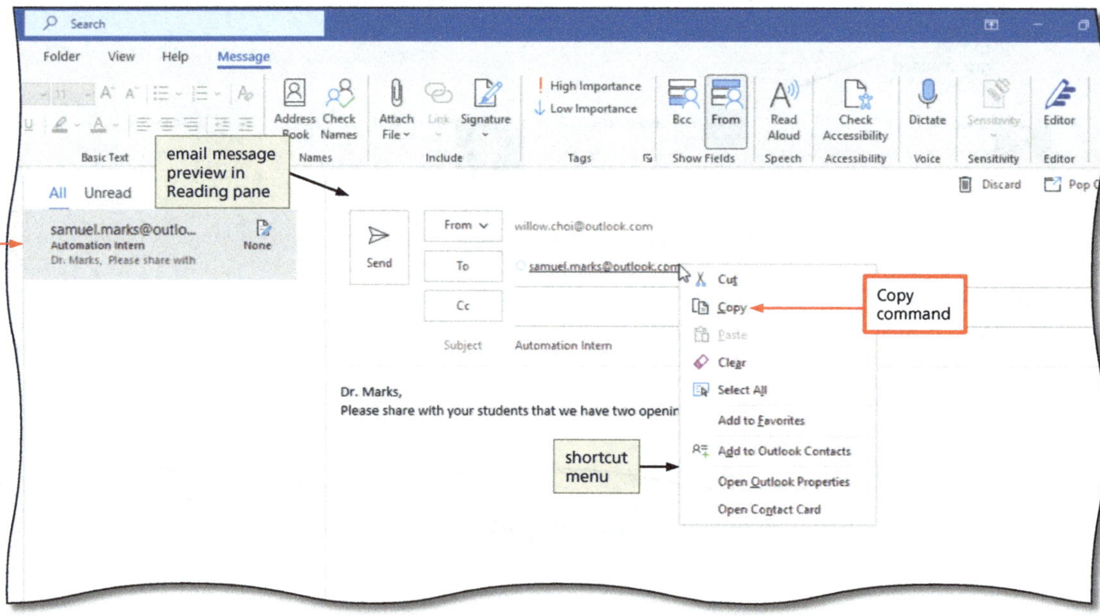

Figure 3–44

3

- Click Copy on the shortcut menu to copy the email address.
- Click Home on the ribbon to display the Home tab.
- Click the New Items button (Home tab | New group) to display the New Items menu.
- Click More Items to display the More Items submenu (Figure 3–45).

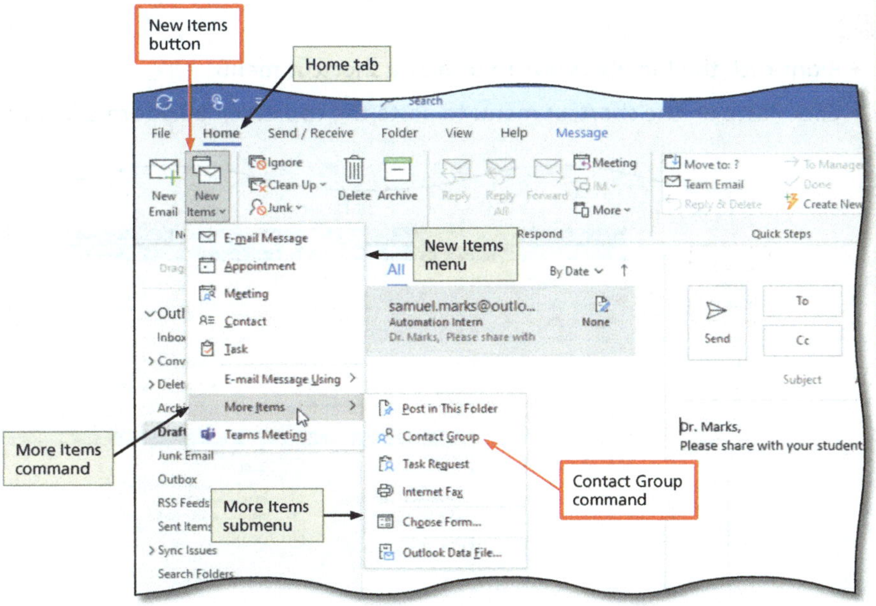

Figure 3–45

4

- Click Contact Group to display the Untitled - Contact Group window.
- Type `Instructors` in the Name box to enter a name for the group.
- Click the Add Members button (Contact Group tab | Members group) to display the Add Members menu.
- Click 'From Outlook Contacts' to display the Select Members: Contacts dialog box (Figure 3–46).

Q&A Why did I click From Outlook Contacts?
You need to display the Select Members dialog box, and you click the From Outlook Contacts menu option to open it. You also could have clicked From Address Book to display the dialog box.

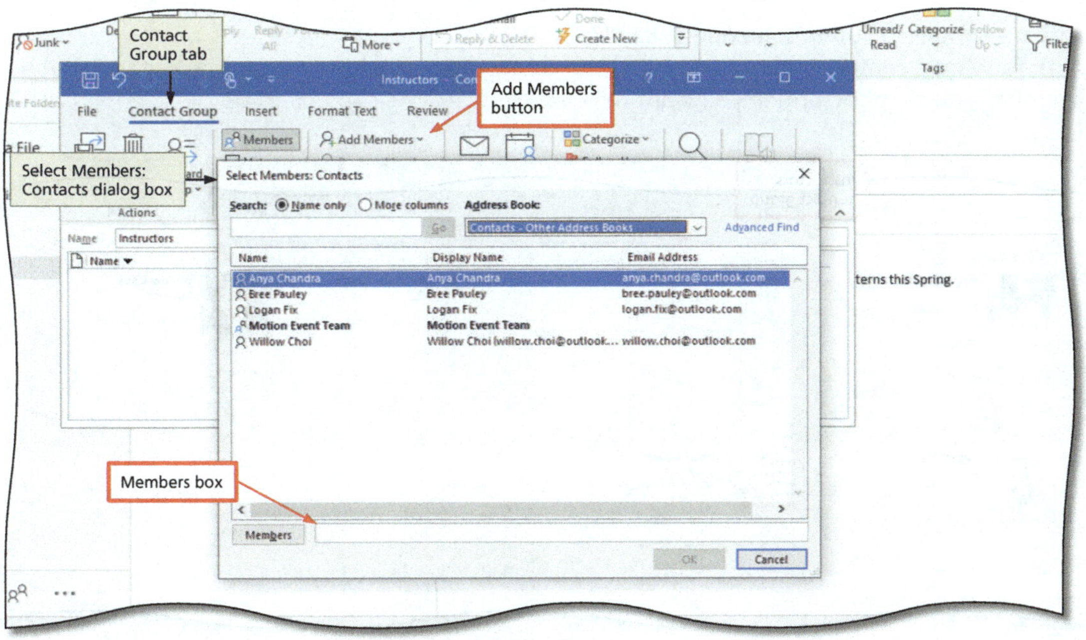

Figure 3–46

5

- Right-click the Members box to display a shortcut menu.
- Click Paste on the shortcut menu to paste the copied email address (Figure 3–47).

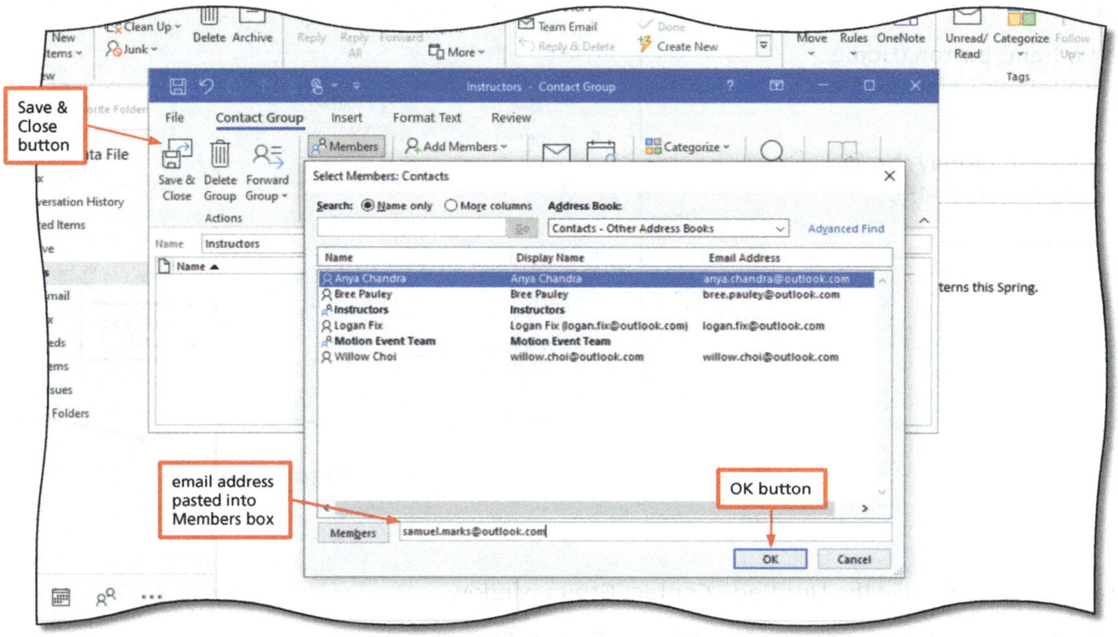

Figure 3–47

6

- Click OK to add the contact to the group.
- Click the Save & Close button (Contact Group tab | Actions group) to save the contact and close the window.
- Click the People button on the Navigation bar to display your contacts (Figure 3–48).

Q&A Can I forward a contact group to someone else?
Yes. You can forward a contact group by selecting the contact group, clicking Forward Contact (Home tab | Share group), and then selecting the option you want to use to forward the contact group.

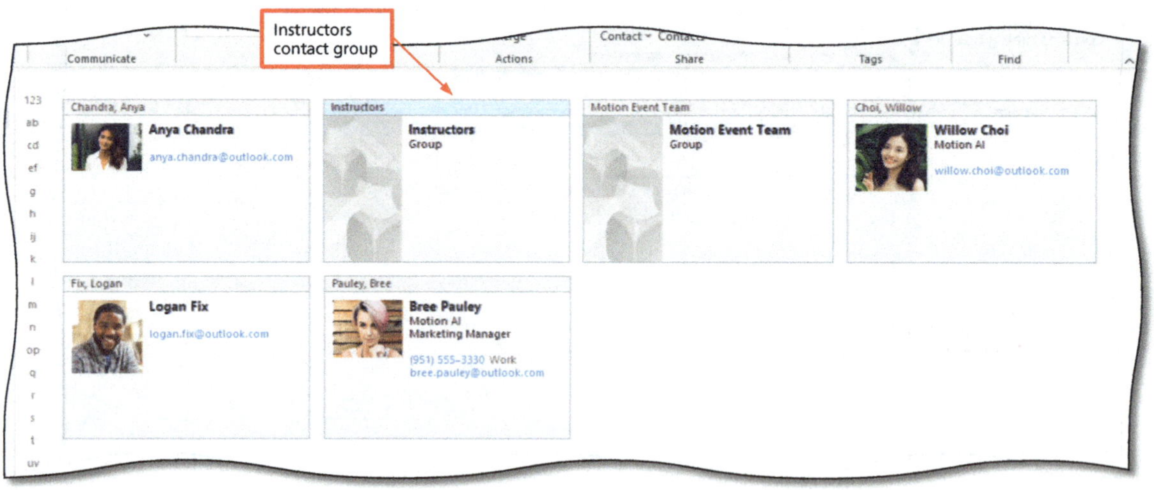

Figure 3–48

To Add a Name to a Contact Group

As you meet and work with people, you can add them to one or more contact groups. Logan Fix is also a self-driving instructor, and you want to add him to the Instructors contact group. ***Why?*** *By adding people to a group, you can send email messages and meeting invitations to groups of people that you contact frequently without having to enter each individual email address.* The following steps add a new contact to the Instructors contact group.

1

- Double-click the Instructors contact group to display the Instructors - Contact Group window (Figure 3–49).

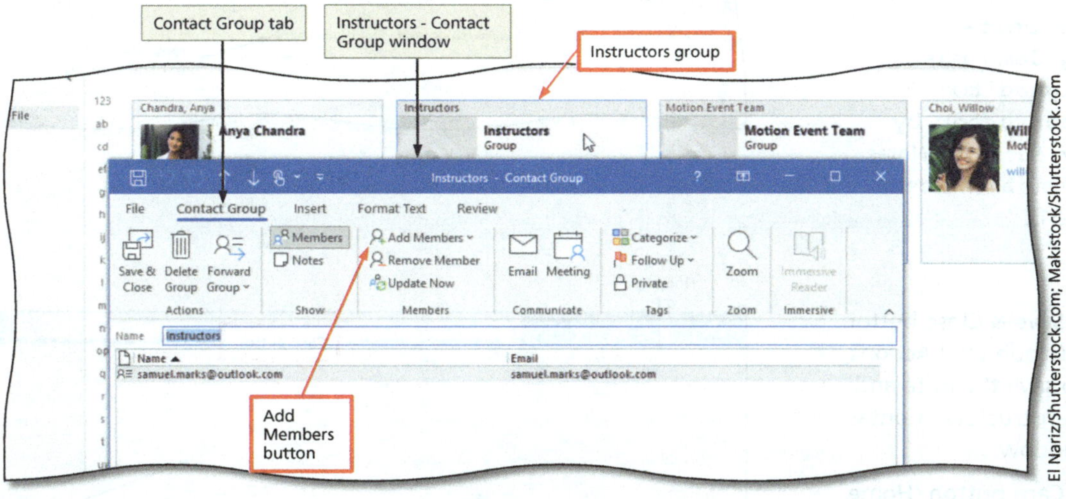

Figure 3–49

2

- Click the Add Members button (Contact Group tab | Members group) to display the Add Members menu.
- Click 'From Outlook Contacts' to display the Select Members dialog box.
- If necessary, click Logan Fix to select his contact record.
- Click the Members button to add Logan Fix to the Members box (Figure 3–50).

3

- Click OK to add Logan Fix to the contact group.
- Click the Save & Close button (Contact Group tab | Actions group) to save the contact and close the Instructors - Contact Group window.

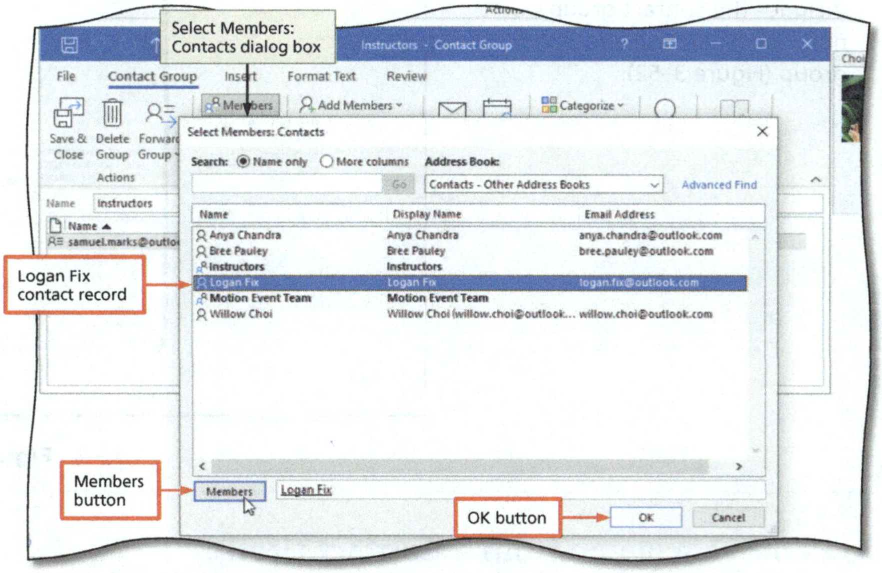

Figure 3–50

To Add Notes to a Contact Group

You can add reminder notes to a contact group. ***Why?*** *As you create groups, you may have trouble remembering who is part of the group and why.* The contact group notes are only displayed in the Contacts list when Card view is selected. You would like to add a note to the Instructors contact group that the self-driving demo must be assigned by January 9. The following steps add a note to a contact group and display the note in Card view.

1

- Double-click the Instructors contact group to display the Instructors - Contact Group window.
- Click the Notes button (Contact Group tab | Show group) to display the Notes page.
- Type **`The self-driving demo must be assigned to each instructor by January 9.`** in the Notes area to create a reminder (Figure 3–51).

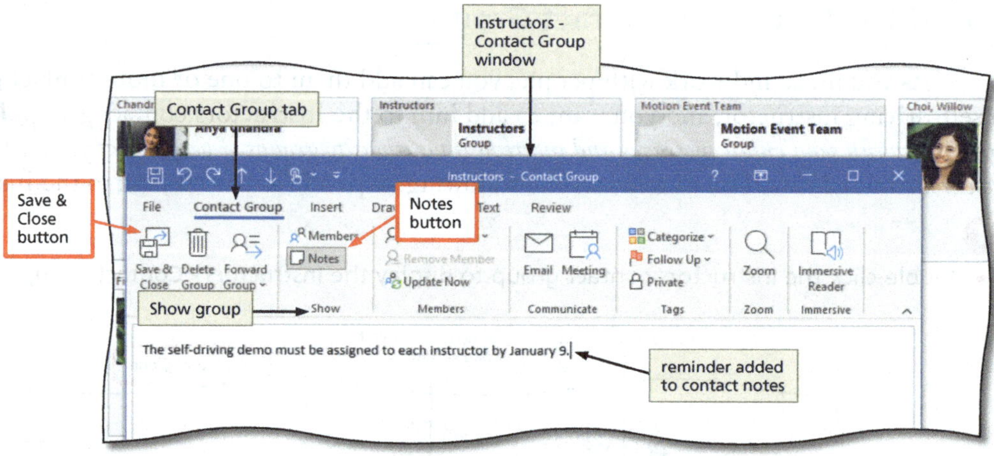

El Nariz/Shutterstock.com; Makistock/Shutterstock.com

Figure 3–51

2

- Click the Save & Close button (Contact Group tab | Actions group) to save the note and close the Instructors - Contact Group window.
- Click the Card button (Home tab | Current View group) to display the contact list in Card view, which in this case includes the contact group note for the Instructors group (Figure 3–52).

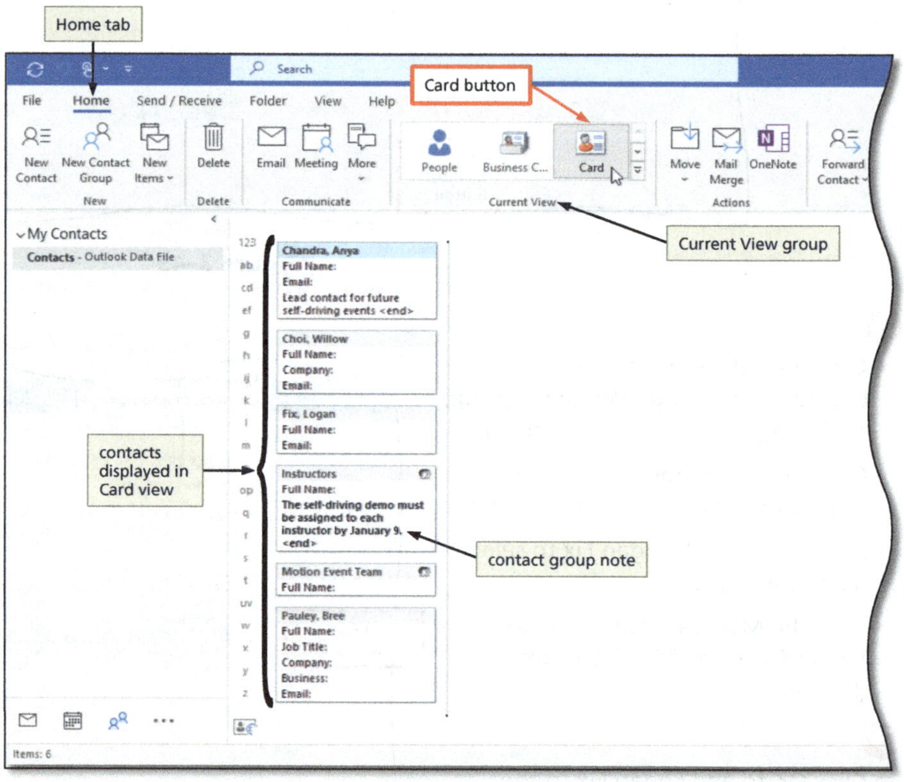

Figure 3–52

To Remove a Name from a Contact Group

Why? Periodically, you may need to remove someone from a contact group. For example, contacts may switch jobs or ask to be removed from your list because they no longer are working on or participating in a company or project. Bree Pauley has switched office locations and will no longer be participating in the Motion Event Team. You have decided to remove her from the Motion Event Team contact group so that she will not receive email messages sent to the group. The following steps remove a contact from a group.

1

- Click the Business Card button (Home tab | Current View group) to display the contact list in Business Card view.
- Double-click the Motion Event Team contact group to display the Motion Event Team - Contact Group window (Figure 3–53).

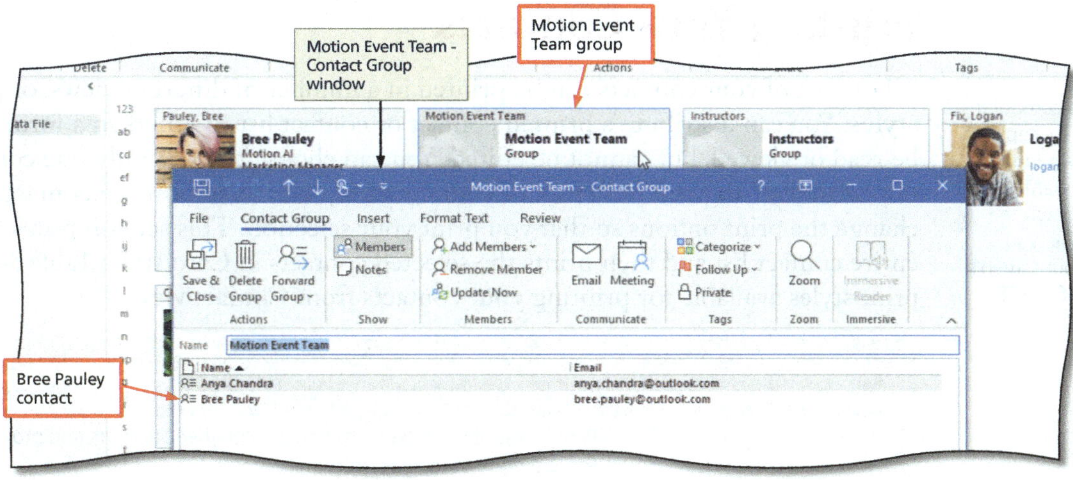

Look Studio/Shutterstock.com; Monkey Business Images/Shutterstock.com

Figure 3–53

2

- If necessary, click the Bree Pauley member to select it.
- Click the Remove Member button (Contact Group tab | Members group) to remove Bree Pauley from the contact group (Figure 3–54).

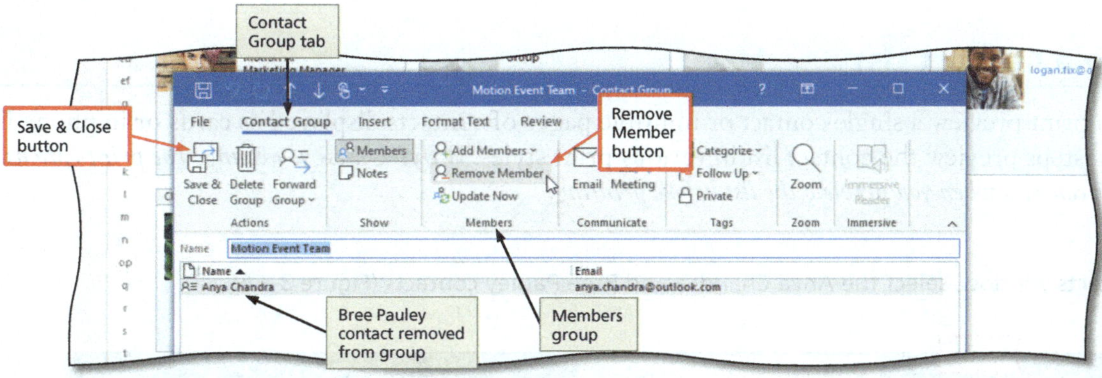

Look Studio/Shutterstock.com; Monkey Business Images/Shutterstock.com

Figure 3–54

3

- Click the Save & Close button (Contact Group tab | Actions group) to save the changes to the contact group and close the window.
- Click the People button (Home tab | Current View group) to display the Contact list in People view (Figure 3–55).

Q&A

When you remove a contact from a contact group, does it also remove the contact from Outlook?

No. The contact remains in Outlook, even after removing it from a contact group.

How can I delete a contact group?

To delete a contact group, select the contact group to delete, and then click Delete (Home tab | Delete group).

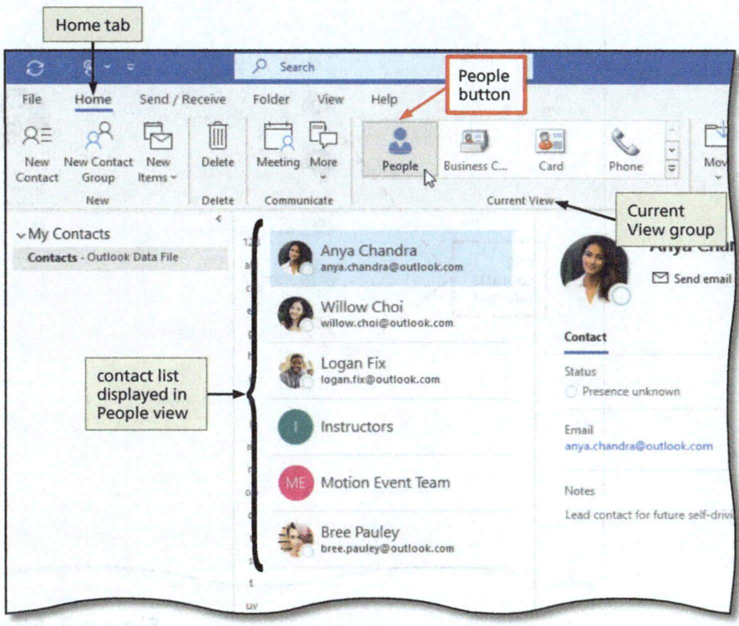

El Nariz/Shutterstock.com; Look Studio/Shutterstock.com; Makistock/Shutterstock.com; Monkey Business Images/Shutterstock.com

Figure 3–55

BTW
Outlook Screen Resolution
If you are using a computer or mobile device to step through the project in this module and you want your screens to match the figures in this book, you should change your screen's resolution to 1366 × 768.

Printing Your Contacts

All or part of your contacts can be printed in a number of different views, or **print styles**. You can distribute a printed contact or contact list to others in a form that can be read or viewed, but cannot be edited. You can choose to print only one contact or the entire list. To print only part of your contacts, select one or more contacts and then change the print options so that you print your selection. This section previews the entire contact list and then prints the selected contacts in Card style. Table 3–1 lists the print styles available for printing your contacts from Contact view.

Table 3–1 Print Styles for Contact View

Print Style	Description
Card	Prints a list of contacts separated by alphabetic dividers and provides a sheet for adding more contact information
Small Booklet	Prints a list of contacts similar to Card style but designed so that it can be folded into a small booklet
Medium Booklet	Prints a list of contacts similar to Card style but designed so that it can be folded into a medium-sized booklet
Memo	Prints a page for each contact, each page formatted to look like a memo
Phone Directory	Prints a list of contacts showing phone numbers only

To Preview a Contact List

You can print preview a single contact or multiple pages of contacts displayed as cards or in phone lists. The following steps preview the contact list in various print styles. ***Why?*** *Unless you change the print options, you will see all your contacts when you preview the list before printing.*

1

- In the Contacts window, select the Anya Chandra and Bree Pauley contacts (Figure 3–56).

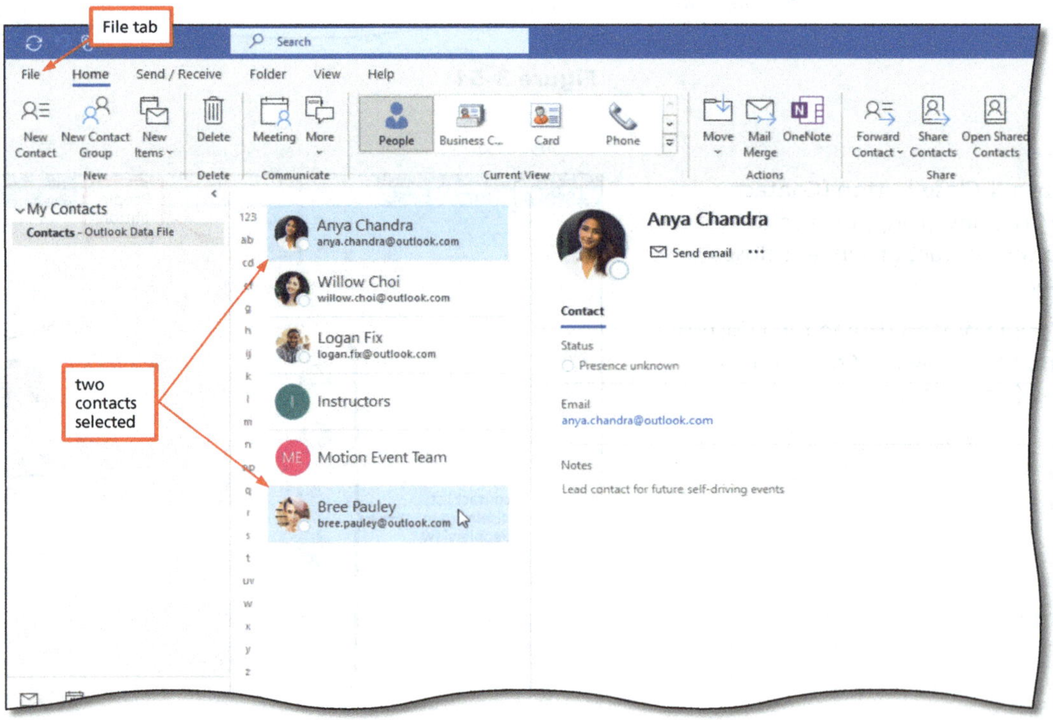

Figure 3–56

2

- Click the File tab on the ribbon (shown in Figure 3–56) to open Backstage view.
- Click the Print tab in Backstage view to display the Print gallery.
- Click Small Booklet Style in the Settings area to change the print style (Figure 3–57).

Q&A Why are all the contacts displayed when I selected only two contacts?
By default, the print range is set for all items to display and print. You can change the Print Options to print only the selected items.

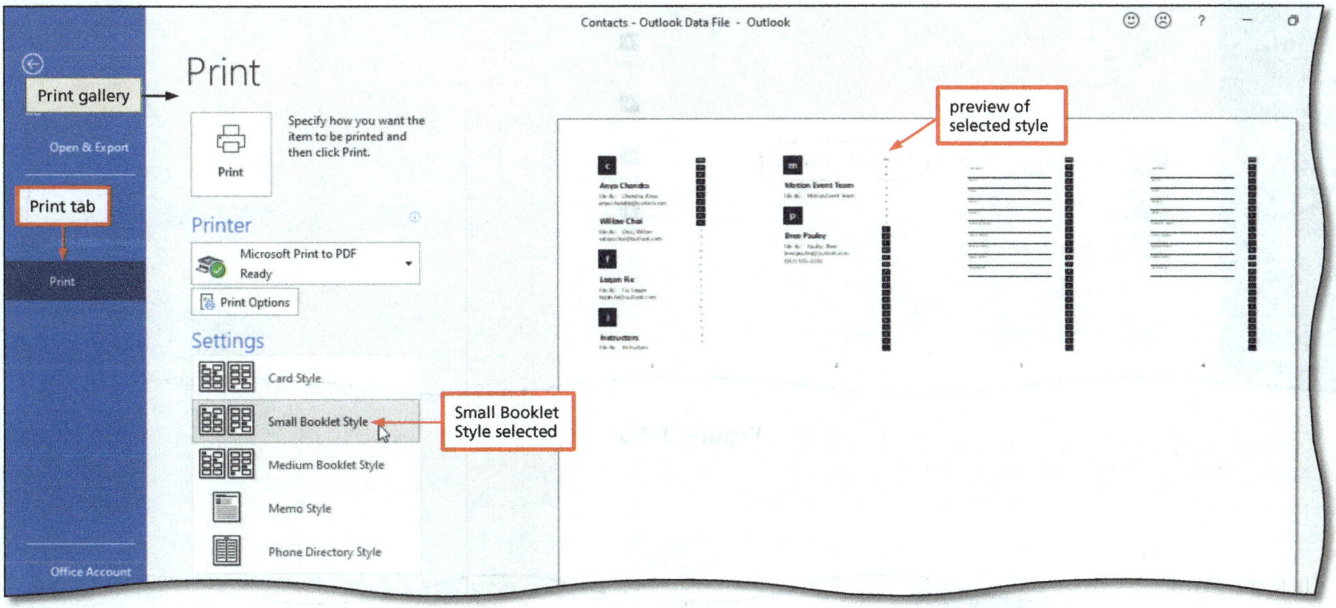

Figure 3–57

3

- Click Phone Directory Style in the Settings area to change to Phone Directory Style (Figure 3–58).

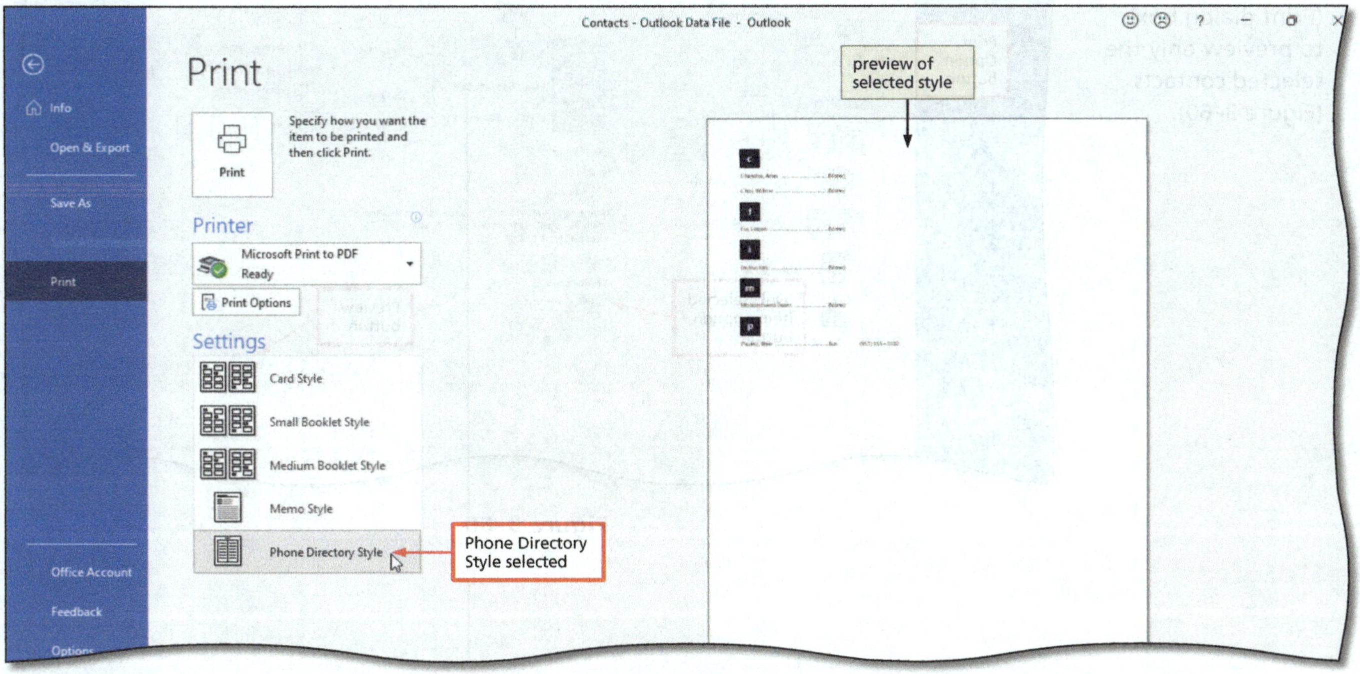

Figure 3–58

4

- Click Card Style in the Settings area to change to Card Style (Figure 3–59).

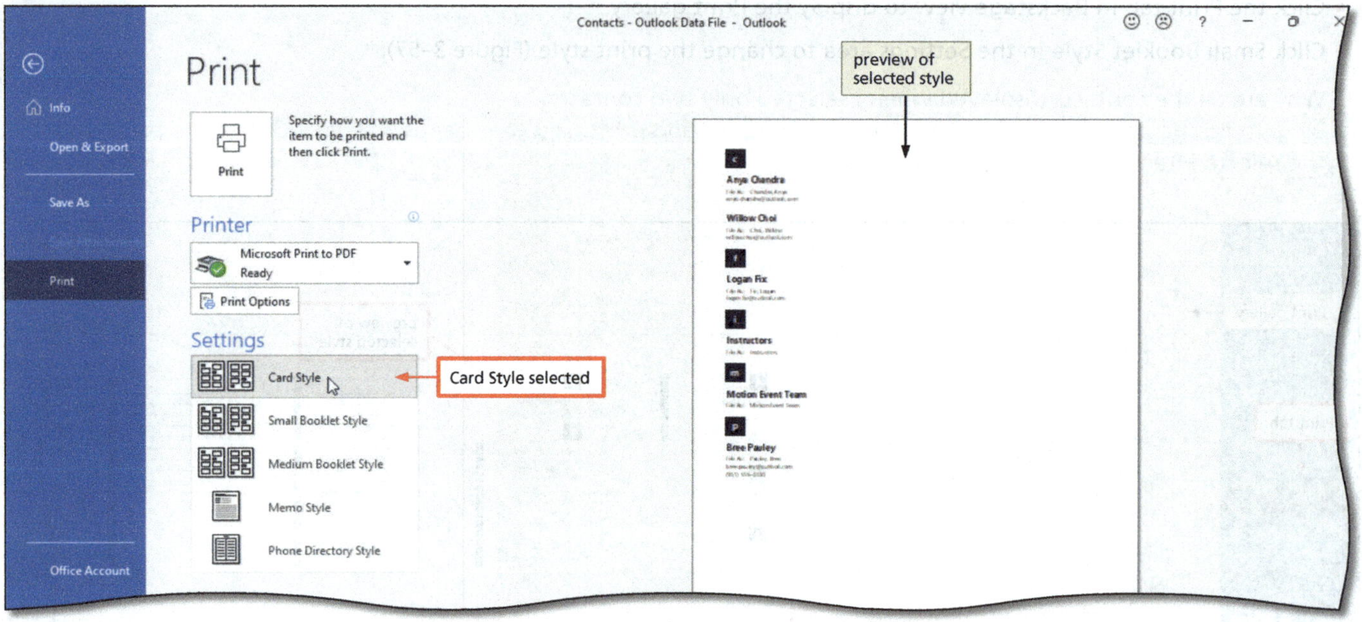

Figure 3–59

5

- Click the Print Options button to display the Print dialog box.
- Click the 'Only selected items' option button (Print dialog box) to preview only the selected contacts (Figure 3–60).

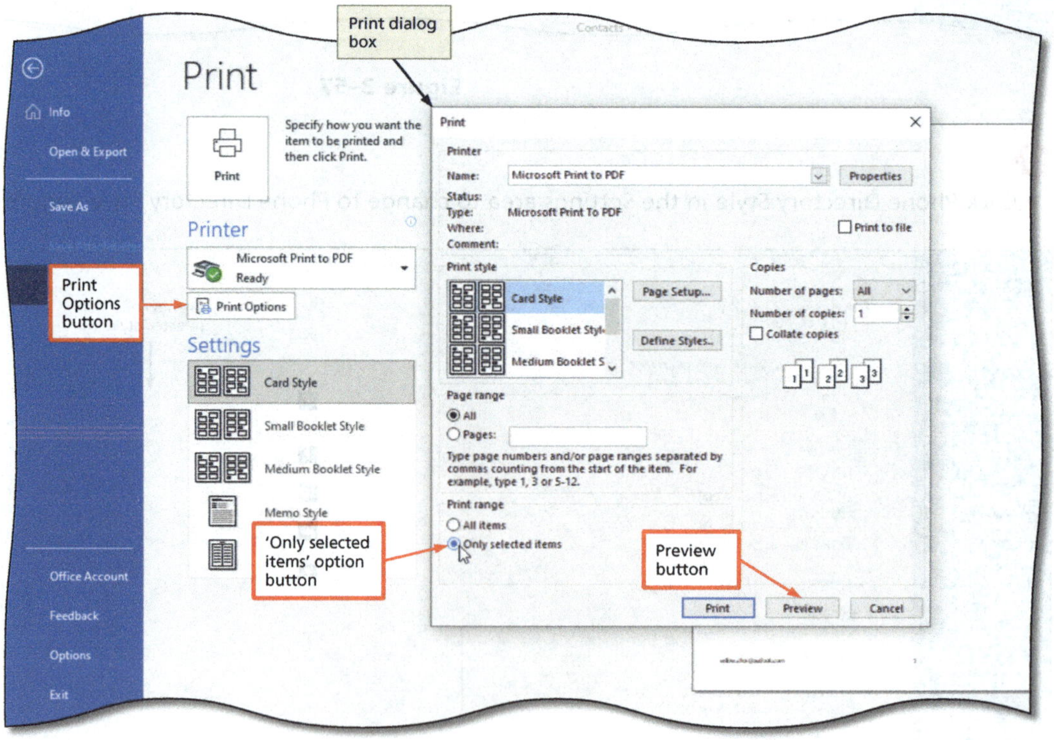

Figure 3–60

6

- Click the Preview button (Print dialog box) to close the dialog box and preview only the selected contacts.
- Click the print preview to zoom in to view the selected contacts (Figure 3–61).

Q&A If I click the other styles, will they only show selected contacts?
No. If you change the style, the preview returns to showing all contacts. To see the selected contacts in a particular style, you select the style and then change the print options.

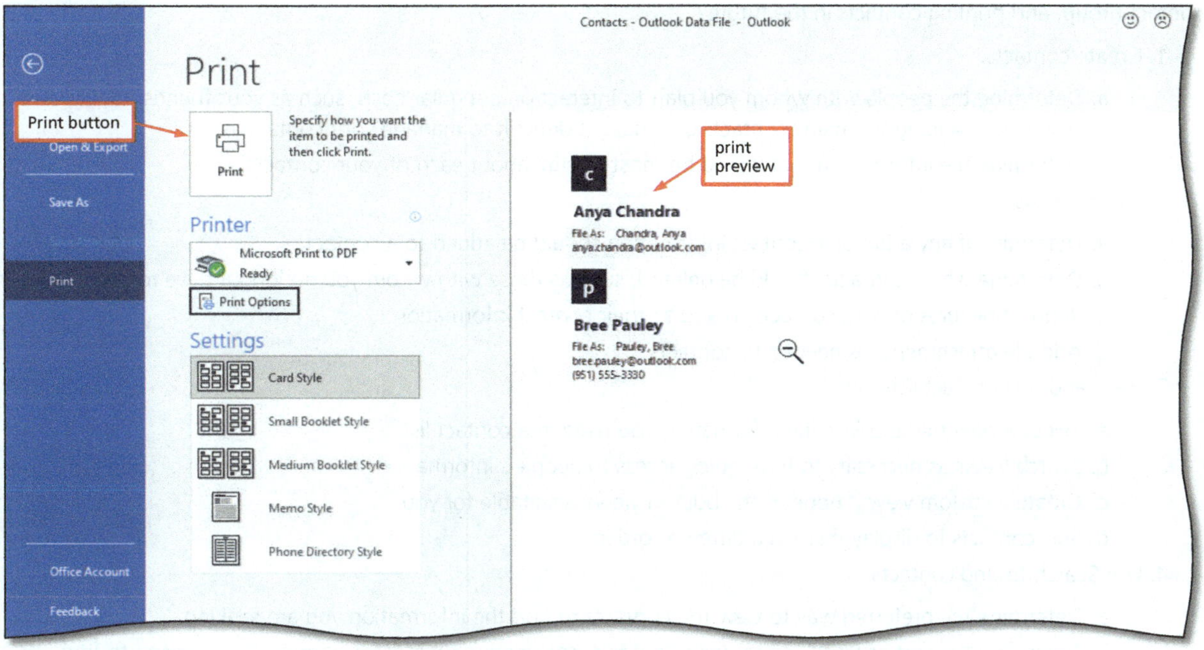

Figure 3–61

BTW
Printing Contacts
Contacts can be printed directly to paper, saved as a PDF file, or sent to OneNote using the Printer button.

To Print a Contact List and Export an Outlook Data File

Why? Before heading to a meeting, you may want to print a list of contacts for reference. The following steps print the selected contacts in Card style, and then exit Outlook.

1. Click the Print button to print the selected contacts.
2. Export the Outlook Data File using `SC_OUT_3_Willow` as the file name.
3. If you have a contact open, click Close on the right side of the title bar to close the Contact window.
4. Click Close on the right side of the title bar to exit Outlook.

Summary

In this module, you have learned how to use Outlook to create a contact list, view and sort contacts, and search for contacts. You learned to create and edit a contact group, add notes to a contact, and print contacts.

CONSIDER THIS

Consider This: Plan Ahead

What decisions will you need to make when creating contacts from friends, family, and coworkers, editing contacts, creating a contact group, and printing contacts in the future?

1. Create contacts.
    a. Determine the people with whom you plan to interact on a regular basis, such as your friends, family, and coworkers. Adding too many contacts can make it difficult to manage your contact list.
    b. Determine the information that would be most helpful about each of your contacts.
2. Edit contacts.
    a. Determine if any additional contact information should be added to a contact.
    b. Determine which contacts should be deleted, such as those with whom you no longer have regular communication.
    c. Request pictures of your contacts to add to their contact information.
    d. Add file attachments as needed to contacts.
3. View and sort contact lists.
    a. Select a view that displays the information you need in a contact list.
    b. Switch views as necessary to have quick access to people's information.
    c. Create a custom view if none of the built-in views is suitable for you.
    d. Sort contacts to display them in a different order.
4. Use Search to find contacts.
    a. Determine the preferred way to view the contacts to find the information you are seeking.
    b. Determine the sort order to use for your contacts, considering what information you are trying to find.
5. Create and edit contact groups.
    a. Plan the relationship of the contacts that are organized under the group name.
    b. Consider a good name for a contact group that will make it easier for you to remember the purpose of the group.
6. Print your contacts.
    a. Plan how best to display your contacts.

CONSIDER THIS

How should you submit solutions to questions in the assignments identified with a symbol?

Every assignment in this book contains one or more questions with a symbol. These questions require you to think beyond the assigned file. Present your solutions to the question in the format required by your instructor. Possible formats may include one or more of these options: write the answer; create a document that contains the answer; present your answer to the class; discuss your answer in a group; record the answer as audio or video using a webcam, smartphone, or portable media player; or post answers on a blog, wiki, or website.

Apply Your Knowledge

Reinforce the skills and apply the concepts you learned in this module.

Note: To complete this assignment, you will be required to use the Data Files. Please contact your instructor for information about accessing the Data Files.

Updating a Contact List

Instructions: Start Outlook. Edit the contact list provided in the file called SC_OUT_3-2.pst, located in the Data Files for Students. The SC_OUT_3-2.pst Contacts file contains six contacts and a contact group for your furniture staging business. Many of the contacts have changed and some are incomplete. You now need to revise these contacts and print them in Card view (Figure 3–62).

Figure 3–62

Perform the following tasks:

1. Open the SC_OUT_3-2.pst Contacts file in Outlook, switch to People view, and select the Contacts file you added, if necessary, to display contacts including Kayla Raines and Naomi Alyssa.
2. Change the company for Kayla Raines to **`Staging with Style.`** Move Kayla's Mobile phone number to the Business box. Change her job title to **`Interior Designer.`** Add an email address of **`kayla.raines@email.com.`**
3. Change the company for Hugo Arenas to **`Show Homes.`** Type **`hugo.arenas@showhomes.com`** as his new email address, and change his phone number to **`555-2220.`** Add the following as his webpage address: **`http://www.showhomes.com/chicago.`**
4. Change Naomi Alyssa's email address to **`naomi.alyssa@showhomes.com.`** Add a Home phone of **`555-9965.`** Add **`Congratulate her for the Design 2023 Award at the next meeting`** as a note.
5. Change the job title for Lauren Mariel to **`Project Manager`** and company to **`Design Realm.`**
6. Change the Staging Staff contact group name to **`#homestaging.`** Add the Hansen Jez and Naomi Alyssa contacts to the contact group and remove the Lauren contact from the contact group.
7. Add a new contact using your name, email address, and photo. Add yourself to the #homestaging group.
8. Print the final contact list in Card Style, as shown in Figure 3–62, and then submit the printout to your instructor.
9. Export the Contacts file using **`SC_OUT_3_Staging`** as the file name. Submit the file to your instructor.
10. Outlook can display your contacts in a variety of views. Which view do you prefer, and why?

Extend Your Knowledge

Extend the skills you learned in this module and experiment with new skills. You may need to use Help to complete the assignment.

Note: To complete this assignment, you will be required to use the Data Files. Please contact your instructor for information about accessing the Data Files. An active email account is necessary to email the contacts to your instructor.

Creating a Contacts Folder

Instructions: Start Outlook. Your school's eSports league is sponsoring a winter sports pass for youths and needs to create a contact list of local schools. The SC_OUT_3-3.pst Contacts file located in the Data Files has no contacts. You will create a new contacts folder, add the names of schools to the new contacts folder, and print the contact list (Figure 3–63). You also will share the contacts folder with others.

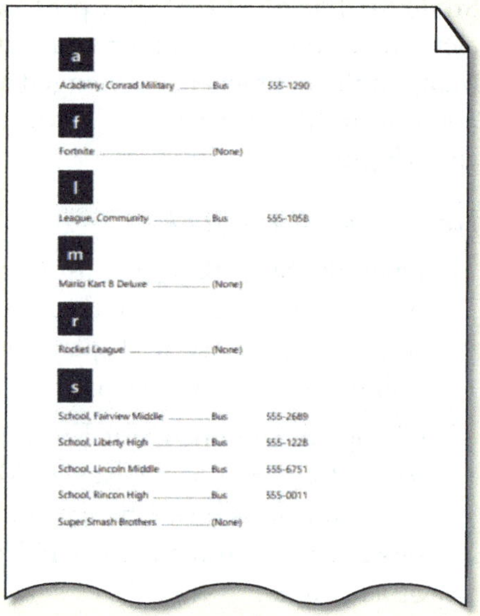

Figure 3–63

Perform the following tasks:

1. Use Help to learn about creating a contacts folder and sharing a contact list.
2. Open the SC_OUT_3-3.pst Contacts file in Outlook, and then create a new contacts folder within it named **eSports Schools.**
3. Create a contact for each school displayed in Table 3–2, including email address, business phone, and notes. Add **eSports League** as the Company for everyone.

Table 3–2 eSports Schools Information

Name	Email Address	Business Phone	Notes	Game
Community League	community@earth.com	555-1058	1v1, Nintendo Switch	Mario Kart 8 Deluxe
Conrad Military Academy	gaming@conrad.edu	555-1290	Solos and Duos any device	Fortnite
Fairview Middle School	lucasw@fms.edu	555-2689	1v1, Nintendo Switch	Super Smash Brothers
Liberty High School	esports@lhs.com	555-1228	3v3 or 1v1, any device	Rocket League
Lincoln Middle School	lincoln@schools.com	555-6751	3v3 or 1v1, any device	Rocket League
Rincon High School	rinconclub@earth.net	555-0011	Solos and Duos any device	Fortnite

4. Create a contact group for each game displayed in Table 3–2. Place the appropriate contacts in the groups.
5. Create a contact using one of your parent's or guardian's last name as a school with the appropriate last name and email address. If you do not want to disclose this email address or if they do not have one, replace it with your email address. Place your picture in the contact record.
6. Print the contact list in Phone Directory Style, as shown in Figure 3–63, and then submit the printout to your instructor.
7. Select all the contacts. Use the Forward Contact button (Home tab | Share group) and click As an Outlook Contact to email the contact list to your instructor.
8. Export the Contacts file using **SC_OUT_3_eSports** as the file name. Submit the file to your instructor.
9. How can you stay more organized by creating separate multiple folders within your contacts?

Expand Your World

Create a solution that uses cloud or web technologies by learning and investigating on your own from general guidance.

Note: To complete this assignment, you will be required to use the completed Module 3 files from this text and outlook.com with a Microsoft email account.

Opening Contacts in Microsoft OneNote

Instructions: Using Outlook Online (outlook.com), you can add contacts that automatically sync with the installed Outlook client when logged into the same Microsoft account. Add the four contacts from Module 3 to your outlook.com contacts, as shown in Figure 3–64.

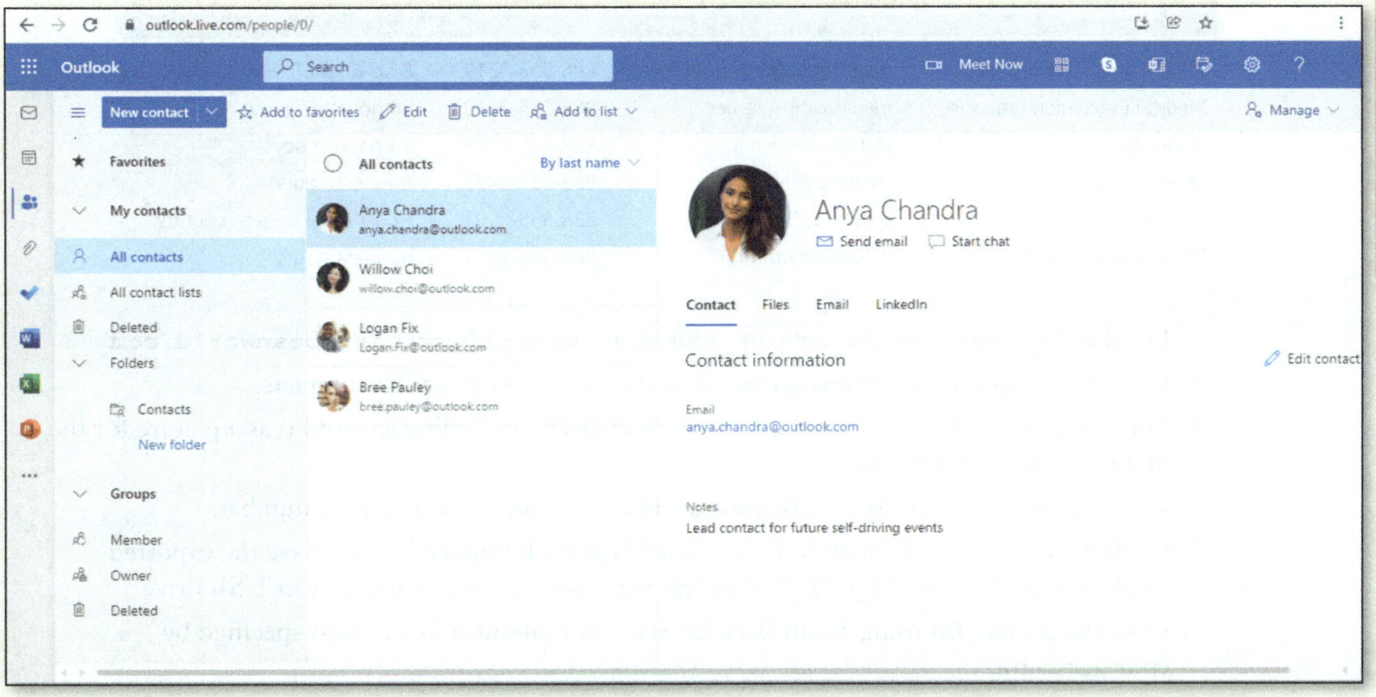

Figure 3–64

Perform the following tasks:

1. If necessary, create a Microsoft account at outlook.com.
2. Open the People option at outlook.com and add four new contacts with first and last names and email addresses from Module 3 for Willow Choi, Anya Chandra, Bree Pauley, and Logan Fix.
3. Click the Manage button and select Export contacts. Click the Export button and save the exported .csv file as `SC_OUT_3_Contacts` on your local computer or USB drive.
4. Submit the SC_OUT_3_Contacts.csv file in the format specified by your instructor.
5. Why would you want your contacts automatically synced between outlook.com and your Outlook installed client? Write at least three reasons in sentence format.

In the Lab 1

Creating Travel List Contacts

Problem: You have agreed to create a contact list for your team at work. The list should include the email and phone contacts for travel services needed for a company sales meeting in the Caribbean. Table 3–3 lists the contact information for each travel service. Enter the contacts into a new contact list.

Perform the following tasks:

1. Start Outlook and create a new Outlook Data File named **`SC_OUT_3_Caribbean`**.
2. Create the contacts in the Contacts window, using the information listed in Table 3–3.

Table 3–3 Travel Contact Information

Travel Contact	Email Address	Business	Notes
Travel Agent Caribbean Blue	travelagent@blueworld.net	888-555-8319	8 AM-6 PM ET
Medical Evacuation Insurance	medivac@insure.net	888-555-2812	24 hours a day
State Department	statedept@us.net	888-555-8178	24 hours a day
Legal Counsel	legaldept@legal.net	888-555-8429	Business hours
Consular Services	sos@world.com	888-555-0101	Hours differ in each country
Travel Health Insurance	insure@health.org	888-555-8111	Business hours

3. For the first contact, list the webpage address as **`http://www.caribbeanworld.com`**.
4. Create a group named **`Insurance`**. Add the two travel insurance contacts.
5. Find an appropriate image for the U.S. State Department online and add it as a picture for the State Department contact.
6. Create a contact for yourself with your email address and mobile phone number.
7. Click the File tab, click Open & Export, and then click Import/Export. Save the exported Outlook Data File as **`SC_OUT_3_Caribbean`** on your local computer or USB drive.
8. Print the contact list using Small Booklet Style and submit it in a format specified by your instructor.
9. What other information might be useful to include in a travel contact list if you plan to share this with the rest of work team?

In the Lab 2

Creating a High School Reunion Contact List

Problem: You are helping to create a high school reunion contact list for your 10-year reunion. Your class officers have decided to email reminders to their class members and need a mailing list of these members to send them emails about the reunion details. You need to create a contact list and add contact groups so that you can send specific information for class reunion attendees (Figure 3–65).

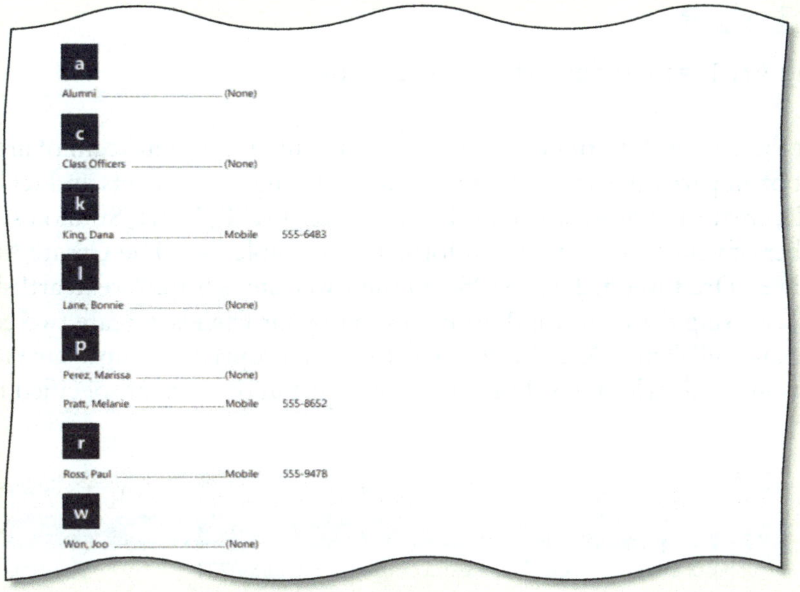

Figure 3–65

Perform the following tasks:

1. Create a new Outlook Data File named **`SC_OUT_3_Reunion_Contacts`**.
2. Create two contact groups called **`Alumni`** and **`Class Officers`**.
3. Enter the contacts in the Contacts list, using the information in Table 3–4.
4. Add the contacts to the appropriate contact group.
5. Add **`Dana has agreed to assist with the catered dinner`** as the second note in Dana King's contact information.
6. Add the Job title of **`Class of 2014`** to each class reunion contact.
7. Print the contact list in Phone Directory style as a PDF file and save the Outlook Data File as a .pst file. Submit both files in the format specified by your instructor.
8. What other information might be useful to include in the reunion contact list if you plan to share this with the rest of your classmates at the reunion?

Table 3–4 Class Reunion Contact List

Name	Email Address	City, State	Mobile Phone	Notes
Dana King	dana.king@earth.com	Clay, IL	555-6483	Active alumni
Bonnie Lane	bonnie.lane@email.com	Waylen, GA	none	Class officer
Marissa Perez	mperez@earth.net	Garland, OH	none	Active alumni
Melanie Pratt	prattm@email.com	Liberty, VA	555-8652	Not sure if this is the correct email
Paul Ross	paul.ross@email.com	Eden, OK	555-9478	none
Joo Won	jwon@email.com	Rawlings, NE	555-2212	Class officer

In the Lab 3

Scheduling Art Teachers for Art Studio Classes

Part 1: At the Create Art Studio, you oversee scheduling for your team of art teachers. You need a contact list of all part-time and full-time teachers. Using the contacts and techniques presented in this module, create an Outlook Data File named SC_OUT_3_Art_Studio.pst and add contacts for each member of your team using the information in Table 3–5. The Create Art Studio is located at 95 Chadwell Dr., Lisbon, TX, 73108 and their website is http://createartlisbon.com. Add three other contacts using the names and information of your friends. Create two contact groups called Part-Time and Full-Time. Add the contacts to the appropriate groups. Save the contact list, print the contacts in Card style, and submit the contact list in the format specified by your instructor.

Table 3–5 Art Team Contacts

Full Name	Email Address	Mobile Phone	Part/Full Time
Ben Cohen	ben@createart.com	555-8221	Full Time
Stan Connery	stan@createart.com	555-2877	Full Time
Nina Inwood	nina@createart.com	555-3846	Full Time
Reagan Jackson	reagan@createart.com	555-6667	Part Time
Aiko Kuro	aiko@createart.com	555-8745	Full Time
Rob Ruiz	rob@createart.com	555-9856	Part Time

Part 2: Should everyone in the company have access to all contact information, or should access to some information be restricted? What was the rationale behind each of these decisions and suggestions? Where did you obtain your information?

4 Creating and Managing Tasks with Outlook

Objectives

After completing this module, you will be able to:

- Create a new task
- Create a task with a status
- Create a task with a priority
- Create a task with a reminder
- Create a recurring task
- Categorize a task
- Configure Quick Clicks
- Categorize email messages
- Update a task
- Attach a file to a task
- Assign a task
- Forward a task
- Send a status report
- Print tasks
- Create a note
- Change the view of notes

Introduction to Outlook Tasks

Whether you are keeping track of the action items after a virtual meeting or working on your school assignments that are due next week, you can use Outlook tasks to manage your to-do list by generating a checklist and tracking activities. Instead of keeping a paper list of the things you need to do, you can use Outlook to combine your various tasks into one list, including reminders and tracking tools, which provides a sense of accomplishment. A **task** is an item that you create in Outlook to track until its completion. A **to-do item** is any Outlook item such as a task, an email message, or a contact that has been flagged for follow-up later.

Creating and managing tasks in Outlook allows you to keep track of projects, which might include work responsibilities, school assignments, or personal activities. Using a task, you can record information about a project such as start date, due date, status, priority, and percent complete. Outlook also can remind you about the task so that you do not forget to complete it. If you are managing a project, for example, you can create a plan and assign tasks to people so that everyone can complete their portion of the project.

Project: Managing Tasks

People and businesses create tasks to keep track of projects that are important to them or their organizations. Tasks can be categorized and monitored to ensure that all projects are completed in a timely fashion.

You can track one-time tasks as well as tasks that recur over a period of time. You also can prioritize tasks so that you can decide which ones must be completed first.

The project in this module follows general guidelines and uses Outlook to create the task list shown in Figure 4–1. The task list in the Willow mailbox for Module 4 includes tasks that are organized using class and internship categories.

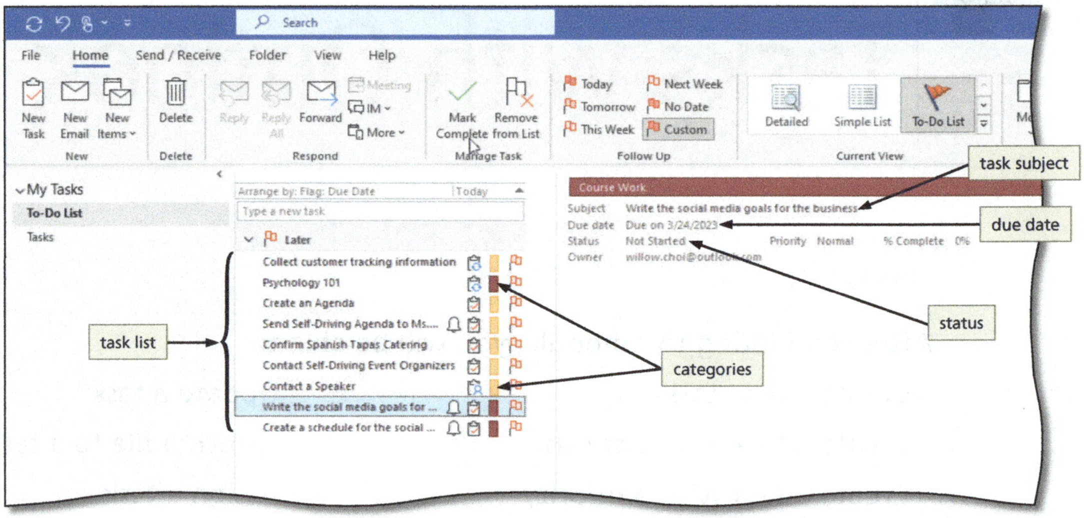

Figure 4–1

BTW

The Ribbon and Screen Resolution

Outlook may change how the groups and buttons within the groups appear on the ribbon, depending on the computer or mobile device's screen resolution. Thus, your ribbon may look different from the ones in this book if you are using a screen resolution other than 1366 × 768.

In this module, you will learn how to perform basic task management tasks. The following list identifies general activities you will perform as you progress through this module:

1. Create a new task.
2. Categorize a task.
3. Categorize an email message.
4. Assign a task.
5. Print a task.
6. Create and use notes.

Creating a Task

The first step in creating a task for your to-do list is to open the Tasks category in Outlook. After you create a list of tasks, you can sync your tasks across multiple devices such as your smartphone and laptop, staying up to date and improving your productivity.

CONSIDER THIS

What advantages does an Outlook task list provide beyond a basic to-do list?

Many business employees use an Outlook task list to detail their hours, business expenses, and mileage. Instead of jotting down how many hours you worked on Monday to report later, remembering the tolls paid on a business trip, or how many miles you must list on your expense report, you can store this information in a task. When it is time to turn in your work hours or expense report, you can easily retrieve the details from your task list.

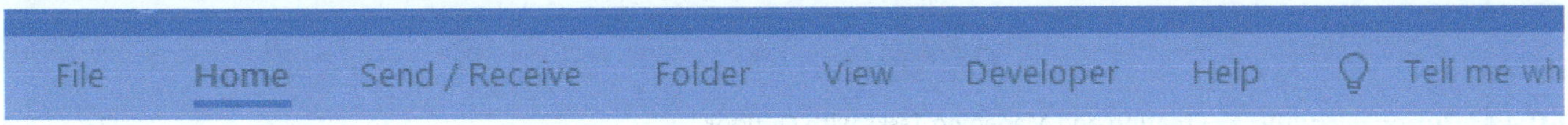

To-Do List Window

The To-Do List window shown in Figure 4–2 includes features to help you manage your tasks. The main elements of the To-Do List window are the Navigation pane, the To-Do List pane, and the Preview pane. The My Tasks folder in the Navigation pane displays the To-Do list link and Tasks folder. Clicking the To-Do list link displays the tasks in To-Do List view, and clicking Tasks displays the tasks in the task folder in Simple List view.

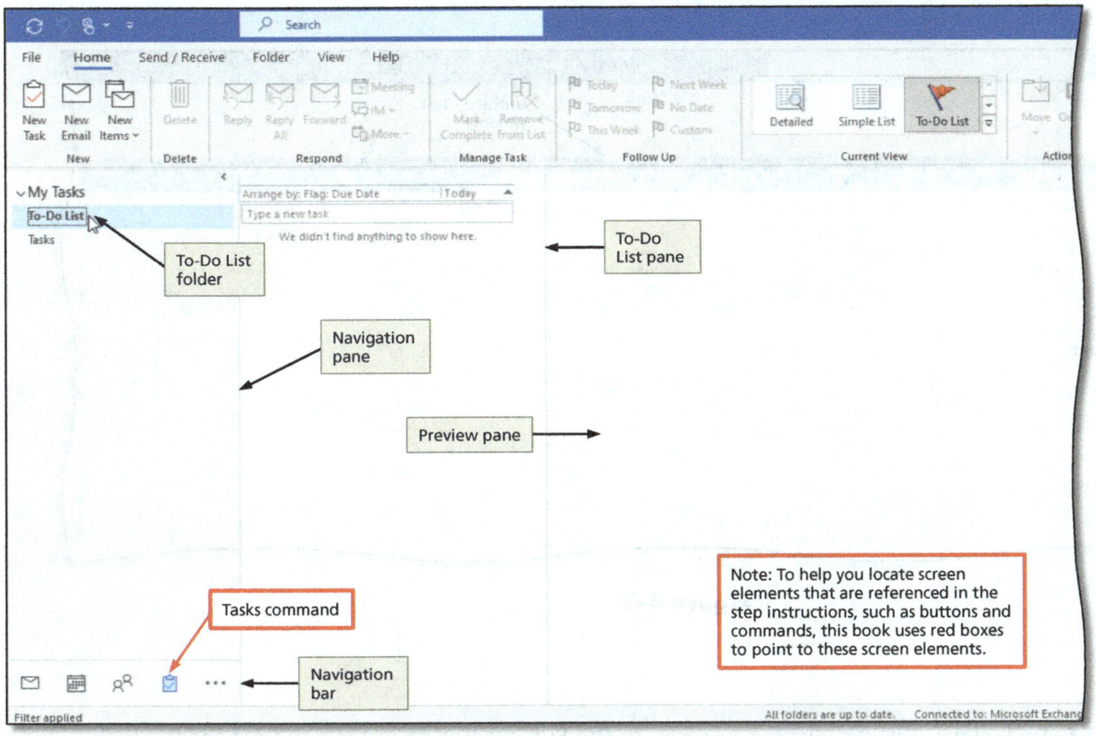

Figure 4–2

Creating a To-Do List

The first step in creating a To-Do list is to select a folder for storing your tasks. By default, Outlook stores tasks in the Tasks folder, but you also can create a personal folder in which to store your tasks, using the technique presented in Module 2. In this module, you will create tasks in the Tasks folder.

To Create a New Task

Willow Choi, an intern at Motion AI Self-Driving, wants to create a task list to keep track of her work events and her college classes. The first task is to invite the organizers of the Self-Driving Event to the rescheduled event at least a month before the meeting now scheduled on March 9 so that she does not forget to complete the task. The following steps create a new task. ***Why?*** *To stay organized, you should create Outlook tasks to make sure you complete all the items on your To-Do list.*

1

- Start Outlook.
- Open the SC_OUT_4-1.pst Outlook Data File from the Data Files for Module 4.
- Click Tasks (shown in Figure 4–2) on the Navigation bar to display the Outlook Tasks.
- Click the New Task button (Home tab | New group) to display the Untitled - Task window (Figure 4–3).

Q&A **Why is my screen different? My Untitled - Task window does not have the two buttons named Assign Task and Send Status Report in the Manage Task group as shown in Figure 4–3.**
If you do not have an email account connected to Outlook (covered in Module 1), you will not have these two buttons.

The New Task button does not appear on the Home tab. What should I do?
Click the New Items button (Home tab | New group), and then click Task. Now the New Task button should appear on the Home tab.

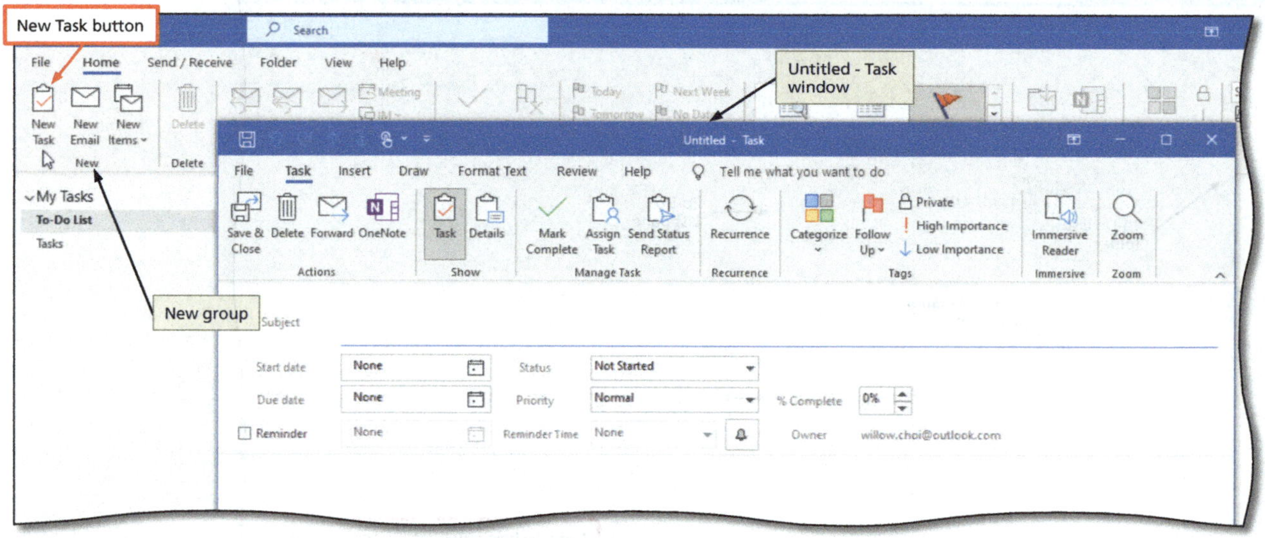

Figure 4–3

2

- Type **`Contact Self-Driving Event Organizers`** in the Subject box to enter a subject for the task.
- Type **`Event rescheduled for March 9`** in the task body area to enter a description for the task (Figure 4–4).

Q&A **Why did the title of the Task window change after I entered the subject?**
As soon as you enter the subject, Outlook updates the Task window title to reflect the information you entered. The task is not saved, however; only the window title is updated.

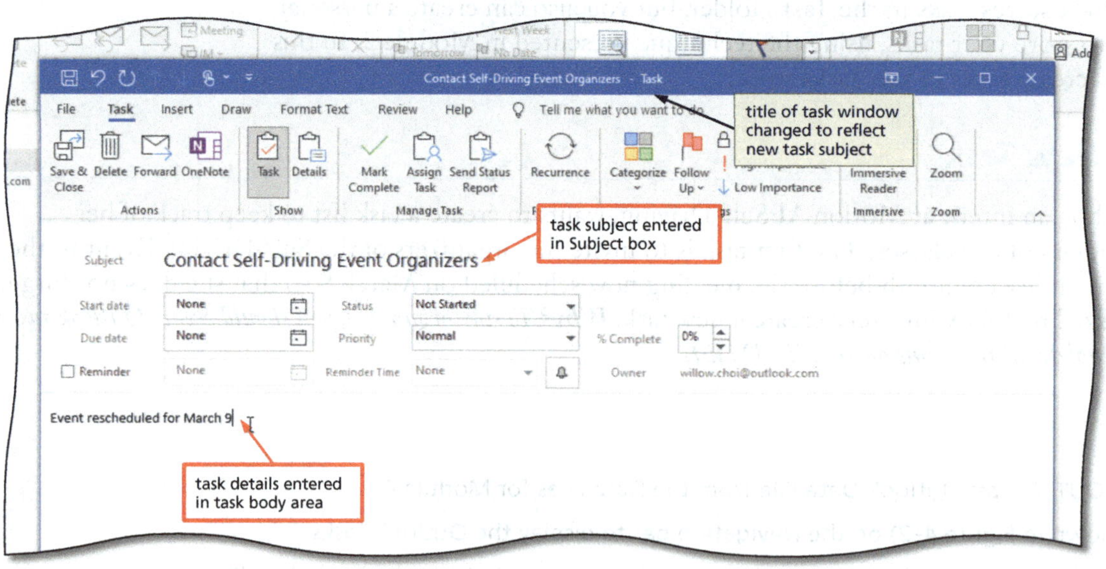

Figure 4–4

3

- Click the Start date Calendar button to display a calendar for the current month (Figure 4–5).

Q&A Why does my calendar display a different month?
Your calendar most likely shows the current month, which may be different from the one shown in the figure.

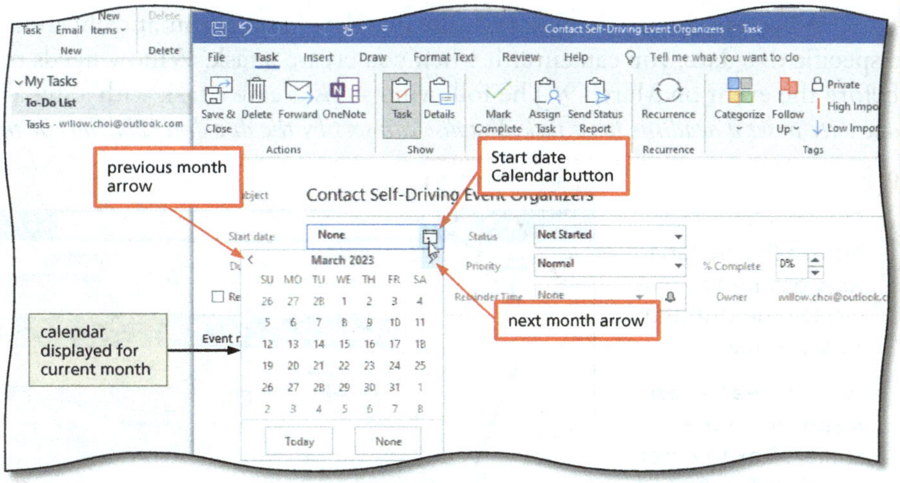

Figure 4–5

4

- If necessary, click the next month arrow or previous month arrow an appropriate number of times to display the calendar for March 2023.
- Click 9 to select Thu 3/9/2023 as the start date (Figure 4–6).

Q&A Why did the due date change?
If you enter a start date, the due date automatically changes to match the start date. You can change the due date if needed.

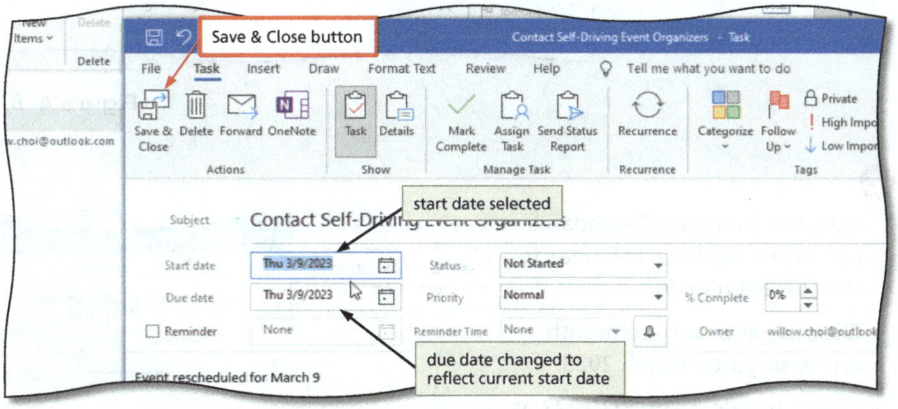

Figure 4–6

Can I just type the date?
Yes, you can type the date. Using the calendar allows you to avoid potential errors due to typing mistakes.

5

- Click the Save & Close button (Task tab | Actions group) (shown in Figure 4–6) to save the task and close the Task window (Figure 4–7).

Q&A My tasks are displayed in an arrangement different from the one in Figure 4–7. What should I do?
Click the Change View button or the More button (Home tab | Current View group), and then click To-Do List.

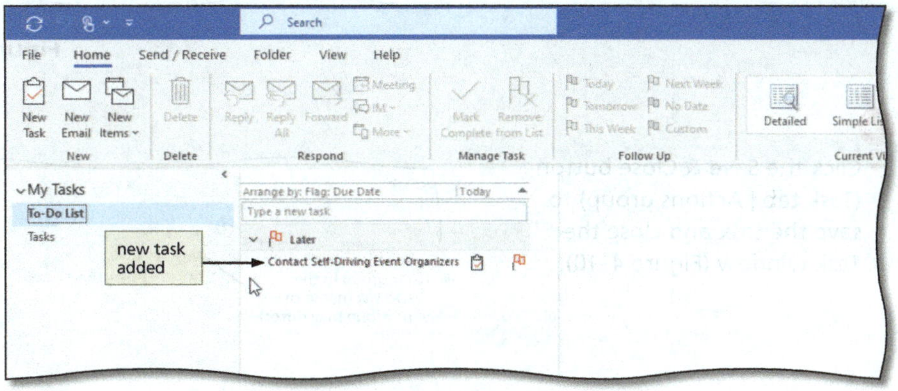

Figure 4–7

Other Ways

1. Press CTRL+N

To Create a Task with a Due Date

When you create the first task, the due date is set automatically after you enter the start date. If you have a specific due date, you can enter it when you create a task. Willow needs to create a meeting agenda the week before the event on March 9. The following steps create a task with a due date. ***Why?*** *You can quickly add a specific due date to set a deadline for a task. You also can sort by the due date, placing the most urgent tasks at the top of your list.*

1

- Click the New Task button (Home tab | New group) to display the Untitled - Task window.
- Type **`Create an Agenda`** in the Subject box to enter a subject for the task (Figure 4–8).

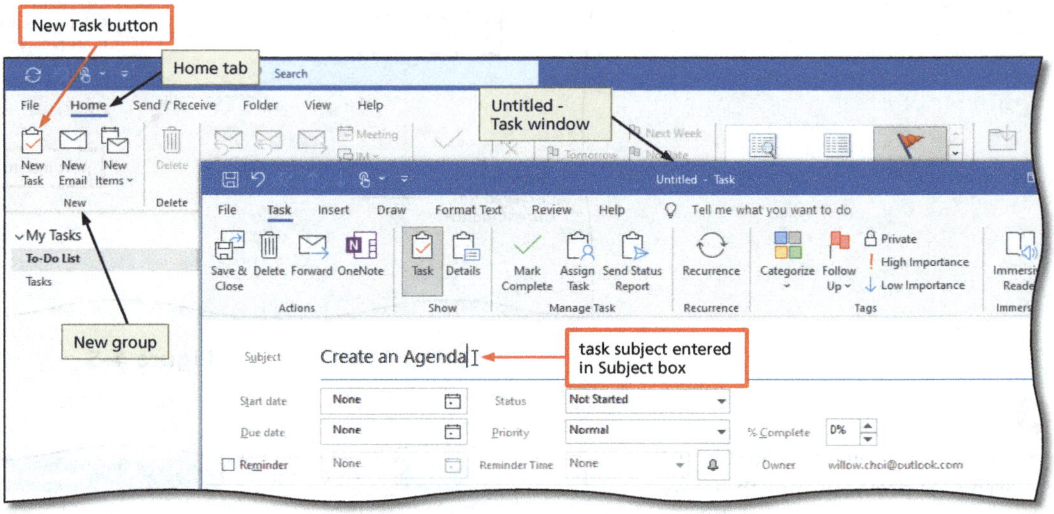

Figure 4–8

2

- Click the Due date Calendar button to display a calendar for the current month.
- Click the appropriate month arrow to go to March 2023.
- Click 2 to select Thu 3/2/2023 as the due date (Figure 4–9).

Q&A My Start date box contains today's date. What should I do?
Replace the date in the Start date box with the word None as shown in Figure 4–9.

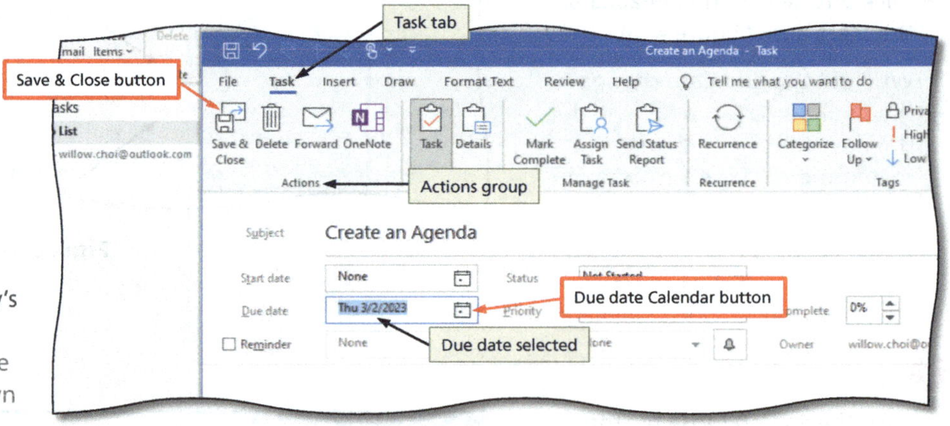

Figure 4–9

3

- Click the Save & Close button (Task tab | Actions group) to save the task and close the Task window (Figure 4–10).

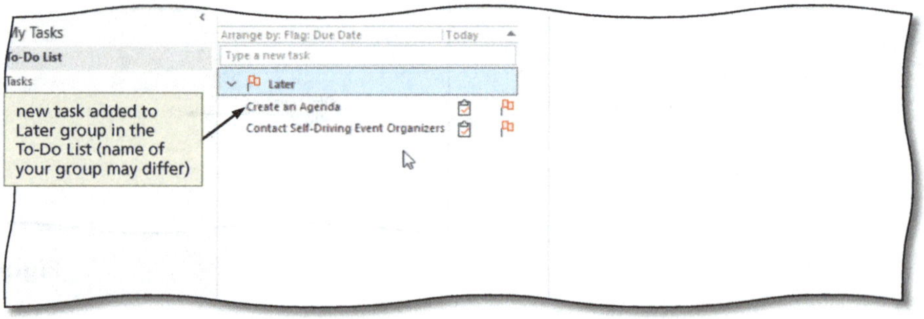

Figure 4–10

To Create a Task with a Status

You can assign a status to a task using any of five status indicators: Not Started, In Progress, Completed, Waiting on someone else, or Deferred. ***Why?*** *You can reflect your current progress by changing the status of a task.* Willow is planning to provide a speaker for the Future of AI event on March 8, 2023 and wants to create a task to remind herself to contact a speaker. She has already started working on a few speaker ideas, so the task status should be set to In Progress. The following steps create a task with a status.

1

- Click the New Task button (Home tab | New group) to display the Untitled - Task window.
- Type **Contact a Speaker** in the Subject box to enter a subject for the task.
- Type **Speaker needed for the Future of AI event** in the task body area to enter a description for the task.
- Click the Due date Calendar button to display a calendar for the current month.
- Click the appropriate month arrow to go to March 2023.
- Click 8 to select Wed 3/8/2023 as the due date (Figure 4–11).

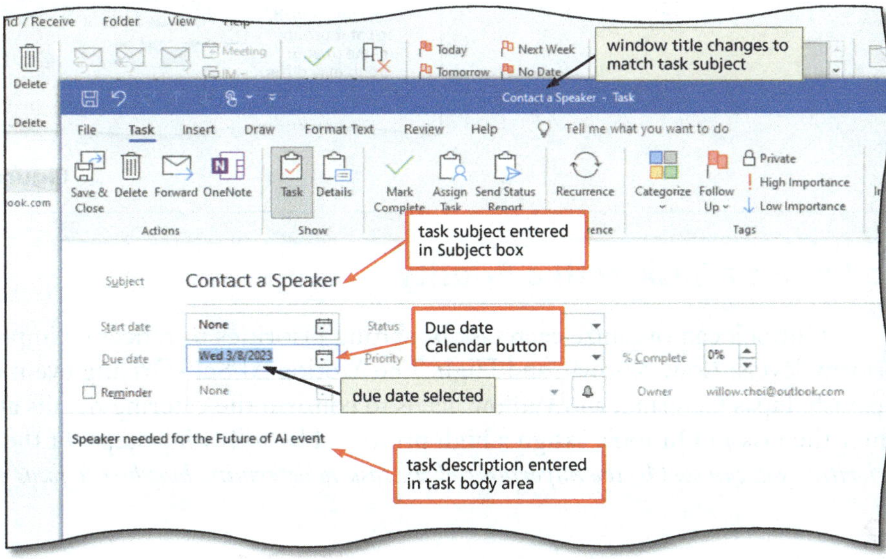

Figure 4–11

2

- Click the Status arrow to display the status options (Figure 4–12).

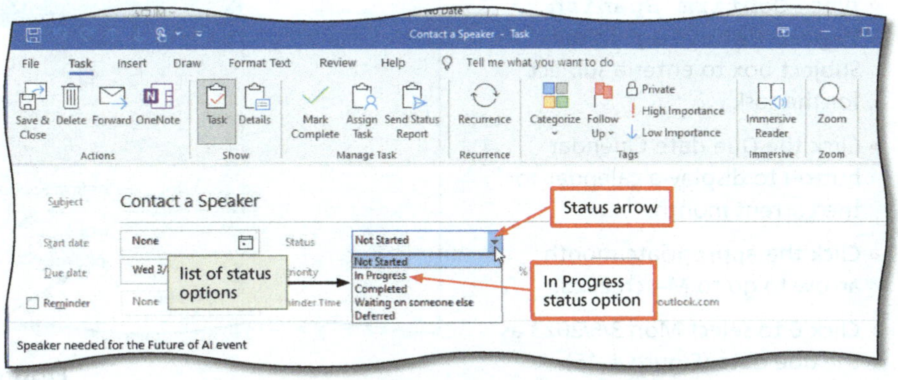

Figure 4–12

3

- Click In Progress to change the status of the task (Figure 4–13).

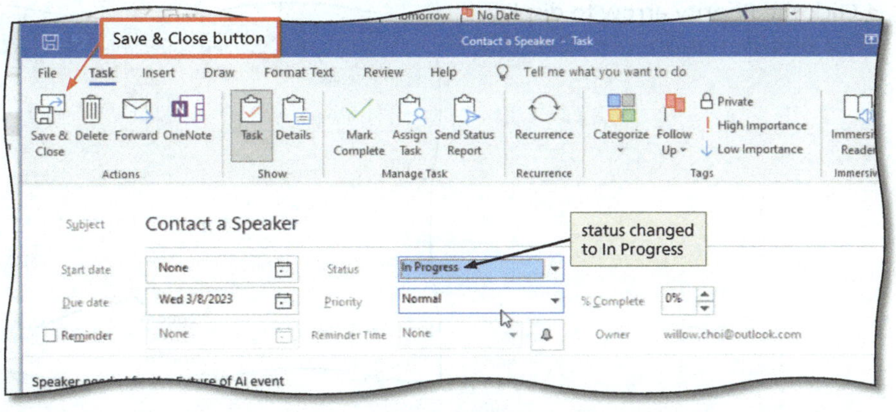

Figure 4–13

4

- Click the Save & Close button (Task tab | Actions group) to save the task and close the Task window (Figure 4–14).

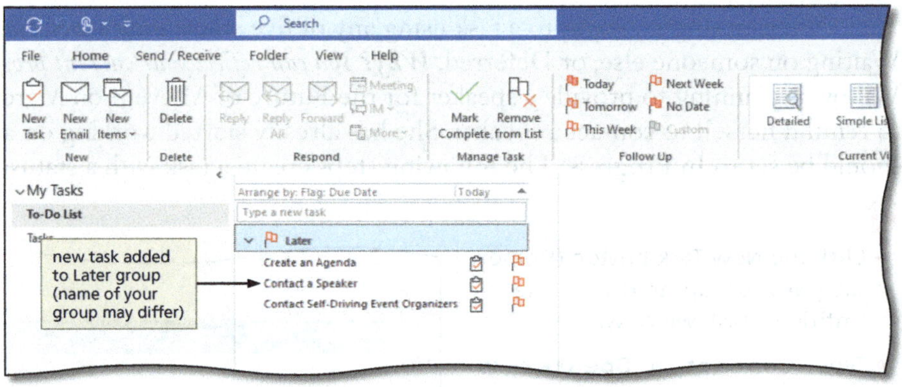

Figure 4–14

To Create a Task with a Priority

Outlook can organize each task by setting priorities to reflect its importance. Outlook allows for three priority levels: Low, Normal, and High. The Motion AI Self-Driving event on March 5 will be catered by Spanish Tapas Catering, and Willow needs to confirm the catering details at least three days in advance. As you enter the task in Outlook, assign a high priority. The following steps set the priority of a task. ***Why?*** *After setting priorities, you can sort by the importance of the task to determine how best to focus your time.*

1

- Click the New Task button (Home tab | New group) to display the Untitled - Task window.
- Type **`Confirm Spanish Tapas Catering`** in the Subject box to enter a subject for the task.
- Click the Due date Calendar button to display a calendar for the current month.
- Click the appropriate month arrow to go to March 2023.
- Click 6 to select Mon 3/6/2023 as the due date (Figure 4–15).

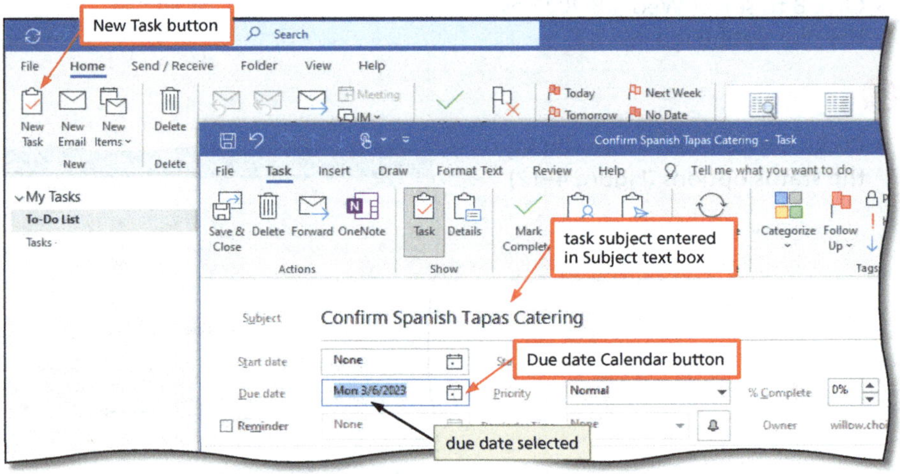

Figure 4–15

2

- Click the Priority arrow to display the priority options (Figure 4–16).

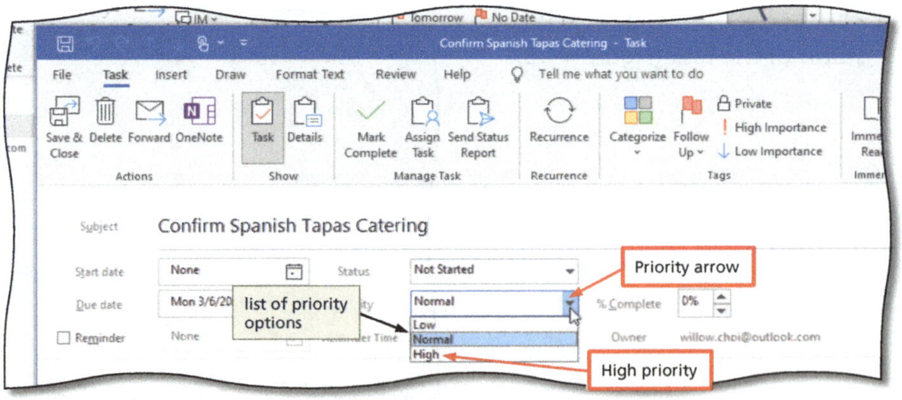

Figure 4–16

3

- Click High to set the priority (Figure 4–17).

4

- Click the Save & Close button (Task tab | Actions group) to save the task and close the Task window.

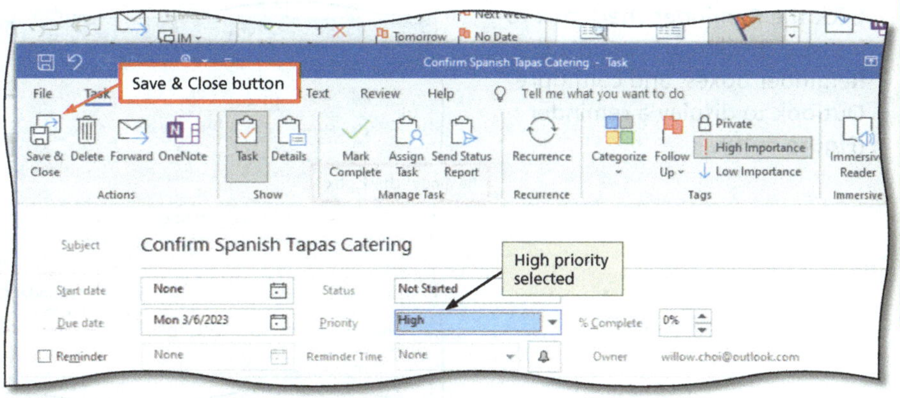

Figure 4–17

CONSIDER THIS

Can a project manager in a business team assign tasks in Outlook to keep track of what work the team has completed?

Outlook provides an easy way for project managers to assign tasks. For example, a manager might want to receive status reports and updates on the progress of a task. If the person assigned to a task rejects it, the manager can reassign the task to someone else and set a high priority for the task.

To Create a Task with a Reminder

To make sure you remember to complete a task, set a reminder before the task is due so you have enough time to complete the task. Ms. Bree Pauley, the marketing director of the Motion AI, asked Willow to send her the self-driving agenda the week before. Willow can create a task with a reminder to respond to Ms. Pauley's request. *Why? By adding a reminder to a task, Outlook can remind you about the task automatically.* The following steps add a task and set the reminder option for a week before the task is due.

1

- Click the New Task button (Home tab | New group) to display the Untitled - Task window.
- Type **`Send Self-Driving Agenda to Ms. Pauley`** in the Subject box to enter a subject for the task.
- Type **`Motion AI Self-Driving detailed agenda`** in the task body area to enter a description for the task.
- Click the Due date Calendar button to display a calendar for the current month.
- Click the appropriate month arrow to go to March 2023.
- Click 3 to select Fri 3/3/2023 as the due date (Figure 4–18).

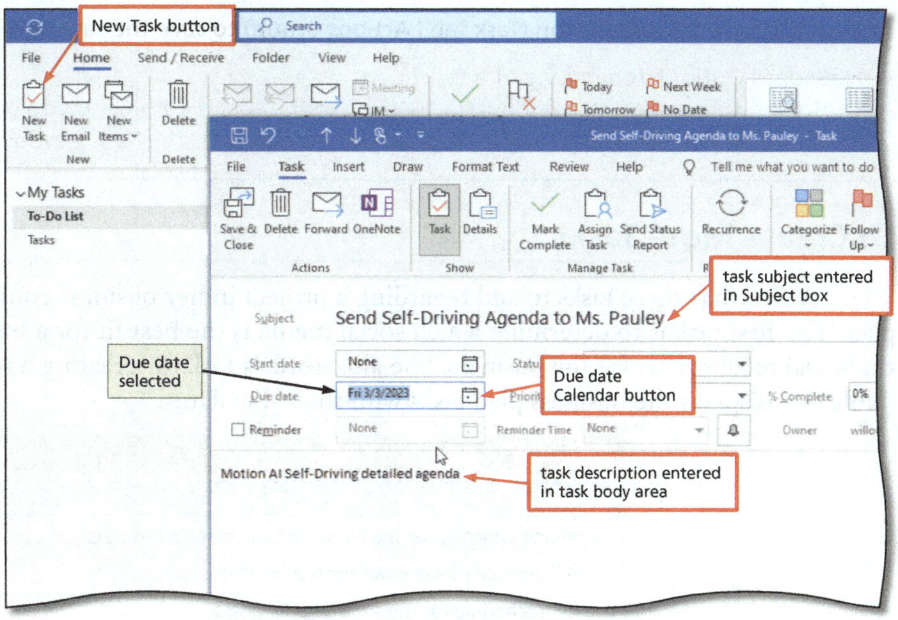

Figure 4–18

2

- Click the Reminder check box to insert a check mark, enable the Reminder boxes, and configure Outlook to display a reminder (Figure 4–19).

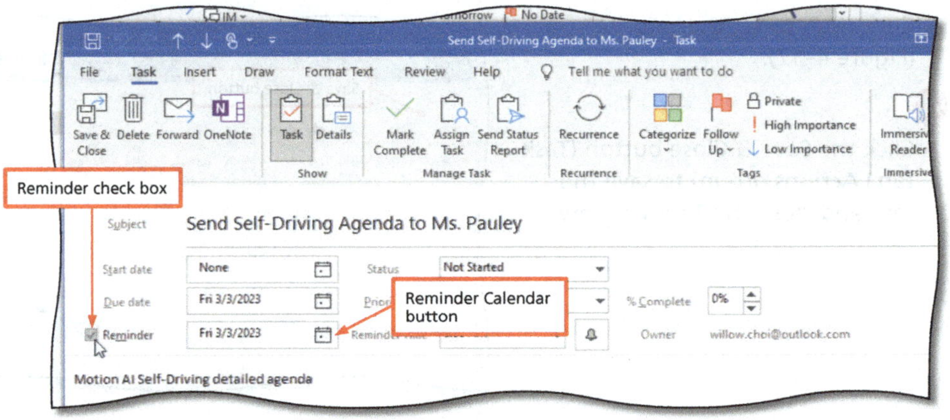

Figure 4–19

3

- Click the Reminder Calendar button to display a calendar for March.
- Click the appropriate month arrow to go to February 2023.
- Click 24 to select Fri 2/24/2023 as the Reminder date (Figure 4–20).

Q&A Can I change the time that Outlook displays the reminder?
Yes. When you set a reminder, Outlook automatically sets the time for the reminder to 8:00 AM. You can change the time by clicking the Reminder Time arrow and then selecting a time. You also can use the Outlook Options dialog box to change the default time.

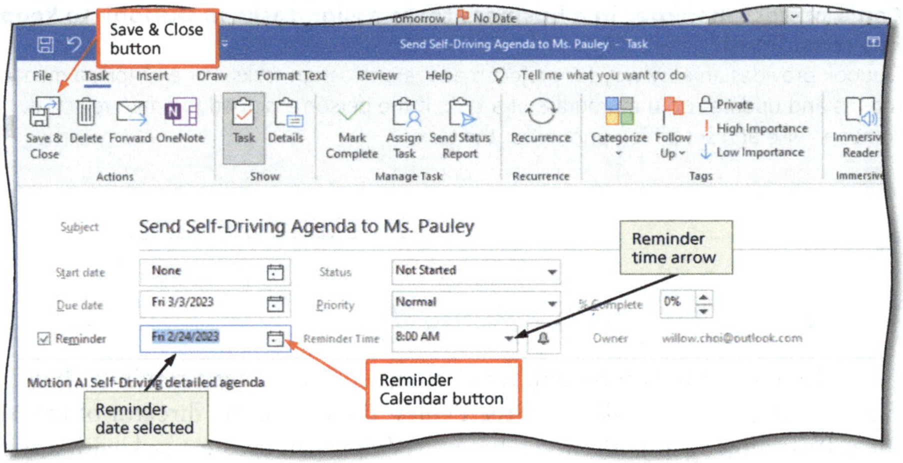

Figure 4–20

4

- Click the Save & Close button (Task tab | Actions group) to save the task and close the Task window.

Q&A How does Outlook remind me of a task?
Outlook displays the Task window for the task at the specified time. If you used the Sound icon to set an alarm for the reminder, Outlook also plays the sound when it displays the Task window.

To Create More Tasks

Willow has three tasks to add regarding a project in her business course to develop a new social media plan. The first task is to determine which social media is the best fit for a business. Another task is to write the social media goals for the business. She also needs a task for creating a schedule for the social media posts. Table 4–1 displays the business plan tasks with their due dates.

Table 4–1 Additional Tasks

Subject	Due Date
Determine which social media is the best fit for a business	3/17/2023
Write the social media goals for the business	3/24/2023
Create a schedule for the social media posts	3/31/2023

The following step creates the remaining tasks in the Task window. ***Why?*** *By adding academic tasks to your list, an item that requires attention will not be overlooked.*

1

- Click the New Task button (Home tab | New group) to display the Untitled - Task window.
- Enter the subject in the Subject box for the first task shown in Table 4–1.
- Click the Due date Calendar button to display a calendar for the current month, and then select the due date for the task shown in Table 4–1.
- Set a reminder for each task one day before the due date.
- Click the Save & Close button (Task tab | Actions group) to save the task and close the Task window.
- Repeat the actions in bullets 1 through 5 for the two remaining tasks in Table 4–1 (Figure 4–21).

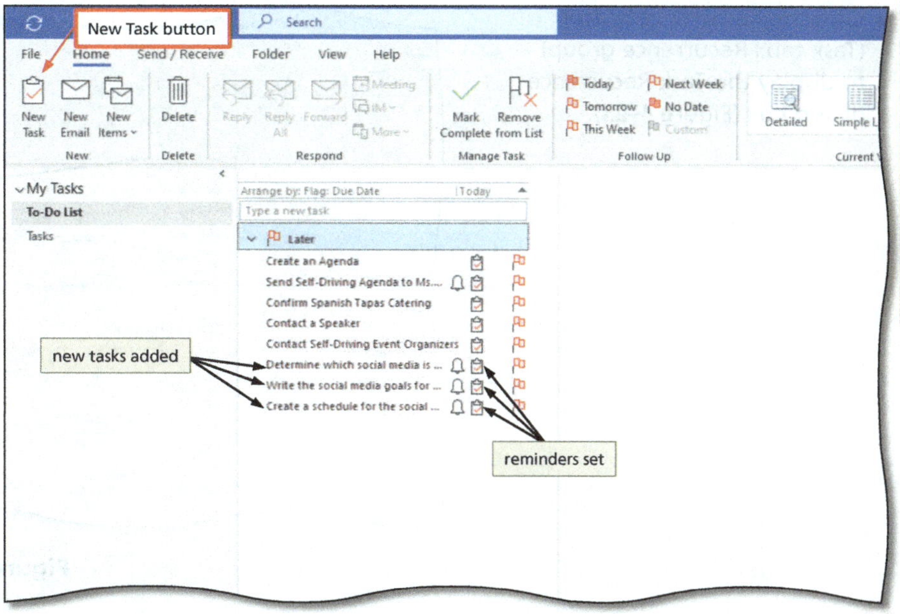

Figure 4–21

To Create a Recurring Task

When you create a task, you can specify it is a recurring task by selecting whether the task recurs daily, weekly, monthly, or yearly. For each of those options, you can provide specifics, such as the day of the month the task occurs. You can have the task recur indefinitely or you can specify the exact end date. Willow has a weekly assignment due in her Psychology 101 college course on Mondays from January 18 until May 10. The following steps add a recurring weekly task. ***Why?*** *When you have a task that occurs at regular intervals, you should set a recurring task to keep you informed.*

1

- Click the New Task button (Home tab | New group) to display the Untitled - Task window.
- Type `Psychology 101` in the Subject box to enter a subject for the task.
- Type `Submit assignment online` in the task body area to enter a description for the task.
- Click the Start date Calendar button to display a calendar for the current month.
- Click the appropriate month arrow to go to January 2023.
- Click 18 to select Wed 1/18/2023 as the start date (Figure 4–22).

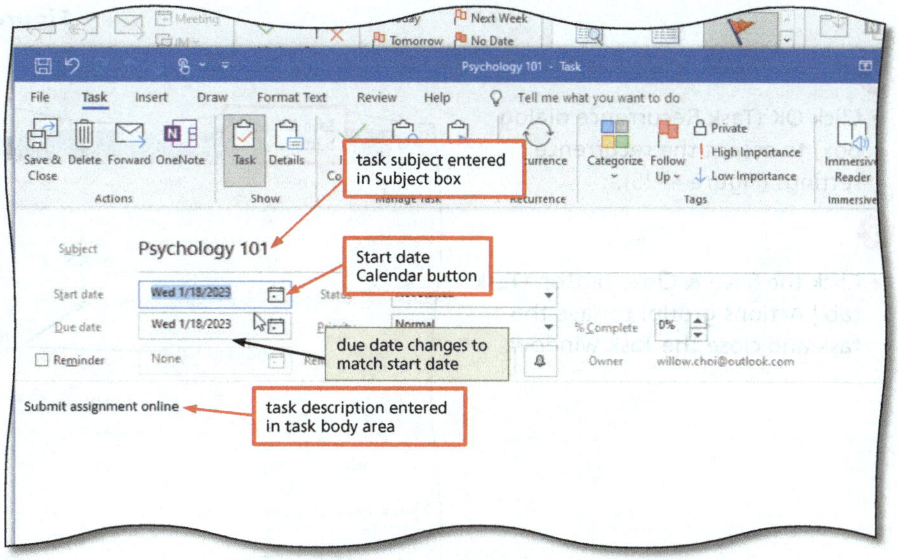

Figure 4–22

2

- Click the Recurrence button (Task tab | Recurrence group) to display the Task Recurrence dialog box (Figure 4–23).

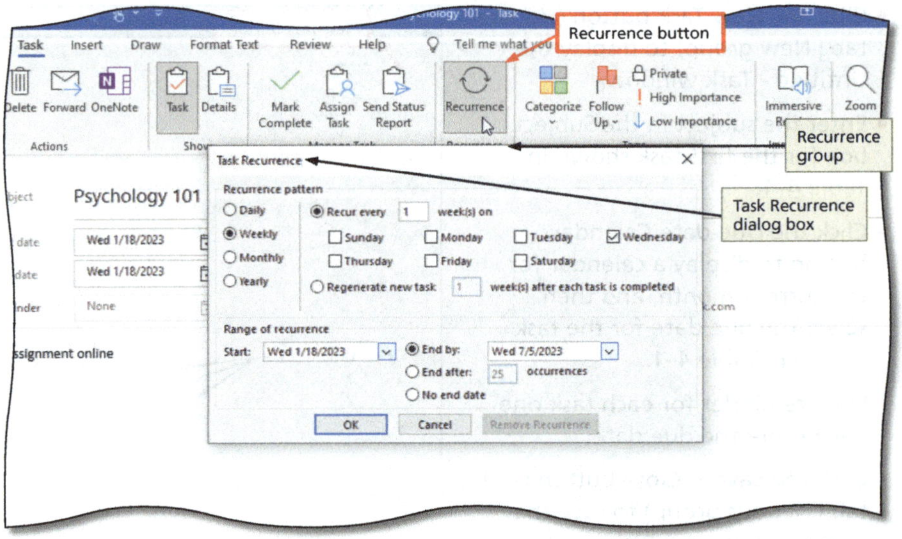

Figure 4–23

3

- If necessary, click the End by option button to select it.
- Click the End by arrow to display a calendar.
- If necessary, click the previous or next month arrow an appropriate number of times to go to May 2023.
- Click 10 to select Wed 5/10/2023 as the End by date (Figure 4–24).

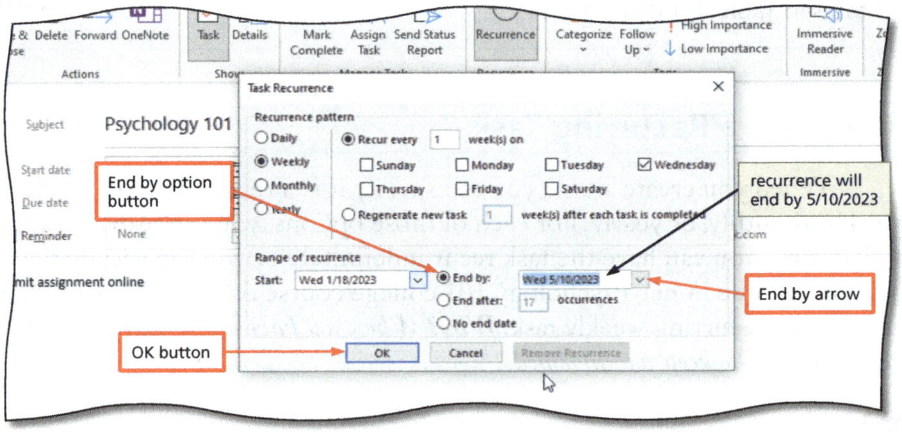

Figure 4–24

4

- Click OK (Task Recurrence dialog box) to accept the recurrence settings (Figure 4–25).

5

- Click the Save & Close button (Task tab | Actions group) to save the task and close the Task window.

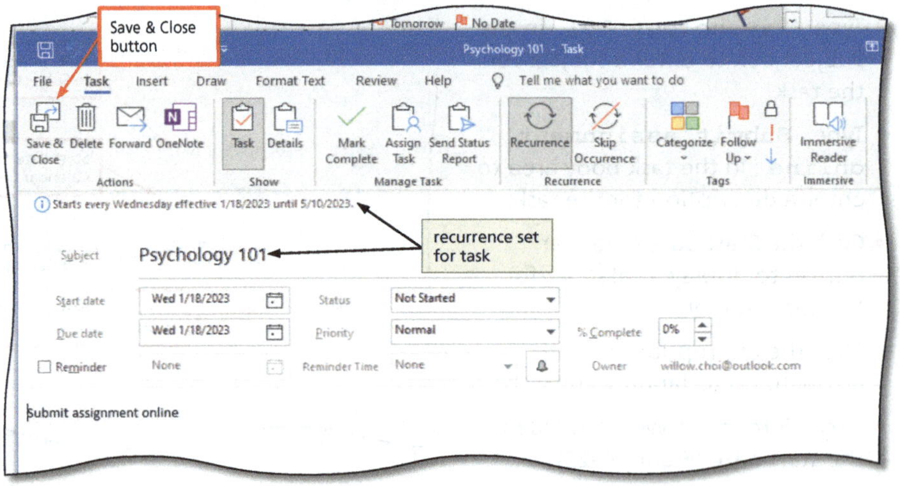

Figure 4–25

To Create Another Recurring Task

Willow also needs a recurring task for collecting the customer tracking information. The sales team will collect information from customers interested in buying an electric self-driving vehicle and send it to Willow every Friday from January 6 until May 19. The following step adds another recurring task. ***Why?*** *When you have a task that occurs at regular intervals, you should add it as a recurring task to keep you informed.*

1

- Click the New Task button (Home tab | New group) to display the Untitled - Task window.
- Type `Collect customer tracking information` in the Subject box to enter a subject for the task.
- Click the Start date Calendar button to display a calendar for the current month.
- Click the appropriate month arrow to go to January 2023.
- Click 6 to select Fri 1/6/2023 as the start date.
- Click the Recurrence button (Task tab | Recurrence group) to display the Task Recurrence dialog box.
- If necessary, click the End by option button to select it.
- Click the End by arrow to display a calendar.
- Click the appropriate month arrow to go to May 2023.
- Click 19 to select Fri 5/19/2023 as the End by date.
- Click OK to accept the recurrence settings.
- Click the Save & Close button (Task tab | Actions group) to save the task and close the Task window.
- Click the Collect customer tracking information task to view the task details (Figure 4–26).

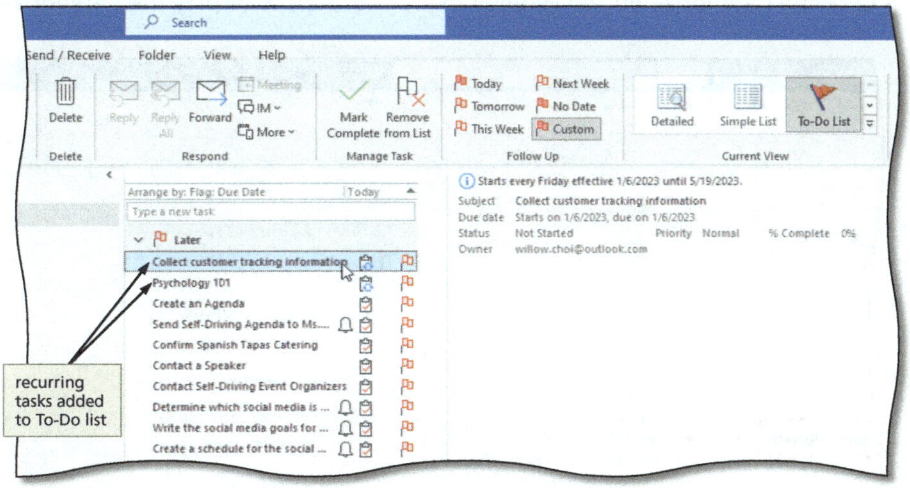

Figure 4–26

To Add a Task Using the To-Do List Pane

If you need to add a task quickly, you can use the To-Do List pane to create a quick task due the day you add it. If you wanted to add a task using the To-Do List pane, you would use the following steps.

1. Click the 'Type a new task' box to select the box.
2. Type a description to enter a description of the task.
3. Press ENTER to finish adding the task and display it in the To-Do list with the current date.

BTW
Task Options
You can modify options for tasks, such as changing the default reminder time for tasks with due dates, changing default colors for overdue and completed tasks, and setting the Quick Click flag. To access task options, open Backstage view, click Options, and then click Tasks.

Categorizing Tasks

Outlook allows you to categorize email messages, contacts, tasks, and calendar items so that you can identify which ones are related to each other and quickly identify the items by their color. Module 2 used color categories to organize calendar items. In the same way, you can use color categories to organize tasks.

Six color categories are available by default, but you also can create your own categories and select one of 25 colors to associate with them. After you create a category, you can set it as a **Quick Click** category, which is applied by default when you click an item's category column in the To-Do List pane. For example, the default Quick Click category is the red category. If you click a task's category column in the To-Do List pane, the red category automatically is assigned to it.

To Create a New Category

***Why?** Custom categories can organize tasks listed in Outlook.* The first category you want to create is the Motion AI category, which you can use for all tasks related to the activities with the self-driving event. When you select a task and then create the category, Outlook applies the category to the selected task. After you create a category, apply it to other tasks as necessary. The following steps create a category and apply it to a task.

1

- Click the `Contact Self-Driving Event Organizers` task to select it.
- Click the Categorize button (Home tab | Tags group) to display the Categorize menu (Figure 4–27).

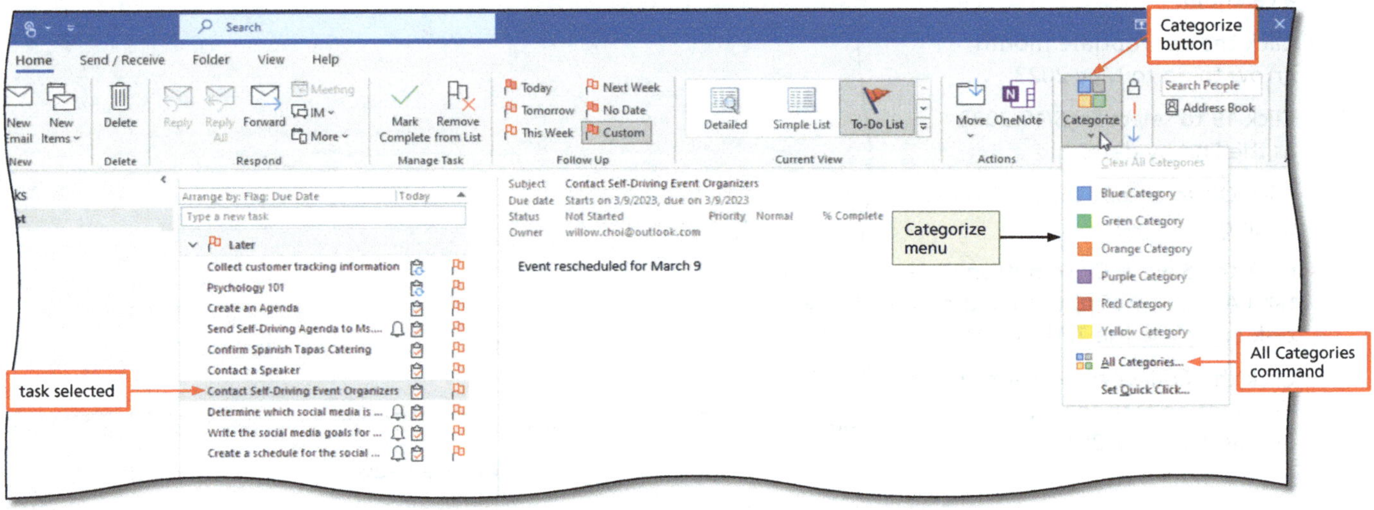

Figure 4–27

Q&A Why do I have to select the Contact Self-Driving Event Organizers task?
To activate the Categorize button, you first need to select a task or group of tasks.

2

- Click All Categories to display the Color Categories dialog box (Figure 4–28).

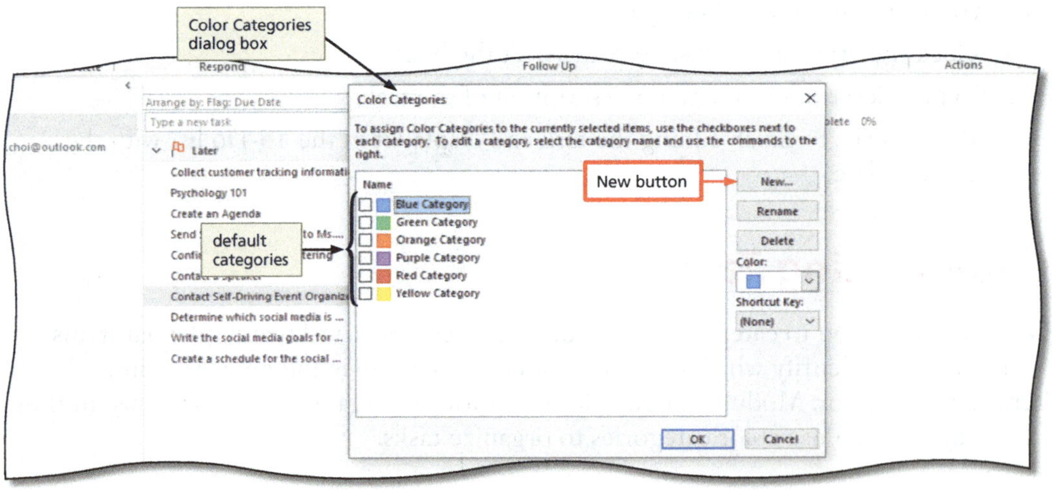

Figure 4–28

3

- Click New (Color Categories dialog box) to display the Add New Category dialog box (Figure 4–29).

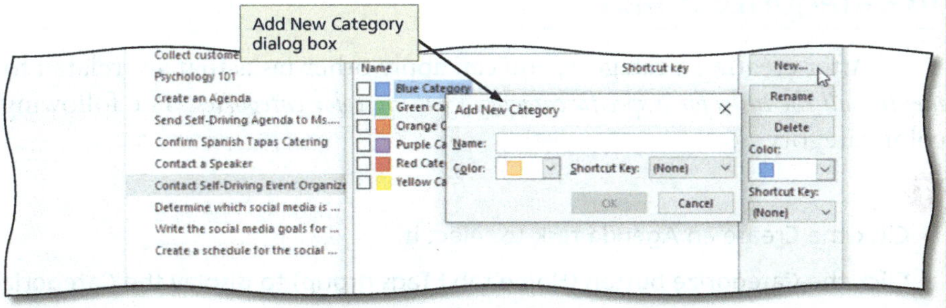

Figure 4–29

4

- Type **`Motion AI`** in the Name box to enter a name for the category.
- Click the Color arrow to display a list of colors.
- Click the Peach square (column 3, row 1) to select a category color.
- Click OK (Add New Category dialog box) to create the new category and display it in the Color Categories dialog box (Figure 4–30).

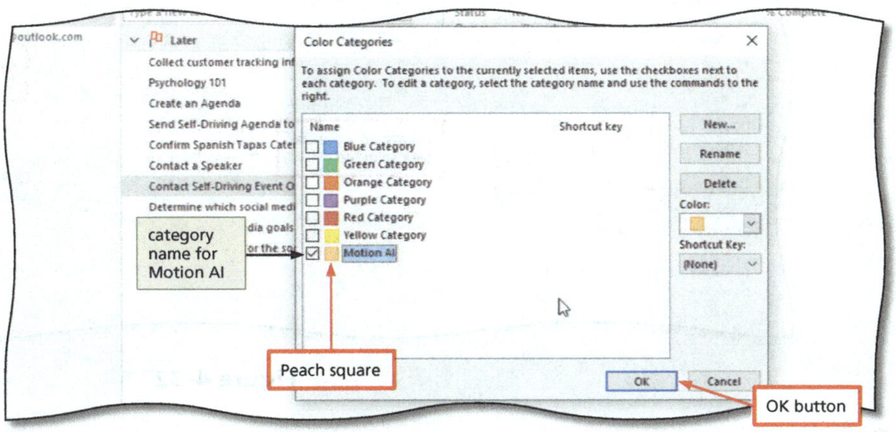

Figure 4–30

5

- Click OK (Color Categories dialog box) to assign the selected task to the new category (Figure 4–31).

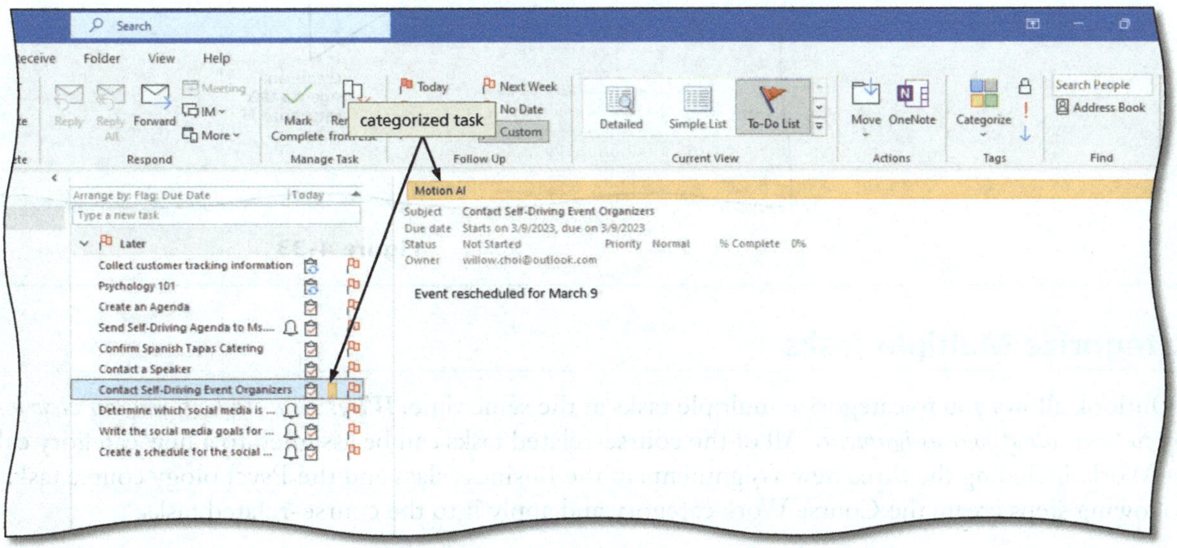

Figure 4–31

To Categorize a Task

After creating a category, you can apply other tasks that are related to that category. ***Why?*** *You can easily identify all the tasks for a specific category by using color categories.* The following steps assign a task to an existing color category.

1

- Click the Create an Agenda task to select it.
- Click the Categorize button (Home tab | Tags group) to display the Categorize menu (Figure 4–32).

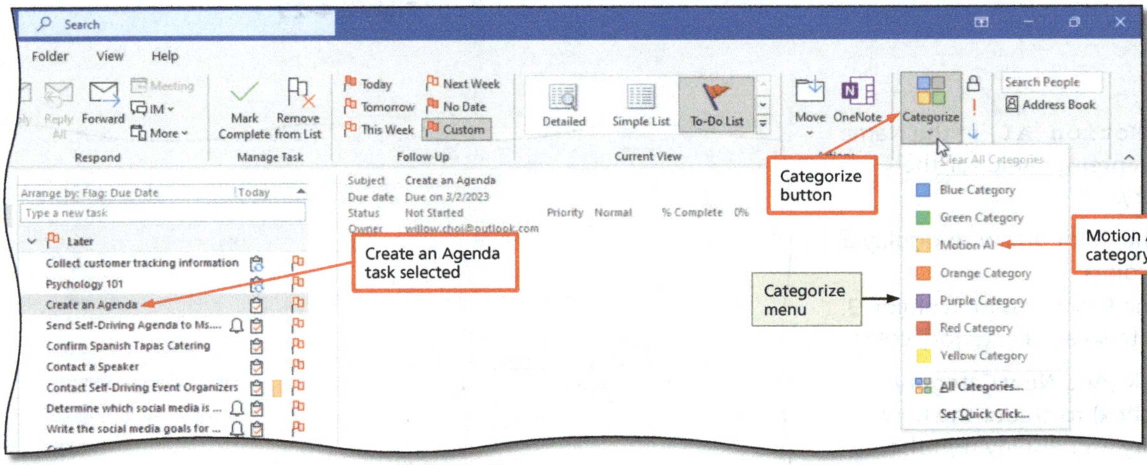

Figure 4–32

2

- Click Motion AI to assign the selected task to that category (Figure 4–33).

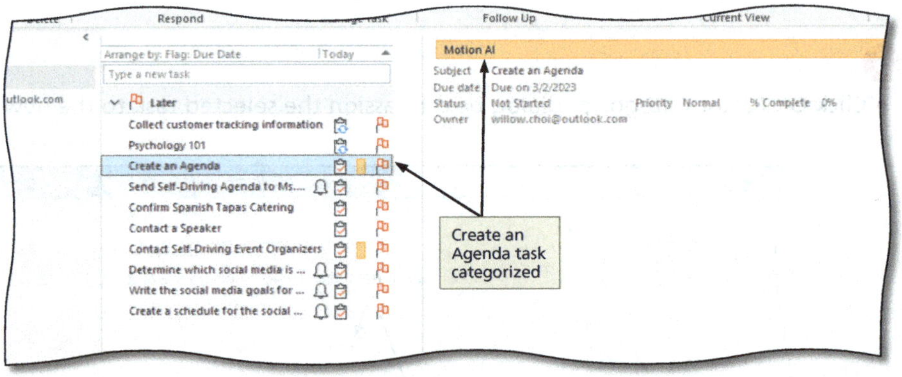

Figure 4–33

To Categorize Multiple Tasks

Outlook allows you to categorize multiple tasks at the same time. ***Why?*** *As a student, you can view a single category to locate all of your assignments.* All of the course-related tasks can be assigned to a new category called Course Work, including the three new assignments in the Business class and the Psychology course task. The following steps create the Course Work category and apply it to the course-related tasks.

1

- Select the Psychology 101, Determine which social media is the best fit for a business, Write the social media goals for the business, and Create a schedule for the social media posts tasks.

- Click the Categorize button (Home tab | Tags group) to display the Categorize menu (Figure 4–34).

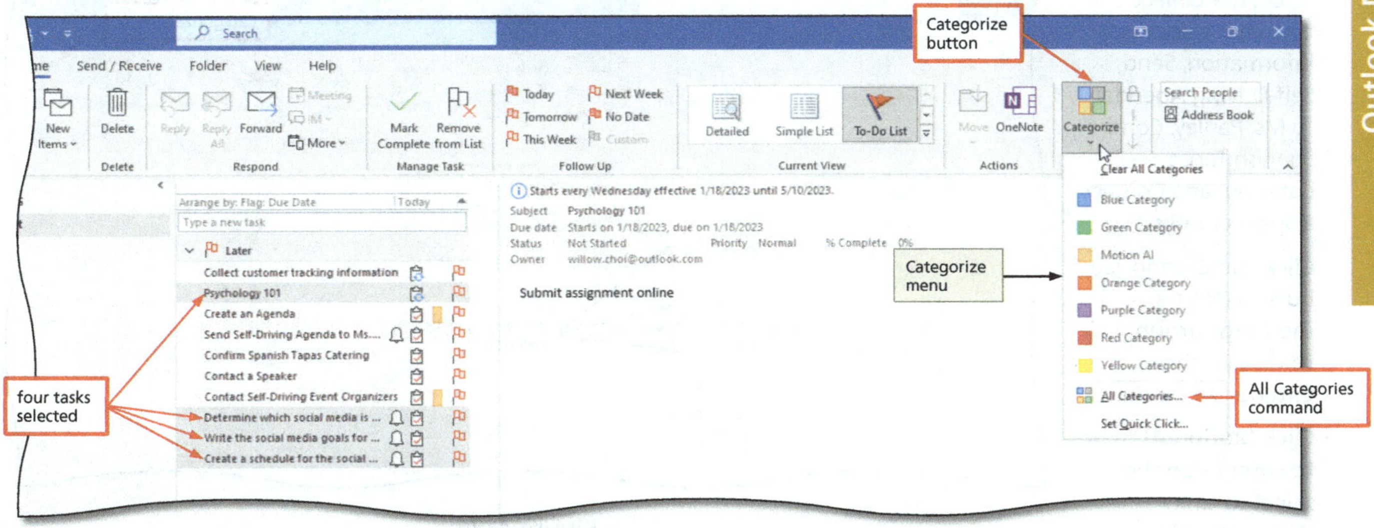

Figure 4–34

Q&A How do I select more than one task?
Click the first task, press and hold CTRL, and then click the other tasks to select them.

2

- Click All Categories to display the Color Categories dialog box.
- Click New (Color Categories dialog box) to display the Add New Category dialog box.
- Type **Course Work** in the Name box to enter a name for the category.
- Click the Color arrow to display a list of colors.
- Click the Dark Red square (column 1, row 4) to select the category color.
- Click OK (Add New Category dialog box) to create the new category.
- Click OK (Color Categories dialog box) to assign the selected tasks to a category (Figure 4–35).

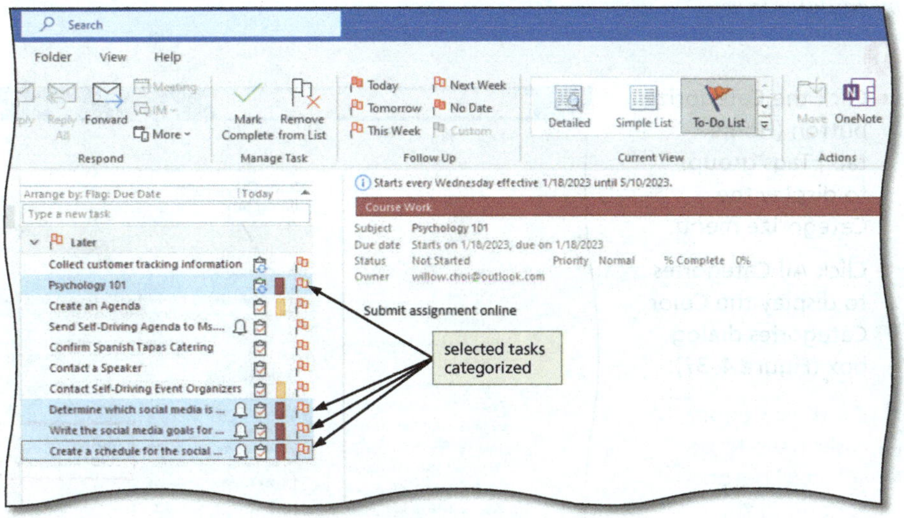

Figure 4–35

To Categorize Remaining Tasks

The following step categorizes the remaining tasks. ***Why?*** *When you sort by category, you will be able to view at a glance which tasks need completion in each facet of your life.*

1

- Select the Collect customer tracking information, Send Self-Driving Agenda to Ms. Pauley, Confirm Spanish Tapas Catering, and Contact a Speaker tasks.
- Click the Categorize button (Home tab | Tags group) to display the Categorize menu.
- Click Motion AI to categorize the selected tasks (Figure 4–36).

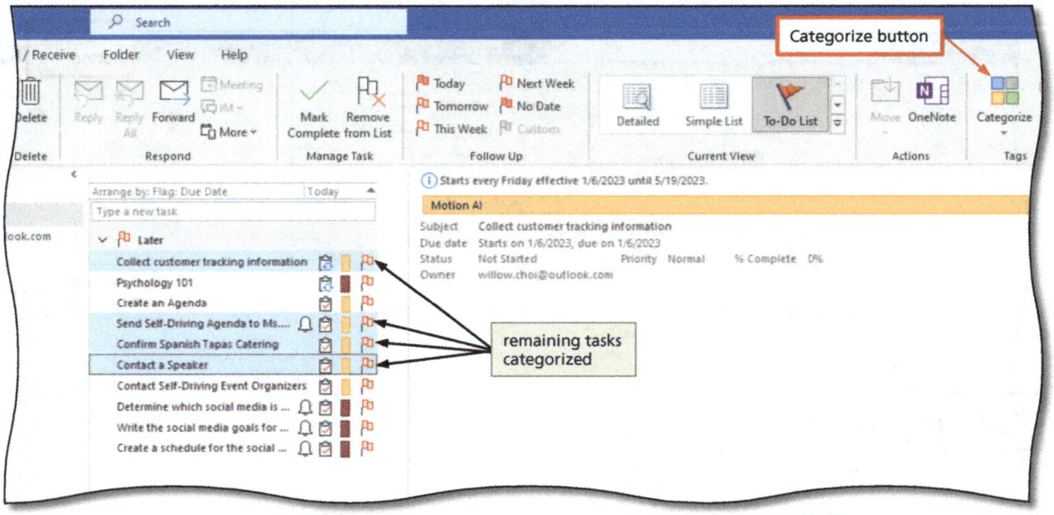

Figure 4–36

To Rename a Category

Willow decides to change the name of the Motion AI category to the Motion AI Self-Driving category. The following steps rename a color category. ***Why?*** *By renaming the color categories, you can assign names that are meaningful to you.*

1

- Click the Categorize button (Home tab | Tags group) to display the Categorize menu.
- Click All Categories to display the Color Categories dialog box (Figure 4–37).

Q&A Do the category tasks have to be selected before renaming the category?
No, any task can be selected. When you change the name, Outlook updates every task in that category.

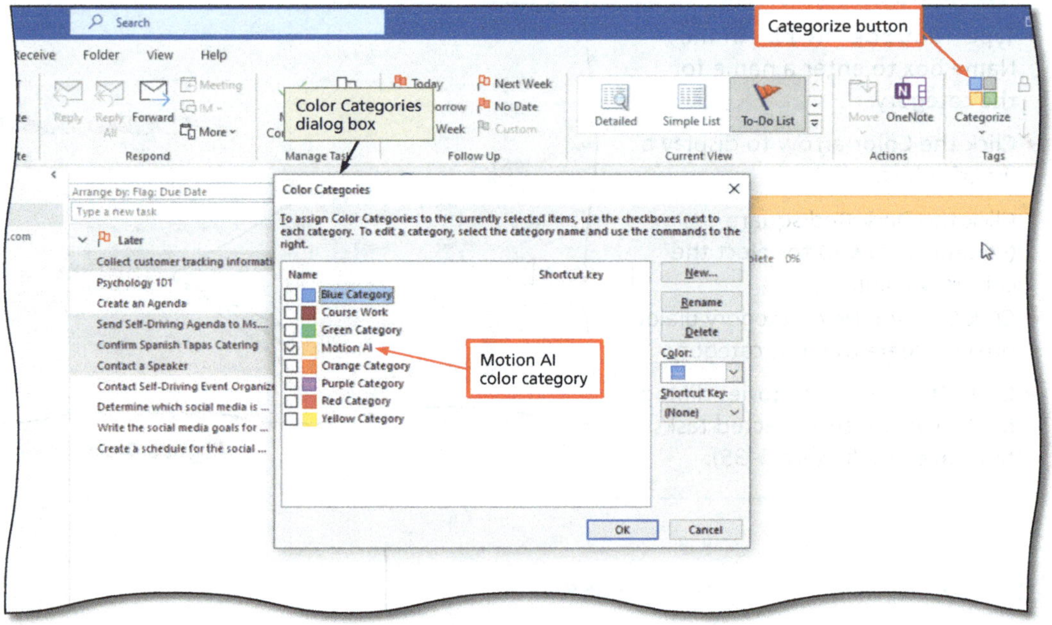

Figure 4–37

2

- Click the Motion AI category to select it.
- Click Rename (Color Categories dialog box) to select the category name for editing.
- Type `Motion AI Self-Driving` and then press ENTER to change the category name (Figure 4–38).

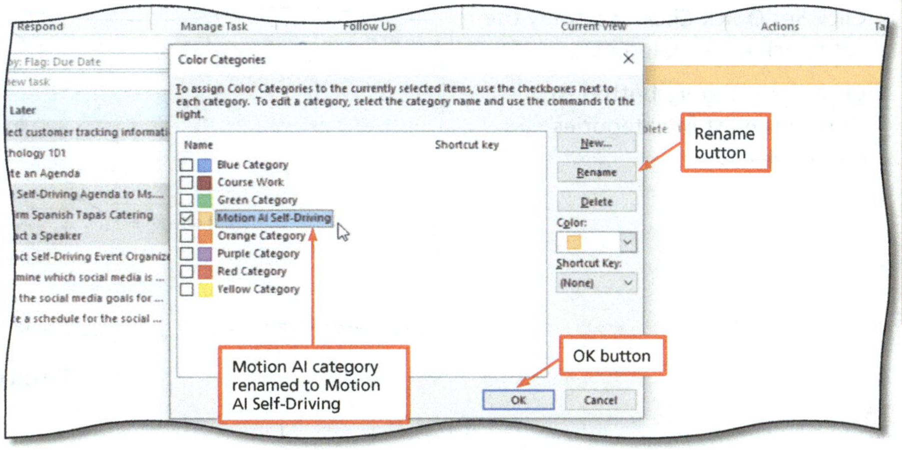

Figure 4–38

3

- Click OK (Color Categories dialog box) to apply the changes (Figure 4–39).

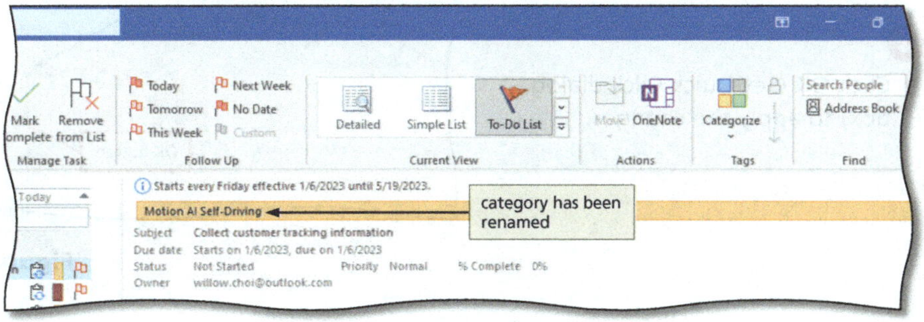

Figure 4–39

To Set a Quick Click

Instead of categorizing tasks using the Categorize menu options, you can assign a task to a category by clicking the category box for a task in the To-Do List pane. If you click the category box, the default category is applied. You can change the default category by setting one as a Quick Click. ***Why?** You can assign a frequently used color category (Quick Click category) by selecting it as your default color category.* Willow realizes that most of her tasks are related to the Motion AI Self-Driving, so she decides to set the default category as the Motion AI Self-Driving category. The following steps assign the default category using a Quick Click.

1

- Click the Categorize button (Home tab | Tags group) to display the Categorize menu (Figure 4–40).

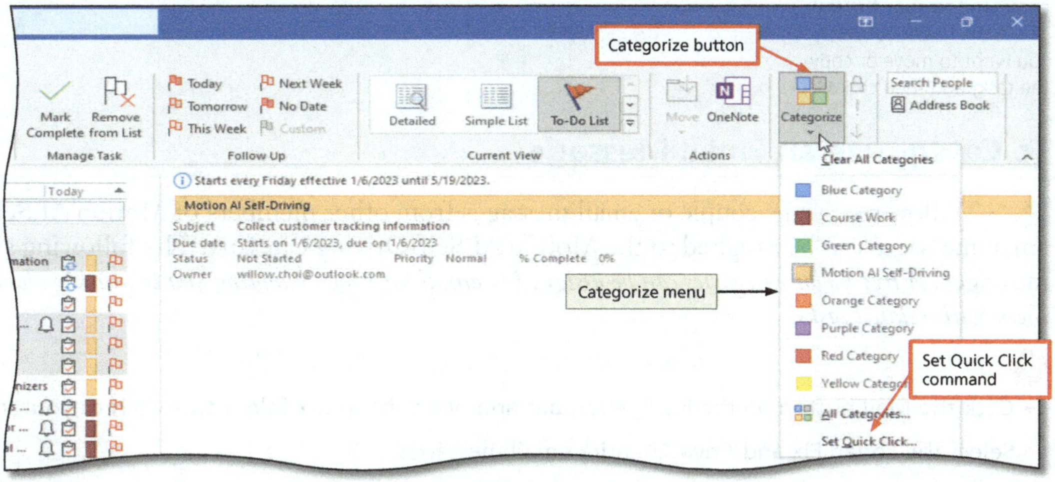

Figure 4–40

2

- Click Set Quick Click to display the Set Quick Click dialog box.
- Click the category button to display the list of categories (Figure 4–41).

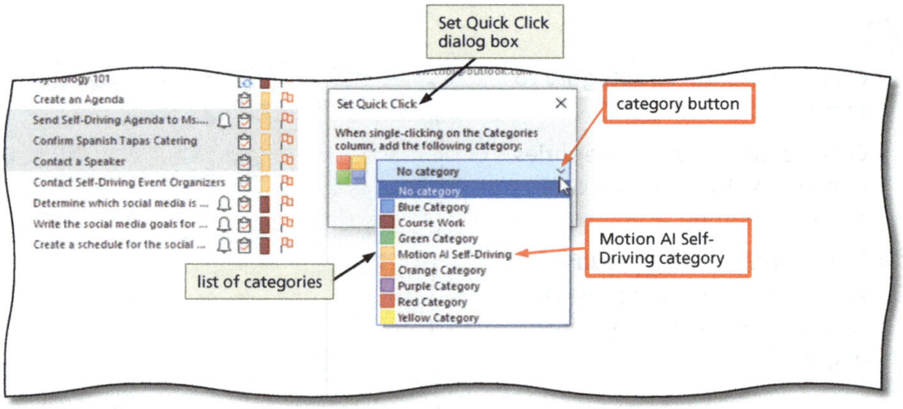

Figure 4–41

3

- Click Motion AI Self-Driving to set it as the Quick Click category (Figure 4–42).

4

- Click OK (Set Quick Click dialog box) to apply the changes.

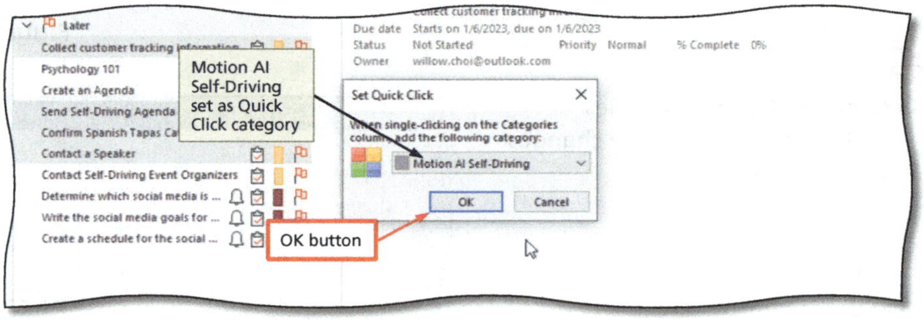

Figure 4–42

Break Point: If you want to take a break, this is a good place to do so. To resume at a later time, continue to follow the steps from this location forward.

BTW
Copying and Moving Tasks
To move or copy a task to another folder, select the task, and then click the Move button (Home tab | Actions group). Click the Other Folder command to move the task; click the Copy to Folder command to copy the task. Select the folder to which you want to move or copy the task, and then click OK.

Categorizing Email Messages

Recall that you can use categories with email messages, contacts, tasks, and calendar items. Any category you create for a task can be used for your email messages. Categorizing your email messages allows you to create a link between them and other related items in Outlook. By looking at the category, you quickly can tell which Outlook items go together.

To Categorize an Email Message

Willow received a couple of email messages from other members of Motion AI Self-Driving. These email messages can be assigned to the Motion AI Self-Driving category. The following steps categorize email messages. ***Why?*** *Color categories can be assigned to email messages, enabling you to quickly identify them and associate them with related tasks.*

1

- Click the Mail button on the Navigation bar and open the Inbox folder to switch to your Inbox.
- Select the Logan Fix and Anya Chandra email messages.

- Click the Categorize button (Home tab | Tags group) to display the Categorize menu (Figure 4–43).

Q&A What should I do if my Inbox email messages are not displayed?
Expand the Inbox folder in the Navigation pane to view the messages.

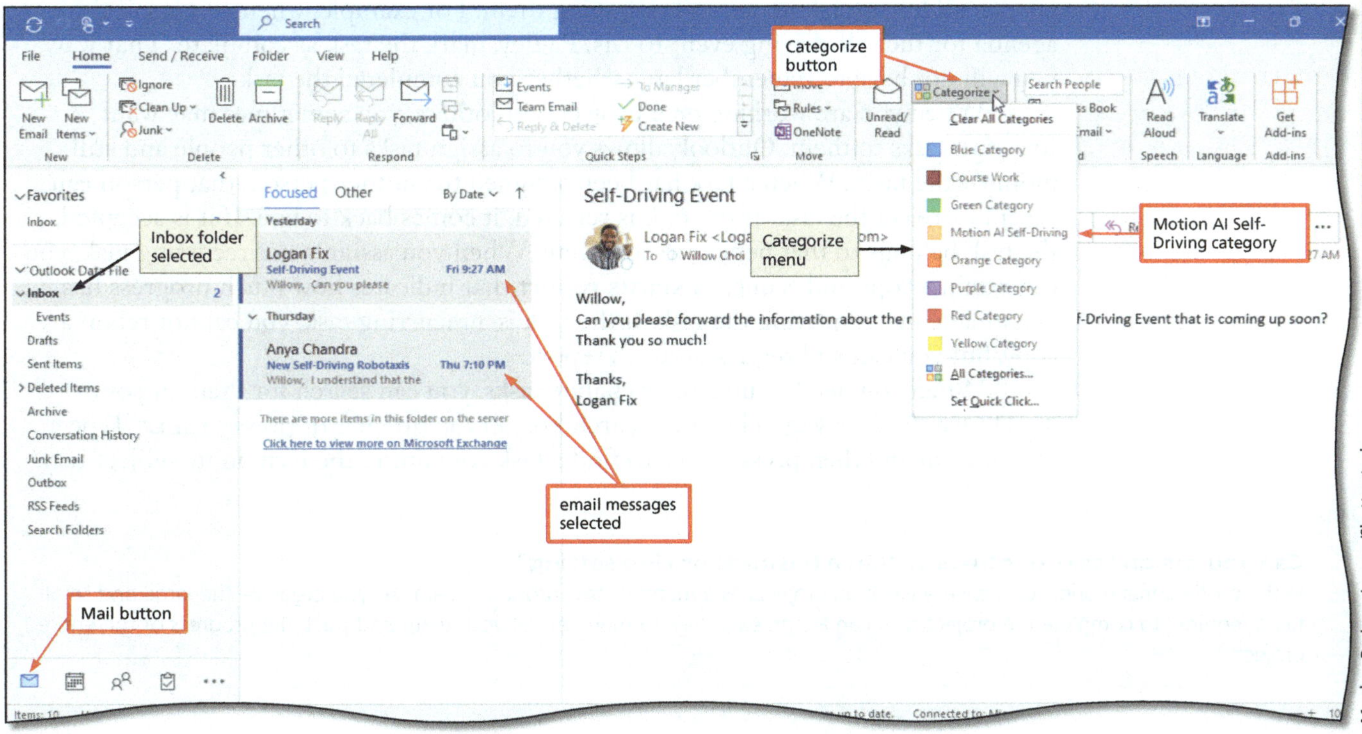

Monkey Business Images/Shutterstock.com

Figure 4–43

2

- Click Motion AI Self-Driving to assign the selected email messages to the Motion AI Self-Driving category (Figure 4–44).

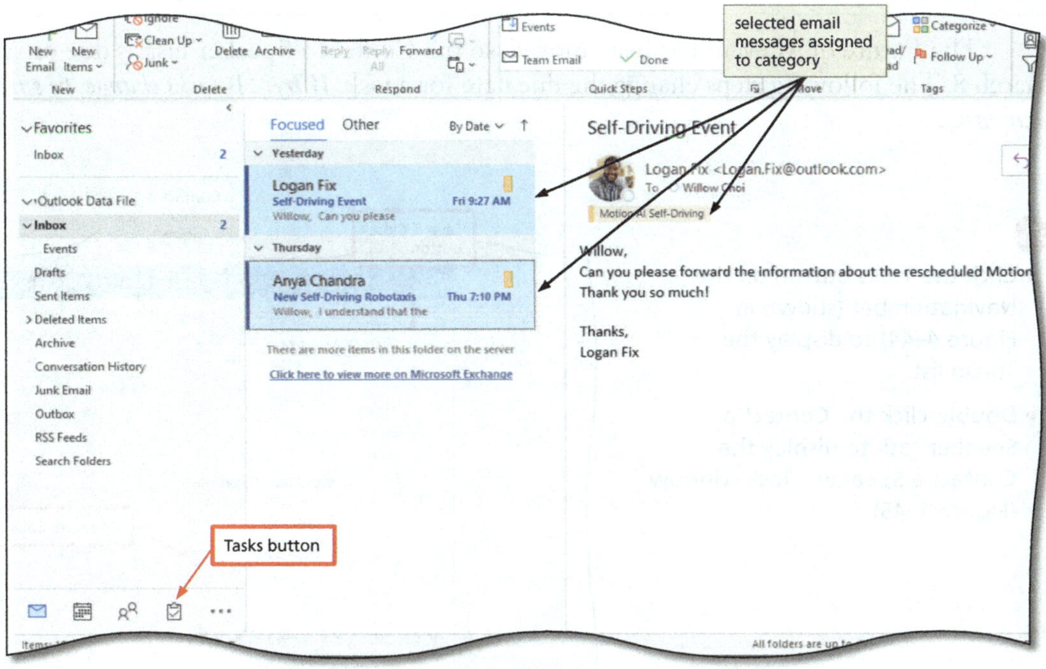

Monkey Business Images/Shutterstock.com

Figure 4–44

Managing Tasks

After creating one or more tasks in your To-Do list, you can manage them by marking tasks complete when you finish them, updating the tasks, assigning some to other people, adding attachments, and removing them. For example, when you email the agenda for the self-driving event to Ms. Pauley, mark the task as complete. That way, you will not have to remember later whether you completed the task.

When you are working on a project with others, you sometimes may want to assign tasks to them. Outlook allows you to assign tasks to other people and still monitor the tasks. When a task has been assigned to another person, that person can accept or reject the task. If the task is rejected, it comes back to you. If it is accepted, the task belongs to that person to complete. When you assign a nonrecurring task, you can retain a copy and request a **status report** that indicates how much progress has been made in completing the task. If the task is a recurring task, you cannot retain a copy, but you can still request a status report.

When you need to update or change tasks, you can search for them in your To-Do list. In Task view, click the Search box on the title bar or press CTRL+E. Type a search term and then press ENTER to find a task containing the term in its subject text.

CONSIDER THIS

Can you assign tasks to others within a business or club setting?

In the professional world, you typically work on projects as a member of a group or team. As you organize the large and small tasks required to complete the project, you can assign each task to members of your team and track the progress of the entire project.

To Update a Task

The Future of AI event has been moved, so the Contact a Speaker task is due on March 10 instead of March 8. The following steps change the due date for a task. ***Why?*** *As tasks change, be sure to update the due dates of your tasks.*

1

- Click the Tasks button on the Navigation bar (shown in Figure 4–44) to display the To-Do list.
- Double-click the Contact a Speaker task to display the Contact a Speaker - Task window (Figure 4–45).

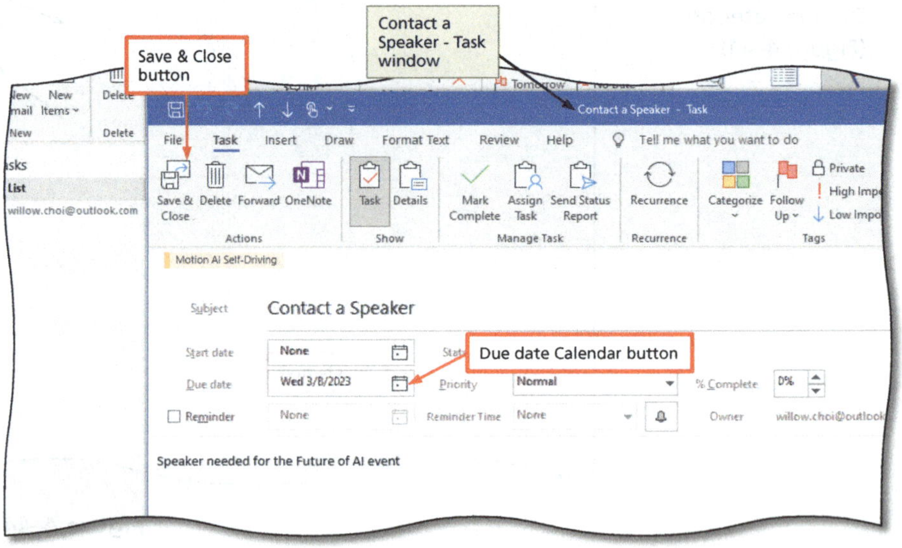

Figure 4–45

2

- Click the Due date Calendar button to display a calendar for March.
- Click 10 to select Fri 3/10/2023 as the due date.
- Click the Save & Close button (Task tab | Actions group) to save the changes (Figure 4–46).

Q&A How do I change the task name only?

Click the task name in the task list to select it, and then click it again to edit the name.

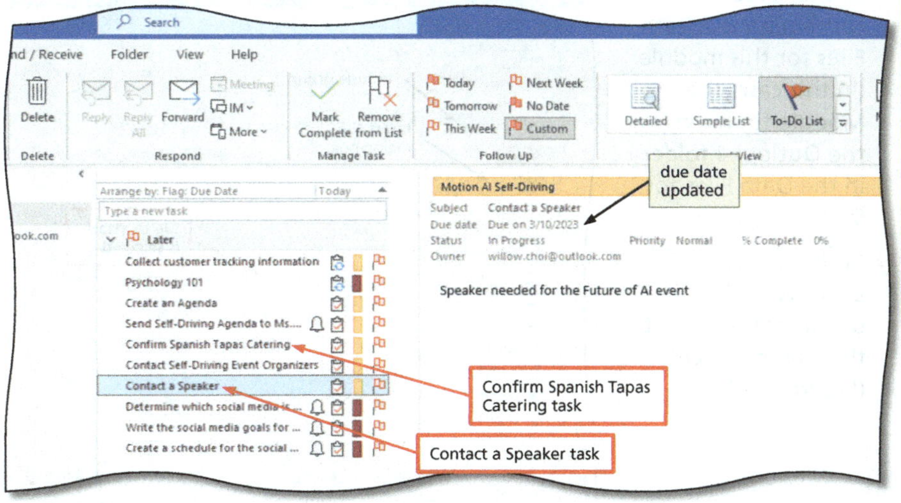

Figure 4–46

To Attach a File to a Task

***Why?** Attaching a file to a task is helpful if you want quick access to information when you are looking at a task.* Ms. Pauley has emailed you an updated Self-Driving Event flyer, which you already have saved to your computer. You decide that you should attach it to the Confirm Spanish Tapas Catering task so that you can share the flyer with the catering staff for room and timing information. The following steps attach a document to a task.

1

- Double-click the Confirm Spanish Tapas Catering task (shown in Figure 4–46) to display the Confirm Spanish Tapas Catering - Task window.
- Click Insert on the ribbon to display the Insert tab (Figure 4–47).

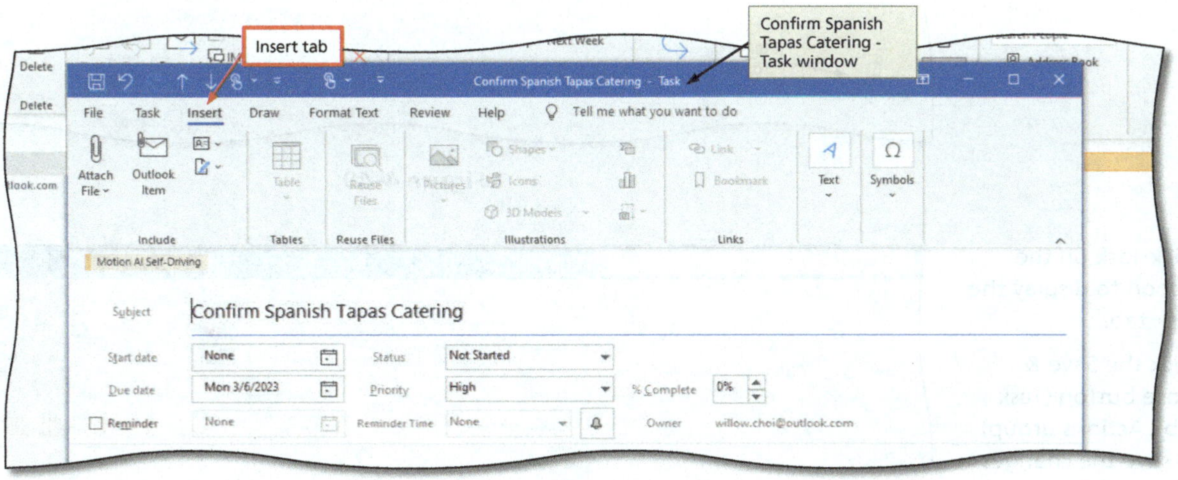

Figure 4–47

2

- Click the Attach File button (Insert tab | Include group) to display a list of recent files.
- Click Browse this PC to display the Insert File dialog box.

- If necessary, navigate to the folder containing the Data Files for this module (in this case, the Module folder in the Outlook4 folder in the Data Files for Students folder).
- Click SC_Out_4_Event (Word document) to select the file to attach (Figure 4–48).

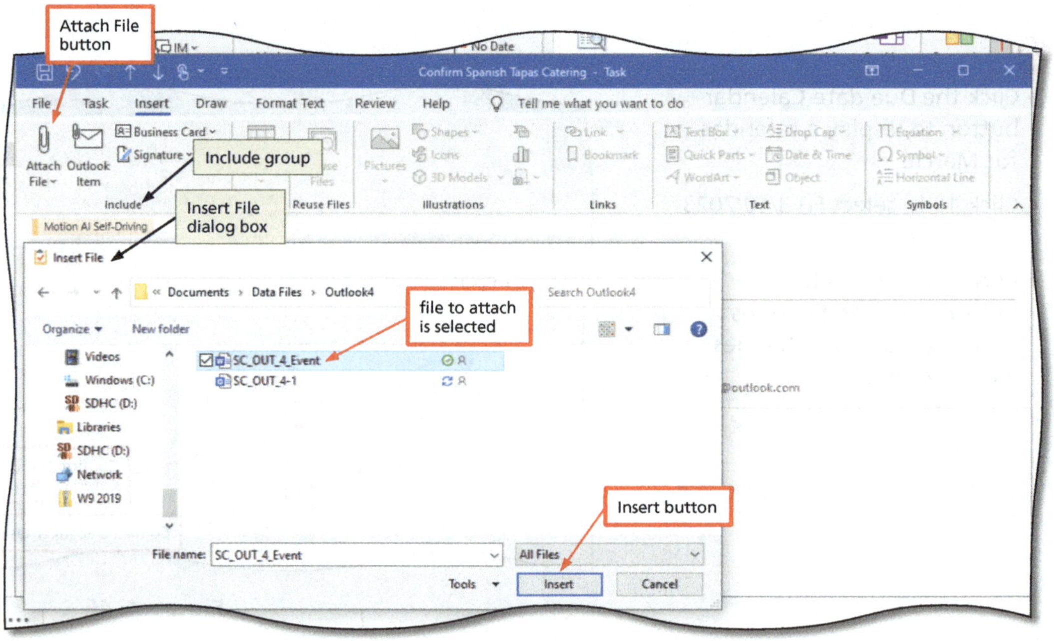

Figure 4–48

3

- Click Insert (Insert File dialog box) to attach the file (Figure 4–49).

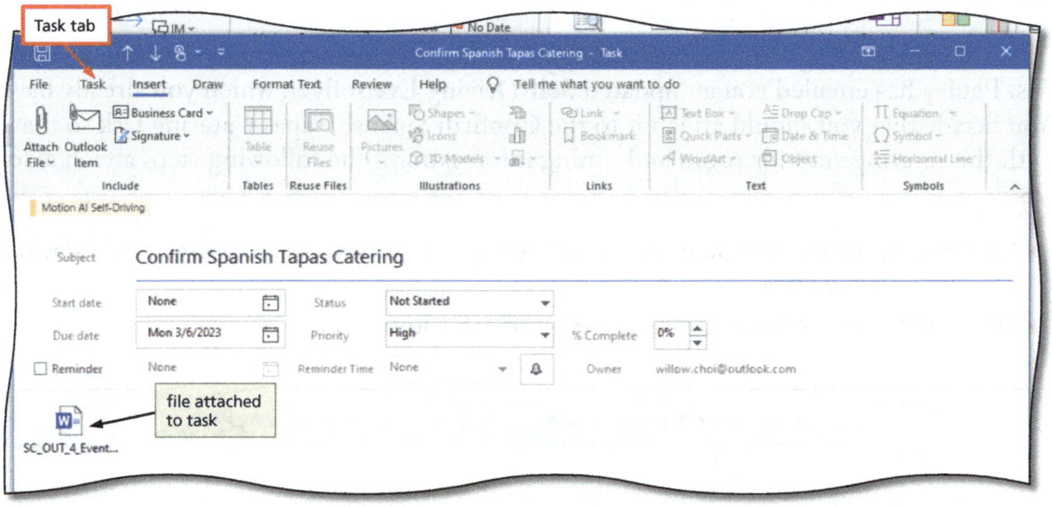

Figure 4–49

4

- Click Task on the ribbon to display the Task tab.
- Click the Save & Close button (Task tab | Actions group) to save the changes (Figure 4–50).

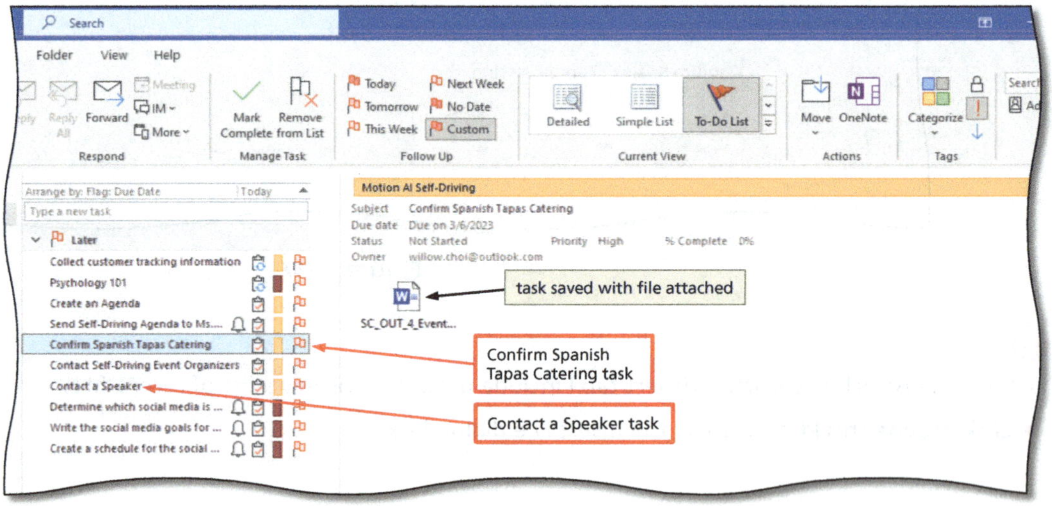

Figure 4–50

To Assign a Task

In addition to creating your own tasks, you can create tasks to assign to others. ***Why?*** *You can assign a task to someone else while ensuring that you retain a copy of the task and receive a status report once the task is completed.* Anya Chandra has volunteered to find a speaker for the Future of AI event. To assign a task, you first create the task, and then send it as a task request to someone. The following steps assign a task.

1

- Double-click the Contact a Speaker task (shown in Figure 4–50) to reopen the Contact a Speaker - Task window (Figure 4–51).

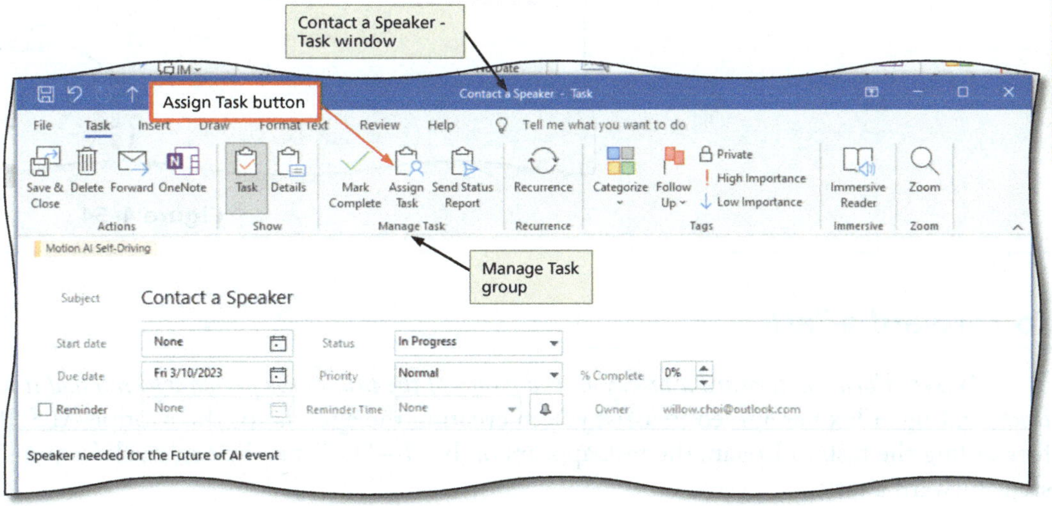

Figure 4–51

2

- Click the Assign Task button (Task tab | Manage Task group) to add the To box to the task to insert an email address (Figure 4–52).

Q&A Why does the Assign Task button no longer appear on the Task tab after I click it?
The Cancel Assignment button replaces the Assign Task button so you can cancel the task assignment if necessary.

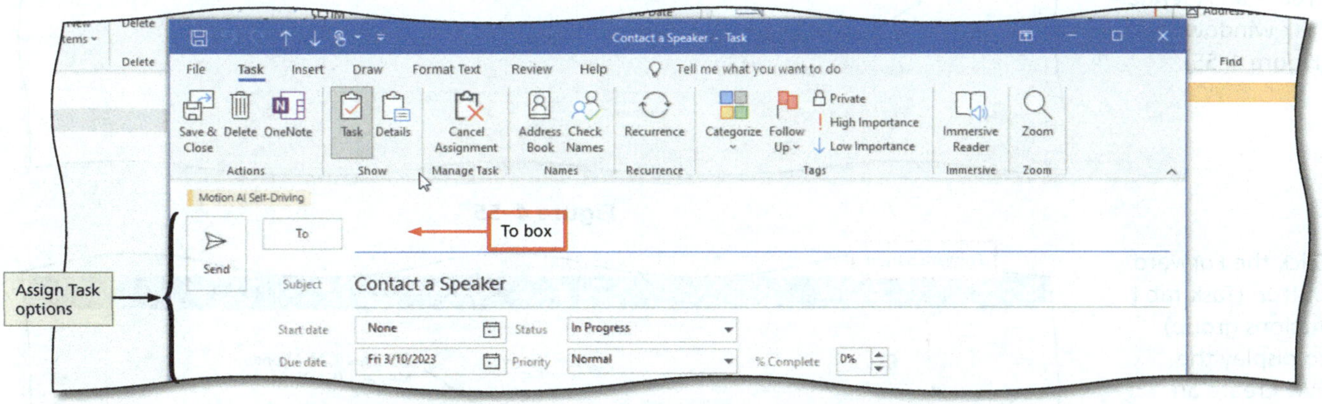

Figure 4–52

3

- Type **anya.chandra@outlook.com** in the To box to enter a recipient (Figure 4–53).

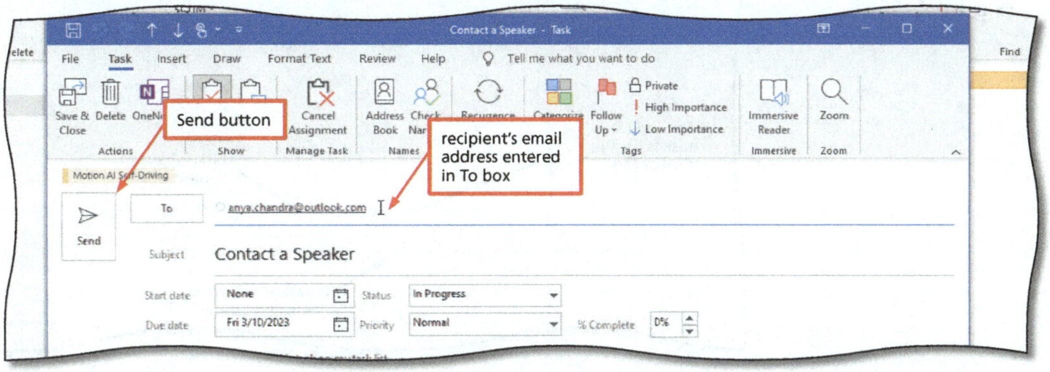

Figure 4–53

4

- Click the Send button (shown in Figure 4–53) to send the task to Anya Chandra (Figure 4–54).

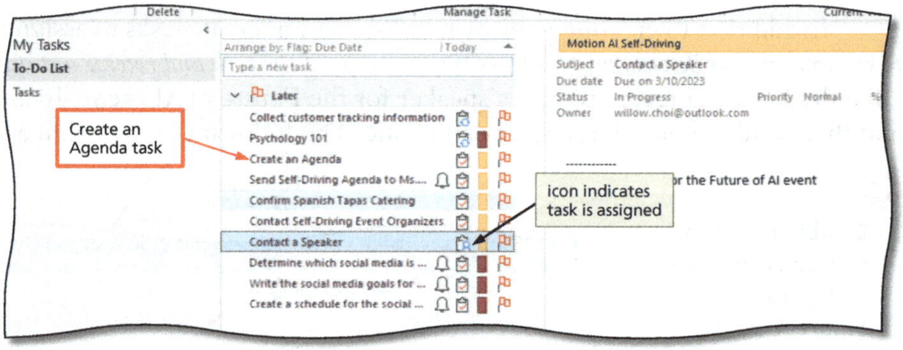

Figure 4–54

To Forward a Task

***Why?** When you forward a task, you send a copy of the task to the person who can add it to their To-Do list for tracking.* Logan Fix has agreed to assist you in creating the agenda for the Motion AI Self-Driving event. By forwarding the task to Logan, the task appears on his To-Do list so he can track it on his own. The following steps forward a task.

1

- Double-click the Create an Agenda task (shown in Figure 4–54) to display the Create an Agenda - Task window (Figure 4–55).

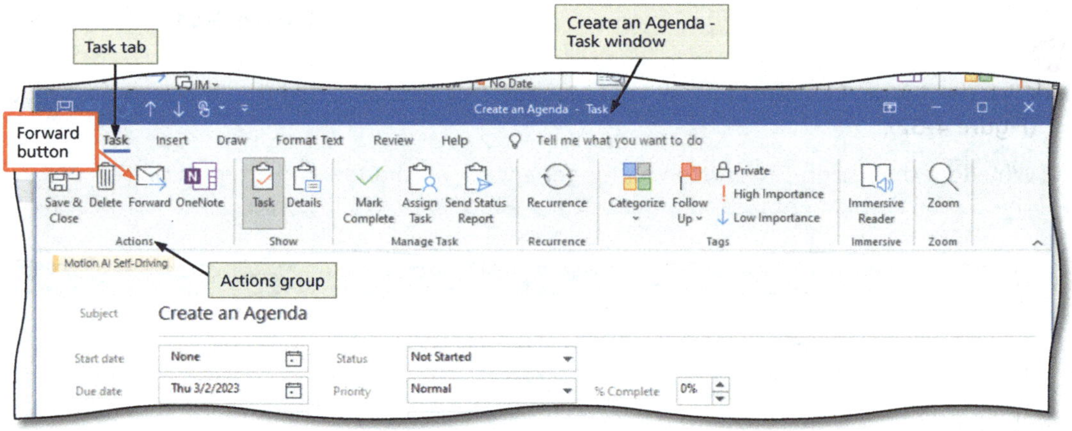

Figure 4–55

2

- Click the Forward button (Task tab | Actions group) to display the FW: Create an Agenda - Message (HTML) window (Figure 4–56).

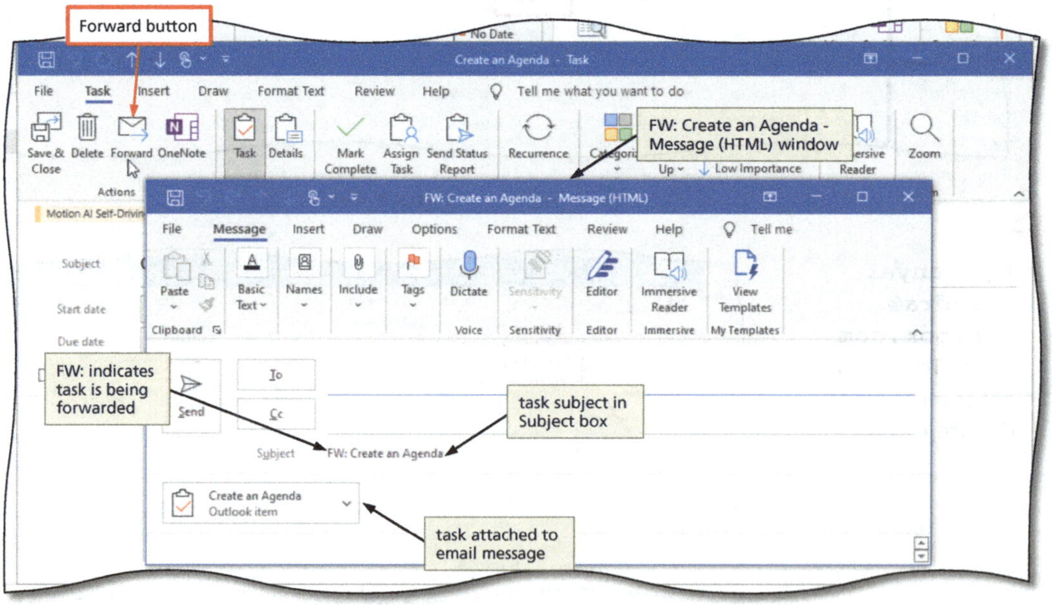

Figure 4–56

3

- Type **logan.fix@outlook.com** in the To box to enter the email address for a recipient.
- Type **Attached is the agenda task for you to add to your to-do list.** in the message body area to enter a message.
- Press ENTER two times and then type **Willow** to complete the message (Figure 4–57).

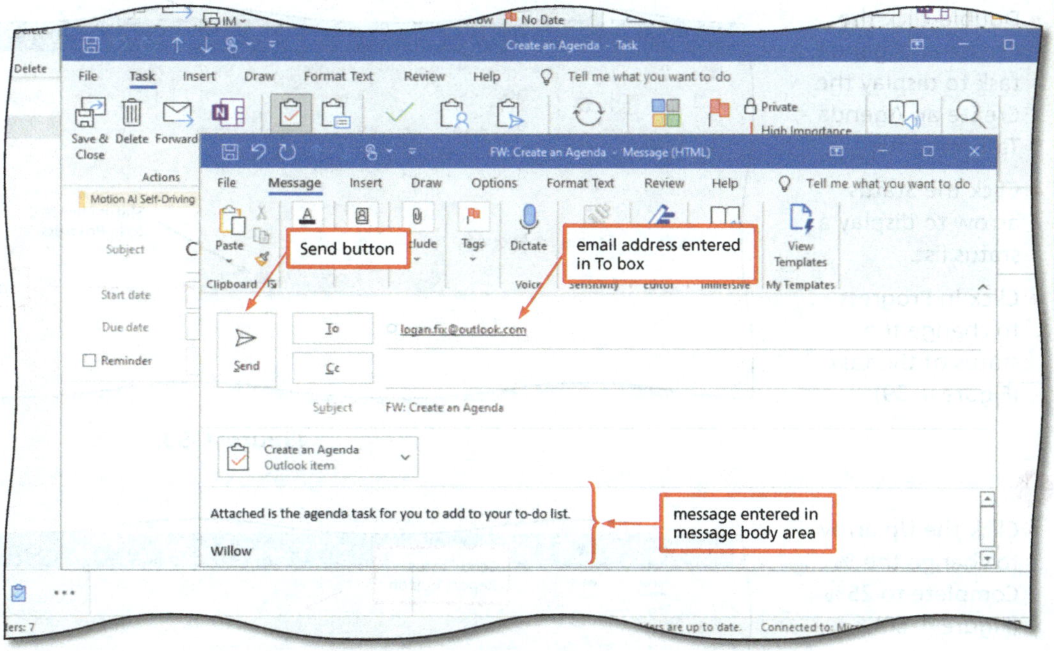

Figure 4–57

4

- Click the Send button to forward the task to Logan Fix.
- If necessary, click the Save & Close button (Task tab | Actions group) to save the changes (Figure 4–58).

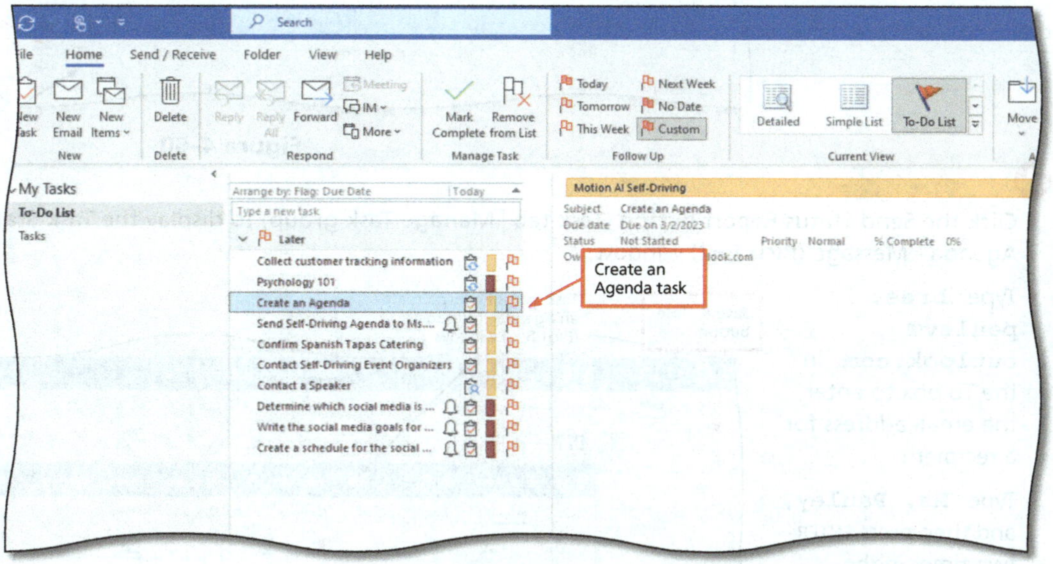

Figure 4–58

To Send a Status Report

While a task is in progress, you can send status reports to other people indicating the status and completion percentage of the task. ***Why?*** *If you have been assigned a task, you can submit a status report before you complete the task to explain why the task has not been completed or why the task needs to be amended.* Ms. Pauley wants to be informed about the agenda for the March self-driving event. Willow has completed 25 percent of the work and wants to inform her that the task is in progress. The following steps create and send a status report.

1

- Double-click the Create an Agenda task to display the Create an Agenda - Task window.
- Click the Status arrow to display a status list.
- Click In Progress to change the status of the task (Figure 4–59).

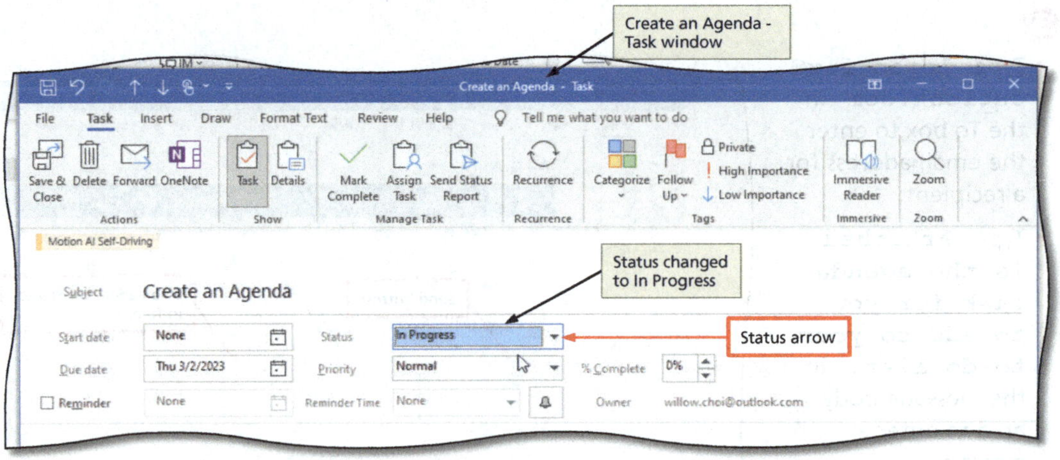

Figure 4–59

2

- Click the Up arrow to change the % Complete to 25% (Figure 4–60).

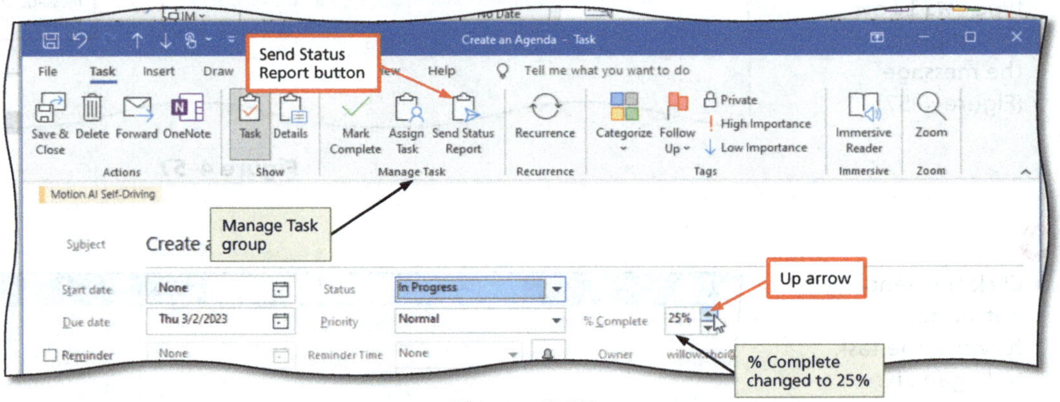

Figure 4–60

3

- Click the Send Status Report button (Task tab | Manage Task group) to display the Task Status Report: Create an Agenda - Message (Rich Text) window.
- Type **`bree.pauley@outlook.com`** in the To box to enter the email address for a recipient.
- Type **`Ms. Pauley,`** and then press ENTER two times in the message body area to enter the greeting line of the message.
- Type **`Here is my first update on this task.`** in the message.
- Press ENTER two times, and then type **`Willow`** to complete the message (Figure 4–61).

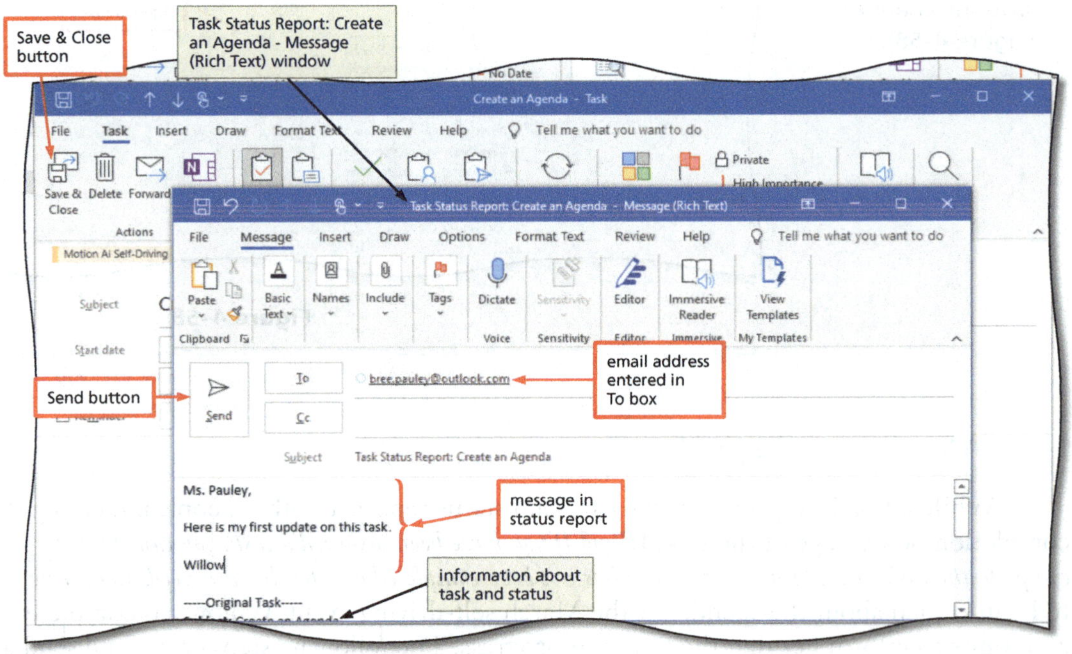

Figure 4–61

4

- Click the Send button to send the status report to the recipient.
- Click the Save & Close button (Task tab | Actions group) to save the changes to the task (Figure 4–62).

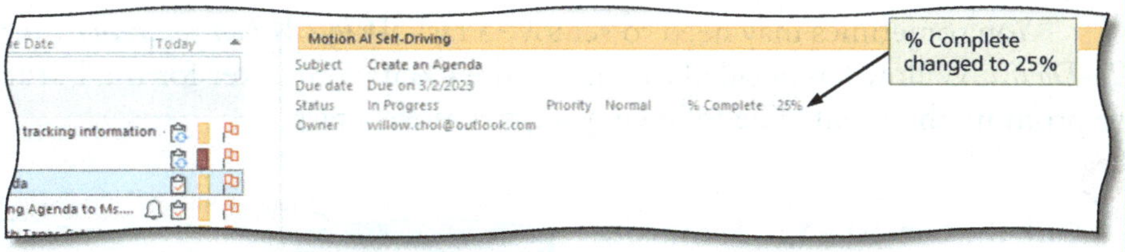

Figure 4–62

To Mark a Task Complete

You have just completed the research for which social media is the best fit for the business task, so you can mark it as complete. ***Why?** Mark a task as complete so that you know it is finished.* The following steps mark a task as complete.

1

- Click the Determine which social media is the best fit for a business task to select it (Figure 4–63).

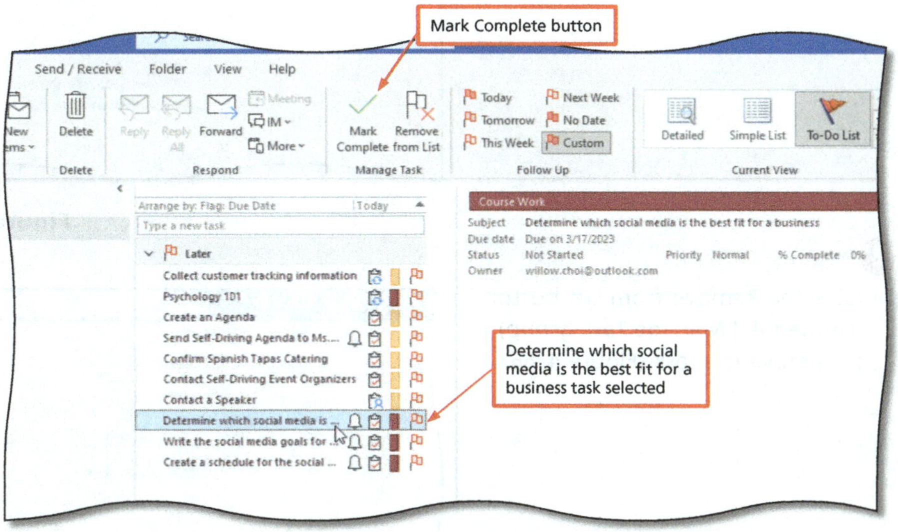

Figure 4–63

2

- Click the Mark Complete button (Home tab | Manage Task group) to mark the Determine which social media is the best fit for a business task as completed (Figure 4–64).

Q&A Why was the Determine which social media is the best fit for a business task removed from the To-Do list?

Once you mark a task as complete, Outlook removes it from the To-Do list and places it in the Completed list. You can see the Completed list by changing your view to Completed using the Change View button (Home tab | Current View group).

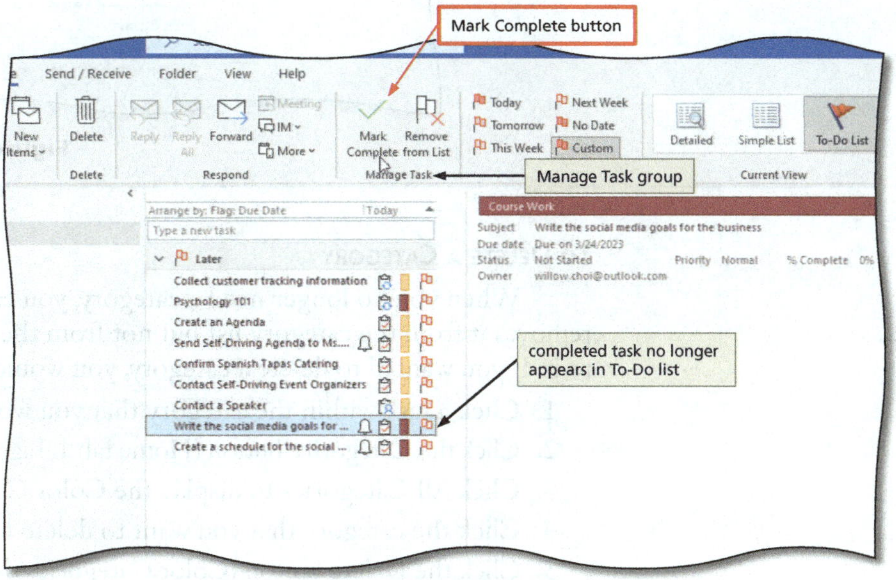

Figure 4–64

To Remove a Task

You sometimes may need to remove a task. ***Why?*** *When you remove a task, it is no longer displayed in your To-Do list.* Willow has decided to remove the Contact Speaker for the Future of AI event task until she has time to promote the event. The following steps remove a task.

1

- Click the Contact a Speaker task to select it (Figure 4–65).

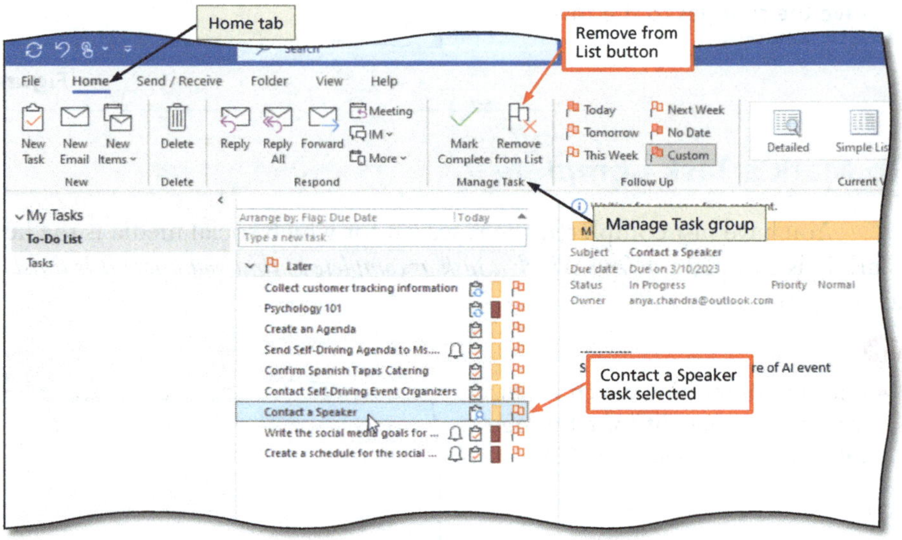

Figure 4–65

2

- Click the Remove from List button (Home tab | Manage Task group) to remove the task (Figure 4–66).

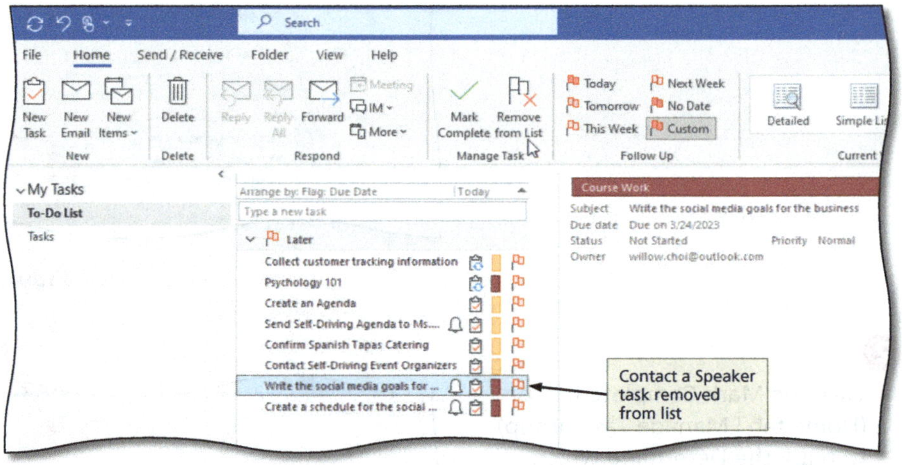

Figure 4–66

To Delete a Category

When you no longer need a category, you can delete it. Deleting a category removes it from the category list but not from the tasks that already have been assigned to it. If you wanted to delete a category, you would use the following steps.

1. Click a task within the category that you would like to delete.
2. Click the Categorize button (Home tab | Tags group) to display the Categorize menu.
3. Click All Categories to display the Color Categories dialog box.
4. Click the category that you want to delete to select it.
5. Click the Delete button (Color Categories dialog box) to delete the color category.
6. Click the Yes button (Microsoft Outlook dialog box) to confirm the deletion.
7. Click OK (Color Categories dialog box) to close the dialog box.

Choosing Display and Print Views

When working with tasks, you can change the view to display your tasks as a detailed list, simple list, priority list, or completed list. Change the view of your tasks to fit your current needs. For example, if you want to see tasks listed according to their priority (High, Normal, or Low), you can display the tasks in Prioritized view. You also can print tasks in a summarized list or include the details for each task.

To Change the Task View

Tasks can be displayed in different customized view layouts. By displaying tasks in Detailed view, you can view all tasks, including completed tasks. The following steps change the view to Detailed view. ***Why?*** *To see the total picture of what you have to accomplish, Detailed view provides all the task details, including task subject, status, due date, and categories.*

1

- Click View on the ribbon to display the View tab.
- Click the Change View button (View tab | Current View group) to display the Change View gallery (Figure 4–67).

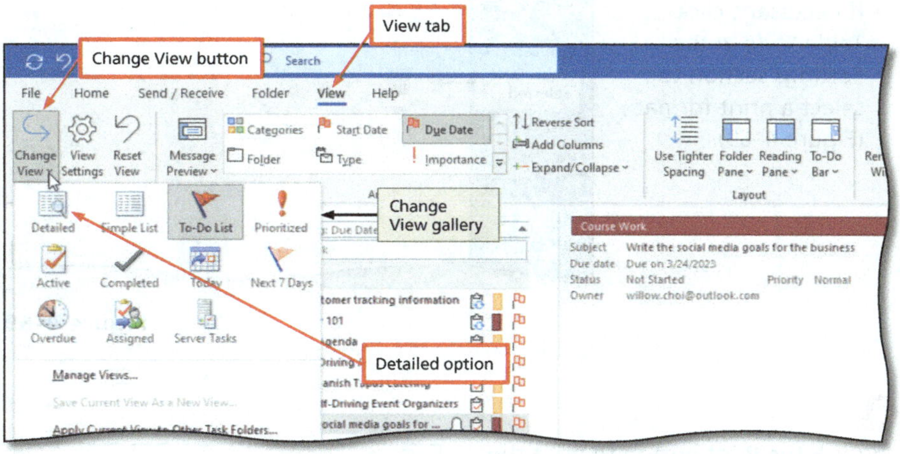

Figure 4–67

2

- Click Detailed to change the view (Figure 4–68).

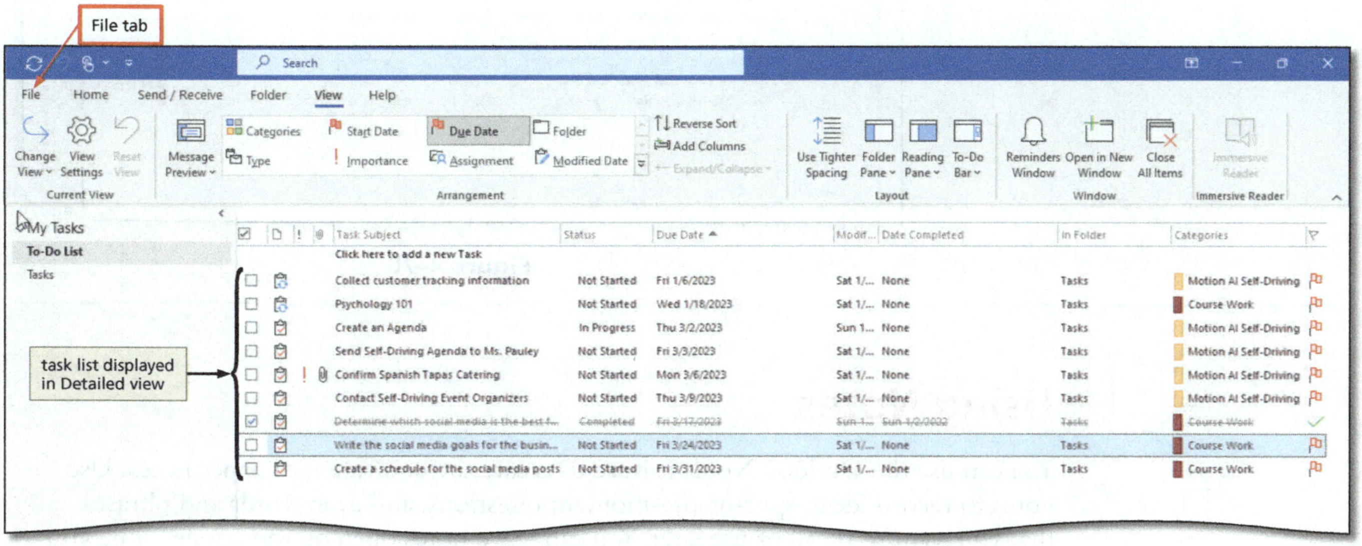

Figure 4–68

Experiment

- Click the other views in the Current View gallery to view the tasks in other arrangements. When you are finished, click Detailed to return to Detailed view.

To Print Tasks

Outlook provides printing options based on the view and tasks you have selected. For example, in To-Do List view, you can select a single task and print in Table Style or Menu Style. In Detailed view, which is the current view, you can print only in Table Style. The following steps print the tasks using Table Style. ***Why?*** *You might need a printed To-Do list to view when you are not working at your computer.*

1

- Click File on the ribbon to open Backstage view.
- Click the Print tab in Backstage view to display the Print gallery.
- If necessary, click Table Style in the Settings section to select a print format (Figure 4–69).

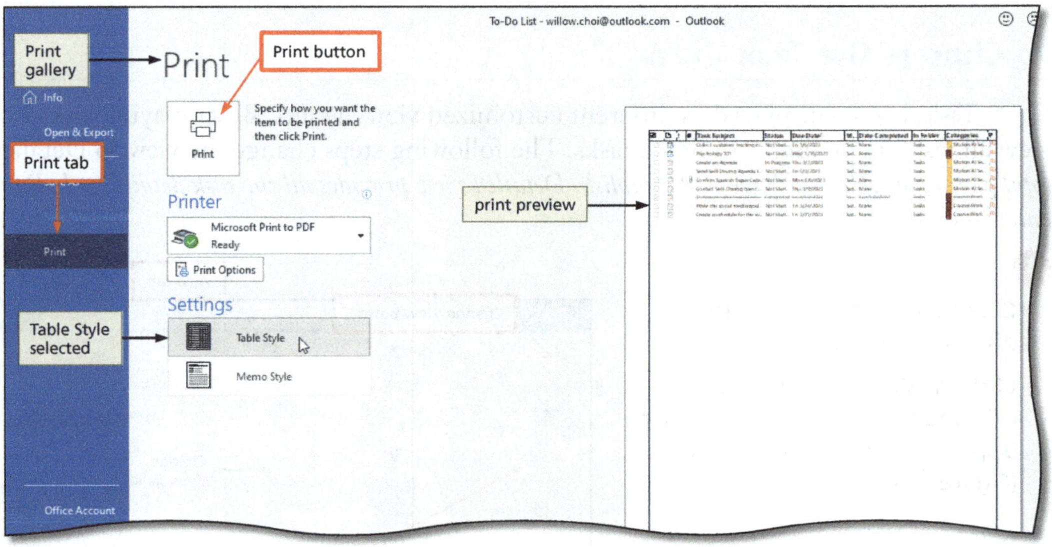

Figure 4–69

2

- Click the Print button to print the tasks in Table Style (Figure 4–70).

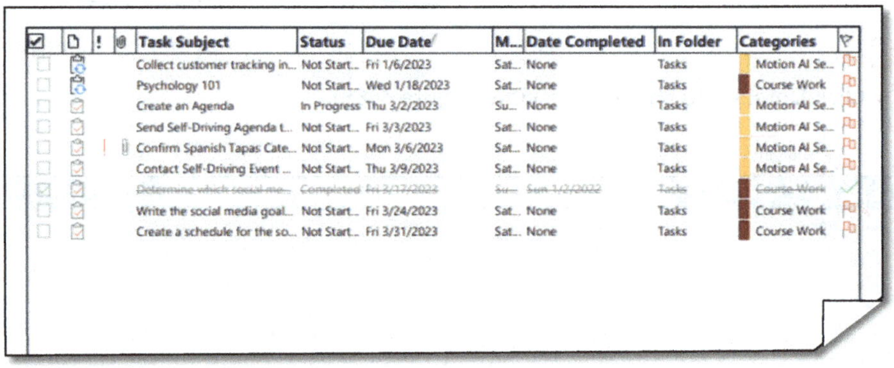

Figure 4–70

Using Notes

You can use the Outlook Notes feature to create the equivalent of paper notes. Use notes to record ideas, spur-of-the-moment questions, and even words and phrases that you want to recall or use later. You can leave notes open on the screen while you continue using Outlook, or you can close them and view them in the Notes window. The Notes window contains the Navigation pane and Notes pane.

CONSIDER THIS

Can I use the Outlook Notes as sticky notes?
Notes are the electronic equivalent of paper sticky notes. You can jot down notes for the directions that you find online to your interview, for example, or write questions that you want to remember to ask.

To Create a Note

Why? *A note can be a reminder from a phone conversation, information you find online for future reference, or even a grocery list.* When you enter text into a note, Outlook saves it with the last modified date shown at the bottom of the note; you do not have to click a Save button. As Willow was surfing the web, she found information that she wants to share with the interns. The following steps create a note reminder.

1

- Click the Navigation Options button (three dots) on the Navigation bar to display the Navigation Options menu (Figure 4–71).

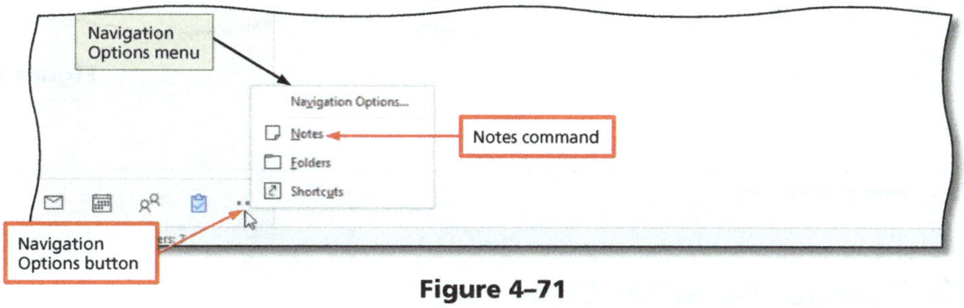

Figure 4–71

2

- Click Notes to open the Notes Outlook window.
- Click the New Note button (Home tab | New group) to display a new blank note.
- Type `The Top AI new jobs include AI Architect, AI Data Scientist, and AI Ethicist` as the note text to enter a note (Figure 4–72).

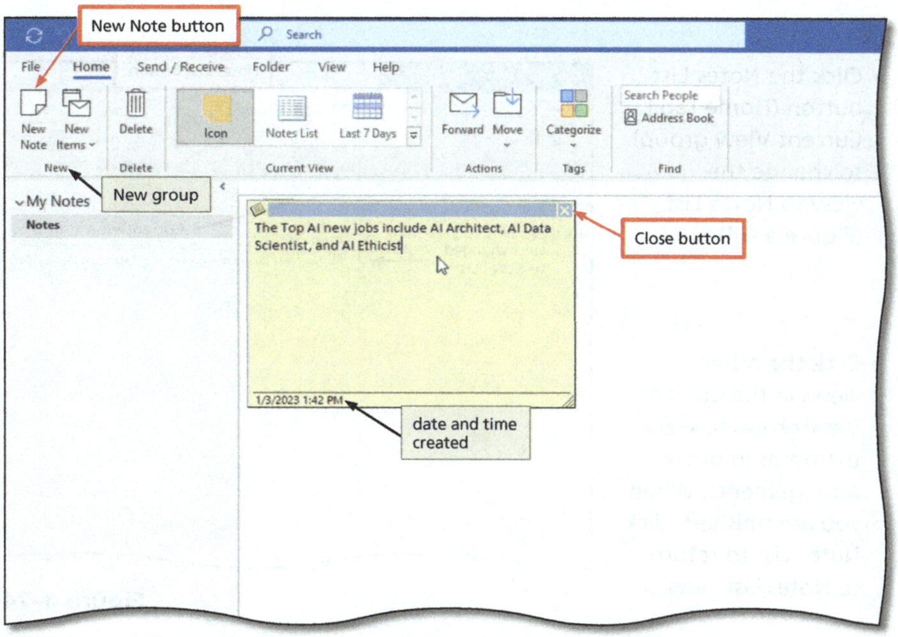

Figure 4–72

3

- Click the Close button to save and close the note (Figure 4–73).

Q&A

Why is my Notes view different from Figure 4–73?
Outlook provides three basic Notes views: Icon, Notes List, and Last 7 Days. Figure 4–75 displays the note in Icon view. To switch to Icon view, click the Icon button (Home tab | Current View group).

Can I print notes?
Yes. First, select the note(s) you want to print. To select multiple notes, hold CTRL while clicking the notes to print. Next, click the File tab to open Backstage view, click the Print tab, and then click the Print button.

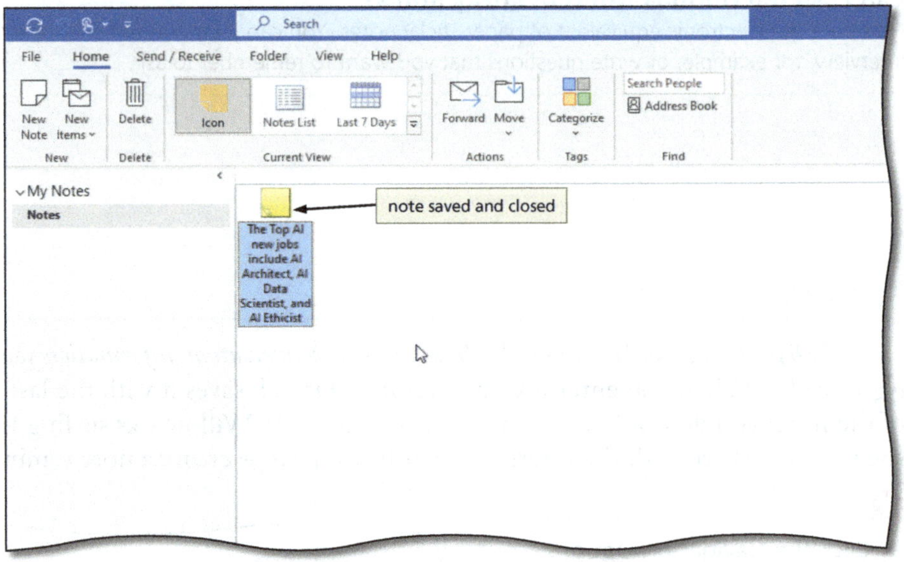

Figure 4–73

Other Ways

1. Press CTRL+SHIFT+N

To Change the Notes View

***Why?** You want to display your notes as a list instead of in the sticky note layout.* You decide to change your notes view to Notes List. The following step changes the view to Notes List view.

1

- Click the Notes List button (Home tab | Current View group) to change the view to Notes List (Figure 4–74).

Experiment

- Click the other views in the Current View group to view the notes in other arrangements. When you are finished, click Notes List to return to Notes List view.

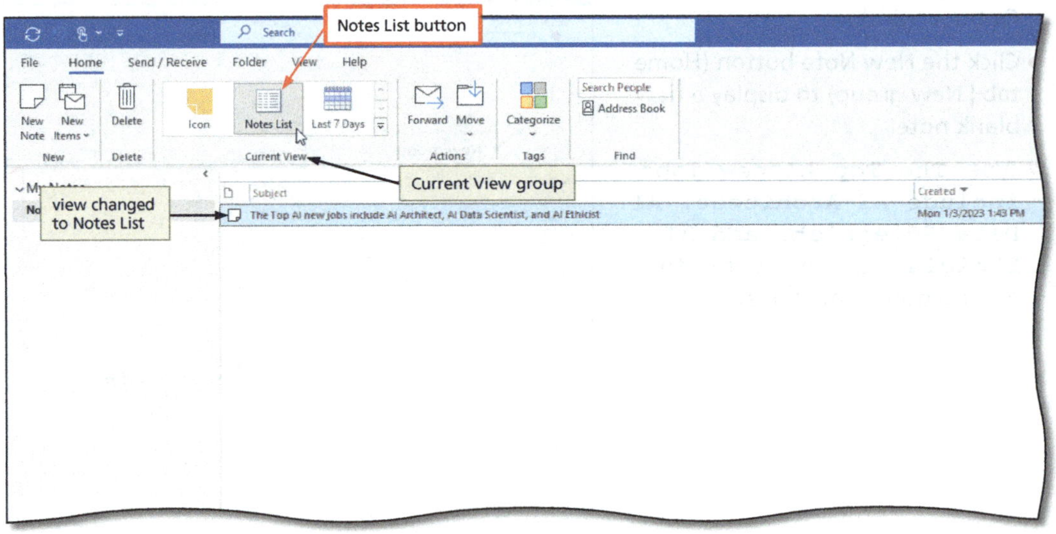

Figure 4–74

To Delete a Note

***Why?** When you no longer need a note, you should delete it.* After sharing the note about jobs in AI you decide to delete the note because you no longer need it. The following steps delete a note and close Outlook.

1

- If necessary, click the note about jobs in AI to select it.
- Click the Delete button (Home tab | Delete group) to delete the note (Figure 4–75).

2

- Export the SC_OUT_4-1.pst file to an Outlook Data File (.pst) named `SC_OUT_4_Willow`.
- Close Outlook.

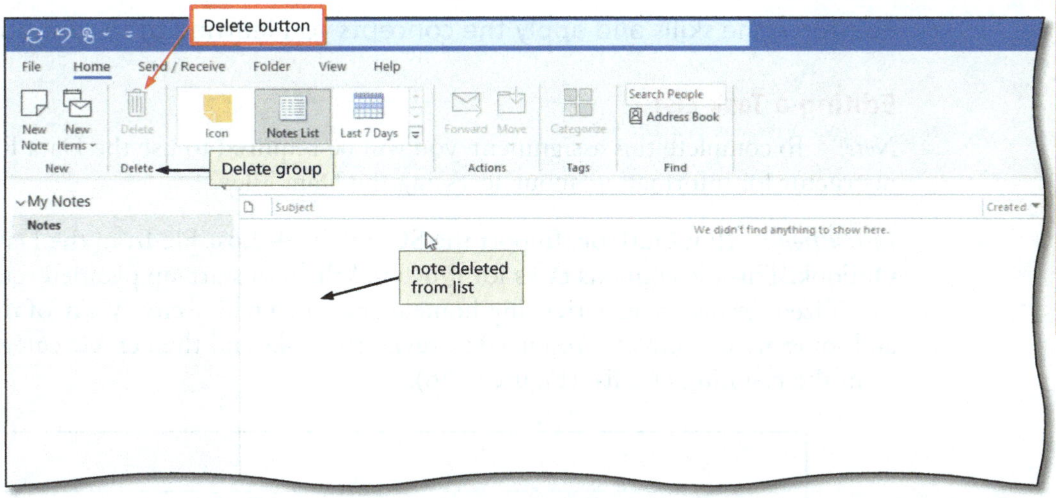

Figure 4–75

Summary

In this module, you have learned how to use Outlook to create tasks, categorize tasks, categorize email messages, manage tasks, print tasks, create notes, and print notes.

Consider This: Plan Ahead

What decisions will you need to make when creating tasks, categorizing email messages, choosing views, and using notes in the future?

1. Create tasks.
   a) Determine what projects you want to track. People use tasks to keep track of the projects that are most important to them.
   b) Determine the information you want to store for a task. For any task, you can store basic information, add attachments, and add detailed instructions.
2. Categorize tasks and email messages.
   a) Plan categories for tasks. To identify and group tasks and other Outlook items easily, assign the items to categories.
   b) Assign emails to the same categories as tasks.
3. Manage tasks.
   a) Determine which tasks may need to be assigned to others.
4. Choose display and print views.
   a) Determine the preferred way to view the tasks to find the information you are seeking.
   b) Determine how you want to view your tasks.
5. Use notes.
   a) Determine what reminder notes would assist you.

CONSIDER THIS

How should you submit solutions to questions in the assignments identified with a ✱ symbol?

Every assignment in this book contains one or more questions with a ✱ symbol. These questions require you to think beyond the assigned file. Present your solutions to the question in the format required by your instructor. Possible formats may include one or more of these options: write the answer; create a document that contains the answer; present your answer to the class; discuss your answer in a group; record the answer as audio or video using a webcam, smartphone, or portable media player; or post answers on a blog, wiki, or website.

CONSIDER THIS

Apply Your Knowledge

Reinforce the skills and apply the concepts you learned in this module.

Editing a Task List

Note: To complete this assignment, you will be required to use the Data Files. Please contact your instructor for information about accessing the Data Files.

Instructions: Run Outlook. Import the SC_OUT_4-2.pst file from the Data Files folder into Outlook. This file contains tasks for Quixote Village, a start-up planned rental community subsidized for people experiencing homelessness in a major city. Many of the tasks have changed and some are incomplete. You need to revise the tasks and then create categories. Finally, you will print the resulting task list (Figure 4–76).

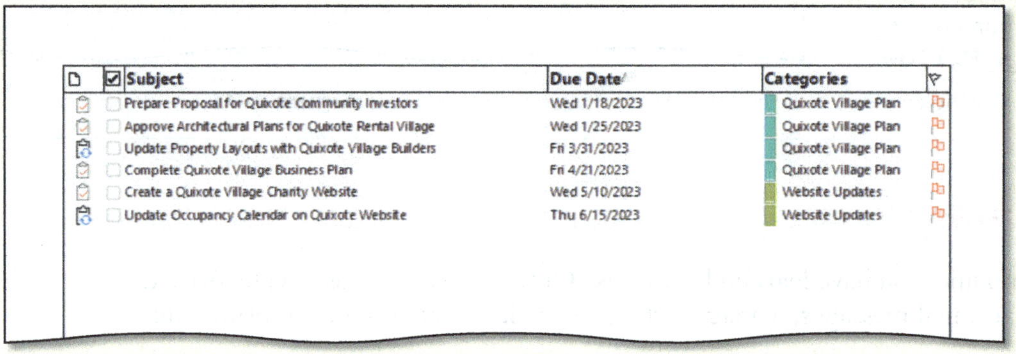

		Subject	Due Date	Categories	
		Prepare Proposal for Quixote Community Investors	Wed 1/18/2023	Quixote Village Plan	
		Approve Architectural Plans for Quixote Rental Village	Wed 1/25/2023	Quixote Village Plan	
		Update Property Layouts with Quixote Village Builders	Fri 3/31/2023	Quixote Village Plan	
		Complete Quixote Village Business Plan	Fri 4/21/2023	Quixote Village Plan	
		Create a Quixote Village Charity Website	Wed 5/10/2023	Website Updates	
		Update Occupancy Calendar on Quixote Website	Thu 6/15/2023	Website Updates	

Figure 4–76

Perform the following tasks:

1. Display the SC_OUT_4-2.pst Tasks folder in the Outlook Tasks window as a To-Do list.
2. Change the task name for the Meet with Quixote Village Community Investors task to **`Prepare Proposal for Quixote Community Investors`**. Change the due date to January 18, 2023. Change the % Complete to 50%.
3. Change the task name of Meet with Quixote Village Building Firm to **`Update Property Layouts with Quixote Village Builders`**. Configure the task as a recurring task that occurs every Friday from March 31, 2023, until August 4, 2023. Set the Priority to High.
4. Add a recurring task titled **`Update Occupancy Calendar on Quixote Website`** that occurs every Thursday from June 15, 2023 until November 30, 2023. Change the status to Waiting on someone else.
5. In the Task body of Update Occupancy Calendar on Quixote Website, type **`Request that the Quixote renter fills out a review.`**
6. Create two color categories. Name the first one **`Quixote Village Plan`** and the second one **`Website Updates`**. Use the colors of your choice. As appropriate, assign two tasks to Website Updates and assign the rest to Quixote Village Plan.
7. Print the final task list in Table Style, as shown in Figure 4–76, and then submit it in the format specified by your instructor.
8. Export the SC_OUT_4-2 Tasks folder to an Outlook Data File (.pst) named **`SC_OUT_4_Quixote_Village`**. Submit the .pst file in the format specified by your instructor.
9. What task categories would you create to categorize the tasks in your personal life? Name at least five categories.

Extend Your Knowledge

Extend the skills you learned in this module and experiment with new skills. You may need to use Help to complete the assignment.

Creating Notes for a Motorcycle Shop

Instructions: Run Outlook. Import the SC_OUT_4-3.pst file from the Data Files folder into Outlook. This file has no notes, so you will create notes, categorize them, and then print the notes.

Perform the following tasks:

1. Use Help to learn about customizing notes.
2. Display the SC_OUT_4-3.pst Notes folder in the Outlook Notes window.
3. Create the following notes for a motorcycle shop:
   - **`Heidi Gonzalez is searching for a 2023 Triumph Trident 660 Matt Jet Black and Silver Ice.`**
   - **`Johnathan Gervasi specializes in riding leather jackets.`**
   - **`Post new stock on the website on Tuesdays.`**
   - **`Several customers have requested a tailor for leather alterations.`**
   - **`Sign Design wants to meet Tuesday to create a new business logo with a vintage feel.`**
   - **`Create an online form for a test ride on pre-owned motorcycles.`**
   - **`Add this note on the website: Due to high service volume, we do not work on bikes produced before the year 2000 during the months of June through October.`**
4. Select the 'Several customers have requested a tailor for leather alterations' note, and then create a color category named ASAP. Use a color of your choosing.
5. Categorize the remaining notes using a new "Action Items" category. Use a color of your choosing.
6. Replace 'Johnathan Gervasi' in the 'Johnathan Gervasi specializes in riding leather jackets' note with the name of your favorite teacher.
7. Change the view to Notes List. Print the notes in Table Style, as shown in Figure 4–77, and then submit them in the format specified by your instructor.
8. Export the SC_OUT_4-3 Notes folder to an Outlook Data File (.pst) named **`SC_OUT_4_Motorcycle,`** and then submit the file in the format specified by your instructor.
9. When is it appropriate to create a note instead of creating a task?

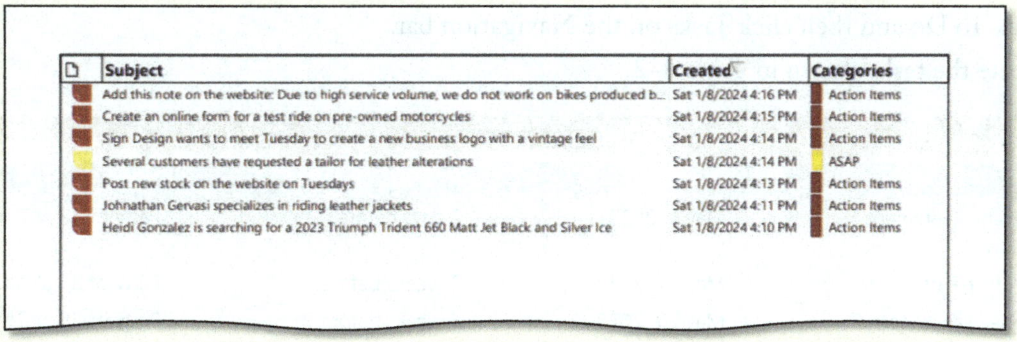

	Subject	Created	Categories
	Add this note on the website: Due to high service volume, we do not work on bikes produced b...	Sat 1/8/2024 4:16 PM	Action Items
	Create an online form for a test ride on pre-owned motorcycles	Sat 1/8/2024 4:15 PM	Action Items
	Sign Design wants to meet Tuesday to create a new business logo with a vintage feel	Sat 1/8/2024 4:14 PM	Action Items
	Several customers have requested a tailor for leather alterations	Sat 1/8/2024 4:14 PM	ASAP
	Post new stock on the website on Tuesdays	Sat 1/8/2024 4:13 PM	Action Items
	Johnathan Gervasi specializes in riding leather jackets	Sat 1/8/2024 4:11 PM	Action Items
	Heidi Gonzalez is searching for a 2023 Triumph Trident 660 Matt Jet Black and Silver Ice	Sat 1/8/2024 4:10 PM	Action Items

Figure 4–77

Expand Your World

Creating an Outlook.com Web-Based Task List Online

Create a solution that uses cloud or web technologies by learning and investigating on your own from general guidance.

Note: To complete this assignment, you will be required to use the Data Files. Please contact your instructor for information about accessing the Data Files.

Instructions: Outlook.com allows you to enter and maintain a task list from any computer with a web browser and an Internet connection. You are to use Outlook.com to create a task list using the information in Table 4–2 for the Dining in Sky Restaurant that hoists diners into the sky on a 100-foot crane. You have six reservations at your restaurant coming up and want to create the tasks along with the reminders for them. The final task list is shown in Figure 4–78.

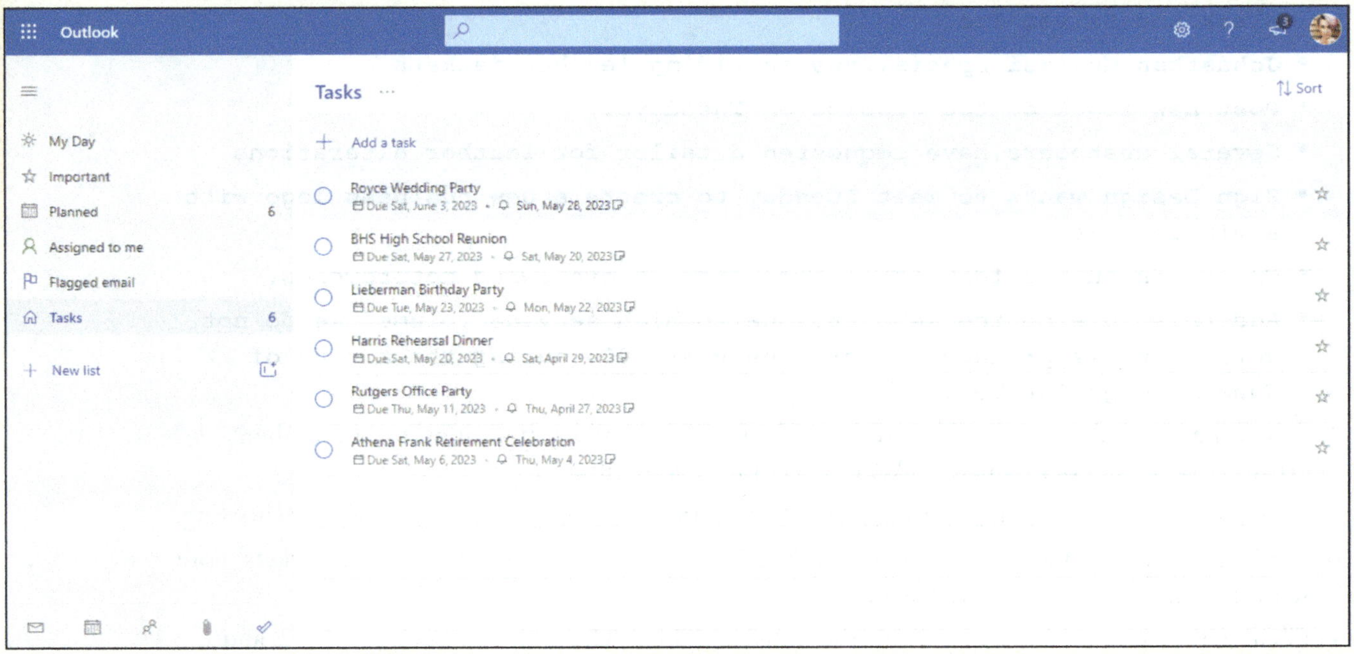

Look Studio/Shutterstock.com

Figure 4–78

Perform the following tasks:

1. Start your web browser and navigate to outlook.com.
2. Sign in to outlook.com. If necessary, sign up for a Microsoft account.
3. Click To Do and then click Tasks on the Navigation bar.
4. Create the tasks shown in Table 4–2.

Table 4–2 Tasks for Dining in the Sky Restaurant

Event	Due Date	Reminder Time	Note
Athena Frank Retirement Celebration	May 6, 2023	2 days before	Party of 12 at 7 PM
Rutgers Office Party	May 11, 2023	2 weeks before	Party of 35 at noon
Harris Rehearsal Dinner	May 20, 2023	3 weeks before	Party of 75 at 8 PM
Lieberman Birthday Party	May 23, 2023	1 day before	Party of 8 at 7:30 PM
BHS High School Reunion	May 27, 2023	1 week before	Party of 60–80 at 8 PM
Royce Wedding Party	June 3, 2023	6 days before	Party of 20 at 6 PM

5. When you finish adding the tasks, submit a screenshot of these tasks in outlook.com to your instructor.
6. When would you want to add your tasks to Outlook.com instead of using Microsoft Outlook? Is there a way to automatically get your tasks in Microsoft Outlook to appear in your Outlook.com account?

In the Lab 1

Creating Managerial Tasks

Problem: You are a manager for the Regency Concert Outdoor Amphitheatre. Table 4–3 and Table 4–4 list the current tasks for your role as manager. Enter the tasks into the To-Do list. The task list you create will look like the one in Figure 4–79.

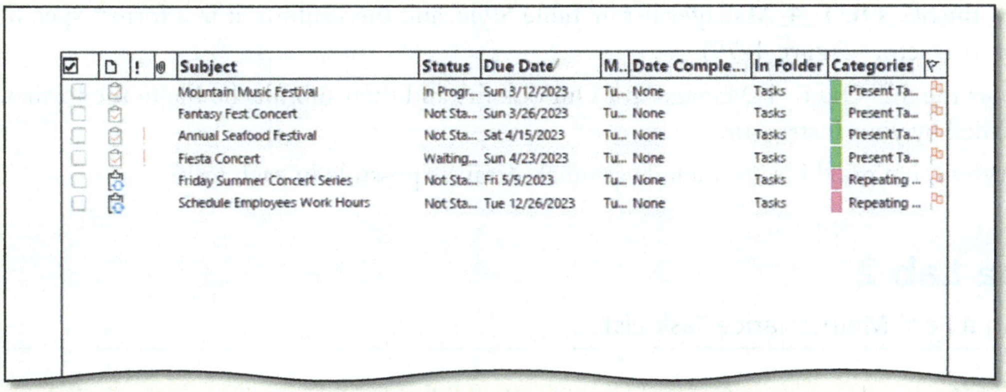

Figure 4–79

Perform the following tasks:

1. Create an Outlook Data File named `SC_OUT_4_Manager`.
2. Create the present tasks using the information listed in Table 4–3.

Table 4–3 Regency Concert Outdoor Amphitheatre Present Tasks

Task	Start Date	Due Date	Status	Priority
Mountain Music Festival	3/9/2023	3/12/2023	In Progress	Normal
Fantasy Fest Concert	3/20/2023	3/26/2023		Normal
Annual Seafood Festival	3/27/2023	4/15/2023		High
Fiesta Concert	4/17/2023	4/23/2023	Waiting on someone else	High

3. Create the recurring tasks using the information listed in Table 4–4.

Table 4–4 Regency Concert Outdoor Amphitheatre Recurring Tasks

Task	Start Date	Due Date	Recurrence
Schedule Employees Work Hours	4/11/2023	End of year	Monthly, second Tuesday
Friday Summer Concert Series	5/5/2023	20 occurrences	Weekly, Fridays

Continued >

In the Lab 1 *continued*

4. Open the Schedule Employees Work Hours task and add the detail in the task body that **`Lia Nguyen cannot work on Monday or Wednesday due to college classes.`**
5. Set a reminder for the Fantasy Fest Concert task for Mon 4/10/2023 at 11 AM (If you receive a message about the current folder not supporting reminders, click Yes to save the reminder.)
6. Create a color category called Present Tasks, using a color of your choice. Categorize the tasks in Table 4–3.
7. Create a color category called Repeating Tasks, using a color of your choice. Categorize all tasks with this category in Table 4–4.
8. Add a note that states **`The First Friday Artist Registry is an opportunity to connect your work with First Friday venues, curators, and general art enthusiasts. Register today and create a profile that will be viewed specifically by people looking for artists to show.`**
9. Print the SC_OUT_4_Manager list in Table Style, and then submit it in a format specified by your instructor (Figure 4–79).
10. Export the SC_OUT_4_Manager.pst Outlook file and then submit the file in the format specified by your instructor.
11. Why is it a good idea to include as much detail as possible in each task?

In the Lab 2

Creating a Pool Maintenance Task List

Problem: You are the owner of a community pool and decide to enter the recommended pool maintenance checklist into Outlook. You need to create a list of all the tasks and categorize them appropriately (Figure 4–80).

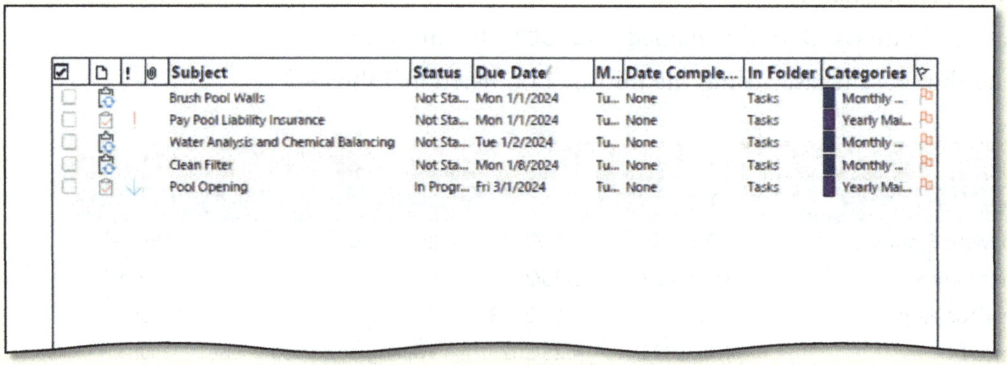

Figure 4–80

Perform the following tasks:

1. Create an Outlook Data File named **`SC_OUT_4_Pool.`**
2. Create the tasks using the information listed in Table 4–5.

Table 4–5 Pool Yearly Maintenance Tasks

Task	Task Body	Due Date	Status	Priority	Reminder
Pay Pool Liability Insurance	Insurance companies recommend liability insurance of half a million with an umbrella policy to bring it up to one million	1/1/2024		High	12/27/2023
Pool Opening	Buy new mesh cover and vinyl liner	3/1/2024	In Progress	Low	

3. Create the recurring tasks using the information listed in Table 4–6.

Table 4–6 Pool Recurring Maintenance Tasks

Task	Task Body	Recurrence
Water Analysis and Chemical Balancing	Add chemicals as needed	Monthly on second day of the month, no end date, starting in 2024
Brush Pool Walls	Brush, skim, and vacuum	First Monday of each month, every 2 months, no end date, starting in 2024
Clean Filter	Backwash and clean out pump baskets	Second Monday monthly, no end date, starting in 2024

4. Categorize the Yearly tasks as Yearly Maintenance by creating a new color category.
5. Categorize the remaining tasks as Monthly Maintenance by creating a new color category.
6. Add a second note, **`Look at the water every day and watch for small variations in clarity and color`**, to the task body of the 'Water Analysis and Chemical Balancing' task.
7. Print the tasks in Table Style, and then submit the task list in the format specified by your instructor.
8. Export the SC_OUT_4_Pool.pst tasks and then submit the file in the format specified by your instructor.
9. Why is it a good idea to update the status of a task as it changes?

In the Lab 3

Creating and Assigning Tasks

Part 1: Your computing instructor has assigned a term paper to be completed by a team of three people. Each person in the team is responsible for researching one job each of the topic "Top Three Jobs According to Glassdoor." The three top jobs are Java Developer, Data Scientist, and Product Manager. After you perform adequate research and write your part of the paper, send it to another team member for a peer review. After all team members have performed a peer review, finalize the content, compile it into one document, and prepare it for submission. Using Outlook, each team member should create tasks for the work they have to perform on the term paper (for example, conducting research, locating recent sources, writing the first draft, sending for peer review, performing a peer review, finalizing content, compiling into one master document, preparing for submission, and submitting the paper). Add as much information to the tasks as possible, such as the start date, due date, priority, status, and percent complete. Categorize the tasks appropriately. Assign the peer review task to the team member who will review your content. Finally, send a status report to all team members showing how much of each task you currently have completed. Submit the task list in a format specified by your instructor.

Part 2: You have made several decisions while creating the task list in this assignment, such as which tasks to create, what details to add to each task, and how to categorize each task. What was the rationale behind each of these decisions?

5 Customizing Outlook

Objectives

After completing this module, you will be able to:

- Add another email account
- Insert Quick Parts in email messages
- Insert easy to understand links in email messages
- Insert pictures in email messages
- Set the default message format
- Create an email signature
- Format a signature
- Assign signatures
- Customize personal stationery
- Configure junk email options
- Create rules
- Configure AutoArchive settings
- Adjust calendar settings
- Subscribe to a news feed

Introduction to Customizing Outlook

Outlook provides many options for customizing your experience when working with email messages, calendars, and other items. From syncing custom email signatures to multiple devices to adjusting how the work week is displayed in your calendar, you can make Outlook fit your requirements so that you can use it more efficiently. For example, a rule is a command that tells Outlook how to process an email message. Using rules, you quickly can categorize or flag your email messages as they arrive so that you can identify at a glance which ones you first want to address. You can change the fonts and colors that are used by default as well. Outlook's customization options can help you become more productive.

Project: Adding a New Email Account and Customizing Options

People often have more than one email account. In fact, some people have more than they can remember. Outlook allows you to manage multiple email accounts. That way, you can read your email messages from all accounts without needing to use several email programs such as one for a Microsoft email account, another for a Gmail account, and a third for a school or work email account.

The project in this module follows general guidelines and uses Outlook to add a new email account and customize Outlook options, as shown in Figure 5–1.

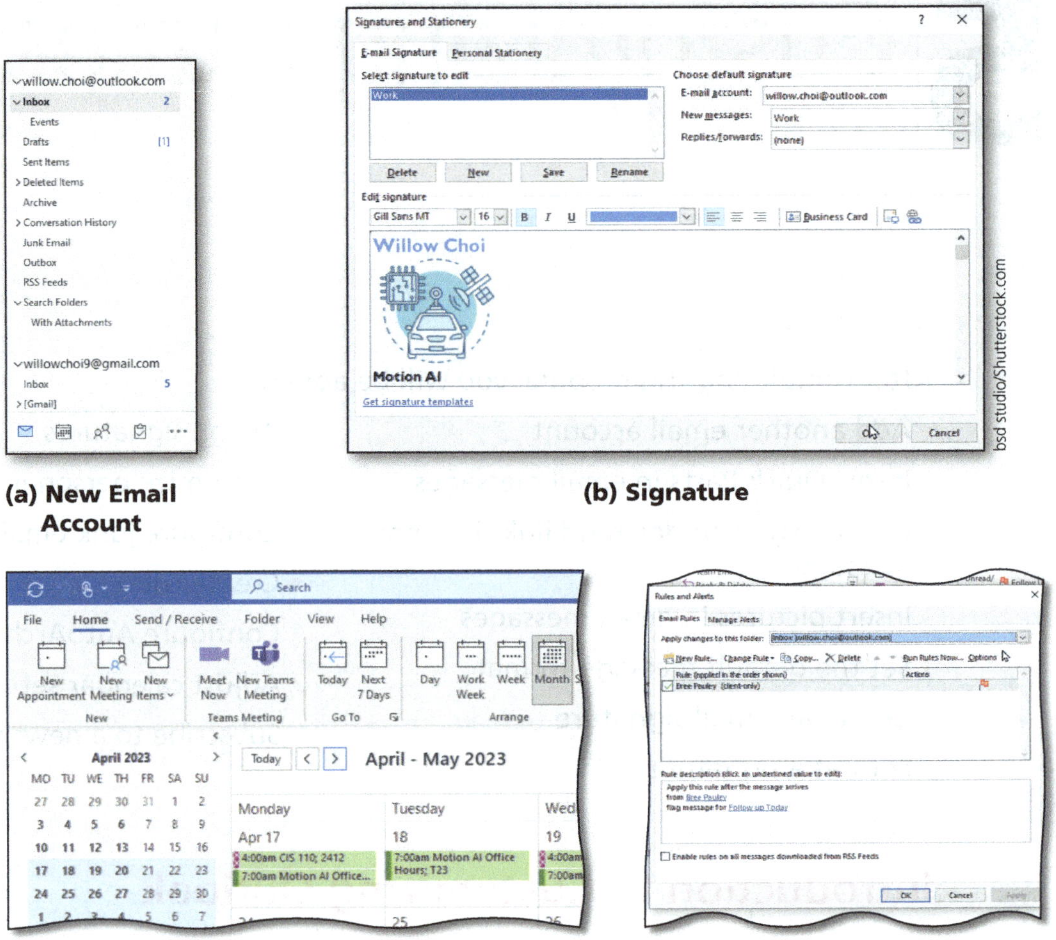

(a) **New Email Account**

(b) **Signature**

(c) **Customized Calendar**

(d) **Email Rules**

Figure 5–1

In this module, you will learn how to perform basic customization tasks. The following list identifies general activities you will perform as you progress through this module:

- Customize email messages.
- Customize signatures and stationery.
- Manage junk email filters.
- Configure rules.
- Change Calendar options.
- Add a news feed.

BTW

The Ribbon and Screen Resolution

Outlook may change how the groups and buttons within the groups appear on the ribbon, depending on the computer or mobile device's screen resolution. Thus, your ribbon may look different from the ones in this book if you are using a screen resolution other than 1366 × 768.

Adding New Email Accounts

As you learned in Module 1, when setting up an email account, you need to know basic information such as the email address and password. For example, in Figure 5–2, the first mailbox is displayed as Outlook Data File (SC_OUT_5_Willow.pst). The second mailbox displayed in Figure 5–2 is an additional Internet-based email account named willowchoi9@gmail.com.

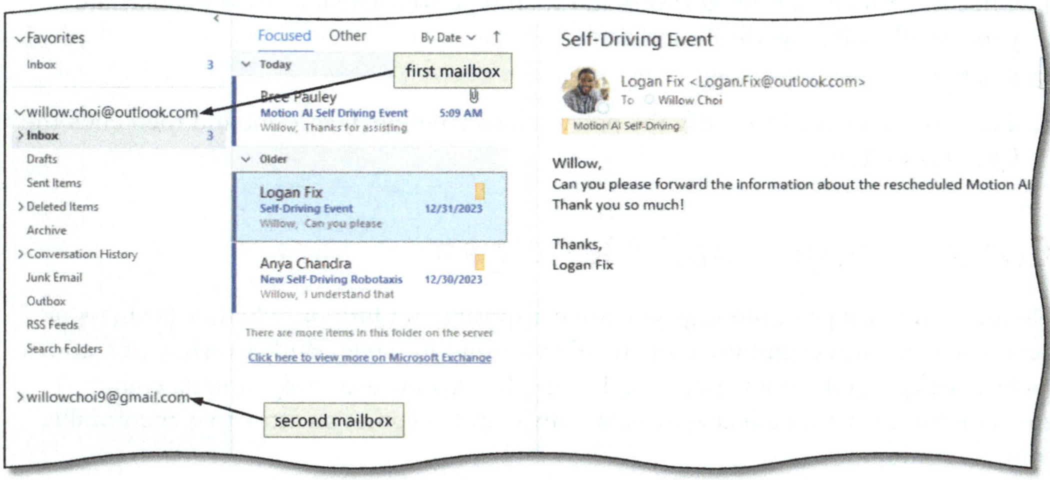

Monkey Business Images/Shutterstock.com

Figure 5–2

After you install Outlook, the Auto Account Setup feature runs and helps you to set up the first email account that Outlook manages. You can add another account and then use Outlook to manage two or more mailboxes.

Depending on your instructor's preferences and your email services, you can perform the steps in this module by opening an Outlook Data File provided with the book and by adding a new email account to Outlook. Before you can add a new email account in Outlook, you must have an account set up with an email service provider that is different from any other account already set up in Outlook. For example, you might have a Microsoft account that provides email service. If you have not configured this account in Outlook, you can complete the steps in this module to do so.

To add a new account, you use the Add Account option in Backstage view to use the Add Account dialog box. If you want to add an account and change advanced settings, you should use the Account Settings dialog box instead.

CONSIDER THIS

My work email address requires additional information to set up my account. Where do I place this server information?

For the work email account you plan to add, make sure you know the account properties and settings before you start to add the account. Gather the following information: type of account, such as email, text messaging, or fax mail; your name, email address, and password; and the server information, including account type and the addresses of incoming and outgoing mail servers. You typically receive the server information from the IT staff at your place of employment. If additional server information is needed, click Manual setup or additional server types when you create an account to add this information.

To Add an Email Account

Willow has a second email address that she dedicates to mailing lists. She uses a second email account (willowchoi9@gmail.com) within Outlook so that she can manage both her primary and secondary email accounts. To follow all the steps within this module, an additional email account is necessary.

If you choose to add an email account to Outlook, you would use the following steps. If you are performing these steps on your computer, enter the name, email address, and password for an email account you own but have not yet added to Outlook.

BTW
Multiple Email Accounts
If you have multiple email accounts configured in Outlook, you can decide which email account to use each time you compose and send a new email message. To select the account from which to send the email message, click the From button in the Untitled - Message window, and then click the desired email account.

1. Start Outlook.
2. Click the File tab and then click Add Account.
3. Click the 'Email address' text box and then type your email address to associate your email address with the account.
4. Click the Connect button.
5. Type your password to verify the password to your email account and then click the Connect button.

Customizing Email Messages

No matter what type of message you are composing in Outlook, whether business or personal, you always can find a way to add your unique style. With a variety of features such as background colors, graphics, designs, links, and custom signatures, your email message starts as a blank, generic canvas and becomes an attractive, memorable communication.

To Add a Link to an Email Message

An instructor named Zion Gibson asked Willow to send him the web address of the Motion AI Self-Driving site. Zion is interested in attending the self-driving event and wants to check the webpage for more information. Willow can send him the web address as a link in an email message. ***Why?** Outlook automatically formats links so that recipients can use them to access a website directly.* To follow the link, the recipient can hold down the CTRL key and click the link, which is formatted as blue, underlined text by default. The following steps add a link within an email message.

1

- Open the SC_OUT_5-1.pst Outlook Data File in Outlook, and then click Outlook Data File in the Navigation pane to display its contents.
- Click the Inbox folder to display the mailbox.
- Click the New Email button (Home tab | New group) to open the Untitled - Message (HTML) window.
- Type **zion.gibson@outlook.com** in the To box to enter the email address of the recipient.
- Click the Subject box, and then type **Motion AI** to enter the subject line.
- Press TAB to move the insertion point into the message area (Figure 5–3).

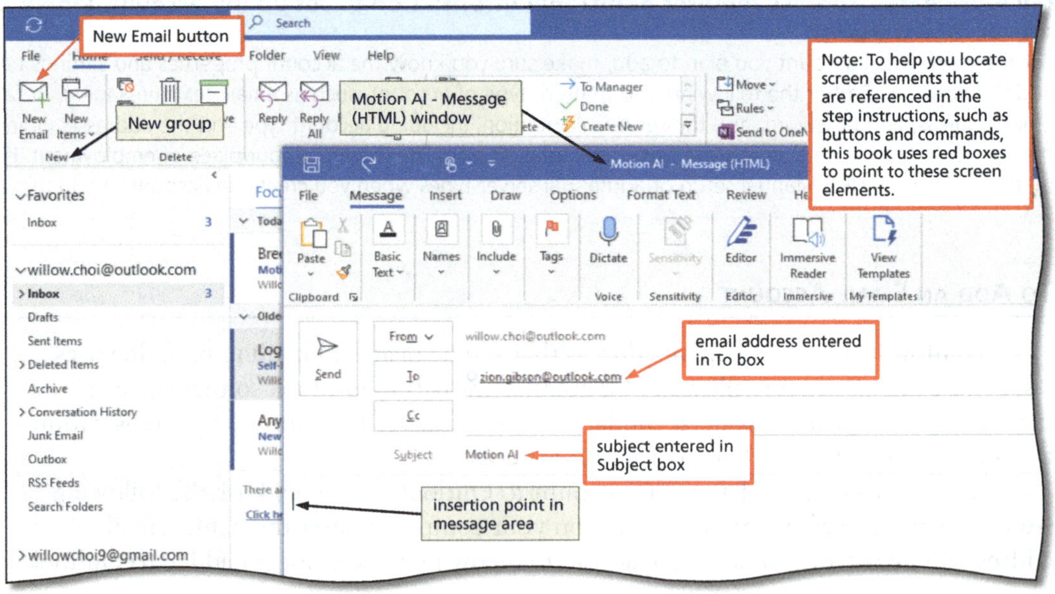

Figure 5–3

2

- Type **Zion,** as the greeting line and then press ENTER twice to insert a blank line between the greeting line and the message text.
- Type **Per your request, the self-driving event site can be found at** and then press SPACEBAR to enter the message text.
- Click Insert on the ribbon to display the Insert tab (Figure 5–4).

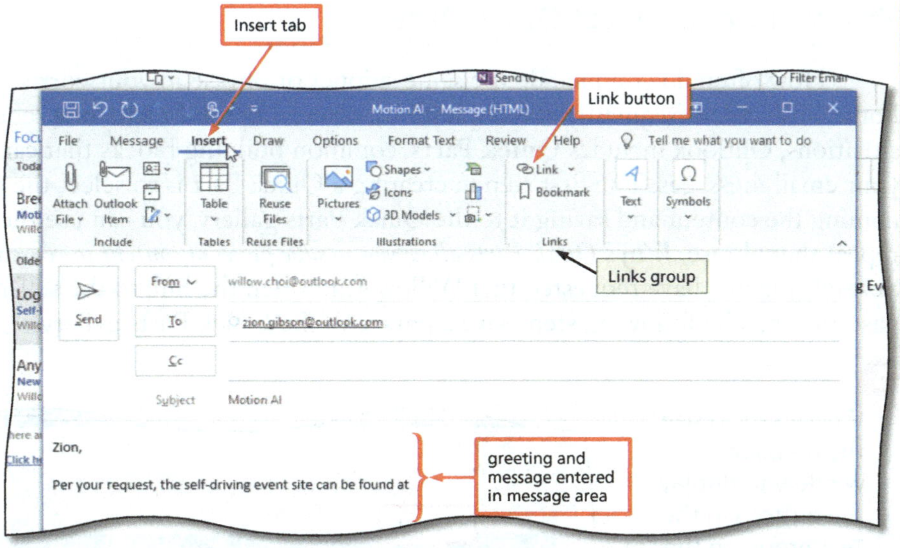

Figure 5–4

3

- Click the Link button (Insert tab | Links group) to display the Insert Hyperlink dialog box.
- In the Address box, type **motionai.com/events** to enter a link to a web address (Figure 5–5).

Q&A Why do I not have to type the https:// part of the web address?
When you insert a link, Outlook does not require the Hypertext Transfer Protocol Secure (https) portion of the address.

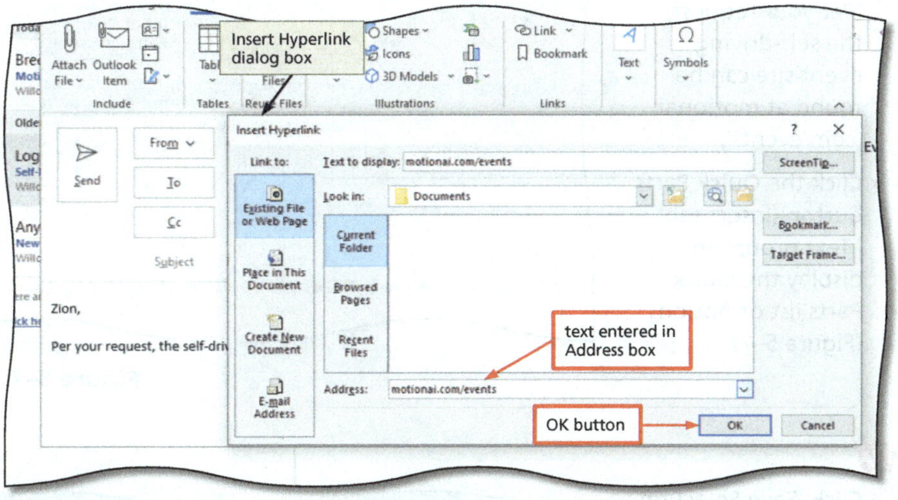

Figure 5–5

4

- Click OK to insert the link in the message body (Figure 5–6).

Q&A When I paste a long file link from my OneDrive account in an email message, how is it displayed?
Instead of a long file link being displayed, friendlier link names in email are displayed. When you include a link to a file in an email, the file name replaces the long link.

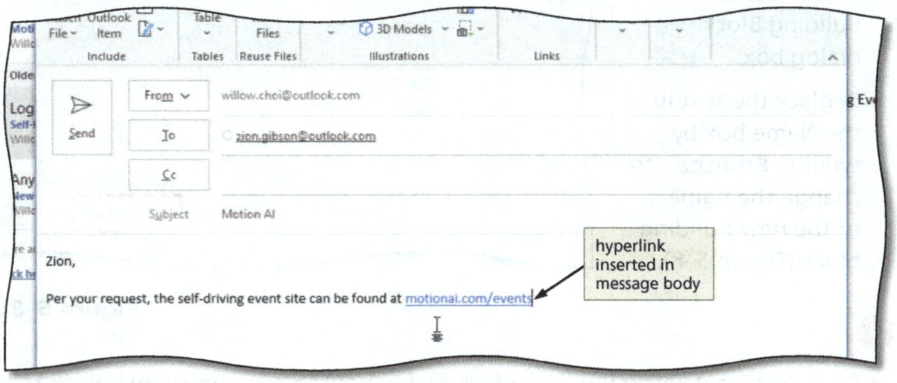

Figure 5–6

Other Ways

1. Press CTRL+K

To Create and Insert Quick Parts

How often do you include the same snippet or phrase in your correspondence, such as directions to your home, answers to frequently asked questions, or even the full name of a school or business? To assist you in these situations, Outlook includes **Quick Parts**, common building blocks that can be recycled and used again within your email messages. The first step in creating a Quick Part is to select the content that you want to reuse. After naming the content and saving it to the Quick Parts gallery, you can use the Quick Part whenever you need to repeat that phrase. ***Why?*** *Quick Parts allow you to save pieces of content to reuse them easily within your email messages.* Several students have requested that Willow send them the link to the self-driving events at Motion AI in the past month. The following steps save a phrase to the Quick Parts gallery.

1

- If necessary, resize the message window to display the buttons in the Text group on the Insert tab.
- Select the phrase 'Per your request, the self-driving event site can be found at motionai .com/events'.
- Click the Quick Parts button (Insert tab | Text group) to display the Quick Parts list of options (Figure 5–7).

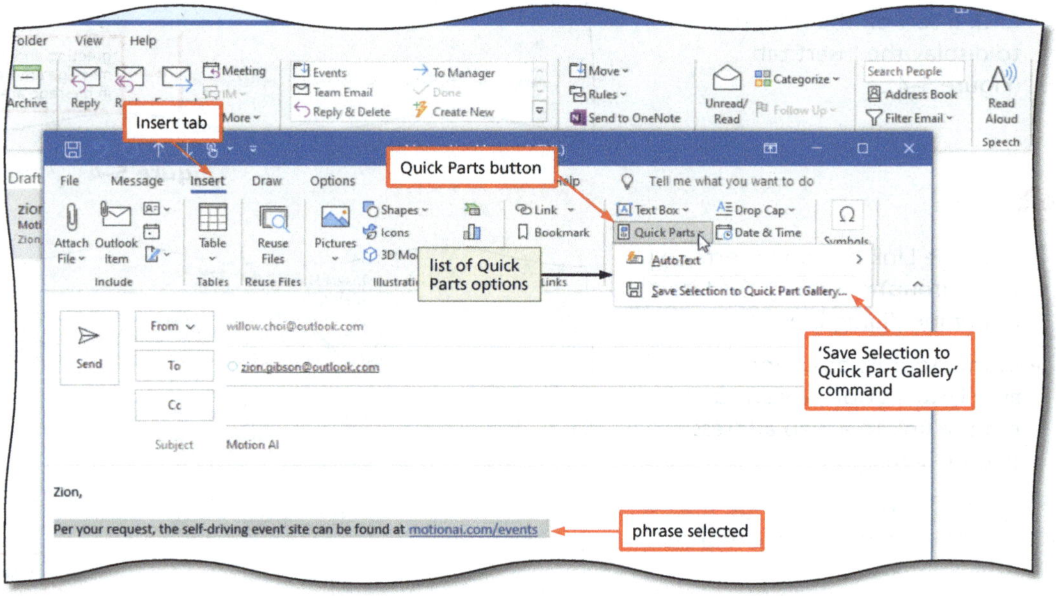

Figure 5–7

2

- Click 'Save Selection to Quick Part Gallery' to display the Create New Building Block dialog box.
- Replace the text in the Name box by typing **Events** to change the name of the new building block (Figure 5–8).

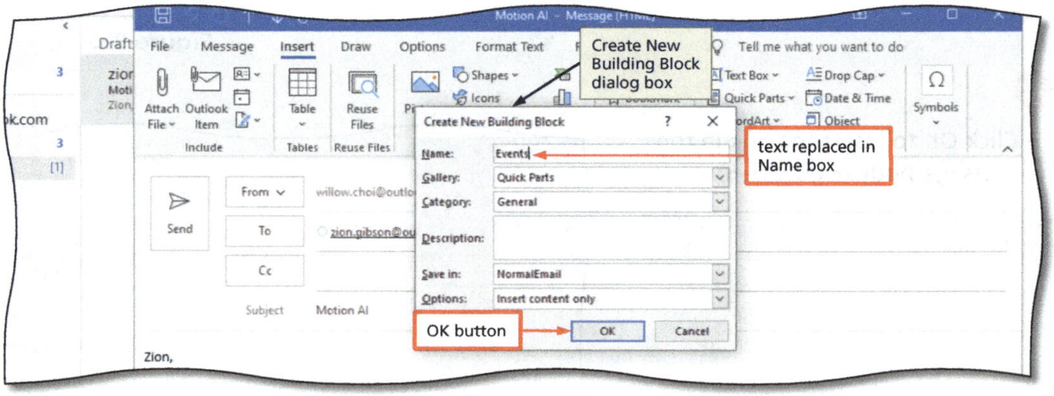

Figure 5–8

3

- Click OK (Create New Building Block dialog box) to add the Events block to the Quick Parts gallery.

Experiment

- Click the Quick Parts button (Insert tab | Text group) to display a list of Quick Parts options. Click Events to insert the building block into the email message. When you are finished, click the Undo button on the Quick Access Toolbar to remove the Events text.

To Insert an Image into an Email Message

As you learned in Module 1, you can attach files to an email message, including image files. Outlook also provides the ability to insert an image directly within the message body of an email message. The images inserted into an email can be your own photographs, but you also have the option of using Microsoft's library of royalty-free images, icons, and illustrations. ***Why?*** *The recipient can quickly view the image without downloading an attachment or saving the picture on their computer.* Willow would like to add a stock image into the body of the email. The following steps insert an image into an email message.

BTW

Adding Alt Text to Images

When you insert an image such as a picture or icon into an email message, add alternative text, or alt text, to the image so that people with limited vision can identify the content. Screen readers narrate the alt text, which typically describes the subject of the image. To add alt text to an image in Outlook, right-click the image, and then click Edit Alt Text on the shortcut menu.

1

- Click after the motionai.com/events web address, and then press ENTER twice to move the insertion point to a new line.
- Click the Pictures button (Insert tab | Illustrations group) to display the Insert Picture From options (Figure 5–9).

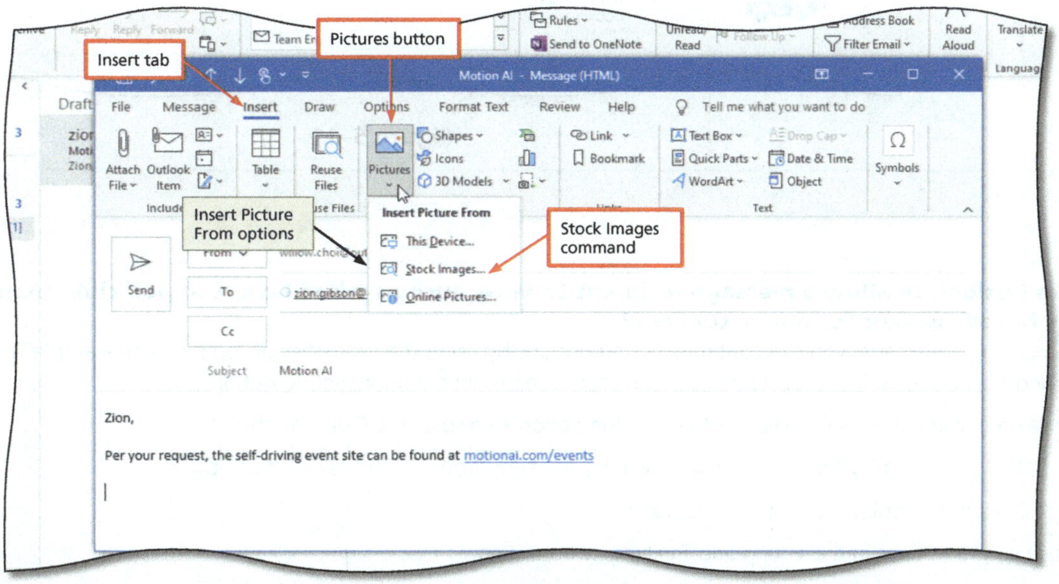

Figure 5–9

2

- Click Stock Images to display the stock image dialog box.
- Click the Icons tab to display the Icons library.
- Type **electric car** in the Search box to display icons of electric cars.
- Click the black electric car with a plug icon (or similar image) to select an icon (Figure 5–10).

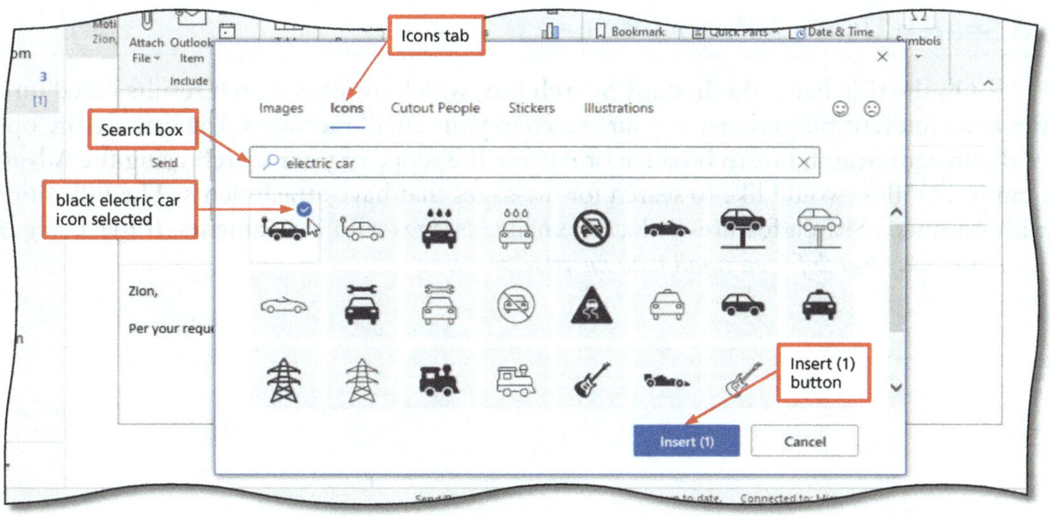

Figure 5–10

3

- Click the Insert (1) button (shown in Figure 5–10) to add the icon image to the message body (Figure 5–11).

4

- Click the Save button on the Quick Access Toolbar to save the email message in the Drafts folder.
- Close the Motion AI - Message (HTML) window.

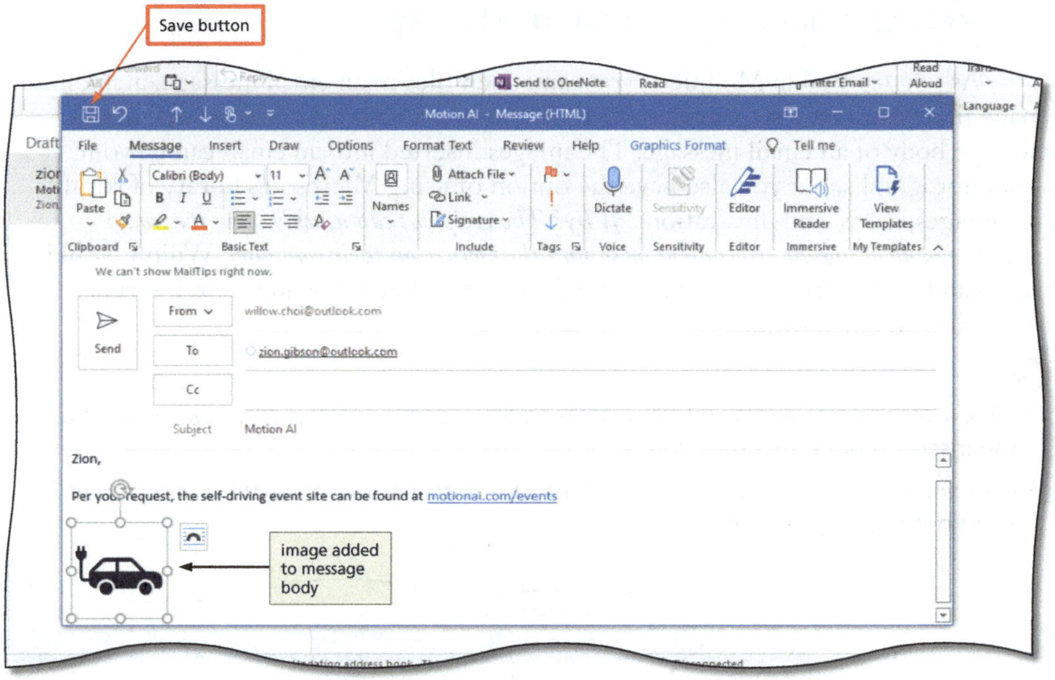

Figure 5–11

CONSIDER THIS

Can I use Outlook to allow a message recipient to vote, such as when I want to poll club members for their preferred speaker for our next event?

When composing a message, you can configure voting options by using the Properties dialog box. For example, you can choose to use voting buttons as well as request delivery and read receipts. To configure voting options:

1. While composing a message, click Options on the ribbon to display the Options tab.
2. Click the Use Voting Buttons button (Options tab | Tracking group) to display a list of options.
3. Click Custom to display the Properties dialog box.
4. Select voting options in the Voting and Tracking options area.
5. Click the Close button to close the Properties dialog box.

To Search Using Advanced Search

On the title bar is the **Instant Search** box, which displays search results based on any matching words and the most relevant files related to your search in your email messages. You can use the options arrow on the right of the Instant Search box to broaden or narrow the scope of your search using the Advanced Search features. For example, Willow would like to search for messages that have attachments. The following steps use Instant Search with Advanced Search features to locate email messages with attachments. ***Why?*** *Using Advanced Search features, you can quickly search for an email with an attachment.*

1

- If necessary, select your Inbox, and then click the Instant Search box to display the Advanced Search arrow.
- Click the Advanced Search arrow to display the Advanced Search options (Figure 5–12).

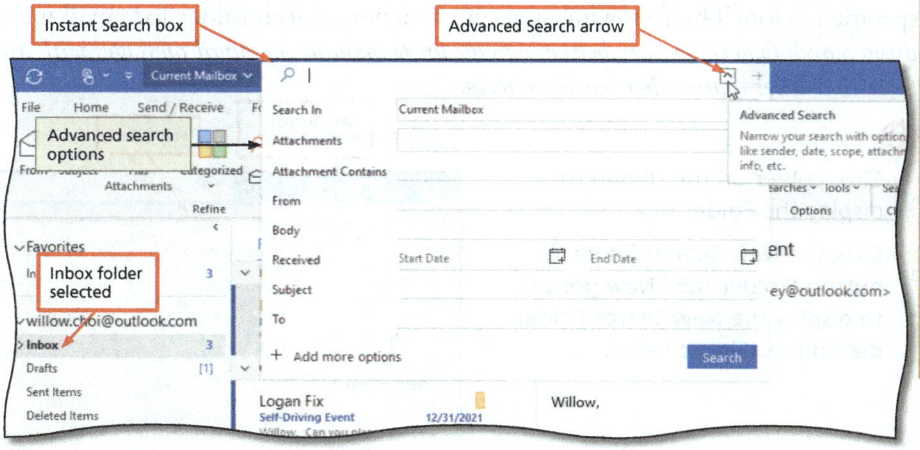

Figure 5–12

2

- Click the 'Choose a value to search for' arrow in the Attachments box to display the Yes or No options.
- Click Yes in the Attachments box to display Yes as your selection to display email messages with attachments (Figure 5–13).

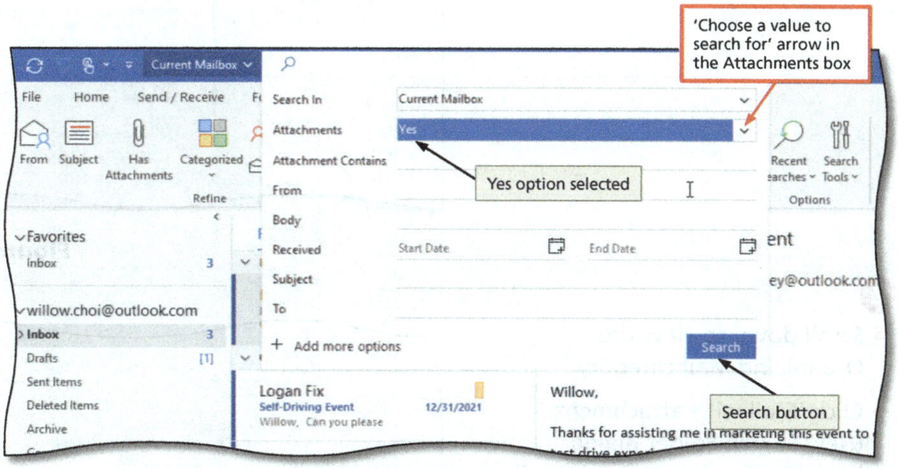

Figure 5–13

3

- Click the Search button (shown in Figure 5–13) to display the Inbox messages that meet the attachment search criterion (Figure 5–14).

4

- Click the Close button (shown in Figure 5–14) to display all the Inbox messages.

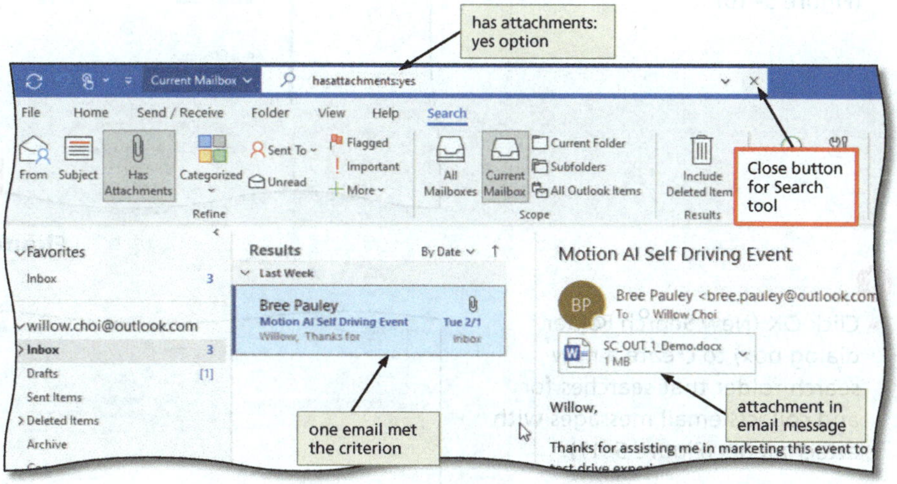

Figure 5–14

To Create a New Search Folder

Use search folders to gather email messages and other items into a folder based on search criteria. For example, Willow wants to place messages with attachments into a separate search folder. You might want to create other search folders to view all messages that you have not read yet or to combine messages from a specific person. The following steps create a new search folder for email messages with attachments. ***Why?*** *By using search folders, you can better manage large amounts of email messages with attachments, from a certain person, and those that meet many other search criteria.*

1

- Click Folder on the ribbon to display the Folder tab.
- Click the New Search Folder button (Folder tab | New group) to display the New Search Folder dialog box (Figure 5–15).

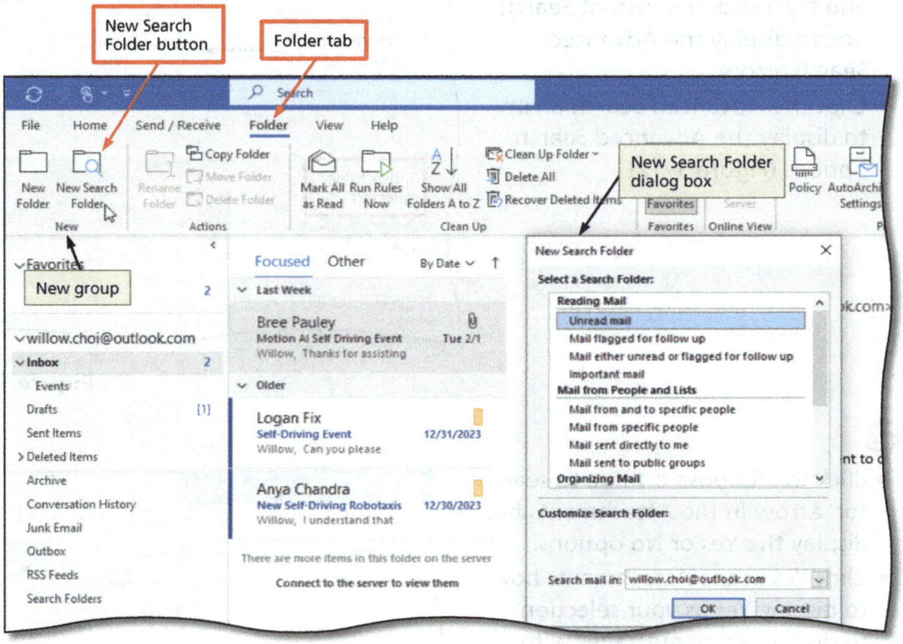

Figure 5–15

2

- Scroll down to view the Organizing Mail category.
- Click 'Mail with attachments' (New Search Folder dialog box) to select the type of email to store in a search folder (Figure 5–16).

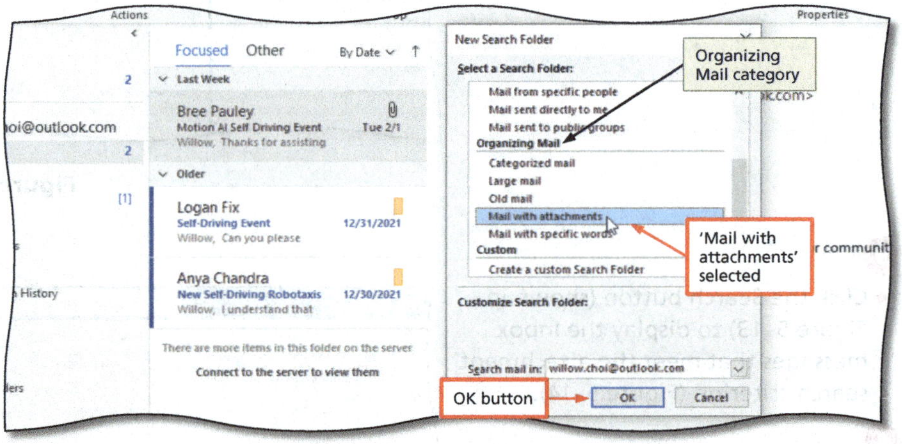

Figure 5–16

3

- Click OK (New Search Folder dialog box) to create a new search folder that searches for and collects email messages with attachments (Figure 5–17).

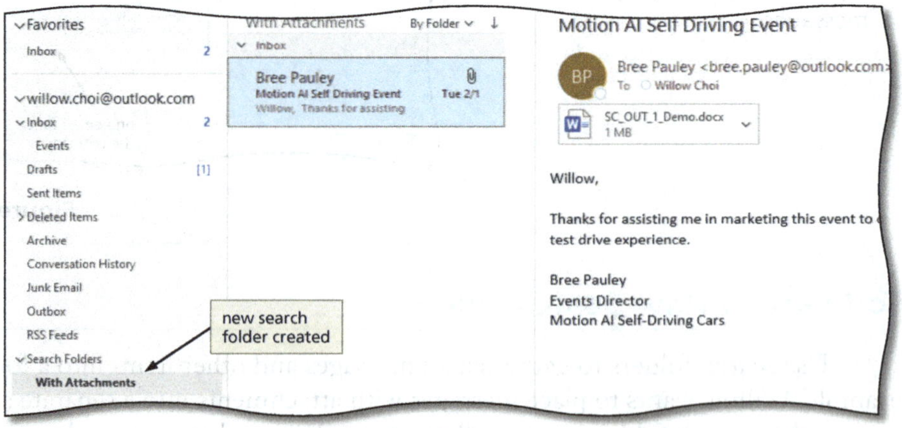

Figure 5–17

To Display Outlook Options

Why? *To customize your Outlook email with default settings such as the message format, you use the Outlook Options dialog box.* The following step displays the Outlook Options dialog box.

1

- Click File on the ribbon to open Backstage view.
- Click the Options tab in Backstage view to display the Outlook Options dialog box (Figure 5–18).

Q&A What options can I set in the General category?

The General category allows you to customize the user interface by enabling the Mini Toolbar and Live Preview, and by changing the ScreenTip style and Theme. You also can personalize Microsoft Outlook by specifying your user name and initials. The Start up options allow you to specify whether Outlook should be the default program for email, contacts, and calendar.

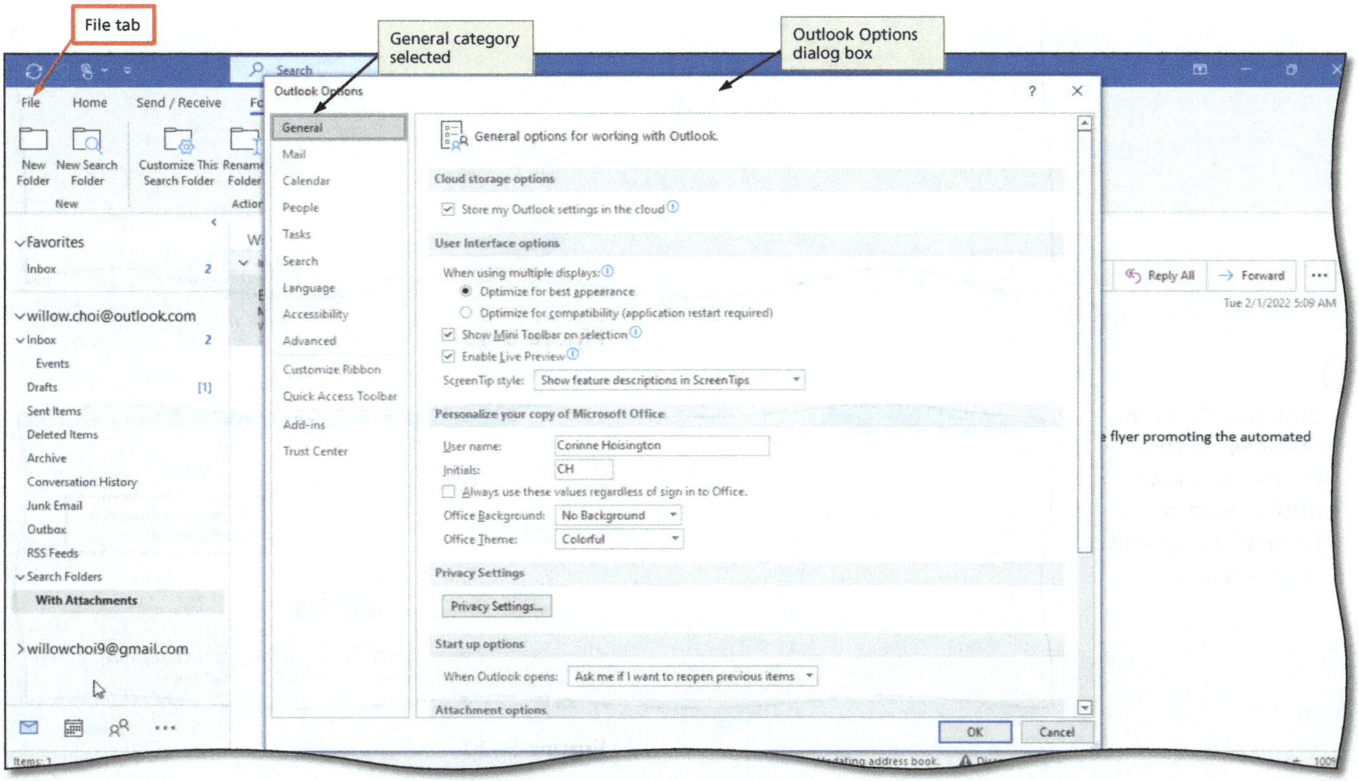

Figure 5–18

To Set the Message Format

Email messages can be formatted as HTML, Plain Text, or Rich Text. As you learned in Module 1, you can format an individual email message using one of these message formats. To make sure that all your email messages use the HTML format by default, set the message format in the Outlook Options dialog box. The HTML message format allows the most flexibility when composing email messages. The following steps set the default message format to HTML. ***Why?*** *Instead of changing each email message to a different format, you can set a default in the Outlook options. All new messages display the default format.*

1

- Click Mail in the Category list to display the Mail options (Figure 5–19).

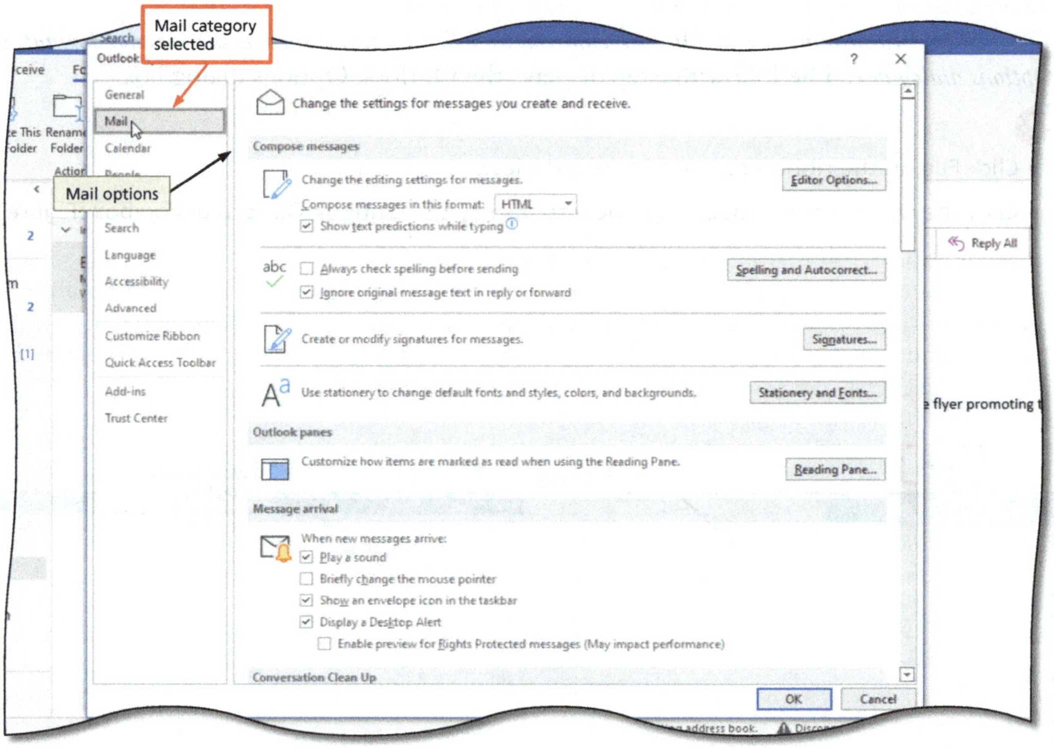

Figure 5–19

2

- Click the 'Compose messages in this format' arrow to display a list of formatting options (Figure 5–20).

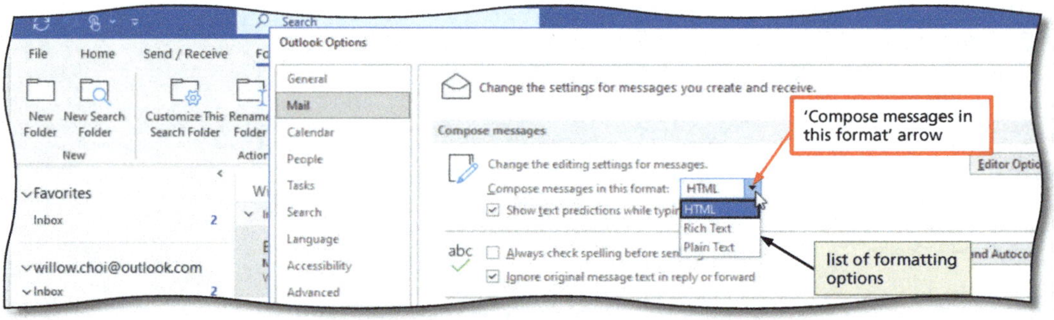

Figure 5–20

3

- If necessary, click HTML to set the default message format to HTML (Figure 5–21).

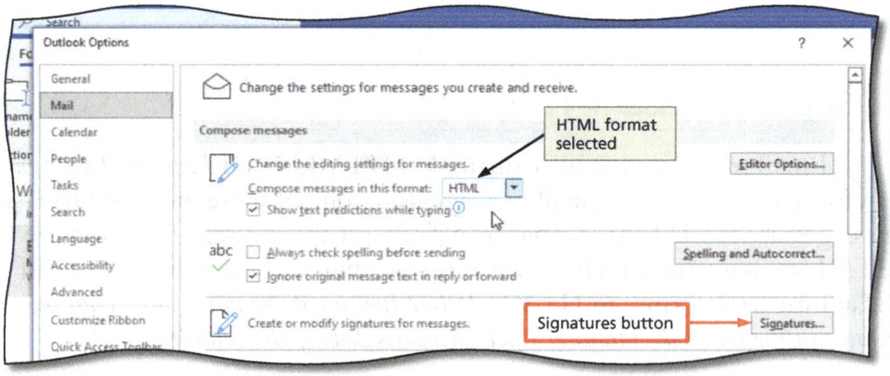

Figure 5–21

Q&A

What if HTML already is selected as the default message format?

Depending on who set up Outlook, the default message format already might be HTML. In that case, you can skip Step 3.

What if I want to choose a different format?

When you display the available message formats, choose the type you want to use. For example, if you want all new email messages to be in the Plain Text format, click the Plain Text option.

CONSIDER THIS

Can I sort my email messages by conversation instead of by date, which is the default setting?

Yes, you can sort by conversation if you prefer to sort your email messages by their subject field grouped by conversation. To sort by conversation:

1. Click View on the ribbon to display the View tab.
2. Click the Show as Conversations check box (View tab | Messages group) to select Show as Conversations.

Your Inbox is re-sorted, linking email messages in the same conversation together. Individual messages that do not belong to a conversation will look the same as before, while those involved in conversations will have a white triangle on the upper-left part of the message header.

If you want to keep unwanted conversations out of the Inbox, click a message in the conversation, click the Ignore button (Home tab | Delete group), and then click Ignore Conversation (Ignore Conversation dialog box). Outlook removes all messages related to the selected conversation and moves future messages in the conversation to the Deleted Items folder.

Creating Signatures and Stationery

You can configure Outlook to add signatures to your email messages automatically. A **signature** is similar to a closing set of lines in a formal letter. It can include your full name, job title, email address, phone number, company information, and logo. You can even include business cards in your signature.

If you have more than one email account, you need to select the account for which you want to create the signature. You can create the signature while you are composing an email message or you can use the Outlook Options dialog box at any other time. If you create the signature while writing an email message, you have to apply the signature to the email message, because Outlook will not insert it automatically. If you create a signature using the Outlook Options dialog box, it is added automatically to all subsequent messages.

Besides adding signatures to your email messages, you can customize the **stationery**, which determines the appearance of your email messages, including background, fonts, and colors. You can pick fonts to use in the email message text, or you can select a theme or stationery design and apply that to your email messages.

To Create an Email Signature

An email signature provides a consistent closing to every email message without requiring you to retype signature lines repeatedly. Willow would like to create an email signature named Work that includes her name, office name, and email address. The following steps create an email signature. ***Why?** An email signature provides your contact information in a condensed format, typically two to four lines.*

1

- Click the Signatures button (Outlook Options dialog box) (shown in Figure 5–21) to display the Signatures and Stationery dialog box (Figure 5–22).

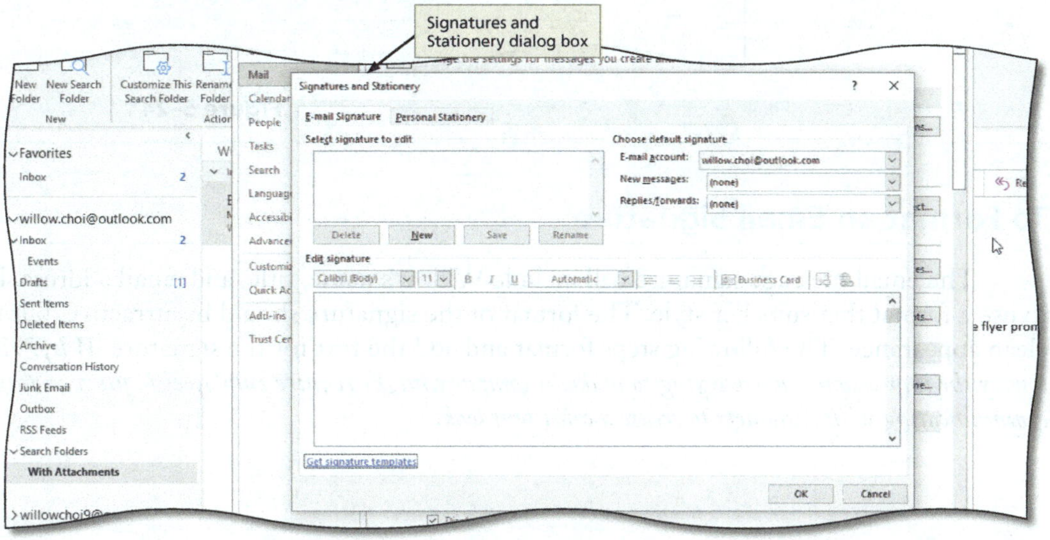

Figure 5–22

2

- Click the New button (Signatures and Stationery dialog box) to display the New Signature dialog box (Figure 5–23).

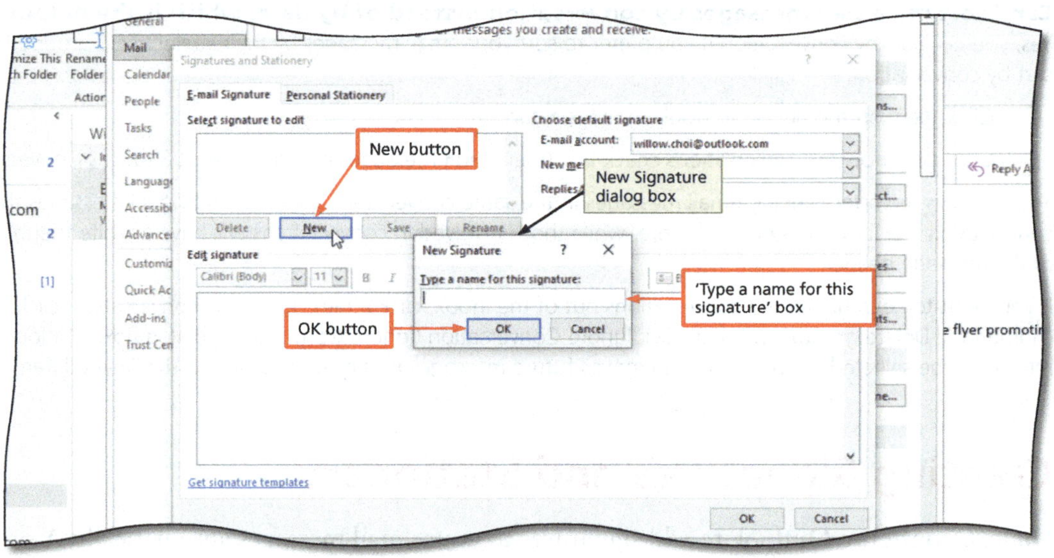

Figure 5–23

3

- Type `Work` in the 'Type a name for this signature' box to enter a name for the signature.
- Click OK (shown in Figure 5–23) to name the signature (Figure 5–24).

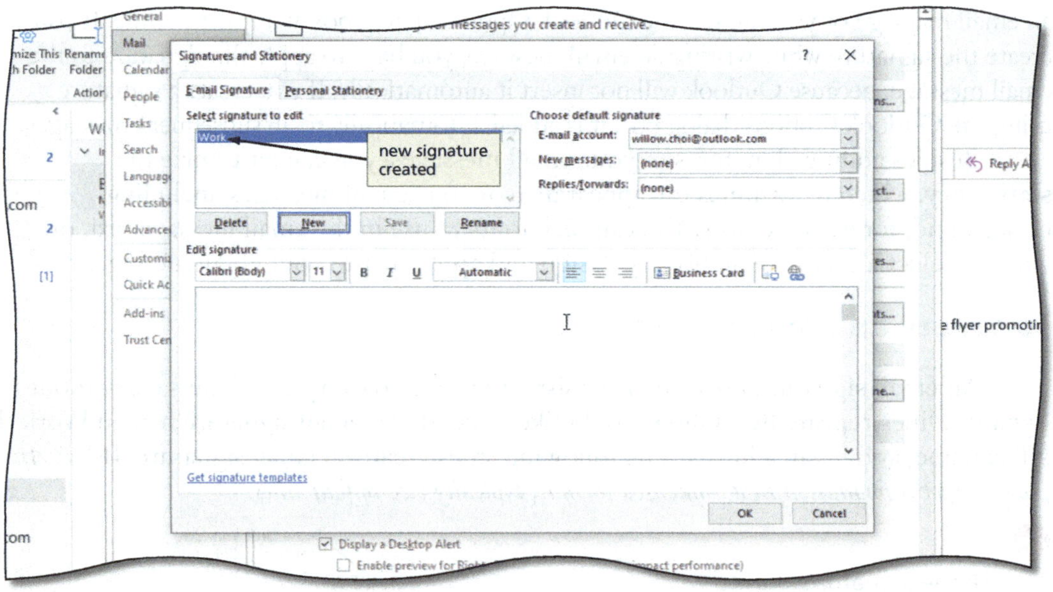

Figure 5–24

To Format an Email Signature

The email message signature will include Willow's name, title, and email address. In addition, she wants to use a format that suits her style. The format of the signature should be attractive, but maintain a professional, clean appearance. The following steps format and add the text for the signature. ***Why?** An email signature should convey the impression you are trying to make. A company might require employees to use a certain email signature when communicating with customers to create a consistent look.*

1

- Click the Font arrow (Signatures and Stationery dialog box) to display a list of fonts (Figure 5–25).

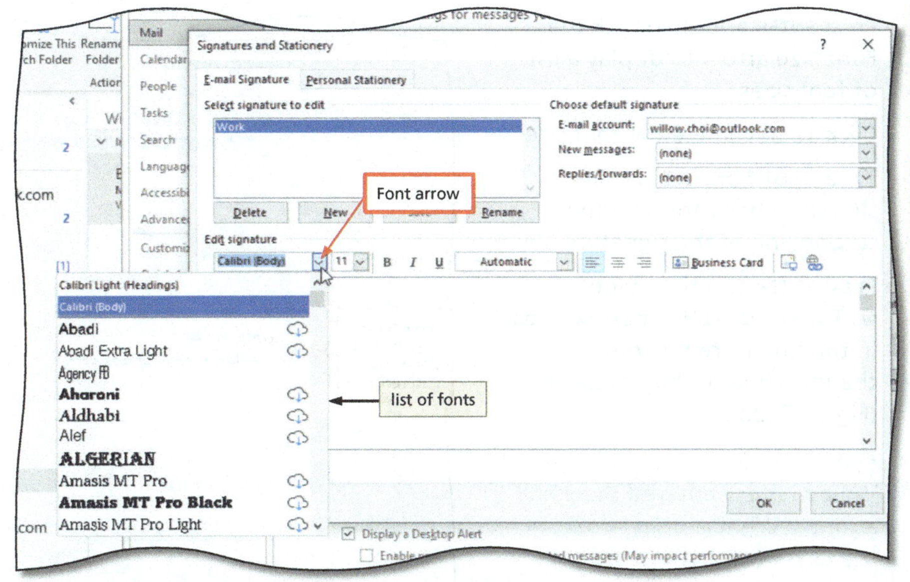

Figure 5–25

2

- Scroll down until Gill Sans MT is visible, and then click Gill Sans MT to select the font.
- Click the Font Size arrow to display a list of font sizes.
- Click 16 to change the font size.
- Click the Bold button to change the font to bold.
- Click the Font Color arrow to display a list of colors (Figure 5–26).

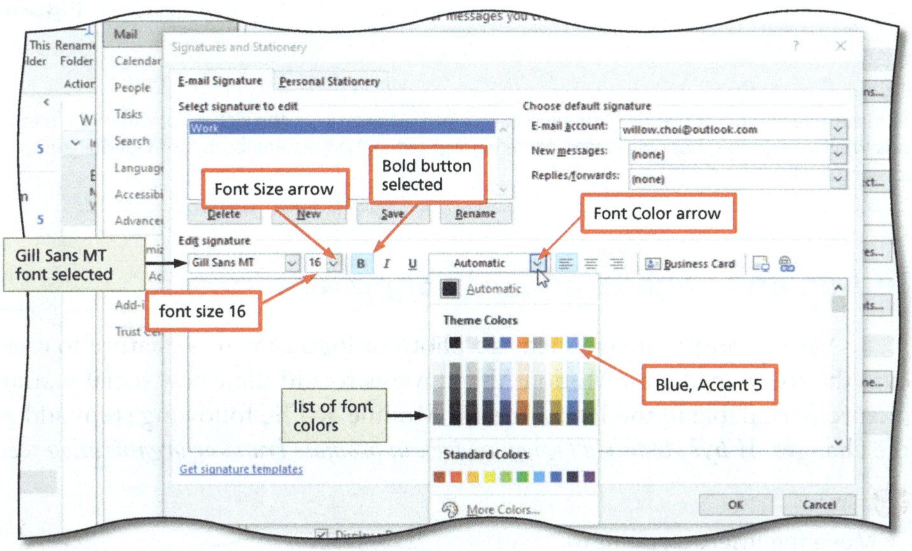

Figure 5–26

3

- Click Blue, Accent 5 (first row, ninth column) to change the font color.
- Type `Willow Choi` in the signature body to enter the first line of the signature.
- Click the Font Color arrow to display a list of colors.
- Click Automatic to change the font color to automatic, which is black (Figure 5–27).

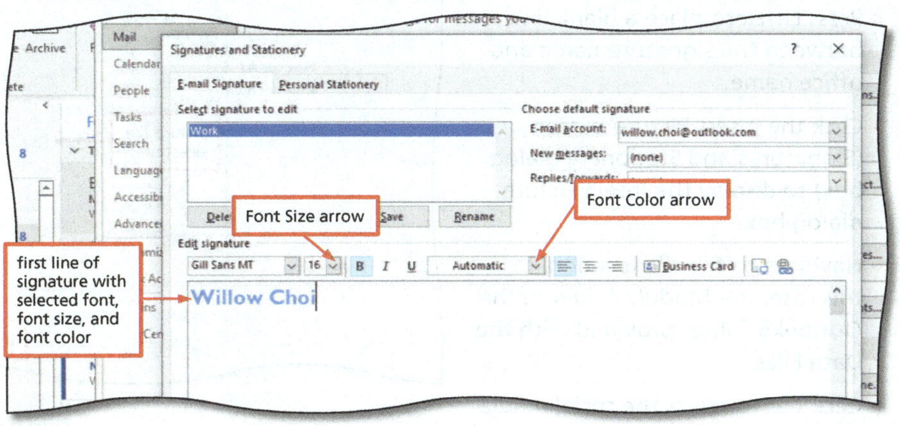

Figure 5–27

4

- Press ENTER and then click the Font Size arrow to display a list of font sizes.
- Click 12 to change the font size.
- Type `Motion AI` in the signature body to enter the second line of the signature.
- Press ENTER and then type `willow.choi@outlook.com` in the signature body to enter the third line of the signature (Figure 5–28).

Q&A Outlook capitalized the W in Willow after I entered the email address. What should I do?
If you want the signature to match the figures in this module, change the W to lowercase.

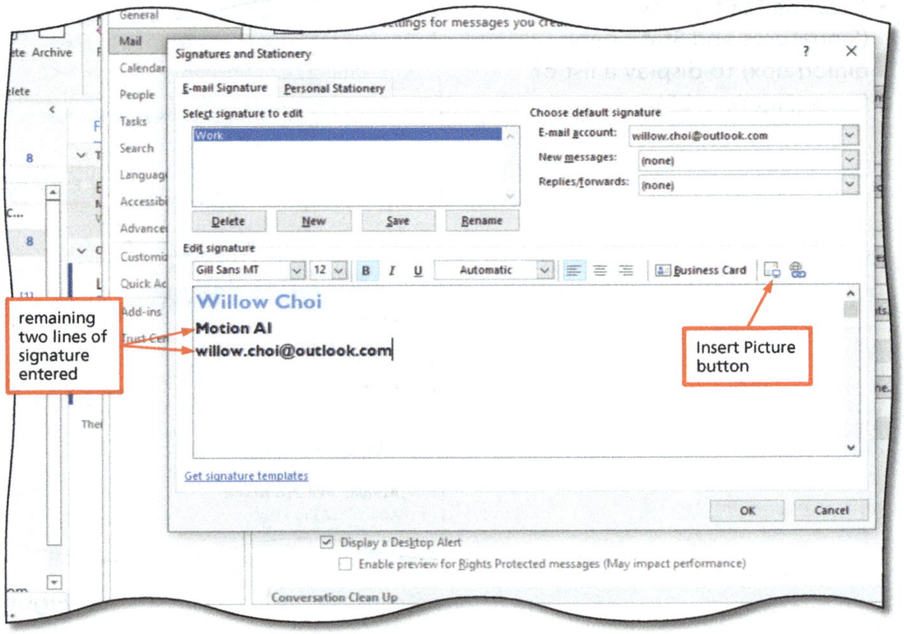

Figure 5–28

BTW
Use @mentions
To make sure you get someone's attention in an email, you can type the @ symbol within the message body, followed by their name (example @ willow). If you do this, not only is their name highlighted in the message body, but Outlook automatically adds them to the To line of the email or meeting invite.

To Add an Image to an Email Signature

You can add an image such as a photo or logo to your signature to create visual appeal. Willow is taking over the social media for Motion AI and wants to add their new social marketing image in her signature. The picture is available in the Data Files for Module 5. The following steps add a logo image to a signature and save the changes. ***Why?** Adding a logo or image can promote brand or organization identity.*

1

- Move the insertion point to the end of the first line of the signature text.
- Press ENTER to place a blank line between the signature name and office name.
- Click the Insert Picture button (Signatures and Stationery dialog box) to display the Insert Picture dialog box.
- Navigate to the file location, in this case, the Module folder in the Outlook5 folder provided with the Data Files.
- Click Car to select the social media image (Figure 5–29).

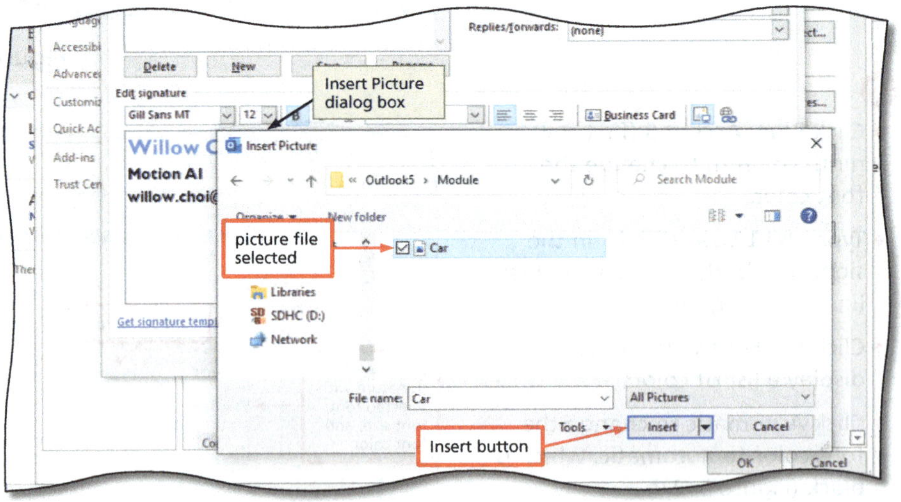

Figure 5–29

2

- Click the Insert button (Insert Picture dialog box) (shown in Figure 5–29) to insert the image into the signature (Figure 5–30).

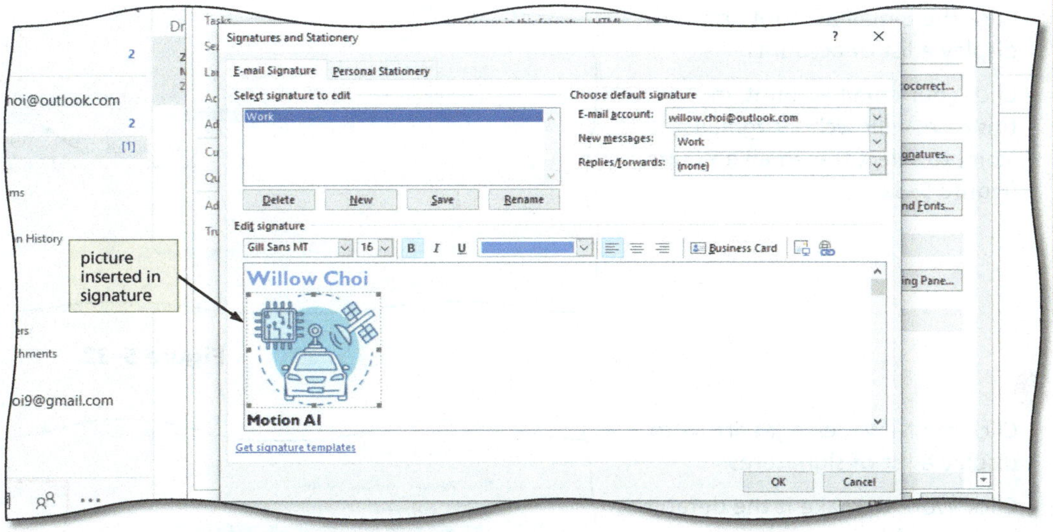

bsd studio/Shutterstock.com

Figure 5–30

3

- Click the Save button (Signatures and Stationery dialog box) to save the changes to the signature (Figure 5–31).

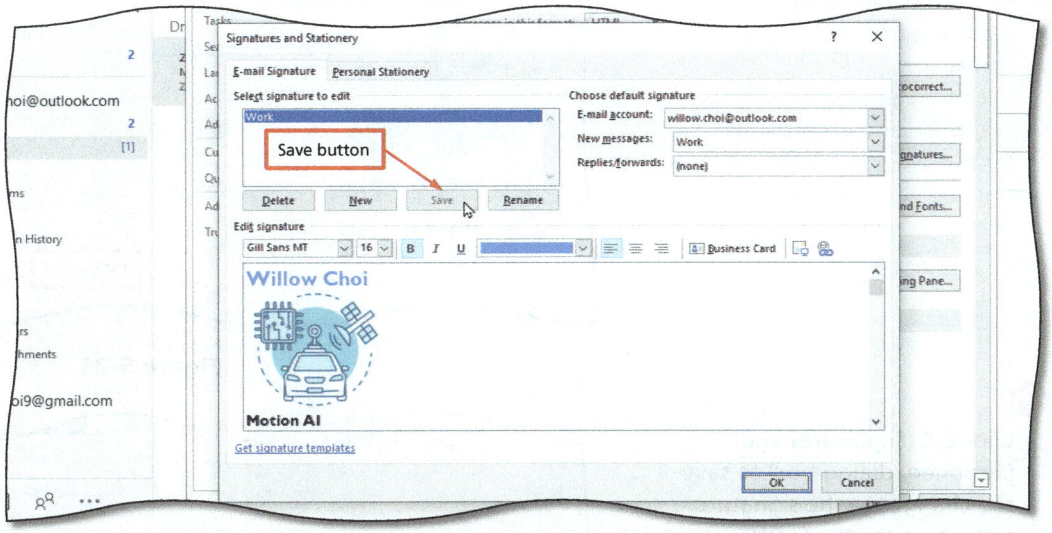

bsd studio/Shutterstock.com

Figure 5–31

To Configure Signature Options

After creating a signature, you need to assign it to an email account. You can associate the signature with as many accounts as you want. You can set two default signatures for a single account: one for new messages and one for replies and forwards. Willow wants to apply her signature for new messages to the email account named willowchoi9@gmail.com (select your own account). The following steps set the default signature for new messages. If you are completing these steps on a personal computer, your email account must be set up in Outlook (see Module 1) to be able to select an email account to apply the signature. ***Why?*** *By associating a signature with a particular email account, your signature automatically appears at the bottom of new messages.*

1

- Click the E-mail account arrow to display a list of accounts.
- Click your email account, in this case, willowchoi9@gmail.com, to select the email account (Figure 5–32).

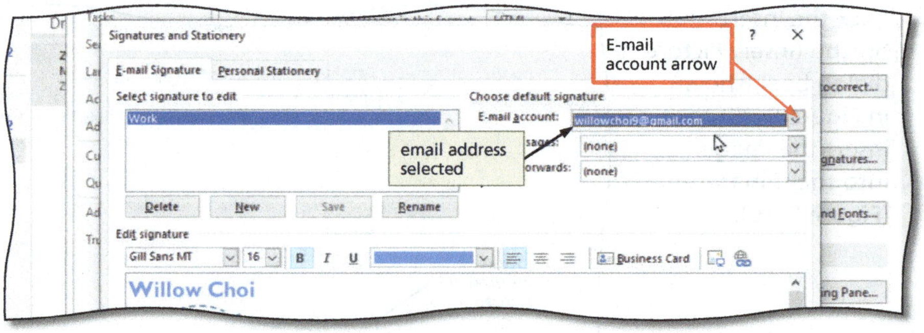

Figure 5–32

2

- Click the New messages arrow to display a list of signatures.
- Click Work to make it the default signature for new messages (Figure 5–33).

Q&A How do I place a signature in all messages including replies and forwards?
Click the Replies/forwards arrow and then click your primary email account to make it the default signature for all message replies and forwards.

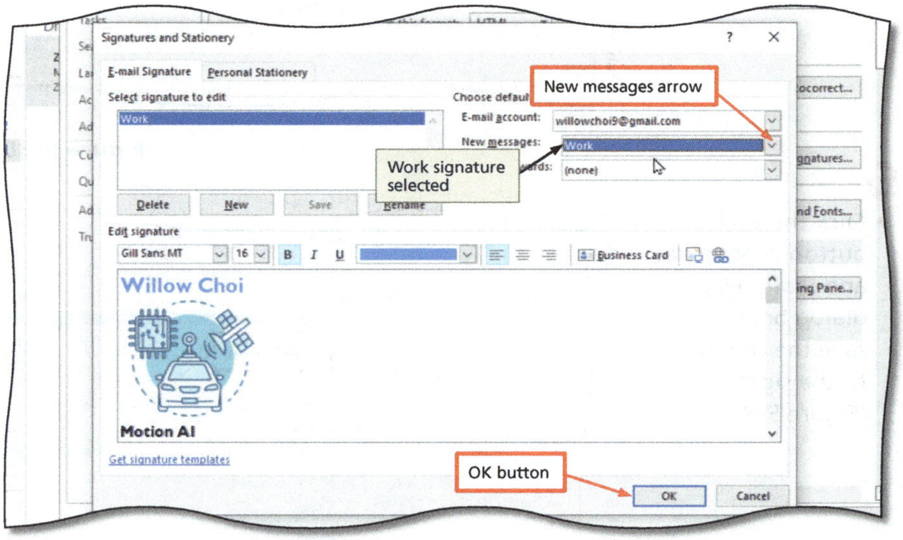

Figure 5–33

bsd studio/Shutterstock.com

3

- Click OK (Signatures and Stationery dialog box) to save the changes to the signature settings, close the Signatures and Stationery dialog box, and return to the Outlook Options dialog box (Figure 5–34).

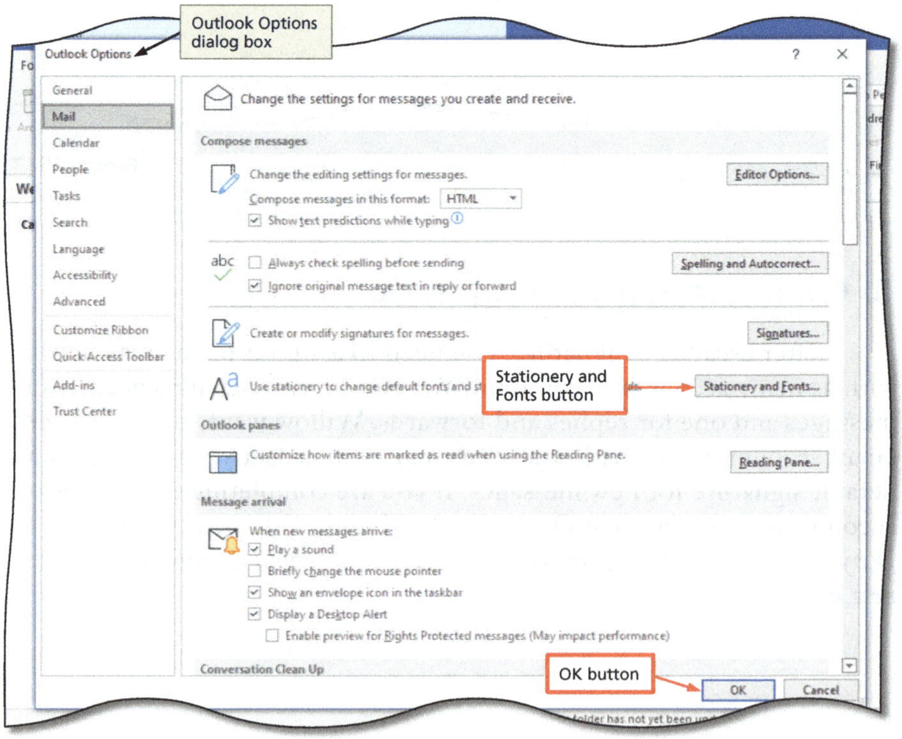

Figure 5–34

To Customize Stationery

Outlook provides backgrounds and patterns for email message stationery and offers themes, which are sets of unified design elements, such as fonts, bullets, colors, and effects that you can apply to messages. Willow decides to use a stationery named Ice, which provides a clean, professional design. The following steps customize the email message stationery. ***Why?*** *Stationery provides a distinctive look for your email messages.*

1

- Click the Stationery and Fonts button (Outlook Options dialog box) to display the Signatures and Stationery dialog box (Figure 5–35).

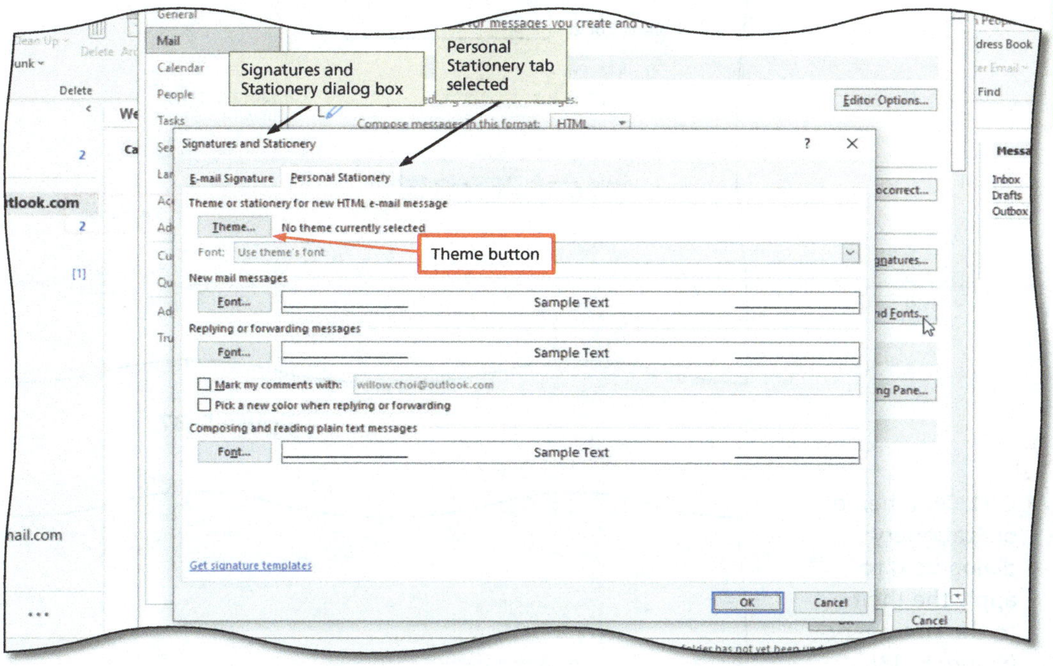

Figure 5–35

2

- Click the Theme button (Signatures and Stationery dialog box) to display the Theme or Stationery dialog box (Figure 5–36).

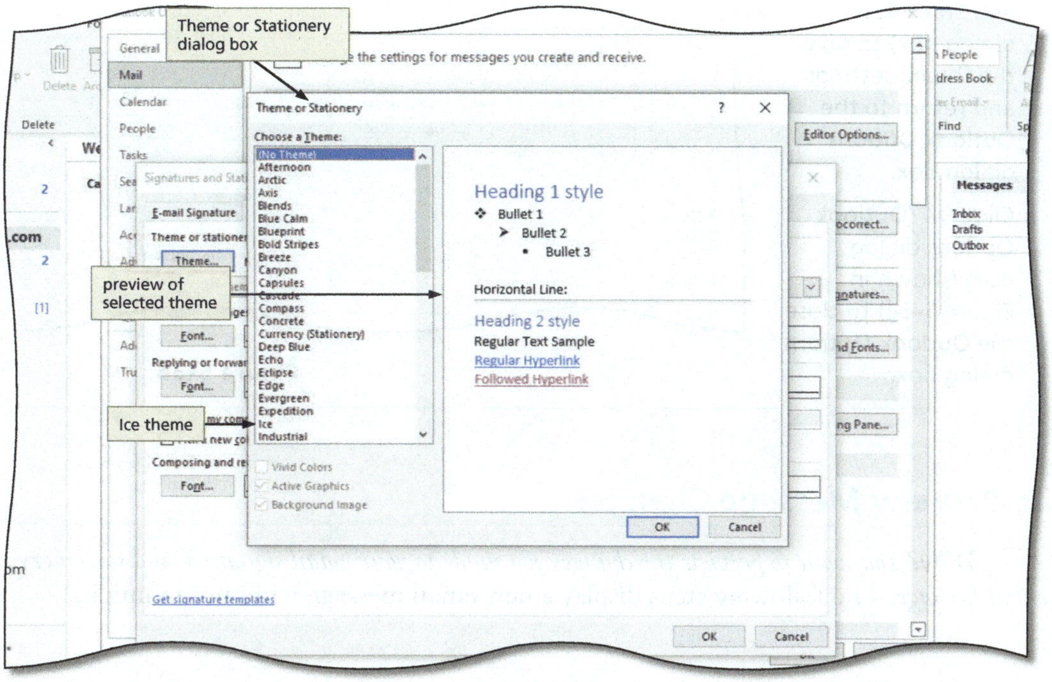

Figure 5–36

3

- Click Ice to select it and display a preview of its formats (Figure 5–37).

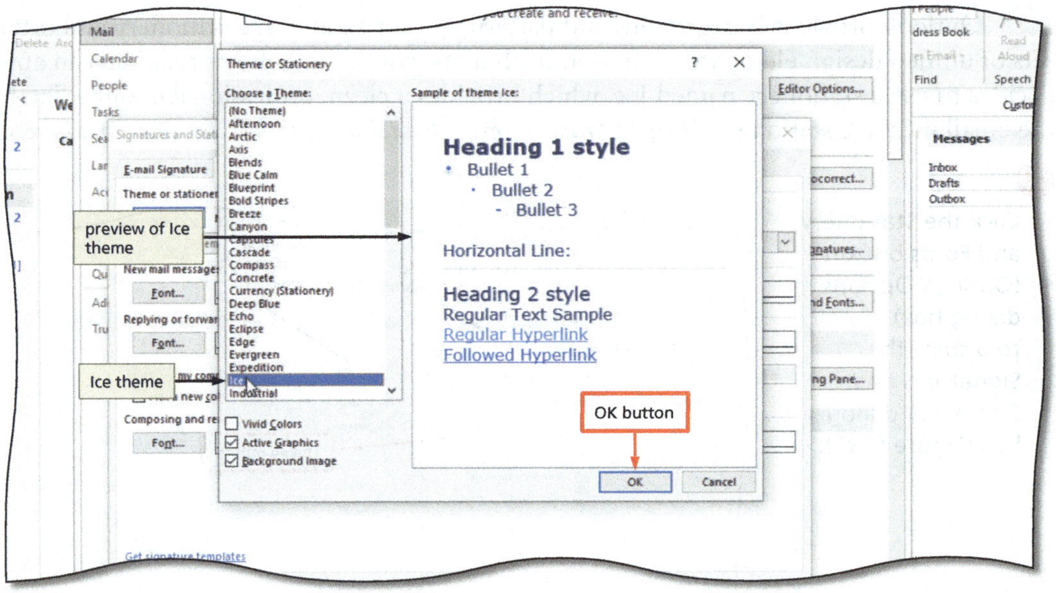

Figure 5–37

4

- Click OK (Theme or Stationery dialog box) to apply the theme to the stationery (Figure 5–38).

5

- Click OK (Signatures and Stationery dialog box) to save the theme settings and return to the Outlook Options dialog box.
- Click OK (Outlook Options dialog box) (shown in Figure 5–34) to close the Outlook Options dialog box.

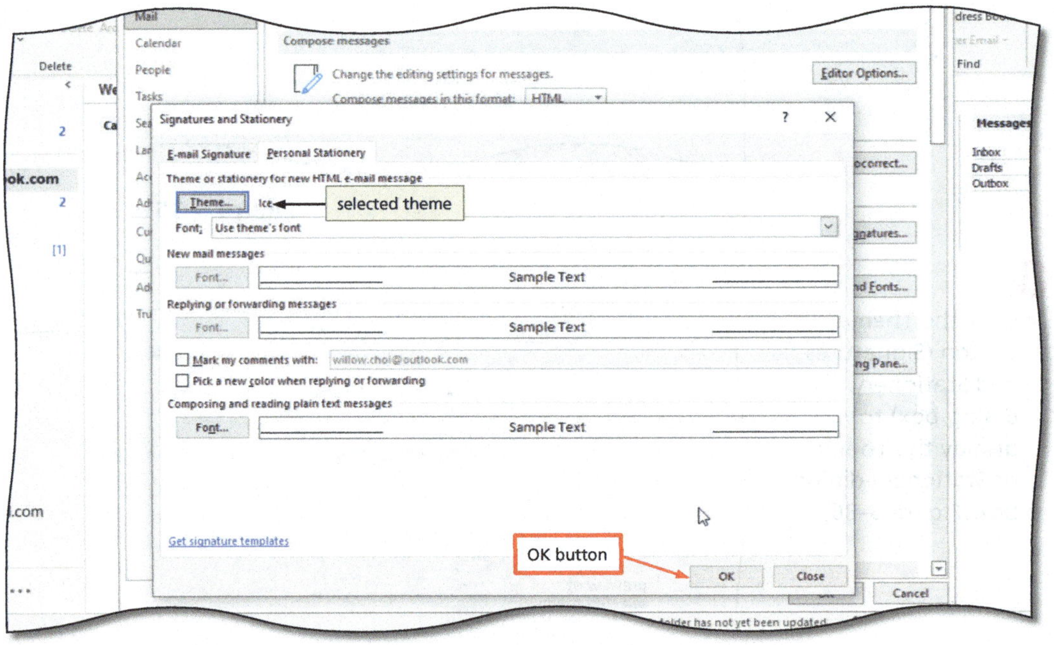

Figure 5–38

To Preview Message Changes

Why? You want to preview the changes you made to your email signature and stationery and see how they look in an email message. The following steps display a new email message without sending it.

1

- Click Home on the ribbon to display the Home tab.
- Click the New Email button (Home tab | New group) to create a new email message (Figure 5–39).

2

- Close the email message without sending it.

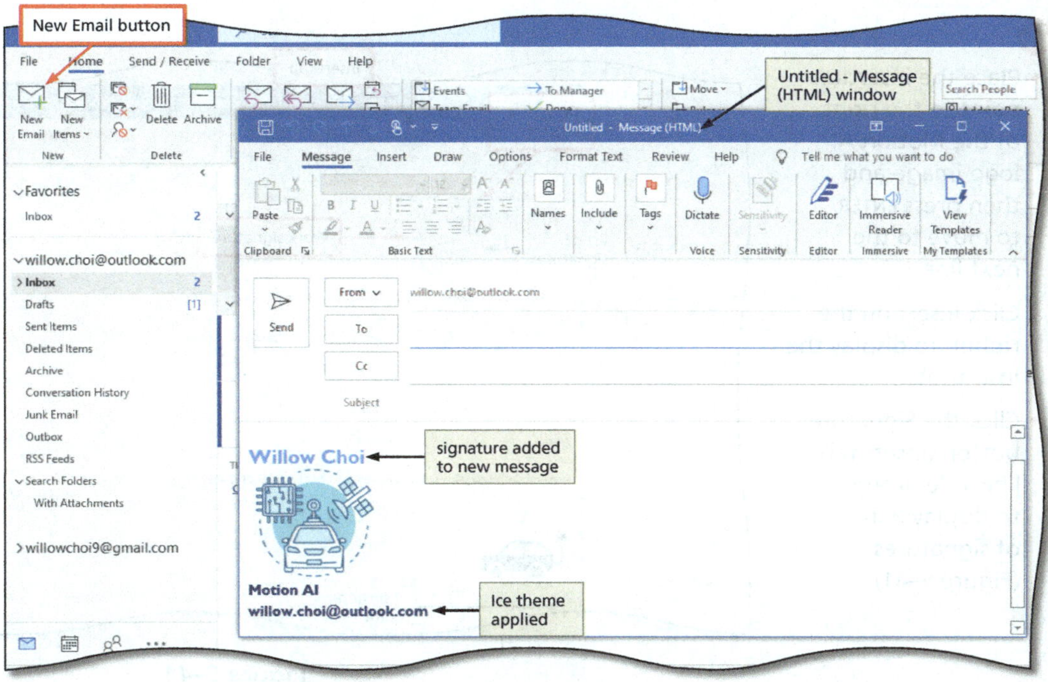

bsd studio/Shutterstock.com

Figure 5–39

To Assign Signatures to a Single Email Message

If you use multiple email accounts, you can set a signature for each account or you can apply a signature to an individual email message. Willow still needs to send the email with the Motion AI events link to Zion and wants to apply the Work signature to that message, which is now stored in the Drafts folder. ***Why?*** *Instead of assigning your email address to one signature, you may want to create different signatures and apply a signature to individual email messages before you send them.* The following steps assign a signature to a single email message.

1

- Click the Drafts folder in the Navigation pane to display the message header for the Motion AI email message in the message list.
- Double-click the Motion AI message header in the messages pane to open the Motion AI - Message (HTML) window (Figure 5–40).

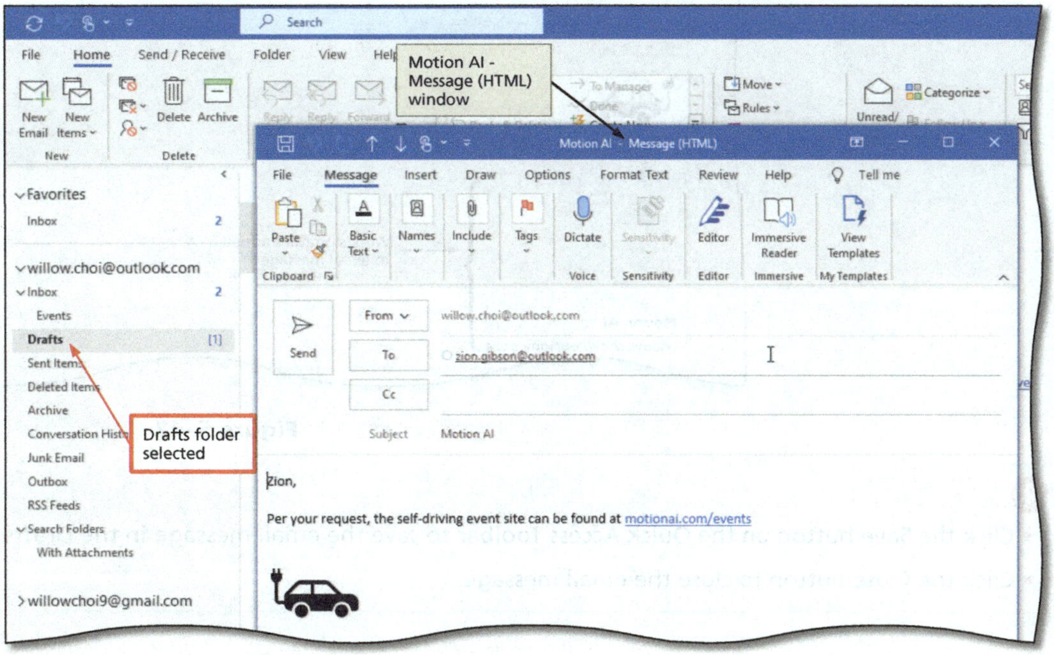

Figure 5–40

2

- Place the insertion point to the right of the Motion AI logo image and then press ENTER to move to the next line.
- Click Insert on the ribbon to display the Insert tab.
- Click the Signature button (Insert tab | Include group) to display a list of signatures (Figure 5–41).

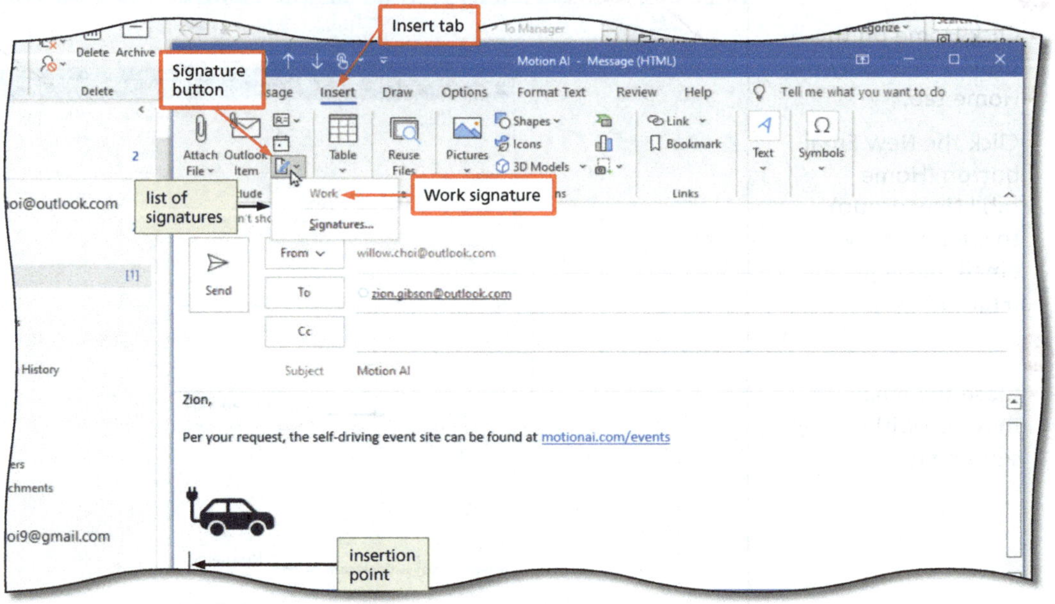

Figure 5–41

3

- Click Work to add the Work signature to the email message body.
- Scroll down to view the full signature (Figure 5–42).

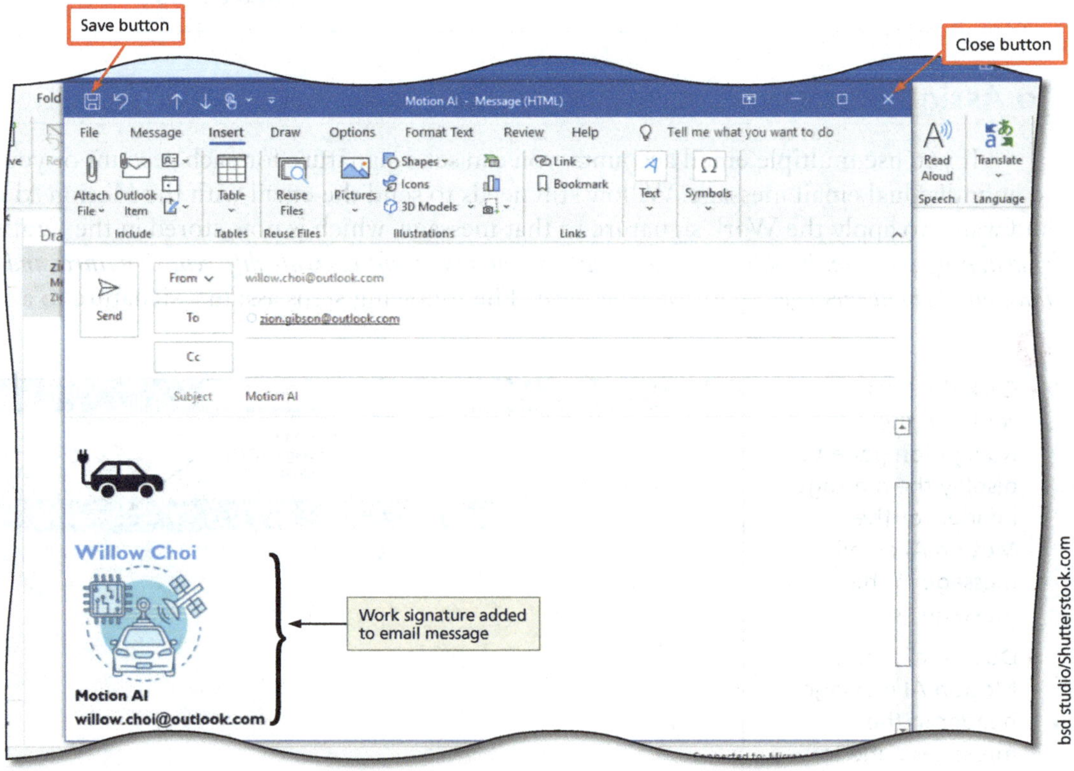

bsd studio/Shutterstock.com

Figure 5–42

4

- Click the Save button on the Quick Access Toolbar to save the email message in the Drafts folder.
- Click the Close button to close the email message.

Break Point: If you want to take a break, this is a good place to do so. To resume at a later time, continue to follow the steps from this location forward.

Managing Junk Email Options

As you learned in Module 1, junk email is bulk email, spam, or other unwanted email messages. Outlook uses a filter to control the amount of junk email you receive. The junk email filter evaluates incoming messages and sends to the Junk E-mail folder those messages that meet the criteria for junk email. You can use the Junk button in the Delete group on the Home tab to override the default criteria when viewing email messages by deciding to block the sender, never block the sender, never block the sender's domain, or never block a group or mailing list.

Using the Junk Email Options dialog box, you can change even more settings (Figure 5–43). Table 5–1 describes the options you can adjust using the Junk Email Options dialog box.

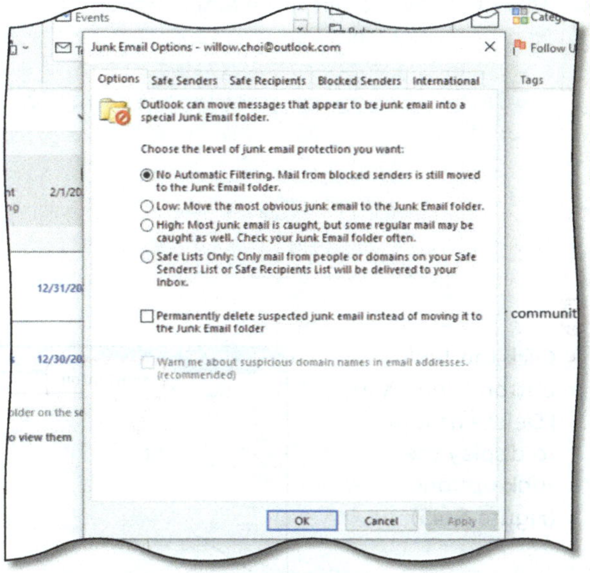

Figure 5–43

BTW

Junk Email

It usually is a good idea to check your Junk E-mail folder regularly to make sure no items are labeled as junk inadvertently. If, after clicking the Junk E-mail folder, you find an email message that is not junk, select the email message, click the Junk button (Home tab | Delete group), click Not Junk, and then click OK.

Table 5–1 Junk Email Options

Tab	Description
Options	Allows you to choose the level of protection (No Automatic Filtering, Low, High, Safe Lists Only), as well as set whether junk email is deleted, links are disabled in phishing messages, and warnings are provided for suspicious domain names.
Safe Senders	Permits the specification of safe email addresses and domains. Email messages from the listed email addresses and domains will not be treated as junk email.
Safe Recipients	Specifies that email messages sent to email addresses or domains in the safe recipient list will not be treated as junk email.
Blocked Senders	Allows you to manage your list of blocked email addresses and domains.
International	Manages which domains and encodings you would like to block based on languages used.

To Add a Domain to the Safe Senders List

The junk email filter in Outlook is turned on by default, providing a protection level that is set to Low. This level is designed to catch only the most obvious junk email messages. Willow feels that too many incoming messages from Microsoft are being sent to her Junk E-mail folder. Microsoft.com can be added to the Safe Senders list, which adjusts the filter sensitivity of Outlook, so the Microsoft messages are sent to the Inbox instead of the Junk E-mail folder. If you are completing these steps on a personal computer, your email account must be set up in Outlook (see Module 1) to be able to select an email account and configure the junk email options. The following steps configure the junk email options for an email account. ***Why?*** *The Junk E-mail folder helps to sort out relevant email messages from junk mail.*

1

- Click your personal email account (in this case, willowchoi9@gmail.com) in the Navigation pane to select the mailbox (Figure 5–44).

Q&A Why did I have to select the email account?
To change junk email options for an account, the account first should be selected. If you selected a different mailbox, you would have changed junk email settings for that account.

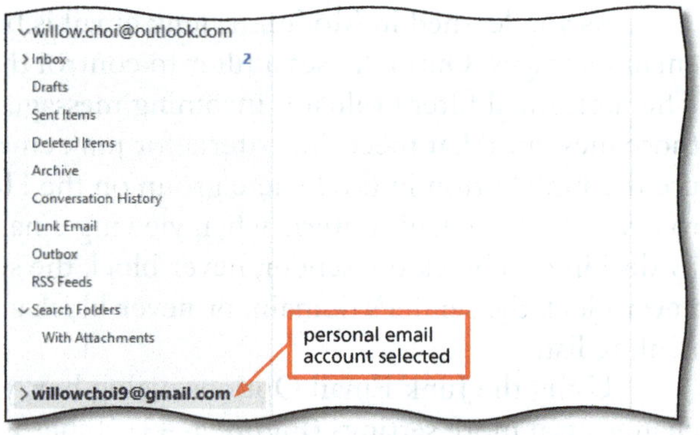

Figure 5–44

2

- Click the Junk button (Home tab | Delete group) to display the Junk options (Figure 5–45).

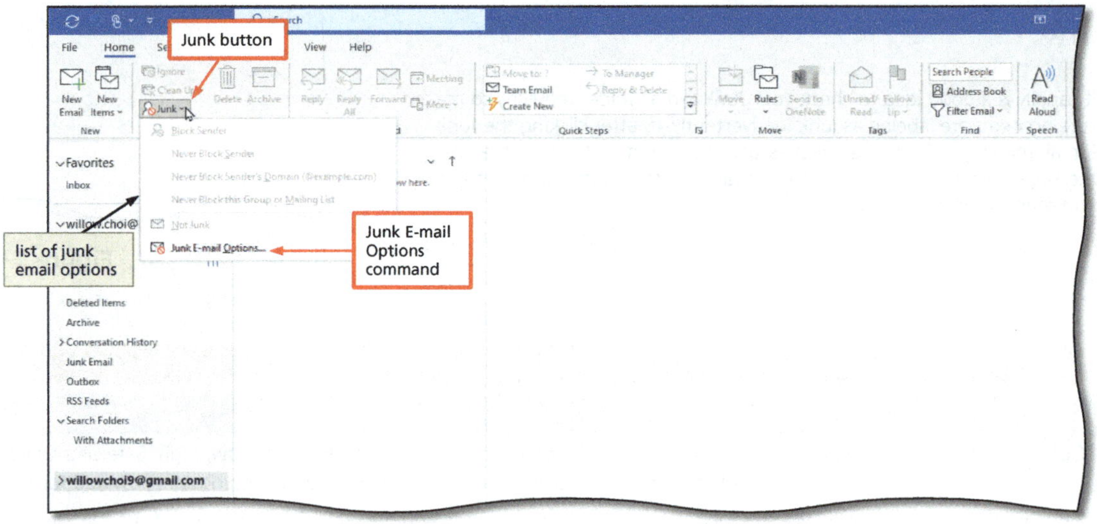

Figure 5–45

3

- Click Junk E-mail Options to display the Junk Email Options dialog box (Figure 5–46).

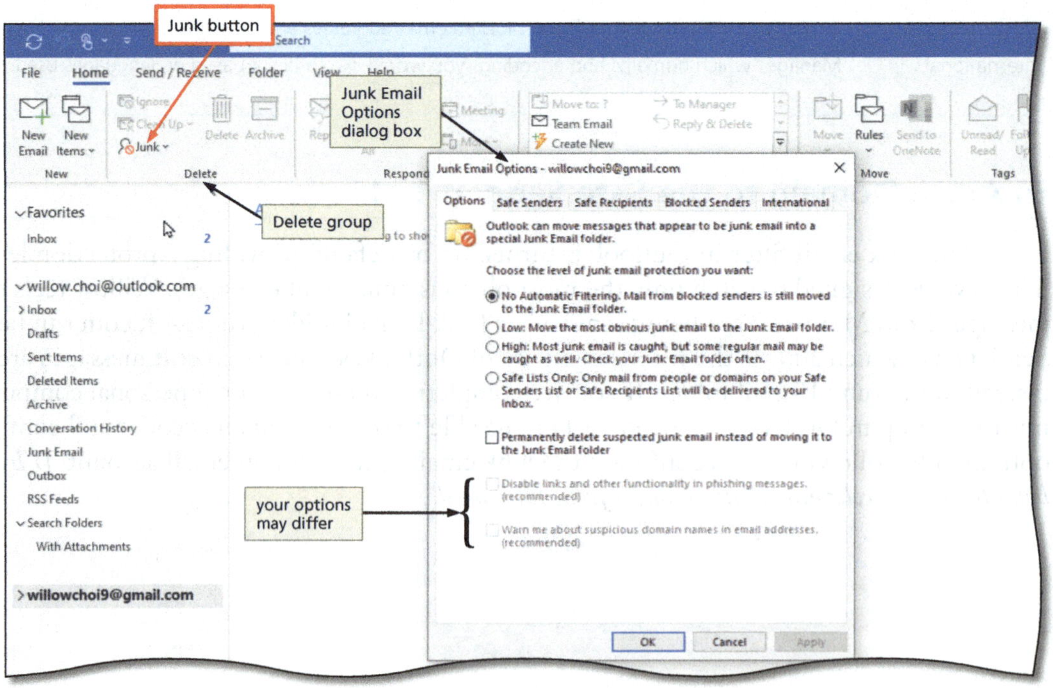

Figure 5–46

4

- Click the Safe Senders tab (Junk Email Options dialog box) to display the Safe Senders options (Figure 5–47).

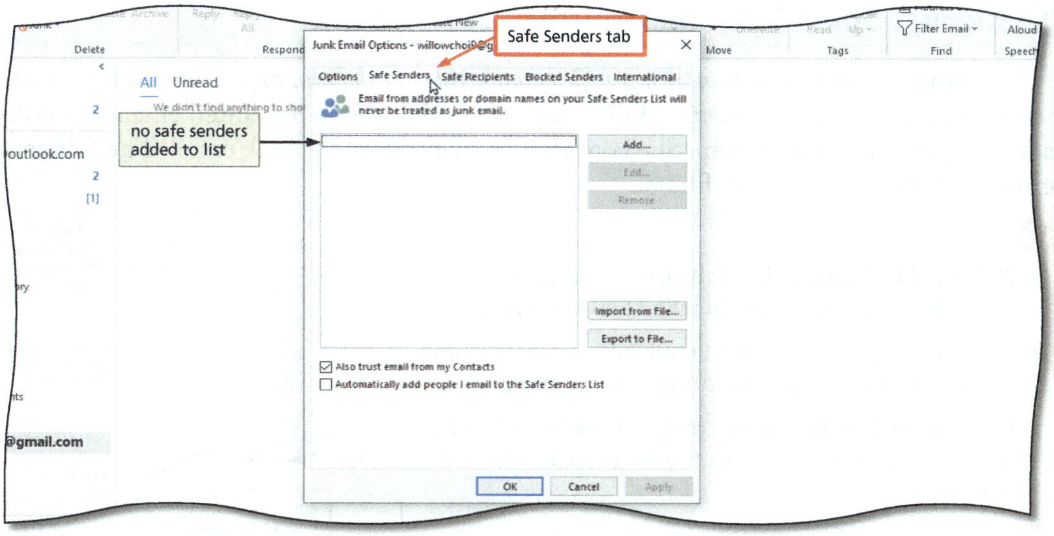

Figure 5–47

5

- Click the Add button (Junk Email Options dialog box) to display the Add address or domain dialog box.
- Type **@Microsoft.com** in the box to enter a domain name to add to the Safe Senders list (Figure 5–48).

Q&A Do I have to type the @ symbol?

Although Outlook recommends that you type the @ symbol to indicate a domain name, you can omit the symbol. In that case, you leave it up to Outlook to determine if your entry is a domain name or email address. Most of the time, Outlook interprets the entry correctly; however, to be certain, type the @ symbol.

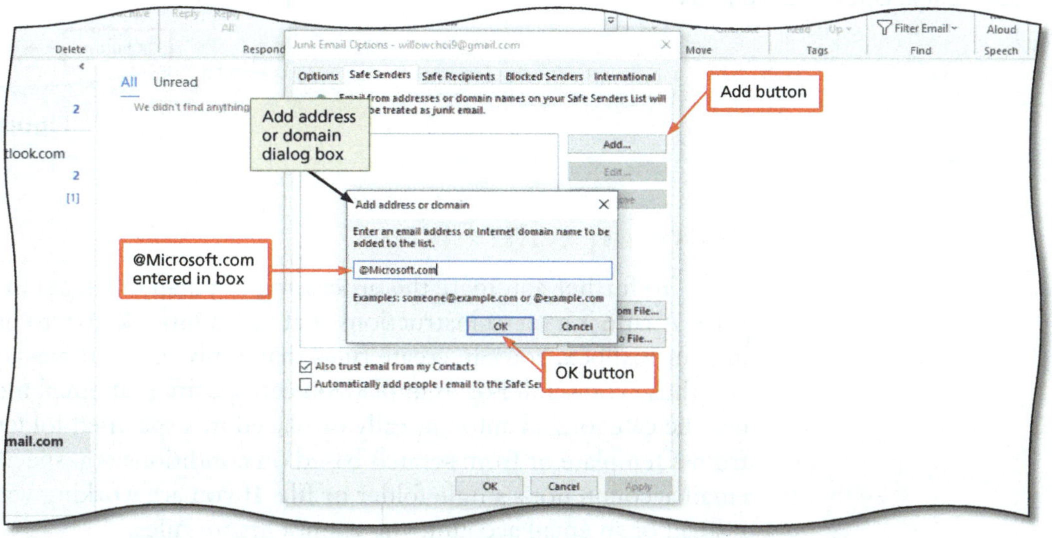

Figure 5–48

6

- Click OK (Add address or domain dialog box) to add the domain to the Safe Senders List (Figure 5–49).

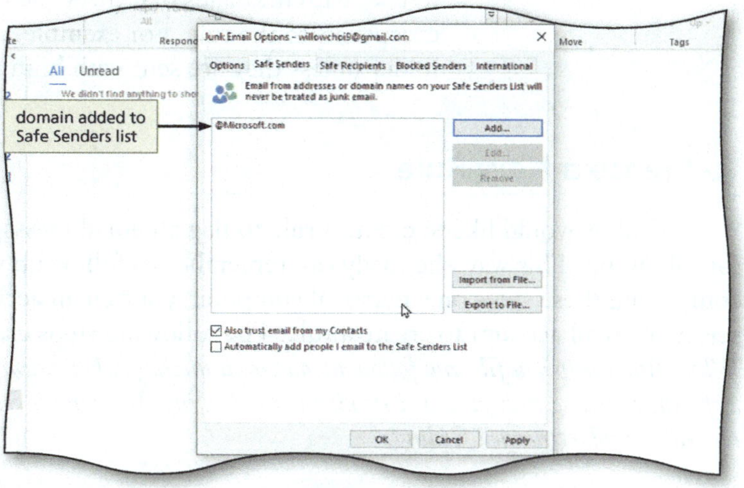

Figure 5–49

BTW
Using the Clutter Feature
If you have a Microsoft 365 subscription, a feature called **Clutter** assists in filtering low-priority email, saving you time to focus on important emails. If you turn on Clutter, the Microsoft 365 Exchange server automatically keeps track of the email messages you read and the email messages that you ignore. Microsoft 365 moves the ignored messages to a folder in your Inbox called the Clutter items folder.

To Block a Specific Email Address

***Why?** You may want to block a specific email address or domain to prevent people or companies from sending you messages you do not want to receive.* Willow has received multiple unwanted emails from the following email address: getrich2@money.com. She considers these messages as junk email. The following steps block a specific email address using the junk filters.

1

- Click the Blocked Senders tab (Junk Email Options dialog box) to display the Blocked Senders options.
- Click the Add button (Junk Email Options dialog box) to display the Add address or domain dialog box.
- Type **getrich2@money.com** in the box to enter the domain name to add to the Blocked Senders list (Figure 5–50).

2

- Click OK (Add address or domain dialog box) to add the domain to the Blocked Senders List.
- Click OK (Junk Email Options dialog box) to close the Junk Email Options dialog box.

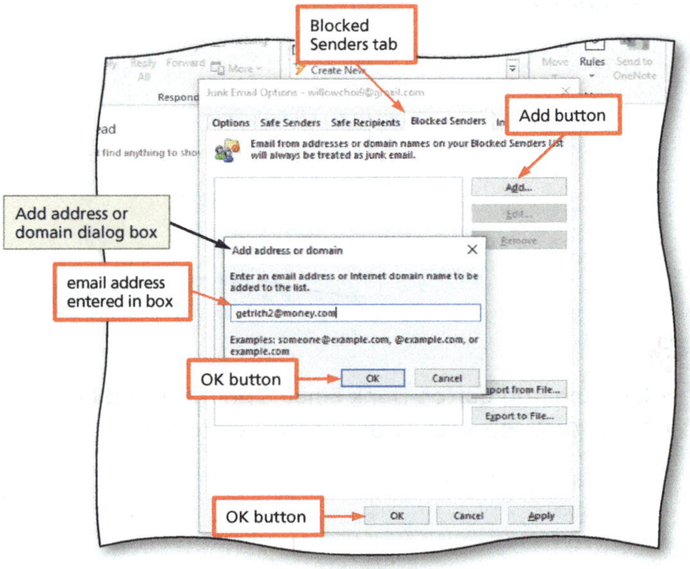

Figure 5–50

Working with Rules

To further automate the processing of email messages in Outlook, you can create rules. A **rule** is a set of instructions that tells Outlook how to handle email messages in your mailbox. You can create rules that apply to email messages you have received and those you send. For example, you can specify that email messages from a particular user be categorized automatically or placed in a specified folder. You can create rules from a template or from scratch based on conditions you specify. Rules apply to an email account, not a single folder or file. If you are working with an Outlook Data File instead of an email account, you cannot create rules.

To simplify the process of creating rules, Outlook provides a Rules Wizard, which presents a list of conditions for selecting an email message and then lists actions to take with messages that meet the conditions. If necessary, you also can specify exceptions to the rule. For example, you can move certain messages to a specified folder unless they are sent with high importance.

To Create a New Rule

Willow would like to create a rule to flag all email messages from the director of Motion AI, Bree Pauley, for follow-up. This way, she easily can remember to follow up with Ms. Pauley on important tasks. If you are completing these steps on a personal computer, your email account must be set up in Outlook so that you can select an email account to create a rule. The following steps create a rule that automatically flags email messages. ***Why?** Rules help you file and follow up on email messages. For example, your instructor can create a rule for messages from a specific course section, such as Introduction to Coding. You can set coding in the Subject line to be flagged for follow-up and moved to a folder named Coding.*

1

- Click the Outlook Data File Inbox to display the Inbox messages.
- If necessary, click the Bree Pauley email message to select it.
- Click the Rules button (Home tab | Move group) to display a list of rule options (Figure 5–51).

Q&A Why is my Rules button missing?
An active email address must be set up in Outlook to view the Rules button.

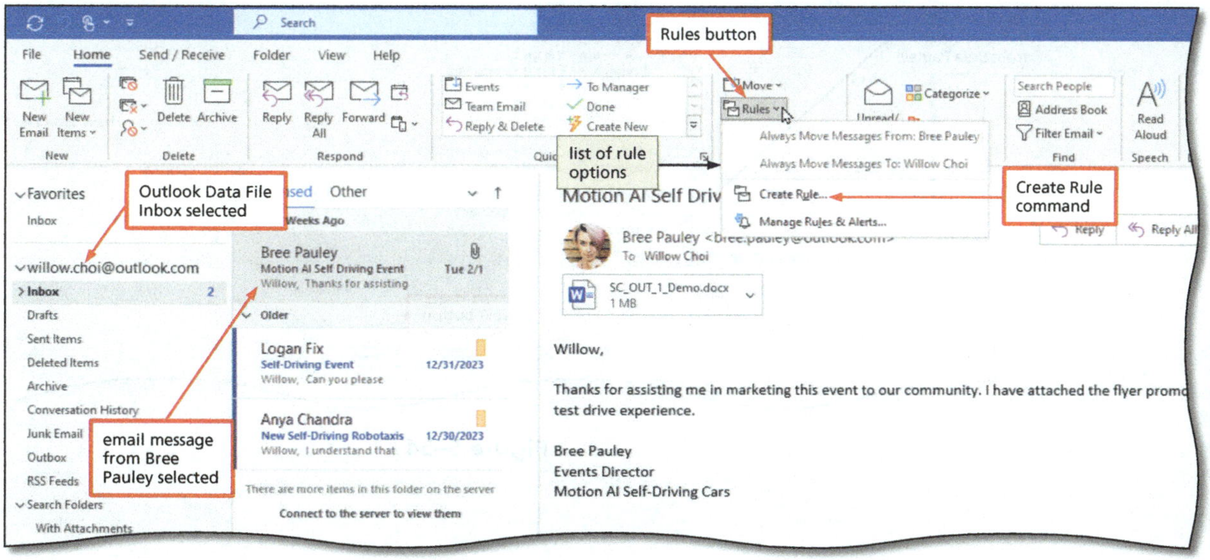

Look Studio/Shutterstock.com

Figure 5–51

2

- Click the Create Rule command to display the Create Rule dialog box (Figure 5–52).

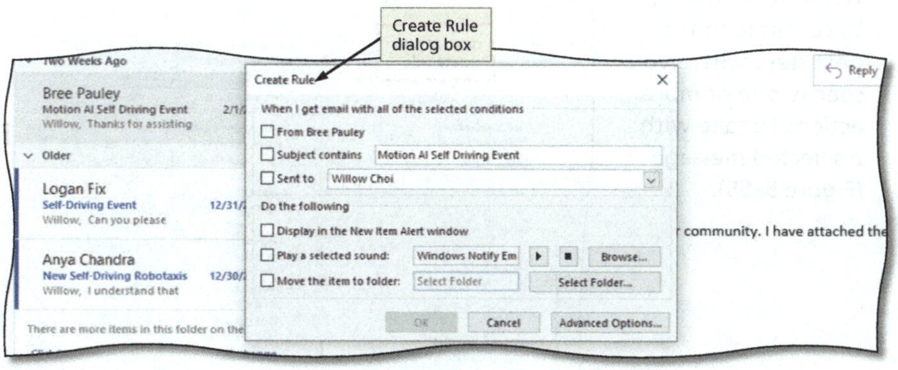

Figure 5–52

3

- Click the 'From Bree Pauley' check box to select it (Figure 5–53).

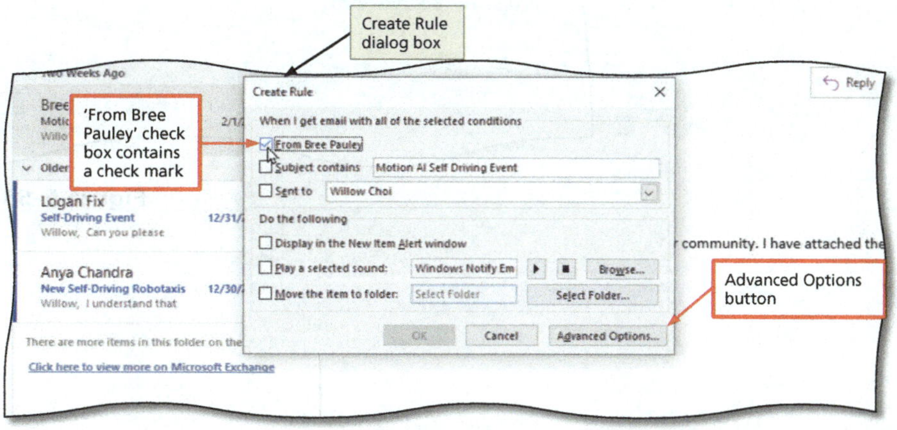

Figure 5–53

4

- Click the Advanced Options button (Create Rule dialog box) to display the Rules Wizard dialog box (Figure 5–54).

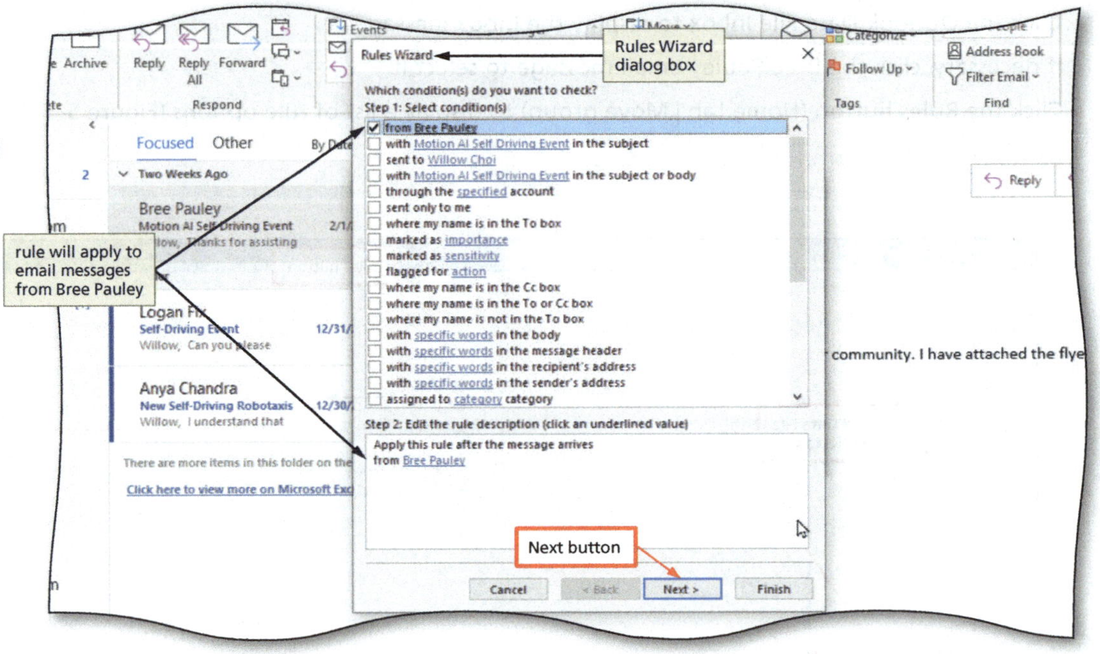

Figure 5–54

5

- Click the Next button (Rules Wizard dialog box) to continue to the next step, where you specify one or more actions to take with a selected message (Figure 5–55).

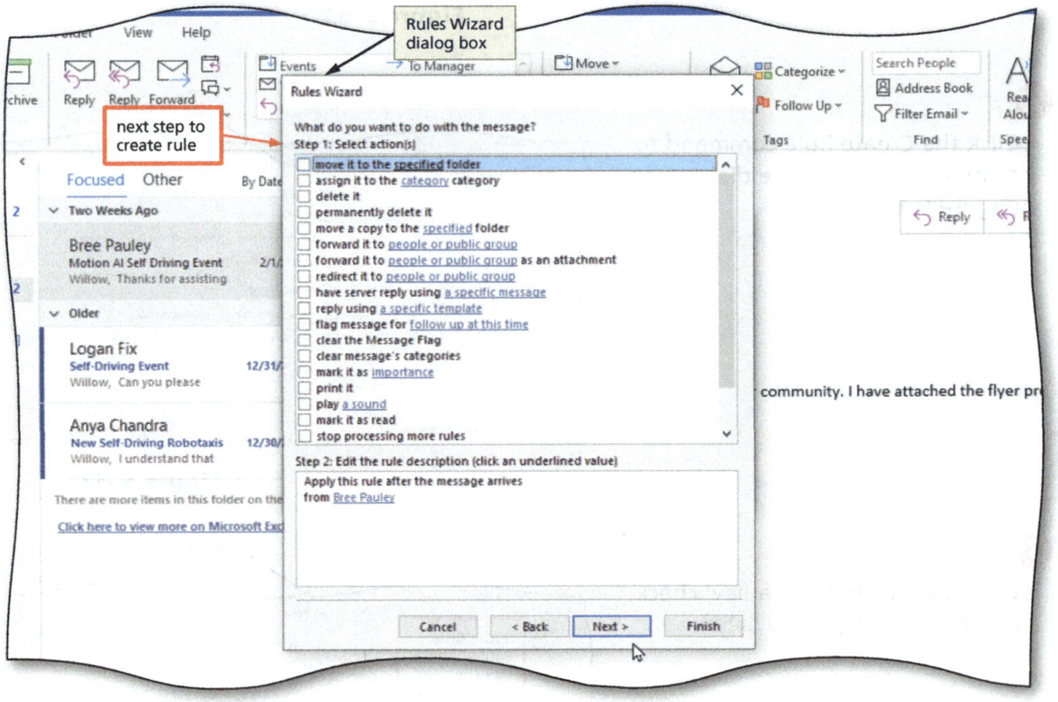

Figure 5–55

6

- Click the 'flag message for follow up at this time' check box to select it.
- If necessary, click the Yes button if a dialog box opens informing you that the rule you are creating can never be edited in previous versions of Outlook (Figure 5–56).

Q&A What is the effect of selecting the 'flag message for follow up at this time' check box?
Messages that meet the conditions you specify, in this case, messages from Bree Pauley, appear in the message list with a flag icon to indicate they need to be followed up.

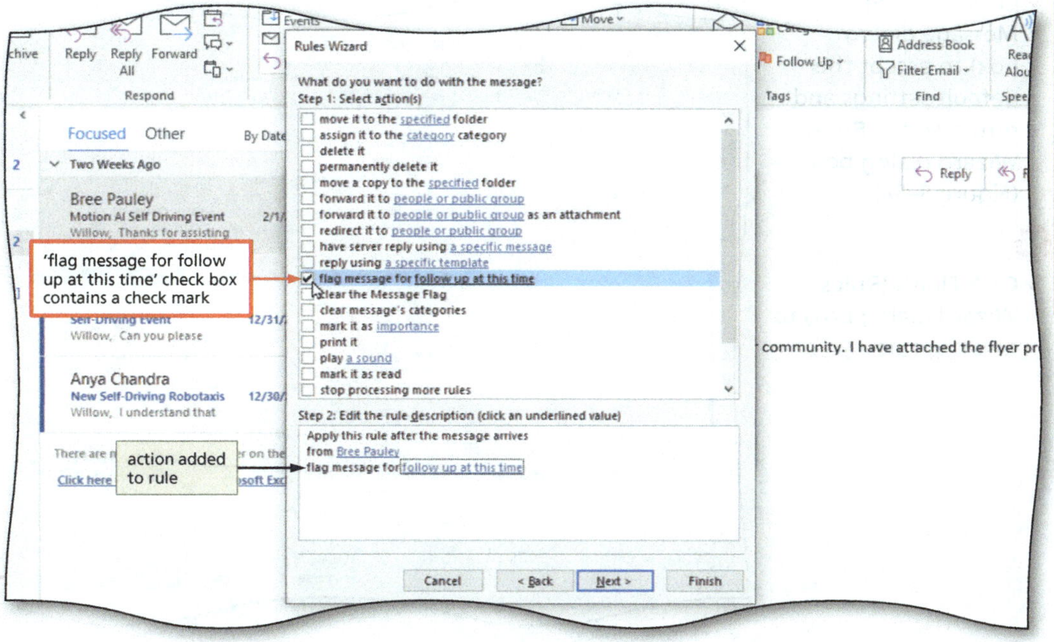

Figure 5–56

7

- Click the 'follow up at this time' link in the Step 2 area to display the Flag Message dialog box (Figure 5–57).

Q&A For what purposes can I use the Flag Message dialog box?
You can flag a message for Follow Up (the default) or for other options, including For Your Information, No Response Necessary, and Reply. You also can specify when to follow up: Today (the default), Tomorrow, This Week, Next Week, No Date, or Complete.

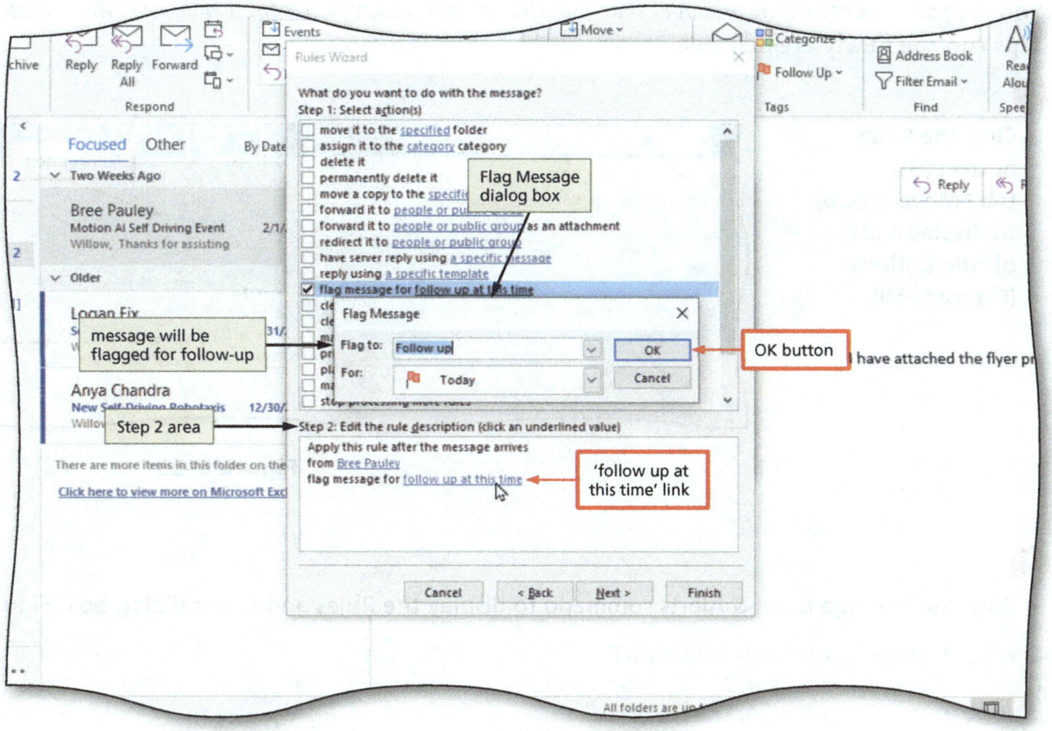

Figure 5–57

8

- Click OK (Flag Message dialog box) to accept the default settings and return to the Rules Wizard dialog box (Figure 5–58).

9

- Click Finish (Rules Wizard dialog box) to save the rule.

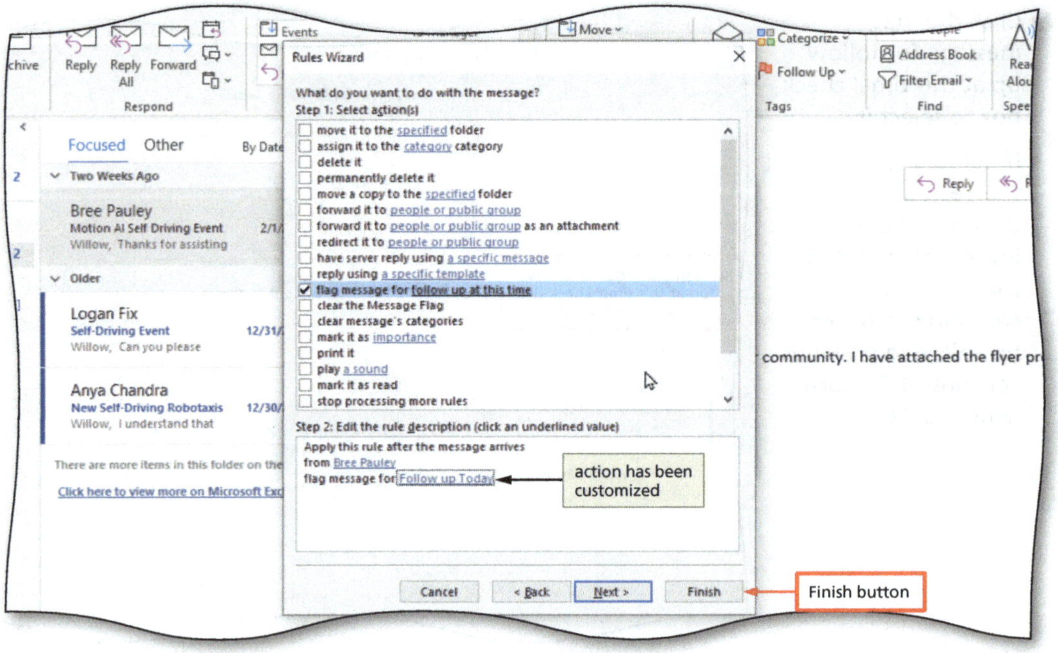

Figure 5–58

To Run Rules

Rules that you create run for all incoming email messages received after you create the rule. ***Why?*** *If you want to apply rules to email messages that you already received, you use the Rules and Alerts dialog box.* The following steps run the newly created rule.

1

- Click the Rules button (Home tab | Move group) to display a list of rule options (Figure 5–59).

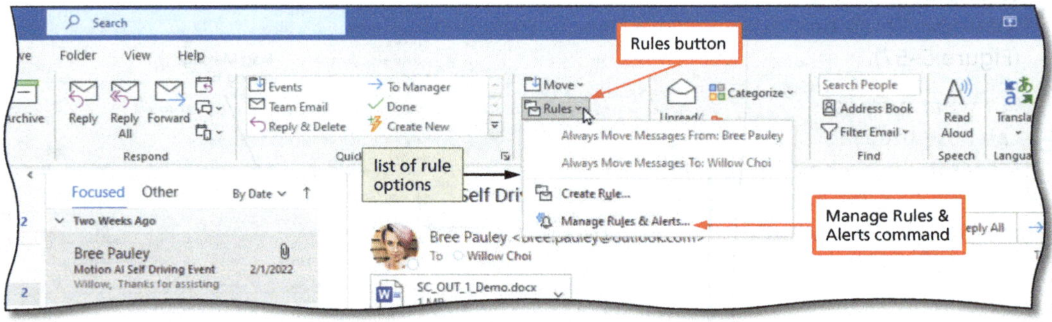

Figure 5–59

2

- Click the Manage Rules & Alerts command to display the Rules and Alerts dialog box (Figure 5–60).

Q&A After I create a rule, can I modify it?

Yes. To modify an existing rule, select the rule you want to modify, click the Change Rule button, and then click the Edit Rule Settings command. Next, make the desired changes in the Rules Wizard. Click Finish after making all necessary changes.

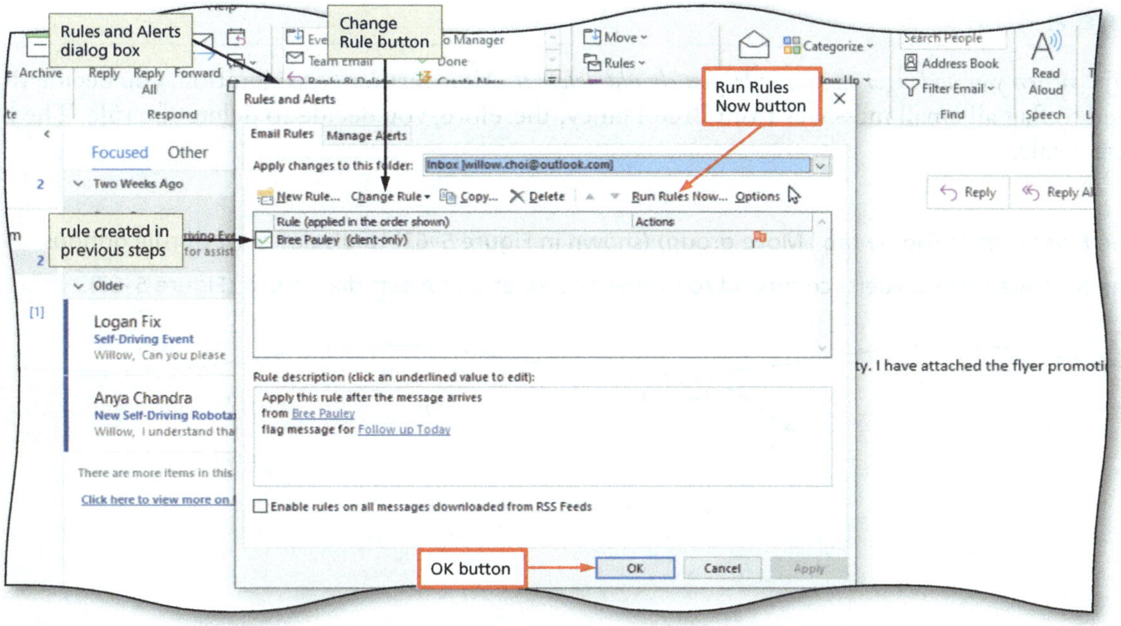

Figure 5–60

3

- Click the Run Rules Now button (Rules and Alerts dialog box) to display the Run Rules Now dialog box.
- Click the Bree Pauley check box to select it and specify the rule that will run.
- Click the Run Now button (Run Rules Now dialog box) to run the rule (Figure 5–61).

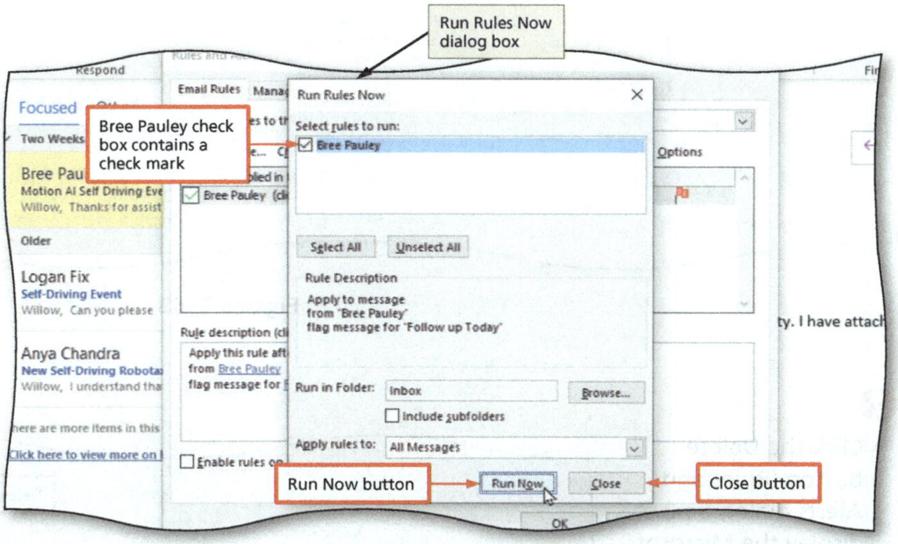

Figure 5–61

4

- Click the Close button (Run Rules Now dialog box) to close the Run Rules Now dialog box.
- Click OK (Rules and Alerts dialog box) (shown in Figure 5–60) to close the Rules and Alerts dialog box (Figure 5–62).

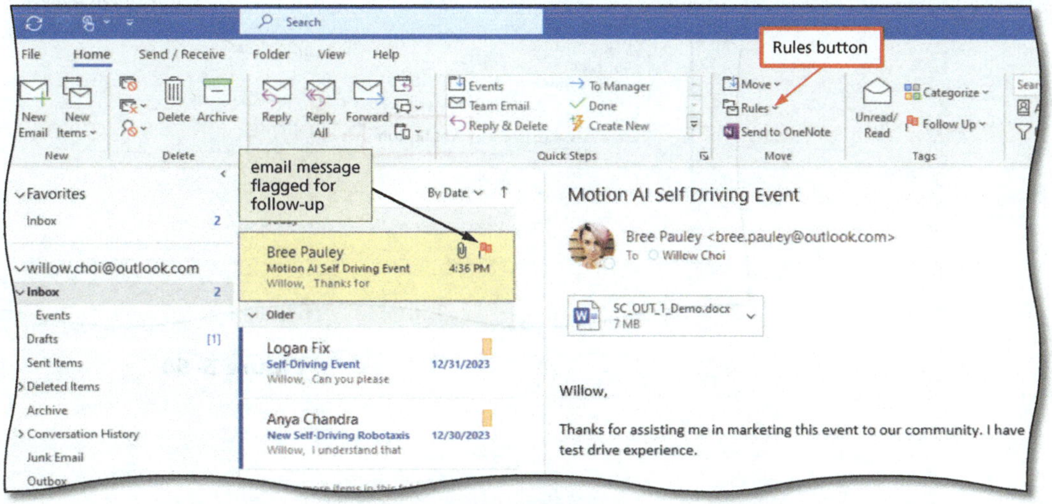

Look Studio/Shutterstock.com

Figure 5–62

To Delete a Rule

Why? *When you no longer need a rule, you should delete it.* After further consideration, you decide that you do not need to flag all email messages from Bree Pauley; therefore, you decide to delete the rule. The following steps delete a rule.

1

- Click the Rules button (Home tab | Move group) (shown in Figure 5–62) to display a list of rule options.
- Click the Manage Rules & Alerts command to display the Rules and Alerts dialog box (Figure 5–63).

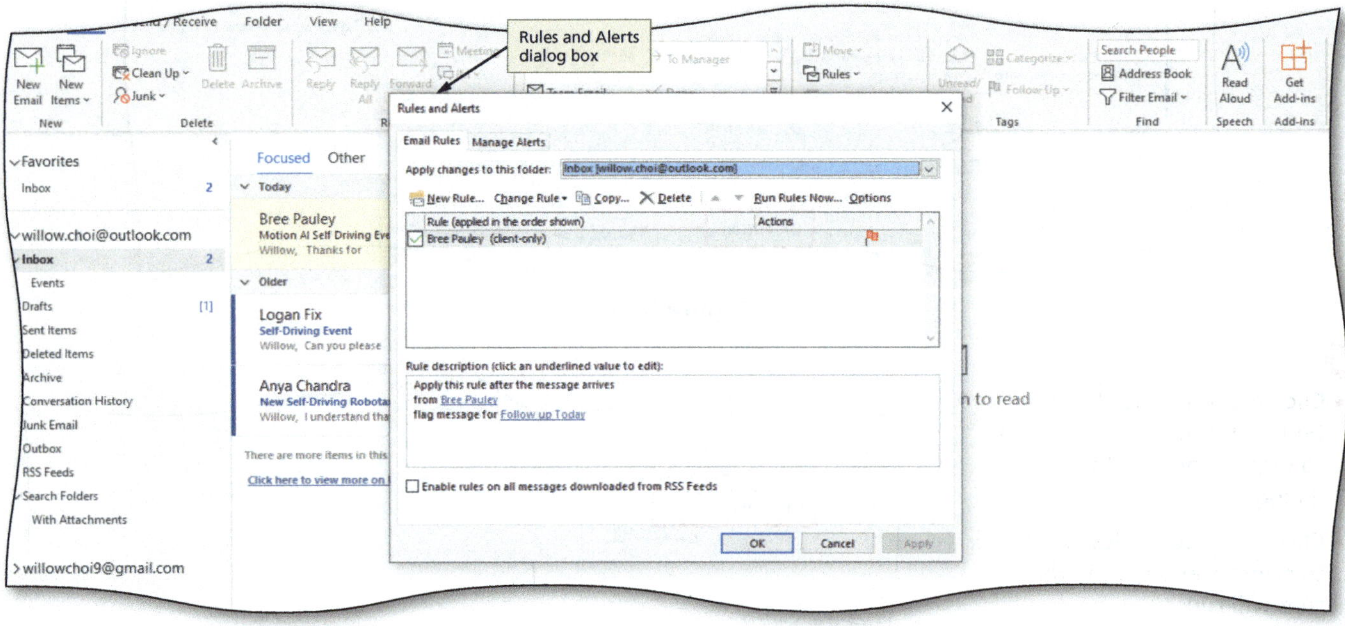

Figure 5–63

2

- Click the Delete button (Rules and Alerts dialog box) to display the Microsoft Outlook dialog box (Figure 5–64).

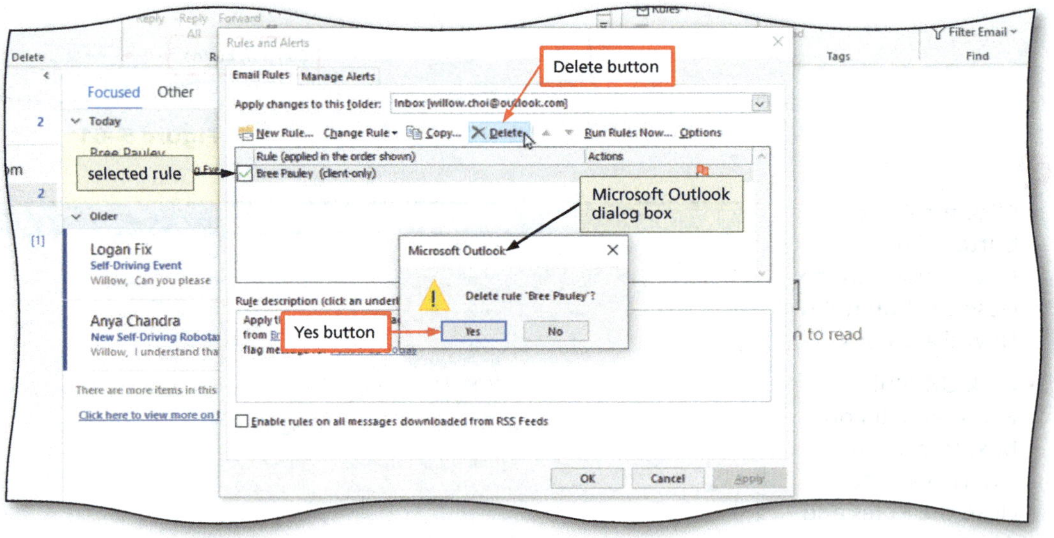

Figure 5–64

3

- Click the Yes button (Microsoft Outlook dialog box) to delete the Bree Pauley rule (Figure 5–65).

4

- Click OK (Rules and Alerts dialog box) to close the Rules and Alerts dialog box.

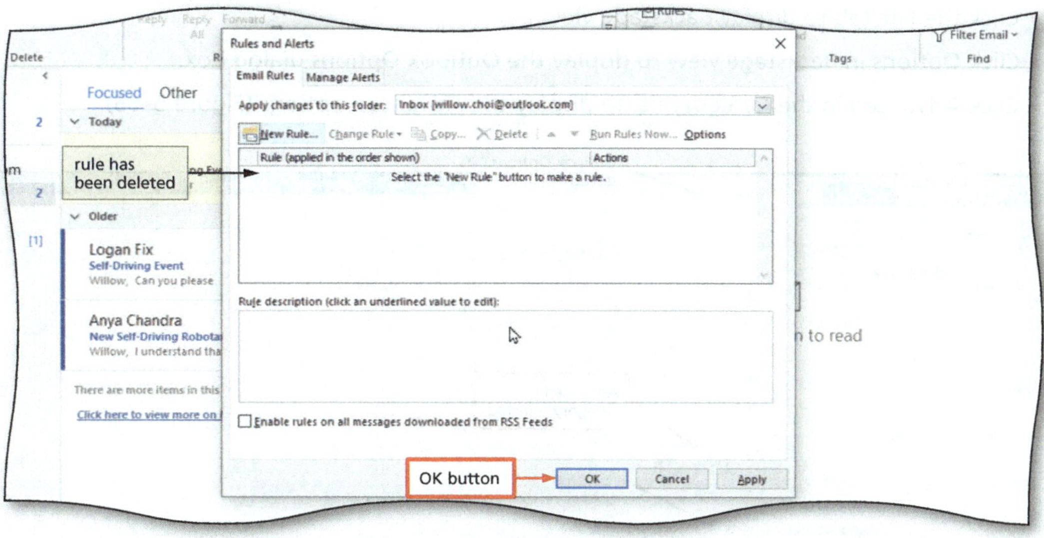

Figure 5–65

To Set Up Automatic Replies

Outlook provides a quick way to set up automatic replies for when you may be away from your email account, such as when you are out of the office; however, your email account must support automatic replies using Microsoft Exchange. If you have a Microsoft Exchange account and want to set up automatic replies, you would use the following steps.

1. Click the File tab to display Backstage view.
2. If necessary, click Info in Backstage view to display account information.
3. Click Automatic Replies to display the Automatic Replies dialog box.
4. Click 'Send automatic replies' to turn on automatic replies.
5. Click the 'Only send during this time range' check box to insert a check mark.
6. Change the Start time to select the day and time for the automatic replies to start.
7. Change the End time to select the day and time for the automatic replies to stop.
8. Select Inside My Organization and enter an email message for email messages to be sent inside your organization.
9. Select Outside My Organization and enter an email message for email messages to be sent outside your organization.
10. Click OK to save the rule for automatic replies.

BTW

Cleanup Tools

In addition to archiving email messages, Outlook provides cleanup tools to help control the size of your mailbox. To access the various cleanup tools, display Backstage view, click the Info tab, click Tools, and then click the desired cleanup tool you want to access.

To Set AutoArchive Settings

Why? *You can have Outlook transfer old items to a storage file. Items are only considered old after a certain number of days that you specify.* Willow decides that she should back up the email messages in her email account. By default, when AutoArchive is turned on, Outlook archives messages every 14 days. The following steps turn on AutoArchive.

1

- Click the File tab to display Backstage view.
- Click Options in Backstage view to display the Outlook Options dialog box.
- Click Advanced in the Category list to display the Advanced options (Figure 5–66).

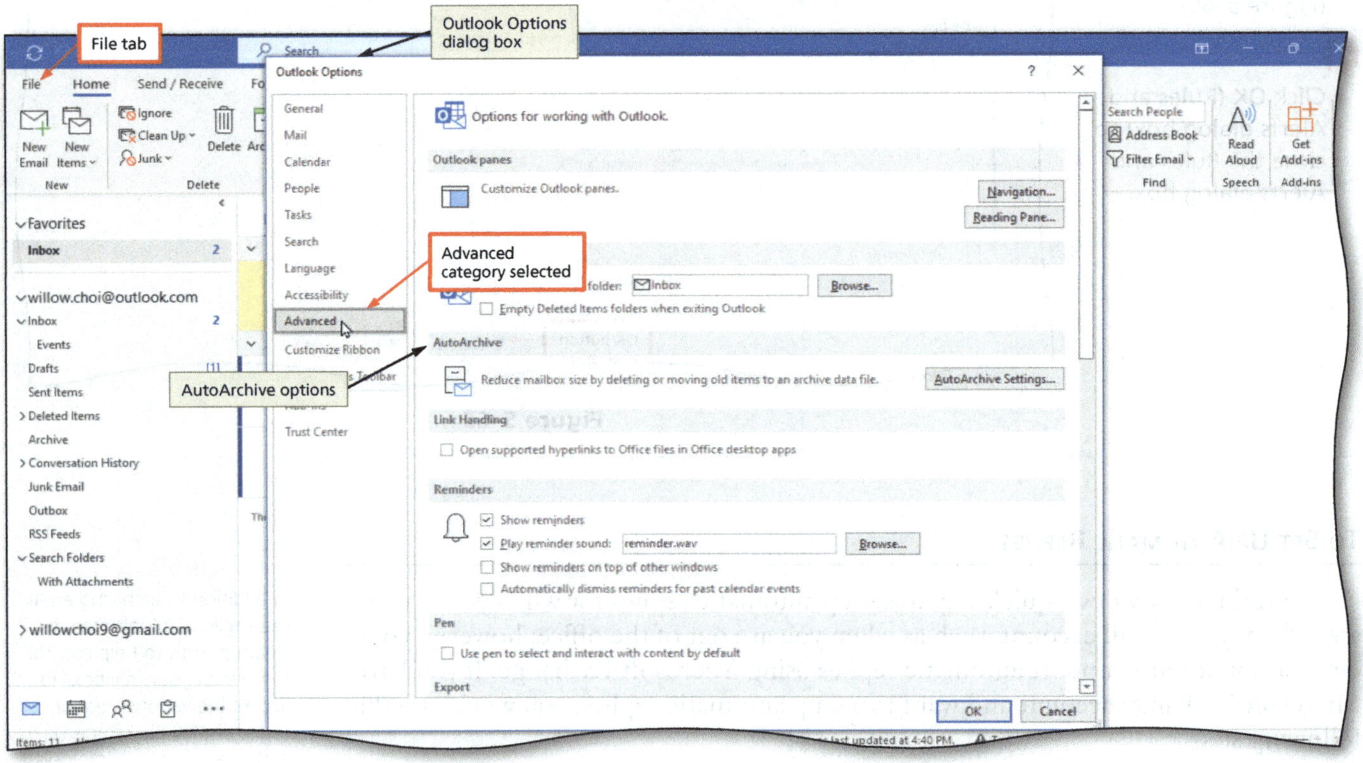

Figure 5–66

2

- Click the AutoArchive Settings button (Outlook Options dialog box) to display the AutoArchive dialog box (Figure 5–67).

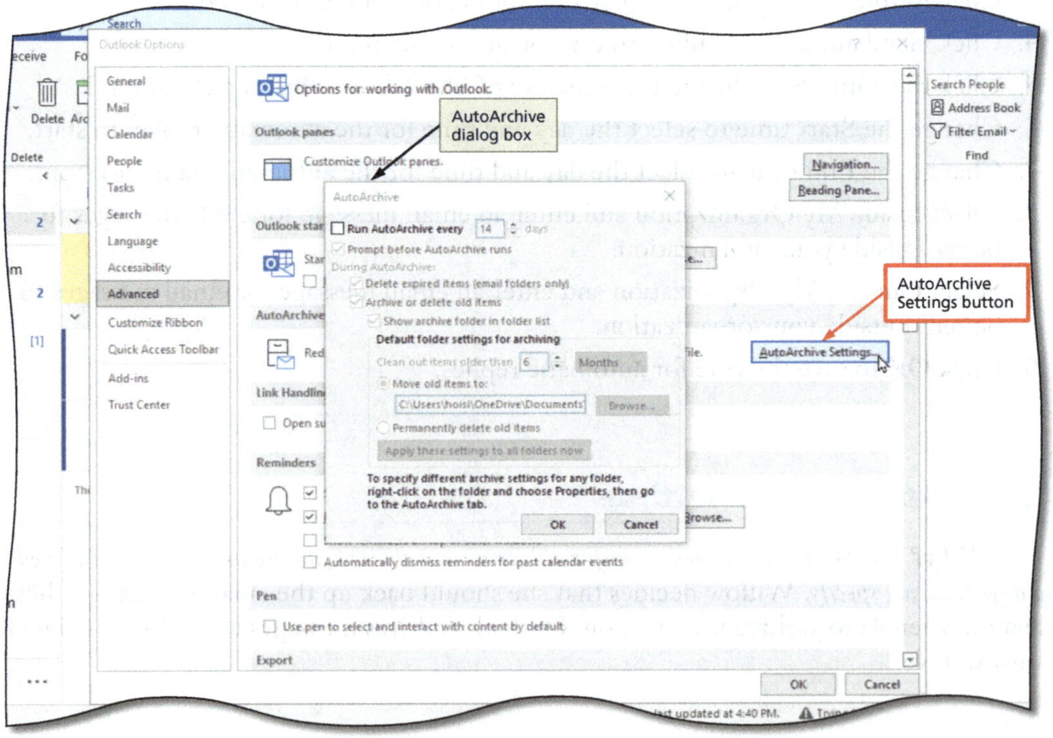

Figure 5–67

3

- Click the 'Run AutoArchive every' check box to select it and enable AutoArchive (Figure 5–68).

4

- Click OK (AutoArchive dialog box) to close the AutoArchive dialog box.

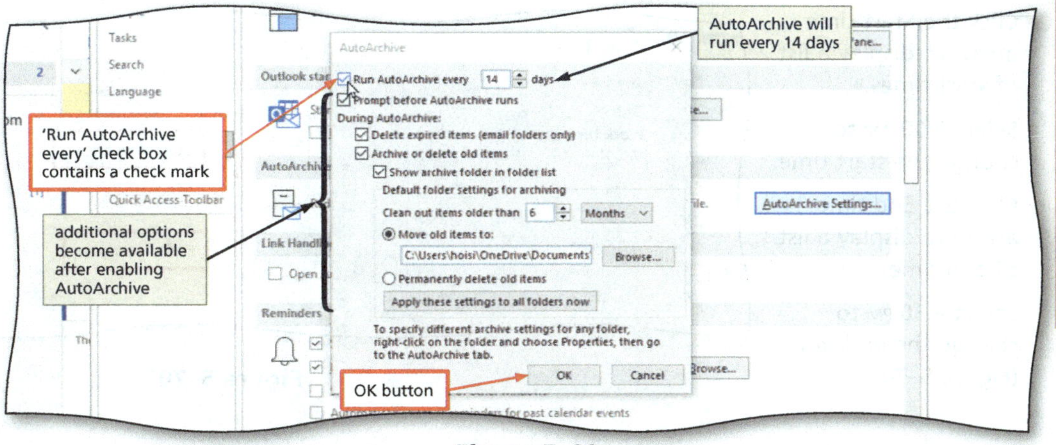

Figure 5–68

Customizing the Calendar

You can customize the Calendar to better suit your needs. For example, you can select the days of your work week and set the displayed time range to reflect the start and end times of your workday. You also can change the default reminder time from 15 minutes to any other interval, such as five minutes or a half-hour. Other Calendar options you can customize include the calendar font and current time zone.

BTW

Advanced Options

In addition to the various Outlook options presented in this module, Outlook allows users to view and change advanced options. To access the advanced options, open the Outlook Options dialog box and then click Advanced in the Category list.

To Change the Work Time on the Calendar

Willow would like to customize the work time on the Calendar so that it reflects her work schedule. She normally works from 8:30 AM to 5:00 PM on Mondays, Wednesdays, Fridays, and Saturdays. The following steps change the Calendar settings to match the work schedule and make Monday the first day of the week. ***Why?*** *By default, the Calendar Work Week is set for Monday through Friday, but you can select which days comprise your work week.*

1

- Click Calendar in the Category list in the Outlook Options dialog box to display the Calendar options (Figure 5–69).

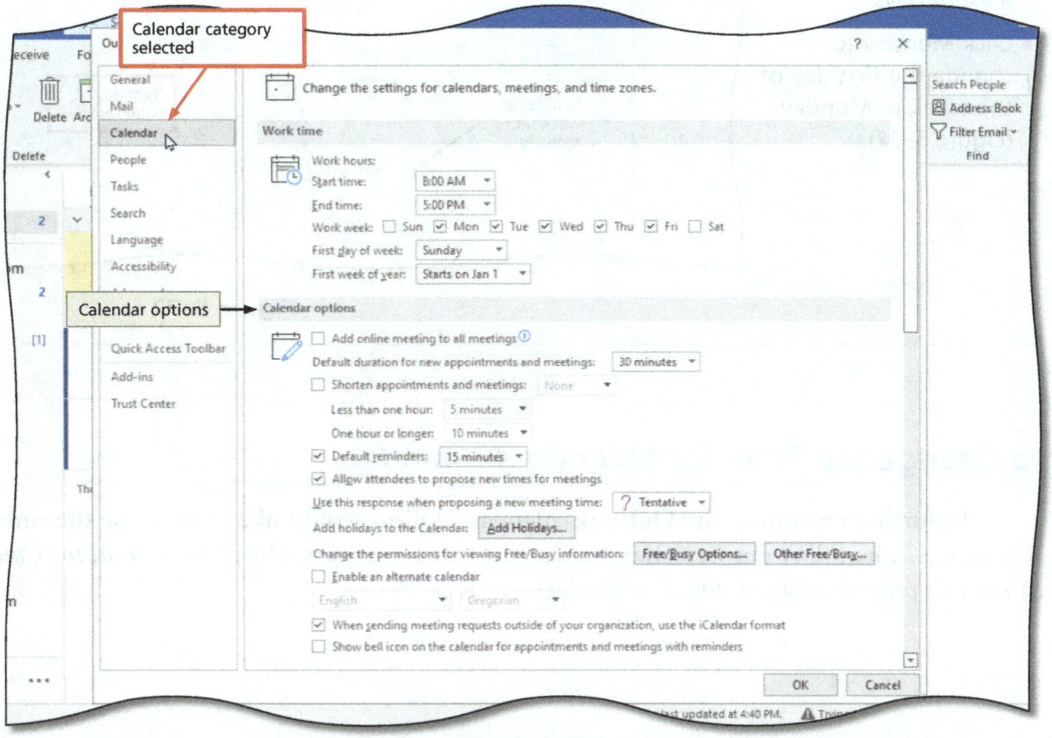

Figure 5–69

2

- Click the Start time arrow to display a list of start times.
- Select 9:00 AM to change the start time.
- Click the End time arrow to display a list of end times.
- Select 4:30 PM to change the end time (Figure 5–70).

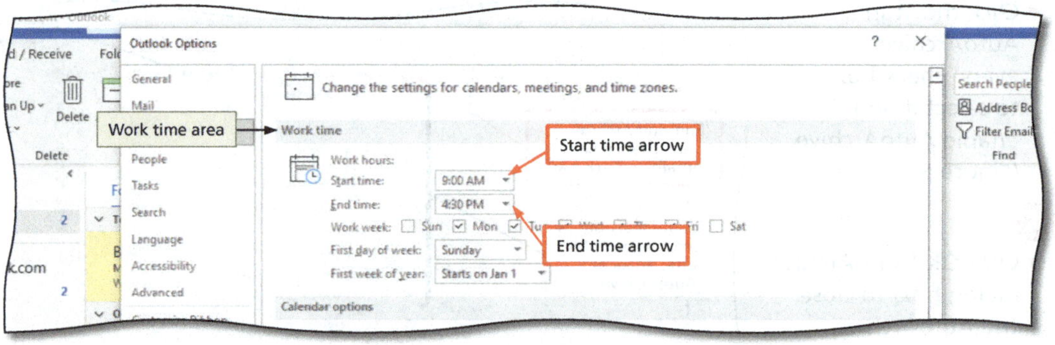

Figure 5–70

3

- Click the Tue check box to deselect it.
- Click the Thu check box to deselect it.
- Click the Sat check box to select it (Figure 5–71).

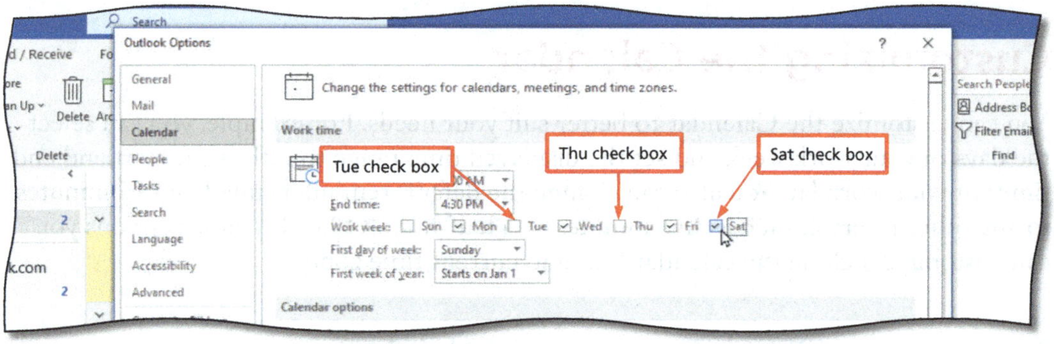

Figure 5–71

4

- Click the 'First day of week' arrow to display a list of days.
- Click Monday to change the first day of the week to Monday (Figure 5–72).

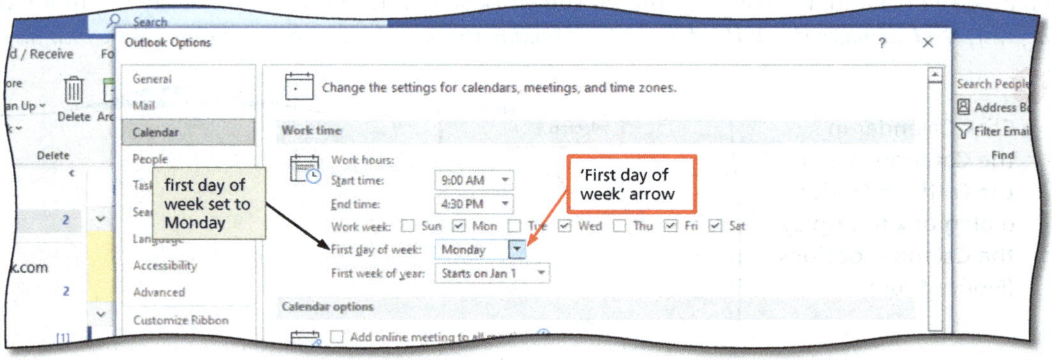

Figure 5–72

To Change the Time for Calendar Reminders

To further customize the Outlook calendar, Willow would like to increase the time for reminders to 30 minutes. The following step changes the time for reminders. ***Why?*** *By default, the Calendar reminders are set for 15 minutes prior to an appointment or meeting.*

1

- Click the Default reminders arrow to display a list of times.
- Click 30 minutes to select it as the default time for reminders (Figure 5–73).

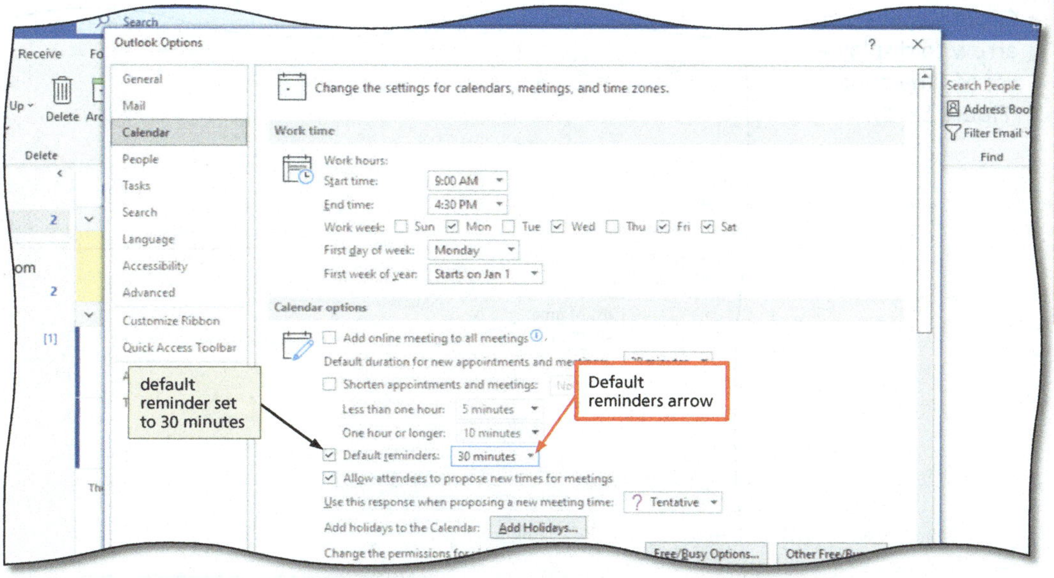

Figure 5–73

To Change the Time Zone Setting

***Why?** When you travel, your time zone may change and your calendar should be updated. If you change the time zone setting in Calendar, Outlook updates your appointments to display the new time zone when you arrive.* Willow is participating in an AI summit this summer with the director, Ms. Pauley, in Kona, Hawaii, and needs to change the time zones accordingly. The following steps change the time zone.

1

- Scroll down until the Time zones settings are visible in the Outlook Options dialog box (Figure 5–74).

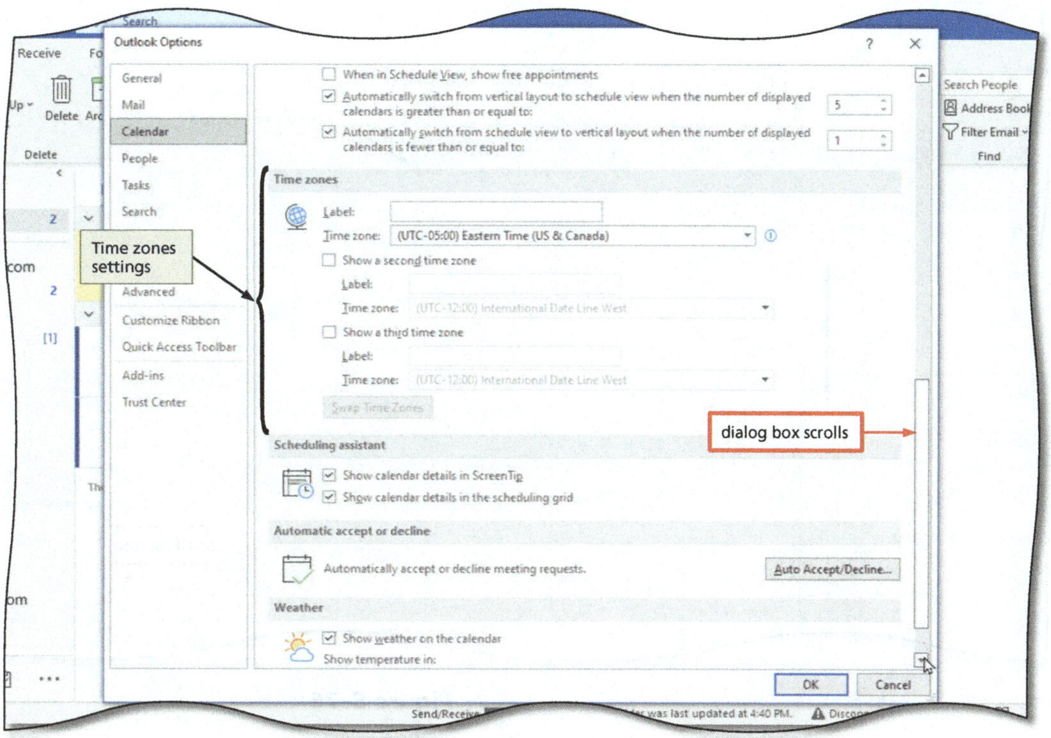

Figure 5–74

2

- Click the Time zone arrow to display a list of time zones (Figure 5–75).

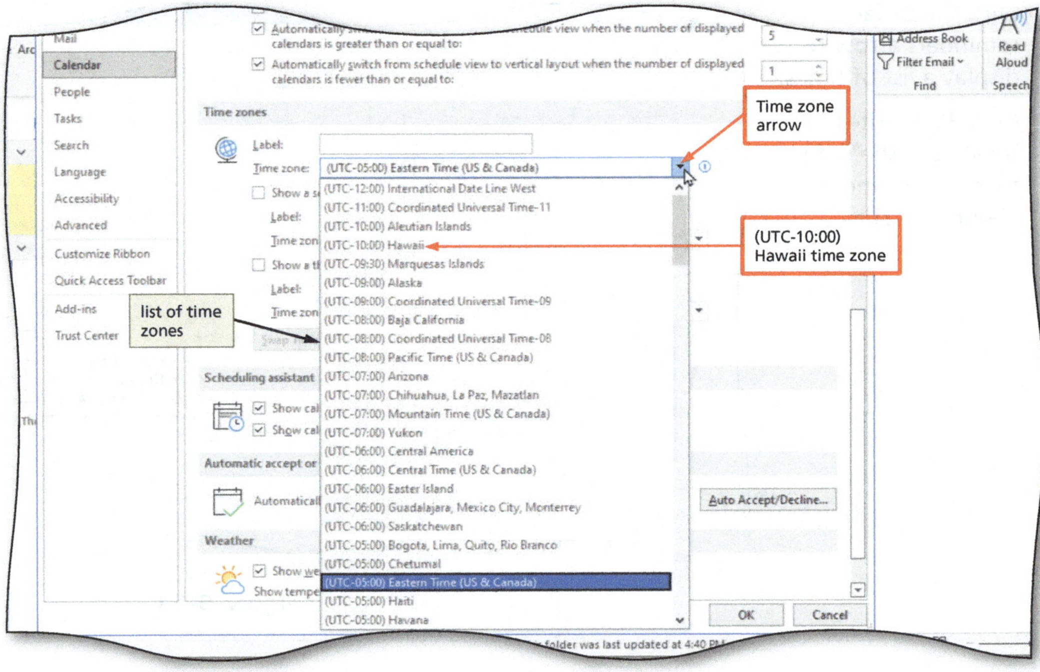

Figure 5–75

3

- Scroll and then click (UTC-10:00) Hawaii to select the time zone (Figure 5–76).

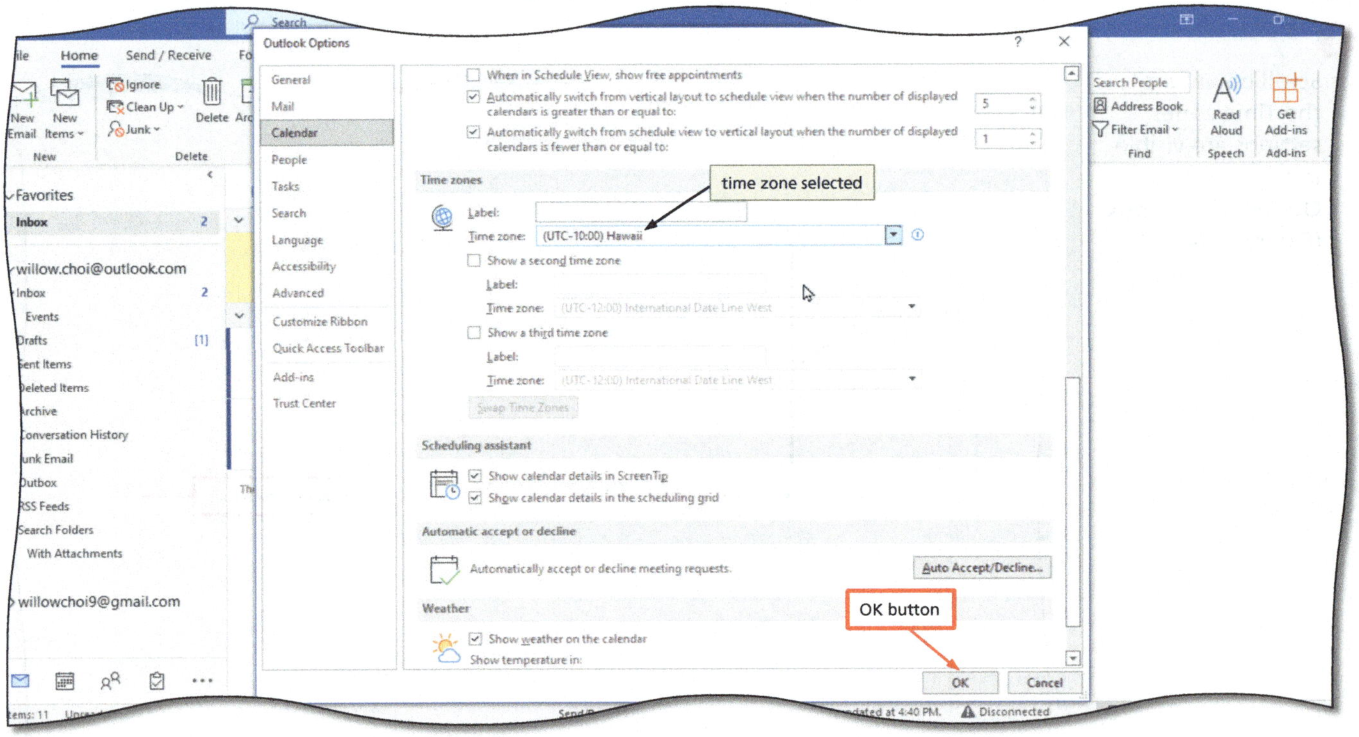

Figure 5–76

4

- Click OK (Outlook Options dialog box) to close the Outlook Options dialog box.
- Click the Calendar button in the Navigation bar to display the Calendar to view the changes (Figure 5–77).

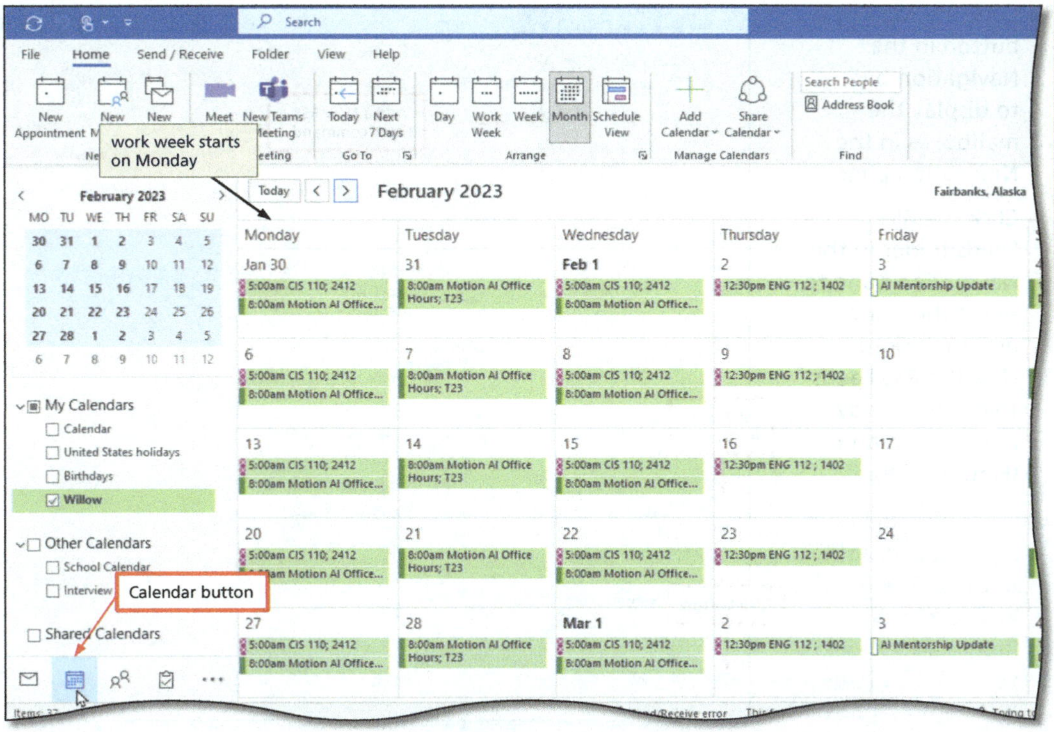

Figure 5–77

Working with RSS Feeds

Really Simple Syndication (RSS) is a way for content publishers to make news, blogs, and other content available to subscribers. RSS feeds typically are found on news websites, political discussion boards, educational blogs, and other sites that frequently update their content. For example, the PBS website contains an RSS feed on the Frontline webpage that allows people to view recent news stories in one convenient location. If you frequently visit websites that offer RSS feeds, you quickly can review the feed content of all the websites in a simple list in your browser by subscribing to their RSS feeds, without having to first navigate to each individual site.

If you want to use Outlook to read the feed, you can add the RSS feed to your account using the Account Settings dialog box. Outlook creates an easy way to manage and work with your RSS feed. Some accounts let you access the feeds from your web browser if they are using a common feeds folder; however, not all accounts allow for this.

To Subscribe to an RSS Feed

Willow subscribes to several RSS feeds in her web browser. To view one of her favorite feeds using Outlook, she needs to set up an RSS feed called 'Microsoft | The AI Blog RSS Feed' about technology news from https://blogs.microsoft.com/ai/feed/. The following steps subscribe to an RSS feed and display the messages. ***Why?*** *The benefit of displaying an RSS feed in Outlook is the ability to combine feeds from multiple web sources in one place. You no longer have to visit different websites for news, weather, blogs, and other information.*

1

- Click the Mail button in the Navigation bar to display the mailboxes in the Navigation pane.
- Click the RSS Feeds folder in the Navigation pane to select the folder, and then right-click the RSS Feeds folder to display a shortcut menu (Figure 5–78).

Q&A What should I do if an RSS Feeds folder does not appear in Willow's mailbox?
Right-click the RSS Feeds folder in a different mailbox on your computer.

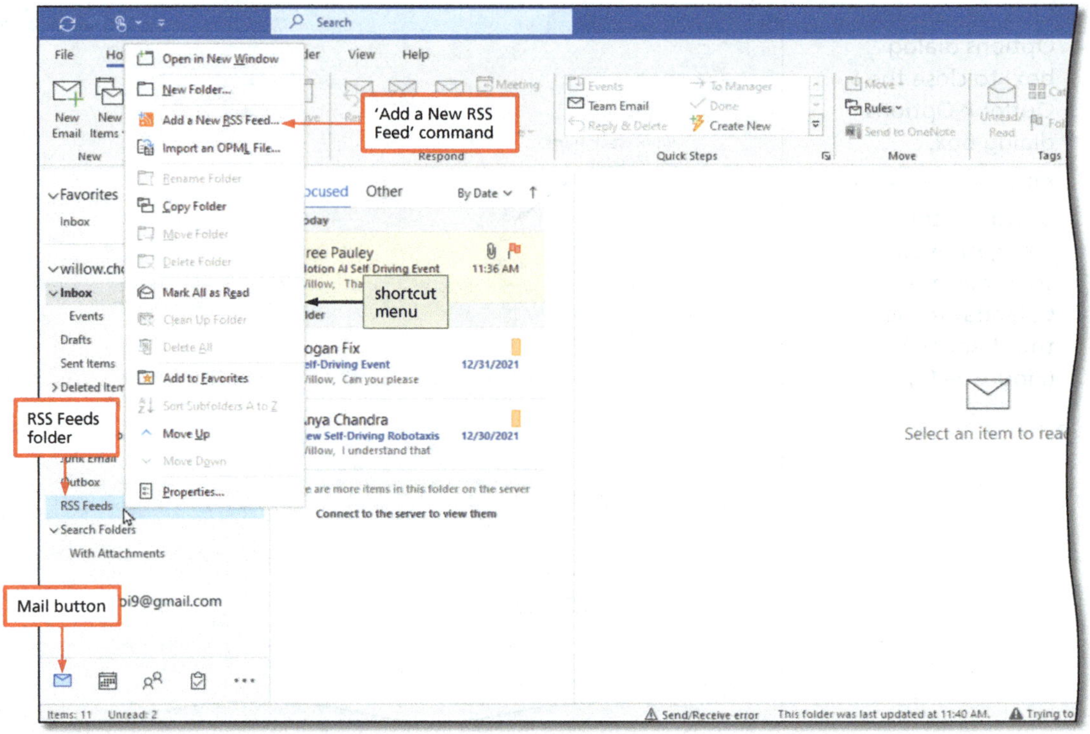

Figure 5–78

2

- Click the 'Add a New RSS Feed' command to display the New RSS Feed dialog box (Figure 5–79).

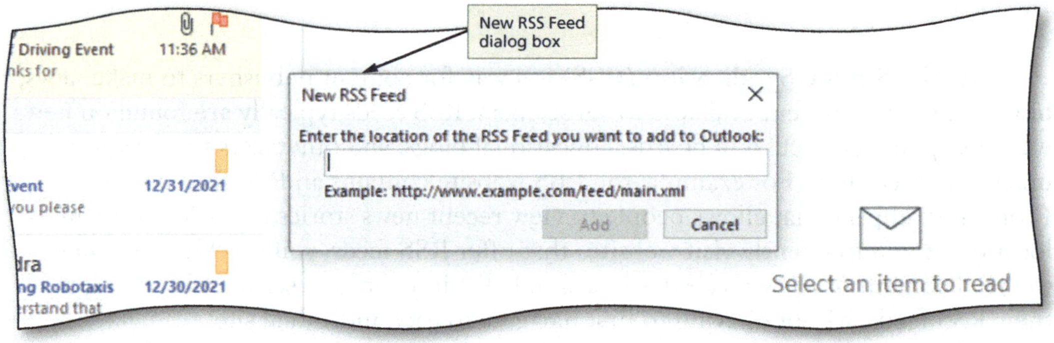

Figure 5–79

3

- Type **`https://blogs.microsoft.com/ai/feed/`** in the text box to enter the address of an RSS feed (Figure 5–80).

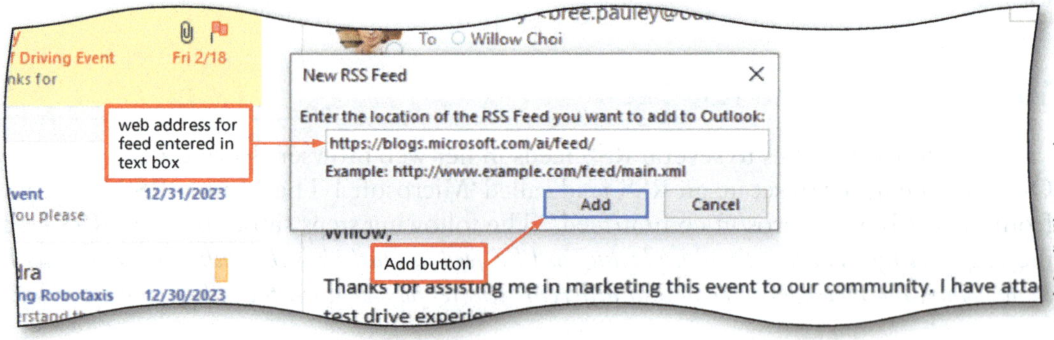

Figure 5–80

4

- Click the Add button (New RSS Feed dialog box) to add the RSS feed to the RSS Feeds folder.
- Click the Yes button (Microsoft Outlook dialog box) to confirm you want to add the Microsoft AI RSS feed (Figure 5–81).

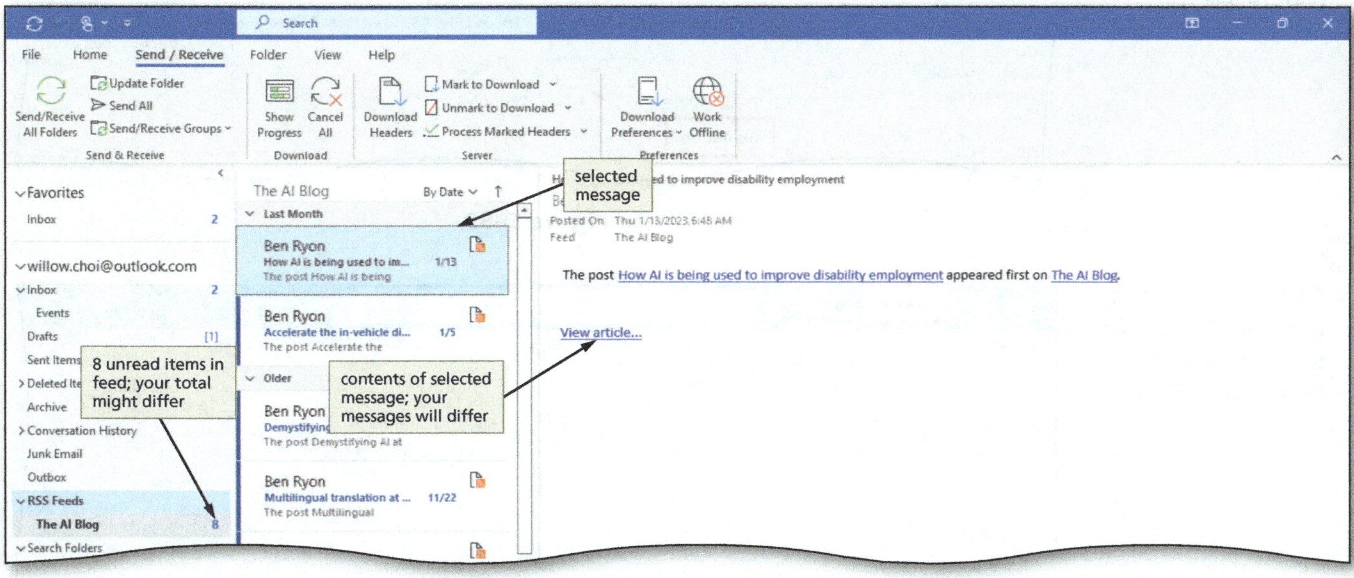

Figure 5–81

Experiment

- Click the different messages to see what has been posted in the RSS Feeds folder.

To Delete an RSS Feed

Why? *When you no longer need to use an RSS feed, you should delete it so that you do not have unwanted messages in your account.* The following steps delete an RSS feed.

1

- Right-click the 'The AI Blog' folder below the RSS Feeds folder in the Navigation pane to display a shortcut menu (Figure 5–82).

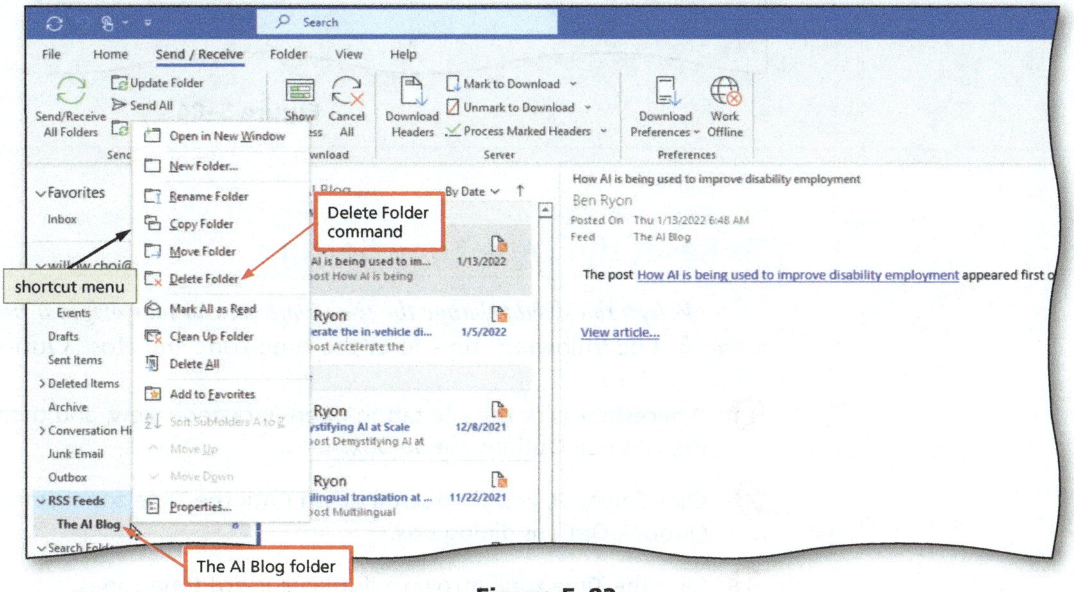

Figure 5–82

2

- Click the Delete Folder command to display the Microsoft Outlook dialog box (Figure 5–83).

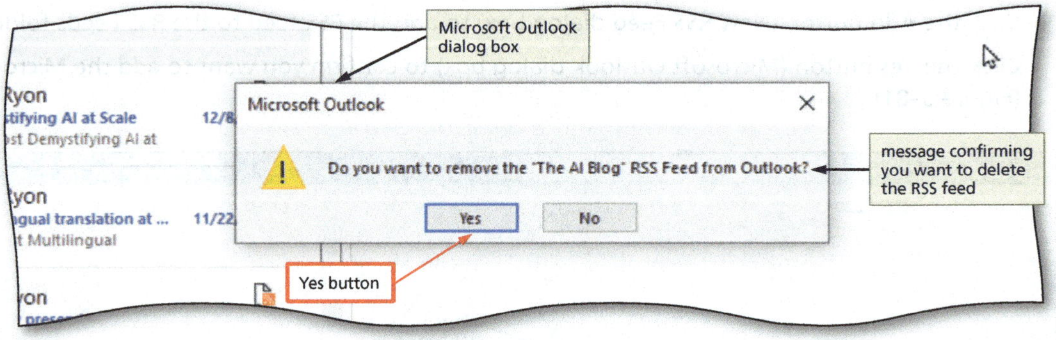

Figure 5–83

3

- Click Yes (Microsoft Outlook dialog box) to delete the RSS Feed (Figure 5–84).

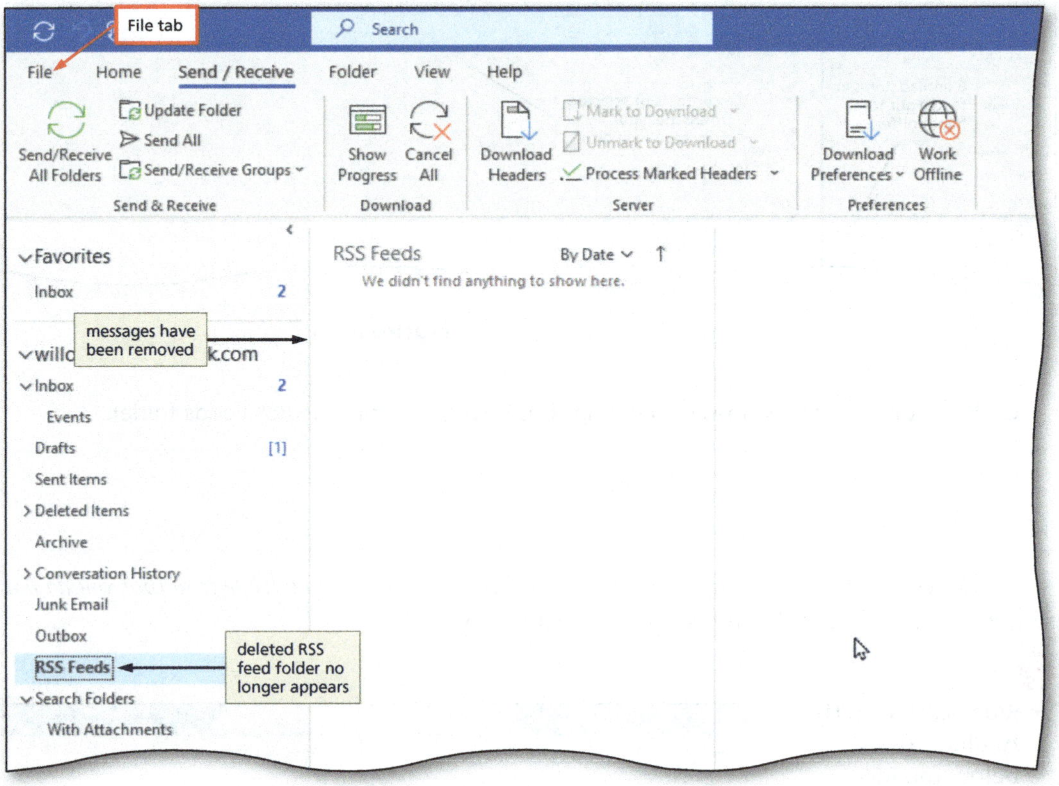

Figure 5–84

To Reset the Time Zone Setting

Why? You should change the time zone back to your original time zone before quitting Outlook. The following steps reset the time zone and close Outlook.

1. If necessary, click the File tab to open Backstage view, and then click Options to display the Outlook Options dialog box.
2. Click Calendar, and then scroll down until the Time zones settings are visible in the Outlook Options dialog box.
3. Click the Time zone arrow to display a list of time zones.

4. Click your time zone to select the time zone.
5. Export the SC_OUT_5-1.pst file to an Outlook Data File (.pst) named `SC_OUT_5_Willow`.
6. Close Outlook.

Summary

In this module, you have learned how to add another email account, customize Outlook options, add signatures and stationery, manage the junk email filter, create rules, customize calendar options, and add RSS Feeds.

CONSIDER THIS: PLAN AHEAD

What future decisions will you need to make when customizing email messages, adding signatures and stationery, managing junk email options, working with rules, customizing the calendar, and adding RSS feeds?

1. Customize Email Messages.
   a) Determine which options you want to customize.
   b) Determine the information to include in your signature.
   c) Determine the layout that you would like for stationery.
2. Manage Junk Email Options.
   a) Determine which domains should be placed on the Safe Senders list.
   b) Determine which specific email addresses should be placed on the Blocked Senders list.
3. Work with Rules.
   a) Plan rules to use with your email messages.
   b) Determine how you would like your email messages to be processed.
4. Customize the Calendar.
   a) Determine the calendar settings you need.
5. Add RSS Feeds.
   a) Determine what news feeds you would like to use.

CONSIDER THIS

How should you submit solutions to questions in the assignments identified with a ✻ symbol?

Every assignment in this book contains one or more questions with a ✻ symbol. These questions require you to think beyond the assigned file. Present your solutions to the question in the format required by your instructor. Possible formats may include one or more of these options: write the answer; create a document that contains the answer; present your answer to the class; discuss your answer in a group; record the answer as audio or video using a webcam, smartphone, or portable media player; or post answers on a blog, wiki, or website.

Apply Your Knowledge

Reinforce the skills and apply the concepts you learned in this module.

Creating a Team Stationery and Personalized Signature

Note: To complete this assignment, you will be required to use the Data Files. Please contact your instructor for information about accessing the Data Files.

Instructions: Start Outlook. One of the top jobs in the world is a user experience (UX) designer who organizes how users experience a webpage or app. You will use the Signatures and Stationery dialog box (Figure 5–85) to create your UX Team stationery and a personalized signature to use when you send email messages to others.

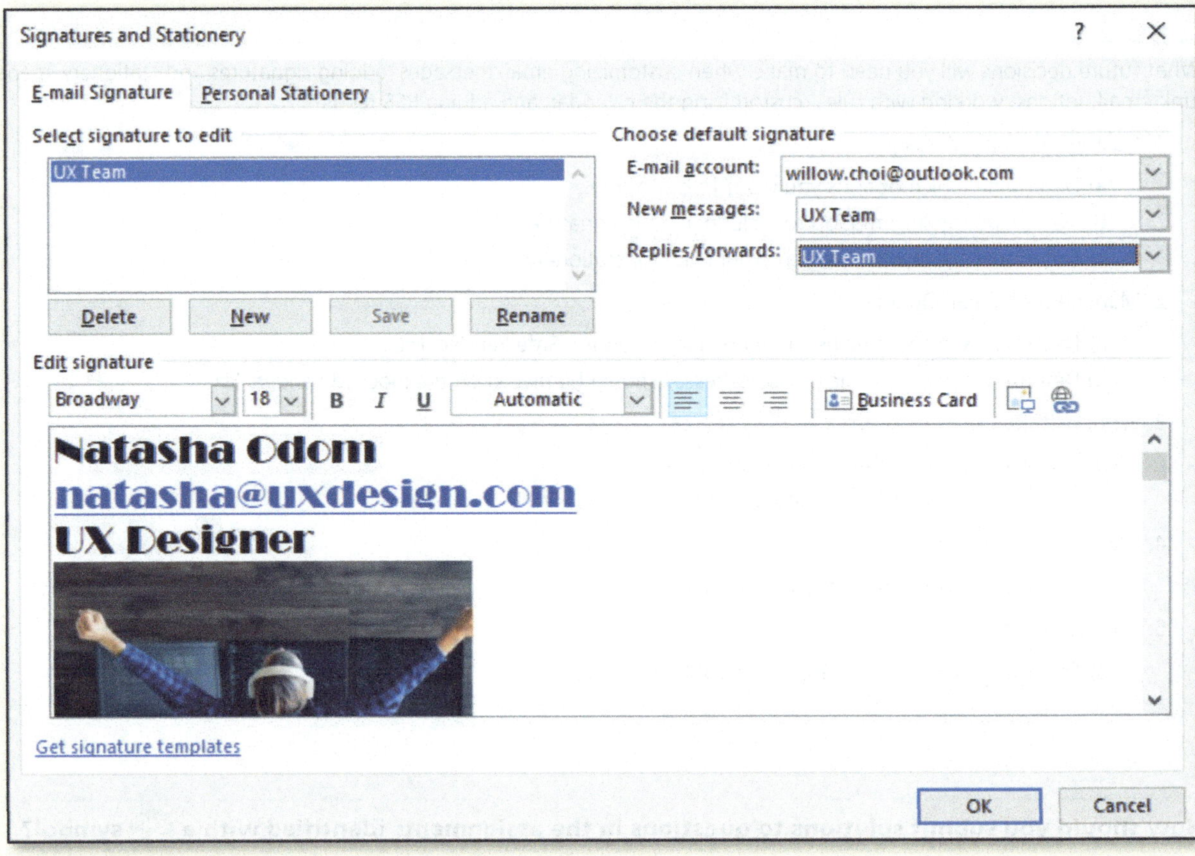

Monstar Studio/Shutterstock.com

Figure 5–85

Perform the following tasks:

1. Display the Outlook Options dialog box, and then display the Signatures and Stationery dialog box.
2. Create a signature using `UX Team` as the name of the company signature.
3. Change the font to Broadway and the font size to 18.
4. On three lines, enter the following information: your name, your email address, and your dream job or field.
5. From the Data Files, add the Coder.jpg picture to the signature on the next line.
6. Set the signature to apply to new messages, replies, and forwards.
7. Select the Studio theme as your stationery.

8. Accept the changes in the dialog boxes and then create a new email message addressed to your instructor to display your new signature and stationery.
9. Submit the email message in the format specified by your instructor.
10. Why is it a good idea to configure Outlook to include a signature in outgoing email messages?

Extend Your Knowledge

Extend the skills you learned in this module and experiment with new skills. You may need to use Help to complete the assignment.

Adding a Second Email Account to Microsoft Outlook

Instructions: Start Outlook. You are going to add a second email account to Microsoft Outlook so that you can send and receive email messages from two accounts. If you do not already have another email account to add to Microsoft Outlook, sign up for a free account using a service such as Outlook.com, Gmail, or iCloud. Once you create the account, you will add the email account to Outlook using the Add Account Wizard shown in Figure 5–86, and then send an email to your instructor.

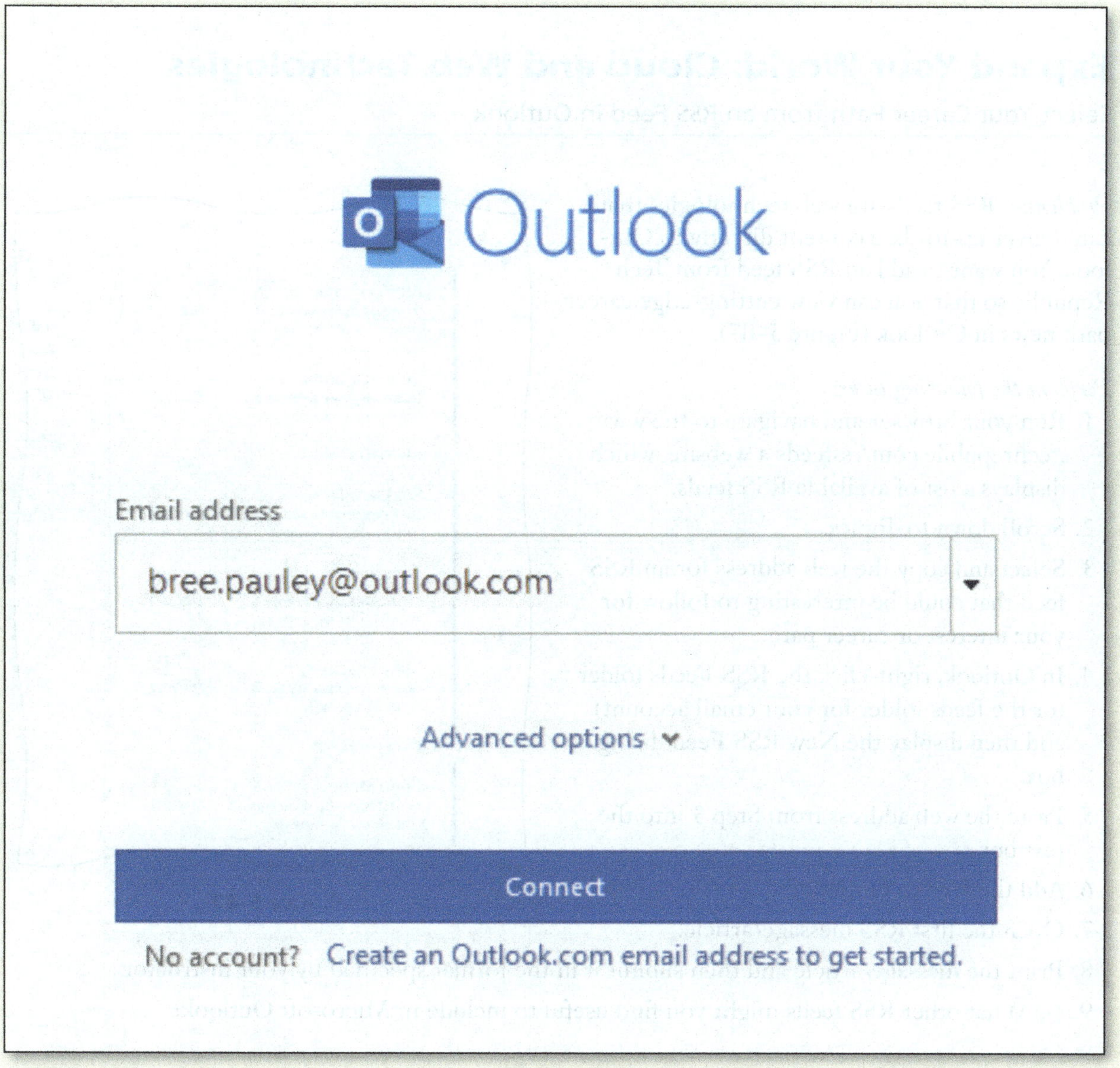

Figure 5–86

Continued >

Extend Your Knowledge *continued*

Perform the following tasks:

1. If necessary, navigate to a free email service and sign up for a free email account.
2. Start Outlook and display Backstage view.
3. If necessary, click the Info tab to display the Info gallery.
4. Click the Add Account button to display the first dialog box in the Outlook account setup.
5. Enter the desired information for the email account you are adding, including email address and password.
6. Click the Connect button to instruct Outlook to automatically configure the account. If Outlook is unable to configure the account automatically, you may need to manually configure the account settings.
7. Open a new email message addressed to your instructor stating that you have configured a new email account in Outlook. Send the email message to your instructor using the account you have just configured.
8. In what circumstances is it helpful to have multiple email accounts configured in Microsoft Outlook?

Expand Your World: Cloud and Web Technologies

Select Your Career Path from an RSS Feed in Outlook

Problem: RSS feeds are web technologies that can deliver up-to-date content directly to Outlook. You want to add an RSS feed from Tech Republic so that you can view cutting-edge career path news in Outlook (Figure 5–87).

Perform the following tasks:

1. Run your browser and navigate to the www.techrepublic.com/rssfeeds a website, which displays a list of available RSS feeds.
2. Scroll down to Topics.
3. Select and copy the web address for an RSS feed that could be interesting to follow for your interest or career path.
4. In Outlook, right-click the RSS Feeds folder (or the feeds folder for your email account) and then display the New RSS Feed dialog box.
5. Paste the web address from Step 3 into the text box.
6. Add the feed to Outlook.

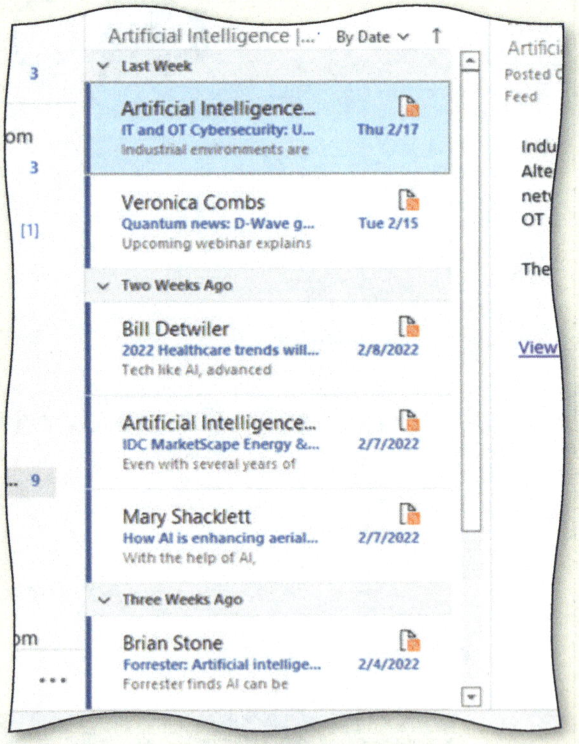

Figure 5–87

7. Open the first RSS message/article.
8. Print the message/article and then submit it in the format specified by your instructor.
9. What other RSS feeds might you find useful to include in Microsoft Outlook?

In the Labs

Design, create, modify, and/or use files following the guidelines, concepts, and skills presented in this module. Labs 1 and 2, which increase in difficulty, require you to create solutions based on what you learned in the module; Lab 3 requires you to apply your creative thinking and problem-solving skills to design and implement a solution.

Lab 1: Creating Multiple Signatures

Problem: You communicate with both instructors and other students via your school email. Your professors ask students to identify themselves clearly in email messages, but you do not want to include the same information in email messages you send to your friends. Instead, you want to include your nickname and cell phone number in your email signature. You will create two signatures: one to use when you send email messages to your instructors, and another for email messages you send to friends. For your instructor's signature email, use one of the templates in the Signature Template file provided in your Data Files. Open the Signature Template file and select one of the layouts. You will use the Signatures and Stationery dialog box to create the signatures.

Perform the following tasks:

1. Display the Outlook Options dialog box, and then display the Signatures and Stationery dialog box.
2. Create a signature using `School` as the name of the signature.
3. Change the font to Broadway, the font color to Blue Accent 1, and the font size to 18.
4. On three lines, enter the following information: your name, the name of your school, and your email address.
5. From the Data Files, open the Signature Template document. Select one of the layouts for your signature file to display your career path or add another photo that you locate online to designate your career interest.
6. Using the School signature, send an email message to your instructor. The email message should specify that the signature is the School signature.
7. Create another signature using `Personal` as the name of the signature.
8. Change the font to Comic Sans MS, the font size to 16, and the font color to one of your choosing.
9. On four lines, enter the following information: your name, your phone number, your email address, and a life quote in quotation marks.
10. Select a theme for your Personal signature.
11. Set the School signature to apply to new messages, replies, and forwards.
12. Using the Personal signature, send an email message to a friend and a copy to your instructor to tell them what you are learning in this class. The email message should specify that the signature is the Personal signature.
13. Do you think it is easier to switch back and forth between different signatures or manually type signature information individually into each email message? Why?

Continued >

In the Labs *continued*

Lab 2: Configuring Junk Email

Problem: You occasionally find email messages you want to read in the Junk E-mail folder for your Outlook email account. You also receive spam from a certain email address. You want to use the Junk Email Options dialog box to make sure you receive email messages from some senders, while blocking email messages from another sender (Figure 5–88). This lab requires that you capture screenshots during the following steps. Your instructor will provide instructions for how to create a screenshot using the Microsoft Word Screenshot tool or the Microsoft Windows Snipping Tool.

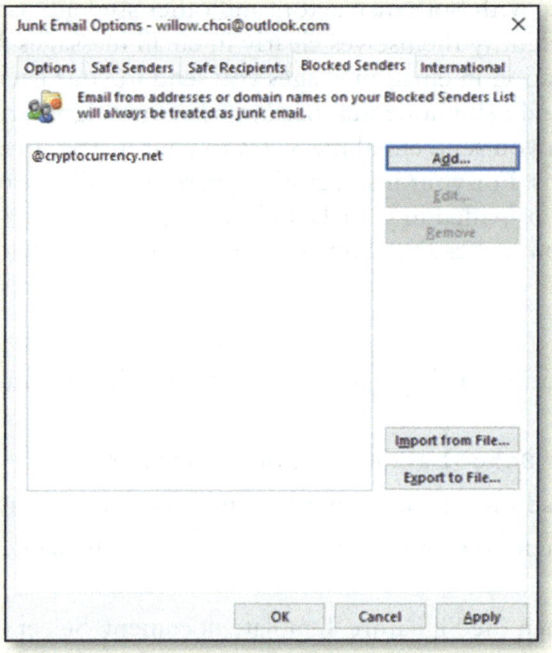

Figure 5–88

Perform the following tasks:

1. In Outlook, display the Junk Email Options dialog box.
2. Add **`@outlook.com`** to the Safe Senders list. Take a screenshot of what is displayed in the Safe Senders list.
3. Add **`naomi22@gmail.com`** to the Safe Recipients list. Take a screenshot of what is displayed in the Safe Recipients list.
4. Add **`@cryptocurrency.net`** to the Blocked Senders list. Take a screenshot of what is displayed in the Blocked Senders list as shown in Figure 5–88.
5. Create a new rule that flags messages for follow-up from your instructor. Flag the message for follow-up today. Take a screenshot of what is displayed in the Rules Wizard setup dialog box after you set up the rule.
6. Submit the screenshots in the format specified by your instructor.
7. What other domains and email addresses might you add to the Safe Senders list? What are some examples of other domains and email addresses you might add to the Blocked Senders list?

Lab 3: Consider This: Your Turn

Apply your creative thinking and problem-solving skills to design and implement a solution.

Creating Rules for Email for School

Problem: This semester you will be receiving emails from many different instructors. To stay organized, create the following folders and rules. This lab requires that you capture screenshots during the following steps. Your instructor will provide instructions for how to create a screenshot using the Microsoft Word Screenshot tool or the Microsoft Windows Snipping Tool.

Part 1: For four of the classes you are currently taking, create email folders for each class and take a screenshot of the four folders. Create four rules to move messages related to the classes to the appropriate class email folder and take a screenshot of each completed rule. Write a rule for the fourth class that flags messages for follow-up for today. Submit the screenshots in the format specified by your instructor.

Part 2: You made several decisions when creating the rules in this exercise, such as which folders to create and how to set up the rule to identify to which class an email message belongs. What was the rationale behind each of these decisions?

Index

Note: **Boldfaced** page numbers indicate key terms

A

B

C

D

E

F

G

H

I

J

L

M

P

Q

R

S

T

U

V

W

Cengage

ISBN-13: 978-0-357-67722-3
ISBN-10: 0-357-67722-6
90000
9 780357 677223